The Empire Project

C000216840

The British Empire, wrote Adam S   t the
project of an empire' and John Dai .....   the
rise and fall of that great imperial project. The British Empire,   is
much more than a group of colonies ruled over by a scattering of British
expatriates until eventual independence. It was, above all, a global phenomenon.
Its power derived rather less from the assertion of imperial authority than from the
fusing together of three different kinds of empire: the settler empire of the 'white
dominions'; the commercial empire of the City of London; and 'Greater India'
which contributed markets, manpower and military muscle. This unprecedented
history charts how this intricate imperial web was first strengthened, then
weakened and finally severed on the rollercoaster of global economic, political
and geostrategic upheaval on which it rode from beginning to end.

JOHN DARWIN teaches Imperial and Global History at Oxford where he is a
Fellow of Nuffield College. His previous publications include *After Tamerlane:
The Global History of Empire since 1405* (winner of the Wolfson History Prize for
2007), *The End of the British Empire: The Historical Debate* (1991) and *Britain
and Decolonization: The Retreat from Empire in the Post-War World* (1988).

THE EMPIRE PROJECT

The Rise and Fall of the
British World-System, 1830–1970

John Darwin

CAMBRIDGE UNIVERSITY PRESS
Cambridge, New York, Melbourne, Madrid, Cape Town,
Singapore, São Paulo, Delhi, Mexico City

Cambridge University Press
The Edinburgh Building, Cambridge CB2 8RU, UK

Published in the United States of America by Cambridge University Press, New York

www.cambridge.org
Information on this title: www.cambridge.org/9780521302081

First published 2009
First paperback edition 2011
Third printing 2013

A catalogue record for this publication is available from the British Library

Library of Congress Cataloguing in Publication data
Darwin, John.
The empire project : the rise and fall of the British world-system, 1830–1970 /
John Darwin.
  p. cm.
Includes bibliographical references.
ISBN 978-0-521-30208-1
1. Great Britain – Colonies – History. 2. Commonwealth countries – History.
3. Imperialism – History. 4. Great Britain – Civilization. 5. Decolonization –
History. I. Title.
DA16.D296 2009
909.09241081 – dc22   2009022115

ISBN 978-0-521-30208-1 Hardback
ISBN 978-0-521-31789-4 Paperback

IN MEMORY OF MY FATHER, G. M. DARWIN

CONTENTS

MAPS

PREFACE AND ACKNOWLEDGMENTS

The British Empire, wrote Adam Smith in 1776, 'has hitherto been not an empire, but the project of an empire; not a gold mine but the project of a gold mine'.[1] A hundred years later, his condemnation might have softened. But, viewed as a political or administrative entity, British imperialism remained just such a project: unfinished, untidy, a mass of contradictions, aspirations and anomalies. Defined as the exercise of *sovereign* power, or the unfettered enjoyment of imperial *rule* (the criteria still favoured by many historians), the British Empire in its heyday was largely a sham. Over much that was most commercially or strategically valuable, it could claim no authority; over much that was useless, its hold was complete. Of the half-dozen states whose loyalty was most vital to British world power in 1914, only one could be given direct orders from London.

Partly for this reason, I have preferred the term 'British world-system' to the conventional 'Empire'. The term was given authority by the shrewdest historian of modern British imperialism.[2] It is also meant to convey (the real theme of the book) that British imperialism was a global phenomenon; that its fortunes were governed by global conditions; and that its power in the world derived rather less from the assertion of imperial authority than from the fusing together of several disparate elements. Amid the colossal expansion of scholarly work on the history of empire, it has been easy to lose sight of the geopolitical facts on which its cohesion depended. I have tried in this book to restore this imbalance but not by reviving the old view from the centre. Instead, I have set out to show how the intricate web of 'British connections' linking Britain to India, to its huge empire of commerce, and to the 'white dominions' – the great auxiliary engines of British world power – was first strengthened, then weakened and finally severed under the stress of geopolitical change. The 'imperial politics' of the British world-system were made and remade by the rollercoaster of economic, political and geostrategic upheaval on which it was tossed from beginning (1830) to end (1970).

In writing this book, I have drawn very heavily on four different traditions in the history of empire. It would be hard to think clearly about British imperialism as a global phenomenon without the extraordinary insights of its greatest modern historians, John Gallagher and Ronald Robinson. In a single short essay, they established once and for all that, despite its many disguises, British imperialism was both global in reach and systemic in structure. It could not be seen as a mere accumulation of colonies; nor could *their* histories make sense on their own. 'Imperialism' in fact was a very flexible force, adapting its method to the time and the place: 'formal' in some places, less formal in others, and at times scarcely visible.[3] I have also relied on what is sometimes regarded as a quite different account of British imperialism, as the instrument of the 'gentlemanly capitalism' evoked by Peter Cain and Tony Hopkins. As I have argued elsewhere, it is easy to exaggerate the historiographical gap.[4] But the crucial contribution that Cain and Hopkins have made is to draw our attention to the massive importance of the City's commercial *imperium* for British power in the world, to its astonishing growth in the late nineteenth century (an age of British decline in many accounts), and to the influence and autonomy that the City enjoyed until its virtual liquidation in the Second World War. Thirdly, I have tried to exploit the insights and ideas of a more recent departure: the attention being given to the socio-cultural attachment between people in Britain and their 'diasporic' relations. 'British World' history has begun to reverse the long neglect suffered by the settler societies in the wider history of empire. It has also helped to restore a long-forgotten perspective of vital importance: the passionate identification of Canadians, Australians, New Zealanders, Newfoundlanders and South African 'English' with an idealised 'Britishness'; and their common devotion to 'Empire' as its political form.[5] Finally, a far older tradition retains much of its value to the historian of empire and the British world-system. The dangers British leaders most feared to their system's stability came from a breakdown in great power relations, a descent into war or the threat of invasion from Europe. That meant that they paid almost obsessive attention to the diplomatic reports of their envoys abroad, and were sometimes easily swayed by alarming accounts of naval and military weakness. In the intricate detail of naval, diplomatic and military history we may find some of the best clues to the British system's success – and its catastrophic collapse.

This book has been a long time in the writing and I have incurred many debts in the course of its making. Nuffield College provides the ideal combination of stimulus and support to its Fellows: there could be no better place in which to undertake an extended programme of academic research. I have been exceptionally fortunate in my colleagues in imperial and global history in Oxford – Judith Brown, David Washbrook, Georg Deutsch and Peter Carey – from whom I have learnt an enormous amount. The experience of teaching so many talented students has been a constant goad to reframe my ideas. For more than twenty years, a cohort of doctoral students has struggled to remedy my ignorance of their fields. I am grateful to them and hope their verdict will be: 'making some progress'. I am especially grateful to the founding fathers of the 'British World' initiative – James Belich, Carl Bridge, Phillip Buckner and Robert Holland – for widening my horizons at a critical time; and to Patrick O'Brien's 'Global Economic History Network', which taught me a great deal. Needless to say, the errors and omissions are mine alone.

A special word is needed here about the *Oxford History of the British Empire*, published in five volumes in 1999–2000. There is no doubt that the appearance of these volumes, spanning the whole history of the Empire from the sixteenth century to the twentieth, was a critical moment in the revival of British imperial history from what had seemed at times an almost terminal decline. All those of us who write (and especially teach) in this field owe a great debt to the editorial team of the series, but most of all to its driving force, William Roger Louis.

The task of writing the book would not have been possible without the librarians and archivists in Britain and abroad on whose kindness and efficiency I have depended so much. Two successive history editors at Cambridge University Press, William Davies and Michael Watson, have combined extraordinary patience with warm encouragement, and proffered shrewd advice. I am most grateful to them. Finally, my family have endured my preoccupation with a task that seemed at times to stretch into eternity: perhaps its completion will come as a welcome surprise!

INTRODUCTION: THE PROJECT OF AN EMPIRE

For more than a century after c.1840, the British Empire formed the core of a larger British 'world-system' managed from London. This book is a study of the rise, fortunes and fall of that system.

The British world-system was not a structure of global hegemony, holding in thrall the non-Western world. Except in particular places and at particular times, such hegemonic authority eluded all British leaders from Lord Palmerston to Churchill. But the British 'system' (a term that contemporaries sometimes made use of) was much more than a 'formal' territorial empire, and certainly global in span. It embraced an extraordinary range of constitutional, diplomatic, political, commercial and cultural relationships. It contained colonies of rule (including the huge 'sub-empire' of India), settlement colonies (mostly self-governing by the late nineteenth century), protectorates, condominia (like the Sudan), mandates (after 1920), naval and military fortresses (like Gibraltar and Malta), 'occupations' (like Egypt and Cyprus), treaty-ports and 'concessions' (Shanghai was the most famous), 'informal' colonies of commercial pre-eminence (like Argentina), 'spheres of interference' (a useful term coined by Sellars and Yeatman) like Iran, Afghanistan and the Persian Gulf, and (not least) a rebellious province at home. There was no agreed term for this far-flung conglomerate. This may have been why contemporaries sometimes found it convenient to fall back on that protean phrase 'the *Pax Britannica*' once it came into use after 1880,[1] as if the 'British Peace' formed a geographical zone.

But, if they found it hard to label this web of British connections with any precision, contemporaries grasped nonetheless that it formed the real source of British world power. In retrospect, we can see that, by the 1840s at latest, the British system was becoming global in three different senses. First, it exerted its presence, commercial or military, in every world region from treaty-port China and the maritime East Indies, through Burma, South Asia, the Persian Gulf, Zanzibar and West Africa, to the Mediterranean, the Caribbean, the River Plate republics, and as far as the Pacific coast of North America, the future 'British' Columbia. Secondly, however clumsy its methods, the point of the system was to promote the integration of these widely separated places: commercially, strategically, politically and – by diffusing British beliefs and ideas – culturally as well. Shared political values, recognisably similar institutions and laws, mutual economic dependence, and common protection against external attack by European rivals or predatory locals, were meant to achieve this for regions and states whether outside or inside the British domain in the constitutional sense. Thirdly, although this aspect was hard to see at the time, the success and survival of British connections depended on something far vaster than the tactics and stratagems of British agents and interests. Economic and political change in Asia, the Qing crisis in China, the geopolitical shape of post-Bonaparte Europe, the unexpected success of the settler republic on the American continent, patterns of consumption, religious renewals and the movements of peoples in migrations and diasporas: all these (and more) opened the way for British expansion, and widened the scope of British connections – but prescribed both their limits and their duration in time. If the British system was global, its fate was a function of the global economy and of shifts in world politics which it might hope to influence but could hardly control.

But was it really a 'system'? There are good grounds for thinking that the British empire of rule, let alone its self-governing or 'informal' outriders, had no logic at all. It looked like the booty of an obsessive collector whose passions had come with a rush and then gone with the wind, to be replaced in their turn by still more transient interests. The result was a pile of possessions whose purpose or meaning was long since forgotten, half-opened packets of quickly waning appeal, and new acquisitions made on the spur of the moment. It was certainly true that by the mid-nineteenth century the West Indian colonies, once the jewel in their crown, seemed to most British observers a troublesome burden, tainted by slavery, ill-governed and impoverished. The small enclaves of rule on the coast of West Africa had an even worse reputation.

London regretted the effort to rule the Southern African interior, and had handed it over to the Boer republics by the mid-1850s. It was also the case that British expansion had no master-plan. It had almost always been true that colonial schemes or their commercial equivalents were devised not by governments but by private enthusiasts in search of wealth, virtue or religious redemption. Sometimes they dragged Whitehall in their wake, to get its protection, secure a monopoly or obtain a licence to rule through a charter or patent. By 'insider-dealing' in the political world, they might conscript Whitehall's resources for their colony-building. Sometimes Whitehall insisted on an imperial claim on its soldiers' or sailors' advice, or to appease a popular outcry. But, once entrenched at their beachhead, the 'men on the spot' were hard to restrain, awkward to manage and impossible to abandon. The result could be seen from the map. The huge swathes of territory scattered all over the globe, whose defence, so it seemed to some late Victorians, was little short of a nightmare.

This is a useful corrective to paying too much attention to the mood of the 'policy-makers', to invoking too often the cool rationality (or constant viewpoint) of the 'official mind', or to being over-impressed by the so-called 'reluctance' of British imperialism. British expansion was driven not by official designs but by the chaotic pluralism of British interests at home and of their agents and allies abroad. The result (by the mid-nineteenth century) was an empire of beachheads and bridgeheads, half-conquered tracts, half-settled interiors, mission-stations and whaling-stations, barracks and cantonments, treaty-ports on the up (Shanghai was the best) and treaty-ports with no future. Its mid-Victorian critics were appalled by its moral and physical cost, and convinced of its commercial and political futility. However, the argument of this book is that, while imposing a system on this chaotic expansion was beyond the power of the imperial government in London, a system emerged nonetheless.

The characteristic of a system is the inter-dependence of its parts, on each other or with the centre of the system, and, as the system develops, the assumption by each of a specific function or role. In the British case, the most obvious forms of such inter-dependence were naval and military. This was not simply a matter of depending on Britain for strategic defence or for military aid in a localised struggle. British ability to provide naval protection or to send reinforcements to the scene of a conflict would have been very limited without the resources the imperial system supplied. It was strategic control of the Cape Colony (whose economic value was derisory before 1870) that secured the naval gateway to Asia from European waters. The prime function of Egypt, occupied by the British in 1882, was to preserve British use of the Suez Canal and protect the 'Clapham Junction' of imperial communications. Malta, Aden, Ceylon, Singapore, Hong Kong, Esquimalt (on Vancouver Island), the Falklands and Halifax, Nova Scotia, formed the network of bases from which the Royal Navy patrolled the world's sea-lanes. India played several roles in the British world-system, but perhaps its critical function was to be the main base from which British interests in Asia could be advanced and defended. Indian soldiers and a British garrison paid for by Indian revenues were the 'strategic reserve' of the British system in Asia. Because India played this role, other British possessions and spheres east and south of Suez were largely exempted from the costs of defence – a fact of crucial importance to their economic viability.

Commercially, too, this systemic inter-dependence became more and more striking. Both colonial territories and 'informal' colonies had to compete for investment and credits from London to expand their economies. They had to find and meet an external demand to earn the overseas income to fund their borrowing needs. They had to produce the specialised exports (staples) that would command the best price in London's commodity markets. In return, with the grand exception of the United States (which had received one-fifth of British foreign invest- ment by 1913), British capital was shuttled by the City of London between the various sectors of its commercial empire (a vast global realm among whose key provinces were Canada, Argentina, India, Australia, Southern Africa, China and the Middle East), employing a calculus of prospective return and speculative gain.[2]

Demographically, also, there were strong systemic influences at work. Britain was the reservoir. Although two-thirds of British migrants went to the United States up until 1900, almost all the rest were dis- tributed between the four main settlement zones of Canada, Australia, New Zealand and South Africa. Indeed, their economic development was usually seen as being closely dependent upon drawing labour and skills from the British supply (South Africa was a partial exception to this rule). In British opinion, the value of migration in creating overseas markets, relieving domestic distress and creating 'Arcadias' free from industrialism, turned the emigrant flow into a form of social renewal and the settlement colonies into prospective 'new Britains'. Nor was 'old' Britain the only well-spring of migration. Between 1834 and 1937, India exported some 30 million people to other British possessions as indentured labour, and perhaps one-fifth remained as permanent settlers. In the tropical empire (which British migrants avoided) they supplied much of the labour and business expertise to promote commercial expansion.

Lastly, the spheres of British expansion were progressively linked by a complex system of communication. From the 1840s onwards, this was provided by subsidised mail services, telegraph wires, undersea cables, an expanding rail network, fast passenger steamers and (in the twentieth century) imperial air routes. They catered for, and stimulated, the growing volume and frequency of the traffic in news, information, private correspondence, personnel and ideas that flowed between Britain and other parts of the system, as well as between those constituent parts. By the late nineteenth century, it has been persuasively argued, an 'imperial press system' had come into being.[3] It supplied London with news as well as buying it back from London-based agencies (a perfect feedback loop), a process accompanied by the circulation of journalists and the diffusion of newspaper practice. The supply of magazines, newspapers and books from Britain was supplemented by a small outward phalanx of teachers, academics and scientific experts. 'Imperial' associations sprang up to pool the experience of businessmen, doctors, surveyors, engineers, foresters, agronomists, teachers and journalists. To an extent we are gradually beginning to notice, the return flows of experience, scientific information and academic talent exerted a powerful influence upon elite culture in Britain.

None of this is to argue that the British world-system was closed or exclusive, let alone self-sufficient. The reverse was the case. Its geopolitical equilibrium required quite specific conditions: a 'passive' East Asia, a European balance, and a strong but unaggressive United States. If those conditions broke down, the imperial archipelago, strung across the world, would soon start to look fragile. British elites – in Canada, Australasia and India as well as in Britain itself – were well aware of this frailty, and more and more so after 1900. Secondly, the British system was also highly exposed to the global economy that took shape with astonishing speed between 1870 and 1914. Britain's overseas earnings derived partly at least from carrying and financing the trade of third parties, brokered through London. The circuit of payments that allowed the huge growth of trade within the British world-system was multilateral in scope.[4] India's deficit with Britain was met by the proceeds of its exports to Europe and the United States. Canada paid its American deficit from its surplus with Britain. One-third of British trade was with European markets and suppliers. Although there was room for debate about what level of protection (if any) would secure the best terms of trade for Britain and its system against the rest of the world, an open global economy not a set of 'mercantilist' blocs seemed the economic corollary of the British system's survival for most of the century after 1840. Thirdly, while the British system promoted certain cultural affinities (most strongly between its English-speaking communities) and proclaimed a liberal ideology (in practice applied by authoritarian means in India and elsewhere in the tropical empire), it was not a closed cultural world. Its external borders were easily permeable, and open to influences from America, Europe and Russia (after 1917), from the intellectual heartlands of the Islamic world, and even from China and Japan (whose revolt against the West was much admired by Gandhi). Internally, too, 'British' culture coexisted uneasily with indigenous cultures and those of non-British settlers. By the late nineteenth century, it faced strong cultural movements in India, forms of cultural nationalism in French Canada, Ireland and among the Cape Afrikaners, and was feebly equipped to attempt a cultural 'mission' among its new African subjects. The angry assertiveness of some British cultural 'messengers' and their periodic fits of despondency reflected not their calm superiority (as is sometimes assumed) but a mood often closer to a siege mentality.

A history of the British world-system must take account of these facts. First, British *possessions* (coloured red on the map) may loom large in the story, but only as parts of the larger conglomerate. Secondly, while the political, economic and cultural history of different colonial (and semi-colonial) territories can be studied up to a point as a local affair, the links between them and other parts of the system exerted a critical if variable influence on their politics, economics and culture. The limits of British concession to Indian nationalism would be inexplicable without the fact of India's contribution to 'imperial defence', just as the goals of the pre-1914 Congress make little sense except as a claim to be treated on terms of equality with the 'white dominions' of the 'British world'. Canada's extraordinary commitment of men in two world wars – the greatest traumas of its twentieth-century history – derived fundamentally from a sense of its shared identity as a 'British nation'. The survival of Afrikanerdom in South Africa – the central fact of *its* twentieth-century history – was the prize for success in fighting the British to a virtual stalemate in 1899–1902, exploiting their fear (as Smuts had foreseen) that keeping their army too long on the veld would endanger too many vital interests elsewhere. Only the parochialism of most British historians has veiled the pervasive effects of Britain's external connections on its institutions and outlook: the huge migrant flows, the vast overseas wealth, the 'imperial' monarchy, the cultural confidence bred by the sense of enduring 'centrality' in a globalised world. Thirdly, 'British connections' were dynamic not static. Their strength and solidity at any particular time were powerfully (perhaps decisively) shaped by the play of economic and geopolitical forces at the global not just imperial level.

But how to write such a history? It plainly cannot be done as a series of parallel histories of regions and colonies, whose distinctive development and ultimate separation form the *Leitmotif* of their story. This is the 'nationalist' historiography in which 'British connection' is an alien force, and a barrier to nationhood with all that it promised. In 'national' histories, links forged by migrations and the flows of goods and ideas retreat to the margins, or form the static backdrop to the national 'project'. But nor can it be done as a grandiose study in 'imperial policy', as if decisions taken in Whitehall, and the thinking behind them, were the dominant force in the fate of the system. Quite apart from the limits to imperial authority imposed by local conditions and external pressures, the 'policy-makers' rarely had a free rein to decide what British (or imperial) interests were, let alone how to preserve them. Least of all will it help to fall back upon a crude stereotyping of conflicting 'imaginaries', in which 'British' conceptions of mastery are contrasted with the values of their indigenous subjects. Although their widely different assumptions about race, gender and class shaped the British connection with almost every part of the world, there was no single pattern of 'hegemonic' assertion and local response. British opinions were not monolithic (since Britain was a complex and pluralistic society) and changed over time. The same could be said of almost every society into which British influence was inserted. Most important of all, discerning the impact of 'imaginings', 'representations' or 'colonial knowledge' requires something more than a sampling of texts: the careful reconstruction of economic and political contexts must be the starting point of enquiry.

Even a book as lengthy as this one could not hope to do justice to the multiple threads that bound different places to Britain and to other parts of its system. Instead, its main focus is upon what might be called 'imperial politics': the almost continual debate over the terms of association by which the various member states (including Britain itself) were bound to the British system. This was not simply the question of whether some form of independence was preferable – for most of the time, this was hardly practical politics. It was more often a matter of the limits of local autonomy; of how far British values (especially representative government) were being respected in practice (a key issue in India); of what place in the system colonial states should aspire to; how much influence they should wield over the general direction of policy (especially in matters of external defence); and whether the benefits and burdens of empire were being shared fairly between them. Politicians in states like Argentina or Egypt, without formal ties to the Empire, but with no means of escape from the British embrace, faced much the same issues. So in their own way did political leaders in Britain, which, together with India, met the main costs of imperial defence. Of course, this debate was not only conducted between organs of colonial and British opinion, or between colonial spokesmen and imperial official-dom. It divided parties and factions in each member territory where religion, ethnicity and regional interests, as well as private ambition, helped determine the outcome.

The theme of this book, then, is the continuous interplay of two sorts of tensions. The first was internal: the chronic disagreements over how the British system should work, usually expressed as political conflict over the connection with Britain or 'British connection'. The second was external. The meaning of 'British connection' – its prestige and appeal, its perceived costs and benefits – was pulled this way and that by the 'exogenous' forces of the global environment. The unpredictable shifts in the shape of world politics; geopolitical change and the rise of new powers; boom, bubble and bust in the global economy; the unforeseen impact of ideological movements and their contagious appeal: their collective effect was to create an 'external' arena of extraordinary turbulence before 1900, and of volcano-like chaos in the twentieth century. On their rollercoaster ride through modern world history, the most powerful units of the British world system were at times flung together by centripetal attraction, at times sucked apart as if about to spin off into separate trajectories. We know of course that, in the great crisis of empire in 1940–2, the system all but broke up and never fully recovered. But, up until then, it had seemed axiomatic that, in one form or another, with more local freedom or less, the bond of empire would hold and the system endure.

What then were the system's most powerful components whose adhesion mattered most to its chance of survival? The most important by far was the imperial centre: the British Isles, yoked together for most of the period in a British 'Union' or by the 'dominion' relationship with Southern Ireland between 1921 and 1948. This composite 'Britain' (more often called 'England' after its dominant element) supplied much of the energy that the system demanded. Its huge financial resources, vast manufacturing output and enormous coal reserves (its so-called 'Black Indies' of a thousand coalfields)[5] made Britain a commercial and industrial titan, whose principal rivals, the United States and Germany, engaged much less in trade or traded mainly with Europe. Even by the late 1880s, Britain disposed of more (steam) horsepower per head than any other state, including the United States.[6] Its large surplus of manpower (the product of birth-rate and prevailing social conditions) fuelled Britain's 'demographic imperialism', the human capacity to stock the settlement colonies and maintain their British complexion, despite a much larger migrant stream to the United States. Britain was also at all times a great power in Europe, and able to use its leverage there as part of the general defence of its interests worldwide. The great strategic bonus of this European role, until the inter-war years, was that the main source of its power in European politics, the world's largest deep-sea navy, could also be used to uphold the oceanic supremacy first grasped at Trafalgar in 1805. Britain also possessed a set of cultural assets whose value is harder to quantify but is of crucial importance. In their institutional form, these were the clubs and societies, associations and leagues, patrons, sponsors and churches (as well as government agencies) through whom information and knowledge of the world beyond Europe was collected, collated, digested and diffused to the public at large or to a more privileged few. Not the least of the attributes that Britain contributed to the overall strength of its system was as a great cultural entrepot.

In the world east of Suez, the indispensable element in British world power was India. Imperial India was more than the countries of modern 'South Asia'. It was 'Greater India': a 'sub-empire' ruled from Calcutta (and Simla), extending from Aden to Burma, and with its own sphere of influence in the Persian Gulf, Southwest Iran, Afghanistan and (for some of the time) Tibet. 'Greater India' might even include coastal East Africa, whose metropole was Bombay until the late nineteenth century, and the 'Straits Settlements' of the Malayan peninsula, ruled from Calcutta into the late 1860s. The agrarian revenues of the Indian 'heartland' paid for a British-officered Indian army and after 1860 for a large British garrison, between a third and a half of Britain's regular army. Of the peace-time strength of the British and Indian armies – together almost the whole regular land force of the British world-system – the Indian taxpayer paid for nearly two-thirds. India's internal market, pegged open by rule, and its return on investment, underwritten by government, was a major contributor to British employment (India was the largest market for Britain's principal export) and to Britain's balance of payments. India's ports and railways (the largest network outside the West), its merchants, migrants and labourers, its British-owned banks and agency-houses, and its strategic position on the marine trunk road to East Asia, made up the engine of Anglo-Indian expansion, an enterprise under both British and Indian management. By the late nineteenth century, it was hard to imagine how this intricate fusion of British and Indian interests could be prised apart without disaster for both.

The third great component of the British world-system was not territorial. It might almost be thought of as a 'virtual India': a vast abstract realm of assets and interests. This was the hinterland of the City of London, a 'commercial republic' bound together by self-interest not rule, but containing within it a fast-growing 'empire' of British-owned property. The jewel in the crown of this empire of commerce was the deep-sea merchant marine, much of it serving non-British customers, but earning a huge income remitted to its owners at home. It was closely paralleled by British-owned railways: like the Great Indian Peninsular and the East Indian Railway, the Canadian Pacific Railway, the Great Southern Railway in Argentina, or the humbler 'Simon Bolivar' in Northern Venezuela. Banks and insurance companies, shipping agents and packers, and a mass of installations including utilities, harbour-works, telegraph companies (like the globe-spanning 'Great Eastern'), plantations, mines, and concessions for oil, also helped to ensure that the profits Britain drew from the growth of world trade were second to none. By the 1890s, the income that was drawn from these overseas assets and the invisible income from shipping and services was equivalent to between 70 and 80 per cent of the earnings from Britain's domestic (merchandise) exports (in 1960, by contrast, Britain's net invisible income was much less than one-twentieth of the earnings from exports). They more than covered the payment gap between British exports and imports (the remotest of dreams in 1960) protected the value of sterling, and built up the 'war-chest' of overseas assets on which British governments drew deeply in both world wars.

The fourth component was the 'awkward squad' of self-governing settlement colonies, called 'dominions' after 1907, or, colloquially, 'the white dominions'. It was a disparate group that comprised Canada, Australia, New Zealand and South Africa (after union in 1910), Newfoundland (whose bankruptcy brought rule by a British commission from 1933 until 1949, when it became a province of Canada), the Irish Free State (from 1921 until 1948 when it became a republic and left the Commonwealth) and Southern Rhodesia (which, after 1923, enjoyed dominion-like status, but without full self-government). To the French Canadian minority, the Afrikaner majority among South African whites, and, in the Irish Free State, loyalty to the 'British connection', was at best conditional, at worst non-existent. But, among the ethnic British majorities in Canada, Australia, New Zealand and Newfoundland, and the large 'English' minority among South African whites, a sense of shared British identity (to be sharply distinguished from any subservience to Britain) was deeply ingrained. Dominion politicians declared over and over again that Canada, Australia, New Zealand and Newfoundland were 'British countries', or 'British nations'. To them and their constituents (since this was a popular not an elite point of view), the 'Empire' was not an alien overlord, but a joint enterprise in which they were, or claimed to be, partners. It was not so much England as the Empire for which they were fighting, said Milner in 1917.[7] Its interests were – or ought to be – theirs. The Whitehall officials who dealt with these 'colonial' leaders found them prickly and unyielding, and took their revenge in disparaging minutes. In fact, the dominions were a critical element in British world power. The remarkable loyalty of the 'overseas British' and their economic efficiency made them the most reliable overseas part of the whole British world-system, contributing a million men for military service in the First World War (as many as India), and more in the Second, as well as (from Canada especially) vital industrial and financial resources.

British world power, to put the matter more starkly, required the cooperation of each of these elements and the resources they offered – material and psychological. When they fell away, collapsed or seceded (as largely happened between 1940 and 1947), that world power soon ended. Three further points, however, need to be made. The first is that those long-favoured categories of 'imperialism' and 'nationalism' as the binary opposites of imperial history are of limited value in making sense of this story. In much of their overseas system, the British could make little use (even if they wanted to) of coercive methods or authoritarian rule. Among those British 'imperialists' for whom 'closer union' with the settlement colonies was the greatest priority, sharing London's command of foreign affairs and defence through a federal system was the favoured solution. Secondly, although 'nationalist' histories make much of resistance, and eagerly trace the genealogy of independence movements back to the earliest phases of colonial rule, most of those who were politically active in colonial societies were far more ambivalent. For some, foreign rule had been a political and cultural bonanza, displacing the power of groups they disliked more. Thus many Bengali Hindus felt liberated from the Muslim regime that Clive had defeated. For others, nationalist activity was primarily 'tactical' – to obtain specific concessions – not 'strategic' – to forge a separate sovereign state. Nor is this surprising. For the third point to make is that, until very late in the day (the early 1940s is the likeliest time), it seemed wisest to assume that British world power would remain exceptionally formidable, that escape from its orbit would be exceptionally difficult, and that, in a world of predatory powers, the imperial frying-pan was not the worst place to be. It was much more realistic to seek the widest autonomy that the British system had to offer than to strive for the grail of an unimaginable sovereignty. With the exception of Jawaharlal Nehru, who dreamt of a Marxist millennium, and of Subhas Chandra Bose, the Indian nationalist leadership of the 1920s and 1930s showed an indifference to the international scene that seems amazing in retrospect.

What difference does it make to the history of British imperialism if we approach it in the way that has just been sketched out? The argument here is that we can take a more realistic view of Britain's imperial power if we keep its main elements in a single field of action. That might also lead us towards somewhat different conclusions on at least five aspects of the imperial past.

First, it might allow us to see more clearly than before that Britain's place in the world was not simply a consequence of Britain's 'own' power and its ability to impose it wholesale on the rest of the globe. Instead, the key to British power lay in combining the strength of its overseas components with that of the imperial centre, and managing them – not commanding them – through the various linkages of 'imperial politics': some persuasive, some coercive, some official, some unofficial. Stripped of those assets that lay outside the direct control of the administrators in Whitehall, British power in the world would have been feeble indeed. The rest depended upon the willingness of political and business elites in different parts of the world to acknowledge the benefits that membership of the British system conferred, and concede – sometimes grudgingly – that its various costs were worthwhile. Of course, that willingness was bound to depend upon the general equilibrium of the whole British system, and Britain's ability to meet its large share of the overall burden.

Secondly, adopting this view allows us to form a clearer impression of the actual trajectory of British world power, both its rise and its decline. In one school of thought, British world power performed a long diminuendo from its brief mid-Victorian triumph.[8] In another, the Edwardian era saw the last fading chance to stave off decline, but one thrown away by the weakness or blindness of the 'weary Titan's' own political leaders.[9] A third proclaims that British power reached its apogee in the inter-war years.[10] A fourth was that the gradual decline of those years was briefly reversed in the Second World War before a final sudden descent.[11] A fifth was that the British clung on by hook or by crook until the final surrender of their 'role' east of Suez in the late 1960s. Each case has its merits. But, if we ask when each part of the British system could contribute the most to its overall power, it seems clear that neither the 'white dominions' nor the mercantile and property empire over which the City presided counted for much before the later nineteenth century, and that the contribution of India, in economic and military terms, also rose in that period. By the inter-war years, in a much harsher environment, there were clear signs of strain, alleviated in part by the weakness of Britain's main rivals until very late in the day. But the real turning point came with the strategic catastrophe of 1940–2. Britain's drastic defeat as a European power, the forced liquidation of the most valuable parts of its property empire, the lapse of its claim to the (more or less) unconditional loyalty of the overseas dominions, and the irrecoverable offer of independence to India to meet the desperate emergency of 1942, marked the practical end of the British system created in the mid-nineteenth century. That empire that hung on after 1945 was built from different (and much more fragile) materials. It relied far more than before upon the efforts of Britain itself, not least the diverting of so much of its manpower into a conscript army and the arduous struggle to earn more from merchandise exports than ever before. It also imposed new burdens on the least-developed parts of the pre-war system. Above all, it depended upon the goodwill and assistance of a far stronger world power, less and less willing to concede even the shadow of parity to its debilitated partner.

Thirdly, a 'systemic' view of British imperialism places Britain itself in a different perspective. It serves to remind us that Britain's attachment to empire should not be taken for granted, and that taking part in the system had variable costs and benefits for different sections of British society. It points up the fact that the overseas elements of British world power were quite different in kind and required quite different types of 'British connection'. To assume that the British at home treated their property empire, the settler societies of the white dominions, and their 'Indian empire', as a single set of possessions, or applied in each case a uniform imperial ideology, would be a basic (but all too common) mistake. For one thing, these different components had built up informal alliances inside British society whose outlook and influence varied considerably. For another, the British interests at play were themselves markedly different. For example, the large fragment of British society with friends or relations in the great emigrant flow to Canada after 1900 had little in common with the narrow elite that championed the interests of the 'Civilian Raj', or with the shareholders and bondholders who had tied up their fortunes with Argentine railways or funds in Peru.

Viewed in this light, it is hard to see how the sometimes furious debate about whether (and how far) Britain itself was 'imperialised' can be settled one way or the other. On the part of some writers, huge claims have been made about the implanting at home of racial, social and sexual values derived from imperial domination abroad. The speculative (not to say intuitive) basis for a good deal of this writing,[12] its flimsy dependence upon a handful of texts, and the methodological error of abstracting fragments of evidence from their broader cultural context, have rightly been criticised – recently and trenchantly in Bernard Porter's *The Absent-Minded Imperialists*,[13] which insisted that enthusiasm for imperial *rule* was confined to a limited section of the upper classes. But it is equally true that, if we define empire more broadly (to include self-governing colonies and zones of economic preponderance), a much wider constituency saw Britain's fate as tied up with its overseas interests and assumed, for example, the unchallengeable right of British migrants abroad to seize and fill up the lands of indigenous peoples. How far these different conceptions and connections of empire helped to 'constitute' British society is indeed a moot point. It can hardly be doubted that the sense of being part of a larger political world extending far beyond Britain was very widely diffused. Only the most obtuse of newspaper readers (perhaps three million adults by 1830)[14] could have failed to notice that external events often intruded upon their domestic activities. Entrenched vested interests, often commanding a loud public voice, could play upon this awareness of a 'greater' Britain on whose power and prestige 'little' England depended. But they could not assume a broad public sympathy for all types of empire and on every occasion. Nor of course did the 'imperial interest' speak with one voice or express a single concern. If Britain was 'constituted' by its empire we should have to consider how far its 'constitution' was shaped by flows of migration (and their return), a sense of pan-British identity, the appeal of free trade (as a source of cheap overseas food), and the claims of evangelical Christianity on the conscience and purse of domestic society, as well as by the vicarious pleasures of lording over 'lesser breeds without the law'. On those grounds alone, the fashionable notion that the least attractive aspects of modern British culture can be traced directly to its unsavoury imperial past, should only appeal to those who like their history kept simple.

Fourthly, while the importance of India and of the 'empire of commerce' are a familiar theme in almost all modern accounts of British world power, the place of the white dominions has been all but ignored by two generations of imperial historiography.[15] At best, the overseas British have appeared in the guise of 'pre-fabricated collaborators', copying the habits and consuming the products of the industrial Britain in whose mould they were formed.[16] In a characteristically witty aside, the most brilliant historian of modern British imperialism dismissed Anglo-dominion relations as a question of 'treaties about halibut'.[17] Revision is long overdue. The dominions cannot be fitted into the Procrustean bed of 'imperial collaboration'. Nor can their contribution to British world power be treated as less important than India's. In four dominions out of five (including Newfoundland), commitment to the British cause in 1914 was a matter not of elite calculation but of popular will. And, unlike the rest of the empire, the dominions were willing and able to sustain a large-scale war effort in manpower and materiel during the system's great crisis, and to do so moreover at their own expense. It was the will and the means to identify their interests with those of Britain, and at huge physical cost, that made the dominions so special. It was only once Britain could no longer make good its claim on their loyalty, or had signalled a new orientation towards Europe,[18] that their attachment began to corrode.

Finally, by thinking in terms of a British system of world power, not of a bundle of territories superintended from London, we can make some better sense of the final strange phase of British imperialism: the zigzags and u-turns after the Second World War. As we have seen, with the loss of so many overseas assets, the independence of India, the dominions' strategic dependence upon the United States, the eclipse of Britain itself as a great naval power, and its renewed vulnerability to external attack, the pre-war British system had almost completely collapsed. Yet there was also the need, and (as it seemed) the scope, to construct a new one, to restore British security and British prosperity. This was why the British pressed into service colonial regions that had previously been of only marginal value in tropical Africa, tropical Asia and the Middle East. The Middle East was a special case. The British had been drawn deeper and deeper into this crossroads sub-continent with its layer upon layer of cultures, religions and peoples. They had rushed in to protect their short sea route to India through the Suez Canal and occupied Egypt in 1882. They fought an arduous war after 1914 to protect the approaches to Egypt and the Persian Gulf against Germany's Ottoman ally. In the year of imperial crisis in 1918 – a 1940 that might have been – they extended their reach as far north as the Caspian to pre-empt a German advance from the broken empire of Russia. In the inter-war years, they clung to much of their takings. After 1945, in far gloomier conditions, they had a powerful motive to hang on regardless. Now the Middle East was a base from which to defend

Britain itself against the daunting threat from the east. But the costs and risks of it all, like the costs and risks of ruling the tropical colonies much more intensely, fell entirely on Britain. The balance of safety became agonisingly narrow. A forward move by a rival great power (hostile or friendly), a show of resistance by local nationalist leaders, an open quarrel with an indispensable ally, a spasm of weakness in an overstrained economy: each was enough to produce symptoms of crisis. Fifteen years after the Second World War, the effort to build a new British world-system had come to little or nothing. By 1960, it was only a question of how to preserve as much influence as possible in a superpower world.

But why begin the history of Britain's world-system in the 1830s and 1840s? After all, Adam Smith, from whose sceptical phrase this book takes its main title, saw the discovery of America and the rounding of the Cape as decisive moments in the history of the world. By the 1770s, when *The Wealth of Nations* was published, the British had won a great North American empire, and were in the process of seizing a second vast empire on the Indian sub-continent. If they had lost much of the first by the mid-1780s, they had certainly gained a good deal of the second. Between 1783 and 1815, they added much more to this haul: Eastern Australia (annexed in 1788); the Cape Colony (taken for good in 1806); Trinidad and Mauritius; Penang (in modern Malaysia); and Malta and the Ionian islands in the Mediterranean. They ejected the French from Syria and Egypt; sent their (Indian) navy into the Persian Gulf; and made an abortive attempt to 'liberate' Buenos Aires from Spanish imperial rule. By 1818, with the final defeat of the Maratha confederacy, their East India Company was the dominant power in South Asia. If the exertion of military power all over the globe is the test of world power, a strong case can be made for this earlier period.[19]

Nor was Britain itself without obvious signs of embracing this imperial and global role. The attempt to reassert British authority over the American colonies had evoked very mixed feelings in opinion at home, while the 'oriental' corruption of the 'nabobs' in India aroused the resentment on which Burke sought to play in the impeachment of Hastings. Adam Smith's famous tract denounced the 'mercantilist' equation between political empire and commercial expansion. But, with the onset of world war in the 1790s, the huge mobilisation of manpower and money for the struggle with France, the vast scope of the conflict – in every continent – swept away any doubt that Britain's survival required a military effort over much of the globe. The old empire of settlement (of which only a rump remained) paled in comparison with the new empire of conquest. What was taken by military force would have to be kept by arbitrary power. The untrammelled authority of British officials, not local self-government by elected politicians, became the constitutional rule.

Of course, this 'empire of authority' of which the great symbol was India remained a key element in British world power almost until its demise. But it would be wrong to see it as the dominant or even representative element. In a longer view, the militarist ethos of 1790–1815 was a transient phase: it soon came under domestic attack once peace and depression set in. The following decades saw the steady restriction of governors' powers except in the poorest or most vulnerable outposts. The 1790s to the 1820s was an age of crisis and strain. It was less the classical era of British world power than its turbulent pre-history, when prevailing conditions remained very uncertain. In the 1830s and 1840s, by contrast, most of the favourable conditions had begun to converge for the growth of the loose decentralised construct that sustained British world power into the 1940s.

The first and most fundamental was the new balance of power and wealth across Eurasia. China's defeat in the first opium war (1839–42), however partial, signalled that East Asia would be a passive actor in world politics for the foreseeable future. The implications were massive. Peking had lost by default the chance to invoke great power diplomacy to restrain its unwelcome new sea-borne neighbour. British interests could press forward in maritime East Asia against only local resistance. The value of India as the base from which to project British power in the East had been strikingly vindicated. At almost the same time, the prolonged 'Eastern crisis' of 1830–41 confirmed the fragility of the Ottoman and Iranian empires, and the wide new scope for British trade and diplomacy in Egypt and the Middle East. The Eastern crisis was also a critical test of the post-Napoleonic order in Europe. What it revealed was not the existence of British hegemony (that luxuriant myth of current historiography) but a pattern of European politics which, while not free from conflict, disfavoured both a grand coalition against Britain (a constant threat between 1778 and 1814) and recourse to a general war. Although their European diplomacy was intermittently stressful, the British were able to distribute their military power across the globe (and lock up much of their army in India after 1860) on the cheerful assumption that domestic invasion was at worst a remote possibility. In the Americas, too, the geopolitical climate after 1830 was much more propitious. The new Latin American states were now fully detached from their old masters in Europe, and thrown open (in theory at least) to British influence and trade. With the anglo-settler republic in North America, relations were more fractious. But the headlong expansion of the 'slave south' (the main source of Lancashire cotton) and the commercial Northeast (with its close ties to London and Liverpool) had created a sufficient degree of mutual dependence to avert renewal of the frontier and maritime warfare of 1812–14, despite the prolonged crisis in Canada and the territorial disputes in Maine and Oregon. An American war, as the British well knew, would have been a strategic catastrophe with global effects.

The other conditions can be listed more briefly. The scale of Britain's industrialisation after 1830 was critical (a simple index of this is the production of pig iron: 1796: 125,000 tons; 1830: 677,000 tons; 1860: 3.8 million tons[20]). Pre-industrial empires required an abundance of coercive force to suppress rebellion and repel external attack. Even close commercial and cultural ties were no guarantee of colonial loyalty, as the Thirteen Colonies had shown. Industrialism changed the context and equation of imperial power. It increased the dependence of 'colonial' economies, and encouraged their development in every world region. It facilitated the global projection of military power far beyond the old limits of wind-powered warships, and greatly cheapened its use once telegraph, steamship and railway could shuttle information and manpower swiftly across vast distances. It turned the demographic imperialism of settler societies from a slow laborious advance into a *Blitzkrieg* invasion, swamping local resistance and transforming faraway natural environments into 'neo-Europes' and 'new Britains'. It hugely reinforced the cultural prestige of the imperial rulers, and (through the new technologies of communication) increased the volume and intensity of their cultural impact. Industrialisation was also closely connected with two other pre-conditions for the growth of Britain's world-system: the great British out-migration and the export of capital. Not until the 1830s and 1840s did the annual trickle of migrants begin

to swell into the flood that helped build a 'British world'. Not till the
1850s and 1860s were the funds coming to hand to build the City's
great property empire abroad. In short, without the geopolitical and
'geo-economic' conditions which Britain was peculiarly well placed to
exploit, but which had scarcely developed before 1830, British expansion would indeed have remained 'not an empire, but the project of
an empire; not a gold mine, but the project of a gold mine'. Without them, the only safe course for Britain would have been, in Adam
Smith's words, 'to accommodate her future views and designs to the
real mediocrity of her circumstances'.[21]

In the story that follows, Part I attempts to describe how a British
system emerged in the long 'Victorian peace' (a relative term to Zulus,
Ashanti, Sudanese, Ethiopians, Egyptians, Aborigines, Maori, Indians,
Burmese, Chinese and others) up to 1914. Part II traces its fate in the
'age of iron' that followed.

Part I

Towards 'The Sceptre of the World': the elements of Empire in the long nineteenth century

1 VICTORIAN ORIGINS

After mercantilism

From the 1830s onwards, the Victorians gradually transformed their sprawling legacy of war and mercantilism into a world-system much of whose fabric survived into the late 1940s. Yet they did not do so to a conscious plan, nor under the influence of a master ideology. Victorian imperialists were drawn from different interests and classes. They were driven by motives that were at times contradictory. Rival visions of empire pulled them in different directions. Nor could they count on a source of irresistible power to carry them forward wherever they chose. British firepower and capital formed a limited stock for which, at any one time, there were competing demands. The scope for enlarging British influence or territory was not just a function of British wishes or needs. It also depended upon many factors and forces outside the control of – perhaps even unknown to – British interests and agents. Hence, much of their handiwork followed the law of unintended consequences. However clear-sighted the prophet, it would not have been easy to foresee the path followed by British expansion between 1830 and 1880. It would have been harder still to envisage the societies that it helped to create both overseas and at home in the British Isles. The imperial system that the Victorians made emerged by default not from design.

Once we concede that there was nothing inevitable about the extraordinary course of Victorian imperialism, we can begin to explore the gravitational field that governed British expansion: propelling it forward in some places; holding it back in others; bending and twisting its impact; raising or lowering its costs; imposing or concealing its contemporary meaning. The starting point must be the play of geopolitical pressures. Victorian Britain was a powerful state, but it was not all-powerful, and much nonsense is talked of Victorian 'hegemony'. Even a minister as aggressive as Lord Palmerston, whose belligerent rhetoric is sometimes naively equated with his conduct of policy, was always acutely aware that British strength had its limits, especially on land. Victorian statesmen avoided confrontation with other strong powers whenever they could. Those who schemed for the extension of colonial territory looked first to the regions where little resistance was feared, or where the British already commanded the main geographical gateways. Secondly, it would be a mistake to imagine that the moves to expand Britain's spheres of rule, protection or semi-free trade were part of a programme or policy invented in Whitehall. Much more important was the pressure exerted by the old networks and lobbies that managed Britain's overseas interests and the new ones that sprang up to promote commercial, land-seeking, emigrant, humanitarian, missionary or scientific enterprise. The annexation of New Zealand, the first 'opium war' against China, and Britain's maritime presence on the west coast of Africa, reflected the strength of these lobbies, and their power to bend the 'official mind' to their will. Yet the fate of these schemes, and of many others besides, was also determined by a third force at work. The 'men on the spot', in the bridgeheads of trade, settlement, religion or rule, had to marshal the 'investments' (of money, men, credit or force) transmitted from Britain and use them to leverage added local resources. How successful they were in exploiting the trade, settling the land, tapping the revenue or enlisting the manpower of the regions around them decided how fast their bridgeheads would grow – and how much appeal they would have to those with influence at home. Indeed, building their 'connection' in London, winning over the press and public opinion, and cementing their ties with a favourable lobby, were a constant concern. The supreme practitioner of this 'bridgehead politics' after 1880 was to be Cecil Rhodes. But he had many precursors.

Left to itself, expansion of this kind was likely to throw up a whole series of 'sub-empires': offshoots of influence, occupation and rule wherever British interests could gain a favourable purchase. By the mid-nineteenth century, there were clusters of British merchants spread around the world from China to Peru, entrenched more or less in the overseas trade of formally sovereign states. There was a clutch of free-ports under British jurisdiction, where British merchants (and others) strove to gather the trade of the neighbouring region: Gibraltar,

Singapore and Hong Kong. There was a mass of (mostly) small settlements scattered across the enormous territories claimed or conquered as British 'possessions' and annexed to the Crown: 'British' North America (comprising the huge tracts 'ruled' by the Hudson's Bay Company west of the Great Lakes as well as 'the Canadas' – modern Ontario and Quebec – and the four maritime provinces); Australia (perhaps one million immigrants along the 'boomerang coast' from Brisbane to Adelaide); New Zealand (a dozen small colonies mainly linked by the sea); and South Africa (where a handful of British in the Cape Colony and Natal lived with the more numerous 'Dutch' in a tense and often violent relation with the black communities within and beyond the colonial frontier). There were the old plantation colonies of the British West Indies, once the jewel in the imperial crown, but (with free trade in sugar and the loss of slave labour) now falling behind their economic competitors (Brazil and Cuba retained their slaves until late in the century). And there was India, still ruled by the Company (until 1858) with its huge 'sepoy' army, a great conquest state whose influence was exerted spasmodically on the arc of territories from Aden (annexed to Bombay in 1839) in the west to Singapore (ruled from Calcutta until 1867) in the east. In what sense, we might ask, was this disparate collection of 'work camps in the wilderness', mercantile agencies, mildewed plantations, treaty-ports and port-cities, coaling stations and bases, fractious semi-protectorates and one huge garrison state to be considered an 'empire'? Yet, by the late nineteenth century, this 'project of an empire' (in Adam Smith's phrase) had become a world-system. Its component parts assumed increasingly specialised roles. They fitted together in ways that maximised Britain's power in the world. How had this happened?

Of the likeliest causes, perhaps three were decisive. The first was the greater integration permitted by technical advance and institutional change. The telegraph, steamship and railway speeded the flows of goods, information and people (as well as military force) between the imperial centre and its outlying parts. The rise of an international capital market in London, and its vast 'information exchange' (of newspapers, news agencies, specialised journals, commercial intelligence and promotional literature) increased the dependence of colonial or semi-colonial regions on this grand metropolis. When competing for markets, money and (in the case of settler countries) men, or if claiming the support and sympathy of the 'imperial factor' in their local affairs, they had to 'sell' themselves as net contributors to the larger 'British world', promising profits, goods or services not on offer elsewhere. The second influence at work was connected with this. The way that empire was imagined by the 1870s revealed the drawing of ever sharper distinctions between the economic trajectory, social development and political status to which different regions could aspire. J. R. Seeley's famous denial that the 'kith and kin' settlements of 'Greater Britain' (the phrase was coined by Charles Dilke in 1869[1]) were an empire at all was one symptom of this. Indian demands for an equal place in what Dadabhai Naoroji called the 'imperial firm',[2] and the angry rejection of a constitutional status below the internal self-government enjoyed by most settler societies, showed how quickly the implications of this were detected elsewhere. Thirdly, from the late 1860s onwards, the British began to think more systematically about the defence of their widely scattered possessions. One committee (in 1867) enquired into the prospects of organising a 'Force of Asiatic Troops for General Service in Suitable Climates' (to replace British garrisons).[3] In the late 1870s, the Royal Commission on Colonial Defence, spurred on by the fear of Russian advance, debated what contribution the colonies should make to their own protection.[4] As the novel conception of 'imperial defence' began to take shape, India's role as the 'imperial strategic reserve' in the world east of Suez became the dominant element in British plans for its future. The pressures of world politics, like those of the new 'world economy' (whose emergence may be dated from c.1870), pushed and prodded the mid-Victorians' forward rush into the late Victorians' world-system

The geopolitics of expansion

Britain's global position after 1815 has often been seen as almost prodigally favourable in geopolitical terms: conferring free movement in almost any direction. It was certainly true that the era of world war between 1793 and 1815 had brought the British some remarkable winnings. They handed back Java and the other Dutch colonies in Southeast Asia as a dowry for the new Netherlands kingdom (modern Belgium and the Netherlands) that was meant to serve as the northern barrier to renewed French expansion. But they kept Ceylon (Sri Lanka), Mauritius and the Cape as a way of preventing the return of French sea-power to the Indian Ocean in any foreseeable future. In the Mediterranean, with their hands on the Ionian islands, and above all on Malta with its Grand Harbour, they could keep their navy in the eastern part of the sea astride the main maritime route to the Straits and Egypt. In the North Atlantic, they already controlled (in Halifax and the British Caribbean) the bases from which to watch the American seaboard. The collapse of Spain, and the client status of Portugal, had now opened the South Atlantic coast to British maritime influence in Brazil and La Plata and (with the occupation of the Falkland Islands in 1833) gave them a guard-post that commanded Cape Horn. In themselves, the territories that the British acquired were not of great value and had small or poor populations. But their geostrategic meaning was huge. Their capture by Britain signalled the end of the mercantilist order that had partitioned Europe's seaborne trade with the Americas and Asia between the closed economic empires of Spain, Portugal, the Netherlands, France and Britain. The age of 'free' trade was about to begin.

If the British had blasted open the path to unlimited commerce with the world beyond Europe, it also looked by the 1820s and 1830s as if the regimes at the far end of their long-distance sea-lanes had become more receptive, or at least more vulnerable, to their trade and diplomacy. In those decades, it seemed as if vast new worlds were now ready to be explored, exploited, colonised or converted. The successive opening up to travel and trade of Central and South America, the Niger, the South African interior, parts of the Middle East (especially Egypt), the Persian Gulf, Central Asia, New Zealand, the North Pacific and China promised a global revolution of which Britain was likely to be the main beneficiary. 'The situation of Great Britain', remarked a parliamentary committee in 1837, 'brings her beyond any other power into communication with the uncivilised nations of the earth.'[5] With command of the sea, a lion's share of inter-continental trade and a long lead in the use of industrial techniques, the British had the means (or so hindsight has often suggested) to make a universal empire along the lines they chose. With little to fear from any European rival, and the means to beat down any local resistance, they would become the hegemon, the invincible power.

A closer inspection makes for a more sober assessment. It was true that, since the naval triumph at Trafalgar, Britain's maritime strength made it hard for any other European state to attack its far-flung possessions by sea. The diplomacy of George Canning (British foreign minister, 1822–7) was intended to exploit this advantage and restrict Britain's European neighbours to the affairs of their continent. Britain alone of the European powers would have position and influence in the world beyond: this was why it was so urgent to establish friendly relations with the newly independent states in Latin America.[6] But, if Canning had hoped that Britain's command of the New World would allow it to cast off the burdens of the Old, his successors (Canning died in 1827) learned a different lesson. His pupil, Lord Palmerston, faced a series of crises in Europe that threatened most of the gains of 1815. After 1830, the Belgian revolt tore in half the Netherlands kingdom – the guard-dog created against French domination of the Low Countries (and the invasion route to Britain). Spain and Portugal, saved from Napoleon by Wellington's army, seemed likely to fall under conservative monarchs who would look to Austria, Russia or even to France rather than to Britain. The Ottoman Empire seemed about to break up, with Egypt and Syria falling to Mehemet Ali (suspected by London to be a client of France) and the rest of the empire – including the Straits – remaining under the sultan, now reduced by misfortune to dependence on Russia. Britain lacked the means to act decisively, however vital its interests in the Eastern Mediterranean. 'It was not in our power, already engaged in the affairs of Belgium and Portugal, to enter into a third business of this kind', the British prime minister told Palmerston in April 1833. 'We had no available force for such a [commitment] and I am quite sure that Parliament would not have granted us one.'[7] Instead, it was laborious diplomacy, the skilful exploitation of Russo-French rivalry and the mutual exhaustion of the local protagonists that brought Palmerston his triumph in 1840–1. Ottoman revival and Mehemet Ali's defeat restored the regional balance and secured the prime British interest in excluding any other great power from a dominant influence in the Eastern Mediterranean or on the land-bridge to India. In much the same way, Palmerston used the hostility of the 'Eastern Powers' (Prussia, Austria and Russia) towards France to entrench the independence and neutrality of the new Belgian state in the 1839 treaty.

The tense diplomacy of 1830–41 showed that British prestige and security, and the safety of their lines of communication with the outer world, depended upon an active diplomacy in Europe, not a passive enjoyment of Europe's internal divisions, let alone the assertion of London's irresistible will. In the world beyond Europe, as much as in Europe itself, British leaders had to reckon with the ambitions of three large states as eager as they were to extend the sphere of their influence. France, Russia and the United States, Palmerston told the House of Commons in 1858, were 'three great...powers...so far independent of naval warfare that even a naval reverse does not materially affect them'.[8] Each had the means to disrupt British influence or cut down its scope. Of the three, it was France that was the most potentially dangerous, although hopes of a liberal alliance – what Palmerston once called 'a Western Confederacy of free states'[9] – periodically lulled British suspicion that Napoleonic ambitions still lingered in Paris. But French influence and interests in Belgium, Spain and Italy, the occupation of Algiers (in 1830) and the special connection with Egypt were a constant factor in British diplomacy. The reputation and size of France's military machine, its volatile politics (with five regime changes between 1815 and 1851), its revolutionary tradition, and the influence derived from its enormous cultural prestige, made for uneasy and often irritable relations. 'Nothing can be settled in Europe or the Levant without war', the Duke of Wellington told Peel (then prime minister) in 1845, 'unless by good understanding with France; nor can any question be settled in other parts of the world, excepting by the good understanding between France and this country.'[10] French public opinion was thought dangerously febrile: 'a certain number of turbulent men, without profession, occupation or principles, idle and thoroughly demoralized, passing their time in reading newspapers and talking politics... give a fictitious character to public opinion', said Palmerston, quoting Guizot.[11] The French government, said Peel, had 'very little control over the popular will, and equally little over its servants, military, naval and diplomatic'.[12] That France was also a naval power, active in the Pacific, Southeast Asia and the Indian Ocean, increased the danger of collision and a storm in the press. A French squadron blockaded the River Plate estuary in the late 1830s. In the second Western war against China in 1856–60, the French presence in East Asia was as large as the British. More serious was the risk that France would exploit Anglo-American tensions. Most frightening of all, at least for a time, was the fear that the application of steam power would allow France to reverse Britain's historic naval advantage and open the way for a *Blitzkrieg* invasion.

Russia was not a colonial power in the maritime sense (except in Alaska, sold in 1867 to the United States). Its naval power outside

Europe was negligible. Russia had been the great counterweight to France in the struggle for Europe before 1815, to Britain's great benefit. By the 1820s, however, the renewal of Russia's southward expansion around the Black Sea, converging on the Straits, had become a major British obsession. The uncertain mood of the Ottoman government (often called 'the Porte' after the great gateway in Constantinople where its main offices were), the restless atmosphere of its European provinces and the open rebellion after 1830 of its over-mighty viceroy in Egypt, Mehemet Ali, all raised the prospect of a sudden implosion of Ottoman power. With the Tsar's armies a few forced marches away, he was likely to take a lion's share of the assets. With control of the Straits, the sympathy of Orthodox Greeks and Armenians (the main mercantile classes across the Near East), and a military grip on Eastern Anatolia, Russia would become the greatest power in the region, and the over-lordship of Persia would follow in due course. 'I take Nicholas to be ambitious, bent upon great schemes, determined to make extensive additions to his dominions and, animated by the same hatred to England which was felt by Napoleon . . .' was Palmerston's verdict in 1835.[13] Whether Nicholas I and his ministers were really committed to the grand geopolitical designs attributed to them now seems unlikely. As an imperial power, Russia suffered from several obvious weaknesses, not least a backward economy, appalling communications, undigested minorities and a brittle and overstretched government.[14] Knowing these defects, the Russians were afraid of encirclement and economic attrition and tried to pre-empt them. But Palmerston was not alone in believing that Russia had entered a critical phase in its pursuit of world power. 'Sooner or later', he told a cabinet colleague, 'the Cossak and the Sepoy, the man from the Baltic and he from the British islands will meet in the centre of Asia. It should be our business to make sure that the meeting is as far off from our Indian possessions as may be convenient.'[15] He hoped to exploit Russia's defeat in the Crimean War (achieved with the help of French military power,[16] not just to drive it away from the Straits but to expel it from the Caucasus, its gateway to Asia and the scene of savage war against the Chechen population. But there and in East Asia, where the Aigun treaty brought them closer to North China in the late 1850s, the Russians were already too strong to be fenced in in this way.

The threat posed by Russia in the Middle East, and, by extension, in Central Asia, acted as a magnet on British grand strategy, sucking the British towards risky forward commitments where their naval advantage was hard to deploy. In the western hemisphere they faced a quite different rival. The American republic was a white settler state, decentralised, populist and territorially avaricious on no less a scale than Russia or Britain. Its leaders were deeply suspicious of Britain and (in the South) fiercely resentful of the British attack on the slave trade and slavery. Britain 'is a great, opulent, and powerful nation', declared Henry Clay of Kentucky, 'but haughty, arrogant and supercilious. Not more separated from the rest of the world by the sea that girts her island than she is separated in feeling, sympathy or friendly consideration of their welfare.'[17] What the British called free trade 'is a mere revival of the British colonial system, forced upon us ... during the existence of our colonial vassalage'.[18] American opinion regarded Britain's colonial presence on the North American continent as an archaic survival, futile and absurd: the 1812 war had been fought in part to expel it. But the Americans' restless expansion was bound to impinge on spheres claimed or controlled by British-backed interests. In Oregon and on the Maine–New Brunswick border, an agreement became urgent in the mid-1840s. The Americans also suspected that the British meant to frustrate the absorption of Texas and California, both of them wrenched from Mexican hands, and had designs on Cuba, whose great harbour at Havana guarded the exit from the Gulf of Mexico, and the maritime highway between the Mississippi valley and Europe. 'We must have Cuba. We can't do without Cuba, [and] above all we must not suffer its transfer to Great Britain', intoned James Buchanan, Secretary of State in the late 1840s.[19] And, as Clay had implied, many Americans resented their dependence upon British industrial goods and favoured a protectionist tariff. Henry C. Carey, the most influential economist in antebellum America, denounced free trade as a disastrous deflection of progress, diverting labour and funds away from local development into costly long-distance commerce.[20]

The British were not helpless against American pressure. Their main point of weakness was the threat of an invasion of Canada (modern Ontario and Quebec) which was weakly defended and almost beyond the reach of reinforcements once winter set in and the St Lawrence River was frozen. But they had a deterrent: the use of naval power to bombard American sea-ports and blockade American trade. In the disputed Oregon country, there were few American settlers, while the Hudson's Bay Company, with its forts and followers, had a significant presence. Yet, although the threats flew and relations at times seemed close to a rupture, three powerful constraints discouraged British aggression. The first was the fear that an American conflict would encourage the other great powers – especially France – to join in against Britain: this was exactly what had happened in the Revolutionary War of 1775–83. Nervousness about France helped to push the British into settling the Oregon question to American satisfaction in 1846.[21] The second was the belief that (as Palmerston pointed out in 1858) British sea-power would be of only limited value if it came to a fight. The best the British could do in periods of tension was to reinforce their Canadian garrison to show they meant business.[22] The third was the sense that an American war, however successful, would be self-defeating. It was no coincidence that the emissary sent to resolve the boundary dispute over Maine was Lord Ashburton, a senior member of the Baring family and a banker with wide American contacts (he had helped to negotiate the Louisiana Purchase in 1803). Blockading American trade would inflict spectacular damage on the British economy. Thus the balance of strength in North America, while far from one-sided, decisively moulded the shape of British expansion. It set strict limits to the territorial growth of British North America and made its prosperity dependent in part on the economic goodwill of its great southern neighbour. Secondly, it ruled out any chance of coercing America into adopting free trade. The commercial and industrial power of the 'Old Northeast', centred on New York, was already a rival to that of Britain itself.[23] A high tariff barrier checked British exports and steadily increased the imbalance of trade in America's favour. And it was from New York, not London or Liverpool, that the trade of the 'Cotton Kingdom' (Lancashire's great partner) was managed.[24] In this richest of continents, the 'imperialism of free trade' had been stopped in its tracks.

Of course, there were places where the British had little to fear from the interference of France, Russia or the United States, although fewer perhaps than appeared at first sight. Palmerston ruled out the invasion of Persia (to stop it seizing Afghan Herat) in 1838 on the ground that it would only drive the shah closer to Russia. Instead, Afghanistan was to be 'saved' by an invasion from India – a costly calamity. Once the Russians were entrenched to the north of Manchuria, their reluctance to support the Anglo-French coercion of Peking eased the pressure on the Manchu court.[25] Even where and when

the British were free to apply their military power, they had to weigh up
its costs against any possible gain. Their great asset was the Navy. Most
of its powerful units had to be kept at home or in the Mediterranean to
watch the French and the Russians. But, with nearly 200 ships, there
were plenty to spare. A squadron blockaded the River Plate estuary
between 1843 and 1846. Brazil was blockaded in the 1850s to enforce
a ban on the slave trade.[26] Twenty gunboats on average patrolled the
West African coast to stop the still-vigorous slave trade. The British
assembled a fleet of forty ships (including numerous steamers) to force
open China's trade in the first opium war.[27] Yet naval power had its
limitations. It could bombard, blockade and police the sea-lanes. But
bombardment was risky and required heavy-weight firepower. A blockade was as likely to damage British trade as to check errant rulers.[28]
The slave trade patrol produced embarrassingly feeble results: in the
four years after 1864, it caught a total of nine slaves. The most striking
success was perhaps against China in 1840–2. This was not because
naval force could be used directly against the Ch'ing government. But,
by entering the Yangtse and seizing its junction with the Grand Canal,
the British could paralyse China's internal commerce and bring the
Emperor to terms.

Away from the sea, the spearhead of power, and its last resort,
was the British regular army. Its strength had drifted upwards from
109,000 in 1829 to 140,000 by 1847.[29] Between 25,000 and 33,000
men were usually stationed in India (the number rose sharply during the Mutiny) as the praetorian guard of Company rule. A smaller
number, perhaps 18,000, were at home in Britain. Much of the rest
was scattered in packets across the colonies and Ireland (where around
18,000 men were normally kept[30]). This system depended, remarked
an experienced general, on 'our naval superiority, and our means of
conveying troops with great rapidity from one part of the world to
another, which multiplies, as it were, the strength of our army'.[31] Even
so, it was thinly stretched. Between 5,000 and 6,000 men defended
Britain's North American provinces. In the Cape Colony, the 400-mile
frontier, where raiding and reprisal were constant between whites and
blacks, was guarded by a single battalion of infantry too encumbered
with equipment to chase cross-border intruders.[32] Its reinforcement was
600 miles away in Cape Town and the whites in the region depended
instead on their local commandos (volunteer bands of notorious ferocity) for defence and revenge. Twelve hundred men sent to New Zealand

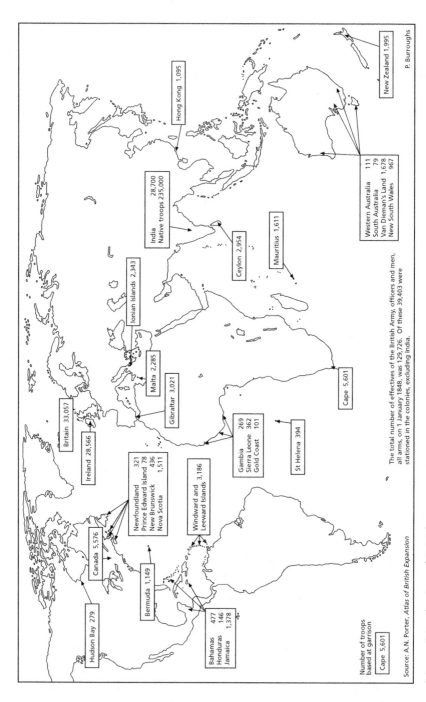

Number of troops based at garrison

| Cape | 5,601 |

| Hudson Bay | 279 |

| Canada | 5,576 |

| Bermuda | 1,149 |

Bahamas	477
Honduras	146
Jamaica	1,378

Newfoundland	321
Prince Edward Island	78
New Brunswick	436
Nova Scotia	1,511

| Windward and Leeward Islands | 3,186 |

| Britain | 33,057 |

| Ireland | 28,566 |

| Ionian Islands | 2,343 |

| Malta | 2,285 |

| Gibraltar | 3,021 |

Gambia	269
Sierra Leone	362
Gold Coast	101

| St Helena | 394 |

| Cape | 5,601 |

| Hong Kong | 1,095 |

| India | 28,700 |
| Native troops | 235,000 |

| Ceylon | 2,954 |

| Mauritius | 1,611 |

Western Australia	111
South Australia	79
Van Dieman's Land	1,678
New South Wales	967

| New Zealand | 1,995 |

The total number of effectives of the British Army, officers and men, all arms, on 1 January 1848, was 129,726. Of these 39,403 were stationed in the colonies, excluding India.

P. Burroughs

Source: A.N. Porter, *Atlas of British Expansion*

Map 1 Distribution of British troops, 1848

in 1845 fought a pitched battle with Maori at Ruapekapeka in the North Island, but lacked the strength to compel their acceptance of British authority.[33] In effect, the army was a collection of garrisons whose main purpose was to protect the colonies from attack by an imperial rival or a revolt from within (as in Ireland, French Canada and British-ruled India). Fifty thousand men were scraped together in 1854 for the Anglo-French assault on Sebastopol, but, with that inglorious exception, the offensive power of the British on land was really pivoted on India, where the Company maintained an enormous army (until after the Mutiny of 1857) of some 200,000 men. The British regiments there could be combined with sepoy battalions to form a respectable force. Of the ten thousand men sent to China in 1842, the larger part were Indians. In the second China war (just after the Mutiny), they made up just under half of the British contingent. It was from India that expeditions could also be mounted into Persia, Afghanistan, Burma and Abyssinia. It was India that made the British a military and not just a naval power – but a military power whose active sphere was almost entirely confined to the world south and east of Suez.

In the 1830s and 1840s, we can see that a certain geopolitical 'logic' was imposing a shape on Britain's place in the world. In the official view from London, Europe bulked largest and posed the most danger. No set of ministers was likely to forget the lesson of what was still called the 'Great War'. Their first priority was to preserve the chief gain of 1815 – and prevent the rise of a European hegemon. For all his bluster, Palmerston stood on the defensive in Europe, watching apprehensively over the Low Countries, Portugal, Spain and the Eastern Mediterranean. In North America, too, the British watchword was caution, lest the populist anarchy of American politics unleash an invasion which they would have to repel – perhaps at a difficult moment. Naval power was deployed on the South American coast in the 1840s and 1850s. But its utility in extending British influence there was open to question. The blockade of Brazil forced a stop on the slave trade but failed to induce a more liberal tariff.[34] There was little enthusiasm for using military power to advance the colonial frontier. When the cost of the South African garrison shot up to over £1 million in the late 1840s (as a result of its frontier wars), London quickly abandoned the highveld interior to the Boer republics. When Whitehall gave way to the urgent request from New Zealand in the mid-1860s, and sent 10,000 men to crush Maori resistance, it did so expecting the cost to be borne by the settler government in Wellington and was enraged when it was not.[35] Only in the sphere where Indian power (both naval and military since the Persian Gulf was patrolled by the Bombay Marine and it was Company steamers that were sent to China in 1842) was available to them could British governments take the lead in advancing British influence. Even there (as we have seen) the limits of action were narrow. Almost everywhere else, the task of building an empire, whether formal or not, fell to private interests at home and to the 'men on the spot'.

Making Empire at home: domestic sources of British expansion

Commerce

'The great object of the Government in every quarter of the world was to extend the commerce of the country', Palmerston told Parliament in 1839.[36] This was not a new doctrine. The close inter-relation between power and profit was proverbial wisdom. Few public men would have denied the connection between overseas trade and Britain's strength as a state. The contribution of trade to taxable wealth, to Britain's ability to subsidise allies in wartime, and to the vital reserve of skilled naval manpower, was well understood. Without overseas trade, empire was redundant, a futile extravagance. Trade was the source of most colonies' revenue and helped to defray the cost of their garrisons. It could also be seen as a great arm of influence. 'Not a bale of merchandise leaves our shores', Richard Cobden declared in 1836, 'but it bears the seeds of intelligence and fruitful thought to the members of some less enlightened community . . . [O]ur steamboats and our miraculous railways are the advertisements and vouchers of our enlightened institutions.'[37] In the 1830s and 1840s, the expansion of overseas trade took on a new urgency. New markets were needed for the swiftly rising production of textiles and ironware, to avert depression, unemployment and strife in industrial districts. Britain's domestic tranquillity required the growth of its trade.

The leading role in promoting the expansion of trade was played not by governments but by merchant houses, especially those based in the largest ports: London, Liverpool and Glasgow. The sum of their efforts might be likened to creating a vast commercial republic, embracing Britain's empire but much else beyond. Its scale can be seen in the statistics for exports whose nominal value had risen from some £38 million in 1830 to £60 million in 1845 and £122 million by 1857. They were matched by the fourfold increase between 1834 and 1860 in the tonnage of shipping that used British ports.[38] From its old concentration in the Atlantic basin, British mercantile enterprise had spread round the world by the mid-nineteenth century. In the late 1840s, a census revealed around 1,500 British 'houses' abroad, nearly 1,000 outside the European mainland, with 41 in Buenos Aires alone.[39] The most notable feature of this commercial expansion, apart from the overall increase in volume, was the shift towards markets in Asia and the Near East (up from 11 per cent of exports in 1825 to nearly 26 per cent in 1860) and in Africa and Australasia (up from 2 per cent to over 11 per cent).

The speed with which British merchants moved out to search for new business, their success in constructing new commercial connections and their dominant position in long-distance trade made Britain *the* great economic power of the nineteenth-century world. This great expansionist movement arose from the junction of favourable forces already apparent by the mid-1830s. British merchants were the immediate gainers from the opening of the trade of Brazil and Spanish America during the Napoleonic War: indeed, wartime Brazil had been virtually a British protectorate. The release of British trade with India (1813), the Near East (1825) and China (1833) from the regime of chartered monopolies encouraged a flood of new enterprise. The rapid development of the American economy after 1815 was another huge benefit. With its favoured position at a maritime crossroads (where the shortest transatlantic route crossed the seaway linking the north and south of Europe), Britain became the main entrepot for the New World's trade with the Old – just as it was for the seaborne trade between Europe and Asia until the cutting of the Suez Canal in 1869. By 1815, London had replaced Amsterdam as the financial centre of Europe, partly because of the wartime blockade of the European mainland, partly because it had been at the centre of a Europe-wide web of war loans and subsidies. The supply of long credit on easy terms from London was the key to business with regions where the local financing of long-distance trade was underdeveloped or lacking. Above all, by the 1830s, with the arrival of power-weaving, the British could undercut competition across the whole range of cotton manufactures (the most widely traded commodity), and break into new markets with products as much as two hundred times cheaper than the local supply.

The main agent of commerce was the commission merchant, usually in partnership. He took goods on consignment from manufacturers at home and a share of the sale price when a buyer was found. In the 1830s and 1840s, there were powerful incentives to search hard for new outlets. Although Britain's industrial output was growing, nearby markets in Europe were either closed altogether against foreign industrial goods, restricted by tariffs or comparatively stagnant. Some manufacturers gave merchants a free hand to sell at cost price or less – a form of dumping.⁴⁰ Armed with cheap credit, equipped with cheap goods, the merchants searched for customers wherever opportunity offered. Of course, the conditions they found were bound to vary enormously, and so did their methods. Henry Francis Fynn, a ship's supercargo, went ashore at Delagoa Bay in 1822 and paddled up-river, looking for ivory to exchange with his trinkets and bolts of cloth.⁴¹ As late as the 1880s, some trade in West Africa was still conducted from ships sailing along the coast, waiting for locals to venture out through the surf.⁴² Few British traders ventured far inland or were allowed to do so by African middlemen resentful of interlopers. Much of Britain's trade with the United States was soon in the hands of American merchants: the role of the British was to supply the finance, to become 'merchant bankers'.⁴³ In Latin America, British merchants sometimes went into partnership with local Creole merchants to widen their contacts and enlist local finance. In Brazil, British merchants quickly established a dominant position in the sugar and coffee trades, Brazil's principal exports.⁴⁴ In Canada, the fusion of the Hudson's Bay Company and its Montreal rival, the North West Company, in 1821 built a powerful nexus of Anglo-Canadian businessmen including Edward 'Bear' Ellice (Palmerston's *bête noire*), Andrew Colville, Sir George Simpson, Alexander Wedderburn (brother-in-law of the Earl of Selkirk), Curtis Lampson (a key figure in the laying of the Atlantic cable and grandfather of the proconsul Miles Lampson, Lord Killearn) and Alexander Matheson, nephew of the co-founder of Jardine Matheson, a Bank of England director, and the biggest fish in the China trade. In India, British merchants were usually partners in one of the 'agency houses' to be found in Calcutta and Madras, whose original purpose had been to remit home the earnings (one might almost say 'winnings') of the East India Company's 'servants'. Agency houses dealt with imports and exports but also acted as bankers to Europeans working in India and managed plantations and processing plants (in jute or indigo) for their European owners. Agency houses spread from India into Burma and other parts of Southeast Asia in the first half of the century. When direct British trade with China (and the right to buy tea) ceased to be an East India Company monopoly after 1833, British houses (with Jardine Matheson in the van) were quickly set up there.[45]

This furious commercial activity had created by mid-century a worldwide network of international business centred on Liverpool, Glasgow and, above all, London. The extension of trade brought with it shipping, insurance and banking, managed and financed by allied mercantile interests or by the merchants themselves. It built up a huge fund of 'commercial intelligence' – market information – and widened the circuits along which it travelled: business letters, reports, local chambers of commerce and globe-trotting businessmen. Since every market was different, there was no single objective and no unified lobby. The main merchant demands were protection from warfare or pirates – largely secured by Britain's command of the seas outside Europe; 'free' trade – meaning the right to trade in overseas markets on the same terms as locals; and 'improvements' – usually investment in canals, roads or railways. British exporters complained bitterly at the miserly spending of the East India Company's government on railways and roads, which they blamed for the shortage of return cargoes from India and the slow growth of their trade. The 'Canadian' interest grasped soon enough that Montreal's future depended on railways, if it was to survive the end of imperial preference in the late 1840s.[46]

The British government's role in building the 'commercial republic' was not insignificant, but it was bound to be limited. As Palmerston claimed, it was keen to advance the sphere of free trade abroad. Through treaties of commerce, it sought to protect British merchants and their property from unfair or discriminatory treatment, and to obtain 'most favoured nation' status – the right for British goods to enter on terms at least as good as those enjoyed by the 'most favoured' foreign state. The treaty system and Britain's naval presence (the world's seas were divided into eight overseas 'stations') gave British merchants unprecedented freedom to trade, but no guarantee of success. 'Free trade imperialism', in the sense of intervention by London, largely functioned in this indirect mode. For five years in mid-century when a detailed count was kept, gunboats were sent to protect commercial interests *outside* the Empire in a bare handful of cases, usually against the threat of violent disorder.[47] But there were three important exceptions to this hands-off policy. First, government subsidy for the carriage of mail encouraged the rapid expansion of scheduled steamship services across the Atlantic, to South America and to India and the Far East. Secondly, as we have noticed already, the Navy maintained a flotilla of some twenty gunboats on the coast of West Africa. Palmerston declaimed on the need to use force there in the interests of trade. 'Cudgels & Sabres & Carbines are necessary to keep quiet the ill-disposed People whose violence would render Trade insecure', ran a vehement minute.[48] But of course the targets of Palmerston's cudgel were the slave traders who tried to drive out the 'legitimate' trade that threatened their own. The gunboats were meant to keep them at bay until the trade in palm oil and other commodities was strong enough to destroy them. Here was a case where commerce sub-served the great moral obsession of Victorian Britain. Thirdly, there was China.

China was much the most striking case where military power was used in the interests of trade. Under heavy pressure from the merchant lobby, and fearing a huge claim to compensate them for the opium that the Chinese had seized, London despatched an expeditionary force in 1840 to demand reparations and win commercial concessions. The treaty of Nanking in 1842 opened half a dozen 'treaty-ports' where British merchants were exempt from Chinese jurisdiction, laid down a maximum tariff that the Chinese could levy on imports and transferred the huge harbour at Hong Kong (then still a village) to the British. After the second opium war (1856–60), the list of ports was extended and the Chinese interior opened to foreign travel. To uphold these rights, the British maintained a fleet of between thirty and forty ships, most of them gunboats, to police the coasts and rivers against pirates, anti-foreign disturbances and uncooperative officials.[49] The commitment seems surprising since the volume of trade remained comparatively modest even late in the century – far below the levels of Britain's India trade. The answer may lie in a curious set of coincidences. Intervention took place at a moment of intense concern about British markets abroad and when the commercial promise of China was wildly inflated (a recurrent phenomenon for more than a century). 'The nation who, but for the existence of certain restrictions on trade, would probably buy the greatest amount of English manufactured goods are . . . the Chinese', claimed Edward Gibbon Wakefield in 1834.[50] Commercial access to China, as it turned out, could only be gained through the consular enclaves and extraterritorial rights to which Peking agreed, both of them subject to constant local attrition. It was India that provided the available means to secure British claims, and India that had a big interest in doing so. British trade in China was largely an outgrowth of the India trade: 'East India' merchants sent Indian opium and cotton to China to buy tea and silk. But the opium itself was a government monopoly, and the revenue from it made up nearly one-fifth of the Indian government's income. The amount exported to China rose astronomically in the 1840s and 1850s.[51] Here, profit and power were inextricably linked. Nor did it seem that the periodic coercion of China would be costly or difficult. When Lord Elgin was sent east in 1857 to demand a new treaty after the breakdown of relations at Canton, he was initially given a mere handful of troops and told to rely upon naval action (to cut the river above Canton and block the Grand Canal) to force Peking to terms. 'It is not the intention of Her Majesty's Government to undertake any land operations in the interior of the country', London grandly declared.[52]

Migrants and missions

The search for new markets in the Outer World was the most obvious expression of British expansion. But it was allied to two others. The first was migration. After 1830, the number of migrants from Britain rose steadily: 1832 was the first year in which more than 100,000 departed for destinations beyond Europe.[53] The United States was much the most popular choice, especially for the huge outflow of Irish after the Famine. But British North America, Australia and (after 1840) New Zealand also attracted a significant number. Perhaps the commonest method was through 'chain migration' when an 'advance party' created the links (and perhaps remitted the means) to bring over friends and family.[54] But migration was also a business, and perhaps even a 'craze'. Migration societies spread propaganda and fired enthusiasm.[55] The 'idea' of migration as a road to self-betterment became increasingly popular. There were also the land companies that sprang up in the 1820s and 1830s, to channel this movement and turn it into a profit. Their aim was to buy land (cheaply) from its indigenous owners (or a colonial government) and resell it (dearly) to settlers whom they recruited in Britain. The Swan River Settlement (in which Robert Peel's brother had an interest), the Australian Agricultural Company, the Van Diemen's Land Company, the Western Australian Company, the Canada Company and the British American Land Company were all of this type. The interest in such ventures was fuelled in part by social

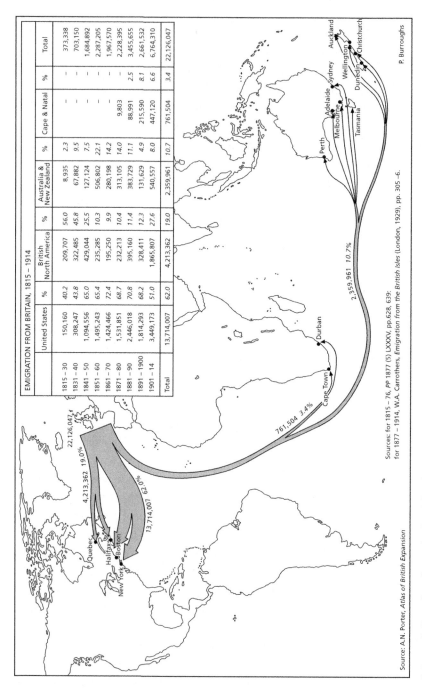

EMIGRATION FROM BRITAIN, 1815 – 1914								
	United States	%	British North America	%	Australia & New Zealand	%	Cape & Natal	%	Total
1815 – 30	150,160	40.2	209,707	56.0	8,935	2.3	–	–	373,338
1831 – 40	308,247	43.8	322,485	45.8	67,882	9.5	–	–	703,150
1841 – 50	1,094,556	65.0	429,044	25.5	127,124	7.5	–	–	1,684,892
1851 – 60	1,495,243	65.4	235,285	10.3	506,802	22.1	–	–	2,287,205
1861 – 70	1,424,466	72.4	195,250	9.9	280,198	14.2	–	–	1,967,570
1871 – 80	1,531,851	68.7	232,213	10.4	313,105	14.0	9,803	–	2,228,395
1881 – 90	2,446,018	70.8	395,160	11.4	383,729	11.1	88,991	2.5	3,455,655
1891 – 1900	1,814,293	68.2	328,411	12.3	131,629	4.9	215,590	8.1	2,661,532
1901 – 14	3,449,173	51.0	1,865,807	27.6	540,557	8.0	447,120	6.6	6,764,310
Total	13,714,007	62.0	4,213,362	19.0	2,359,961	10.7	761,504	3.4	22,126,047

Sources: for 1815 – 76, PP 1877 (5) LXXXV, pp.628, 639;
for 1877 – 1914, W.A. Carrothers, *Emigration from the British Isles* (London, 1929), pp. 305 – 6.

P. Burroughs

Source: A.N. Porter, *Atlas of British Expansion*

Map 2 Migration from the British Isles, 1815–1914

anxiety. 'Colonisation' was a way of relieving economic distress, directly by removing unneeded labour, indirectly (as Edward Gibbon Wakefield argued) by creating new consumers abroad. It was no coincidence that some of the most ardent free traders (like Sir William Molesworth) were also drawn into the colonisation business. The South Australian Association was a highly successful lobby that won government support for a new settlement colony to which more than 10,000 migrants were sent in its first few years. Even more daring was Wakefield's New Zealand Association (1837), which successfully forced the British government's hand into annexing the islands.[56] Its patrons included some of the greatest and best, among them Lord Durham, cabinet minister, ambassador and the special commissioner into the Canadian rebellions of 1837–8. It promised, among other things, to save 'the native inhabitants' from the evils inflicted by the disreputable Europeans already in the country.[57] Not all were convinced. 'This beautiful compound of the mercantile and the merciful', sneered *The Times*, 'will occasion a brisk demand for religious tracts and ball-cartridges.'[58]

The colonisation movement, unofficial and private as well as organised and official (the Colonial Land and Emigration Commission was set up in 1840 mainly to subsidise migration to Australia from colonial land revenues), advanced in parallel with the great expansion of trade. It threw out dozens of settlements, often small and isolated, whose strongest links were with their parent communities in the British Isles, the source of their manpower, exiguous capital and religious identity. Tiny outposts, like those of the Scots on Cape Breton, lonely New Plymouth in New Zealand's North Island,[59] the even more lonely Kaipara,[60] as well as the larger and better known colonies in Upper Canada, New South Wales, Victoria, Otago and Canterbury, were all part of a web of human connections to which almost every part of the British Isles was linked. If commercial expansion helped breed a demand for 'free' trade, demographic expansion evoked a cry for 'free' land. The right of the British to settle abroad became as much part of their 'birthright' as the right to trade without let or hindrance. In the twenty-one years after 1850, an annual average of more than 200,000 people migrated abroad.[61] By that time, the idea of overseas settlement as amounting almost to a providential duty was becoming deeply entrenched. 'The great object and purpose of England in colonising was the multiplication of her race', declaimed W. E. Gladstone in

1852. 'Whatever course of legislation tended most to the rapid expansion of population and power, in [Britain's] colonies, necessarily tended
to enhance the reflected benefits that she was to derive from their
foundation.'[62] There was a wide consensus in Britain, claimed Edward
Cardwell thirteen years later, about 'the great advantage of having
these free, industrious and enterprising communities sharing their own
blood, their own language, and their own laws, settled over the whole
world'.[63]

Migrant and mercantile interests could mobilise a wide if
fragmented constituency to support the extension of British influence. So, for different reasons, could missionary societies. The most
important of these were the Baptist Missionary Society, founded in
1792, the inter-denominational London Missionary Society (1795), the
(Anglican) Church Missionary Society (1799), the British Foreign and
Bible Society (1804) and the Wesleyan Missionary Society (1813).
Launched on a wave of evangelical enthusiasm, the societies were carried by the surge of popular religiosity and the patriotic feeling of
wartime. It was 'artisans, petty shopkeepers and labourers who made
up the bulk of the missionary workforce'.[64] 'Is it presumptuous', asked
the annual report of the Church Missionary Society in 1812, 'to indulge
the humble and pious hope that to Great Britain may be entrusted the
high commission of making known the name of Jesus to the whole
world?'[65] In 1813, in a signal victory, the societies forced the East India
Company to fund a church establishment and admit missionaries freely
to its territories on the sub-continent. By 1821, the societies had a collective income of over £250,000 a year.[66] By 1824, the Church Missionary
Society alone had sent abroad more than 100 missionaries.[67] By 1848,
it had over 100 stations and had recruited some 350 missionaries.[68]

Between the 1820s and the 1840s, the missionary frontier was
as dynamic as the mercantile. In South Africa, a survey between 1838
and 1840 counted eighty-five stations, most of them run by the London
Missionary Society or the Wesleyans.[69] In New Zealand, where Samuel
Marsden had arrived in 1814, well before annexation in 1840, more
than sixty stations were active by the 1840s.[70] In the same decade,
missionary enterprise in West Africa was carried along the coast from
its old bridgehead in Sierra Leone to Yorubaland in modern Nigeria,
where a station was founded at Abeokuta, and into the Niger delta at
Calabar.[71] Johan Krapf landed at Zanzibar in January 1844 to open
the campaign for souls in East Africa. By that time, the greatest prize

of all seemed within reach. The first resident Protestant missionary in China had been Robert Morison, who was sent to Canton in 1807 by the London Missionary Society.[72] But the real missionary–king of the China coast was the anglicised German Karl (Charles) Gutzlaff. Gutzlaff had gone first to the Dutch East Indies where he made contact with Chinese traders whose junks still carried much of the commerce of Southeast Asia. In 1831, he made the hazardous journey up the China coast (then forbidden to European travellers) as far north as Tientsin, the port for Peking, and ingratiated himself with the local authorities by his medical skills. By the time he returned to Macao (to which European traders were required to withdraw at the end of the trading season in Canton), he had acquired a wider knowledge of contemporary China and Chinese than any other Westerner, and a brimming faith in the scope for conversion. His *Journal of Three Voyages along the Coast of China* (1834) was a sensation. A Gutzlaff Association was formed. It was Gutzlaff's ingenious formula of the medical missionary, and the glamour of bringing China to Christ that inspired the young David Livingstone: only the opium war and the temporary cessation of missionaries to China diverted him to Africa in 1841. But, with the treaty of Nanking in 1842, a new era had opened for missionaries as well as merchants: the following year, the Protestant mission organisations in East Asia met in Hong Kong to share the field between them.[73] The total of Chinese converts was tiny (six in 1842, 350 ten years later[74]); enthusiasm at home was to flag before it revived; and the missionary effort (as much American as British, Catholic as well as Protestant) was battered by the storms that swept over South and Central China in the 1850s. But it was missionary enterprise as much as commercial that defined the British presence in the Ch'ing empire.

By the later 1840s, the missionary societies had mapped out a vast field of operations. 'Contrast... the present openness of the whole world to missionary enterprise', exulted the Church Missionary Society, recalling the era when India had been barred, New Zealand 'shunned' and the Caribbean blacks 'crushed'.[75] At home they could draw on a reservoir of popular sympathy organised through the evangelical societies into a private army of millions, 'ready', said a correspondent in *Blackwood's* in 1824, 'to take the field at a moment's notice'.[76] The *Missionary Register*, one of several missionary organs, had over 120,000 subscribers in 1826.[77] Exeter Hall was opened in 1831 for the annual meeting of the societies, whose attendance ran into the thousands. Gentlemanly evangelicals were found in cabinet and Parliament. Missionary publications – autobiography, propaganda and travel (like John Phillip's *Researches in South Africa*, 1828) – shaped public knowledge of remote places. No one did more to arouse public enthusiasm than David Livingstone (1813–73), the missionary-explorer of South Central Africa. Livingstone's ardent evangelism, his epic crossing of Africa (1852–6), and his passionate attack on the Arab and Portuguese slave trades, evoked intense public sympathy. Livingstone's own writings, full of danger and hope, and his keen sense of publicity, reinforced the effect. By the late 1850s, he was a great public figure. His lectures at Oxford and Cambridge led to the founding of a new Anglican mission, the Universities Mission to Central Africa. His vehement campaign against the East African slave trade forced the government in London to fund a 'Zambezi expedition' to open the river to 'legitimate' trade. Livingstone himself was received by the Queen. At a great farewell banquet of over 300 guests in February 1858, he lectured his hosts (some of the great men of the day) on their self-evident duty. 'Should we be able', he told them, 'to open a communication advantageous to ourselves with the natives of the interior of Africa, it would be our great duty to confer upon them the great benefits of Christianity which have been bestowed upon ourselves' – a demand greeted with cheers.[78] 'Were your lordship in power', he wrote to Lord Palmerston the following year, 'I would strongly urge free trade to be secured on the Zambezi.'[79]

Of course, missionary enterprise could be an awkward partner with other forms of British enterprise. Missionaries often depended on traders – Gutzlaff had sailed on ships selling opium. In New Zealand, they sold muskets and speculated in land. Sometimes, they took public office or acted as intermediaries between colonial rule and indigenous peoples. But, in other ways, their 'version' of empire conflicted with the interests of merchants, settlers and officialdom, and their networks of information and lobbying competed with those of their secular rivals for public support. For more than most outsiders, missionaries depended upon the goodwill of their hosts. They needed local sponsorship, better still an invitation from authority.[80] Missionary strategy envisaged not the indefinite tutelage of subject peoples but the rapid creation of a native clergy. In West Africa, the most dynamic missionary leaders were the part-African Thomas Freeman and the Yoruba Samuel Crowther.[81] Christian conversion worked best where missionaries helped to rebuild local communities fragmented by ethnic conflict or the fall-out from European expansion. 'The great bane of Africa', wrote the South African missionary statesman, Dr John Phillip, 'is the minute fractions into which its tribes have been broken up by the Slave Trade; we have here materials for a viable building but nothing can be done towards it till the fragments are joined together. The Gospel is the only instrument by which this means can be accomplished.'[82]

British protection should be extended over neighbouring peoples (he had the Xhosa in mind), but they should become British subjects and their lands secured against settler incursion. Britain's true interest lay in fringing its borders with independent black nations sharing a common Christian civilisation.[83] Far from conceding that the missions depended on empire, Phillip insisted that the reverse was the case. Missionaries, he urged, 'are . . . extending British interests, British influence and the British empire . . . [E]very genuine convert . . . made to the Christian religion becomes the ally and friend of the colonial government.'[84] To much missionary opinion, the greatest obstacle to conversion was the contamination of their flock by the vices and desires of itinerant traders and land-hungry settlers. 'The White Man's intercourse has demoralised them, his traffic has defrauded them, his alliances have betrayed them, and his wars have destroyed them', the Aborigine Protection Society told Lord Glenelg in 1838. 'They have thus lost the virtues of the savage without acquiring those of the Christian.'[85] 'The great intercourse with the Shipping', raged the New Zealand missionary Henry Williams in 1831, 'is the curse of the land.'[86] For many missionaries, then and later, spiritual salvation could only be assured by physical segregation.

Mercantile, migrant and missionary interests in mid-Victorian Britain were eager to enlarge the commercial, colonised and religious spheres where British enterprise was dominant and British influence unchallenged. Their restlessness, aggression, economic dynamism and spiritual 'energy' were given force and direction by the peculiar conjuncture that formed early and mid-Victorian society. This was, first of all, a society in the throes of unprecedented mobility, stimulated in part by the differential effects of economic change (driving people off the land, expanding towns and cities) and accentuated by the new means of travel. By 1870, every sizeable town in Britain had a railway station, and the network itself (at 13,000 miles) was the densest in Europe. Industrialism had created the means as well as the motive for migration – within Britain, beyond Britain – on a scale undreamt of before the 1830s. It transformed the geographical space within which people in the British Isles could imagine their lives. Secondly, while Britain had long been a 'polite and commercial' society, the growth of new industries alongside old trading connections, the rapid integration of the national economy (partly through railways), and the appearance of new urban societies where social bonds and identities were being remade, created a more intensely competitive and commercialised society, or perhaps more accurately one where a competitive and commercial ethos was ever more widely diffused. We should not listen too much to the lamentations of contemporaries regretting the end of deference (or migrants in exile bemoaning the rise and rise of conspicuous consumption[87]), but the census records give some indirect indication of how quickly commerce was expanding as an occupation. In 1851, there were just under 44,000 'commercial clerks'; twenty years later, the number had more than doubled (as had the number of merchant seamen). Thirdly, the velocity with which information and ideas could circulate, as well as the volume that the 'information circuits' could carry, was also increasing dramatically. Letters and packets that were transported by steam and at hugely reduced cost were part of the story and so was the telegraph. Newspapers and 'monthlies' extended their reach. By 1870, the leading London dailies sold together some 400,000 copies, and dailies were printed in forty-three provincial towns. The number of books published rose by 400 per cent between 1840 and 1870.[88] Societies sprang up to disseminate knowledge (like the Royal Geographical Society, founded in 1830), drawing their subscribers in part from those with utilitarian, not to say mercenary, objects in mind. The scope for publicity, advertisement and pressure-group politics were all enlarged with this industrial production of knowledge. Lastly, economic and social change, far from making Victorian Britain a more homogeneous society, reinforced its pluralism, empowered its interest groups and intensified the sense of spiritual and cultural as well as social struggle. The arena of struggle was, at least partly, to be found abroad. The search for escape from social oppression and hardship, the projects of those who envisaged ideal societies in distant 'new Britains', the hopes of those who sought spiritual uplift by saving the heathen, and the enthusiasms of those pursuing humanitarian goals, scientific knowledge or private adventure supplied much of the energy for 'British expansion'.

This is not to argue that Victorian society was dynamic enough by itself to carve out a world empire. It did not have to be. The new social energy that it generated was injected into the husk of an older empire and supercharged the commercial networks that had already grown up in the Atlantic basin. Both left their mark. Victorian imperialism was thus a curious fusion of mercantilist ambitions and free trade assumptions, 'nabob' morality and Evangelical high-thinking, an eighteenth-century 'estate' and nineteenth-century 'improvements'. There is a second limitation on what Victorian society could achieve by itself. It projected its influence all over the world and with particular force into those regions where it met less resistance from an organised state, an existing 'high culture' or a developed economy. But the scale and scope of British world power was bound to depend not only on the manpower, money and produce that flowed out from Britain, but also on the extent to which they could leverage more local resources. It was at the 'bridgehead' that the question was settled: how and in what form the agents of British expansion could command a hinterland, build a new state and harness its wealth to the imperial project.

Bridgeheads of empire

The most visible evidence of Britain's power in the world by the mid-nineteenth century was the extraordinary scale of its territorial possessions in North America, the South Pacific, Southern Africa and India. At opposite ends of the globe lay two large bundles of settlement colonies: six in North America (Newfoundland, Nova Scotia, New Brunswick, Prince Edward Island, 'Canada' – modern Ontario and Quebec – and British Columbia) and seven in Australasia (New South Wales, Tasmania, Western Australia, South Australia, Victoria, Queensland and New Zealand). In both these vast regions, it was Britain's naval and military power that was the main safeguard against foreign invasion – American, French or, less plausibly, Russian (although fear of Russian attack reached fever pitch in Melbourne during the Crimean War). But neither British strength nor wealth was the primary cause of their rapid development as semi-autonomous colonial states with standards of living as high if not higher than the 'mother-country' at home.

The key role had been played by their colonial elites, even before they had wrested full internal self-government from the Colonial Office in London. The North American colonies had had a headstart. Halifax (founded 1749) and Montreal (captured 1760) had attracted merchants from the Thirteen Colonies to the south. After 1783, they were reinforced by loyalist exiles who brought mercantile knowledge as well as artisan skills and a hunger for land. New Brunswick developed quickly as a producer of timber, the main source of wealth, employment and population growth. The leading lumber firm in Saint John, that also built ships and traded with the British West Indies, was founded by refugees from New York.[89] Samuel Cunard, founder of the shipping line and a dominant figure in Nova Scotia's economy by the 1830s, was the son of a Pennsylvania loyalist whose burgeoning business empire he inherited. The commercial success of British North America's port-cities attracted merchants from Britain. Hugh Allan arrived in Montreal from Glasgow in the 1820s as the junior partner in the family ship-owning business. He quickly built up a substantial share in Montreal's export trade (the main staple was timber) and secured the mail contract for Liverpool. His business empire embraced railways and telegraphs as well as shipping, banking, insurance and even manufacturing.[90] Allan was one of a group of Montreal entrepreneurs whose interests were continental in scale. Their burning ambition was to conscript British capital for the building of railways that would make Montreal into a commercial metropolis to rival New York.[91] Their achievement lay in harnessing their British connections to the ruthless exploitation of local opportunities, a task that required both commercial and political skills.

Their counterparts on the other side of the world faced the same challenge. Australia's transformation from a remote prison farm heavily dependent on imperial subsidy was mainly the work of local free settlers and merchants who created a pastoral industry and forced the abandonment of London's attempts to restrain inland expansion. Invoking the rule that the aboriginal peoples had no rights of ownership (the *terra nullius* doctrine), 'squatters' seized the colony's principal asset, its far-reaching grasslands, bargaining with the Crown – their nominal possessor – for the lowest land charge. While both South and Western Australia had been founded directly by private interests from Britain, Victoria and Queensland were settled by migrants from the two original colonies, New South Wales and Van Diemen's Land (later Tasmania). John Macarthur (1767–1834), who introduced the merino sheep, his son James (1798–1867), who made a Lombard Street marriage, and

William Charles Wentworth (1790–1872), explorer, trader, pastoralist, lawyer, politician and 'booster', were the key political architects of the pastoral interest and inveterate opponents of London's 'autocracy'.[92] Thomas Mort (1816–78), whose statue now stands near Sydney's Circular Quay, created much of the financial and mercantile apparatus on which the wool trade depended. In New Zealand, where London's annexation had been openly grudging, imperial policy was to restrict the area of settlement to a handful of enclaves. The sale of land by indigenous Maori, formally acknowledged by the treaty of Waitangi as owners of the soil, was to be strictly controlled. In the South Island, where the number of Maori was low (perhaps as few as 5,000 in the 1840s), there was direct settlement from Britain in Otago and Canterbury. But, in the North Island, local men did most to make New Zealand into a settler state. Isaac Featherston, superintendent of the Wellington province, eagerly pushed its boundaries inland to the Wairarapa and Manawatu.[93] Auckland interests pressed for occupation of the Waikato valley, the scene of major Anglo-Maori conflict in the mid-1860s.[94] But the crucial figure was Donald McLean, the government land agent and, not coincidentally, a major landowner himself in the Hawke's Bay province.[95] McLean's aggressive purchasing policy[96] stoked the settler appetite for land until the crisis was reached in the 1860s. The Maori wars that followed decided the question: henceforth New Zealand was to be a white settler state.

In all of these cases, settler control of the colonial state was a critical factor in local success. It was conceded by London in the 1840s (in British North America) and 1850s (in Australia and New Zealand) with almost complete local autonomy, as 'responsible government'. It was the colonial state that decided what land could be granted, at what price it was sold, and where and from whom it should be bought for resale. The colonial state's revenues could be used to subsidise railways, or pay for their building. The colonial state had the power (conceded by London after 1859) to protect local enterprise by tariffs against competition from Britain. In South Africa, the local equation was radically different. Here, the (British) settler bridgehead was feeble. As in New Zealand, it faced a tough local opponent: the African peoples along the Eastern Cape frontier. But the injection of migrants and capital that made New Zealand dynamic (with a white population of 300,000 after a mere thirty years of colonisation) was lacking at the Cape. A desultory trade in wool was the best it could manage. Regarding the colony as a financial black hole after the costly frontier wars of the 1840s, London pulled back. For the next thirty years, no proconsul in Cape Town had the military means to command the northern interior, and there was no local entrepreneur with strong British connections to create a business empire on the necessary scale. Instead, the initiative passed to the Afrikaner frontiersmen, the trekkers or Boers. It was they, not the British colonial state, who seized the interior's resources of labour and land to create their trekker republics, not so much states as loose federations of their paramilitary bands, the notorious commandos.[97] So great was the Boers' distaste for fixed boundaries that they treated map-makers as spies.[98] Only where sea-power gave the British a foothold could they make their influence felt. They annexed Port Natal. When the trekkers (who had arrived before this imperial riposte) departed in dudgeon for the highveld interior, a precarious beachhead of traders and farmers grew up under the eye of the Zulu kingdom across the Tugela. This was Natal, the puny and troublesome offspring of the original Cape Colony.

But no settler bridgehead was a rival to India in power and importance in the mid-nineteenth century. Here a unique set of circumstances had permitted the growth of an exceptional Anglo-Oriental imperialism. More completely than anywhere else, the British in India had been able to take rapid command of local resources and turn them to their use. It had been the East India Company's victory at Plassey over the Bengal nawab, Siraj ud-Daulah, that had laid the foundation. Within eight years of Plassey, the Company had assumed the *diwan*, the right conferred by the Mughal ruler in Delhi to collect the land revenue of the subah of Bengal. In Bengal and the Carnatic (and wherever its rule was imposed), the Company inherited a long-established revenue system whose yield could be diverted to fill its deep pockets. It could also exploit India's commercial economy, for India had been, in textiles at least, the workshop of the world in the eighteenth century. Indian bankers advanced some of the credit on which the Company's campaigns against other Indian rulers had depended.[99] India's exports of opium, a Company monopoly, came to supply nearly one-fifth of its income.[100] India could also supply, through its market of military labour,[101] a wellspring of manpower not already attached to clan or feudal allegiance. The Company state could build up an army of nearly a quarter of a million men. It could also afford to hire from the Crown (at a cost of more than £1 million a year) between twenty and thirty thousand British troops to stiffen its sepoys and act as a check upon unrest in its army.

With a revenue of around £30 million a year by the early 1850s (perhaps half that of Britain), the Indian government had a freedom of action no other colony matched. London constantly frowned on its expansionist tendencies, fearing disaster and financial collapse. One viceroy was sacked for defying its veto but usually Calcutta had its way in the end and the area ruled by the Company Raj was extended relentlessly. What drove the Company forward was partly the fear that its brittle regime could not take the strain of a turbulent zone on its external frontier or in the autonomous states that divided the tracts of Company rule.[102] To less sympathetic observers, the real cause could be found in the unreformed nature of the Company state. Denouncing the war against Burma in 1852, Lord Ellenborough, a former governor-general himself, ascribed the Indian government's aggression to the influence of 'certain . . . British merchants . . . in concert and connexion with the press at Calcutta, the movements of which I have always viewed with anxiety and distrust [because] the desire to push forward trade and make a money speculation is the feeling which actuates the press at Calcutta'.[103] But they were not the only culprits, since the pressure for war came from 'a large part of the civil and the whole of the military service'.[104] Jobs, plunder and perquisites – not a sense of imperial purpose – formed the compass they steered by. Indeed, it was not hard to see the Company's 'servants' in India as a selfish and self-appointed oligarchy whose ranks were replenished increasingly from the sons of old Company men.[105] 'We require some change which shall enable Englishmen to enter the service of the Indian government by other channels than one small college', argued *The Times*[106] – a reference to Haileybury, the Company's training school. Nor was this the only complaint. Manchester cotton merchants, hungry for markets, lambasted the Company's miserly spending on railways and roads: between 1834 and 1848, it had spent less than one half per cent of its revenues on improvements like this.[107] The Company's local mercantile allies, who often acted as agents in its officials' private affairs, were suspected of trying to keep out the competition from home – with the Company's help. No British exchange bank was allowed to start up in India until 1851, and then by mischance.[108]

It was thus hardly surprising that, when the Company's failings were put on brutal display at the time of the Mutiny in 1857, it found few friends in Britain. The Mutiny had been a stunning shock to the Company: its intelligence system had failed almost completely.[109] The British were lucky that the Mutiny (or 'Great Rebellion') was not universal. Instead, it was largely confined to the Upper Ganges valley, although its effects spread out into the lightly ruled tracts of upland Central India. The main centres of revolt were in Delhi, where the Mughal emperor had been the Company's pensioner, and in Awadh (Oudh), whose Muslim nawab had been brusquely displaced by the British in the previous year. The Mutiny released some of the bitter resentments that the headlong expansion of Company power had built up over decades. The Company's apparent alliance with the Christian missions, and its disparaging treatment of the Mughal ruler and court, alarmed and enraged North Indian Muslim divines. Fear that the Company meant to treat other princely states as it had treated Awadh pushed the Nana Sahib, a Maratha prince, into open revolt. Agrarian unrest was fed by the hardship of once-prosperous peasant communities caught between the exactions of landlords and the loss of army employment, as the British revised their zones of recruitment. But it was the sepoy mutiny of May 1857, first at Meerut forty miles from Delhi, that set off the explosion. It revealed – or seemed to – that the Company's power could be easily broken.[110]

But the British hung on and assembled an army in the newly conquered Punjab. They had recaptured Delhi by the end of the year. A large British army, rushed out from Europe, smashed its way up the Ganges, exacting savage revenge for the murder of British women and children and imposing what was seen (by many British observers) as a white reign of terror. Although resistance smouldered on for more than a year, the real back of the revolt was broken in months, largely because there was little to hold its disparate elements together. The Mutiny had been, nonetheless, an extraordinary crisis. It demolished at a blow much of the mid-Victorians' complacency and challenged their self-confidence. As soon as the worst was over, the Company was called to account.

The reaction was penal. The Company state was abolished by Parliament with hardly a whimper. Its enormous army was cut down by half. Under the new regime, civilian values were meant to prevail. Railway construction to open up India to Lancashire's wares became an urgent priority. The result was a paradox. In theory, the great garrison state that the Company's servants had made would now be the springboard for British expansion across southern Asia. India's wealth (in money and men) would be pledged more completely to the imperial cause. And so it was – up to a point. But there was a price to be paid. When the Company's army was shown to resemble not so much the sword of Achilles as his vulnerable heel, the effect on the disposition of Britain's own military manpower was bound to be large. 'The Government of India', a pre-Mutiny Viceroy had warned, 'unlike the Colonies of the Crown, has no element of national strength on which it can fall back in a country where the entire English community is but a handful of scattered strangers'.[111] Since creating a large British 'colony' in India was out of the question, the gap had to be filled by a military force. From the Mutiny onwards, it became axiomatic that the number of British soldiers in India must never be less than half the strength of the Indian army: even with a reduced sepoy army, that meant a far larger contingent than in pre-Mutiny days. The reward (for Britain's taxpayers) was great; the strain on the army unremitting. In the emergent world-system, India's place had been set – as Britain's great 'barrack in an Eastern sea'.

Britain's empire of trade, like its settlement and Indian empires, also depended upon the success of expatriate Britons – in digging themselves into the local economy, enlisting local support, and enlarging the scale of export production and the consumption of imports. As we have seen, British merchants and their 'houses' were spread around the globe by the 1840s and were well placed to exploit the great expansion of trade that set in after 1850. But the extent to which they held the commercial initiative varied considerably. In Brazil, several large British firms held a commanding position in the coffee and sugar trades, and Brazil remained Britain's best Latin American customer until the end of the century. But the growth of British commercial influence really set in only after the rise of the Sao Paulo 'coffee economy' in the late 1860s, and the building of the Santos–Sao Paulo railway in 1868.[112] In Argentina, where British merchants had been on the scene early, their influence, and that of their *porteno* allies, had been checked by the long reign of the *caudillo* Rosas (1828–52). The British naval blockade in 1846–8 had made matters worse, and it was an internal shift within the Argentine's politics that really opened the way for commercial expansion after mid-century. Likewise in Peru, where the mercantile house of Anthony Gibb pioneered the export of guano (the dung of sea-birds, an agricultural fertiliser), British hopes of freer trade were forced to hold fire until the dominant Peruvian faction had discovered the fiscal appeal of international commerce.[113] In the Levant and Middle East, the free trade agreement that Palmerston had exacted in 1838 opened the Ottoman Empire to British merchants and encouraged the formation of Anglo-Greek firms, like the Rallis or Rodocanachis.[114] But it was the collapse of Egypt's attempt to be a textile producer, its switch to becoming a vast cotton plantation, and the 'cotton famine' that arose during the Civil War in America, that gave British merchants their niche in the trade of Alexandria, Egypt's main port-city. In Southeast Asia, British control of Singapore after 1819, and its free-port status, made it the base from which British merchants could seek cargoes and customers across a wide maritime region. Opium and guns were their early stock-in trade.[115] Improved sailing ships (especially the clipper) gave them an advantage over junk-using Chinese, and the Navy's onslaught on Malay *orang laut* (sea-people) as a pirate community removed some of their local competitors. But it was still merchant entrepreneurs from South China who controlled local trade and the production, from which expatriate interests were largely excluded.[116] And then there was China.

In China, the British had tried using direct military force to drive their trade into a huge commercial economy with all the allure of a modern eldorado. Two treaties imposed at the bayonet's point gave British merchants (and other Westerners) a privileged position at numerous ports of entry (the number reached ninety-two by 1914) on China's coasts and rivers – the so-called 'treaty-ports'. In Shanghai, which commanded the immense Yangtse basin, the 'land regulations' of 1845 set aside a zone where foreign residents could buy or lease property, forming a settlement with its own municipal council. British merchants and others were free to import goods at a modest tariff of 5 per cent by value, and were exempt from interference by Chinese officials. Their rights were protected by a small army of consuls – perhaps forty in all – whose influence was backed by the threat of a gunboat's arrival in case of a quarrel. From 1854, when its pressing need of a revenue to counter the Taiping insurgency secured Peking's approval, a Chinese 'Imperial Maritime Customs Service' was set up with a European staff to regulate the collection of tariffs and duties. Under these conditions, British merchants could purchase the teas and silks in demand in the West, and exchange them for cotton goods and opium, the largest import, whose traffic was formally legalised in 1858.[117] But, although a number of

British firms, including Jardine Matheson, Dent's and Butterfield and Swire, set up on the coast, it was far from clear by the mid-1870s how much China could promise. The inland trade remained in the hands of Chinese merchants, sometimes acting as *compradors* for the treaty-port British. Indeed, by the late 1860s, the consuls were reporting that British merchants were being driven out of the inland trade altogether, and that many treaty-ports were redundant.[118] Inland residence (i.e. away from the treaty-ports) was the merchants' panacea, but the consuls rejected this as a vast extension of their administrative burdens and practically unenforceable, a view strongly endorsed in London.[119] Behind the barriers of its language and its complex currency system, and without Western-style banks or commercial property law, China was 'singularly successful at checking foreign economic penetration', remarks a modern authority.[120]

The response of the British was a straw in the wind, and not just in China. Where they held the advantage was in commercial services. Jardine Matheson and Swires both became ship-owners. Their shipping lines 'Ewo' and 'Taikoo' plied China's coastal waters and rivers. They provided insurance and banking and dealt in bills of exchange. A new British interest arose on the coast with the formation in 1864 of the Hongkong and Shanghai Banking Corporation, designed to attract Chinese capital as well as British. This trend was mirrored elsewhere in the world. It was strengthened by the technological changes that favoured British business: the spread of the steamship to South America, West Africa and (with the opening of the Suez Canal) to the Indian Ocean and East Asia; and by the telegraph as a vector of credit as well as price information. As the exchanges between the different compartments of the global economy grew swifter and easier, the business of managing them became more and more profitable. A new kind of empire was now in the making.

The Victorian pattern established

The years from the 1830s to the 1870s were the critical phase of Britain's emergence as a global power in command of a world-system. This was partly a matter of geographical range. Before 1830, Britain had been overwhelmingly an Atlantic power with a great eastern outpost. By the 1870s, the scale of British activity in the Pacific, East Asia,

Southeast Asia, the Middle East and East Africa, as well as Latin America, showed that almost no part of the world outside Europe and the United States was immune from their interference. But it was also a measure of the rapid maturing of Britain's connections with the three different kinds of empire that mid-Victorian expansion had made: the 'sub-empires' of settlement, trade and rule. It was by drawing them into a closer relation (more of function than of form) and exploiting the different benefits that each had to offer, that the British preserved in the more competitive world of the late nineteenth century the geopolitical vantage won in 1815.

The transformation of British society had been vital to this. Before 1830, powerful networks and interests had championed the claims of the old 'mercantilist' empire and defended its privileges. The abolition of slavery and the demand for free trade had threatened to sweep them away. But the economic and social development of mid-Victorian Britain was not hostile to empire. Instead, it hugely strengthened Britain's ability to act as the mainspring of a new global system.

It was the scale and the speed with which the British adapted to the promise of global expansion that gave them their chance. First, the British Isles had become by the 1860s and 1870s a great emigrant reservoir. By the mid-1870s, over eight million people (three-quarters of them British and Irish) had left British ports for destinations outside Europe. The habit of migration had become deeply entrenched since the first great rush in the 1830s. 1.3 million left in the 1850s, 1.5 million in the 1860s and a further 1.2 million in the first half of the 1870s. Nor, after 1870, was it chiefly an Irish phenomenon.[121] The British were not the only Europeans to migrate, but they did so earlier, in larger numbers and more persistently than any other people in Europe. Nor of course did most British migrants go to Britain's settlement colonies: instead, two-thirds went to the United States (there were only two years between 1853 and 1899 when the American share fell below 50 per cent). But the American magnet had a broader effect. It helped to make Britain an emigrant society, in which the appeal of mobility and the moral legitimacy of settling a 'new' country were widely accepted. It helped to inspire the idea, trumpeted in Charles Dilke's *Greater Britain* (1869), that the British were a 'world-people'. 'In 1866 and 1867', ran Dilke's famous opening sentence, 'I followed England round the world.' The idea 'which has been ... my fellow and my guide ... is a conception, however imperfect, of the grandeur of the race, already girdling the earth.'[122] It was the most positive proof that the migrant societies growing up in the settlement colonies had a viable future as non-dependent communities. And America, as much as Britain's own settler states, encouraged the British 'at home' to see themselves as an 'old' community recreating itself in new lands overseas – a vital part of their colonising ideology.

Secondly, Britain had become an open economy with the adoption of free trade in the 1840s and 1850s (the repeal of the Navigation laws in 1850–1 almost completed the process). The motives behind this have been fiercely debated. They may have owed more to the political need to rebalance commercial and agrarian interests than to commercial calculation.[123] But, once enacted, free trade reinforced Britain's role as the world's principal entrepot, the market-place to which the world's goods could be carried without commercial restriction. It removed any limit on the City's development as the eyes and ears of the new world economy, its banker, insurer, shipping-agent and dealer. It allowed British merchants to open commercial relations with any part of the world and offer its produce to the widest selection of buyers through the London exchanges. Thirdly, Britain had become an investing economy, with an investment income that grew fourteen-fold between 1830 and 1875 from under £4 million to £58 million.[124] The mobilisation of savings that 'railway mania' had encouraged, as well as domestic prosperity, created a fund for investment abroad, at first in government bonds and then, increasingly, in the building of railways and other infrastructure in India, the Americas and Australasia. Here was the basis for not just an empire of trade, but also an empire of overseas property.

Lastly, it was not just a matter of investment, trade and migration. Social and economic change in Britain had speeded the shift towards a more diverse, pluralistic and open society. While the Anglican aristocracy and gentry continued to dominate parliamentary politics, they were forced to accommodate urban, commercial, industrial, non-conformist, Catholic and even working class interests. The Evangelical and humanitarian pressure groups, already very active by the 1830s, recruited fresh allies among the newly enfranchised. Much of the appeal of Gladstonian liberalism (whose influence extended far beyond the ranks of the Liberal Party) lay in its promise of a political system, attuned to the moral concerns of the whole range of classes, and free from the bias of legalised privilege – so-called 'Old Corruption'. The result was to create within British society vocal support for liberal and universalist values, and their diffusion abroad. This was an 'alternative Britain' to which those disenchanted with its more masterful face could turn for assistance. No single version of empire ruled over opinion in Britain: it was precisely the nature of the British world-system that it embodied a number of alternative visions of British expansion. 'All ranks, all classes are equally interested', said the historian-polemicist James Anthony Froude of Britain's colonial expansion. Manufacturers wanted new markets, landowners would welcome the colonial safety-valve for rural discontent. 'Most of all is it the concern of the working men' who had the chance to emigrate.[125]

Left to themselves, the different visions of empire espoused by mercantile, humanitarian, missionary, settler, scientific, official and military interests might have led to political stalemate. The loathing of radicals for Palmerstonian bellicosity (as the last reckless gasp of an obsolete aristocracy); the mistrust of India as a source of corruption and the forced militarisation of British society (a large British garrison there would mean conscription at home warned the radical professor Goldwin Smith[126]); the grumbling unease at the violence and cruelty of colonial rule (the Royal Commission into the Jamaican disturbances of 1865 described their suppression as 'barbarous, wanton and cruel');[127] the indifference of those concerned with the settlement colonies for the future of India, and *vice versa*: these and other divisions might have undermined any consensus on the British world-system. Parties and governments might have feared all or any expansion as too acrimonious, putting at risk their domestic priorities. A different tradition of political liberty (one less anchored in property rights), or (at the other extreme) a run of defeats in colonial warfare, might have changed the terms of debate altogether. In practice, however, the scope for real disagreement was surprisingly narrow.

One reason for this was that the conflict of interests was more apparent than real. Manchester free traders might dislike Palmerston's wars.[128] But they wanted to 'open up' India to their cottons and safeguard their access to markets in China. There was no more ardent free trader than Sir John Bowring, the governor of Hong Kong who hoped for a British protectorate over much of South China.[129] Missionary leaders distrusted colonial officialdom. But they looked to London for help against predatory settlers, and to extend its imperial umbrella over their new fields of activity. Scientific and humanitarian lobbies had to convince British opinion that its real interests were global, and should not be frustrated by local obstruction that was stuck in the past. The rapprochement of interests was also ideological, and sprang from a common commitment to 'progress' – the real moral warrant of Victorian imperialism. Thus authoritarian rule on the 'crown colony' principle (where the executive controlled an appointive legislature) was originally justified as necessary when the 'British' were too few and 'free people of colour too numerous'.[130] But it acquired a new moral purpose as the way of restraining an oppressive minority of white settlers or planters. Both positions assumed that only *enlightened* British rule, not its coarse local variant, could redeem Asians and Africans from their slough of stagnation, or worse. It was precisely on these grounds that John Stuart Mill, the scourge of colonial crimes in Jamaica, excused the denial of representative government to the people of India.[131] Humanitarians and missionaries might decry the mistreatment of indigenous peoples. But they were wholly committed to the moral obsessions of Victorian society, and its strictures on gender, the place of the family and the treatment of women.[132] Few mid-Victorians would have resisted the claim – however romantic their views – that 'commercial' societies like their own were richer and stronger because their institutions and mores favoured the advancement of knowledge and technology. The common ingredient of most of these attitudes was a vulgar conception of 'race' – not a scientific racism but a catch-all presumption that variations in skin-shade, religion and climate were an accurate predictor of civilisational capacity. Some Victorians discovered by personal experience the limitations of this theory, but not very many.

These trends in British society were part of the story. They were matched by the changes in Britain's spheres of expansion. The sudden death-crisis of the Company state gave London the chance to impose British priorities on a self-centred expatriate Anglo-Indian regime. The remnants of the Company's old merchant-warrior ethos were thrown on the scrap-heap. India was now to be much more thoroughly integrated into Britain's pattern of trade and investment – a process accelerated by the cutting of the Suez Canal and the extension of the telegraph and submarine cable. But, as quickly became clear, the military foundations of the new British Raj also demanded a closer strategic connection, and imposed willy-nilly a general revision of imperial defence. Once London had to find more than 70,000 soldiers for the Indian garrison (and perhaps more in an emergency – 90,000 had been needed during the Mutiny), the strain on the rest of its imperial commitments became overwhelming. 'In truth', remarked Gladstone, 'England must keep a military bank on which India can draw checks at pleasure.'[133] To make the books balance, British troops were withdrawn from New Zealand and Canada – occasioning a furious protest from the New Zealand ministers. By 1872, the War Office expected that, of the British troops stationed abroad, fifty-seven of its line battalions (the infantry backbone) would be garrisoning India, with a mere thirteen in the rest of the colonies.[134] In return, London expected that both the British and Indian troops stationed in India would form Britain's strategic reserve in the world east of Suez, to be charged on the Indian budget except for the 'extraordinary' costs of an expedition or war. In political terms, the effect was far-reaching. Henceforth, any concession London might be willing to make to Indian self-rule had an iron limitation. No change could be made that imperilled India's military budget (the largest item of spending), nor the huge remittance it made for the hire of its garrison. And, as the demand from Lancashire for more Indian railways (and thus more Indian customers) was felt more directly, the burden of Indian debt also rose steeply. India was locked into the British 'system' far more completely than under the Company Raj.

In the settlement colonies, the signs were less obvious. They enjoyed internal self-government (except at the Cape) by mid-century, keeping at bay the concern of London-based interests for their indigenous peoples, a potent source of friction. Their white populations had grown. They contained large urban centres. Their economic and cultural institutions were comparable to those of provincial Britain. But in two important respects they were being bound more closely to the old 'Mother-Country'. To compete in the global economy required heavy investment in the infrastructure of transport, and ever greater reliance on the shipping and sea-lanes that carried their products to Europe. Both drove them into a deeper dependence on London and Liverpool, and sharpened the sense that their credit and capital were only as strong as their reputation in Britain. The colossal priority of economic development made it even less likely that they would cease to depend on British sea-power for strategic protection. Secondly, as the scale of their societies grew, their points of contact with British institutions and interests, the circulation of persons as well as ideas, and Britain's significance as the model of modernity (as well as a warning of its costs and risks), also grew rapidly. The only alternative to 'British connection' was a painful march back into colonial isolation or, in the Canadian case, to embrace annexation to the next-door republic. Neither appealed much. Something similar was happening in the invisible empire of commerce and credit. At the London end of the axis, the growth of the capital market centred on the stock exchange, the rise of specialised financial entrepreneurs, the spread of risk through limited liability, and the increasing volume of economic information available through cable and telegraph, increased the capacity of the imperial centre to trade and invest in overseas countries. At much the same time, improvements in transport brought by steam technology drove prices down and exposed local merchants, like those in Latin America, to fiercer competition from abroad. Combined with the need to raise more and more capital for railways, harbours and urban improvements, the result was to strengthen British-based enterprise (including banks and insurance companies) over local concerns that lacked their resources and network of contacts. The foundations were laid for what one writer has called the 'Londonisation' of international commerce.[135] London built up its property empire and amassed an income from services. In Latin America, the escape into autarky became a subject for romance.

By the mid-1870s, a set of conjunctures and crises, scarcely imaginable some forty years earlier, had largely reshaped Britain's place in the world. More by default than by any design, they endowed Britain with the military, economic and demographic resources to sustain a world-system, given reasonable prudence. How that system was challenged, defended, reinvented and broken the chapters that follow are meant to explain.

2   THE OCTOPUS POWER

After 1870, the global conditions in which a British world-system had first taken shape began to change rapidly. Between then and 1900, the political and economic map of the world was redrawn. New imperial powers, including Germany, Italy, the United States and Japan, entered the stage; old ones ballooned in size. Africa, Southeast Asia and the Pacific were partitioned leaving only patches of local sovereignty: Ethiopia, Liberia, Siam. The great Eurasian empires of the Ottomans, Qajars and Ch'ing hovered on the brink of collapse: their division between rival predators seemed imminent and inevitable. The old political landscape of mid-century, with its separate spheres, was being fused into a single system of 'world politics'. At the same time, industrialisation, the huge rise in the volume of trade, the wider reach of inland transport, the deepening penetration of capital, the tidal wave of European migration and the lesser flows of Asian, were creating a global economy in which even basic foodstuffs were ruled by a world market and world prices.[1] In this more intensely competitive setting, hitherto 'remote' societies were brusquely driven to 'reform'. In many, the hope of building a new model state to beat off outsiders and suppress internal revolt, was forlorn at best and ended in crisis and colonial subjection. Meanwhile, in those societies already under colonial rule, or where European influence was being felt more acutely, political and cultural resistance came to seem much more urgent, and the appeal of 'nationalism' (in various forms) began to rise sharply. Even at home, or among overseas British communities, new kinds of mass politics reflected the sense of ever deeper exposure to external forces, and the need to create greater social cohesion by reform or exclusion.

    An early source of alarm was a Near Eastern crisis that threatened to bring Russian power to the Straits (and thus the Mediterranean)

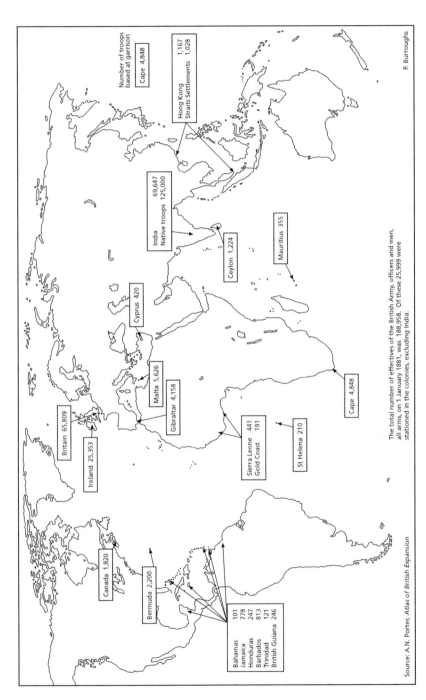

Number of troops based at garrison

Cape 4,848

Hong Kong 1,167
Straits Settlements 1,028

India 69,647
Native troops 125,000

Ceylon 1,224

Mauritius 355

Cyprus 420

Malta 5,626

Gibraltar 4,158

Britain 65,809

Ireland 25,353

Sierra Leone 441
Gold Coast 191

St Helena 210

Cape 4,848

Canada 1,820

Bermuda 2,200

Bahamas 101
Jamaica 778
Honduras 247
Barbados 813
Trinidad 121
British Guiana 246

The total number of effectives of the British Army, officers and men, all arms, on 1 January 1881, was 188,958. Of these 25,999 were stationed in the colonies, excluding India.

P. Burroughs

Source: A.N. Porter, *Atlas of British Expansion*

Map 3 Distribution of British troops, 1881

and make the Ottoman Empire a client state of the Tsar. It was rapidly
followed by a general crisis in Egypt, and by a British invasion intended,
said London, to restore order in Cairo before an early withdrawal.
There was no withdrawal. Instead, within less than three years the
British became party to an extraordinary plan for the territorial partition of Africa. Under the rubric of 'effective occupation', a bundle of
treaties made with African rulers would justify a protectorate or even
a colony. Whether intended or not, the result was a 'scramble', and
the rush to partition was echoed in other parts of the world. But what
had led British governments to react in this fashion? What risks did
they run? How would opinion in Britain respond to the mass of new
liabilities that scrambling imposed? Would it relish the triumphs that
'new imperialism' brought home, or remain sourly indifferent to these
baubles of empire? Was this burst of expansion a sign of irrepressible
confidence in Britain's 'manifest destiny' or the gloomy precaution of a
power in decline and its hag-ridden leaders? Had British greed wrecked
their diplomatic position in Europe and united their rivals in shared
animosity? Some people thought so. 'We have not a friend in Europe',
wrote a cabinet minister as Britain plunged into war in South Africa,
'and ... the main cause of the dislike is ... that we are like an octopus
with gigantic feelers stretching out over the habitable world, constantly
interrupting and preventing foreign nations from doing that which we
in the past have done ourselves.'[2]

The new geopolitics

Even in the 1870s, the alarm had been sounded about the speed with
which the world was 'filling up'. 'The world is growing so small that
every patch of territory begins to be looked upon as a stray farm is by a
County magnate', wrote the editor of *The Times* in 1874, in language
he thought ministers might understand.[3] By the 1890s, the idea was
becoming a commonplace. Frederick Jackson Turner (in an American
context), and five widely influential writers, Charles Pearson (1893),
Benjamin Kidd (1894), Alfred Mahan (1900), James Bryce (1902) and
Halford Mackinder (1904) all regarded the closing of the settlement
frontier and the demarcation of the world's land surface as the beginning of a new epoch.[4] Coupled with the growth of almost instantaneous
communications, what the Canadian imperialist George Parkin called
'a new nervous system' of the cable and telegraph,[5] they had brought

about a phase of unprecedented delicacy in great power diplomacy. 'In the post-Columbian age', declared Mackinder,

> *we shall again have to deal with a closed political system, and none the less it will be of world-wide scope. Every explosion of social forces, instead of being dissipated in a surrounding circuit of unknown space and barbaric chaos, will be sharply re-echoed from the far side of the globe and weak elements in the political and economic organism of the world will be shattered.*[6]

Mackinder's suggestion that the end of the open frontier of territorial expansion would have important effects upon domestic and international politics had already been anticipated by Pearson and Kidd. Now that the temperate lands had been filled up, argued Pearson, the pent-up force of surplus population would force governments in Europe to assume an ever larger role in social and economic life. Kidd believed that the closing of the temperate frontier of settlement had coincided with the arrival of a 'new democracy' in Europe, social as well as political, whose economic demands could only be satisfied by the exploitation of the tropics – 'the richest region of the globe'.[7] Both writers assumed that only large, well-organised states could survive in an age of increasing competition for resources.

These large predictions also reflected powerful cultural and racial assumptions. Pearson, whose views had been shaped by the antipathy to Chinese immigration in the Australian colonies where much of his career was spent, imagined a future in which the 'higher races' would have been driven back upon 'a portion of the temperate zone'.[8] He prophesied the rise of Afro-Asian states 'no longer too weak for aggression', with fleets in the European seas, attending international conferences and 'welcomed as allies in the quarrels of the civilised world'.[9] No doubt his readers could feel their flesh creep as the 'yellow peril' grew closer. But to most writers it was the relentless pressure of Europeans upon other peoples and civilisations that seemed more obvious. The Anglo-Saxon, despite his humanitarian sentiments 'has exterminated the less-developed peoples... even more effectively than other races', remarked Kidd sarcastically.[10] Tropical peoples could offer no resistance to Europe's 'absolute ascendency'. 'Europe has annexed the rest of the earth', remarked the historian-politician James Bryce, 'and European ideas would prevail everywhere except China.'[11]

The close contact between advanced and backward peoples marked a 'crisis in the history of the world'.[12] Isolation was no longer an option: extinction or absorption was the fate of many tribes or peoples, and the 'backward nations' were condemned to be a proletariat. Nor was there any way of preventing Europeans from annexing and settling 'countries inhabited by the coloured races': the best that could be hoped for was to regulate relations between whites and blacks, Indians and Chinese to minimise friction and keep 'some races ... at the highest level of efficiency'.[13] To an acute observer of Indian civilisation, it seemed certain that the old cultural realm of Hindu polytheism was under siege from external forces, and that a 'moral inter-regnum' would intervene before the Hindu reformation was complete.[14] Lord Salisbury referred bluntly to 'dying nations'.

It was hardly surprising that, among non-European writers, the irresistible advance of the Europeans was regarded with a mixture of awe at their technical prowess, and mistrust of their political motives. The overweening racial arrogance of Europeans was widely noted by Indian,[15] Chinese – 'Westerners are very strict about races and they look upon other races as enemies', said the influential mandarin-scholar K'ang Yu-Wei)[16] – and Afro-American observers. Europeans would make little progress in spreading Christianity in Africa, thought the highly educated black West Indian Edward Wilmot Blyden. They were hindered by climate but also by their supercilious view of African cultures.[17] Islamic intellectuals were divided between those who argued against any compromise with the subversive teachings of the West and those who insisted that a new synthesis could be found between its technical and scientific knowledge and a modernised Islam.[18] Underlying much of this academic commentary was the sense of an impending cultural struggle to reshape the non-European world. For the ruling elites of Afro-Asia's remaining independent states, international politics after 1880 were a race against time to achieve 'self-strengthening' before the might of the European powers imposed 'protection', annexation or partition upon them.

On all sides, world politics were coming to be seen as a vortex in which only the strong would survive, and then at the price of a discipline and organisation at variance with older traditions of diversity and individualism. Among Europeans, the sense of intensifying competition was sharpened by crucial changes on their own continent. After the 1870s, the brief experiment of free trade was swept away and, in almost every large power except Britain, agriculture protected and industry built up behind tariff walls. At the same time, the political geography of the continent was reshaped by the emergence of Germany and Italy as great powers and (after 1880) would-be colonial powers as well. The old triangular imperialism of Britain, France and Russia had become hexagonal. Since the European 'dwarfs' (as the Dutch described themselves) could not always be disregarded, imperial diplomacy sometimes became octagonal – even before the rise of American and Japanese power in the Pacific. Henceforward, it became hard to resist the claim that the principle of equitable compensation on which the peace of Europe was held to depend should be extended to any region where a European power had enlarged its possessions. For the British, the shock of change was particularly severe. British opinion had blithely assumed that, in the new world economy of rising trade and rapid transport, international free trade would guarantee their commercial ascendancy. Secondly, they had every reason to fear that their large, loose, decentralised confederacy, with its wide zones of informal influence and fluid primacy, would be especially vulnerable to a new imperialism of partition.

The intensifying pressure to modernise in a world more and more subject to a global economy and to a single system of international politics thus threatened a double revolution in which old (Afro-Asian) states would disappear and a new, more fiercely competitive group of (European) empires would emerge. Its first epicentre was in the Near East. The Ottoman Empire had been under siege since the 1770s but it had shown a remarkable capacity for survival. In the Crimean War, Russia, its main enemy, had been hurled out of the Black Sea. The empire had been cautiously 'reformed' to strengthen its army and centralising bureaucracy. But, in such proximity to Europe and with large Christian populations in its western provinces, this was bound to be difficult. Drawing closer to Europe through trade and technology risked upsetting the delicate balance of its internal politics. Borrowing heavily in the West to improve its rule was a gamble on economic forces over which it had no control. In 1875, disaster came. The Ottoman government declared itself bankrupt, defaulting on large loans in London and Paris. In the political turbulence that followed, reprisals against its Christian subjects (the 'Bulgarian Horrors') became a *cause célèbre* in Europe. Amid a wave of passionate sympathy for 'fellow Slavs', Russian intervention in 1877 led swiftly to full-scale invasion and the imposition of a treaty (at San Stefano outside Constantinople) which openly reduced Turkey to a client-state. With the loss of their European provinces (the richest part of their empire) and an indefensible frontier in Thrace, the Ottomans had reached the brink of final collapse. Russia's control over the Straits and her predominance in the Eastern Mediterranean – the nightmare of British diplomacy since the 1780s – was only a matter of time.[19]

Disraeli's government reacted angrily but indecisively. A fleet was sent to lurk in the approaches to Constantinople and an Indian army contingent sent to Malta. London grandly urged the Turks to stand firm and embrace reform. But, with France still traumatised by defeat in 1871 and no sign of animosity between the Russians, Germans and Austrians, there was no chance of repeating the diplomatic triumph of 1856. After much huffing and puffing, the result was a 'strategic retreat' in British policy, carefully disguised by Disraeli as a diplomatic victory.[20] The British took Cyprus, theoretically to guard Turkey's Asian provinces against further Russian encroachment, and staved off the 'Big Bulgaria' which might have brought Russian influence to the Aegean. But Salisbury (who became Foreign Secretary in 1878) was under no illusion that the 'Eastern Question' was settled.[21] Indeed, the wholesale confiscation of Ottoman Europe and Russia's advance in the Caucasus, acquiring Kars, Batum and Ardahan, suggested that Turkey's decay had entered the terminal phase. In every court in Europe, Salisbury told his ambassador in Constantinople, 'the Empire is looked upon as doomed'.[22]

This was the larger context in which the governments of both Disraeli and Gladstone tried to exert political and financial discipline on Egypt whose default had followed on the heels of Turkey's in 1876. Away from the Balkan cockpit, it was easier for Britain and France (the main source of Egypt's loans) to exert their joint influence through the so-called 'Dual Control' over Cairo's finances. The real difficulty was that the drastic reduction of government spending to meet the 'coupon' owed to the bondholders was bound to offend the powerful vested interests upon whom the Khedive's regime depended: landowners; the bureaucracy; above all, the army. It was hardly surprising that, while Ismail had been anxious to restore his credit and regain access to money-markets in the West, he also used every means to loosen the foreign control at the heart of his government. But, when France and Britain secured his deposition by the Ottoman Sultan (his formal overlord) in June 1879, in favour of the more pliant Tewfik, the whole khedivial structure began to disintegrate. By September 1881, an alliance of discontent had made Colonel Arabi, a senior army officer, the dominant power.[23]

The scale of Egyptian debt, Egypt's importance as the closest and most dynamic of Europe's new Afro-Asian trading partners and her strategic value as the 'highway' to the East (drastically increased with the completion of the Suez Canal in 1869) all made an Anglo-French accord with the ruling power in Cairo of the greatest urgency. But the prospects of an agreement with Arabi were always bleak. The Anglo-French officials of the 'Dual Control' regarded his movement as a road-block in the path of financial reform. Without the wholehearted backing of a 'native' government, they feared the shrivelling of their influence. Their hostility was loudly echoed by the large European community (nearly 100,000 strong) who lived under extra-territorial privilege and largely exempt from taxation. They were regarded by Arabi's following as a parasitical class responsible for Egypt's misfortunes.[24] The atmosphere of mistrust was deepened by the efforts of Tewfik to restore his authority, and by the natural suspicion on the Arabist side that sooner or later the Western powers would act against him and (as in Cyprus and Tunis) impose their rule. Under these conditions, reconciling autonomy, stability and financial reform would have needed a miracle.

For the British and French governments did not regard Egypt as a sovereign state whose independence had to be respected at all costs. Nor was this just a British view. 'L'Egypte a une importance politique qui lui interdit l'indépendance' was the terse Russian summary.[25] Its uncertain status as an autonomous part of the Ottoman Empire, its protected European 'settlers', and the Khedive's acceptance of the Dual Control made it a region where international interests and influence were already uniquely entrenched, and where local rights were closely circumscribed. On this view, they were bound to regard Arabi's demand of 'Egypt for the Egyptians' as a dangerous and retrograde slogan. The result was an escalating campaign of pressure and threat to deflate his prestige and restore the Khedive as the prime mover in Egyptian politics. In June 1882, the appearance of a French and British fleet at Alexandria, Egypt's premier port and its window on Europe, led to a massacre of Europeans. In July, Admiral Seymour's bombardment of the city merely raised Arabi to the zenith of his fame as the champion of Egyptian rights against the alien oppressor.

The Gladstone cabinet was now in a quandary. A change of government in France had ruled out joint action. To do nothing would be to acquiesce in Arabi's supremacy. But did Britain's interests really justify a unilateral military intervention, courting international resentment, and risking domestic outrage at the shameless reversal of Gladstone's Midlothian principles of 1879? Gladstone was in two minds, if not more. But a strong 'war party' in the cabinet insisted that Egypt was on the verge of anarchy, that Arabi was goading a murderous xenophobia, and that only prompt action – an invasion – could save Britain's vital interest in the free passage of the Canal. With his mind on Ireland, Gladstone accepted defeat, and the vote for war credits passed triumphantly through the Commons. In September, an expeditionary force of 31,000 British and Indian troops swept Arabi aside at Tel el-Kebir and placed Egypt under a 'temporary occupation' that was to last for more than seventy years.

The real motives for this crucial decision, with its vast unforeseen consequences for Britain's world position, have been fiercely debated ever since. Was the Canal really in danger at the moment in July when the cabinet authorised an invasion? Was there any risk of France striking a separate bargain with Arabi and subverting British influence? Was Arabi the monster of anarchy that he was painted? Were British ministers as indifferent to the laments of the bondholders as they claimed? Was strategy rather than economics the true compelling force that drove the British into Egypt? Scepticism on all these fronts has been vigorously expressed.[26] But the closest archival study of the decision shows convincingly that even those who came to favour invasion were extremely hesitant until the massacre at Alexandria, and all hope of persuading the Turkish government to 'restore order' had vanished. The bombardment of Alexandria was a 'calculated risk' to frighten Arabi and his followers into retreat, taken in the knowledge that he might then disrupt the Canal.[27] The invasion was prepared on the assumption that this last effort to coerce the Arabists might make the Canal, hitherto untouched by disorder, a scene of confrontation.

Disentangling the motives at work in a group of ministers struggling to make sense of a faraway crisis and distracted by bitter simultaneous divisions over rural disorder in Ireland is a rough and ready task. But several points stand out clearly. It is unlikely that those in favour of military intervention drew a sharp distinction between Britain's wider interests in Egypt and her strategic interest in the Canal. It would have been quite illogical to do so. The Canal lay some distance from the Delta towns, but its commercial centres at Port Said and Suez could not be insulated from wider popular unrest.[28] Even Gladstone acknowledged that 'the safety of the Canal will not coexist with illegality and military violence in Egypt'.[29] Nor, as Arabi's own actions showed, would the Canal be safe if the conflict between his regime and the Western powers intensified. The Canal was much the largest tangible British interest in Egypt, and its fate was bound up with the question of who ruled in Cairo.

But, in that case, if the Canal was so critical, why not come to terms with Arabi and ease the tension that endangered its use? Why jeopardise a vital interest by the clumsy attempt to suppress a movement whose capacity for harm was limited? Plausible or not, such an argument would have made little impression on the group of ministers for whom the Canal's safety loomed so large. Their leader, Lord Hartington, was Secretary of State for India; he would have liked to have been Viceroy in 1880.[30] Lord Northbrook at the Admiralty was a former Viceroy, deeply suspicious of the loyalty of India's Muslims. Charles Dilke, junior minister at the Foreign Office, a close friend of Joseph Chamberlain and a key member of the 'forward party', shared the widespread post-Mutiny view that British rule in India was inherently fragile. For all these ministers, India was not only the second centre of British power but the prism through which they surveyed non-European politics. To have compromised with Arabi would have threatened the prestige on which authority in India was held to depend. To have done so after the Alexandria massacre, with its horrible evocation of the Mutiny, would have been inconceivable. Of all the ministers in the Gladstone cabinet, those most alarmed about the Canal (because of India) were those least disposed to treat with Arabi (because of India). They were the most susceptible to alarmist reports about a coming anarchy and the least likely to see Arabi as a 'national' leader fighting fairly for freedom.

But, in the end, what carried the Gladstone government over the edge into invasion was the weakness of the arguments against it. When Disraeli's cabinet had debated how to check Russia's advance in 1877, the colossal risk of a war without allies was so divisive that 'in a cabinet of twelve...there are seven parties'.[31] But, at the time that military intervention was considered in July 1882, it was clear that a brief occupation to 'restore order on behalf of Europe' would present few diplomatic complications and had the approval of both the Ottoman Sultan and the Khedive. The cost would be modest, and would be met partly by India. There was little danger of defeat. Power would revert to the Khedive, not pass to a British governor. On the other hand, if the crisis worsened, the Canal were blocked and more Europeans killed, the government's credit would suffer badly and it would come under irresistible pressure to invade in much less favourable conditions. The 'geopolitical calculus' in short was overwhelmingly for intervention and its champions too resolute to be outmanoeuvred by Gladstone.

The occupation was the single most important forward move-ment made by Britain in the age of partition which set in after 1880. There is no convincing evidence that it was undertaken primarily to recoup the fortunes of British investors in Egyptian bonds. But, equally, it is too schematic to argue that it was merely the culmination of a long-standing interest in the safety of the route to India: a pure question of strategy. The complex reaction to Egyptian politics in London did not spring from the wish merely to *conserve* the existing strategic link with India, still less to recover funds sunk before the crash of '76. The leading ministers, and the wider public who had celebrated Disraeli's purchase of Canal shares in 1875,[32] recognised that Britain's stake in the Canal (and therefore in Egypt) was growing rapidly. An entire shipping sys-tem was being built around it,[33] and the commercial and military value of India was rising steeply. The canal was not the symbol of a decaying mid-Victorian pre-eminence, but of the dynamic expansion of late-Victorian Britain. That, perhaps, was why its defence united Whigs and Radicals (like Chamberlain and Dilke – who had urged annexation in 1878[34]) in Gladstone's cabinet. In the same way, the hard line towards Arabi reflected the late-century view that economic and social progress was too urgent to be obstructed by Afro-Asian regimes whose capacity for self-improvement was now regarded with ever heavier scepticism. In the decade after 1882, Egypt became the test case for arguments about 'progressive imperialism' and the matrix of a new imperial consensus on politics and strategy in the era of *Weltpolitik*.

The logic of partition

Whatever the logic behind occupation, the Liberal ministers soon found that they had entered Egypt on a false prospectus. Intervention had been meant to achieve a brisk reconstruction of Egyptian politics, locking out 'disruptive' elements and allowing Tewfik to organise a government committed to financial and political 'reform'. Once a safe regime was firmly installed in Cairo, repaying its debts under the eye of the international *Caisse de la Dette*, the British could revert to their old policy of influence and their old partnership with France. But nothing went according to plan. It soon became clear that facile constitutional schemes (like the Dufferin report of 1883) would collapse as soon as the British garrison left Cairo. The internal crisis brought by economic change and deepened by foreign interference, was much too severe to be solved by a Whig formula. Amid all the promises of British withdrawal, Egyptian politicians were understandably reluctant to ally themselves to a transient force. Then, within a year of the British invasion, the Mahdist revolt in Egypt's vast southern colony of the Sudan – a possession which meant as much to Cairo as India to London – threatened to destabilise Egypt's politics still further and spread rebellion in its upper provinces.[35] As these complications were rubbed in by Evelyn Baring, the British Agent at Cairo, the date for withdrawal receded until, by 1889, the occupation, however 'temporary', had become indefinite.[36]

The British now feared to leave because they were convinced that a chaos worse than that of 1882 would follow. The logic of intervention had become the logic of control. The strategic and diplomatic cost of this discovery was bound to be high. Turning Egypt into a virtual colony broke every rule of imperial expansion. Thus far, Britain's movement into the Outer World beyond Europe had served to insulate her interests more and more from the play of intra-European rivalry. Except in India (which had its own army and paid for British 'help'), access to Britain's colonies and spheres was by the open sea, the element where her strategic advantage was greatest. This pattern of maritime expansion allowed the British to localise their conflicts and even to choose between fighting limited or unlimited wars. But Egypt was an exposed salient on the rim of Europe, a great hostage to diplomatic fortune. As the Ottoman Empire sank towards collapse, the eastern Mediterranean became the cockpit of European politics. It was one thing to organise a diplomatic defence of Turkey in the style of Palmerston, quite another to protect a territorial stake as large and important as Egypt. The British dared not lower their guard lest a sudden crisis bring on partition and wreck their status in Cairo. The price was relentless pressure on their naval power, already strained by technical change

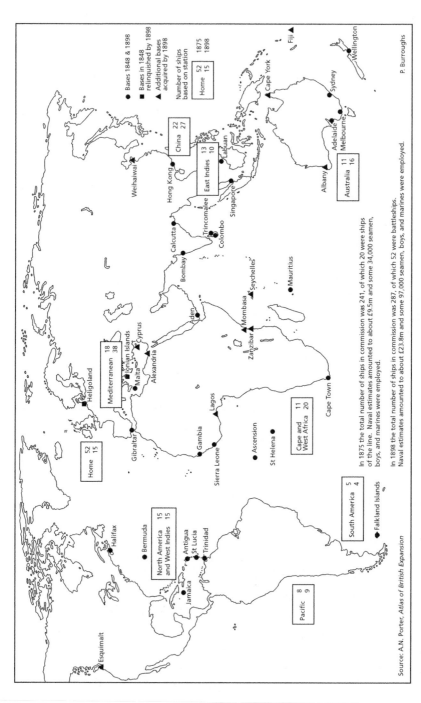

Bases 1848 & 1898
Bases in 1848 relinquished by 1898
Additional bases acquired by 1898

Number of ships based on station

	1875	1898
Home	52	15

China 22 27

East Indies 13 10

Labuan

Hong Kong

Weihaiwai

Mediterranean 18 38

Ionian Islands

Malta

Cyprus

Alexandria

Heligoland

Gibraltar

Home 52 15

Gambia

Lagos

Sierra Leone

Ascension

St Helena

Cape and West Africa 11 20

Cape Town

Aden

Bombay

Calcutta

Trincomalee

Colombo

Singapore

Zanzibar

Mombasa

Seychelles

Mauritius

Fiji

Wellington

Sydney

Adelaide

Melbourne

Albany

Australia 11 16

Cape York

Esquimalt

Halifax

Bermuda

Jamaica

Antigua

St Lucia

Trinidad

North America and West Indies 15 15

Pacific 8 9

South America 5 4

Falkland Islands

In 1875 the total number of ships in commission was 241, of which 20 were ships of the line. Naval estimates amounted to about £9.5m and some 34,000 seamen, boys, and marines were employed.

In 1898 the total number of ships in commission was 287, of which 52 were battleships. Naval estimates amounted to about £23.8m and some 97,000 seamen, boys, and marines were employed.

P. Burroughs

Source: A.N. Porter, *Atlas of British Expansion*

Map 4 The Royal Navy and its stations, 1875 and 1898

and the building programme of France. Between 1885 and 1890, the Royal Navy kept six first-class battleships in the Mediterranean. In the fretful 1890s, the number rose to ten and, by 1902, to fourteen.[37] The naval 'scare' became endemic and drove spending higher and higher: from £10.6 million in 1882 to £24 million by 1899. Even so, after 1893, fear of naval inferiority in the Mediterranean Sea was a governing factor in British policy. The sense of being dragged willy-nilly into a dangerous, expensive and inflexible commitment explains much of the continuing anger of the Gladstonians (until the mid-1890s) at what they regarded as the Egyptian folly.

Strategic insecurity placed a huge premium on diplomatic finesse. From the beginning, the British found themselves paying a diplomatic ransom for the occupation, and Egypt became, bizarrely, the fulcrum of their world policy. Having claimed a European mandate to reorganise Egypt's finances, the British were pressed by France and Germany (both with seats on the international *Caisse* which controlled part of Egypt's budget) to compensate the bondholders without delay. They pressed for wider international supervision of Egyptian finances, denounced the charge the British levied on Cairo for the cost of their garrison and threatened an international enquiry into the fiasco of the Sudan campaign. The British were to pay dearly for the privilege of staying. The result of this pressure was soon visible. To appease the Germans (who had less at stake financially), Gladstone referred a crop of colonial disputes to a congress in Berlin in 1884. There Bismarck wielded his *baton Egyptien* to good effect. To break the Franco-German combination and escape the general displeasure of Europe, the British abandoned a shoal of colonial claims. At a stroke, Bismarck gained an embryo empire in West, East and Southwest Africa and in the Pacific. To his lackey, the filibuster king of the Belgians, Leopold II, fell a giant crumb from the diplomats' table: the Congo basin. The British took their reward in the easing of financial and diplomatic pressure on Egypt.[38]

This was just the first round, for the partition of Africa, like the reform of Egypt, had hardly begun. The real task of managing Britain's ungainly new commitment fell to Lord Salisbury, the supremo of foreign policy between 1886 and 1892 and from 1895 to 1900 when he was both Prime Minister and Foreign Secretary. (He remained Prime Minister until 1902 but gave up the Foreign Office in 1900). Salisbury was greatly helped by the ruthless skill with which Evelyn

Baring (later Lord Cromer) created a 'veiled protectorate' in Egypt to minimise open dissent. Baring's 'system' preserved the fiction of Egyptian autonomy. But it rested on the tacit knowledge of the Egyptian ruler that defiance would mean deposition; on the studied manipulation of Egypt's internal stresses; and on the systematic infiltration of the government by British 'advisers' who were Baring's eyes and ears. With unrivalled political intelligence, a British garrison (of 6,000 men), a reorganised local army under British officers, and an extraordinary hold over his political masters in London (a measure of their trust), Baring was able to restore Egypt's solvency (by 1890) and ride out the crises of his eccentric regime.[39] Salisbury's other advantage lay in the chronic mistrust between France and Germany and the gradual emergence of two rival diplomatic groupings: Germany, Austria-Hungary and Italy on one side; France and Russia (after 1892) on the other. But he faced the constant risk that another crisis in the Near East might unite the continental powers behind a scheme of partition whose victim (apart from the Sultan) would be Britain's strategic link with India.

By outlook and training, Salisbury was well suited to this game of diplomatic poker. He took a disenchanted, ironic view of human motive. He mistrusted enthusiasm and laughed at nationalism ('the philological law of nations'[40]). But he had thought deeply about state-craft and saw the virtue of an active policy in Europe.[41] 'Sleepless tact, immovable calmness and patience'[42] he deemed the secret of success; the diplomat's victories were 'made up of a series of microscopic advantages....' 'Serene, impassive intelligence' was the mark of the statesman.[43]

Salisbury regarded foreign policy as a realm of technical exper-tise ill-suited to wayward cabinets let alone the rough and tumble of electoral politics.[44] He preferred to work in secrecy with a small group of aides. From his room in the Foreign Office or at Hatfield, his country house near London, he kept a close, obsessive watch on the cauldron of Near East diplomacy and the manoeuvres of his European counterparts. He held the threads of policy tightly in his grasp. In the 'inner zone' of British policy, the security corridor to India, his authority was not eas-ily challenged. The 'official' interest in India and Egypt was under his command; occupation had soothed the Egyptian bondholders. Public hostility to Turkey aroused by new Armenian 'Horrors' was the main constraint. But, in the 'outer zone' beyond, where diplomacy grappled with unofficial colonialism, his grip was less sure.

Yet Salisbury's whole policy depended upon the careful balance between the needs of Egypt and the Near East, where Britain was most vulnerable, and British interests in other regions of the Outer World. In essence, his technique was to use the open spaces and 'light soil' of tropical Africa to appease France and Germany, soften their irritation at Britain's unwarranted primacy in Cairo and stave off an anti-British coalition among the continental powers. This was easier said than done. By the 1880s, unofficial or commercial interest in African hinterlands was growing rapidly. In Senegal and the Upper Niger, the military sub-imperialism of the French colonial army was on the march.[45] Rival groups of traders, missionaries and private imperialists were soon jostling each other and scrambling for 'treaties' granting commercial, mineral or religious rights. Worse still, they were remarkably deft at rallying public support at home for ventures easily repackaged as crusades against slavery or for the promotion of Christianity through commerce.

To Salisbury, the result seemed a nightmare of misguided if not fraudulent expansionism. At best it might be managed: it could not be suppressed. Left untended, it threatened to wreck the fingertip delicacy with which he steered between the rival great power combinations. It might drive him into unwelcome friendships and towards unwanted confrontations. Many years before, ruminating on the sources of friction in European politics, he had argued that, when a state had become 'permanently anarchical and defenceless', its neighbours for self-preservation must impose a 'tutelage of ambassadors . . . or . . . partition'.[46] This insight he now applied to anarchic, defenceless Africa. The aim of policy must be to damp down the quarrels of Europe's frontiersmen by an equitable partition of spheres before they could inflame opinion and damage the interests that really mattered. To this most detached observer of human foibles, with his gloomy view of the burdens on British power, it seemed obvious that the diplomatic defence of Egypt depended upon a cartographic fantasy: the parcelling-up of Africa.

Salisbury may have been the grand architect of African partition, applying his diplomatic method to regions as remote and unknown, he once said, as the 'far side of the moon'. But he had to tread carefully round vociferous 'interests' at home, and ruthless empire-builders on the ground like Goldie and Rhodes. Without the means (and perhaps the confidence) to counter their mastery of the

press, he took a fatalistic view of public opinion. 'I once told Salisbury', wrote the German ambassador, 'that it seemed to be the Government's duty to lead public opinion. He replied that this was harder than
I appeared to realise.'[47] Whatever his reservations about the methods
and mentality of the private imperialists, he had little choice but to press
on behalf of their claims. He mixed the careful palliation of Germany
(exchanging Heligoland for Zanzibar) with the brutal coercion of Portugal (both in 1890). Portugal's claims in what is now Zimbabwe were
dismissed with a growl – in favour of Rhodes. The contest with France,
which had greater strength on the spot and, after 1892, an alliance with
Russia, required much more finesse. Salisbury could not afford to let the
French *officiers soudanais* and their ragtag black army hem in British
interests on the West African coast and deny them their hinterland;
or risk an armed struggle between them and Goldie's pale imitation
of the East India Company (Salisbury was scornful of Goldie's Clive-
like pretensions). Nor could he permit a French forward move into the
southern Sudan, in case their arrival coincided with the expected collapse of the Mahdist regime in Khartoum. A French-ruled Sudan would
have wrecked Cromer in Egypt. In the West African case, despite much
bad-tempered diplomacy and some sabre-rattling in the bush, Salisbury
largely achieved the partition he wanted. In the Sudan, his victory was
much more complete. There Kitchener's (Anglo-Egyptian) army, with
its light railways and steam launches, decisively smashed the Mahdist
regime and captured Khartoum (in September 1898). With Marchand's
tiny force at Fashoda hugely outnumbered, and the Royal Navy assembling in the English Channel, Paris abandoned its claim to the Upper
Nile Valley.

Salisbury's triumph had been three-fold. He had secured
Britain's position in Egypt, the strategic hinge of Anglo-Indian defence,
without drawing down on his head a continental coalition. The price
he had paid in African claims had been surprisingly light, guarding his
flank against an outcry at home. Above all, he had avoided the diplomatic and military setbacks that dogged Disraeli and Gladstone and
threatened electoral disaster. But, by the late 1890s, for all his success
at Fashoda, it was no longer so clear that his deft combination of British
strength on the ground, with an agile diplomacy and Britain's naval
deterrent could protect British interests against the threat of attrition.

The main reason for this was the sudden emergence of a new
epicentre of extra-European upheaval. China's shattering defeat by
Japan in 1895 signalled a political bankruptcy as complete as that of

the Ottomans twenty years before. The break-up of the Ch'ing empire seemed imminent. Even more alarming from the British point of view was the formation of the 'Far Eastern Triplice' – a coalition of Germany, France and Russia – to strip Japan of her spoils and impose their own terms for China's survival. Britain's commercial interests were centred on Shanghai and the Yangtse valley but spread out all over China. Neither Kwangtung in the south (the hinterland behind Hong Kong) nor North China and Peking could easily be given up. But with France looking north from Indochina, Russia south from the Amur, and German interest in Shantung, the British faced a squeeze and Salisbury a dilemma. He could fall in with an agreed partition and make the best terms he could. He could challenge the other powers to an open competition for the spheres and concessions which the Chinese offered in return for loans. Or he could hang back and wait, hoping the crisis would pass.

Salisbury's instinct was to wait. An early agreement with Britain isolated and the Triplice in harmony would be expensive and perhaps unacceptable to his colleagues and public opinion. An open competition risked extending the Triplice to the Near East, exposing the core of his system to the danger he tried most to avoid, and at a moment when the Armenian crisis and Anglo-French rivalry in Africa were coming to a head. 'In Asia there is room for us all', he soothed in November 1896.[48] But delay was not an easy option. Salisbury's caution was out of tune with the mounting excitement among the British in China and their sympathisers at home. The Asia-Pacific had replaced the Near East and tropical Africa as the platform for imperial publicists and commercial alarmists. The young George Curzon, patrician, politician, scholar, traveller and 'coming man', proclaimed the Far East to be the only region left where British manufacturers could find and keep an open market.[49] In the *Transformation of China* (1898), Archibald Colquhoun insisted that only in China could Britain hope to expand her Asian commerce and strengthen her position. The *Times* correspondent in China, George Morrison, regaled his foreign editor with dire warnings of French and Russian advance, while Chirol raged back against Salisbury's 'infirmities' and the 'blundering and lying in which Downing Street excels'.[50] Inside the Cabinet, Joseph Chamberlain pressed for a more forceful policy:[51] outside it he intrigued for an ill-fated German alliance. Under this barrage, Salisbury moved crabwise. Peking was asked to promise that no territorial rights would be granted away in the Yangtse valley. Russian, French and German acquisitions were

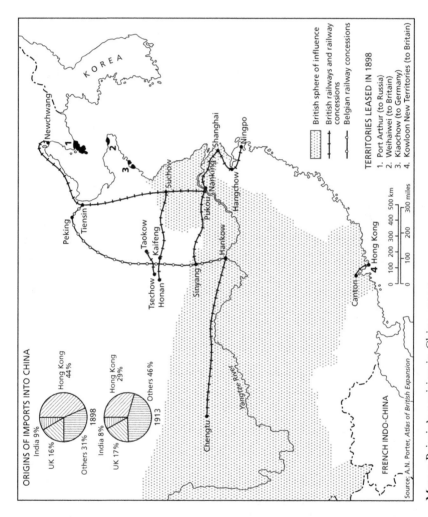

ORIGINS OF IMPORTS INTO CHINA

Hong Kong 44%
India 9%
UK 16%
Others 31%
1898

Hong Kong 29%
India 8%
UK 17%
Others 46%
1913

KOREA

Newchwang

Peking
Tientsin

Taokow
Kaifeng
Tsechow
Honan
Sinyang
Suchow
Pukow
Nanking
Shanghai
Hankow
Hangchow
Ningpo

Chengtu

Yangtze River

Canton
Hong Kong

FRENCH INDO-CHINA

British sphere of influence

British railways and railway
concessions

Belgian railway concessions

TERRITORIES LEASED IN 1898

1. Port Arthur (to Russia)
2. Weihaiwei (to Britain)
3. Kiaochow (to Germany)
4. Kowloon New Territories (to Britain)

0   100 200 300 400 500 km
0   100   200   300 miles

Source: A.N. Porter, Atlas of British Expansion

Map 5 Britain's position in China, 1900

'balanced' by a British base at Wei-hai-wei in North China and the extension of Hong Kong into the 'New Territories'. But Salisbury also tried to reduce the danger of friction with Russia (his main fear) by acknowledging her claim to priority in Manchuria in the Scott-Muraviev agreement in 1899. If Russia, as France's ally, had nothing to gain from quarrelling with Britain, so he reasoned, there was little danger of Anglo-French antagonism in the Near East and Africa spilling over into war. This was an approach already vindicated by the French retreat in the Fashoda crisis and the successful resolution of Anglo-French differences in West Africa. But, in the middle of 1900, as Britain became ever more deeply embroiled in the South African War, the Boxer Rising and its xenophobic challenge to all foreign interests in China threatened to unite Britain's rivals in a general partition of the Ch'ing empire. 'Her Majesty's Government', Salisbury told his minister at Peking with gloomy understatement, 'view with uneasiness a "concert of Europe" in China.'[52]

As it turned out, the Chinese were too resilient and the Europeans too divided to permit a replay of the African partition. Japan's victory over Russia in 1905 removed a Chinese share-out from the European diplomatic agenda. But the Boxer crisis in 1900 had brought the new geopolitics of British power to a climax. It signalled the birth of what became the grand dilemma of imperial strategy in the twentieth century: how to safeguard British interests simultaneously in Europe, the Middle East and East Asia. With the great enlargement of scale brought by the new wave of rivalry and confrontation in Asia and the Pacific, Salisbury's delicate system of checks, balances, blandishments and threats, with its pivot in Egypt, seemed to have reached its term. In the world now imagined by Pearson, Kidd and Mackinder, and by Chamberlain, Milner or Curzon, old diplomacy was not enough. The tide of world politics, that had run so long in Britain's favour, now seemed to have turned against her.

Managing empire

Managing a worldwide empire under these new conditions threw a heavy burden of political management onto administrative institutions in London that had grown up haphazardly since the early part of the century. 'The external affairs of Great Britain', remarked a sarcastic observer, 'are distributed without system between the Foreign, Colonial and India Offices. Their provinces overlap and intersect each other... like the divisions of some of the northern counties of Scotland.'[53] In fact, responsibility for the faraway spheres of rule and influence that made up the British system was scattered across half a dozen departments. The shadow of the Treasury with its 'Gladstonian garrison' of bureaucratic skinflints lay over them all. The Foreign Office enjoyed primacy in external affairs as the guardian of Britain's stake in the cockpits of Europe – the centre of the world. It supervised relations in the 'informal empire' including Egypt (even after its occupation in 1882), the Sudan (even after conquest in 1898), China and the early protectorates in West and East Africa. The Colonial Office ruled over a jumble of 'crown colonies' (where local representatives had an advisory role at best), dependencies and protectorates; and reigned over the self-governing settler colonies, who resented this *mésalliance*. In the Mediterranean, parts of tropical Africa and even in China (Hong Kong was a crown colony) it was the recalcitrant junior partner of the Foreign Office, with its own view of priorities. The India Office had been constructed in 1858 out of the East India Company and the old Board of Control to preside over an Indian 'empire' enlarged by 1885 to include all of Burma as well western outposts in the Persian Gulf and at Aden. Control over imperial defence lay with the Admiralty and the War Office. The former regarded itself (like the Foreign Office) as the real guarantor of imperial safety and despised the army as a motley of colonial garrisons without strategic value.

Of course, the vast proportion of public business in the colonies and India lay 'below the line' and never came to the attention of officials or ministers in London. The self-governing colonies were almost entirely exempt from imperial scrutiny. In theory, the Colonial Office could disallow their legislation if it was deemed to infringe the imperial prerogative in external affairs, defence or constitutional change. In practice, this power was rarely needed and hardly ever used. Crown colony governors reported to the Office, but, even with the telegraph (still very expensive) and more frequent mails, its officials were ill-equipped to oversee their rule. Colonial governors were, by convention, masters in their own house. They could be rebuked or recalled for misdemeanours or acting *ultra vires*, but, provided they stayed solvent, kept order and avoided war, remote control from London was lax. The

Colonial Office acted more as a regulator, monitoring colonial laws, expenditure and personnel, than as a policy-making department, certainly before Joseph Chamberlain's arrival in 1895.[54] Much the same was true of the India Office, which faced a single 'super-governor' in the Viceroy. The Viceroy, selected almost invariably from the political elite at home, not from the ranks of British officialdom in India, had his own network of political friends, and his status approached that of a cabinet minister. As a temporary autocrat of tsar-like magnificence, the liege-lord of 600 feudatory states and an Asian ruler with his own army and diplomatic service (for India's frontier regions), he was hard to coerce and practically irremovable.[55] The vast stream of paper that poured westward annually to fill the archives of the India Office was less a measure of its control than a relic of Parliament's obsession since the age of Burke with the misuse of Indian revenues by the home government for patronage or foreign war. In fact, the torrent of administrative minutiae enthusiastically supplied by Calcutta dulled parliamentary curiosity about India to the point of anaesthesia – and was meant to.[56] The formal debates on the Indian budget were notoriously ill-attended.

Despite this pattern of devolution by accident and design, there were many issues that rose 'above the line' and required a decision in London. Any serious breakdown of internal order would mean reinforcing the colonial garrison from the pool of British infantry battalions – the reserve currency of imperial power. Using up this scarce resource (much of it already deployed in India) raised awkward questions about the balance between British commitments in Asia, North America, the Mediterranean and Southern Africa. Any constitutional alteration had to be inspected in case it implied new costs for the British taxpayer or had implications for other dependencies or imperial defence. Action by a colonial government which impeded British trade invariably set off an alarm at Westminster. London had to swallow the tariffs imposed by self-governing colonies, but vetoed any attack on free trade in India and the dependencies. Any aspect of imperial rule, or of the advancement of British interests in the informal empire, which produced international complications and raised the prospect, however remote, of conflict with a European power, attracted immediate scrutiny in London. More than anything else, it was the addition of new imperial liabilities carrying higher costs and the risk of friction with rival powers which exercised policy-makers in the late-Victorian period.

As a result, the problem of imperial expansion has come to be the main window through which we peer at the late-Victorian idea of empire. It raised in an acute form the question of what purpose the formal empire and the larger British system were meant to serve, on what grounds they should be extended, and for whose benefit. The response of British leaders was bound to reflect, however subliminally, their understanding of world politics, their notions of strategy, their grasp of economic realities, their views of race and culture, their sense of national community, their hopes of expansion and fears of decline. The tortuous decision-making imposed by conflicting priorities at home and abroad and the periodic sense of crisis, gives a powerful insight into the mechanisms through which primacy in a huge and unwieldy world-system was reconciled with representative government in an age of growing social anxiety. Indeed, the intricate connection sometimes revealed between domestic politics and imperial policy raises the hardest question of all: how far Britain had become by 1900 an 'imperialised' society, founding its values, culture and social hierarchy mainly upon its role as the centre of an imperial system.[57]

Not surprisingly, the process by which the central issues of imperial expansion were resolved politically has long been the focus of an intense debate. The older historians of late-Victorian imperialism emphasised crude motives of economic gain, diplomatic prestige, racial arrogance or electoral calculation as the dynamic behind the willingness of successive British governments to extend the formal empire of rule, practise the diplomacy of brinkmanship in the Middle East, Southeast Asia and China, and resort to a costly and humiliating colonial war in 1899. But, since the 1960s, explanation has been dominated by the powerful model put forward by Robinson and Gallagher and taken up by a large school of disciples.[58] Robinson and Gallagher rejected most previous explanations as naïve conjecture or special pleading. They insisted that the motives for imperial aggrandisement had to be sought in the largely private thoughts and calculations of the decision-making elite who sanctioned territorial advance and chose between the forward policies that were urged upon them. They denied that the documentary evidence revealed any serious pursuit of economic goals and claimed instead that the overwhelming motive for intervention, annexation and acquisition was strategic: to defend the territories and spheres accumulated in the flush times of mid-century, above all the vast, valuable, vulnerable empire in India.

This conclusion, resting upon a close study of the African partition, was also based upon a radical reinterpretation of the place of
empire in British politics and the outlook of the ruling elite. Whereas
previous writers had stressed the growth of 'popular' imperialism and
the anxious desire of party leaders to propitiate it with jingo excess,
Robinson and Gallagher argued that public attitudes towards empire
were mainly shaped by dislike of the financial burden it implied and
distaste for the moral risks it imposed. The best kind of empire was
informal (and therefore free from patronage), costless and peaceful.
Expansion might be tolerated if it recouped its expenses and avoided
disaster. But the Midlothian election in 1880 showed how the electorate
would punish a government caught red-handed in imperial misadven-
ture. Thereafter, they argued, ministers would only agree to a forward
policy *in extremis*, as a painful remedy to stave off the general attrition
of their world-system and its defences. Far from bowing to popular
pressure or the pleading of commercial and financial interests, the 'official mind' – a key concept in their model – based its grudging decisions to advance on gloomy estimates of strategic and electoral danger.
They mistrusted jingoism on principle and loathed all forms of imperial
enthusiasm. The policy-makers' rule of thumb decreed that, far from
staging a forward march from the bastions of mid-Victorian imperialism, the British were condemned by secular change to run faster to stay
in the same place.

In other hands, this ironic portrait of late-Victorian high policy
broadened into a definitive view of British imperialism after the turning
point of 1880. Reactive, defensive, gloomily conservative, it was built
on regret for the golden age of mid-Victorian primacy and obsessive
concern for the protection of India. Britain was a *status quo* power
drawn into reluctant expansion by the crises in her spheres of influence, felt most acutely where strategic not economic interests were at
stake.[59] But, at the height of its influence, this 'pessimistic' interpretation was robustly challenged in a critique which pointed unerringly
to its least plausible components. These were the implication that the
mid-Victorian era had seen the apogee of British imperial power; the
suggestion that late-Victorian expansion was economically sterile; and
the view of the policy-makers as a Platonic elite guided by abstract
principles of national interest. Cain and Hopkins[60] insisted instead that
politicians, officials and the commercial and financial world of the City
of London were united by a common ethos of 'gentlemanly capitalism'.

The Victorian ruling elite sprang from a marriage of landed and commercial (not industrial) wealth, and its members were to be found as
much in banks and finance houses as in Whitehall or the Houses of
Parliament. A common education, shared values and linked fortunes
meant that governments and their advisers were instinctively sympathetic to the interests of trade, but especially finance. The key decisions
of late-Victorian forward policy, like the occupation of Egypt in 1882,
the policy of spheres in China and the war against the Boers in 1899,
were taken not on strategic criteria but to promote (or defend) Britain's
financial stake. Far from marking the gloomy defence of a reduced
inheritance, imperial assertiveness reflected an aggressive commercial
and financial expansion and the deliberate channelling of new economic
energy into a periphery which had to be 'remade' for the purpose. And
behind this advance stood not a doubting, sceptical public opinion but
a powerful vested interest enthroned at the heart of government.

The sheer scale of Britain's global activity from China to Peru,
the inevitable intermingling of political and economic interests, the different conjunctures of international affairs and the economic cycle and
the shifting cast of actors make any overview a heroic abstraction. But
there are obvious ways in which neither grand model quite fits the
evidence. Thus the furious arguments *within* the political elite after
1880 over Ireland, Egypt and South Africa show how useless it was
to appeal to an agreed version of the 'national interest' as the lode-
stone of imperial policy. The 'national interest' was not a text to be
consulted; it was a trophy carried off by force of rhetoric or the canny
appeal to public sentiment; at best, it was an oracle of Sibylline ambiguity. However much it yearned for seclusion in a 'hidden city' barred
to the uninitiated, the 'official mind' was forced to accept the discipline of popular government. Delegations had to be seen; newspapers
read; questions answered; support rallied; public emotions appeased;
opponents (and colleagues) outmanoeuvred, by fair means if possible.
No policy-maker cultivated a more Olympian detachment than Lord
Salisbury, the 'great Unapproachable'.[61] But, even Salisbury acknowledged that diplomacy must defer to popular prejudice. 'The loss of
Constantinople', he told Lord Randolph Churchill in 1886, 'would be
the ruin of our party ... The main strength of the Tory party ... lies in
its association with the honour of the country.'[62] When governments
were divided and control over imperial policy was disputed between
ministers, as happened frequently between 1880 and 1900, indecision

and the tendency to sniff the popular breeze were all the greater. The normal state of the 'official mind' was not cool certainty but chronic schizophrenia.[63]

This endemic turbulence made it all the less likely that any government would risk identifying itself openly with a single economic interest, however powerful. In fact, the relations between government and business in the imperial sphere were marked not by a sense of common purpose but by deep mutual mistrust and a conscious disparity in outlook and values. Businessmen raged against diplomatic ignorance of commercial realities. Ministers and officials sneered at the obtuseness of private entrepreneurs. The Royal Niger Company became Salisbury's *bête noire* in the quest for Anglo-French agreement in West Africa. 'Goldie' (its head), complained Salisbury, 'is a great nuisance. His knowledge of foreign relations must have been acquired in a music hall.'[64] Proconsuls jeered at the dubious ethics of their business counterparts. Salisbury's contemptuous dismissal of the British commercial population in Johannesburg ('a people for whom we care nothing'[65]) is well known. To the exponents of 'chartered imperialism', the efficiency of their 'company states' organised along semi-commercial lines and answerable to shareholders, stood in dynamic contrast to the 'cumbrous machinery' of colonial administration.[66] The hallmarks of colonial rule were heavy taxation, wasteful expenditure and vaunting official ambition. But, in official eyes, unofficial imperialists and the business interests behind them showed a myopic disregard for the framework of order that was needed to make their commercial inroads tolerable to indigenous populations and home opinion.

At bottom, there was a fundamental divide that could not be bridged by agreement on the logic of capitalism. If matters came to a crisis, the incentives and obligations that shaped business decisions were very different from those at work in politics and government. Status, merit, honour and success were judged very differently in these two worlds. Lost battles did not break banks but they could break governments. Trade monopolies made business sense but political trouble. Conscripting semi-servile labour – African, Indian, Chinese – lowered commercial costs, but (if discovered) could raise the home political temperature to boiling point. A diplomatic rebuff (unless of directly commercial significance) was of little moment in the City, but at Westminster it was the noose from which a government could be hanged. In theory, diplomacy and commerce might march in step, but at the first sign of trouble each followed quite different rules of engagement. It was grudging respect for each other's utility, not identity of outlook, that drove them into wary collaboration.

These objections suggest that there is no need to choose between two starkly different views of late-Victorian imperialism. It is possible instead to reconstruct the workings of the 'official mind' to take better account of the untidy reality. The starting point is to recognise that, as in earlier periods, the initiative for British imperial expansion rarely if ever lay with governments, ministers and officials in London. The Colonial Office, remarked one ardent unofficial imperialist, could not be a creative force: it was 'the "governor" of the steam-engine, not the boiler'.[67] The energy for advance had to come from elsewhere. After 1880, much as before, expansion was incremental and its agents usually local men (both official and unofficial) who enjoyed backing at home from the array of public and private bodies with interests on the periphery of empire. With the acceleration of trade and investment, and the ready means of switching capital from one region to another, it was not surprising that the speed with which the frontier of European influence was driven forward was getting faster and faster. Nor that zones of longstanding sensitivity (like the Near East) should have seemed at greater risk from a sudden shift in their political and economic fortunes. But the hinterlands into which British interests ventured differed widely in two crucial ways. In some cases, the unofficial presence had grown strongly enough, or rallied sufficient local support, to establish a visible British interest; in others, it had not. Some of these 'bridge-heads' enjoyed highly placed or well-organised sponsors at home, with backstairs influence or the means of publicity; others were much less well endowed.

The real task of the 'official mind' was to decide which of these interests deserved official support and in what form. For that purpose, arcane criteria of the 'national interest' were of little use – except as rhetorical cover. What counted was whether those who wanted to drag the 'imperial factor' after them, or enlist its support in their local struggles, could peg out their claim not just in Africa or Asia but on public attention in London. Newspaper coverage and a talent for propaganda were vital. At the height of its difficulties in the 1890s, the Royal Niger Company, struggling against commercial rivals, bureaucratic hostility and French advance, won the backing of the *The Times* in a series of planted articles.[68] Its chairman, complained a British diplomat in

West Africa, 'is on the spot [i.e. in London] and has a ready and clever tongue'.[69] Even to official agents in the field it often seemed that the best plan was to act first and wait for public opinion to rally behind. It was no good asking the Foreign Office for permission in advance, advised Milner in 1895. 'The people on the spot must take things into their own hands, when, if the occasion of the decisive move is well chosen, public opinion here will surely approve.'[70] But that meant careful attention to rousing public feeling and the artful depiction of a 'forward policy' as the defence of an existing (and valuable) interest. Even the great Lord Cromer was not above using the press 'to work for a "forward game"', and outflank his nominal master, Lord Salisbury.[71] 'Just like all British governments', Cromer was reported as saying. 'they will act more or less in a hand to mouth way on the spur of the moment, but they will not think out and adopt a steady policy.'[72] Of course, the weaker the vanguard of British influence and the more exposed it was to local or international attack, the harder it would be to extract a commitment from the policy-makers. Nor was there any point 'firing into a continent' (in Conrad's graphic phrase): there had to be sufficient local agency to be the 'transformer' that would inject British power into local circuits. Reasonable certainty was needed that the cost would be minimal or could be recouped. The vital decision London had to make turned most of all upon a geopolitical calculus, in which the international risks of intervention were weighed against the local means of British leverage and the extent to which opinion at home had been mobilised for action.

It was hardly surprising that policy made under these conditions was often erratic and inconsistent, lurching forward, falling back, plunging from inertia to frenzy. The longer decisions lingered in the arena of opinion bounded by Westminster, the City and the Clubland of St James, the more likely they were to be improvised, opportunistic and unpredictable. The effects of this were felt more severely in some regions than in others. In the 'inner zone' which followed the Anglo-Indian 'security corridor' from Gibraltar to Bombay, the official interest was dominant. Here matters could often be settled privately between London and Calcutta, and strategy was a trump card. But, in the vast 'outer zone' beyond, the official interest was much weaker, and official concepts more protean. Here, even the master of *Realpolitik* could lose his way. Even Lord Salisbury became, as we have seen, the target of savage private criticism from insiders who saw in his chessboard diplomacy not a master-plan but muddle and sloth. It might indeed be argued that the whole pattern of Britain's territorial aggrandisement after 1880 had less to do with any grand strategy, than with the latent strength of the bridgeheads of influence and occupation established before the era of partition and the all-but-irresistible pressure on governments to support them, where practicable, against their enemies. But that is not the whole story. The most striking feature of the period after 1880 was precisely the uncertainty about how the 'national interest' could be defined in an era of such disorienting fluidity. But, if policy-makers, proconsuls, private imperialists, press and public opinion all displayed periodic signs of hysteria, it was partly because geopolitical disorder abroad seemed to be matched by the unnerving fluidity of the domestic political scene.

The late-Victorians and empire

Indeed, to many 'imperialists', alarmed by signs of imperial weakness, it was evident that the dangers abroad found an echo in disturbance at home. Far from providing a stable platform for the defence of a world-empire, British society was in the throes of upheaval. Far from springing to the defence of its vital interests, it was distracted by sectional strife. Far from recognising its need for resources overseas, it was at odds over the share-out of wealth at home. Partisan struggle sapped imperial will. This gloomy connection had been made by Lord Salisbury. In a notorious essay published in 1883, and brusquely titled 'Disintegration', he prophesied the imperial doom that would follow the rising clamour for radical reform.[73] The radicals' assault on 'churchmen, landowners, publicans, manufacturers, house-owners, railway-shareholders [and] fund-holders' was symptomatic of the sea-change in British politics. Its effects were magnified by the democratisation of the electorate. The ballot was a 'regime of surprises'; the voters paid only fitful attention; ministerial power was held 'on a capricious and precarious tenure'; the House of Commons had become the instrument of 'sudden revulsions of feeling' unimaginable in earlier times. The result was a social war – 'civil war with the gloves on'. Society was atomising into hostile fragments. 'The temper that severs class from class is constantly gaining strength.' Patriotism was dead or dying. 'The national impulses which used to make Englishmen cling together in face of every external trouble are beginning to disappear.' Pride in the 'stupendous achievement of thousands ruling over millions' (a reference to India) had shrivelled. Instead, Britain was faced with the 'loss of large branches and limbs of our Empire, and . . . the slow estrangement of the classes which make up the nation to which that Empire belongs'. And, of course, it was Ireland that was 'the worst symptom of our malady': to abandon the Union would be an avowal 'that all claims to protect or govern anyone beyond our own narrow island were at an end'.

Salisbury's polemic was partly designed for his own party's consumption. But his acrid vision of democratic politics was shared (from a different angle) by his political opponents while his gloomy portrait of the decline of authority chimed with the prognostications of Herbert Spencer, the most influential social theorist of the age. Spencer had argued that social progress meant the advance from a 'militant' to an 'industrial' society: from rule by a prescriptive warrior elite towards voluntary cooperation between the myriad of specialised interests thrown up by economic and technological development. Iron- ically, at the same time as Salisbury was fulminating against disintegra- tion, Spencer was warning (in *Man versus the State*) against collectivist interference with the free play of social competition.[74] But Salisbury's fear that a mass electorate would turn its back on the *arcana imperii* of British world power, repudiate imperial obligations and thwart the exercise of consistent policy, became almost a political commonplace. John Morley, the radical editor and parliamentarian, had opined in 1880 that a working-class electorate would refuse to go to war.[75] Joseph Chamberlain thought that 'fighting can never again be popu- lar with the people'.[76] 'The old ways of diplomacy are unsuitable to the new Electorate', he told a friendly editor in 1885.[77] Even after the fall of the Gladstone ministry in 1886, Salisbury's colleague, Lord Ran- dolph Churchill, then high-priest of 'Tory Democracy', insisted that British policy was by its nature 'always more or less a policy of hand to mouth' since the government of the day 'depends upon a Parliamentary majority . . . assailed and swayed by an enlightened, but at the same time by a capricious, public opinion'.[78] Defending Constantinople, he told Salisbury, could not be done as it had been in the Crimean War or in the Eastern crisis of 1876–8: 'I doubt whether the people will support that method.'[79]

The implication was that the imperial burden had become dangerously heavy at a time when British politics were inflamed by the social, ethnic and religious antagonisms unleashed by domestic

radicalism and Irish Home Rule. For governments of either party, foreign or colonial entanglements brought with them the risk of war,
embarrassment and expense in a period of exceptional instability in
domestic politics. It was this that made veterans of either party like
the Liberal Harcourt and the Conservative Hicks-Beach so wary of
new commitments in Egypt and sub-Saharan Africa. Harcourt feared
the entrenchment of British power in Egypt and the slide towards a *de
facto* protectorate. He opposed the annexation of Uganda. Hicks-Beach
warned Salisbury that spending on empire would rouse opposition at
home and increase the pressure on the landed interest already beleaguered by agricultural depression.[80] For both men, an expanding empire
was an open-ended risk, an unlimited liability. Meeting its demands
would drive both parties into conflict with their natural supporters,
wreck the interests for which they stood and exhaust their electoral
credit. Keeping the parties afloat in rough democratic seas meant reducing to the minimum their exposure to the high winds of competitive
imperialism and its fearsome corollary, great power rivalry in Europe.
But to ardent imperialists like Milner and his circle it was precisely
this cringeing attitude to public opinion, the influence of 'wire-pullers'
and party hacks, and the elevation of party over empire that explained
the weakness and vacillation they saw in British policy. A decadent,
hysterical elite, too timid to lead, too selfish to abdicate, blocked the
constructive programme that was needed to fuse domestic and imperial
politics and to educate the masses. From the opposite end of the political
spectrum, the radical journalist J. A. Hobson warned that the irrational
instincts of mass opinion made it an easy prey to propaganda and
delusion.[81]

As we shall see, the imperialists protested too much and raised
a false alarm. But it is easy to see why they were anxious. If domestic opinion turned against the defence of empire, the imperial system
might unravel with astonishing speed. A 'premature' withdrawal from
the exposed salient of Egypt would signal an immediate shift in the
Mediterranean balance of power. The steady advance of British influence all along the seaborne approaches to India would go into reverse.
The long-range defence of its landward frontier against encroaching
rivals in Persia, Central Asia and Tibet would look less sure. It was
a cliché of Anglo-Indian officialdom that a strong frontier policy was
the touchstone of British rule in northwestern India, and the best warrant for Muslim loyalty. A second 'mutiny', however modest, would

re-open the Indian question in British politics with a vengeance. In China and at the Cape, British interests, influence and prestige also depended upon the assumption that force would be used to prevent their attrition. Failure to win parliamentary support for naval expansion would be just as dangerous. Naval primacy, at whatever the cost, was the ultimate guarantee that the British could underwrite their own claims and those of their innumerable clients and subjects. Its loss or disavowal was bound (amid much other damage) to rouse the separatist tendency latent in the colonial politics of the 'white dominions' or, in the special case of Canada, to weaken the argument against political union with its southern neighbour. In the domino theory of empire that Salisbury had invented (but which was taken up by many Unionists), the fate of Ireland was crucial. Its strategic position across the Atlantic approaches to Britain,[82] and its symbolic value as a proving ground of British institutions meant that Ireland was the exposed nerve of both domestic and imperial politics. The concession of Home Rule, and the failure to uphold the Union and 'tame' Irish nationalism, would be, on this view, the starting-gun for the implosion of British world power.

It is hard to tell how large a shift there was after 1880 in British attitudes to empire. There were no opinion polls to record public feeling on issues of empire and world power. In the election campaigns of the period, 'imperial' questions were absorbed into more urgent debates over Ireland in 1886, or wartime 'loyalty' in 1900. 'Imperial sentiment' played second fiddle to anti-Irish feeling, patriotic enthusiasm and the anxiety over employment and living standards at home. There is, anyway, much anecdotal evidence that, except in moments of unusual excitement, imperial questions stirred little public interest. It is true that contemporaries detected a persistent strain of jingoism in popular politics – a reserve tank of xenophobic prejudice. But to politicians like Salisbury jingoism was not a useful political fuel but a blind force, 'a strain of pure combativeness' at the base of society.[83] It was a far cry from the traditional attachment to the national interest whose decay he had lamented. It had little to do with the intelligent cultivation of 'empire-mindednesss' or a new sense of imperial identity. Radical commentators attributed any sign of popular support for overseas expansion, conquest or adventure to the crude emotions stirred up by manipulative politicians and an unscrupulous press: behind both stood the sinister shape of financial influence.[84] Playing upon the irrational instincts of an ill-educated urban mass, they created a jingo 'false-consciousness', transient and febrile. Working-class voters whose real interest lay in social reform and a redistribution of wealth were bought off with the fool's gold of imperial glory. Many historians have followed a similar line: that it took disillusionment with the South African War of 1899–1902 to prick the bubble of jingo-imperialism and usher in the sober age of liberal reform after 1906.

Indeed, a close study of popular culture suggests that the attractions of empire had little appeal except to those in the middle and upper classes to whom it might offer some material benefits – a career or a dividend. However stark they might seem in our selective rear view, the literary, musical or visual celebrations of empire were lost in the mass of non-imperial production. The efforts of imperialists to educate and inform testified not to their confidence in the imperialism of the masses, but to their fears of indifference or even downright hostility. Even after the trauma of the South African War, and perhaps because of it, this feeling persisted. 'One must unfortunately explain to these d___d fools', wrote Milner of his audiences in 1906, 'why we want... an Empire, and it pinches one in dealing with the methods of maintaining it.'[85]

Certainly, if the records of policy-making are any guide, *mass* enthusiasm for empire-building, whether spontaneous or manufactured, was considered a will o' the wisp. Far from bowing to a surge of popular imperialism or trying to drum up votes by derring-do on the imperial frontier, ministers of both parties viewed public opinion with deep mistrust. They feared (in Salisbury's words) a 'jingo hurricane' that could drive them on the rocks: an ill-conceived foreign adventure (like the relief of Gordon at Khartoum) ending in disaster. They were just as frightened of new commitments for which support at home might die away, leaving them helpless in the political doldrums. Both would be a huge electoral liability. But, equally, they could not afford to treat every demand for intervention or annexation with patrician contempt. Still less could they hope to 'manage' all public discussion of imperial issues, or reduce it to a soothing murmur of approbation. As a recent study has shown, a large part of the public interest in empire was expressed through pressure groups and associations lying outside the formal arena of parliamentary politics or straddling the usual lines of party loyalty. It connected with new political issues (like women's rights) and mobilised enthusiasts for a new kind of social politics.[86]

Working-class opinion might have been indifferent to the glories of the Raj, or the 'civilising mission' in tropical Africa. But it could hardly have been so to the value of overseas markets, some like India sustained by colonial rule. And their habit of migration displayed the tacit belief that British people were entitled to occupy the lands of others, provided their resistance was not embarrassingly stiff. This 'demographic' imperialism might not have been glamorous. But no British leader would have dared question its claims. In late-Victorian politics, 'empire' had come to mean more than the aggressive pursuit of new places to rule.

This suggests that we need a more complex explanation for the receptiveness of British opinion towards the huge growth of imperial liabilities after 1880 and the willingness to accept a large and growing burden of imperial defence. One obvious starting point is the capacity of interests connected with empire and Britain's spheres of overseas influence to maintain an influential presence on the domestic scene and win the political support necessary for their projects. In the past, the East India Company, the anti-slavery movement, the evangelicals, the China traders and the philanthropic businessmen of the South Australian or New Zealand Companies in the 1830s, had all enjoyed moments of special leverage in British politics. But they had all been vulnerable to the charge of 'old corruption' and to the ebb tide of public altruism. By the 1880s, however, imperial interests had dug deeper into domestic society and built a wider network of alliances. They also adapted with striking success to the new scale of popular politics and even to its language.

Behind this reinforcement of empire on the home front lay three great changes. The first was the sheer scale by the 1880s of overseas enterprise and settlement: a mass of overlapping mini-empires of traders, investors, migrants, missionaries, railway companies, shipping companies, mining ventures, banks, botanists and geographers. 'In every large seaport or manufacturing town in this Kingdom', pronounced the explorer H. M. Stanley in 1884, 'an enterprising shipowner or . . . manufacturer . . . should know something of geography.'[87] New geographical societies in Edinburgh and Manchester were followed by those on Tyneside (1887), Liverpool (1891) and Southampton (1897).[88] Britain's huge stake in the foreign trade of the extra-European world made commercial and political conditions from China to Peru the object of anxious scrutiny in a host of industrial districts now dependent on far-flung markets. Lancashire cottons might still be Britain's premier export. But, for a wide range of other industries, commercial geography had gone global. From the Black Country round Birmingham, Walsall exported three-fifths of its manufactures, the greater part to India and the settlement colonies.[89] Newcastle exported 30 per cent of its steel, almost all to 'India and the Colonies'.[90] 'The Colonies and India particularly afford very large markets for the products of the district', reported the Sheffield chamber of commerce in 1885.[91] To businessmen around the country, emigration and railway building were favoured panaceas for the falling off in trade. Capital exports soared after 1880, doubling British foreign investment by 1900 (and quadrupling it by 1913). Migration from Britain also showed a strong upward trend. From 1880 to 1893, the numbers leaving for extra-European destinations never fell below 200,000 a year, peaking at 320,000 in 1883. For six of the thirteen years after 1901, it exceeded 300,000 a year, before reaching a new peak of 470,000 on the eve of the First World War.[92] There were also many more 'sojourners' who spent their working lives abroad as soldiers, officials (in the new tropical dependencies), policemen, doctors, teachers, forestry experts, engineers and businessmen. Railway and steamship lines recruited their technical and managerial staff in Britain. The British India Steam Navigation Company alone employed 800 'Europeans' (i.e. British) – almost as many as the Indian Civil Service. Schools, universities and newspapers in India and the white dominions looked to Britain for professional expertise. In 1899, there were more than 10,000 British missionaries around the world.[93] By the end of the century, a career overseas, punctuated by home leave and ending in retirement at Cheltenham, Bournemouth, Bedford or other spots favoured by climate or schooling, had become a familiar pattern in middle-class life. Just as serial migration, punctuated by returns, was a feature of many working-class communities from Scotland to Cornwall.[94]

The volume of trade, migration and investment flowing overseas was symptomatic of the increasing integration of the domestic and international economy. It pointed to the growing attraction that its settler and colonial possessions exerted on the sea-power of the Old World. That had long been true of the United States. Indeed, much informed opinion by the 1880s was convinced that an introverted, militarised and dynastic Europe would be eclipsed by its dynamic offshoot beyond the Atlantic. In the 'world of fifty years to come', wrote the historian J. R. Green in 1880

how odd, how ludicrous, will be the spectacle of France
and Germany . . . still growling and snarling over their little
Alsace! To me all these Bismarcks and Dizzys and
Andrassys are alike anachronisms . . . whose mighty
schemes and mighty armies are being quietly shoved aside
by the herdsmen of Colorado and the sheepmasters of New
South Wales.[95]

By the last decade of the century, however, the role of the United States as the great recipient of migrants and capital was rivalled more and more by Britain's settler empire and India. New 'Americas' were rising in Canada, Australia and New Zealand. Britain's colonial societies acquired a new scale and sophistication. Their communications improved; they became more open to external influence; their economies were oriented more firmly to international markets. The scope of colonial government expanded. New functions were assumed – in transport, education, public health, conservation and public works. The effect was to reduce the social and cultural distance between the Mother Country and what had once been a string of settler outposts and an oriental garrison state. The points of contact were multiplied. Tastes and lifestyles converged – even in India where family life became more common for the British and a 'western education' more common among Indians: between 1881–2 and 1901–2 there was a threefold increase in the number of Indians being taught in English at schools and colleges.[96] A subtle but decisive shift occurred in British attitudes to the colonies of settlement. For Seeley, Froude and Dilke,[97] who commented authoritatively on 'Greater Britain', they had become the future sources of strength, an extension of Britain, the basis of a 'world-state'. Canada, thought Dilke, would support a population as large as that of the United States; Australia a 'white population which may be counted by hundreds of millions'.[98]

Thirdly, after 1880, the channels through which images and information from the colonial and semi-colonial world reached public attention in Britain became wider and deeper. Not surprisingly, the growing mass of external activity and connections required an ever more extensive network of domestic agencies – to mobilise its funds, recruit its personnel, process its information and trumpet its virtues. Settler governments began to compete more actively for capital and emigrants through British newspapers[99] and their high commissions in London.[100] From the late 1860s, *The Times* had carried a long monthly article surveying Australian affairs. A vast audience of would-be emigrants, investors, subscribers and recruits (not to mention their friends and relations) had to be addressed through pamphlets, prospectuses, brochures, religious literature and travel books (some deliberately designed like Trollope's to promote emigration). The demand for foreign news went up. A specialised press arose to meet (for example) the needs of 'Anglo-India' in Britain.[101] A tidal wave of print formed the backwash of empire. In Britain more than anywhere else, the new culture of worldwide mobility coincided with the coming of mass literacy (after the Education Act of 1870) and the appearance (after 1884) of mass politics.

It was in fact no accident that the promoters, lobbies, pressure groups and vested interests of empire and the wider 'British world' should have flourished in late-Victorian Britain. Their insistence that Britain's future lay in a deepening engagement with overseas communities, especially with those already bound by political ties to the Mother Country, chimed with some of the strongest social and cultural tendencies of the age. Late-Victorian society was decisively reshaped by the economic revolution in its food supply. From the 1870s onwards, the volume of imported food, grain especially, rose with dramatic speed – by three times between 1872 and 1903.[102] Farmers on cheap or 'free' land in North America could undercut the agrarian economies of the Old World. Without the burdens of rent, tax and intensive husbandry (necessary on 'old' soils), all they needed to compete was cheap bulk transport and an organised commerce. By the 1870s, an extensive rail network and a streamlined market (including a huge 'futures' market in Chicago[103]) brought the output of the American Midwest straight to the consumers of Europe. With their vast Atlantic traffic, accessible ports, dense communications and large population, the British Isles were the obvious market for American food. Here, politics were as critical as economics. It was the decision, unique among Europe's larger states, to preserve free trade and the open economy which threw open the British market to unlimited competition from foreign foodstuffs.

The results were dramatic. As farm prices fell so did rents and wages. As agricultural depression set in through the 1880s, rural communities (especially in the 'wheat countries'[104]) shrivelled. The distinctiveness and diversity of rural life began to atrophy. A tide of migration flowed towards the towns and cities. As a more uniformly urban society took shape, it adopted new social and cultural habits. Processing industries for imported food catered for a 'national' market, setting the trend towards mass retailing and the use of advertising to mobilise consumers. The falling price of food pushed up the living standards of families in work and created larger disposable incomes for new consumer goods: including 'exotic' foodstuffs, leisure, sport and 'cultural products' like newspapers, books and magazines. The literate urban consumer, with new tastes and interests shaped by marketing and the printed word, was a key figure in the remaking of late-Victorian society.

These changes in society at large were mirrored in the reshaping of the elite. The drastic fall of rents cut away the income of the landed class, or of that portion mainly dependent on agricultural receipts. Wealth and power within the aristocracy shifted towards those whose agrarian incomes were buttressed with earnings from finance, commerce or public employment.[105] The titled 'guinea pig' became a familiar figure on the boards of companies: by 1896, one-quarter of the peerage held directorships.[106] The pressure for inter-marriage with wealthy but non-landed families became more acute. The marriage market, like the food market, was opened up to American imports. New creations in the peerage marked the arrival of a neo-aristocracy for whom landed property was less a source of income and authority than an item of (very) conspicuous consumption and a leisure amenity. The independent 'country gentlemen', the traditional ballast of the parliamentary system against its 'faddists', placemen and adventurers, shrank in numbers and influence. New lifestyles, new sources of income, new social and geographical horizons,[107] and perhaps a new urgency in wealth creation in the speculative nineties were all signs that the upper class was being recreated behind the facade of aristocratic continuity.[108] To many contemporaries the outward sign of this change was the galloping expansion of the financial world, the brutal display of new wealth and the pre-eminence of London – that 'vortex of gigantic forces' as H. G. Wells called it[109] – as the centre of culture, fashion and commerce.

Late-Victorian society was thus far from being dragged willy-nilly behind an alien imperial juggernaut. Imperial-minded interests, lobbies and pressure groups took easy root in a soil well harrowed by the side-effects of international economic change. 'Empire' was acceptable to a broad swathe of opinion because it appealed both to those alarmed by the stresses in late-Victorian Britain and to those exhilarated by its new possibilities. The stresses were real. Rather than surrender

free trade, the ark of their social covenant[110] as well as the talisman
of national wealth, the late Victorians tolerated the external pressures
transmitted inwards by their open economy. They accepted the rising mobility of capital and labour. But there were deep misgivings.
Social commentators warned against a 'rootless' and 'volatile' urban
proletariat,[111] and sighed with regret for a more stable and 'rooted'
agrarian age.[112] The evidence of urban poverty recorded by observers
like Booth and Rowntree suggested that the uneven distribution of
wealth was a serious threat to the social fabric. Nervousness about
a growing 'under-class' was coupled with alarm at the rise of a new
asocial plutocracy, fattening on the profits of financial speculation.[113]
Both raised fears about a decline of civic virtue in an era of incessant
change. Both implied the need for a stronger state: to remedy social
abuses and hold society together. Indeed, a new state did appear in
late-Victorian Britain employing four times as many public servants by
1914 as it had in 1870.[114] To all these various concerns, some version of 'empire' offered hope: emigration (including child emigration)
as a specific against unemployment and urban degradation; a grand
imperial monarchy as the focus of popular conservatism and loyalty
to established institutions – the object of the million-member Prim-
rose League, which remained 'vague, amorphous and sentimental in
its imperialism';[115] a grander imperial state whose need for strength
abroad would be the counterpart of social reform at home; an imperialised civic virtue that would rise above the petty squabbles and shabby
compromises of the party system.

Late-Victorian imperialism grew out of this set of interlocking
alarms and assumptions. It was bolted together by the recognition that
Britain could not escape the process that we might call 'early globalisation' – the rapid dismantling of the economic and cultural barriers between Europe and the rest of the world. Contemporary opinion
regarded it as irresistible and 'progressive', but also risky. Unlike its
late-twentieth-century counterpart, late-nineteenth-century globalisation accelerated at a time when colonialism was already entrenched in
Afro-Asia and when half a dozen states had the means and the will
to carve out new colonial zones in its wake. This 'globalisation in an
imperial setting' prompted an ambivalent British reaction: enthusiasm
for the spread of commerce, 'civilisation', religion and (sometimes) settlement; anxiety that a fiercer and fiercer imperial competition would
leave Britain worsted or set off a war. The polemical exchanges between

self-styled 'imperialists' and their more sceptical critics were sharpened by this sense of double jeopardy. Britain could not turn her back on the new international economy. Her commercial life demanded it; her living standard (increasingly) depended on it. But, at the same time, the gross extension of her vital interests in a boisterous world, and the growing dependence on foreign food, foreign trade and foreign income made it harder and harder (or so it seemed) to balance the demands of security and prosperity.

Virtually all shades of opinion agreed, however, that, in whatever form, Britain must choose the Open Sea and not the Closed Door. Autarkic retreat to the Home Islands was not an option. 'Many men have dreamt that it would be a pleasant thing to close the capital account of empire and to add no further to its responsibilities', Salisbury told an audience in Bradford in May 1895. 'That is not the condition which fortune or the evolution of the world's course has assigned to the development of our prosperity'.[116] Like it or not, Britain's place lay at the centre of the world, a position graphically emphasised on a conventional map. 'As commerce has grown more world-wide', remarked Chisholm's *Commercial Geography* (first published in 1889), 'as the New World has become more populous and more wealthy, the advantage of situation has come to belong to the British Isles, which are nearly in the middle of the land-surface of the globe'.[117] In the Columbian epoch, insisted Halford Mackinder, the foremost geographer of the day, 'Britain gradually became the central, rather than the terminal, land of the world'.[118] Centrality derived from Britain's double openness, towards Europe and towards the 'ocean highways'; from her having an eastern and a western shore; and from the dual qualities of 'insularity' and 'universality'.[119] But most of all it sprang from the part played by sea communications in a global system of economics and politics. 'The unity of the ocean', said Mackinder, 'is the simple physical fact underlying the dominant value of sea-power in the modern globe-wide world.'[120] The significance of Britain's geographic position and the logic of naval supremacy were both 'rediscovered' in the 1880s and 1890s. Fear of French, Russian and (later) German competition coincided with a great widening of maritime horizons towards East Asia (as a commercial jackpot) and the Pacific (as a sea and cable route). Naval 'scares' became a recurrent feature, and rival experts fumed and quarrelled. But there was no mystery about the entrenchment of seapower in the late-Victorian and Edwardian imagination. As the barrier to invasion from Europe, the guarantor of trade routes and food supply and the guardian of possessions and spheres more far-flung than before, the Navy seemed the key to Britain's place and prosperity in the new and uncertain 'globe-wide world'. 'It is the Navy', intoned a Liberal minister in 1894, 'which delivers us . . . from the curse of militarism.'[121] This was all the more so with the rise of other world-states. 'In the presence of vast Powers, broad based on the resources of half-continents', warned Mackinder in 1902, 'Britain could not again become mistress of the seas. Much depends on the maintenance of a lead won under earlier conditions.'[122]

The third element in the late Victorians' reinvention of empire was a new view of migration. It was no longer regarded simply as the providential evacuation of waste (as in the eighteenth century) nor as the convenient redistribution of labour and consumption recommended by Malthus and Edward Gibbon Wakefield. By the 1880s, emigration was an established social function in the English 'heartland' as much as the Celtic periphery.[123] Its value was still seen in part as an overflow for unwanted labour and a safety valve for poverty and despair. Emigration had become respectable: an acceptable choice for single women;[124] a means of redemption for abandoned children.[125] As the reaction against the consequences of industrialisation gathered pace in Britain, it acquired a new virtue. Emigrant communities in the Empire became the healthy alternative to the urban decadence of industrial Britain. This view increasingly coloured attitudes towards the white dominions by the 1890s. It was combined with the hope that the emigrant British would reinforce the solidarity of the settler countries with imperial Britain, an idea whose influence was still strong fifty years later in the report of the Royal Commission on Population.[126]

Lastly, the late Victorians accepted, though with much less enthusiasm, that their dependent empire of rule was bound to grow larger and to last indefinitely. To the mid-Victorians, their Indian Raj had been a grand exception, justified by John Stuart Mill as a rescue from chaos. But a powerful strand of radical opinion had never been reconciled to this oriental despotism. That was why the extended occupation of Egypt had been so controversial in the 1880s: it seemed to entrench the Indian mode of empire with all its risks and vices. It threatened to drag Britain into another Raj, and more mutinies, in a little India that was dangerously exposed to foreign interference. But, if Egypt occasioned much liberal unease, it also became the battering ram against liberal arguments. A series of powerful imperialist tracts, of which the most influential was Milner's *England in Egypt* (1892), insisted that Egypt was too anarchic to be left to itself. To do so would be to invite international crisis and threaten British interests. Cromer's regime as consul-general in the 'veiled protectorate' offered proof that financial acumen could calm the diplomatic storm. The old Egyptian hands clinched their argument with a shrewd appeal to liberal prejudices. Their veiled authority, they insisted, was the best trustee of foreign interests, the true guardian of peasant Egypt and the real engine of material progress.

Egypt was the proving ground for arguments originally formulated in post-Mutiny India to justify a Raj based not on consent but on force. To many Liberals, the 1880s were an intellectual watershed.[127] The gloomy evidence from India that progress was advanced by authority more than by persuasion[128] was driven home still more painfully by what seemed the failure of liberalism in Ireland against religious bigotry and backward-looking sectionalism. In the imperial sphere, this Indo-Irish disillusionment was the solvent of mid-Victorian liberal confidence. It paved the way for the rapprochement between liberalism and the authoritarian tradition of colonial rule brilliantly evoked by Milner. But it was not the only factor at work. The rapidity of global partition after 1880 served notice that under what a later generation would call 'the strenuous conditions of the modern world' there was little room for states that had failed the test of 'social efficiency'.[129] These 'dying nations' were a danger to themselves, a helpless prey to European predators and a source of friction between the emerging 'world states'. They could not be left in festering decay. Nor, without affronting the tenets of free trade, could they be allowed to preserve their seclusion, closing off their resources to outside enterprise.[130] The real question was not whether some form of external supervision was needed but the terms on which it should be imposed. In the British case, the prominent missionary and humanitarian lobby, the commercial allies of the 'open economy' and the powerful administrative elite associated particularly with India created a large potential constituency for a 'new imperialism' along these lines. Traces of evangelicalism, free trade, Ireland and India were fused in a new doctrine of administrative trusteeship – the 'imperial idea' whose clash with opposing democratic ideals imparted, said Mackinder, 'a singular richness and resource to the modern British nation'.[131]

These were the overlapping, half-contradictory versions of empire that were by 1900 deeply embedded in Britain's political culture. Each had its stage army of supporters. Each was, at least minimally, compatible with the others. Collectively, they represented an overwhelming coalition committed to the British world-system. They explain why 'empire' was so protean a concept in late-Victorian Britain, and why the meaning of 'imperialism' was so elusive. But the diversity of interests, opinions and language mobilised behind 'empire' also explains why no single imperial ideology emerged and why the politics of empire in Britain often appeared more divisive than it really was.

Towards 1900

'I quite agree with you', wrote Lord Milner to Cecil Rhodes in August 1898, 'that there is an enormous change in British opinion with regard to schemes...involving risk and expenditure in Imperial expansion, during the last few years. Things have been going very fast indeed – in the right direction.'[132] Milner was writing on the eve of the conquest of the Sudan, at the height of Chamberlain's aggressive partition diplomacy in West Africa, and with his own struggle with Kruger very much in mind. The 'forward policy', reviled by the Gladstonians in 1880, had become habitual. The British system, hitherto content to leave its interests in large areas of the world under loose, if not negligible, supervision, had become formalised. With the coming of world politics, the British had played a central role in the partition of the globe. They had taken the largest slice of the territorial share-out – and were soon to have more.

This great expansion had not occurred because British leaders subscribed to new theories of economic imperialism nor because they thought that their electorate would be appeased by circuses abroad. Nor had it arisen, for the most part, from any deep-laid strategic design. It cannot be explained merely as a defensive reaction against the proactive imperialism of rival powers. But it was not random. The pattern of annexation and occupation closely reflected the distribution of existing commercial and strategic interests. The crucial variables that determined the scale of British intervention were usually the leverage those interests could exert at home, the agency they could command 'on the spot', and the diplomatic risk involved in the assertion of a territorial claim. With so many springboards of expansion around the world in place before 1880, it was hardly surprising that the late Victorians should have responded to the new geopolitics with an octopus-like ubiquity.

Yet even this can hardly explain the relative ease with which the British had piled up territorial gains in Afro-Asia by 1899. Here, paradoxically, they had benefited from the very circumstance that had seemed to threaten their older, looser world system. The imperialism of their European rivals may have been eager, but it was not single-minded. The continental great powers regarded the balance of power in Europe, and the *status quo* it guaranteed, as the magnetic pole of their diplomacy. Their outlook was conservative. None of them was prepared to risk its security or status in Europe for the sake of a foreign adventure. France had shrunk from confrontation over Egypt in 1884 (mistrusting German support) and accepted humiliation over Fashoda in 1898. Russian policy towards Turkey, Persia and China was far more cautious than British alarmists allowed. Germany dreaded the realignment implicit in an Anglo-French entente: Germany was happy to see the British in Cairo, noted the Belgian Foreign Office in 1898, because it drove a wedge between Britain and France.[133] Revealingly, no two *European* powers went to war over a colonial issue between 1880 and 1914. For similar reasons, the continental powers found it difficult to combine against the ubiquitous British despite widespread European resentment against them. Where partition had been stalled by great power disagreements, the unexpected tenacity of the intended victim, or the intervention of a third party (Japan's role in East Asia), Britain's strategic (in the Middle East) and commercial (in China) interests had been the principal beneficiary.

Even where partition had been imposed, in Africa, Southeast Asia and the Pacific, its impact upon the British system had been much less severe than the Gladstonians had feared. Egypt had been a huge strategic burden. But the conquest and rule of tropical Africa had been astonishingly cheap. For all the colonial powers in Africa, an agreed partition was the means to ending local rivalry, and reducing the military and administrative costs of faraway colonialism to the minimum. The settling of claims allowed their paper empires to be lightly governed and lightly guarded: internal 'pacification' of the indigenous, not external, defence against each other, was the prime expense. The British, whose acquisitions weighed most heavily (in population if not acreage), gained most from this consensual colonialism. Thus far it had allowed them to absorb a vast new territorial empire without suffering any drastic imbalance in their world-system or risking its stability. Between the 1880s and the century's end that system turned out to be more resilient than contemporaries had sometimes feared and more successful than historians have usually allowed. By design and good fortune, but often by virtue of their prior claims on the spot, the British had been able to shield their most valuable interests against the effects of geopolitical change. They had also been able (as we will see in the next chapter) to turn the new world economy to their commercial advantage. But none of this would have been possible without a comparable process of change in Britain itself.

The real imperial issue in late-Victorian politics was thus not whether empire was desirable, nor even whether it should be defended. On both questions, a broad consensus emerged. Where opinion, and sometimes parties, divided was over how these objects should be secured and, more to the point, what extra burdens (if any) should be loaded onto Britain. What claims should the enterprise of building and entrenching a British world-system be allowed to make upon a complex industrial society with its own domestic priorities, its social and cultural divisions, and its liberal tradition? As we have seen, much of the intensity with which imperial questions were debated by the political elite after 1880 arose from its anxiety about the remaking of the political kingdom in the British Isles. The new mass electorate (after 1884), the revival of the Irish Question and the new 'social politics' of the 'great depression' together transformed the political landscape. Viewing their overseas commitments through the prism of rising domestic uncertainty, it was inevitable that ministers and officials should often dislike the expansionist moves into which they were forced by outside pressures or the logic of partition diplomacy.

In fact the political mood had proved surprisingly benign. After the Third Reform Act, which doubled the United Kingdom electorate and enfranchised some 60 per cent of adult males over twenty-one,[134] the radical impetus so widely anticipated seemed to wither away. The political Armageddon for which Salisbury had planned did not materialise. As Prime Minister for much of the period between 1886 and 1902 (there was Liberal ministry in 1892–5), Salisbury had envisaged a Fabian defence of the Union, empire and aristocracy. Instead, the more conservative mood in Mainland Britain was sharpened by sectarian feeling in areas like South Lancashire where Catholic Irish immigration had been heavy. The shift towards single member seats in the Third Reform Act allowed the Conservatives to capitalize on 'Villa Toryism': the middle and lower middle class suburban property-owners on whose fears the party played skilfully.[135] The fall of Parnell and his death in 1891 seemed to take much of the steam out of the Irish nationalist challenge, so that defending the Union came to seem practicable as well as necessary: the ideal combination from Salisbury's point of view. The mood of social crisis declined. Strong public finances underwrote heavier spending on defence. The Liberal cabinet of 1892–5 agreed to spend more on the Navy (a decision that led to Gladstone's retirement), stand firm in Egypt and annex Uganda. When Salisbury returned to power in 1895 after the Liberal interlude, a new political era opened up. The Unionist coalition, with over four hundred seats, overawed its divided Liberal opponents. The Union was safe (for the moment). Salisbury could pursue his cautious diplomacy of imperial coexistence and risk the small wars and confrontations that rose in the Sudan, West Africa, Siam and Venezuela with domestic equanimity. Here at last was the climate in which imperial enterprise might hope for a fair wind from opinion at home. Now was the moment to reconstruct British politics and erase the obsolete conflict between domestic reform and imperial defence. This was the aim behind Rosebery's efforts to rebuild Liberalism after Gladstone.[136] It was the target of Chamberlain's cautious moves towards protection and imperial federation after he had entered Salisbury's cabinet in 1895. Indeed, to some of Chamberlain's more ardent supporters, the time was ripe to push aside the 'old gang' – the timid aristocratic leadership of Unionism – in favour of a dynamic chief who would grasp the challenge of mass politics in the coming age of competing 'world-states'.

But before the South African War it was hard to proclaim that the British position was in imminent danger. The British had been the great beneficiaries of the imperialism of coexistence to which the great powers subscribed tacitly. In the aftermath of Fashoda, the French and Russian foreign ministers pondered gloomily how British assertiveness in the colonial sphere could be restrained.[137] Far from falling apart, the British world-system was being drawn together more closely. Britain's imperial functions – as strategic guardian, colonial ruler, demographic reservoir, market-place, merchant and lender – were more deeply engrained in public attitudes, social behaviour and economic choice:

the latter was evident in the rising volume of foreign investment and company formation. The settler countries had become larger and more important markets for British goods and capital. Through migration, trade and the exchange of ideas, they made closer links with Britain, the metropole of their culture as well as their commerce. In India, the rapid growth of an export economy made the Raj a better market for British goods and a huge commercial debtor whose earnings elsewhere in the world, when remitted to London, plugged a vital gap in Britain's balance of payments. In trade, currency and military organisation, India was being adapted step by step to an imperial role, a future envisaged (if with different emphases) by both civilian rulers and Congress nationalists.[138] In the commercial empire, where British property and investment was not protected by sovereignty, the scales were being tipped more heavily against autarky or default. The widening use of gold as the standard of currency value reinforced the trade-promoting effects of the multilateral payments system pivoted on London. The management of overseas assets – once fraught with numerous perils – became safer and more straightforward in the age of swift telegraphic connections. The City could control its commercial empire with a speed and precision undreamt of by its mid-Victorian financiers.

Thus in an age conventionally seen as the zenith of predatory imperialisms, the British seem well placed to prosper. The Diamond Jubilee of 1897 expressed patriotic self-confidence. The Spithead review of the Fleet seemed proof that it was justified. But, there was, nonetheless, an undertow of anxiety. Global competition brought an endless round of commitments and confrontations whose risk and scale were hard to measure. Britain was a power without allies, and often without friends. A 'scrimmage at a border station' might unleash a war and threaten invasion. The danger of arrogance and complacency in the Jubilee year was the theme of Kipling's 'Recessional', published in *The Times*. Unless it paid heed, Britain would follow past empires into collapse and oblivion:

> *Far-called our navies melt away;*
> *On dune and headland sinks the fire:*
> *Lo, all our pomp of yesterday*
> *Is one with Nineveh and Tyre!*
> *Judge of the Nations, spare us yet,*
> *Lest we forget – lest we forget.*

The urgency of modernising – and unifying – the Empire to meet the challenge of other 'world-states' was obvious to Chamberlain and his followers. 'The tendency of the time', cried Chamberlain, 'is to throw all power into the hands of the greater empires, and the minor kingdoms – those which are non-progressive – seemed to be destined to fall into a secondary and subordinate place.'[139] The folly of vacillation or appeasement was the cry of those who denounced any compromise on British claims in China or the Middle East. To the self-proclaimed 'imperialists' the climax of the struggle was near. The world would soon be made anew and on lines very different from the old order of cosmopolitan free trade and an open maritime frontier. In the age of world states, politics, economies and society would have to be organised on an imperial scale and for imperial purposes. The deeper thinkers suspected that even sea supremacy was not enough to guarantee the survival of the British system.

The outbreak of the South African War in October 1899 thus served to catalyse a variety of hopes and fears in Britain whose political fall-out lasted for much of the following decade. But the most immediate effect of the war was geostrategic. For a decade or more, Salisbury and his Liberal shadow Lord Rosebery had perfected a diplomacy of opportunism. But British success had rested upon the skilful evasion of any large or lasting conflict that would soak up their limited manpower. In South Africa, however, Salisbury stumbled into a war that quickly became more than a colonial expedition. The European chancelleries rubbed their hands with glee. At last, perhaps, the British system could be brought to heel and a European price extracted for its global claims. In a world that was all but partitioned, where the undivided zones of East Asia and the Near East were cockpits of Great Power rivalry, and where the naval and military strength of the contending 'world states' seemed more finely balanced than ever, a new era of world politics was about to begin.

3 THE COMMERCIAL REPUBLIC

The striking expansion of Britain's geostrategic commitments and of its spheres of influence, occupation and rule had a less visible counterpart. There was at the same time a great widening and thickening of the web of commercial relations between Britain and many other parts of the world. This 'commercial republic'[1] centred on the City of London, became one of the vital constituents of the British world-system that the late Victorians erected on its mid-Victorian foundations. Indeed, there was an obvious link between its extraordinary growth and the comparative ease with which the British world-system survived the stresses of geopolitical change after the mid-1870s. Britain's prosperity appeared to rise in direct proportion to the scale of its overseas trade and the increase of its invisible income. Income tax, estate duty, excise and postal receipts increased government revenues by nearly 50 per cent between 1870 and 1897.[2] The favourable balance of payments (largely the product of invisible income) kept sterling attractive and replenished the sources of investment abroad. The stream of outward-bound wealth, greasing and fuelling overseas commercial connections, was a powerful addition to British world influence. It secured Britain's claims on a huge range of assets, most of them safely remote from the great powers in Europe. It helped to sustain the flow of migration, Britain's demographic imperialism. Last, but not least, it preserved Britain's lead in communications technology, especially the telegraph and undersea cables that made London (and Britain) the information hub of the world.

But Britain's position in the new world economy could not be taken for granted. It required adaptations of practice and outlook that were just as far-reaching as those that tested political nerves in Whitehall and Westminster. The scale of commercial activity as 'new regions' were drawn into the 'high-pressure zone' of the Atlantic economy; the intricate network of multilateral payments on which trade growth depended; the demand for finance, both credit and capital; and the competitive threat posed by new industrial producers: all posed new challenges to the commercial apparatus that the mid-Victorians had fashioned.

The most obvious difficulties arose from the struggle to enter new hinterlands, open new markets and create new commodity trades. Exploiting 'new' lands and their productive capacity, and bringing their produce to market more cheaply than a generation before, were the great driving forces behind the late-century expansion of trade. But they required a huge effort to pay for new systems of transport and maintain the momentum of technological change. That meant the mobilisation of capital in ever increasing amounts, and finding the means to transfer it cheaply and quickly between regions, sectors and firms. It meant devising the tactics and recruiting the men that were required to drive deeper into previously closed or self-sufficient economies, sometimes against the determined resistance of entrenched local interests. It increased the importance of managing two kinds of risk: the political risk that an obstructive, enfeebled or hostile regime would frustrate or despoil a foreign-owned enterprise; and the financial risk that those who had borrowed – on public or private account – would simply default. There was also the threat, widely discussed in the 1870s and after, that large parts of the world beyond Europe would be walled off by tariffs – an economic partition to match the diplomatic division of spheres in Southeast Asia and Africa, and (as seemed increasingly likely) the Near East and China.

These actual or possible barriers to trade were a forceful reminder that success in the new global economy depended on being able to meet the transaction costs it imposed. As Douglass North pointed out, in modern large-scale economies, the costs of coordinating productive activity usually exceed the cost of production itself.[3] Settling the terms of exchange for different commodities, grading their quality, and securing the claims to property rights over them (a complex operation in tradeable goods) were elaborate tasks. The long train of agents that brought products to market, and then to the consumer, cost time and effort to manage. The key to success was commercial intelligence. 'Information', remarked one profound economic observer, 'is one of the principal commodities that the economic organisation is engaged in supplying.'⁴ The risks and transaction costs of global trade and investment were lowest where (more or less) reliable information was cheap and accessible. Their burden was lightest where commercial institutions responded most quickly to new products, new markets, new forms of exchange and the need for new kinds of investment. It was here that London's long lead as the world's principal entrepot conferred a crucial advantage. It was why it became the headquarters of the new global economy. No other port city enjoyed the double advantage of lying so close to such densely used sea-lanes, while being the capital of a wealthy state and the centre of its internal communications. No other port-city was the political centre for so many dependencies, or formed the arena where so many lobbies – imperial and colonial – contended for backers or paraded their claims. The benefits accruing to Britain were huge. Yet, as we shall see, there was no simple equation between the interests of the City with its web of commercial relations and those of British imperial power. In theory at least, the power that the City enjoyed sprang not from authority but from the leverage conferred by the need for its services, and the economic reciprocities it had helped to create. But one of the critical questions was how far the commercial republic really depended upon its 'imperial alliance'; and whether its rapid acquisition of a huge property empire, and the income drawn from it, now made it a hostage to geopolitical fortune.

The mercantile cosmopolis

British economic success in the late nineteenth century rode on the back of the colossal growth in world trade whose value increased tenfold between 1850 and 1913. British enterprise was still better placed than any competitor to promote this expansion of trade and profit from it. Technology (especially the application of steam power), capital (accumulated from industrial and commercial success), institutions (already developed to serve a highly integrated industrial and commercial economy) and personnel (both commercial and technical) equipped it to exploit overseas opportunities all over the world. This was particularly true of the building of infrastructure on which much British effort was concentrated. Railways were the key to opening up hinterlands without access to navigable water, dragging them from subsistence into commercial production. The world's railway mileage rose from 66,000 in

1860 to 465,000 in 1910 (and 674,000 in 1920).[5] Shipping tonnage more than doubled in the same period (and travelled more rapidly). Telegraph cables lengthened from approximately 8,000 miles in 1872 to reach 325,000 miles by 1922. British interests owned, managed or controlled all these enterprises on a grand scale: the vast proportion of railways outside the United States and Continental Europe and some 40% of registered shipping by the early twentieth century. By then, 40% of the world's telegraph cables were in the hands of a single British concern, the Eastern Telegraph Company and its associates.[6]

Trade followed construction. Building railways overseas required locomotives, rolling stock and iron rails. New customers appeared as commercial production extended. The demand for British exports rose on both accounts. It was true that, as new industrial competitors arose in Germany and the United States, Britain's share of the world's manufactured exports drifted down from 38% in 1880 to 30% in 1913.[7] More generally, Britain's share of world trade fell from 25% in 1860 to 20% in 1900 and 17% by 1913.[8] But these figures disguised a large absolute rise in the value of British exports and a remarkable increase in the share of Britain's total production that they represented. In 1856, the ratio of exports to gross domestic product had been 14.6%. By 1873, it had reached 18.3%. In 1913 it was 25%.[9] British imports also grew rapidly as dependence upon foreign food supplies became greater and greater. Indeed, the imbalance between exports and imports widened steadily after 1880 despite the falling cost of food and many raw materials from an average of around £97 million in 1880–9 to £160 million after 1900.[10] In production and consumption Britain had become more dependent upon international trade and more international in outlook than ever before. Free-trade capitalism had reached its highest stage.

But the most spectacular change was the extent to which British-based interests profited from the surging growth of international trade and the scale on which they acquired assets abroad. A huge proportion of the world's trade passed through London by the early twentieth century, not so much physically but rather in all the commercial and financial operations that international commerce required: ship-broking; insurance; the grading of products; and sale. Sterling was the currency of trade, and the 'bill on London' the usual (because most convenient) form of payment. By 1913–14, 60 per cent of bills on London were for transactions entirely between foreign buyers and sellers.[11] London was the world centre for commercial information, the listening post for commercial opportunities in every continent. London prices were, for most goods, the world's prices. Not surprisingly, British companies took the lead in providing the information and services that world trade needed, especially in shipping and insurance. Despite the huge fall in the cost of seaborne freight (by some 50 per cent between 1870 and 1913[12]), the income from these 'invisible' exports rose steadily from £80 million a year to nearly £170 million by 1913.[13] Large as this figure was, more than covering the trade gap, it was outstripped by the income drawn from assets built up abroad.

A marked tendency to invest overseas was already visible before 1880. Partly it arose as British merchants mobilised capital at home to create the kind of 'fixed' assets – like docks or warehouses – that would expand their business on the spot. British lenders, who readily bought government bonds ('consols') at home, also willingly placed money in the bonds issued by foreign states. A disinclination to risk savings in domestic commercial ventures, and the low level of government borrowing at home after mid-century, drove the surplus incomes of the wealthy abroad. The major impetus came from the construction of railways overseas, which, unlike most commercial or industrial ventures, required a very large immediate investment before any return was forthcoming. British confidence in railway technology, the early development in Britain of a market in railway shares and the prominent role of British railway contractors overseas combined to make this an especially attractive outlet for surplus British funds. As the international railway boom developed in the 1870s, a huge stream of British capital flowed abroad. Between 1870 and 1913, British investment in Indian, colonial and foreign railway companies rose fivefold to £1.5 billion – around 40 per cent of all British overseas investment. There was a similar rise in the sums invested in government bonds (both inside and outside the Empire) – often to fund state railway construction or other kinds of infrastructure. By 1913, a third category of foreign investment was growing even faster: overseas companies controlling utilities (like gas- or waterworks), banks, real estate, mines and plantations, but rarely industry.[14] The result was an overall increase in the value of Britain's assets abroad from under £1,000 million in the early 1870s to around £2,000 million by 1900, and £4,000 million by 1913.[15] Almost all of this was placed outside Europe and 44 per cent of the world total of foreign investment was in British hands.[16] Altogether these overseas assets produced an income worth more than one-fifth of all Britain's overseas earnings.[17] They made up some 34 per cent of all British assets at home and abroad. A forward glance will reveal the true scale of this astonishing mountain of wealth. By 1937, the effects of war loss and depression had driven that proportion down to 18 per cent and by 1973 to 3 per cent.[18] In 1990, British overseas investment, having staged a major recovery, reached the impressive figure of £100 billion. But, measured against the overall rise of Britain's assets, this was no more than one-seventh of its value in 1913.[19]

The head and centre of this far-reaching financial and commercial activity was the City of London. Essentially, the City was a cluster of markets attracting buyers and sellers from all parts of the world. Some of these markets were organised as 'exchanges' like the Wool Exchange (established in 1875), the London Metal Exchange (1882), the Baltic Exchange (for grain cargoes) and the Coal Exchange. Mincing Lane was the market for commodities like sugar, cocoa, coffee and spices, with regular auctions at its sale rooms. A large number of City firms dealt in the import or re-export of commodities, sometimes for immediate sale, sometimes as options or 'futures'. Many tended to specialise by country or type of produce, and one entirely in the import of hair.[20] Because the commodity trades usually required the advance of credit to faraway producers, and because of the lapse of time before the harvest came to market, the dealers in London were also lenders.[21] They, in turn, required the services of specialised finance houses, 'accepting houses' or merchant banks, who could tap the reservoirs of short-term borrowing drawn to the City from bank deposits throughout the country. The merchant banks, headed by the great houses like Rothschilds, Barings (the 'sixth great power' until its crash of 1890),[22] J. S. Morgan, Kleinworts and Schroders, but including many that were far smaller and more specialised, lent money on their own account but were usually the agents through whom large loans or an issue of securities were negotiated by public or private borrowers. Including the Bank of England and the joint stock banks catering for the ordinary public, they made up the 'Inner City' of high finance.[23] London was also the headquarters of more than forty British-owned overseas banks like the Bank of London and the River Plate or the Chartered Bank of India, Australia and China, with branches in Bombay, Calcutta, Rangoon, Singapore, Hong Kong, Shanghai, Manila and Batavia (modern Jakarta). By 1900, banking had become increasingly cosmopolitan and British banks faced competition

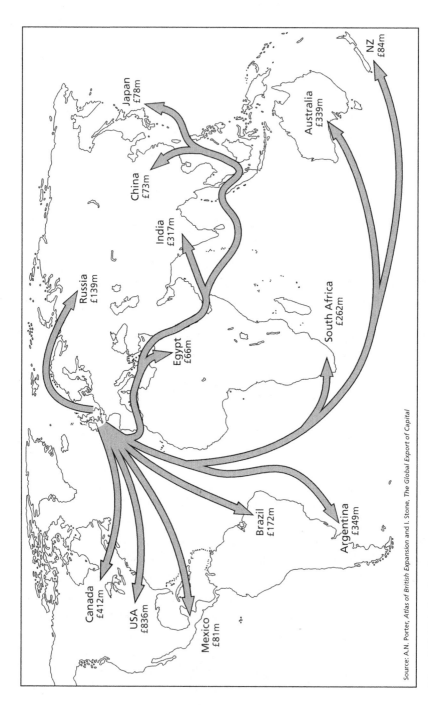

Canada £412m
USA £836m
Mexico £81m
Brazil £172m
Argentina £349m
NZ £84m
Australia £339m
South Africa £262m
Japan £78m
China £73m
India £317m
Egypt £66m
Russia £139m

Source: A.N. Porter, *Atlas of British Expansion* and I. Stone, *The Global Export of Capital*

Map 6 British foreign investment to 1914

from foreign banks in London serving the commercial needs of their own traders.

But the most dynamic element in the commercial life of the late-Victorian City was the Stock Exchange.[24] Until mid-century it had been largely concerned with the sale of government bonds. Thereafter, railway shares and loans to foreign states rapidly widened its business. In the 1880s and 1890s, expansion was frantic. Membership (the entitlement to deal) grew from 1,400 (1871) to over 5,500 by 1905. By the early 1900s, one-third of all quoted securities around the world were traded in London and around 60 per cent of the Stock Exchange's share listings were for overseas enterprises.[25] In the search for capital, most roads led to London. The Exchange itself was informally divided into sections including Consols; the 'Yankee' market (American railways); Home rails; and, in the 1890s, the 'Kaffir Circus' for South African gold shares. Stockbrokers developed specialist expertise in lines of business or regions. In 1898, the *Stock Exchange Year Book* listed over 650 railway companies, a large proportion of them overseas; more than 1,000 firms engaged in mining or 'exploration'; and several thousand loosely described as 'investment, trust and finance' – a category which included Cecil Rhodes' 'British South Africa Company' with its private empire north of the Limpopo. As the communications revolution seemed to throw open more and more commercial opportunities in the non-European world, and distant prospects were gilded by gold discoveries on the Rand, in Australia and at the Yukon, the Stock Exchange became the great arena where private savings were mobilised for investment overseas. Circling round it were the ubiquitous company promoters, scrupulous or predatory, whose role was to convert a commercial idea into a marketable security. Their skill in the 'financial arts', remarked the radical economist J. A. Hobson, was often exercised to 'scoop out' the real assets of an enterprise while selling on its 'shrivelled carcase' to a bamboozled public.[26]

Proximity to the Stock Exchange and merchant banks, and access to the flows of market information was the reason why many British-owned overseas firms based themselves in the City. This was especially true of overseas railway companies with their constant thirst for new capital. Finsbury Circus was the favoured address of British-owned Argentine rails like the Buenos Aires Great Southern or the *Oeste*. Similar needs made the City the world headquarters for mining enterprise.[27] Large shipowners like Cunard, British India, Peninsular and Oriental and Shaw Savill (trading to Australasia) were drawn to London by its ship-chartering market. London was the principal centre for insurance. Railway, mining and shipping enterprise also required the services of non-financial expertise: consulting engineers and other technical specialists. In short, there was scarcely any large commercial or financial venture linking Britain (and much of Continental Europe) to the 'new economies' of the wider world that, in one aspect or many, did not pass through a London agent. In a vast swathe of the world outside Europe, commercial development and even financial solvency turned upon decisions made in the City. Here was a plenitude of influence that matched that of Whitehall and Westminster, the political capital of the British system.

Indeed, the great commercial and financial emporium centred on London (with the lesser marts of Liverpool and Glasgow) was more than just an adjunct to British world power. It was the great cosmopolitan intermediary between the British domestic economy and the outside world. It might almost be seen as an autonomous partner attached to the British world-system by sentiment, self-interest and domicile, but largely indifferent to the strategic or administrative preoccupations of its political managers – except where they impinged directly on its economic prospects. It had grown up willy-nilly over the remains of the old mercantile system liquidated after 1846. Its well-being was acknowledged as a vital national interest. Its leaders and spokesmen periodically emphasised its contribution to British wealth. It shaped powerfully the conception of the British interest in India. It massively – perhaps at times decisively – reinforced the allegiance of the white dominions to their faraway motherland. It was the conduit for the large British investment in the United States, half-rival, half-associate in a world of voracious imperialisms. But the commercial power it exerted was no mere extension of Britain's imperial influence and authority. The managers of the commercial empire, especially the City elite, had wide autonomy and fiercely resisted outside regulation. Their priorities were rarely the same as those of the political and official world at the far end of the Strand. It was true that many bankers were drawn from the same class as the political and administrative elite. But many other interests were represented in the City, and in parts of it capitalism was anything but gentlemanly.[28] Even in the most respectable quarters overseas business was carried on with little regard to the 'national interest', partly because, with so little inclination to think analytically, such a notion existed only in the haziest form.[29]

For their part, officials and politicians were inclined to treat the commercial cosmopolis as an allied but not necessarily friendly power. Its independence was warily recognised. But its political judgment was laughed at;[30] and its morals widely distrusted. The sensational growth in the wealth and social power concentrated in the City after 1890 aroused alarm as well as satisfaction. On both Left and Right, the appearance of a new City-based 'plutocracy' was regarded with deep suspicion.[31] On both political wings, the 'cosmopolitan' outlook of the financial world was equated with rootlessness, restlessness and the readiness to sacrifice public good for private gain. The cosmopolitan financier, indifferent to any consideration but profit, was the villain in J. A. Hobson's radical unmasking of the hidden forces behind imperial expansion and the South African War. His famous analysis of the export of capital, on which the City prospered, insisted that its social function was to perpetuate poverty and 'under-consumption' at home by rewarding the 'over-saving' of the rich.[32] The Tariff Reformers blamed cosmopolitan indifference to the domestic industrial economy for the hostility of the financial world towards their programme of imperial unity. In his 'City' speech in January 1904, Joseph Chamberlain warned his audience not to forget that 'the future of this country and of the British race lay in our colonies and possessions...the natural buttresses of our Imperial State'.[33] His economic expert, W. J. Ashley, gloomily forecast Britain's future as a declining rentier state: 'the history of Holland is to be repeated.'[34]

There were other grounds for doubting the congruence of the interests of the City with those of nation or empire. The Barings crisis in 1890 and the American crash in 1907 showed that the City's huge exposure to overseas markets could destabilise the whole financial system. Some observers warned that the speculative manias and fraudulent promotions bred by the Stock Exchange could damage Britain's real interests overseas and unsettle her imperial ties.[35] But, down to 1914, this criticism made little headway. Economic orthodoxy proclaimed the unalloyed benefit of a large foreign portfolio and even Leftish opinion came to concede that the City's influence in world affairs was benignly pacific.[36] Nor was there yet much sign of conflict between the City's cosmopolitan functions as the owner and manager of a vast property empire outside British sovereignty and its role as the emporium for 'Imperial' trade between Britain, the dominions, India and the Crown Colonies. Quite the contrary. London easily mobilised the vast stream of capital that flowed to Canada after 1900. Its multilateral payments system made it much easier for Britain to profit from India's surplus on foreign (i.e. non-Empire) trade, remitted to London as the 'home charges'.[37] Its foreign investments stimulated British production of cotton, ships, locomotives and coal – for bunkering and as the outward freight that made British shipping so widely profitable.[38] It made Britain the 'telegraph exchange of the world',[39] and hence 'British' news the most widely circulated. Its vast income stream lifted the social and cultural prestige of the British metropolis to its zenith.[40]

New frontiers of commerce

In all these ways, the City (with the smaller cosmopolises in Glasgow and Liverpool) was the grand ally of the (formal) Empire. Its own sphere of unofficial or 'semi-colonial' expansion was also growing rapidly after 1880. Here it was engaged in turning the sketchy 'informal empire' of mid-Victorian times into prosperous new tributaries of its great commercial republic. Four great zones lay at the edge of the 'developed' world but beyond the imperial frontier: tropical Africa, the Middle East, China and Latin America.

None of these was wholly unfamiliar to British merchants and lenders, but none had lived up to its early promise. By the 1860s and 1870s they had become much more appealing. In part this was a side-effect of accelerated commercial development elsewhere. As new regions were 'colonised' by banks, railways, shippers and brokers, merchant houses scoured remoter neighbourhoods for fresh trades where competition was less harsh and windfall gains more likely.[41] Technology was on their side. With the rising volume of long-distance trade, seaborne travel became faster, cheaper and more regular, lowering the start-up costs of merchant enterprise. After 1870, the Suez Canal changed the geography of shipping in the Indian Ocean in Europe's favour. The expanding telegraph network carried the 'information-head' of market intelligence into ever deeper hinterlands, reducing business risk. With a weekly steamer service even the mystery and horror of the West African coast was tamed.[42] Secondly, merchants and lenders could hope to profit from the increasing readiness of previously conservative, secluded or simply disorganised states to embrace financial and administrative modernisation – sometimes by 'quick-fixes' like the Reuter's Concession in Iran where most of the modern commercial sector was handed over (if only briefly) to a single foreign entrepreneur.[43] Thirdly, British-based enterprises were well placed in the later nineteenth century to piggy-back on older mercantile pioneers. It was usually local men who first opened the trade paths in 'backward' regions, plugging them into larger commercial circuits. But, once their trade was worth the taking, they were often no match for interlopers with cheaper credit, better shipping and vastly superior commercial intelligence of markets and prices. Europeans were sometimes 'trade-makers', but they were just as likely to be 'take-over' merchants, squeezing out or subordinating older practitioners – nowhere more so than in Africa.[44]

In principle, this extension of commercial activity ought to have been self-reliant – much more so than in early Victorian times. In the age of contract, the diplomatic glove, let alone the mailed imperial fist, should have been redundant. The momentum of commercial change was greater, its rewards more visible, its necessity more accepted. Businessmen had access to more capital and better information. In the era of the limited company, it was easier to transfer capital to regions promising quicker profits. And, as the tide of economic change lapped higher in the non-Western world, finding local partners should have been as straightforward as squaring 'progress'-hungry rulers. And, up to a point, it was.

In practice, it was much less clear that, even in its own semi-colonial sphere, the City could dispense with political Empire. There were three reasons for this. In some parts of the semi-colonial world, the limited scope of political institutions threw upon the trader the onus of defending his property and commercial rights by agreement if possible, by force if necessary. Produce, markets and especially labour were prizes for those with the strength to seize and hold them. But, to enforce his 'contractual' claims in the face of other foreign interlopers, the trader needed either the protection of his government or a licence (like a charter) to make treaties, levy taxes and dispense 'justice'. Secondly, there were parts of the extra-European world where foreign trade or investment were concessions in the gift of patrimonial or bureaucratic regimes. Here the merchant existed on sufferance or by favour. His status and prospects depended upon the help of diplomatic intermediaries without whose protection the privileges (freedom from taxation, arrest and bureaucratic harassment) that made his business profitable would lapse. Thirdly, there was the question of how the merchant (or investor) could secure himself against default, when the debtor was also the ruler. As trade and finance moved deeper into the Outer World and their stakes grew higher, these 'political' risks loomed large in their calculations.

For a late-Victorian government, however, smoothing the merchant's path and standing guard for the investor were not to be undertaken lightly. Each threatened it with complications, embarrassment and expense. Each laid it open to accusations of favouritism or worse. But, where commercial interests could mobilise wider support or claim some higher purpose, they were not so easily brushed aside. They might even be useful to some diplomatic ploy. The result was a frontier of commercial expansion in which the role of government varied between a maximum (annexation) and a minimum (diplomatic inertia). It was a revealing irony that annexation was most likely where local and international conditions made it easiest, not where its economic dividend looked most promising.

British business in Africa

Tropical Africa represented the extreme case. Here was a vast region between the Sahara and South Africa where British (and other European) traders had scarcely ventured beyond the West African coast. Access to the hinterland was barred by physical obstacles or the obstruction of suspicious 'middlemen'; there were no modern states to lend to nor landed property to mortgage; and commercial information about the interior was often, literally, at the exploratory stage. Even more daunting, perhaps, was the fact that, in the 1880s and 1890s, tropical Africa's commodities – such as they were – were of marginal interest to industrialising Europe, and the principal commercial export, palm-oil from West Africa, sank to its lowest price level in that period.[45] Indeed, tropical Africa had a declining share in the trade of an expanding world economy. Yet none of this deterred British entrepreneurs from striking into the interior to carve new business empires out of the African bush.

This paradox, and Africa's subjection to a diplomatic rather than a commercial partition, have led some writers to argue that the motive for commercial activity was only superficially economic, or better described as 'meta-economic' – driven less by hope of commercial gain than by a vision of how Africa should be fitted for a commercial future.[46] But there was no doubt that those who launched new business ventures into Africa were eager for profits and needed them to attract both capital and publicity. The peculiarity of tropical Africa lay in the harshness of its physical and commercial environment away from the beachheads where Europeans had sheltered hitherto. It was no coincidence that military drop-outs, imperial visionaries, down-at-heel aristocrats and redundant explorers found a berth in African commerce. Nor that the projects for exploiting the interior needed to appeal to a broader constituency of investors in Britain – those who wanted an 'ethical' investment to spread the Gospel and stamp out the slave trade as well as those who gambled on a lucky strike. For a century past, British opinion had regarded Africa as an object of charity and as an Aladdin's cave.

In the last quarter of the nineteenth century, British enterprise entered the African interior by three different routes: from South Africa, from India and from Europe. In West Africa, there was a direct connection from Britain to the 'Coast' – a vast maritime zone stretching from Sierra Leone to the Congo. British commerce was most active on the Gold Coast, at Lagos – the gateway to the Yoruba states – and at the Niger delta, the so-called 'Oil Rivers', where the palm-oil trade was concentrated.[47] In 1841 and again in 1858–64, the British government had supported attempts to open the Lower Niger as far as the Benue confluence at Lokoja as part of its anti-slave-trade policy.[48] Both efforts had failed, and, apart from a consular 'presence' (as consul in West Africa 1861–3, Richard Burton had made the offshore island of Fernando Po his base) and a periodic gunboat, the British oil traders at the Niger mouth carried on their business under the skimpiest kind of informal empire.[49]

The new departure of the 1880s seems to have sprung less from hopes of commercial expansion than from fears of collapse. Between 1876 and 1881 the price of palm oil fell by more than 16 per cent and was to fall further.[50] To protect their position, four of the oil companies trading up-river merged to form the United Africa Company in 1879. The architect of the merger was George Goldie (1846–1925), a failed soldier without obvious talents or prospects.[51] Goldie came from a gentry family on the Isle of Man with family interests in one of the merged companies. A visit to West Africa in 1877–8 had suggested how the oil traders' difficulties could be solved. Goldie revived the old idea of opening the Niger as a thoroughfare for direct trade with the Hausa emirates upstream, cutting out the African middlemen who skimmed the profits. It was obvious enough that this was beyond the means of four struggling companies, amalgamated or not. Goldie's solution was ingenious. In 1881, he reorganised the company on a grand scale as the 'National African Company' with a nominal capital of £1 million (far in excess of its modest assets) and offices in Ludgate Hill. He recruited as directors a reputable private banker from the City, a major cotton merchant from Manchester with West African interests (James Hutton) and, as chairman, Lord Aberdare, a former minister, a confidant of Gladstone and president of the Royal Geographical Society. Goldie's real purpose was to obtain a charter for his company, and transform it from a frail commercial bark into an armoured cruiser. A charter from the imperial government would entitle his company to act as its agent in the Niger interior. It would give him the right to acquire territory, levy taxes and maintain a private army to enforce the company's rights. Events played into Goldie's hands. By the early 1880s, the Gladstone government was so alarmed that a French occupation of the Niger would drive out British trade that it reinforced its consular supervision and then, in 1885, declared its own protectorate in the Niger delta. Granting a charter to the importunate Goldie and his influential friends in 1886 solved the tiresome problem of how to pay for this unprepossessing imperial annex.

Goldie's genius was to turn a rickety British enterprise into an Afro-European hybrid, well adapted to its frontier habitat. Behind its European mask, the Company was a modern-day forest kingdom, ruling the trade paths like Ashanti or Dahomey. It gathered treaties and cessions from African rulers in the Niger hinterland and diverted the interior trade into its own forts, factories and steamers. The charter strictly forbade monopoly, but this was a dead letter.[52] As a result, Goldie's relations with the independent Liverpool companies still trading in the Delta through African middlemen were bitter. With the middlemen themselves, the Company was virtually at war. By the early 1890s, under growing pressure from French and German competitors, the Company became even more openly a crudely organised state, conducting private diplomacy, waging private war, levying private taxes and paying its way through a commercial monopoly backed by force. It was a risky, but successful, formula. Except for 1886–8, the Company paid a steady dividend, often well over 6 per cent[53] and attracted many small shareholders.[54] By 1894, it had bought out the remaining Liverpool traders on the river (though not in the Delta). But its main achievement was to turn its ramshackle collection of claims and treaties into an 'asset' which the imperial government dared not renounce.

Goldie achieved this through careful politicking and a ruthless publicity campaign. He recruited Frederick Lugard, a half-pay officer lionised for his exploits against Arab slave traders in East Africa. Lugard was a brilliant publicist. Within a few months in 1895–6 he published thirteen major articles reciting British claims, interests and achievements in tropical Africa.[55] *The Times* came to Goldie's aid. Goldie himself rushed out to lead the fight against the Company's toughest African enemies. As the West African competition grew fiercer, Chamberlain sought the Company's help to drive the French from the hinterlands of Lagos Colony and the Gold Coast while the Company's own military weakness became more and more glaring.[56] By 1898, both the French and British governments were eager to settle the local feud in the Niger valley for fear of its wider repercussions. As Goldie had long realised, an imperial partition in West Africa meant that he would have to be bought out, to appease the French, the 'colonial' interest in Lagos (whose black merchants reciprocated his hatred) and Liverpool. The pay-out was a bonanza: at £865,000 nearly three times the Company's real assets. The Company lost its charter and its royal prefix and reverted to lawful trade.

In East Africa, the impetus behind British commercial activity came not from London or Liverpool but from India. With the cutting of the Suez Canal and the new short steamship route between Europe and India, opening up 'branch lines' into the Persian Gulf and East Africa became much more attractive. The pioneers of this new trade were Mackinnon Mackenzie, a British merchant house based in Calcutta. Its senior partner, William Mackinnon (1823–93) was now manager of the shipping line *British India* and keen to extend its business into new ports and hinterlands. His partner, George Mackenzie, spent several years reconnoitring the commercial prospects of the Persian Gulf.[57] In the 1870s, Mackinnon had tried to lease a stretch of the

East African mainland opposite Zanzibar as a bridgehead for a new business empire.[58]

This came to nothing, but Mackinnon's choice had not been accidental. Zanzibar was already part of an Indo-Arab trading world and Indians were well established as merchants and moneyed men on the East African coast. Zanzibar itself had long been considered part of British India's sphere of influence. By the mid-nineteenth century, its merchants had built a commercial system that linked together the huge country between the Zambezi, the Great Lakes and the Indian Ocean at a time when European traders were barely in evidence. Zanzibar became a great emporium for ivory and the entrepot of the whole coast. Here was a goose ripe for plucking. Secondly, after Stanley's epic trans-African journey in 1874–7, much more was known about the undeveloped wealth of the lacustrine interior and Uganda, which Stanley described as the 'pearl of Africa'. Thirdly, Mackinnon, like many other Scottish merchants, was deeply affected by Livingstone's call for the reclaiming of Africa by commerce and Christianity at his famous Cambridge lecture in 1857.[59]

Livingstone's death and burial in 1874 in Westminster Abbey (a measure of his saintly status) was the trigger for a new effort to plant a large missionary centre, 'Livingstonia', on Lake Nyasa, where slave-raiding was at its most intense. Mackinnon was heavily committed to the African Lakes Company, set up in 1878 to support the mission project. But his own plans for commercial philanthropy stalled until the German 'occupation' of East Africa in 1885 transformed the politics of the East Coast. With the large inland sphere conceded (for Egyptian reasons) by London in 1886, it was obvious to the British consul in Zanzibar (and even more to the Sultan) that the island state was doomed to commercial strangulation and a gradual slide into German control. So Mackinnon revived his scheme for a coastal lease, this time with the Sultan's support, and formed his East African Association to bring the Ugandan pearl to market.

Mackinnon's scheme was ambitious and attracted some heavy-weight support. Among his directors were Goldie's friends, James Hutton and Lord Aberdare. There were two ex-consuls and a brace of generals. There was Lord Brassey, the greatest railway contractor of the age. Reborn as the Imperial British East Africa Company, the Association gained its royal charter on the nod in 1887. With its mainland lease, and its right to tax, make treaties and acquire territory, it seemed the perfect commercial vehicle to carve out an informal empire north and west of the German sphere. Uganda would be ruled in all but name from its office in Pall Mall. When German competition threatened its Uganda hinterland, it successfully pressurised a sceptical Salisbury into demanding its inclusion in the new British sphere in East Africa agreed with Germany in 1890. When Salisbury wavered, Mackinnon and his fellow directors threatened to resign and close the Company down.[60] In reality, the Company's position was desperately fragile. Its capital was modest – only £250,000 had been subscribed. Its outgoings were heavy. Worst of all, unlike Goldie's company, there was no established trade to divert and no convenient route to the interior. Uganda lay three months' walk away over a dangerous path skirting the warlike Masai and Kikuyu. Stanley told Mackinnon that he would need 500 men and a railway. Salisbury and his man on the spot, Gerald Portal, thought the Company a shambles and Mackinnon a dilettante.[61]

The result was a fiasco for which company and government blamed each other. With the Barings crash in 1890, no more capital could be gleaned in London, and the Company faced bankruptcy. It abandoned hope of a private empire by Lake Victoria: only a government take-over could supply the political infrastructure needed for its commercial and philanthropic aims. After a bitter Cabinet struggle, a publicity campaign in which Lugard and Stanley were prominent, and a face-saving mission of inquiry, Uganda was annexed in 1894 and 'British East Africa' (modern Kenya) in 1895. Like Goldie, the East Africa Company's backers had successfully exploited public anxiety (about the fate of Christian missionaries and their converts) to goad the government into a forward policy. Like Goldie, they were helped by its grudging recognition that an administrative take-over was the only answer to the runaway competition of traders, missionaries and soldiers whose well-publicised jostling might derail their diplomacy in Europe and the Mediterranean. Unlike Goldie, however, Mackinnon's group profited little from the government buy-out. They were paid off with half of their costs, mostly at Zanzibar's expense.[62]

In the classic case of the African Scramble, private imperialists with their commercial roots in London, Liverpool, Glasgow or India were usually at cross-purposes with the agents of official policy. In West and East Africa, the chartered companies were meant to limit imperial liability while protecting a commercial interest. In both cases, they proved more successful at increasing the liability than in guarding the interest. Both were as much political as commercial enterprises whose 'virtual' assets could only be realised if the transaction costs of external protection were transferred to the imperial government. It was the peculiarity of tropical Africa in the 1890s that the technical, administrative and financial cost of transfer was so low; the mobilisation of public interest sufficient; and the diplomatic argument so pressing: conditions which favoured a sudden, swift and complete partition. Only in Southern Africa was private imperialism strong enough to resist the imperial take-over, build a state – and start a war.[63]

The Middle East and East Asia

In the Middle East and China, commercial conditions were quite different. Here, where three old empires struggled to modernise, diplomatic rivalry was intensified by the prospect of their collapse and partition. In Turkey and China, profit from trade was outshone by the lure of investment in government loans secured on state revenues or the grant of concessions for railways or other enterprises. Merchants and investors were forced to depend upon the mediation of diplomats who had an entree to the inner bureaucratic world where such transactions were finalised. Nor, in the cockpit atmosphere of great power diplomacy, could they impose their commercial claims where these conflicted with the interests of strategy or prestige.

The Middle East was particularly risk-laden. By 1880, both the Ottoman Empire and Egypt (its autonomous tributary) were bankrupt and their politics in crisis. The Ottoman government had lost some of its most valuable provinces in the treaty of 1878. In 1881, after six years of default, a new loan regime was created to regulate its borrowing under international supervision and repay the bondholders. The 'Ottoman Public Debt Administration' and its foreign managers controlled a large part of Turkey's public revenues, and directed to all intents its public investment. But, despite their previous interest in Ottoman bonds, British investors played a much smaller role in financing Turkey's new-style public debt than their counterparts in France where more than half the total was held by 1913.[64] The commercial promise of the Anatolian hinterland – the scene of numerous railway schemes in the 1890s – was meagre compared with that of the Americas or South Africa. Worst of all, British lenders faced fierce competition from French and German banks represented on the Debt Administration. Success required furious diplomatic lobbying since the allocation of loans and the concessions they brought with them were a barometer of great-power influence at the Ottoman court. While the Foreign Office was keen to encourage British investment as a diplomatic instrument, the need to reach an accommodation with France or Germany made it an unreliable champion of the City's interests at the best of times.[65]

Egypt was a special case. Before the bankruptcy of 1876, it was the most dynamic zone on the European periphery, attracting trade and investment by the speed with which its great programme of public works was extending the cotton production of the Nile delta. The Suez Canal, the engineering marvel of its day, symbolised the importance to the international economy of Egypt's openness to foreign interests and influences.[66] The eagerness with which the landholding elite responded to new commercial opportunities contrasted favourably with much of Afro-Asia.[67] But the long crisis that followed default, and reached a climax in the revolution of 1881, threatened this steady transformation of Egypt into a satellite economy of Europe. Whatever its constitutional programme, Arabi's following, the 'Urabiya, drew upon widespread popular resentment against European artisans, merchants and landowners.[68] The outcry of this 'semi-colonial' community was amplified by the press and the local agents of the British government. It contributed, as we have seen, to London's belief that a xenophobic Islamist movement was about to roll up British interests: economic, political and strategic.

With the 'temporary occupation' of 1882 and its tacit prolongation by 1890 into the indefinite future, Egypt was drawn more firmly than any other part of the Middle East into Britain's commercial orbit. The British dared not annex, and they were forced to respect the clumsy international machinery of the *Caisse de la Dette*, Cairo's version of the Ottoman Public Debt Administration. But, as the real (if hidden) force in the Egyptian government after 1883, the British consul-general Evelyn Baring (Lord Cromer) shaped a financial regime that turned Egypt into a pocket India.[69] Free trade, public works and an ironclad guarantee against default made it a happy hunting ground for banks and land companies financed in London. By 1897, 11 per cent of Egypt's cultivable land was owned by foreign nationals, with heavy concentration in the Delta provinces.[70] But the existence of this quasi-colonial regime can only partly explain the £66 million of British capital invested by 1914.[71] The exceptional growth of cotton output and the fertility of new lands reclaimed for cultivation made Egypt the richest and most productive economy in the Middle East.[72]

In Egypt, British commercial interests benefited from official London's determination to exclude rival powers from the Nile Valley after 1882 and from Britain's ability, at considerable diplomatic cost, to maintain a monopoly of influence in Cairo. Commerce and empire were in harmony. In China, the commercial and diplomatic interests interlocked quite differently. Here British merchants (like Swires or Jardine Matheson) dominated foreign trade by 1880. But progress in tapping the vast hinterland behind the treaty-ports had been slow. Exportable commodities were sparse. With a population larger than India's, China took only 8 per cent of Britain's cotton exports (in 1896) to India's 27 per cent. The result was an involution of the trading frontier back towards the treaty-ports as the large British firms diversified into services like banking, shipping and utilities.[73] British visitors were inclined to blame a treaty-port culture of sloth and complacency. The intrepid Isabella Bird demanded more 'capital, push, a preference for business over athletics, a working knowledge of the Chinese language and business methods and a determination to succeed'.[74] But, marooned at the edge of a vast non-Western world, British traders needed more than the spirit of enterprise to transform their economic environment. Less ambitious men hoped for the reform of China's pre-modern currency and the abolition of internal tariffs, the *likin*. But the real challenge was to persuade the Chinese authorities to sanction a railway programme: the one sure instrument of commercial progress.

The 1890s brought a breakthrough, or so it seemed. China's shock defeat by Japan in 1895 brought a new urge to 'self-strengthen', and a new need for loans.[75] The difficulty was that, as in the Ottoman Empire, the allocation of loans, and the concessions that went with them, was bound up with speculation about a future partition. A loan might become a mortgage on the property of a bankrupt. To negotiate a loan under these conditions required forceful diplomacy at Peking, as much as commercial intelligence in Shanghai or financial backing in London. To British commercial interests on the spot, it was obvious that any reasonable allocation should reflect their pre-eminence. 'Our true heritage in Asia is all Southeastern Asia up to the Yangtse valley', wrote the *Times* correspondent in Peking to J. O. P. Bland, who was to play a leading role in pressing for railway concessions.[76] China was now ripe for modernisation under British guidance, urged the young Charles Addis, the rising star of the Hong Kong and Shanghai Bank.[77]

But, as we have seen, official London was reluctant to risk the diplomatic confrontations to which the aggressive pursuit of British commercial interests might lead. The Hong Kong Bank was encouraged to arrange separate spheres of concession-hunting with the Deutsche Bank. An agreement was reached with Russia in 1899 to refuse official support for British concession-seekers in Manchuria in return for Russian self-denial in the Yangtse. Peking was persuaded to grant a fistful of railway concessions in 1898 to match those granted to Russia and France.[78] But a concession was one thing; transforming it into a finished railway quite another. That required constant diplomatic pressure on the Chinese authorities. With the outbreak of the South African War in October 1899, followed by the Boxer Rebellion in 1900, it became harder and harder to drive the concessions through the provincial bureaucracies whose cooperation was essential. To Bland, who aspired to be the Chinese Rhodes, the solution was obvious. 'Either we must adopt the methods of our successful competitors or go under... [T]he Russians pay their Chinese friends well to block our roads.' What was needed was 'a Government institution like the Russian Bank which should engineer commercial and financial undertakings', and a candid recognition 'that the obtaining of a concession in China meant certain payments to the officials concerned'.[79] But, as he constantly complained, there was no diplomatic will in London for this or for the negotiation of railway zones in which the concessionaires would have security against the interference of the provincial authorities.[80] By 1903, not a mile of line had been laid.[81] Nor, though they toyed with the idea at the height of the Boxer Rebellion, would the policy-makers contemplate declaring a Yangtse protectorate – a Chinese Egypt – for which a strong group of China merchants had campaigned,[82] to safeguard the prime region of British trade behind Shanghai.

The British government's real decision was to ally itself with the strongest commercial force in China, the Hong Kong and Shanghai Bank. It was a marriage of true convenience. The Bank was an exchange bank, an investment bank and a bank of issue, as well as being Whitehall's financial agent in China.[83] It transacted business throughout China and hoped for more. It had no interest in a policy of spheres, still less in a Yangtse protectorate.[84] It was anxious for good relations with the Chinese government, not least because any loans it might float would have to be secured on its revenues and not on those of the provinces.[85] It was also well placed to dominate the international banking consortia which official London favoured as the instrument of development without spheres. With the Bank on its side, Whitehall could fend off complaints from the City and claim plausibly to be defending Britain's commercial stake in China. The Bank in return gained official support against its rivals in London and its critics among the British community in China.

The results were mixed. The defeat of the Boxers, the Anglo-Japanese alliance of 1902 and the defeat of Russia in 1905 might have been expected to open the golden age of Anglo-Chinese railway-building. In fact, the City proved reluctant to invest in China. The Foreign Office and the Bank argued over who should be admitted to the loan consortium: after the *Entente cordiale* of 1904, French participation became a diplomatic necessity.[86] In the face of Chinese resistance, there was little prospect by 1908 of enforcing the kind of concession in which foreign interests kept full control over the construction and operation of a railway, as well as its finance. To Bland, that had seemed vital.[87] As Peking lost control of its provinces and the 'rights recovery' movement gathered pace among the provincial gentry, the grandiose schemes for the opening of China to the trade of the treaty-ports and Hong Kong were quietly shelved. British trade and investment was more rooted than ever within the safe haven of the treaty-ports and diversified there into industry and services. The Bank fell back upon its favoured policy of promoting the international loan consortia through which it hoped to maximise its influence. But, within five years, the Chinese revolution and the outbreak of the First World War changed the political and economic landscape beyond recognition.

Despite the scale of Britain's commercial interests and the expected value of the China market, the modest scope of British action in the crucial decade after 1895 stood in marked contrast to the intervention, partition and annexation favoured in Egypt and Africa. This was not because official policy was inflexibly committed to a united and independent China, as the flirtation with a Yangtse protectorate showed. Nor because British interests were thought strong enough to fend for themselves. In the Chinese interior, that had never been true. The reality was that in China Britain's power was too limited, her unofficial protégés too weak, her international rivals too strong and the Chinese 'host' much too resilient for a solution along African or

Egyptian lines to be imposed.[88] The larger aim of promoting British commercial interests throughout China by official pressure was even more impractical. After 1905, the more perceptive of the China hands recognised that the future lay not in attempts at the colonial subordination of China, still less in partition, but in 'normalising' her relations with the West, especially through currency reform, the greatest single barrier to trade.[89] European financial cooperation, thought Addis, would be the instrument of modernity.[90] It was a banker's dream. But, in the time of troubles that lay ahead, it was a vision to which British leaders would return with almost desperate faith.

Latin America: the swing to the West

Up to 1914 (and long after), foreign-owned business in China remained the step-child of diplomacy or was confined to the shelter of treaty-ports. By contrast, Latin America was a fair field of commercial enterprise, offering exceptionally favourable conditions after 1880 for the growth of a vast business empire pivoted upon London. Latin America was far away from the great geopolitical faultline that ran from Vienna through Constantinople to Teheran and Peking. Latin American states were defective by European standards, but after c.1850 they were far more robust and commerce-friendly than almost anything to be found in tropical Africa.[91] There was neither the need nor the opportunity to engage in the costly privatised state-building to which Goldie, Mackinnon and Rhodes had resorted. Nor was there a great imperial bureaucracy, like that in China, to confine the commercial intruder to a coastal enclave. Latin American elites, far from resisting a disruptive alien culture, eagerly embraced European models of 'order and progress' and identified with Europe's colonising drive elsewhere in the world. They saw themselves as the vanguard of civilisation among their benighted countrymen, especially where those countrymen were Indian or black.[92] Amid the enthusiasm with which they opened their economies to the outside world, the clumsy apparatus of semi-colonialism erected in China would have been an absurd irrelevance.

Three other circumstances shaped the economic connection between Britain and Latin America. No Latin American state in 1880 remotely compared with the United States in population, accessible resources, commercial infrastructure or industrial development. There was neither the means nor the will to challenge Britain's financial, commercial and industrial superiority by building a manufacturing base behind tariff walls. Secondly, Latin America's mineral wealth and its rich zones of tropical, sub-tropical and temperate agriculture promised a huge stream of primary products at the very moment when Europe's urban and industrial transformation was moving into high gear. Finally, Latin American governments, notably in Brazil, Argentina and Uruguay, were now ready to exploit their natural resources with a vast immigrant workforce drawn from the stagnant rural economies of Italy and Spain.

British businessmen were perfectly placed to exploit this dynamic new commercial frontier. They could move out from the old mercantile bridgeheads first occupied during or before the 1820s. They commanded an ample reservoir of commercial credit and a versatile shipping network. They were attuned to the commodity markets in London and well supplied with commercial intelligence. Above all, they enjoyed ready access, through merchant banks and the Stock Exchange, to a stream of capital. Credit, capital and commercial know-how were their supreme comparative advantage for, though none of these was entirely lacking in Latin American economies, local businessmen preferred familiar assets like land or housing to riskier long-term projects subject to the ebb and flow of foreign markets.[93] As the Latin American economies were drawn more fully into the web of international trade, their commercial association with Britain grew closer and closer.

The results were impressive. In 1880, Britain exported goods worth some £17 million to Latin America. By 1890, the figure had risen to nearly £29 million, and had surged past £50 million by 1910.[94] By that date, British purchases had grown even faster to exceed £70 million. By the eve of the First World War, around 10 per cent of British trade was with the Latin American states. But much more striking than the growth of trade was the astronomical rise in British investment. In 1875, when Latin American borrowing was already under way, the total had been £175 million. Thirty years later, it had increased four-fold, and by 1913 stood at nearly £1,200 million[95] (these figures must be treated as orders of magnitude since the amount of private investment, as opposed to quoted securities is necessarily conjectural). By 1913, two-thirds of that total was invested in enterprises rather than government bonds (the reverse had been true in 1885). Perhaps half of all British investment was in railways, and there were British-owned railways in every South American country and in Mexico, Guatemala and Costa Rica. More British capital was poured into docks, harbours, tramways and utilities to serve the booming cities, including Buenos Aires, the 'Paris of the southern hemisphere'.[96] 'Nowhere in the world', remarked James Bryce of Buenos Aires, 'does one feel a stronger sense of exuberant wealth.'[97] In this benign environment, British businessmen like the Johnston family in Brazil,[98] the banker George Wilkinson Drabble in Argentina,[99] Colonel North, the 'nitrate king', in Chile[100] and the great contractor Weetman Pearson (later Lord Cowdray) in Mexico[101] could build up their interests on an imperial scale.

In fact, British interests were scattered prodigally across Central and South America. Even in inhospitable states like Paraguay and Venezuela, there were British-owned railways like the Paraguay Central and the Bolivar.[102] Sixty per cent of Colombia's network was British-owned.[103] In Peru, where the government had defaulted on its railway loans in 1879, a British holding company, the Peruvian Corporation, administered the country's railways, guano deposits and certain utilities under the 'Grace Contract' of 1890.[104] In Chile, British capital controlled one-third of nitrates production – Chile's principal export and its main source of public revenue – by the 1880s.[105] In fact, British capital was concentrated in Mexico, Chile and along the Atlantic coast in Brazil, Uruguay and Argentina. Mexico ranked third in 1913, with some £132 million in railways, mines and the oil concessions into which the Pearson interests had diversified – a figure broadly equal to that of American investment.[106] In Uruguay, British commercial predominance was proverbial. 'All of the industrial enterprises . . . of any importance are in English hands', remarked the British minister in 1881.[107] Transport, communications, utilities, insurance, banking, meat-processing and ranching were largely British-owned or managed by 1900,[108] and the Uruguayan president ruefully described himself as the 'manager of a great ranch whose board of directors is in London'.[109] In Brazil, the growth of British banks and insurance companies followed in the wake of the large trading houses dealing in coffee and sugar. The British-owned Sao Paulo Railway, the great trunk route into the coffee-growing heartland, was the most profitable British railway anywhere in South America.[110]

But it was in Argentina that British interests had flourished most of all. Argentina was the miracle economy of the age and the most dynamic in Latin America.[111] Its seemingly boundless resources prompted comparisons with the United States. Between 1880 and 1913, its population increased fourfold to eight million, nearly half the increase being due to immigration. Its production of cereals grew by forty times. In 1913, it was by far the world's greatest exporter of maize. It became a major supplier of frozen meat and the second largest producer of wool. Its railway network by 1910 covered more than 17,000 miles of line[112] and was still growing rapidly. The maize and wheat lands west of Buenos Aires were crisscrossed by the densest railway system in South America. By 1913, Argentina had long since overtaken Brazil as Britain's main trading partner and dominated British trade with the continent. Not surprisingly, this exceptional growth and the close commercial tie with Britain were reflected in the volume of British capital directed to the country. In 1880, British investment had stood at £20 million; a decade later at £157 million;[113] and by 1913 at £360 million – as much as in India. More than half this sum had been placed in the railway system, the key to export-led growth. The Buenos and Great Southern, the Buenos Aires and Pacific, the Central Argentine, the Western, the Central Cordoba and other British lines made up 70 per cent of Argentina's network.[114] After 1900, the Southern returned a consistent dividend of 7 per cent.[115] The railway companies were also linked to docks and harbour companies and to shipping lines. Other British capital went into water, gas and tramways. And, by the late nineteenth century, British banks like the Bank of London and South America dominated the finance of trade.

The British stake in Argentina's development was huge. But, both there and elsewhere in Latin America, it was based on a tacit accommodation with local elites. Even in Colombia, a congressman could urge that 'we ... offer Europe raw materials and open our ports to manufactures to facilitate trade and the advantages it brings'.[116] The 'open economy' favoured the political, commercial and cultural aspirations of a dominant landed class, nowhere more so than in Argentina where *estanciero* supremacy had been consolidated in the pampas war against the Indians – the sordid prelude to the economic miracle. Import substitution occurred and capital was accumulated locally. But any deliberate policy of large-scale industrial development faced insuperable difficulties in the transitional phase. It could hardly be undertaken without the protection of tariffs. But tariffs would produce a slackening of trade, reducing exports and foreign income. The inflow of capital would tail off threatening an adverse balance of payments and destabilising the whole economy and its fragile superstructure. Hence, while development 'towards the interior' had its advocates and appealed to important local interests, they were rarely strong enough to challenge the agrarian class and its commercial allies before 1914.

Even so, in a region of such rapid economic and social change, where political institutions were relatively weak, foreign interests could not escape the side-effects of instability and sometimes faced frontal attack. The Peruvian Corporation representative in Lima, Clinton Dawkins, complained bitterly of breaches of the 1890 agreement under which the loan default was being paid off: the Peruvian president was 'bestially stupid'.[117] With its guano running out, its nitrates lost and silver's value in steep decline, Peru was going to ruin 'not by degrees but by sheer strides'.[118] In Chile, the civil war of 1891 threatened British nitrate interests with a government take-over. In Brazil, political upheaval in the 1890s and a policy of industrialisation choked off foreign capital and wrecked the exchange rate.[119] Worst of all was the great crisis of 1890 in Argentina. Reckless over-investment by the great banking house of Barings crashed into the reckless inflation of its paper currency by the Argentinian government. As Argentina's ability to meet its fixed payments on railway and government loans (payable in gold not paper) came into question, panic spread in London about the value of British holdings, the solvency of Barings and the stability of the City's whole enormous stake in international lending.[120]

The instinct to punish default by diplomatic intervention and a blockade of cruisers had not entirely disappeared, but on the British side it was widely recognised as clumsy and inappropriate. Diplomatic pressure in Chile was abandoned when it was realised that local British opinion was as divided as the Chileans over the rights and wrongs of the civil conflict.[121] In Peru, Dawkins (an ardent imperialist) jeered at the 'absurd notions' of his London board 'about diplomatic interference, British squadrons, Johnny Atkins and all that fustian'.[122] In the aftermath of the Barings crisis, Lord Salisbury curtly dismissed the idea of official involvement in a stabilisation agreement as 'dreams'.[123] In fact, political coercion was redundant, if not counter-productive. Subtler means lay to hand. The British could exploit their 'structural' advantages as the source of credit, capital and information.[124] Nationalisation in Chile was resisted as fiercely by Chilean as by British owners.[125] Elsewhere, the penalties of financial default were felt as keenly by the South American elites as by their British creditors. It meant an indefinite stoppage of new capital whose inflow had become essential not just to the growth of the export economy but to the efficient working of the export-import cycle, with its dependence on credit and its exposure to volatile price movements. Credit starvation heralded a total breakdown of the commercial economy, with a revolution close behind. Hence the focus of South American diplomacy in London in the troubled 1890s was not the Foreign Office but New Court, the Rothschild offices in the City. It was Rothschilds who negotiated the Romero agreement with Argentina in 1893,[126] and a loan to stabilise the Brazilian exchange in 1898.[127] For both countries, the price was a sharp deflation, and the strengthening of British-based banks and railway companies over local competitors. The adoption (or re-adoption) of the gold standard with its fixed parities by Peru (1897–9), Argentina (1899), Mexico (1904) and Brazil (1906)[128] was further evidence that they were willing to accept the financial discipline imposed by the City.

To the official classes in Britain, Latin America was the dark side of the moon. 'South America . . . is quite out of the currents of the world', wrote Dawkins wistfully, hankering after official preferment in Egypt or India.[129] The continent was a diplomat's graveyard. But, by 1913, it was the brightest jewel in the City's crown, the richest province of its business empire and the great white hope of the investing classes. It was the perfect illustration of the third dimension of British power, springing not from conquest or settlement but from collaboration in the pursuit of wealth. By 1913, Latin America was providing around a quarter of Britain's overseas property income. It employed nearly a quarter of Britain's long-distance shipping fleet[130] and contributed heavily to her invisible earnings. Its expanding railways were the perfect vehicle for British financial, technical and managerial expertise, as well as being large consumers of British coal – whose bulk export was the key to the profitability of British shipping: 85 per cent of outward cargoes to Brazil were coal.[131] The British commercial and professional communities in Latin America were small in numbers, but wealthy, well-educated and influential.[132] In a continent (increasingly) of European immigrants, and in cities like Buenos Aires where foreigners made up three-quarters of the adult population by 1914,[133] their cosmopolitan origins and outlook were no handicap. In Buenos Aires in 1909, there were 7,113 British among 7,444 Germans, 27,000 French, 277,000 Italians and 174,000 Spanish.[134]

In a wider perspective, the remarkable florescence of British commerce in Latin America around 1900 can be seen as part of a 'swing to the West' – a subtle rebalancing of Britain's global interests and commitments between Europe, the Americas and the Eastern world. The huge flow of capital towards Argentina had its counterpart in the great migration of men and money to Canada in the decade before 1914 and the dramatic growth of Anglo-Canadian trade. British investment in the United States also surged upwards from £500 million in 1899 to £800 million by 1914.[135] The Anglo-American rapprochement and the careful accommodation of British interests in Central America to American regional predominance[136] was part of this new Atlantic pattern. By 1913, the Americas accounted for one-fifth of Britain's exports, one-third of her imports, more than half of her overseas investment and almost three-quarters of her oceanic shipping. Here, far away from the cockpits of imperial rivalry, was a vast zone of safety, stability and wealth: some compensation for the strain of defending British interests in Asia or, after 1910, for the strategic burden in Europe.

Of course, in Latin America at least, this happy conjuncture could not be taken for granted. The growing size and scale of British enterprise bred resentment.[137] The nativist reaction of the early 1900s in Argentina and elsewhere revealed the strains of nation-building under conditions of hectic growth and foreign influence.[138] Ultimately, the 'order and progress' in which the British had invested so heavily rested upon the primacy of the local agro-commercial elites. In turn, their fate and their readiness to comply with external financial discipline depended on the booming demand for their commodity exports and London's ability to supply the capital on which growth and stability relied. In 1914, with appalling suddenness, this great experiment in business empire came to a grinding halt.

Commerce or empire?

The union of commercial and imperial muscle was the foundation of the British world-system. The vast scale of British trade, the fleets of merchant shipping, the treasure chest of overseas investment and the resources it commanded were widely seen as the real embodiment of British world power. They supplied the economic energy to sustain the show of empire and pay for its defence. They formed the invisible chains that bound the visible empire of dependencies and settler states to their far-off metropole. They provided the means to expand the sphere of British influence and turn the 'undeveloped estates' of empire into imperial assets. In a world in which a handful of imperial 'superstates' was expected to hold sway, they were the guarantee of premier status, and of independence.

Yet the project of a free-standing commercial republic, no longer reliant on political, diplomatic or military support, had made little headway outside the favoured zones of South and Central America. Even there, it depended to a degree upon British political and cultural prestige. 'The educated Englishman who arrives in Latin America', remarked a traveller in 1913, 'must generally assume the prestige as well as the burden of his empire.'[139] Elsewhere, beyond the developed world of the United States and the 'white dominions', commerce needed empire more than ever. This was especially true in the Eastern world south and east of Suez where a large proportion of British trade and investment was still to be found. Eighteen per cent of British investment was in India and East Asia: the total for Asia, Africa and Australasia was 41 per cent. In India, the largest market for Britain's largest export, cotton textiles, colonial rule pegged open a market that would otherwise have been snapped shut by tariffs and homemade competition. It was decisive in the early and rapid construction of railways, underwritten by colonial revenues and pressed forward at London's command. The contrast with China, whose disorganised network was barely one-sixth the length of India's by 1913, was telling. Indeed, there, the security of British investment, the organisation of foreign trade and the prospects for commercial development seemed to require the enforcement of the 'unequal treaties' and the defence of the colonial and semi-colonial enclaves scattered the length of the China coast. To its British residents, treaty-port Shanghai was as much a part of the Empire as Sydney or Cape Town and entitled to the same protection[140] – a claim which the policy-makers acknowledged down to the 1930s. To the champions of tariff reform after 1903, it was precisely this reliance on force to open new markets in Asia and save old ones that condemned free trade. 'Not feeling quite strong enough to keep the door open in Europe by threat of force', Leo Amery told Milner, '[England] tries to do so elsewhere by forcibly retarding the expansion of other powers. The policy has increased our armaments and our territory enormously in the last twenty years.'[141]

Experience of India, China, the Middle East and Africa also kept alive, in the heyday of *laissez-faire*, a variant of political or imperial capitalism that had little in common with the rational entrepreneurship imagined by Joseph Schumpeter in his *Imperialism and Social Classes* (1919). To businessmen like Goldie, Mackinnon, the Liverpool traders on the Niger, the *taipans* of the China coast and railway promoters like Bland, it was self-evident that political power should be used if necessary against the threat of monopolistic rivals and to clear the path of local 'obstructions'. To them, commercial development, local progress and the imperial interest were bound up inseparably, and the cavils of diplomats and administrators either myopic or self-serving. It was a short step from this to the harder face of political capitalism in those parts of Afro-Asia where resources were scantier, the resistance tougher and the environment harsher. In sub-Saharan Africa, especially, coercion became the fastest means of accumulating wealth. Force was used to uphold a commercial monopoly against local competition (on the Niger); and to appropriate land and cattle (in East and Central Africa). Coercion ensured the supply of labour from African societies whose manpower was scarce and valuable. The threat of collective vengeance became the shield behind which traders, settlers and miners could practise a quasi-coercive production system with remarkable security and at negligible cost.[142] With the rise of a vulgar 'ethnic Darwinism' in the later nineteenth century, these cruder forms of political capitalism could also be dignified as instruments of 'moral and material progress'.

In all these ways the commercial republic was heavily dependent upon the well-being of the British world-system as a whole. To its fiercer critics it seemed ever more reliant on profits extracted by coercive methods and regions exploited by political power. This was too pessimistic. What was beyond doubt was the extent to which the vast commercial system pivoted on London needed the support of its British host: to guard its long lines of communication and the vulnerable installations of trade; to preserve free trade, the magnet of commerce and finance; and to maintain the advanced industrial base whose products it traded. In return, it supplied much of the influence and wealth that late-Victorian opinion had come to see as its birthright.

4 THE BRITANNIC EXPERIMENT

Perhaps the most striking feature of Britain's global expansion was the limited influence exerted over its course by the imperial government in London. Most of the energy behind British expansion was private, not public. Of course, it was true that it usually needed a mixture of private and public resources: capital, manpower, but also protection against external and sometimes internal opponents. Governments could withhold that protection and refuse to annex when the political risks they entailed seemed out of proportion. They could also strike bargains with rival imperialists that frustrated the plans of British settlers, merchants or missionaries. But only up to a point. The promoters of British expansion could usually mobilise both public and private 'investment' at home (both material and emotional), and use it to leverage additional resources on the local or colonial 'spot'. It was this combination that made them so versatile; and that versatility was what made the British presence so ubiquitous.

The result by the later nineteenth century was the creation of a British world-system. Its system-like character can be seen in two ways. First, private and public activity had combined (most visibly in the strategic and technological achievement of long-distance sea-lanes) to encourage the growth of a single vast network centred on Britain, to distribute credit, capital, goods, information, manpower and protection on a global basis, and not into a set of closed 'mercantilist' zones each with its own rules. The result was to lower the cost of defence and reduce the transaction costs of a global pattern of trade. Secondly, by a series of incremental adjustments, the main spheres of British enterprise came to play different but complementary roles in the larger process of British expansion. The shipping and property empire, much of it active in non-British territory, provided an income that sustained high levels of imports, the domestic balance of payments, and new exports of capital. The 'sub-empire' of India assumed after c.1870 a primarily (but not exclusively) military function, meeting the ordinary costs of almost two-thirds of the Empire's regular land forces: its British garrison and its own Indian army. By contrast, the settlement colonies were not expected to pay for their *strategic* defence and were allowed (unlike India) to protect local industry. Their contribution instead was to borrow and trade on a scale (proportionately) far greater than India. And, increasingly, by the end of the century, they began to take up the part of Britain's most reliable allies, bound to her 'system' by deep ties of self-interest and self-identification.

The Britannic idea

This 'Britannic' solidarity was a crucial dimension of the British world-system, and one of the keys to its tenacious survival in the twentieth century. It would have greatly surprised the early Victorians. Indeed, it is easy to see why opinion in Britain in the earlier part of the century had shown little enthusiasm for the settlement colonies. They seemed liabilities scattered broadcast across the world. With the exception of the two 'Canadas' (modern Ontario and Quebec) and New South Wales, their populations were tiny and their prospects uncertain. Far from forming solid territorial blocs, British North America, British South Africa and the British South Pacific were fragmented and fissiparous. The Canadas had been forced into uneasy union in 1840, but the 'Lower' or Maritime provinces remained stubbornly separate: indeed, overland travel between them and the Canadas was dauntingly difficult.[1] In the 1850s, six separate governments ruled over the one million or so settlers in Australia, while geographical separation (on a much smaller scale) encouraged a similar trend in New Zealand. Although London had recognised that local self-government ('responsible government') could not be resisted in most settlement colonies (but not in Cape Colony), their financial fragility and proneness to faction – rather than party-based politics – cast doubt on how far self-reliance could be carried.[2] Worse still, in too many cases, the risk of foreign invasion or local 'native' wars had made them a drain on Britain's limited military manpower. In the 1840s, frontier conflicts in South Africa and New Zealand, as well as the tension provoked by the Oregon crisis with the

United States, dispersed British forces from one end of the world to the other.

Nevertheless, by around 1850, a more positive estimate of the settlement colonies had begun to take root. The 'Colonial Reformers' attributed the colonists' failings to interference from London, not the inherent defectiveness of colonial societies. Edward Gibbon Wakefield's idea that the British were especially adapted to colonise became more influential. The irresistible flow of Gladstonian rhetoric was deployed in support of British colonisation. 'The object [of colonization]', he began to tell audiences, 'was to reproduce the likeness of England, as they were doing in Australia, New Zealand, North America and the Cape, thereby contributing to the general happiness of mankind.'[3] Far from being seen as tiresome dependants, they were increasingly thought of, in some circles at least, as little Americas, from whom separation was certain at some foreseeable point. In the world of free trade, the balance of colonial costs and benefits could only be negative. But there was also gradual acceptance that the settler communities could be a valuable adjunct to British wealth and power, and a 'healthy' extension of British society.

Three separate developments may have strengthened this view. The first (and perhaps the most important) was the effect of railway construction. Railways connected large British interests to settler expansion. Railway-building offered much more definite proof that the colonies could achieve dense and continuous settlement, replicating the pattern of British society at home, and sustaining a similar level of institutions and culture. Above all, perhaps, investment in railways created loud vested interests with an obvious motive in selling the colonies' future to British opinion.[4] The second development was the growing belief from mid-century onwards that industrialisation in Britain had imposed high social costs some of which could be redeemed in the colonies. This was the idea that colonial life, free from the contagion of urban industrialism, offered a physically and morally healthier climate. Here British social virtues could be preserved and revived; the perils of decadence, degeneration and 'Caesarism' – a populist dictatorship – averted.[5] This perception coincided with the steady advance of emigration (and return migration) to become key social features not just of the Celtic 'periphery' but of English society as well. Thirdly, with the rising sense of a world that was linked by fast and regular movement – by wire, steamship and rail – the settlement colonies came to look less like the random results of demographic opportunism and more like the links in an imperial 'chain', part of a system of global power. The message of John Robert Seeley's *Expansion of England* (1883), that the settlement colonies should be seen as an organic extension of Britain not part of the burdensome empire of rule, was the cogent expression of an emerging idea, not a sudden new insight.[6] The late Victorians experienced an enlargement of their mental horizons, and also perhaps in their sense of identity.

In late-Victorian Britain, this shift of attitudes was part of a new imperial outlook. It was matched by a change in the colonies of white settlement, soon to be called the 'white dominions'. There too the imperial idea was transformed and made popular. Yet, by the latter part of the century, in all the settlement colonies, there was a growing sense of self-conscious nationhood and (especially after 1900) a buoyant view of their economic future as 'young nations'. This paradox was resolved by the special quality of settler nationalism. In Canada, Australia, New Zealand and (as we shall see) among the British minority in South Africa, national identity was asserted by rejecting subservience to the British *government*, but by affirming equality with Britain as 'British peoples' or 'nations'. It was this 'Britannic nationalism' which underpinned the commitment of all the white dominions to the imperial enterprise, and the British world-system, until its eventual disintegration in the 1940s and 1950s. It was not an unthinking observance of old imperial loyalty, nor an unconsummated passion for an impractical imperial federation. It was stronger, subtler and deeply rooted in the needs of the dominions themselves. Socially, it derived from the feeling that creating modern large-scale societies demanded institutions and habits – private and public – on the model already familiar in Britain, the great exemplar of a 'modern' community, but improved and adapted to local requirements. Politically it sprang up when two great imperatives converged in the later nineteenth century: the urge for expansion and need for cohesion. Expansion in an age of rival empires and 'world-states' could only be secure under the aegis of British power, and so long as the imperial centre acknowledged the claims of its Britannic outposts. So Britannic nationalism meant asserting settler influence at the heart of the empire. Secondly, as settler society grew more urban and industrial, more divided by wealth and class, more conscious of deficiencies of education and welfare, Britannic ethnicity offered the promise of social cohesion, and a charter for social renewal. A reformed and purified local Britishness went hand in hand with – was the domestic counterpart to – a grander role as 'British nations', partners, not subjects, of imperial Britain.

Canada

The oldest self-governing settler societies in the British Empire were in British North America. They were also the first to federate – as the Dominion of Canada in 1867. With the acquisition of Rupertsland – the vast northern domain of the Hudson's Bay Company – in 1869, adhesion of British Columbia (in 1871) and Prince Edward Island (in 1873), Canada became a transcontinental state rivalling in territorial scale the great republic to the south. But in wealth and population it was puny. There was the rub. A *second* transcontinental state in North America flew in the face of commercial and geographical logic. Along its whole length, the new dominion was bound to feel the immense gravitational pull of American enterprise. The builders of confederation embarked upon a staggeringly grandiose venture for a small colonial community, deeply divided by ethnicity, region and religion, and already strung out along a ribbon of cultivation between Lake Huron and Halifax. Measured by ambition, the 'Fathers of Confederation' (principally John A. Macdonald and George Brown) were among the greatest of Victorian empire-builders, planning a vast new colony anchored by 'British connection',[7] loyal to the British Crown and drawing on British migrants and capital to fuel its expansion. They looked forward to the day, declared George Brown in the confederation debates in 1865, 'when one united government under the British flag shall extend from shore to shore'.[8]

From the beginning, the politics of the new dominion were dominated by two interlocking priorities. The first was to make the new federal constitution workable. That meant reconciling the Maritime provinces to the burden of debt that the old Canadian provinces (now Ontario and Quebec) had accumulated building railways and canals, and to the tariff that had been imposed to pay for them. It meant the careful management of Quebec with its French Canadian majority and its vocal minority of English Canadians in Montreal and the 'Eastern Townships'. Federation had separated the two Canadian provinces previously locked in legislative union, but did little to reduce the mutual antipathy of Protestant Ontario and Catholic Quebec. It meant heading off the opposition among Ontario farmers to the railway and banking interests from whose headquarters in St James Street, Montreal, the first prime minister, Sir John A. Macdonald, was widely believed to take his orders and his party funds. It meant an uphill struggle to broaden the power and authority of the new 'general government' in Ottawa against provincial pressure for devolution or even (in the case of Nova Scotia) for secession.

These teething problems were constantly entangled with the second great issue that absorbed both Macdonald and his Reform (or 'Grit', later Liberal) opponents: how to make good the dominion's claim to the vast western empire beyond the Great Lakes, the key to its future as a separate 'British' North American state. The imperial government in London had been eager to transfer 'Rupertsland' to Canada, believing that the Hudson's Bay Company could no longer rule a vast inland colony now thought ripe for agricultural development. But the conveyance was not as easy as it seemed. For one thing, the best organised community in the west, the mixed-race (French and Indian) *Metis* in the Red River Valley (near modern Winnipeg), objected to a transfer that they feared would bring a flood of British settlers from Ontario.[9] Under the charismatic leadership of Louis Riel, they staged the first of two northwestern rebellions whose suppression required the despatch of imperial troops under Sir Garnet Wolseley, the ubiquitous generalissimo of the Empire's smaller wars. The *Metis* were routed and the new province of Manitoba set up.[10] But, as Macdonald well knew, a much greater challenge awaited. Only with a railway across the continent could he hope to transform the northwestern interior from an economic desert into a great agrarian asset – and Canada from a stagnant eastern colony into a dynamic continental state.

In the first decade of confederation, there was little to show for the high hopes of 1867. Macdonald's first attempt to commission a railway across the continent was a failure, and the ensuing 'Pacific scandal' blew him out of office in 1873. His Reform party opponents, suspicious of the Montreal capitalists, and hobbled by economic depression, made no headway. Canada was in the doldrums. The immigrants it did attract were as likely to pass on to the United States as to stay; many more Canadians moved south of the border in search of better times: nearly one million between 1881 and 1891.[11] Macdonald came back to office in 1878. In the thirteen years that followed, he fashioned a surprisingly durable political regime, presided over the completion of the east–west railway and pushed through Canada's transformation into a separate northern economy with a tariff wall to guard its railways, trade, finance and infant industry. Together, the 'Macdonaldian state', the Canadian Pacific Railway and the 'national policy' turned the prospectus of confederation into something like reality. The question was whether the 'Canada' that Macdonald had made could survive the disappearance of his master touch.

By the time of his death in 1891, Macdonald had been the dominant figure in Canadian politics for fifty years. In the black arts of patronage, 'Old Tomorrow' was a virtuoso, reconciling Canada's complex dualities – English and French, monarchy and populism, liberal and clerical, protestant and catholic, provincial and federal – by the systematic use of every office under federal control in a spoils system for party purposes.[12] Perhaps instinctively, he grasped the irreducible conditions of Canadian unity. British institutions and a shared allegiance to the British Crown formed the only ideological glue between the regions and peoples that made up the federation. The mercantile and financial nexus at Montreal was the natural (indeed only) focus of a 'northern economy'. The transcontinental hinterland, and a railway to serve it, offered the only escape from the economic failure and encirclement that threatened Eastern Canada. Macdonald's 'national policy' had fused these into a rough and ready programme and a loyal political following. Together, they were robust enough to overcome the challenge of 'reciprocity' in 1891 – the call for commercial union with the United States championed by the Liberal opposition. 'The old flag, the old policy and the old leader' (Macdonald's slogan in 1891) fended off the critics of the 'northern economy', despite deepening depression and the lack of any sign that the west would relieve it. But, by the mid-1890s, the political system that had been built round Macdonald's personal ascendancy was on the brink of collapse. The provinces were in revolt and determined to win back from the centre some of the rights and revenues conceded in 1867. More ominously still, the coalition that Macdonald had forged between Montreal business, the protestant and loyalist tradition in Ontario and the clerical conservatives (the *Bleus*) in Quebec – the electoral basis of Conservative predominance since the 1870s – began to break up. The growth of mass politics in Quebec weakened the elite on whom Macdonald had relied.[13] The vitriolic disagreement between Ontario and Quebec politicians over the execution of Louis Riel (convicted of murder after the second northwest rebellion

in 1885) and over separate schools for Manitoba Catholics[14] widened
the breach and exposed Macdonald's successors to criticism from all
sides. When the Conservatives were swept away by a new system-
builder, the Liberal Wilfrid Laurier, the result was not only a new party
regime. To many Canadians, a new definition of the Canadian state
and its bond with Britain now seemed necessary.

The challenge had already been posed by the radical historian
Goldwin Smith, sometime professor in Oxford, now the resident sage
in Toronto. In his widely read *Canada and the Canadian Question*
(1891), Smith denounced the dominion as the artificial product of tariffs, (subsidised) railways and political corruption. The 'primary forces'
in Canadian life, he insisted, were pulling it towards a continental
future as part of the United States – a future Smith welcomed as the
fulfilment of Anglo-Saxon race unity. Towards French Canada and its
claims, he displayed, by contrast, a mixture of contempt and dislike.
French Canadians were irredeemably backward. But English Canada
alone was too weak to swamp, swallow and digest them. Continental
union with the United States, among other benefits, would break the
obstacle they posed to social progress.[15]

Smith's argument may have been extreme, but he evoked many
of the prejudices of Protestant, Liberal Ontario against the Macdonald
state and Quebec. His book drew a carefully argued riposte from O. A.
Howland, a Toronto lawyer from one of the city's leading families.[16]
The 'natives of this country' said Howland, would not accept the
extinction of their 'separate nationality'. The St Lawrence river system gave Canada the means for a separate statehood, but within the
Empire – 'a term which should be transferred from the island of Great
Britain to the whole of our modern union of constitutionally governed
English nations'.[17] 'The free men of the Empire', he went on, claimed
'equal Imperial citizenship, whether our homes are in Great Britain,
or Canada or Australia.'[18] As part of the Empire, Howland insisted,
Canada would enjoy greater freedom and security than the United States
could offer. It would keep its own constitution and escape the crushing
embrace of Chicago and New York. And, within fifty years, the Empire
would 'comprise not less than three mighty states . . . more than equal
in population and resources to the United States [in 1860] . . . What
Armageddon of history would threaten the integrity of that vast
alliance?'[19]

In Howland's tract, we can see the emerging themes of Britannic
nationalism in its Canadian version. As elsewhere in the settler colonies,

this was a complex political emotion. Its appeal ranged far beyond the small minority who looked forward to an imperial federation or called themselves 'imperialists'. In Canada, it was a cross-party sentiment that was strongest between 1890 and 1920, but continued to shape the English-Canadian outlook until c.1960. It was an echo of Macdonald's old war cry: 'A British subject I was born, a British subject I will die.'[20] It affirmed that Canada was a 'British' country in allegiance, institutions and values. But it was not to be mistaken for the Macdonaldite Toryism which Britannic nationalism rejected as a shabby, inadequate compromise bringing internal disunity and external impotence. Indeed, just because it was based on the endless 'squaring' of rapacious interests, chief among them the clerical conservatives of Quebec, Macdonald's 'system' – so its critics maintained – would bar, not open, the way to a Britannic future.

In the early 1890s, a variety of political fears coalesced into the informal programme at whose heart lay the 'Britannicising' of Canada. The election of 1891 and the wide appeal of commercial integration with the United States showed that Smith's attack on the idea of Canada could not be taken lightly. If Canada was to survive as a 'separate nationality', patriotic sentiment would have to be founded on something more durable than Macdonald's fixes, fudges and fiddles. Politics must be cleaned up and modernised. Political leadership should be based on a covenant with the people and be seen to respond to their needs. This was the Gladstonian model whose influence in and beyond the English-speaking world has been insufficiently recognised.[21] Its realisation was made all the more urgent by recognition that urbanisation, industrialisation and (after 1900) the flood of immigration had created new social problems and demanded new moral and social action, including factory laws, education and temperance. A populist gospel of social duty, moral uplift and physical improvement laid stress, as elsewhere across the 'British' world, upon ethnic solidarity: 'Britishness' was to be the building block of a more efficient, better-disciplined as well as more mobile society.

To the champions of reform, it seemed obvious that a new-style dominion must be built up as a protestant, secular state, guided by a progressive liberalism and governed (through its parliamentary institutions) by an enlightened public opinion. Equally, that, while Canada's 'separate nationality' could only be guaranteed as a 'British' nation, national dignity and self-esteem demanded an equality of status with Britain in what Howland had provocatively called a 'federal Republic . . . united under a hereditary president'.[22] But equality of status meant not indifference to the wider concerns of Empire, but much fuller participation in them. Only in that way could Canadians guard their national interests against the danger of Anglo-American agreement at their expense. 'Britannic nationalism' in short meant neither subservience to Britain nor a repudiation of Canadian nationhood. It was a programme to achieve a Canadian nation by drawing more deeply (if selectively) on recent British political practice, and by asserting Canada's claims (as Britannic nation not colonial dependency) on the imperial centre in London.

Much of the bitterness in Canadian politics after 1890 sprang from the fear that the pursuit of Britannic nationhood for Canada would be frustrated by French Canadian opposition. Until the 1890s, the willingness of English Canadians to 'tolerate' the 'peculiar institutions' of French Canada – especially the entrenched power of the Catholic church – rested on the assumption that Quebec was (largely) an inward-looking 'reserve' whose population (a minority in the dominion) would not obstruct the 'progress' of the British majority. That was the English-Canadian version of the 'compact' of 1867. The Riel affair, the fillip it gave to French Canadian feeling, and the emergence of the *parti national* under Honore Mercier first belied this hope. The Jesuit Estates Act (1886) that Macdonald refused to veto seemed to show that in Quebec the clerical influence so hateful to Ontario Liberals and protestants was growing more assertive. It led to the virulently protestant Equal Rights Association in Ontario.[23] Then, in the 1890s, as settlers moved into Manitoba from Ontario, a furious row broke out over the right of the province's Catholic, French-speaking minority to maintain separate schools against the will of the provincial government. In Ontario especially, the dithering of the Macdonald government was ample proof that it was willing to sacrifice the vital ingredients of nationhood – secular education and popular democracy – to the corrupt dictates of its coalition with the Quebec *Bleus*. Indeed, the 'schools question' seemed the crux of Canada's future. Settlement of Western Canada, long delayed by depression, was expected to break the deadlock between English and French Canada. Vast, new, and English-speaking, provinces in the West would form, politically, a 'Greater Ontario'. But not if their politics were fractured and corrupted by the entrenchment of clerical and French-Canadian influence.

Indeed, Ontario was the heartland of Britannic nationalism which was rooted in the province's Liberal and protestant ethos. It was the creed of the Orange Order, the most powerful association in the province.[24] In Ontario, the shift from agrarian society towards urbanisation and industrialisation had gone furthest and fastest, and the need for new kinds of political solidarity was felt most deeply. Ontario politicians and publicists like Clifford Sifton (soon to be Laurier's main Liberal henchman in English Canada), Newton Rowell and John Willison, editor of the great Liberal organ, the *Toronto Globe*,[25] were adamant that British values must prevail in Ontario, and Ontario values in Canada. 'Upon the English and Protestant people', declared Sifton in 1895, 'most largely rests the duty of developing that province [Manitoba] in a manner consonant with British institutions – to take all this heterogeneous mass and make [it] into one.'[26] And nowhere did the Britannic programme strike a louder chord than in Toronto, the provincial capital. Toronto aspired to be the true capital of a modern, progressive (and therefore British) Canada.[27] By the 1890s, industry and the mining boom in Northern Ontario were boosting its wealth and self-confidence. It was no coincidence that its social elite combined an intense civic consciousness with political views resembling those in Howland's manifesto. The new class of bankers (like G. A. Cox and Byron Walker), financiers like Pellatt[28] and general merchants like Flavelle[29] were eager to give Toronto the institutions of a dynamic, cohesive urban community. A university, to be a national university for Canada,[30] a modern hospital, a museum and an art gallery were key elements in the grand design. So too were a new railway to the West to rival Montreal's Canadian Pacific;[31] the westward expansion of Walker's Canadian Bank of Commerce – by 1915 nearly half the bank's branches were west of the Great Lakes;[32] and the takeover of Manitoba by Ontario men. When Lord Milner was invited to Canada to preach the doctrine of closer imperial union, his old friend Glazebrook, now a Toronto banker, pressed the claims of the city in revealing terms:

The vital and most important part of Canada is the West ... [I]t is there ... that the new type of Canadian is being developed. Toronto is really ... the eastern extremity of the North-West; the new enterprises of the West are being financed in Toronto, and the type of man in the West shades off as you go East into the Ontario type.[33]

The outbreak of the South African War in October 1899 was the occasion for an outburst of this Britannic sentiment. Laurier's Liberal government, resting on electoral support in both Ontario and Quebec, tried to steer a middle course. It expressed sympathy with the Uitlander grievances in Johannesburg. But Laurier was also determined to avoid direct involvement in the war and not to send a military contingent.[34] This stance infuriated much Ontario opinion. Laurier's Liberal allies in the province begged him to take the lead. 'We must not let this patriotic feeling be headed by the Tories', one warned him. 'You must head it and guide it yourself.'[35] Under intense pressure from Ontario Liberals, Laurier caved in – to the outrage of his most ardent supporters in Quebec. Was Canada returning to 'l'état primitif du colonie de la Couronne', demanded his erstwhile protégé, Henri Bourassa.[36] 'The English Canadians have two countries', complained the Montreal paper *La Presse*, 'one here and one across the sea.'[37] But the weight of opinion bore down inexorably on Laurier. 'You will not, you cannot deny', a fellow Quebecois told Bourassa,

> *that the will of an overwhelming majority of the Canadian people expressed through its press, the mouthpiece of a free people . . . not only justified but practically compelled the action of the Executive . . . Canada cannot be indifferent to anything which may affect the honour and prestige of the British flag.*[38]

The choice for French Canada, Laurier himself told Bourassa, was whether to march at the head of the Confederation or to retreat into isolation.[39] French Canadians had to choose between English and American imperialism. The contingent was sent.[40]

For Laurier's 'system' and for the leadership of both main parties, Liberal and Conservative, in French Canada, the rise of Britannic sentiment was a dangerous challenge. As prosperity and immigration increased from 1896, the simultaneous rise of the West and of 'industrial Canada' threatened to dominate Quebec and unravel the compromise of 1867.[41] Laurier had always parried the claim that Canada was a 'British' country, preferring to argue that while Canada 'must be British' that meant 'British in allegiance and Canadian in sentiment'.[42] Laurier's popularity in Ontario rested partly on his reputation as an anti-clerical in Quebec, partly on his regard for 'provincial rights' and

partly on the belief that he was best qualified to reconcile French Canadians to a progressive 'Britannic' future. He was a French Canadian
'moderniser' whose constant professions of imperial loyalty reassured
Britannic sentiment in English Canada. That and the same laborious
attention to federal patronage that had kept Macdonald in power for
so long were enough to win a Liberal majority in the elections of 1900,
1904 and 1908. But behind these electoral successes an earthquake was
under way in Ontario. There, much Liberal opinion had been incensed
by Laurier's apparent willingness to entrench separate catholic schools
in the two new prairie provinces set up in 1905.[43] Then, in 1910, the
navy question and reciprocity blew apart the alliance of Quebec and
Ontario Liberalism, and signalled the partial and uneasy triumph of
'Britannic' politics in Canada.

Since 1902, Laurier had tenaciously opposed the call by the
Australian and New Zealand governments for closer participation in
the making of British defence and foreign policy – fearing that any
deeper imperial commitment would revive the damaging controversy
with Bourassa in 1899. But, in 1909, with the rising alarm over
German naval rivalry, Laurier found that more was required than professions of imperial loyalty. As the 'naval scare' spread like a virus along
the telegraph lines and through the news agencies, the newspapers of
English Canada took up the call for a Canadian contribution to imperial
defence.[44] Canada should give two dreadnoughts to the Royal Navy,
declared the *Manitoba Free Press*, the voice of prairie Liberalism.[45]
Laurier's Conservative opponents took up the cry, urging immediate
help in Britain's naval 'emergency'. Laurier's response was canny. His
naval service bill in January 1910 proposed a small Canadian navy,
under Canadian control. As Laurier conceded, Canada's constitutional
status meant that, if Britain was at war, Canada would follow automatically. But the extent of Canada's contribution would be for ministers
in Ottawa to decide.

Laurier's formula was shrewdly calculated to appease Britannic
sentiment among Liberal supporters. He also knew that Conservative
demands for direct subvention to the Royal Navy would divide their
supporters, especially in Quebec. Instead, by conceding his 'tin pot
navy', Laurier intended to consolidate his unwieldy coalition across
Quebec, Ontario and the West. It was a drastic miscalculation. In
Quebec, the navy bill became the hated emblem of English-Canadian
hegemony in Canada and of the growing dominance of 'English'

capitalism in the province where urbanisation and industrialism threatened to deracinate the *Canadiens* crowding into the anglicised cities.[46] To Bourassa, whose nationalism was rooted in religious and social conservatism, and to the Quebec Conservatives with their clerical connections, the enemy became 'imperialism'; the collaborator Laurier; the stake the survival ('*survivance*') of French Canada as a distinct, Catholic society.[47]

On its own, the navy question might have weakened Laurier but not unseated him. His second miscalculation was more dangerous. Historically, the Liberals were the party of free trade, who had opposed the protectionism of Macdonald's 'national policy'. After the defeat of reciprocity in 1891, Laurier had given up the idea of regional free trade with the United States, adopting instead a tariff preference towards Britain in 1897 – a shrewd sop to freer trade and Britannic feeling. But there were powerful economic interests that still hankered after free entry into the American market for Canada's staple products. Above all, there was the West. By 1910, the three prairie provinces were growing at phenomenal speed as immigrants and capital flooded in to develop the wheat economy.[48] Here was a 'new' Canada whose support would be decisive in the political struggle hitherto confined to the three sections of eastern Canada. The grievances of the prairie West against high land prices, high transport costs and grain prices lower than those just across the American border[49] became focused in 1910 in a campaign against the tariff – as Laurier learnt at first hand during a prolonged tour of the region. When the American government offered mutual free entry in natural products, Laurier jumped at the chance to win over the West and the farming interests in Eastern Canada eager to sell to or export through the United States. It might offset the Western dislike of his naval programme.[50] Being confined to natural products, reciprocity posed, apparently, no threat to the industrial interests in Eastern Canada sheltered by the national policy tariff. And, in an era of 'good feelings' between Britain and the United States, the danger of an imperialist backlash seemed slight. Opposition to reciprocity he dismissed contemptuously as 'froth'.[51]

Instead, the result was indifference in Quebec where the naval question was all[52] but an explosion of rage in Ontario. The signal was given by Clifford Sifton, Laurier's sometime lieutenant in English Canada, and the proprietor of the *Manitoba Free Press*. Sifton denounced reciprocity as a threat to Canadian nationality.[53] He was quickly followed by the 'Toronto Eighteen', the cream of Toronto's Liberal elite, the bankers, financiers and merchants at whose head stood Byron E. Walker and Zebulon Lash.[54] Their defection began a full-scale revolt in Ontario against official Liberalism. Laurier's opponents made play with the claim that the limited reciprocity on offer would soon be extended, under American pressure, to complete free trade. It was a short step to argue that 'British connection' was in danger and Canada's own freedom at risk. 'On the day British connection fails us', roared the *Montreal Star*, 'Canadian independence is lost.'[55] Rejecting reciprocity meant 'self-reliance and allegiance to the Empire'.[56] Critics at the time were quick to see the campaign against reciprocity as naked self-interest masquerading as imperial loyalty.[57] Indeed, it was true that, as Canada's industrial zone, Ontario depended heavily on the 'national policy'. The Toronto plutocracy was bound to fear that freeing the West to trade south rather than east would endanger the new rail links being built from Toronto to the West and (consequentially) the prospects of the Canadian Bank of Commerce of which Walker was president. But it was also no coincidence that the Liberal defectors included those most ardently committed to the union of Ontario and the West as the heartland of a British Canada: Sifton, Walker and John Willison. To weaken prematurely the ties binding the prairies to Eastern Canada would shatter this dream. Reciprocity had been rejected in 1891 at a time when the West was unoccupied, Willison told a Toronto audience. Now it was filling up with Americans and a multitude of foreigners (i.e. non-British immigrants). 'Even the very optimistic will admit that the national problem is very different from that which we faced even ten years ago... [I]t is a mighty problem to fuse these [new people] into a common citizenship.'[58] When reciprocity was defeated, Sifton told the Ottawa *Citizen*: 'the national development of Canada along British lines will go on.'[59]

The result was a disaster for Laurier. Instead of fighting a Conservative party divided over the navy, he fought it with a Liberal party divided over trade. In riding the tiger of Britannic sentiment on the navy question, he lost Quebec. By unintentionally confronting it over reciprocity, he lost Ontario. His place as premier was taken by Robert Borden and his careful policy by an eager commitment to help with Britain's naval 'emergency' and claim a voice in London's defence and foreign policy. To Laurier, it was obvious that he had been defeated by the insurgent force of Britannic sentiment. He told the South African premier, Louis Botha, that the defection in Quebec had been large 'though not abnormal'. But, in Ontario, 'it was not a defeat, but a landslide. In the latter Province the jingo spirit was the cause.' He went on: 'You are quite right in supposing that there will be a revival of the Jingo element.'[60] Botha had sympathised, as well he might: 'I very much fear that the result will be a revival of the jingo spirit in all parts of the British Empire.'[61]

Between 1890 and 1914, the most forceful and articulate champions of Canadian nationhood were those who insisted that Canada's future lay as a British or 'Britannic' country. Only as a British country, they argued, could Canada forge a cohesive identity at home – around a common language, institutions and history. Only as a senior partner in the Britannic association (i.e. Empire) could Canada transcend its colonial status and begin to take responsibility for the defence of its national interests. This Britannic nationalism was less than the full-blown imperialism of those who favoured imperial federation;[62] but much more than support for 'British connection'. 'British connection' was politically anodyne. In French Canada, loyalty to the monarch and to British institutions as the guarantee of liberty was proverbial. Even Henri Bourassa, the scourge of British imperialism, proclaimed his loyalty to 'British connection'. But, to the Britannic nationalists, if it meant no more than the sectional compromises invented by Macdonald and refined by Laurier, then it was a feeble substitute for a real nation-state. Their priority was uniting the three great English-speaking sections: 'backward' French Canada could stumble on behind, perhaps, in due course, to be annexed in spirit. It would, perhaps, be wrong to exaggerate the extent to which Canadian opinion was preoccupied with nation-building and the imperial tie, especially in an age of such rapid economic change. But the linked crisis over the navy question and reciprocity showed that Britannic nationalism was the strongest political sentiment in Canada. It was fanned by economic buoyancy and the sense of a tightening commercial, strategic and demographic bond with Britain. In 1911, with the Borden premiership, it seemed to hold the initiative. Its finest hour, and its greatest trial, were yet to come.

'Britannic' Australia

The Australian communities, wrote Edward Shann in 1930, *festooned along a coastline of ten thousand miles are nowadays strangely uniform in social structure. In each port... you will find a group of importers' warehouses, some big wool-stores, a railway terminus, a wharf-lumpers' union and a number of public houses tied to breweries. If there is a capital-city in the near-background, it is inhabited largely by a civil service connected with Crown lands, public works and education. Its environs will boast some industries engaged on the simpler manufactures or on the repair and maintenance of the mechanism of land transport. Ships, if they can, seek cheaper repair elsewhere... Over the range is the scene of the peculiarly Australian work done by a scattered population of miners, farmers and station-hands, who turn out staple raw-products on a rough, grand scale with labour-saving machinery...*

Brooding over the coastal capital and browbeating... the mercantile and professional classes... stand the federated trade unions. Their Trades Hall is the scene of a fluctuating contest between the capable leaders of three groups: (i) the shearers, miners and timber-workers of the bush, (ii) the town artisans, and (iii) the transport workers and public works employees. These contend for mastery... through the primaries or 'selection-ballots' that name the labour candidates for the local or national parliament... The farmers, with some aid from pastoralists and the middle class, are learning political organization from the workers, but are still clumsy and inarticulate. This social structure varies little with the minor staples that differences in local climate may add to the dominant wool and wheat. The Australian communities have set in these forms with a surprising uniformity. In the politics of each the drive comes mainly from a hard-eyed, hard-headed, hard-mouthed working democracy.[63]

Shann was describing (in prose reminiscent of Joseph Conrad) a society that had crystallised in the 1890s when Australia entered her imperial age. In the 1850s, the Australian colonies had been transformed economically by the gold rush, politically by self-government and socially by the end of convict transportation (the exception to all three was Western Australia). In the thirty years after 1860, they had expanded (at 5 per cent a year) in an atmosphere of boom.[64] The population rose from one to three million, some 40 per cent of the increase by immigration. The number of sheep rocketed from 40 million in 1870 to 106 million twenty years later.[65] Wheat farming sprang up in South Australia. Pastoralism and mining developed in the vast spaces of Queensland.[66] Huge deposits of silver, lead and zinc were found at Broken Hill in New South Wales.[67] An infant manufacturing economy emerged behind Victoria's tariffs, and Melbourne (as the local metropolis of gold) became the financial capital of the Australian colonies.[68] British investment rushed in. Railway mileage tripled in the decade after 1870 to 4,000 miles and reached 10,000 miles in 1892.[69] With the opening of the Suez Canal in 1869, and the arrival of the submarine cable in 1872, Australia's long isolation seemed less forbidding. But Europe was still thirty days' steaming away,[70] and up to the 1890s most Australian trade was carried slowly but cheaply in sailing ships.[71]

In fact, between 1860 and 1890, distance and democracy had combined to fashion a highly distinctive pattern of Australian development. Rapid commercial expansion might have been expected to favour the local concentration of wealth and power. But Australia's remoteness from Europe and its huge internal distances worked in the opposite direction. Trade and capital were not funnelled through a single gateway as happened in Canada but entered by a string of ports each with its own agricultural, pastoral and mineral hinterland and its own system of roads and railways. The high cost of transit from Europe cut immigration to a relative trickle (compared with the North American flood)[72] and the high risk of railway construction in Australia's empty interior deterred the private capital that came forward in the Americas. As a result, the political economy of development fell largely under state control. The colonial governments alone had the revenue (from land sales) to meet its demands and bear its risks. Half of Australian borrowing abroad (that is, on London) was by public authorities rather than private enterprise.[73] That might have meant less had colonial ministries been the servants of a mercantile elite. But, since the 1850s, all the eastern colonies save Tasmania had had manhood suffrage. There was little enthusiasm in these colonial democracies for the subsidy of new migrants whose arrival would drive down wages. Separate colonial electorates created a vested interest in separate colonial development, so that Australia's economy like its railways remained fragmented. The political influence concentrated in each colonial capital helped to ensure

that public spending flowed disproportionately to boost its rail connections and port facilities, tightening its grip on a 'private' hinterland
behind and discouraging inter-regional connections.[74] Colonial politics revolved, predictably, not around issues of class, status or religion,
but around more homely quarrels over 'log-rolling' – using political
influence to roll public money towards particular persons, interests or
localities. Factions not parties dominated the colonial parliaments – a
pattern only partly mitigated by disputes between the 'squatter' interest with its vast sheep runs and aristocratic pretensions and those who
favoured close settlement and small farms.[75]

Australian experience between 1860 and 1890 seemed to show
that colonial autonomy could be successfully practised despite political fragmentation, heavy dependence on a narrow range of staple
exports and a small population recruited almost exclusively from British
migrants. Australia remained a geographical expression, although a
sense of common origins, cultural and occupational similarities and
a high degree of labour mobility between colonies encouraged literary depiction of a distinctive Australian 'type' or identity common
to all. Australian unity remained a vague aspiration. Inter-colonial
cooperation was chiefly visible in the common antipathy to Chinese
immigration – the occasion of joint inter-colonial declarations in 1881
and 1887 – and in a gradually rising alarm at the arrival of German
colonialism in the South Pacific in the same decade.

The 1890s brought a dramatic change. The rapid growth of
previous decades was violently checked. Having borrowed easily from
London in the 1880s when City lenders were awash with money, Australian governments, banks and businesses found their credit running
dry. Borrowing had outstripped (for the moment) the capacity to gen-
erate new income to service the debt. The Barings crisis in Argentina,
where export growth had failed to match the rising cost of foreign loans,
helped shatter confidence in Australia's prospects.[76] British investors
turned away. Australian banks watched their London deposits dwindle, enforcing a drastic monetary contraction in the colonies. Banks
and businesses failed. Unemployment soared, throwing (the figures are
imprecise) perhaps one-third of skilled workers into the street.[77] With
no system of welfare as a safeguard, the 'workingman's paradise' in
Australia had become a gloomy dystopia of depression.

Partly for this reason, the 1890s were the critical phase in the
making of Australian political consciousness. A tradition of labour

militancy, laced with imported socialism and republicanism, had grown up in the booming eighties, most vigorously on Queensland's raw frontier of mining and pastoralism.[78] Boom conditions sharpened the contrast between those with access to imported capital and the means to corner the supply of natural resources and those who depended on their labour.[79] With the fierce contraction of trade, labour discontent turned to bitterness and desperation. Wage cuts and lay-offs provoked large-scale strikes among shearers, seamen and miners across much of Eastern Australia in the early 1890s.[80] But direct action made little headway against hostile governments and employers who could draw on the great pool of unemployed. The real legacy of the depression was the emergence of labor parties to speak for organised labour in the colonial parliaments. In New South Wales, Labor won 35 seats out of 141 at the election of 1891.[81] Elsewhere, the rise of labour as a political force produced a series of concessions to populist demands: reducing the parliamentary term to three years (in Queensland and Western Australia); abolishing the property qualification for members (Western Australia and Tasmania); manhood suffrage where it had not already been conceded; new factory legislation; new taxes on land and income; the extension of wage boards and arbitration courts to set pay and resolve disputes.[82] Under the blast of economic hardship, the instinct of Australian communities was to protect, as far as they could, the living standards of more prosperous times and the egalitarian ethos inherited from the 1850s.

This defensive mood was aggravated by deepening racial anxiety. The fear of cheap 'Asiatic' labour willing to work for low wages was common to white settler societies all round the Pacific and even beyond. Economic rivalry, cultural difference and settler democracy were a lethal combination. The resentment of white workers was inflamed by the suspicion that Chinese immigrants, indifferent to Christian ethics, would be a source of moral, social and political corruption; worse still, that they would be pliant tools of big employers. Social cohesion and the enforcement of respectability, fragile growths in migrant societies, seemed to demand the ruthless suppression of visible distinction and a rigid adherence to 'common' ideals – a tendency that Tocqueville had noticed in the United States in the 1830s. The racism of white labour was fiercest in Queensland where a tropical climate, a plantation system and the arrival of Polynesian as well as Chinese labour threatened to split the colony between a 'white' south and a 'black' north.[83]

Depression exacerbated this race antagonism. Australia's Chinese population was tiny: perhaps 2 per cent of the adult male population in 1891.[84] Chinese labour was largely excluded from agriculture, pastoralism and mining. But, in a number of trades, it made up 20 per cent or more of the workforce.[85] As unemployment rose, these Chinese made an easy scapegoat for economic failure. The rights of labour mutated swiftly into the racial privilege of white workers and the demand that, at whatever cost, Australia should be reserved for the white man.

In fact, Chinese entry had been closely restricted since the 1880s. But, in the 1890s, depression-induced nightmares of a vast reserve army of Asian labour poised to rush the Australian barricade fused with the geopolitical unease set off by the French and German colonial presence in the South Pacific. This intrusion was resented in part as frustrating the ambitions of Australian 'sub-imperialists'.[86] But its underlying threat was much more serious. If the South Pacific became the scene of colonial and naval rivalry (or the horse-trading of imperial powers), the Australian colonies, so precariously dependent on sea transport for their local communications and long-distance trade, would be dangerously exposed to disruption if not invasion. Their capital cities, into which one-third of the population was now crowded, had no defence against naval attack.[87] In the mid-1890s, as great power competition in China accelerated, a new factor catalysed Australian anxiety. Japan's victory over China in 1895, its annexation of Taiwan, and the rise of Japanese migration in the Pacific region signalled the emergence of an *Asian* great power and brought home the true extent of Australian vulnerability in the new fluid era of world politics.

Depression and its populist aftermath, racial panic and strategic alarm, thus formed the context in which the great project for an Australian federation was carried through in the 1890s. Together, they exerted a crucial influence on the 'founding fathers' and their design. The originator of the federal project was Sir Henry Parkes, the grand old man of New South Wales politics. Parkes was a long-standing advocate of federation. He regarded the non-executive 'federal council' set up in 1881 to encourage inter-colonial co-operation as a dead-end. In 1889, he invited the premiers of Victoria, Queensland, Tasmania and South Australia and New Zealand to a convention to plan a federal parliament of two houses and a federal executive.[88] Parkes evoked an Australia of 'one people, one destiny'. He was eager for federation to promote Australian defence, control the entry of 'aliens', harmonise the railways and create a local Australian court of appeal. But his vision of Australian nationhood was heavily tinged with 'Britannic nationalism'. For Parkes, Australian unity derived 'from the crimson thread of kinship [that] runs through us all'.[89] Under federation, he urged, 'we should have an outline of empire such as we could never hope for as isolated colonies; and our place would be admitted in the rank of nations, under the noble and glorious flag of the mother land.'[90] For Parkes, Australia's nationhood would rest on an affirmation of British origins and undergird her destiny as the dominant local power in the South Pacific.

Parkes' ideas chimed with the widespread sense that the Australian colonies were too small (in population) and weak for an age of agglomeration.[91] Arguments of this sort had been behind the enthusiasm for *imperial* federation shown by politicians like Alfred Deakin and Edmund Barton in the 1880s.[92] By the 1890s, imperial federation no longer seemed feasible. Even Australian federation seemed a Sisyphean task. The first attempt to promote its acceptance among the colonial parliaments reached stalemate, partly because of the opposition of free traders (strong in New South Wales) who feared Victoria's protectionism would become universal, and the labour parties who feared the coercive power of a federal government in the pocket of wealth. But, with signs of wider public support (at the Corowa convention), political momentum revived. After a meeting of the colonial premiers in 1895, opposition fears were allayed by the promise of an elected convention to draw up the federal constitution. The constitution itself made large concessions to the provincialism of the colonies. The Canadian model for a strong central government was rejected.[93] The separate colonies (now to be 'states') retained wide powers over their economic development, immigration and taxation: the centre was largely confined to defence and external relations (both under imperial supervision), commerce (trade, tariffs and currency) and the control of aliens. In what may have been a concession to radical sentiment, the new federation was christened the 'Commonwealth' of Australia.

Looking back from an era when the old imperial links between Australia and Britain have withered away almost completely, some historians have been tempted to see in federation the imagining of a distinctively Australian nation that had shrugged off its colonial status. Only sentimental attachment to the mother-country, and a desire not to hurt her feelings, suggests one, prevented the move to whole-hog republican independence.[94] But this is a misreading of the intentions of the 'founding fathers' and also of the special quality of Australian nationalism. The makers of federation had no desire to 'cut the painter' and few illusions about the danger of doing so. Deakin and Barton had been enthusiasts for closer imperial ties, not separation. Kingston had denounced the idea that any British-born person should not have full rights in the new federation.[95] John Forrest of Western Australia was to die at sea in 1918 on his way to take his seat in the House of Lords. Sir Samuel Griffiths praised the federal scheme as 'designed by Her Majesty's loyal subjects to serve as a further and lasting bond of union between the Australian colonies and the Mother country'.[96] The federalists had also been keen to include New Zealand in the new 'nation'. Their preoccupation with defence and Asian immigration reinforces the impression that they were less concerned to assert a new Australian identity in the world at large than to exert a stronger Australian influence on the imperial centre in London, where sovereign power on immigration, foreign policy and defence ultimately resided. Australian nationalism, as reflected in the federal idea, was not so much a demand for independence as a recognition that closer integration in the British 'world-system' was the price of growth, and perhaps of survival.

That is not to say that Australian leaders had settled for an indefinite future of dependence. Far from it. If federation was envisaged as a new phase in the imperial relationship with Britain, it was because empire on the British model was compatible with an enlarged sense of Australian nationhood; indeed, symbiotic with it. Acceptance of federation and allegiance to the Australian nation it created grew out of a convergence between two very different traditions in colonial Australia. 'Imperialism' was the viewpoint of those who (apart from attachment to the monarchy, 'British' institutions, and cultural and social models drawn from Britain) insisted that Australia could not be a self-sufficient faraway country in the South Pacific.[97] Its only imaginable future lay in a programme of social, economic and cultural enlargement. Expansion (of any kind) required a continuous transfusion of capital and labour from Britain (and thus conditions that would attract them) as well as the guarantee of strategic protection against rival European imperialisms or the 'Asiatic' threat. Set against imperialism was the isolationist tradition. Isolationism was endemic in settler societies but peculiarly strong (among British colonies) in Australia. Convict alienation from the imperial gaoler; the tyranny of imagined distance; the digger democracy of the goldrush era; the influence of republican radicalism imported from 'home'; the dislike for cosmopolitan capital and the class divisions it encouraged: all these combined to diffuse a pervasive suspicion of imperial motives and truculent faith in a self-sufficient 'island-continent' with its promise of escape from the Old World's conflicts.[98] Amidst the urban despair of the 1890s, it found expression in the myth of the 'Bush': an Australian nation forged in an Australian environment.[99] Its loudest voice was the *Bulletin*.[100] 'No Nigger, no Chinaman, no lascar, no Kanaka, no purveyor of cheap coloured labour', it raged in a characteristic outburst, 'is an Australian.'[101]

Convergence between imperialism and isolationism was possible in the 1890s because both sides accepted that the cohesion of Australian society in a period of great social stress depended upon the defence of a racially exclusive egalitarianism.[102] The social and labour reforms of the 1890s which helped reconcile Labor to federation were matched by the recognition that isolation could no longer ensure racial exclusion and a 'white Australia'. Even the *Bulletin* abandoned republicanism in 1896.[103] Federation registered the fusion of imperialism and isolationism in a new ideological compound. This 'imperial nationalism' was not a reversion to colonial deference, but the optimal pathway up from an inadequate colonial autonomy. Empire membership left wide scope for achieving much of the old isolationist agenda. It permitted tariffs, state-control of economic development, and the elaborate apparatus of wage arbitration. It also promised greater influence over imperial decisions and the best hope of realising Australia's 'manifest destiny' in the South Pacific. Australia's 'imperial nationalism' asserted her claim on the resources and sympathy of the pan-British world, and her right to direct the local energies of the British world-system. It drew proudly on the civic and commercial self-confidence of British communities around the world and the belief that 'Britishness' conferred the cultural attributes of civilisational progress. Far from yielding to the primacy of Downing Street, it quietly insisted that Australian Britishness was more vigorous, manly and forward-looking than the home-grown variety[104] and (in its own large sphere) the natural standard-bearer of the imperial purpose. Australian nationalism was not a repudiation of imperialism but its confident vanguard.

Of course, these distinctive features of Australian nationalism, catalysed by strategic and demographic anxiety,[105] created inevitable differences between the outlook of the new Commonwealth and official opinion in Britain. The Australian colonies contributed over 16,000 volunteers to the imperial cause in the South African War. But there was a strong dissenting tradition which suspected the part played by British finance and was deeply uneasy at an imperial war against free white men in Southern Africa.[106] After 1902, Milner's recourse to 'Chinese slavery' in the Transvaal was fiercely criticised by all shades of Australian opinion.[107] There was bound to be friction between the ideal of a 'White Australia' and the needs of an empire in which white settlers formed only one element in a complex political and strategic equation. Thus Australian governments were keen to contribute to naval defence. But a sense of remoteness, and of London's European priorities, sharpened the case for a local army and a local (not imperial) navy to guard home waters in case of need.[108] Australian governments hoped to shape imperial policy in the South Pacific but got scant encouragement from the Colonial Office, still their channel of communication with the imperial government.[109] Australian prosperity revived after 1904, seeking capital and immigrants from Britain. But protection and 'socialistic' legislation went down poorly in the City.[110] And Australian politicians were deeply suspicious of the imperial 'embrace': the sweet life of London 'society'. To wear court dress at the coronation, said the Labor Prime Minister Andrew Fisher in 1910, was more than his job was worth.[111] Yet the significance of all this should not be exaggerated. Before 1914, and long after, to Australian opinion of almost any hue, independence outside the imperial framework would have meant not the fulfilment of Australian nationality but its certain negation. Their nationalism was the fuel, just as federation was the vehicle, for finding Australia's true place in the system of empire.

'New Britain' in the South Pacific: New Zealand

Among the British settlement colonies, New Zealand was the extreme case, and remains the most fascinating. It was the most remote from Britain, perched far out on the Pacific frontier of Australasia. Much of its terrain was harsh or poor. The value of its grasslands – its principal wealth – depended overwhelmingly on the demand for food and wool on the other side of the world. But, despite this, it had grown with astonishing rapidity into a settled society: from a few thousand immigrants in the 1840s to over a million whites seventy years later.[112]

(Over the same period, the indigenous Maori population had fallen by two-thirds to less than forty thousand.) This demographic invasion had been accompanied by a drastic transformation of the pre-colonial environment into a land of European grasses, trees, flowers and animals.[113] No less remarkable was the apparent strength of white New Zealand's attachment to imperial Britain. Remoteness was no bar. Of all the settlement colonies, New Zealand became the most committed to closer imperial relations, and regarded itself as the most 'British' of the white dominions. But it would be a great mistake to see this as an unthinking loyalism, or as the calculating 'super-patriotism' of a far-flung outpost. Nor was it a retrograde diversion from the high road to a Pacific 'destiny apart'.[114] Quite the reverse. As we will see, the emergence of a distinct New Zealand nationality at the end of the nineteenth century was at the heart of New Zealand's 'imperialism'. Indeed, 'imperialism' and 'nationalism' were the two faces of a single identity.

Cook had been the first European to gain an accurate knowledge of New Zealand's coastline in 1769, circumnavigating these 'high, slender, irregular islands'.[115] But, from then until British annexation in 1840, 'Old New Zealand'[116] had been a disorderly maritime frontier where some hundreds of European and American whalers, sealers, traders and timbermen sojourned, settled, trafficked and intermarried among the Maori. Old New Zealand was part of a 'Tasman world' linking the New Zealand islands with the convicts, commerce and sheep farms of Eastern Australia. Where trade had ventured, missionaries soon followed (the first was Samuel Marsden in 1814), and in 1833 the British government sent James Busby (dragging with him a prefabricated cottage) to keep order among the escaped convicts, boisterous seamen and grog sellers who congregated at the Bay of Islands, the great natural harbour in the north of New Zealand. Busby's regime was ineffectual, and a stream of missionary complaints flowed back to London. Meanwhile, New Zealand had attracted a group of promoters who hoped to plant British emigrants on land bought (cheaply) from Maori and resold (less cheaply) to incoming settlers. The New Zealand Company (with its aristocratic directorate) countered missionary objections by insisting that 'systematic colonization' would bring order to the chaotic relations between Maori and European in the islands, aiding not hindering the civilising and converting of the tribes.[117] Unwilling, or unable, to block the Company, the imperial government trailed reluctantly after it. In 1840, it annexed the islands and, by the Treaty of

Waitangi, asserted its authority over the resident Europeans and (more ambiguously) the Maori chiefs.[118]

Annexation was the beginning of a thirty-year struggle to widen the original settler beachhead (at Wellington) and construct a viable colonial state. Distance and expense, the shortage of capital, the difficulty of acquiring more land, the antagonism between the early governors (anxious to restrain settler expansion) and the Company (eager to satisfy it) and friction with the Maori chiefs dimmed its early promise. But, by the 1850s, the location of grasslands free of the dense New Zealand 'bush' (patois for forest) in the Wairarapa, Hawke's Bay and parts of Taranaki[119] and the planting of new settlements on the Canterbury plains and in Otago on the South Island gradually turned New Zealand into a second New South Wales built on wool. In the early 1860s, the discovery of gold at Gabriel's Gully in Otago brought a rush of immigrants, and the white population climbed to 267,000 by 1871. Meanwhile, London had conceded self-government in 1852, but withheld from the settler politicians control over relations with the Maori, whose land could only be bought through the agency of imperial officials – a rule laid down in the treaty.

Until the 1860s, it seemed as if New Zealand might develop not as a full-blown settler state but as 'one country, two systems'. In the South Island where there were few Maori and around the fringes of the North Island, were a series of settler enclaves, largely confined to the grasslands and the flat coastal plains and linked together not by roads but by sea. Across much of the North Island stretched a Maori 'protectorate', where Maori *hapu* and the 'pakeha-Maori' who lived among them farmed and traded largely free from outside control.[120] But it was an uneasy equilibrium. Maori chiefs sold land. More settlers moved in. The pressure to keep up a brisk market in land sales – the settlers' fastest route to a speculative fortune – was intense. By the late 1850s, Maori unease was turning towards resistance. On the edge of the settler enclave in Taranaki, the 'King' movement sprang up to unite Maori behind a common leader and the refusal to part with more land.[121] Far away in London, the Colonial Office was baffled and irritated by the growing racial friction and accepted its governor's advice that more settler responsibility for dealing with the Maori would curb their aggression.[122] The result was confusion as settler leaders in the North Island pressed forward, demanding imperial protection against a Maori 'conspiracy'. A forceful new governor, George Grey,

with previous experience in the colony, tried to reassert his authority
over the Maori chiefs and conciliate the settler politicians by conquering
the Waikato region, south of Auckland. The New Zealand wars ground
on through the 1860s as some 10,000 imperial troops and a large body
of settler volunteers fought the 'fire in the fern' – with very mixed
success and a heavy reliance on Maori allies (the so-called *kupapa*)
hostile to the Kingites.[123] By 1870, when the imperial contingent was
eventually withdrawn, Maori still controlled much of the North Island's
hilly interior. Their tenacity had bought a breathing space and perhaps
a measure of grudging toleration.[124] But they had failed to check the
steady expansion of the settler world around them.

The main consequence of the wars was to marginalise the Maori
and snuff out what was left of the fragile vision of 'racial amalgamation' as the basis of New Zealand society. Henceforth, New Zealand
was to be unambiguously a settler state. But it was, as yet, a small
and backward one. The 1870s, however, were a turning point. In a
period of rising trade and easy money, colonial New Zealand became
a prosperous and successful settler community, able to attract a steady
flow of capital and migrants from the distant metropole. The agents
of this transformation were local men, immigrants who had enough
capital and connections to build up small fortunes in land or trade.[125]
They were the runholders whose sheep ranches spread out over the
Canterbury plains; and the merchants who made Dunedin (for a time)
the colony's main port and manufacturer, and the headquarters of the
Union Steamship Line (founded in 1875) that supplied much of New
Zealand's coastal and maritime connections.[126] In the North Island, the
leaders were provincial notables like Isaac Featherston, who opened up
Wellington's hinterland in the Wairarapa; Donald McLean and J. D.
Ormond, who dominated Hawke's Bay;[127] or the Richmond-Atkinson
clan in Taranaki.[128] These men were pocket versions of Cecil Rhodes,
building empires but on a smaller scale. They mobilised capital and
commercial enterprise to push forward from the coastal plains into the
bush:[129] building railways, recruiting settlers, laying out townships.[130]
The exception was Auckland, which grew fitfully into a small Pacific
entrepot, exploiting its magnificent harbour, the timber trade in kauri
pine and the short-lived gold rush in the Coromandel. From the start,
Auckland was a merchant not a settler enclave.[131]

But the main architect of the new settler state was Julius
Vogel (1835–99), a colonial politician in the same mould as Sir John

A. Macdonald. Whether as finance minister, premier or agent-general in London, Vogel was the most influential figure in New Zealand's affairs for much of the 1870s and 1880s.[132] The son of a Jewish small businessman in London, Vogel had gone to the Australian gold fields as a youth, but found his métier as a newspaperman not a digger. In 1861, he came to Otago to try his luck in its golden prosperity. By 1870, he was a leading South Island politician who pressed on his colleagues a bold plan for rapid economic development. Vogel's scheme was simple but audacious. He proposed that the settler government should raise a large loan in London to finance a programme of railway-building and subsidised immigration. 'Let the country but make the railroads and the railroads will make the country', he declared.[133] As the railways were built, and newcomers poured in, the government's land reserves would be sold off at a profit, output and exports would swell, the loans would be paid off, and the colony would rise to a new plateau of prosperity, with more of the amenities of an 'old' country. A virtuous circle of growth and improvement would be set in motion. Vogel's prospectus was seductive. But his real genius lay (like that of Cecil Rhodes) in convincing investors in Europe (including the Rothschilds) that New Zealand was a colonial eldorado. Vogel was a visionary who sailed close to the wind and a speculator on his own account who died in near-poverty. But his economic programme was transformative[134] and, by driving through the abolition of the provincial system (where control of public lands still inconveniently lay), he created a unitary colonial state in 1876.

In fact, 'Vogelism' contained many of the ingredients used by later governments to fashion a distinctive role for New Zealand in the British system of empire. Vogel had insisted on the urgency of attracting British immigrants and capital to ward off stagnation and regression. As agent-general in London, he used his pen freely to advertise the colony's charms. He saw that New Zealand must compete with many other calls on British investment and grasped (though not the first to do so) that its special claim must be based on assertions about its likeness to Britain. 'The ambition of the New Zealand settlers', he announced in his journalistic days, 'has been to make in the Southern Hemisphere an exact counterpart of Great Britain in the Northern.'[135] With Vogelism, the myth of New Zealand as the replica of Britain – but without the 'warts' of industrialism – entered the political mainstream, and lodged there firmly for a century. Vogelism proclaimed that the main business of government was development: borrowing, buying, building, recruiting and settling. Everything was secondary to the prime task of expansion and colonisation. But Vogel was not content with a purely domestic vision of New Zealand's future. More vigorously than any contemporary, he pressed the colony's claim to be 'Queen of the Pacific'. New Zealand's manifest destiny was to be the centre of a great Polynesian dominion[136] – a maritime version of Canada – incorporating Fiji and Samoa as well as many smaller islands. Vogel wanted to promote this scheme through a government-backed company based in Auckland, a pale (and abortive) shadow of Macdonald's alliance with the Canadian Pacific Railway. London's hostility to his plans strengthened Vogel's belief in the need for imperial federation to amplify Wellington's voice at the imperial centre, and assert New Zealand's right to act as the local manager of the imperial enterprise in the Pacific. Indeed, it was Vogel's intense vision of New Zealand's special role, its unique tie with Britain, and its claim to a Polynesian sub-empire that turned him against entry into an Australian federation, mooted in the 1880s and favoured by some New Zealand politicians.

Here was an embryonic view of New Zealand as a distinct nationality, a new British nation in the South Pacific, with its own empire in miniature. But, at the end of the 1880s, New Zealand entered an economic and social crisis. The depression and financial panic felt in Australia crossed the Tasman Sea. Discontent among urban workers in the docks, railyards and workshops of the larger towns combined with farmers' grievances. By 1890, it seemed, the frontier had closed. The unlimited supply of land for the farmer-settlers had run dry. The key resource that had allowed New Zealand to avoid the social tensions of the Old World was exhausted. Of course, the shortage was an optical illusion. Thousands of acres were 'locked up' in the possession of the pastoralist 'gentry' who had built up great sheep runs in the palmy days of mid-century. In 1891, a new generation of populist politicians came into power calling themselves Liberals and appealing to labour. They were led by John Ballance (premier, 1891–3) and his charismatic successor, 'King' Richard Seddon (premier, 1893–1906), a former pub-keeper from the South Island's west coast, a gaunt region of gold and coal mines. Seddon and his lieutenants, John McKenzie and William Pember Reeves, knew that, in a country where every (white) man had the vote, equal opportunity for all (white) men was the unwritten Magna Carta of New Zealand politics. Reeves swiftly introduced new laws to regulate wage-bargaining, factories and the conditions of labour.[137] The spectre of the workhouse – that grim symbol of social failure in Victorian Britain – was lifted by the coming of old age pensions. The state took on wide new social responsibilities, later trumpeted by Reeves in his *State Experiments in Australia and New Zealand* (1902).[138] Meanwhile, McKenzie pressed forward with 'bursting up the great estates': buying out the runholders (many of them eager to sell) and parcelling up the land for closer settlement – a programme soon reinforced by the vigorous purchase of Maori land in the North Island.[139]

The enlargement of the Liberal state, and its espousal of 'state socialism', has sometimes been seen as the founding of a new political tradition in New Zealand, coinciding with the moment when the local-born at last outnumbered the incomers from Britain.[140] But, if this is true, it is only half the story. The real purpose of Liberal reform was not to build a socialist state but to protect New Zealand against the social warfare and class-conflict of the Old World. The Arcadian promise, New Zealand's gift to Old Britain, had to be kept. The prospect of social mobility within a broadly equal society had to be preserved[141] if need be by state action. None of this meant that Seddon and his followers wanted to turn New Zealand into an isolated Pacific utopia, proudly separate from a decadent motherland. When Reeves opposed the return to Vogelism – large-scale borrowing for rural development – he was packed off to literary exile as agent-general in London.[142]

A new nationality *was* being forged in New Zealand but its roots did not lie in socialism or a self-conscious Pacific identity.[143] The social crisis of the 1890s had gone deeper than material hardship. It evoked a widespread dissatisfaction with the rough and ready society of colonial New Zealand. The drive to modernise settler society fused with the struggle to preserve its egalitarian ethos. Both seemed to require a clean-out of its darker corners, a campaign for social (and racial) 'hygiene', and a new spirit of social conformity. From this grew a demand for temperance (women's suffrage in 1893 was a by-product of the abortive crusade for prohibition), improved education, better policing, more protection for children, young women and mothers, as well as the expulsion of the alien and unwanted.[144] In 'God's own country',[145] there was no place for sloth or larrikinism. The ugly face of the new emphasis on social uplift and discipline was 'white New Zealand': the exclusion of non-white migrants like the small Chinese

minority who had come to the mining towns of the South Island.[146]
A new social ideal was in the making: the small independent yeoman
farmer or 'cow-cockie'. It was given reality by the technological revolution in New Zealand agriculture. By the mid-1890s, the technique
of refrigeration, the spread of large freezing works and the growing
demand for frozen meat and dairy produce in Britain was transforming the New Zealand economy. Mutton and butter matched wool as
the premier export.[147] The area under white occupation increased by
50 per cent between 1896 and 1911, and the volume of production
by 60 per cent.[148] The colonisation of New Zealand entered a second
phase, lasting into the 1930s when settlers were still struggling to carve
out dairy farms 'up on the roof' in the old Maori 'King Country' of
central North Island.[149] Crucially, this new agrarian bonanza assured
the economic success of the Liberals' drive to make New Zealand a land
of small farmers. It consolidated the 'rural myth'[150] that belied the scale
of New Zealand's port-cities, the growth of a unionised workforce, the
industrial basis of agricultural production and the extreme dependence
on faraway urban consumers.

The result was to bring a new depth and meaning to the old
tenets of 'Vogelism'. The familiar idea of New Zealand as an Arcadia
recreating an idyll of rural England was energised and transformed by a
vision of social renewal. New Zealand was not to be an archaic Britain
but a distinct, progressive experiment in Britishness. New Zealanders
reinvented themselves not as a colonial fragment but as a modern,
rural British (or 'Britannic') nation in the South Pacific, which had
successfully erased the economic inequalities and social divisions of the
class-ridden motherland, partly by transplanting what was best and
brightest from 'Home'.[151] The future lay not in gradual separation
from the mother-country but in more and more vigorous reciprocity
with her: the exchange of goods, men and ideas to press ahead with the
full colonisation of the New Zealand landscape, still half-conquered
and half-alien.[152] This was the ideology of 'dominionhood', the shift
from colonial to 'dominion' status consummated in 1907, and marked
by local adoption of 'the Dominion' as the country's colloquial name.
It reflected a new confidence that New Zealand had something positive
to add to the grand project of making a 'British world'. It was hardly
surprising, then, that Seddon should also have revived the imperial and
sub-imperial planks of Vogel's platform and imbued them with a blunt
no-nonsense populism.

Indeed, since Vogel's time, the pace of diplomatic competition in the Pacific had quickened and with it the New Zealanders' sense of vulnerability. The idea that New Zealand could escape involvement in the quarrels of the Old World – once favoured by Seddon's old rival, the South Island lawyer Robert Stout[153] – now seemed fanciful in the age of *Weltpolitik*. The Anglo-German agreement on Samoa in 1899 was the final straw: clinching evidence of London's blindness to destiny – and New Zealand's interests.[154] Seddon revived Vogel's scheme for a Polynesian dominion. His well-publicised Pacific tour in 1900 was meant to jog London's elbow and assert New Zealand's claim as the real trustee of the British interest in the South Pacific. Seddon's imperialism was the counterpart of his nationalism. It identified 'Empire' not with the territorial possessions of the imperial government but with the territorial interests of the overseas British. Sympathy for the Uitlanders in the Transvaal was its natural expression. Seddon had no doubts about the justice of the British cause in South Africa and regarded the outbreak of the Boer War there as a welcome sign that London could be made to defend its beleaguered subjects.[155] It was a tendency he was eager to encourage by New Zealand participation. 'The flag that floats over us', he told the New Zealand parliament, 'was expected to protect our kindred and countrymen who are in the Transvaal.' It was 'our duty as Englishmen' to support the Uitlanders' struggle. 'We are a portion of the dominant family of the world', he went on,

> *we are of the English-speaking race. Our kindred are scattered in dispersed parts of the globe, and wherever they are, no matter how far distant apart, there is a feeling of affection – that crimson tie, that bond of unity existing which time does not affect – and in the end will become indispensable.*[156]

But New Zealanders took part not at London's command but as 'partners' in the Empire, 'sharing the profits and knowing the advantages'.[157] Seddon's rhetoric was at once a manifesto of 'Britannic nationalism' and a claim to full membership in the management committee of the British world-system. His great ally, John McKenzie, was an advocate of imperial federation. His successor as premier, Melbourne-born Sir Joseph Ward (premier, 1906–12), was to urge an 'imperial parliament of defence' at the Imperial Conference in 1911 – but to no avail.[158]

New Zealand's commitment to empire was thus neither cynical nor deferential, still less an aberration from the path to nationhood. Its vehemence and certainty reflected the uniquely close fit between the geopolitics of this white colonial settlement in the South Pacific and the peculiar trajectory of its economic development. The influence of both reached their height at the moment when the localised outlook of mid-Victorian New Zealand began to be reshaped by the rise of its late-Victorian 'Britannic' ideology of modernity, discipline and expansion. Unlike Canada or Australia, there was much less of a tradition of isolationism to challenge the ideal of the 'imperial nation'.[159] There was no ethnic interest to appease: the Maori had no quarrel with the imperial connection declared the MP Honi Heke in October 1899.[160] Instead, more completely than in any other dominion, a new sense of nationhood fused with a new conception of empire as the vehicle of local safety and national ambition. But it was an empire that was expected to embody not just the interests of the United Kingdom, but a broader 'Britannic' ideal.

Building the British world

By the end of the nineteenth century, it was no longer a pipe-dream that the main settlement colonies, with Canada in the van, might form the heart of an overseas 'British world', a vast zone held together not by rule or coercion but by common political values, and cultural attraction as well as (in this case) by racial solidarity. Nor that a sense of shared 'Britannic' nationality, a collective insistence on a shared 'Britishness', provincial but equal (or even superior), would induce spontaneous identification with the fortunes of Britain, and even a willingness, in a real emergency, to spend blood and treasure in the common British cause. In the first forty years of the twentieth century, this 'Britannic' identity was tested and proved in the hardest of trials. Indeed, many contemporaries learned to take it for granted as a fact of political life. Dismissed, disparaged or simply ignored by the 'nationalist' historians of the ex-'white dominions' in the 1960s and after, its pervasive, foundational importance has been rediscovered in more recent years.[161] For historians of the British Empire, its key contribution to the strength and survival of the British world-system can hardly be doubted.

There was a further dimension of the 'Britannic experiment' which we should not overlook. The settlement colonies, John Robert Seeley declared, were really 'a vast English nation' merely dispersed by distance.[162] Seeley wrote in an age when the distinction between 'Britain' and 'England' was usually elided, when Scotsmen (or 'Scotchmen') sometimes called themselves 'English', and when Scotland itself could be referred to as 'North Britain'. But Seeley knew perfectly well that the making of empire and what he called 'Greater Britain' were the handiwork of all the four nations that comprised the British 'Union' – to the cohesion of which he was passionately committed.[163] Seeley seems to have assumed – what much recent scholarship has confirmed – that the opportunity, power and prestige brought by empire reinforced the appeal of a composite 'British' nationality in the Home Islands themselves. Welsh, Irish and Scots took pride in an empire they had helped to create, cherished their links with their overseas countrymen, and identified their 'regional' interests – merchant, migrant and missionary – with the empire's success.[164]

In the settlement colonies, distinct Scots and Irish identities were emphatically visible. Scots made up a significant proportion of emigrants to Nova Scotia and Upper Canada (Ontario). A ring of Scots families supplied most of the mercantile leadership in Canada's premier port-city, Montreal.[165] The Presbyterian church, the 'Caledonian' societies and a fondness for curling forged strong social bonds. In Australia, too, Scots Presbyterians played a prominent part in the professions and business. Scots made up nearly a quarter of New Zealand's population by the end of the century.[166] And, although the main tide of Irish migration had turned to the United States by the 1850s, an earlier stream of Protestant Irish from both North and South had decisively shaped Upper Canada's political life, not least through the influence of the Orange Lodge in the province.[167] Catholics were more numerous in the Australian colonies where one-quarter of the population was of Irish descent in 1900,[168] and in New Zealand where they made up three-quarters of the Irish total and some 13 per cent of the whole population.

Even more than at home, Scots and Irish 'colonials' adopted a 'British' allegiance even if they preserved a strong sentimental attachment to their ethnic identity. There were several reasons for this. The mobile conditions of colonial life discouraged the formation of closed or exclusive communities. The parochial disputes of faraway homelands had diminishing relevance. But perhaps the most important factor of all was the inclusive character of colonial political life. Responsible (or parliamentary) government was open to all (men) without regard to religion. And, although the distinction between Catholic and Protestant remained an important divide, it was not wide enough to subvert Catholic attachment to British institutions. In three Catholic Irishmen, Thomas D'Arcy McGee (1825–68), an ardent champion of confederation in Canada, (Sir) Charles Gavan Duffy (1816–1903), sometime premier of Victoria, and Charles Coghlan (1863–1927), first prime minister of Southern Rhodesia, strong nationalist feeling was combined with a 'Burkean reverence' for parliamentary government and (at least outwardly) deep loyalty to the Crown.[169]

5 'UN-BRITISH RULE' IN 'ANGLO-INDIA'

British rule in India had always been an awkward compromise between principle and practice. The early Victorians had declared that the purpose of the Company Raj was the political education of Indians and their preparation for eventual self-government. Fifty years on, progress towards this goal was barely perceptible. At the end of Company rule in 1858, the Queen's Proclamation had reassured Indians that race discrimination would play no part in the new colonial regime. But this was hard to square with the status of even educated Indians in the politics and social life of the late-Victorian Raj. The third contradiction was even more telling. The British had founded their rule on the promise of social and economic improvement: what the annual reports of the Indian government were to call 'moral and material progress'. Yet, even at the end of the century, India remained prey to devastating famines, terrifying epidemics and contagious diseases whose sphere was widening not contracting. Literacy (even in local languages) remained (at around 10 per cent) embarrassingly low. But, while social progress seemed stalled, the Indian government spent more and more on the army, and especially on that part of it 'borrowed' from Britain. It was hardly surprising, then, that the terms of India's association with the British world-system became more controversial after 1880. But it was India's *growing* importance to the imperial system, as much as the grievances of its social elites, that shaped its late-Victorian and Edwardian politics.

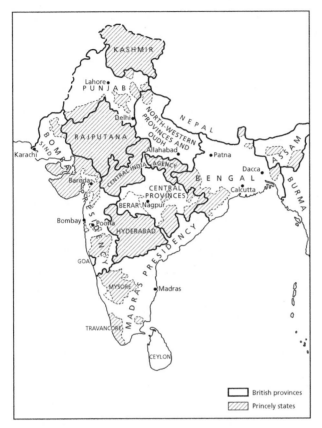

Map 7 The Indian Empire

Imperial India?

In the later nineteenth century, the value of India as the second centre of British world power became more than ever an axiom of British thinking. This was partly because, in the aftermath of the Mutiny of 1857, Company rule was replaced by the direct control of the London government, a transition glamorised a few years later by the proclamation of Victoria as 'Queen Empress of India' or *Kaisar-i-Hind*. But mainly it reflected the rising contribution that India made to the world-system whose consolidation in the age of world politics after 1880 we have been tracing. Without India as one of its four grand components, the British world-system would have been without some of the most vital sources of its security, stability and cohesion. And part of the motive and much of the means for the acquisition of so many lesser dependencies in Afro-Asia would have been lacking.

India's contribution to British world power was not left to chance or self-interest. It was deliberately shaped by British rule. After 1870, the Indian economy was developed rapidly as a major producer of export commodities: wheat, raw cotton, jute and tea, among others.[1] It also became an ever more important market for British exports, especially cotton textiles and iron and steel. At a time when many other markets were being sealed off by tariffs, India was wedged open by imperial *fiat*.[2] The British officials who ran the Indian government could levy import duties; but they could not *protect* Indian producers of textiles against outside competition because London insisted that any tariff be matched by a local excise. In this way, India, which bought some 25 per cent of Lancashire's export production, took the largest share of Britain's largest export up to 1914. Simultaneously, the growth of its own exports, mainly destined for European or American consumers, earned the foreign exchange that, when remitted to Britain, helped square Britain's own balance of payments. For, while Britain was usually in deficit to Europe and the United States, India was always in deficit to Britain. This was partly a matter of borrowed capital, much of it by government to build railways, and much of it at London's urging – since longer lines meant wider markets.[3] But it also grew from the 'Home Charges' that London imposed on India to pay for the British troops that were stationed there, as well as the pensions of British officials and the cost of the India Office, the Whitehall department from which Indian affairs were supervised.

In the later nineteenth century, then, India's economic value to Britain – and to Britain's ability to service its world-system – was great and growing. The expansion of the Indian economy widened British markets, increased the demand for British capital and helped India bear more easily the cost of its second great imperial contribution – to imperial defence. Even before 1857, the Company had maintained a sizeable army in India to uphold its power and expand its territories. It had 'borrowed' British troops at a charge from the home government. After the Mutiny, the Indian troops were cut down in number to between 120,000 and 140,000. But, at the same time, the all-British contingent was enlarged so as to be roughly half the size of the Indian. As we have seen, providing 60–70,000 British soldiers for Indian service (with inevitable 'wastage' for disease) was a major strain on the British military system and enforced considerable adaptation. But there was also a benefit. By the late nineteenth century, when the Empire's standing armies totalled some 325,000 men, two-thirds of this number was paid for by the Indian taxpayer. For the rule was that every British soldier, once embarked for India, had to be paid, pensioned, equipped and fed by the government of India, not of Britain. And there was an irresistible tendency, as time went on, for more and more British soldiers to be kept in India at Indian expense. How valuable this was politically can be grasped by asking how readily the British parliament would have agreed, at a time of rapidly rising naval costs, to maintain an army nearly three times as large as that for which the Treasury had actually to pay. How valuable it was strategically can be illustrated by the frequency with which troops were despatched from India after 1860 on operations that had little or nothing to do with India's own defence – to China (1860, 1900–1), Ethiopia (1867–8), Malaya (1875), Malta (1878), Egypt (1882), Sudan (1885–6, 1896), Burma (1885), East Africa (1896, 1897, 1898), Somaliland (1890, 1903–4), South Africa (1899, but white troops only) and Tibet (1903).[4]

India's commercial and military contributions were both functions of British rule which facilitated, or enforced, a distinctive pattern of economic development and financial spending. India made a third contribution that was less directly the result of colonial control. Across the whole face of the 'British world', Indian manpower and commercial expertise helped open new regions to British influence and make colonial government financially viable. Indian labour made plantation agriculture possible in Malaya, Southeast Africa and the Pacific. It built the railway to Uganda. Indian peasants streamed into British Burma and made it the rice bowl of Southeast Asia.[5] Indian retailers and merchants, with lower overheads than their European counterparts, built a commercial infrastructure in places too exacting for the 'nation of shopkeepers'.[6] Indian policemen, clerks and orderlies served as far away as China.[7] In much of the tropical world east of Suez, 'British' expansion was really an Anglo-Indian enterprise: here was a field almost as much of Indian as of British colonisation. It was Winston Churchill as a junior minister who picturesquely evoked East Africa as 'the America of the Hindu'.[8]

Between 1880 and 1914, these commercial, military and demographic connections (and others) sharpened the dominant tendency in late-Victorian and Edwardian India: its ever-closer integration into the British world-system. 'Advancing civilisation', remarked the Indian Currency Committee in 1893, 'brings with it constantly increasing demands for Government action and enterprise.'[9] Irrigation schemes and, above all, railways, were a heavy call on Indian revenues. Financing them drove the government of India ever more frequently to the capital market in London. As a result, the proportion of its public debt that was held there rose from a mere 7 per cent in 1858 to 60 per cent by 1914.[10] Servicing this debt became an ever-increasing burden, especially when silver, the basis of India's currency, depreciated sharply against gold in the later nineteenth century. As a guarantee against default on the 'Home Charges', the government of India was forced after 1898 to maintain a gold fund in London, managed by the India Office, whose operation regulated the supply of money in India – and thus the general level of economic activity there.[11] This was integration with a vengeance. The 'silver problem' exacerbated the growing burden of Indian military spending, especially that part of it needed to 'rent' the British garrison from London. Between 1884 and 1897, India's military expenditure increased by 45 per cent – a colossal figure.[12] Much of this was due to the fall in silver's value. But it also reflected increases in both Indian manpower (up by 20,000) and the size of the British contingent (up by 10,000).

Behind this martial expansion lay the diplomatic and geostrategic imperatives that seemed to be drawing India ever more closely into London's embrace. The new geopolitics of the later nineteenth century envisaged a handful of 'world states' whose global pre-eminence would be based on their coordination of territories, resources and populations. At the same time, Asia (especially East Asia and the Pacific) was becoming the focus of European (and American) economic and diplomatic rivalry. 'I am one of those', Lord Curzon told an enthusiastic audience on the eve of his departure as Indian Viceroy in 1898,

> who think that the Eastward trend of Empire will increase
> and not diminish ... [T]he strain upon us will become
> greater not less. Parliament will learn to know East Asia as
> well as it now knows Europe [and] Asiatic sympathies and
> knowledge will be ... the interest of the whole nation
> (Cheers).[13]

Both these developments pointed to a steady rise in the imperial importance of India, the springboard and citadel of British influence in Asia – the 'pivot and centre', in Curzon's phrase, 'of the British Empire'.[14] But they also made India more vulnerable. In the 1870s, the British had been alarmed by the threatened disintegration of the Ottoman Empire exposing their sea communications with India to Russian and French interference. In the 1880s, the advance of Russia into Central Asia had produced a crisis (over Penjdeh in 1885). In the 1890s, the impact of Russia's colonial presence there began to sink in: the threat of a Tsarist encirclement of Persia east and west of the Caspian Sea; and a forward move towards the Persian Gulf and India's maritime frontier. As the risk of Anglo-Russian confrontation over China grew greater, so did the danger of a Russian jab towards India. When '[Russia's] Siberian railway is ready', argued Lord Salisbury in 1900,

> she will want to be mistress of the greater part of China: and if Afghanistan is unprotected she can force us to give way in China by advancing upon India. She won't try to conquer it. It will be enough for her if she can shatter our Government and reduce India to anarchy.[15]

The meaning for Anglo-Indian relations was clear. India must play a larger but also more obedient part in imperial strategy. It must take up the burden of forward defence in Persia and the Himalayas – but not in ways that risked a great power conflagration.[16] It must reorganise its ramshackle armies, concentrate them in the Northwest and recruit from the Sikhs, Punjabis, Pathans, Baluchis and Gurkhas who were suited to the northern climate.[17] It must acknowledge its function as the strategic reserve of the British Empire in the East.[18] It must contribute to the costs of the Royal Navy.[19] Its diplomatic agents in the Middle Eastern borderlands must faithfully echo the shifts and twists of London's European diplomacy – especially the intermittent search for an accommodation with Russia pursued by Salisbury and Lansdowne. And it must guard against the political disruption of its military system. 'I dread the day', the Secretary of State warned Viceroy Elgin, 'when the northern or fighting races from who we draw recruits take to reading the vernacular press.'[20]

This steady tightening of the economic and strategic bond between Britain and India was symptomatic of a deeper force for integration whose effects were not so easily managed. Like other parts of the extra-European world, India became more and more accessible to European influences as the frequency, speed, volume and cost of communications with the West were transformed by the telegraph, railways, steamships and the opening of the Suez Canal.[21] Information from, or about, India became available in Britain in greater quantity, and from a much wider variety of unofficial sources, especially the English-language newspapers owned by private British interests in the sub-continent. Political, scientific and literary ideas from Europe circulated more rapidly and much more cheaply in India, reaching – and disturbing – wider audiences. Christian notions of religious community and personal ethics posed a sharper challenge. European styles – in speech, humour, dress, deportment, leisure and family life – became more widely known and imitated. But the results of all this were not simply to make India more culturally attuned to Britain. Far from it. Instead, three contradictory tendencies were at work. First, the larger flow of news and information back to Britain, much of it originating in the Anglo-Indian press, helped entrench in 'Home' opinion a negative view of Indian political aspirations and a condescending attitude towards the 'exotic chaos' of Indian society. This was the outlook of the British settler community writ large. Secondly, it heightened the sense of destiny among Western-educated (or 'anglo-literate') Indians about their role as the intermediaries between India and Europe, as the standard-bearers of modernity and as the natural legatees of British rule whenever it might end. For who could doubt that India must adapt, and be adapted to, a West-centred world? Thirdly (however), the flood of European attitudes, ideas, images, habits and prejudices pouring into India evoked an anxious, angry, defensive response from those who feared that the social and moral foundations of Indian society – Muslim or Hindu – would be washed away in the process.[22] For a wide section of the traditional educated class (including some who had acquired an 'English' education) the close encounter with imperial Britain was the signal for a campaign of cultural rearmament. Religion must be renovated; social discipline reinforced; moral order reasserted; language reformed; literature reinvented; history rewritten; the nation (or nations) remade. It was in this uneasy atmosphere that the terms of India's connection with the emerging British world-system became the object of a subdued (by later standards) but fierce political struggle between 1880 and 1914.

The Civilian Raj

At bottom, this was a question of how far the 'Civilian Raj' would be diluted by the admission of Indians into its executive and legislative branches. The 'Civilians' were members of the Indian Civil Service, recruited by an examination held in Britain and almost exclusively British in origin. They formed an administrative cadre that numbered around 1,000 who had signed the 'covenant' of faithful service, and for whom the 700 or so most senior posts in the central and provincial governments were reserved, including the key position of district officer in the 250 districts of British India.[23] The Civilians were a bureaucracy whose medium was the official minute, memorandum, report and inquiry. But they bore only a superficial resemblance to civil servants at home. In practice, they formed a ruling oligarchy whose authority was limited only (and in theory) by the oversight of the India Office in London; and by the presence in India of a Viceroy, two governors (in Bombay and Madras) and one or two members of the Viceroy's executive council, all habitually appointed from outside the ranks of the Service and (supposedly) immune to its prejudices. In pay, status, prospects and pension, the Civilians (whose name in print was invariably followed by the honorific letters 'ICS') stood at the summit of the European official hierarchy: above the army, medical service, police, forestry service and education: and far above the lowly Railway and Public Works departments.

In the thirty years that followed the end of Company rule in 1858, the Civilians had consolidated their power. Their internal solidarity had been reinforced, not least by the virtual exclusion of qualified Indians. Their authority was enhanced by the new emphasis on administrative and financial stability rather than the forcible annexation of princely states – a practice that had given Company rule its aggressive, militaristic character. Through the census, the *Imperial Gazetteer of India* completed in 1881, the great *Statistical Survey* with its 114 volumes and 54,000 pages, the ethnographic studies of 'tribes and castes', and the district 'histories' compiled by energetic officials, the Civilian Raj extended and codified its administrative knowledge and imposed its categories on an untidy social reality.[24] More fundamental, perhaps, was the virtual demolition of supra-local political ties between Indians, partly achieved by Company expansion before 1857, and completed after the Mutiny with the final abolition of the Mughal throne (the surviving princely states were closely supervised and political contact between them forbidden). For thirty years thereafter, British India resembled the *Agraria* imagined by Ernest Gellner:[25] a congeries of districts without horizontal connections (for the provinces were merely administrative confections without economic or cultural rationale).

Their only links were vertical: through an alien bureaucratic hierarchy with whose high culture, language and ethnic origins they had nothing in common – but whose authority they could not hope to challenge. It was this localisation and differentiation of Indian politics that was faithfully recorded in the Civilians' gazetteers, surveys and censuses: indeed, they were the warrant and charter of the Civilian Raj.

Entrenched in India, the Civilians were protected in the rear by political sympathy in Britain. Unofficial information from India upheld the necessity of authoritarian rule, at times with hysterical urgency. The mild extension of judicial powers proposed for Indian (i.e. non-British) officials under the Ilbert Bill in 1883 produced an explosion of settler rage that soon found an echo in the British press. British commercial interests in India, with their City connections, had little love for the Civilian Raj but even less for any alternative. The new regime established in London to supervise the Indian government after 1857 saddled the Secretary of State for India with a 'Council of India', largely composed of retired Civilians. It formed the centre of an extended network of 'Old India Hands' whose mandarin scholarship and constant intervention in the correspondence columns largely informed 'public opinion' on late-Victorian India.[26] Then, at a crucial moment in the 1880s, the intellectual basis of Gladstonian Liberalism was challenged by a powerful phalanx of Liberal thinkers, including several, like Henry Maine and Fitzjames Stephen, with Indian experience. Their part in the Liberal split over Irish Home Rule in 1886 eventually helped to turn the authoritarian bureaucracy of British India from an embarrassing exception to Liberal practice into an authentic (though not uncontested) expression of the Liberal ideal.[27]

These benign conditions strengthened the Civilians' claim to be the ideal 'collaborators' of British imperialism in India. Of course, no contemporary would have used such a term. What makes it appropriate in historical analysis is that the Civilians did not see themselves as, nor were they in reality, mere *agents* of the British state. They were 'Anglo-Indians'[28] – the political hinge between Britain and the indigenous communities of the sub-continent. 'Anglo-India' had its own interests, its own ethos, its own patriotism, its own shrines (at Lucknow and Cawnpore) and martyrs, its own ideology, its own state. Its self-image was energetically disseminated by the late-Victorian Civilians who piled up an astonishing literature of antiquarian history, sociological enquiry, ethnographic description, political commentary and biographical memoir, as well as the vast collective labour of the district gazetteers – a literary self-creation as remarkable as that of any conquest state in history. In a standard text on Indian administration, Sir George Chesney's *Indian Polity*,[29] Anglo-India's claim to political autonomy was stridently asserted. 'The Indian administration', said Chesney, 'must not be placed at the mercy of the erratic dictates of a chance majority in the House of Commons.'[30] India 'should not...be subjected to treatment which the...Commons would not venture to adopt towards the smallest self-governing colony'[31] – a claim that anticipated the later demand of the Indian National Congress for self-government on the model of the 'white dominions'. From retired Civilians poured a stream of reminiscence proclaiming India's incapacity for self-rule and the Civilians' role as the platonic guardians of the peasant mass. In 1899 came the first volume of Sir William Wilson Hunter's *History of British India*. Hunter was, with Sir Alfred Lyall, one of the great scholar-mandarins of the late-Victorian Raj. He had masterminded the *Imperial Gazetteer*. He became Curator of the Indian Institute in Oxford, founded to prepare trainee Civilians for life in India. He wrote for *The Times*. In planning his history on a monumental scale, Hunter confronted head-on the issue of India's place in the imperial story. The aim, he told his agent, was to show that the growth of British India 'stands out as an epic of the British nation – the fibre of its fibre, the express image of its innermost character... [I]t will make the world understand the British race – adventurous, masterful, patient in defeat and persistent in... its designs.'[32] These qualities had made England 'the residuary legatee of the inheritance painfully amassed by Europe in Asia'.[33]

It was, perhaps, no accident that, as the Civilians came under challenge in India, the value of *their* rule to Britain's imperial system, and its legitimacy as an authentic expression of the British genius, were reiterated more and more vehemently by the officials themselves and by their political allies at home – and by no one more eloquently than Lord Curzon whose *The Place of India in the Empire* (1909) was a sustained plea to acknowledge that Britain without India would be a third-class power. In retrospect, we can see that this whole vast literary enterprise was part of the secret of Anglo-India's tenacious grip on the British imagination, unmatched by any other dependency. Of course, it had also its unofficial laureate of genius in Kipling. And ironically its tropes, values and categories exerted a persistent fascination for

Indians themselves. Yet, ultimately, its political survival depended upon brokering the rival demands of the British at home and its indigenous subjects. The Civilian Raj had to persuade British opinion that it was indispensable and Indian opinion that it was irremovable. But, as India's imperial value rose and the stresses of its commercial, strategic and cultural entanglement with Britain were felt more deeply in the sub-continent, the position of this foreign ruling elite was bound to grow more vulnerable to criticism and more open to attack.

For the moment, however, 'Anglo-India' seemed an essential partner in the late Victorians' imperial enterprise. Indian unity was becoming more urgent, for commercial and strategic reasons. The Civil-ian Raj looked its best guarantee. Tariff-free access was becoming more vital. The Civilians would, grudgingly, maintain it. Indian rev-enues must be driven up to match the rising cost of imperial defence and expenditure in the localities held down. What other regime would match the fiscal parsimony of the Civilians' localised despotism? For their part, the Civilians resented the escalating demands imposed by London on their brittle system. They contested the issue of tariffs and the burden of military costs – but only so far.[34] The concession they won in return was to be free to fashion a political system that paid scant regard to the shibboleths of Liberal Britain. They repudiated represen-tative government (except in a grossly bowdlerised form), the market economy (through restraints on the sale of land) and liberal individual-ism (in favour of caste, religious or tribal identity). To some disgruntled observers, the Civilians' aim was to make parliamentary control from Britain a nullity and rule without restraint. And, to some, they had already achieved this goal. For William Wedderburn, himself a former Civilian, but now a supporter of Congress and an MP, the Secretary of State, far from being the master of the official hierarchy in India, was only its 'mouthpiece and champion ... the apologist of all official acts'.[35]

The political struggle in India between the 1880s and the out-break of the First World War thus had implications that went far beyond conceding greater representation to the gentlemanly nation-alists of the Indian National Congress. It was really a struggle between rival groups for the support of imperial Britain in ruling India. It was a struggle between the Civilians' 'Anglo-India' and the 'British Indians' of the Congress who were determined to supplant it. For the Civilians it was vital to maintain their status as the indispensable collaborators, and to preserve the wide freedoms this had brought them. To dissuade their London 'partners' from any backsliding, they must meet Britain's requirements in India and pay the 'imperial dividend'. They must polish the image of Indian contentment and repress disorder. Above all, they must discredit any rival claiming a real share in governing the subcontinent. They had, in short, to find a means of adapting India to its changing place in the imperial system without pulling up the roots of their Civilian Raj.

Indian politics

Before 1880, the main threat to the Civilian Raj seemed to lie in the princely states and their aristocratic sympathisers in British India: great landowners like the *taluqdars* of Oudh (modern Awadh). They alone had the means to challenge British rule. It was against this danger that the army was partly deployed. It was to strengthen the Raj's hold on princely allegiance that the British Queen became 'Empress of India' in 1876.[36] It was to conciliate this 'traditional elite' that the Raj adopted a neo-feudal public style and 'Indianised' some of its outer trappings – like army uniforms. But, by the 1880s, a more insidious challenge was beginning to threaten the Civilians' power.

From its very outset, British rule had relied heavily upon Indian manpower, military and civil. To fill up the lower ranks of its bureaucracy government had gratefully recruited Indians equipped with a Western education. It smiled upon the English-style schools and colleges that sprang up by local initiative in Calcutta and Bombay. It was convenient to appoint a handful of Indian notables with an 'English' education to the central and provincial legislative councils where the executive was temporarily transformed into a law-making body. In this way, an Indian element was assimilated into the highest level of the autocracy without threatening the local arrangements at district level where the revenue was derived and patronage distributed. After 1880, however, the gravitational pull drawing India into the world economy and the British world-system steadily undermined this post-Mutiny settlement.

It did so in two ways. The more obvious was through a double revolution of rising costs and expectations. A combination of the falling value of silver and the upward trend of defence expenditure, exerted, as we have seen, a continuous strain on the Indian budget after 1880. At the same time, government also came under pressure to play a more active role in developing the economy and providing for social improvements. In Bengal, for example, in the forty years after the Mutiny, the provincial administration acquired sixteen new departments, among them those for forests, mines, factories, vaccination and municipalities. To meet these new needs, government had to borrow more and tax more. But its room for manoeuvre was limited. Land revenue (calculated on the productivity of the soil) formed the bulk of its income. It was notoriously difficult to increase. An income tax was risky.[37] One hopeful solution lay in raising more revenue at the local level for local improvements. Even here, if British rule was not to seem *more* oppressive, it was desirable that new levies should be made as far as possible on Indian initiative and with Indian support. That pointed towards wider participation by Indians on district boards and municipalities. On the other hand, if the principle of elective authority was conceded there, and Indians organised themselves to compete for it, how long would it be before they pressed for the extension of that principle to the provincial or even 'All-India' level?

This was only one side of the late-Victorian coin. India's deepening association with Britain was, as we have seen, cultural and intellectual as well as material. By the 1880s, it had thrown up a local class literate in English, familiar with British ideas and deeply loyal to the new educational and social institutions that had shaped its outlook and opportunities. Though small by Indian standards, this anglo-literate community (700,000 adult males could read and write English by 1901)[38] dwarfed the non-military British population in India (c.100,000). It filled the highest bureaucratic ranks to which Indians could be promoted. It quickly overran the senior profession open to talent – the law – and expanded sideways into education and journalism. Because it depended not on local patronage or district-level politics, but on the expansion of government, education and trade at the provincial level and above, it was quick to form associations that spanned the provinces. For the tiny group of Indians resident in London, it was natural to think on an All-Indian scale. The East India Association, founded in 1866, was the first approximation to a national body for Western-educated Indians – though it was dominated by Bombay merchants and largely ignored in Calcutta and Madras.[39] Behind all this clubbing together lay a bid for influence over government and a claim for recognition. The climax of this gradual mobilisation was the founding of the Indian National Congress in Bombay in 1885.

Historians have been disdainful of this 'early' Indian nationalism and condescending towards its achievements. The outward deference of its leaders to their British masters is easily ridiculed. Their ambitions seemed modest compared with later demands for '*purna swaraj*' (complete independence) or '*swaraj* in one year'. They were mocked by their British critics as a 'microscopic minority' greedy for jobs and influence. It was true of course that the Congress nationalists seemed obsessed with equal access for anglo-literate Indians to the Indian Civil Service, and with getting seats on the legislative councils, where, it was alleged, they would promote the dominance of urban commerce over the rural cultivator. It was true, no doubt, that self-interest helped hold the Congress together. But the timidity of its demands has been exaggerated, and the shrewdness of its 'moderation' misunderstood. The Civilians would have had little to fear from a disparate collection of job-hunters and 'wire-pullers'. What they did learn to fear about the early Congress was the dual onslaught it launched on the ideological basis of the Civilian Raj and on the Civilians' claim to serve the best interests of Imperial Britain. As the tougher and more percipient of the Civilians acknowledged, 'early' Indian nationalism presented a deeper and subtler challenge to Anglo-India than the huffing and puffing of an alienated intelligentsia. It pointedly reaffirmed its imperial loyalty to disarm the Civilian tactic of dismissing all opposition as subversive. It insisted that the apparatus and institutions of British India were the foundation of any future Indian state. But it claimed that the Civilian Raj was a dangerous perversion of the imperial purpose in India and a betrayal of the Queen's Proclamation of 1858 with its promise of no discrimination. The 'un-Britishness' of Civilian rule was an affront to Victorian liberalism, a dangerous experiment in authoritarianism and a bar to India's becoming a commercially progressive and politically contented member state of the Empire.

This was a seductive appeal to British opinion at home, though one that was fiercely contested by the official and unofficial propaganda of Anglo-India. But the more insidious threat that the early nationalists posed derived from their local roots in Indian society. For they were not an isolated anglophone elite vying for colonial preferment but part of a larger movement of educated opinion. There was a close if ambivalent relationship between those who insisted that membership of the legislative councils and the Civil Service was all-important, and those who drew on Western ideas for a broader project of cultural or national renewal. This wider 'cultural' nationalism, diffused through educational institutions and charged with religious and historical symbolism, was the vital link between the hyper-elitist preoccupations of the Congress leadership and the far wider constituency of Indians literate in the vernacular languages (like Bengali, Marathi, Tamil or Hindustani) rather than English. But, as we shall see, right up to 1914 this connection was often fraught and unmanageable, an embarrassment to Congress leaders as well as a source of strength.

Bengal had been the bridgehead of British power in India and the pivot of their expansion across the sub-continent. Not surprisingly, it was also there that the British impact was felt most deeply. The Bengal Presidency (as the province was called) was a huge multi-ethnic territory stretching over three modern Indian states as well as Bangladesh. Illiterate cultivators formed the bulk of its population. Many of them were Muslims. Many were Oriya or Assamese, not Bengali. Many in wooded or hilly tracts were 'tribals' who did not follow the rituals and conventions of Hindu caste society. Political consciousness in this vast conglomerate was concentrated in the literate elite or *bhadralok* (the 'respectable people'). The Hindu *bhadralok* was neither princely nor aristocratic. It had little in common with the pre-conquest ruling class. In many ways it was the stepchild of colonial rule, a social group that had sprung up to service the colonial state and exploit its opportunities. Its badge of membership was higher education. It had made Bengal society, in the sardonic words of an official report, 'a despotism of caste tempered by matriculation'.[40]

The *bhadralok* were concentrated in Calcutta, the imperial capital of British India and its commercial metropolis, where some 60 per cent of British investment in India was managed. Calcutta dominated Bengal, commercially, administratively, educationally. There the *bhadralok* could supplement the rentals of absentee landownership by a career in the literate professions: administration, law, journalism and education. The city was a forcing-house for the *bhadralok*'s belief in itself as a vanguard class, the makers of a new Bengal liberated (in the past) from Muslim rule and (in the future) from Civilian power. Their ethnic consciousness was sharpened by the presence of the Calcutta Europeans, the large non-official community dominating the city's commercial life and virulently hostile to '*babu*' ambitions through its newspapers (like the *Englishman*), clubs and associations. *Bhadralok* solidarity was rooted in its schools, colleges, newspapers and societies, and voiced by the cadre of new professionals that had formed in a maturing provincial society. By the 1870s, a vigorous literary and religious movement was imparting a keener sense of cultural identity and social purpose. Bhudev Mukerji, Bankim Chandra Chatterji (the first modern Bengali novelist) and Swami Vivekananda showed how foreign ideas could be scrutinised, annexed or rejected in the creation of an up-to-date literary and religious tradition.[41]

The most influential figure in Bengali politics between the 1880s and 1914 was Surendranath Banerjea. Banerjea became the hero of *bhadralok* nationalism and the scourge of the Civilian Raj. Famously, he had overcome the barriers of prejudice and secured appointment in the Indian Civil Service only to be dismissed a few years later on what was widely seen as a trumped-up charge. Instead, Banerjea became an educator – with a devoted student following – and a journalist whose paper, the *Bengalee*, was the organ of *bhadralok* aspirations. Banerjea's programme perfectly expressed the ambivalence of *bhadralok* nationalism towards British rule. Like many educated Bengalis, Banerjea was deeply dissatisfied with what he regarded as the tainted legacy of the Indian past. In a speech on 'England and India' in 1877, he denounced the effects of caste, the practice of child-marriage, the customary ban on the remarriage of widows, and the *zenana* system (the seclusion of married women).[42] England's mission in India, he declared, was to help eradicate the evils of Indian society, to help 'in the formation of a manly, energetic, self-reliant Indian character', and to introduce the 'arts of self-government'. This was a liberal programme, to be enacted with British encouragement by Indian protégés – the Western-educated class (the exact audience to which Banerjea was speaking). It was meant to 'regenerate and civilise' (Banerjea's phrase) India as a liberal society. Self-government, he insisted, would not mean separation. When Britain, 'the august mother of free nations', conferred self-government, it would clear the way for the 'perpetual union of the two countries'.[43] Abolishing race distinctions and 'conferring on us . . . the franchise of the British subject [would] pave the way for the final and complete assimilation of India into the Empire of Britain'.[44]

The precondition of this happy outcome was, of course, recognition by the British of the claims of the *bhadralok* elite. This was Banerjea's cause. In the 1870s, his 'Indian Association' pushed aside the landlord-dominated 'British Indian Association' to become the largest political movement in Bengal. When the Calcutta city government became elective in the 1870s, the Indian Association quickly moved in. By the late 1880s, it had over 100 branches in the Bengal Presidency and beyond. *Bhadralok* resentment of European racial arrogance, painfully visible in the furious outcry against the proposal in 1883 to allow Indian magistrates to try European defendants, helped fuel the movement. So did the growing anxiety that educated Bengalis would be frozen out of bureaucratic employment elsewhere in North India as the British began to favour local regional elites instead. The dominance of European firms in Bengal's main industries – tea, jute, coal and cotton – and export trades was bound to make public employment and its political control the focus of *bhadralok* concern.

This was where Banerjea's nationalism came full circle. *Bhadralok* loyalty and the achievement of a liberal India bound to Britain in 'perpetual union' could only be guaranteed if the Civilian Raj was broken and its administrative citadel surrendered to a new local garrison. 'All India is of one mind on this great question', Banerjea had declared in 1878.[45] But how was he to overcome the entrenched resistance of the senior Civilians and the bitter hostility of the Calcutta Europeans and their vociferous press? Neither he nor his *bhadralok* followers had any taste for mobilising the masses – so much of them ethnically, culturally or religiously alien. If mass politics did come to the vast, unwieldy Bengal Presidency, how long would a Calcutta-based, anglo-literate and privileged Hindu 'vanguard' stay in control? To fight the Civilian Raj, it seemed better to spread wide rather than dig deep. It was hardly surprising, then, that, when the chance came to join forces with like-minded Bombay politicians in an All-India national 'congress', Banerjea and the Indian Association quickly signed up.

Dadabhai Naoroji, the pioneer of an All-India political movement, was a merchant from Bombay and a member of the small Parsi community that stood apart from the Hindu majority. The Parsis were a cosmopolitan business elite, conscious of their wealth and culture and determined to share in the government of Bombay City and the Presidency. The rapid growth of the city as its railway system reached deeper into the hinterland, the expanding trade in raw cotton and the new textile industry, helped create a confident business class largely free from the commercial dominance of European firms so evident in Bengal. Shrewdly, the Parsi elite founded its claim upon its Indianness, but was equally careful to insist that its object was partnership in what Naoroji had called the 'Imperial firm'. British supremacy, declared Sir Pheroze-shah Mehta, the Parsi godfather of Bombay city politics as also of the early Congress, was 'the indispensable condition of Indian progress'.[46] Like the *bhadralok* politicians of Bengal, Mehta and his friends had little time for populism. But he was just as determined to overthrow the Civilian Raj. 'The English official', pronounced Mehta caustically, 'moves among the natives, isolated even when not unsympathetic, igno-rant even when inquisitive, a stranger and a foreigner to the end of the chapter.'[47]

The advantage that Mehta and the Bombay group enjoyed over Banerjea was their alliance with an inland elite whose hold on popu-lar sympathy could be used as a tactical weapon against the Civilians. On the plains north of Bombay city and behind the Western Ghats on the Deccan plateau lay a different cultural world, the Maratha country or Maharashtra. Here the elite were Chitpavan brahmins, the scribal class that had been the mainstay of the Maratha Confederacy organ-ised by Sivaji against the Mughals in the seventeenth century, and only defeated by the British in 1818 after a bitter struggle. For the Maratha brahmins, the British Raj was a conquest state in a much fuller sense than for the *bhadralok*. In the 1870s and 1880s, cultural nationalism in Maharashtra meant coming to terms with the ubiquity of British insti-tutions and practices while re-establishing contact with the Maratha past. For the new cadre of anglo-literate Marathas, thrown up by the expansion of English-language education, cultural revival and social cohesion demanded a new view of the Maratha past, freed from the condescension of Civilian history where the Confederacy was cast as a predatory *banditti*. The pre-conquest polity was now imagined as the prelude to a new Maratha nation, in which the language and concepts of European liberalism would be selectively grafted onto the indigenous stem. The master-mind of this project was the historian and philosopher M. G. Ranade, described by a British official in 1880 as the 'Parnell of the Deccan'.[48]

The Maratha brahmins were far better placed than the Ben-gal *bhadralok* to mobilise a wider following against the Civilians. Ranade and his protege, G. K. Gokhale, were cautious. They preferred to emphasise the loyalty of the elite to British ideas of government and Western notions of social progress, and, in Gokhale's case, to build bridges towards the Parsi 'nationalists' in Bombay city. But, to

B. G. Tilak, like them a Western-educated brahmin, a more drastic confrontation with the Civilians seemed necessary. Tilak was later portrayed as the champion of traditionalism, the 'trusted and accredited leader of Conservative and religious India in the paths of democratic politics'.[49] In fact, Tilak's attitude to caste rules and orthodox piety was perfunctory.[50] He sent his daughter to an English-language high school and corresponded with British academics on Sanskritic literature. His ultimate goal was not, perhaps, very different from the liberal model of nation-state favoured by Banerjea or Mehta. But he was more willing than they were to experiment with popular religiosity and folk patriotism as the building blocks of a political movement. In the 1890s, he agitated against raising the age of consent for marriage; promoted the cult of Ganapati, a regional deity; and evoked the Marathi folk hero Sivaji – all in the effort to ground the arm-wrestling with the Civilians in a wider sense of cultural grievance. None of these campaigns went very far. But the hostility with which the Civilians regarded him (Tilak was gaoled for sedition in 1897 and exiled for six years to Burma in 1908) was matched only by the nervousness of his political compatriots. To them, Tilak's appeal to religious conservatism, his baiting of the British and his championing of a Maratha hero regarded elsewhere in India as a barbaric freebooter[51] threatened to wreck their fragile interprovincial coalition and destroy the mantle of respectability on which their dealings with the Civilians (and their credit in Britain) depended so heavily.

Elsewhere in British India, especially in the vast southern Presidency of Madras, we can see a similar pattern of provincial politics bringing to life movements that, for all their local differences, were broadly united behind the common demand for a real voice in the provincial legislatures and the appointment of Indians to the Civil Service. The new political leaders were deeply conscious of the need for social and cultural renovation. They accepted much of the British critique of an atomised Indian society lacking the beliefs and institutions for social progress. But they fought shy of popular politics fearing a religious backlash against their reformist project and the Civilians' accusation that they were accessories to a second Mutiny. They preferred to concentrate on a constitutional and administrative platform that would maximise their power and influence. The radicalism of their strategy should not be disparaged. Diluting the Civilian oligarchy with anglo-literate Indians would have broken the back of the Civilian Raj (not least by choking off its British recruitment). The new politicians were neither imperialist poodles nor the protagonists of full-blooded independence. Instead, they favoured the making of a self-governing 'middle nation'[52] in which the institutions and structures of the conquering power would be manned and moulded by the representatives of a revitalised indigenous culture. The object was not rebellion nor separation from Britain but partnership in a reformed and decentralised imperial association. Indeed, there was much to be gained, they thought, from an alliance with the strongest liberal power, the richest commercial state and the great entrepot of progressive culture. This was the programme of 'British Indian nationalism', a bold assertion of India's rightful place in a new imperial order. Its struggle with the Civilian Raj occurred at a critical moment in the shaping of the British world-system, in whose ultimate fate British rule in India was to be so deeply implicated.

The struggle

It was the resentment of anglo-literate Indians at the racial arrogance of unofficial Europeans in their campaign against the Ilbert bill that triggered the formation of an 'All-India' national congress. The Ilbert agitation had shown how vulnerable the Viceroy's government was to lobbying by a handful of European residents. The Congress would redress the balance. The Congress was just that: an annual meeting of the provincial associations representing the anglo-literate elite and voicing its distinctive (and elitist) demands. It had no mass support – and no desire for it. On the face of it, this 'microscopic minority' held no fears for the Civilians. Yet, within a few years, the Civilian Raj had been partly reconstructed to appease its demands.

Three arguments forced the Civilians to take '*babu* politics' more seriously in the 1880s. First, it was well understood that the Raj needed more cooperation from local men, and those who represented their interests, if the growth of government was not to stall. Like many governments of the period, the Raj found itself pressed to regulate more closely and intervene more frequently in the cause of social and economic improvement. More rules must be made; more revenues raised. As a result, it needed to cultivate local notables and secure the endorsement of the educated elite. The Civilians might dislike the '*babu*' politicians: but, in the project to govern India more closely, to impose codes for famine relief, forest management, irrigation works or plague control, they were vital allies through whom progressive opinions would trickle down into the vernacular world of the *mofussil*. Secondly, the obverse was just as important. The Civilians could coerce disorder; but they were poorly armed against public criticism. In a regime whose security was stretched thin, and where prestige seemed the key to obedience in the army, police and bureaucracy, unrelenting hostility from the newspapers was a corrosive force. Smothering it by any means short of outright censorship (which London was expected to veto) became a Civilian obsession. That too pointed towards some accommodation with the Congress politicians whose links with the Indian press were invariably close. Thirdly, by the mid-1880s, the Civilians had become increasingly nervous of 'Home' opinion. The advance of the radicals, whose threat to British power, Lord Salisbury (a former Secretary of State for India) had excoriated,[53] did not bode well for the Civilians and their political autonomy. The artful campaign of Naoroji, Banerjea and Ranade, with its appeal to 'Gladstonian' values, and its reassuring loyalism, was bound to trouble Liberals conscience-stricken by interference in Egypt and coercion in Ireland. More repression in India might bring down London's wrath and end by clipping the Civilians' wings. It was an apt coincidence that the Indian Viceroy at this uneasy moment was an Anglo-Irish landowner, the Marquess of Dufferin. Dufferin knew better than most how the shifts of mood in Westminster could subvert the oligarchies of the Empire.[54]

The Viceroy and his advisers decided that bureaucratic discretion was the better part of imperial valour. Two enquiries probed the limits of concession. One committee of senior Civilians considered the Congress demand for a reform of the legislative councils. A second committee under Sir Charles Aitchison took up the question of Indian appointments in the Civil Service, the *arcana imperii* of Civilian power. On the first issue, the Civilians found some scope for compromise. After all, they calculated dourly, enlarging membership of the councils, and adopting less restrictive rules about what could be discussed, queried or debated, could be worked to their advantage. New allies might be recruited and, in a larger forum of public discussion, the officials would be able to rebut the criticisms levelled against them in the press. But, on the second question, the Aitchison committee returned a telling negative. With minor qualifications it rejected any change in the rules of the entry competition or in the numbers of senior posts reserved for members of the Indian Civil Service. Indian ambition would have to be content with a larger provincial service – the intended instrument of bureaucratic expansion. To the Congress leaders, however, even half a loaf was welcome. With larger legislatures in the provinces, and modest advances in scrutiny, interpellation and debate, they hoped to follow the path to self-government carved out by settler politicians in Canada, the Cape Colony or New South Wales. When the proposals gained London's approval in 1892, the Congress reacted with joy.

In fact, of course, the 1892 Councils Act was not the end of the Congress campaign but the beginning of its political struggle. In 1895, Surendranath Banerjea, presiding over the annual Congress meeting, laid out its political programme: 'the goal of our aspirations, the promised land of equal freedom and equal rights with British subjects'.[55] There should be more elected members: Bengal had only seven for 70 million people. Debate and scrutiny should be wider and freer. The military budget should be cut down. And (the old cry) the employment of a 'foreign element' in the public service (the British Civilians) was 'morally wrong, economically disastrous and politically inexpedient'. British rule, declared Banerjea, must be liberalised so that India could 'find its place in the Great Confederacy of Free States, English in their origins, English in their character, English in their institutions, rejoicing in their permanent and indissoluble union with England'.[56] The educated class in his province, wrote the lieutenant-governor of the North-West (after 1900 'United') Provinces, were thoroughly discontented – not because they wished to overthrow British rule but because they wanted to administer it themselves.[57]

On their side, the senior Civilians were just as determined that the act should be the end of concession and the start of stricter political discipline. As usual, London devolved the detail of reform to the Indian government. The Civilians took full advantage. Their own view of India as a jumble of conflicting castes, communities and interests formed the working principle of the new representative system. The enlarged legislatures were not to represent territorial constituencies but sets of 'interests' defined and approved by the Civilians. Their members might be chosen by the interests concerned, but they sat in council as the nominees of government, not by popular vote. The councils met only briefly: that of Bengal (the largest province) for nine days a year. Discussion and questions were permitted (up to a point) but without control over financial supply, and faced by an irremovable executive, the scope for collective action was minimal, and the formation of parties a dream. In the last resort, the deck of interests could always be shuffled to throw up a different 'hand' of members. But, for all these administrative safeguards, the number of Congressmen on the councils crept steadily upward.

Reform was thus the goad for Civilian reassertion. Sir George Chesney, one of the committee that had drafted the councils scheme, made a blunt avowal. In the third edition of his *Indian Polity* (1894), he rejected the schemes of Congress as 'absurd'.[58] His book was a forceful restatement of the need to entrench the autonomy of the Civilians, as much from Whitehall and Westminster as from Indian opinion. Another old India hand, Sir William Hunter, was sympathetic to Congress but dismissed the 'numerical principle of representation'.[59] Among the senior Civilians in India, insistence upon the ethnic (and thus ineradicable) basis of India's social divisions, and the incompatibility of the caste system with any form of representative government, became the hallmark of the new official scholarship. Ethnographic and census studies along these lines made Herbert Risley a rising star in the 1890s.[60] In the Punjab, where large-scale irrigation works were forming a new 'hydraulic society' in the 'canal colonies',[61] the dominant school among the Civilians insisted on the 'tribal' basis of rural society and the need to prevent urban and commercial castes from buying land and social influence in the countryside.[62] Elsewhere in India, the Civilians actively sought new allies among the provincial elites.[63] In North India, the 'Mutiny syndrome' could still be readily invoked.[64]

The lesson of all this was clear enough. The Civilians were determined to challenge what they saw as the absurd and potentially dangerous pretensions of the anglo-literate elite to be representative of India at large. Opinion at home had to be reminded of Indian 'realities'; and Indian politics corrected to put the Congress in its place. Lord Elgin was too much a Gladstonian to be sympathetic. But his successor as Viceroy (in 1899), Lord Curzon, brought a different outlook. Curzon was of landed family but modest means. He had made his way by academic talent, intense ambition, hard work and a ready pen. In the early 1890s, he had entered politics with a reputation for expert knowledge of Asia, especially of Central Asia and Persia (Iran) where Anglo-Russian competition was greatest. He was the protege of Lord Salisbury whom he served at the Foreign Office.[65] By 1898–9, Salisbury was deeply alarmed by Russia's diplomatic advance towards India. A Viceroy in tune with his thinking and with Curzon's local knowledge would secure London's grip on Indian frontier policy. By an added irony, Curzon was also expected (in London) to bring a more sympathetic and imaginative approach to Indo-British relations and soften the rule of the dour Civilians.

As Salisbury had intended, Curzon brought to India an intense concern for its central Asian borderlands – the viewpoint of a Mughal emperor. It was a crucial change of perspective. Like some latter-day Mughal, Curzon saw Indian politics as the rightful preserve of princes and landowners bound by neo-feudal allegiance to the imperial crown. He attached great importance to the education and training of the princes as a governing class in imperial service.[66] 'The native chief', he said, is 'my colleague and partner.'[67] India's vast treasury of ruins, monuments, forts and palaces excited his imagination. Curzon had a life-long passion for architecture as the visual key to both history and politics. To maintain and restore the monuments of India was to link the Raj to its Mughal past not to '*babu*' modernity. To build new landmarks – like the Victoria Memorial Hall on the Calcutta maidan – was to make the imperial monarchy (and not the British Parliament) the focus of Indian loyalty.[68]

Curzon's strategic preoccupations and his 'Mughalist' outlook chimed well with the Civilians' wish to curb the ambitions of the Congress politicians. Curzon was readily persuaded that the inroads of *babu* politics must now be reversed, and nowhere more urgently than in Bengal on the doorstep of the Indian government. The opening salvoes were directed at two bastions of *bhadralok* influence: the Calcutta city government and Calcutta University. The elected majority on the Calcutta Corporation was removed. The autonomy of the University was cut down.[69] But the Civilians' real target was the Bengal Legislative Council and the growing *bhadralok* influence in provincial and All-India politics. They found a neat, if drastic, solution. The sprawling Bengal Presidency had long been the target for administrative surgery. It was over-centralised in Calcutta. Oriya-speakers in the west and Muslims in the east were no match for Calcutta Hindus in catching the attention of government. Assam, separated in 1874, was too small to maintain its own cadre of Civilians. The administrative answer had always been to divide Bengal. Now there was the will to do so. There was little doubt about the motive. 'Bengal united is a power', remarked

Risley, now (as Home Secretary) the director of political strategy. 'Bengal divided will pull in several different ways. That is one of the merits of the scheme.'[70] Curzon faithfully repeated this logic to London. 'The Bengalis', he told the Secretary of State,

> like to think of themselves as a nation... If we are weak
> enough to yield to their clamour now we shall not be able
> to dismember or reduce Bengal again, and you will be
> cementing and solidifying on the eastern flank of India a
> force almost formidable, and certain to be an increasing
> trouble in the future.[71]

By the time the final version of the plan was sent to London for approval, the aim of partition had become still more explicit. Calcutta, said Curzon,

> is the centre from which the Congress party is manipulated
> throughout the whole of Bengal, and indeed the whole of
> India. Its best wire-pullers and its most frothy orators all
> reside here... They dominate public opinion in Calcutta;
> they affect the High Court; they frighten the Local
> Government; and they are sometimes not without influence
> on the Government of India... Any measure... that would
> divide the Bengali-speaking population; that would permit
> independent centres... to grow up; that would dethrone
> Calcutta from its place as the centre of successful intrigue,
> or that would weaken the influence of the lawyer class, who
> have the entire organisation in their hands, is intensely and
> hotly resented by them. The outcry will be very loud and
> very fierce.[72]

It was an accurate prophecy. The Bengal Congressmen and their allies elsewhere in India rightly saw the partition driven through in 1905 as a frontal attack upon the claim of the anglo-literate class to a political voice, and as a blatant attempt to stir up other religious or ethnic groups against them. To rub salt into the wound there was no pretence of consulting the legislative council: partition was by Viceregal *fiat*. The result was a furious outcry which widened steadily beyond the educated class. The *swadeshi* campaign was meant to boycott British goods (especially textiles) in favour of local products as an expression of Bengali patriotism. It was taken up by student groups and hastily formed clubs or *samitis*. Soon there were signs of its being enforced by caste associations and through coercive means.[73] Marches, demonstrations and the singing of *Bande Mataram* as a national song were an open challenge to the colonial power. The Civilians grew uneasy: some had doubted the partition plan all along. But so too did their opponents. For all his outrage at the Civilians' ploy, Banerjea drew back from a violent confrontation with the Raj. As the tempo of agitation increased, he looked instead for some accommodation with the embattled government. Relief was to come from a surprising quarter.

Curzon's endorsement of partition had sprung from his urgent geopolitical vision: of the coming struggle for Asia. Throughout his term of office, he argued fiercely for a 'forward' policy to contain the Russian threat and safeguard India. Pressing his views on the British cabinet, he claimed that he spoke for Indian opinion.[74] Without India, he was to argue a few years later, Britain was scarcely a first-class power.[75] In Curzon's geostrategic universe, it was intolerable to have Congress snapping at his heels, denouncing India's foreign wars and blaming the size and cost of the Indian army for poverty, plague and famine. If India was to take what the Viceroy saw as its rightful place in the British system, its internal politics must be brought in line with its imperial duty. But, by a painful irony (to Curzon at least), his insistence upon the imperial status of the Indian government was to bring about his downfall. Ministers in London were already annoyed by Curzon's presumption: in foreign policy they expected India to pay, to be seen but not to be heard. They resented his opposition to the appeasement of Russia. When Curzon was drawn into a bitter row with Lord Kitchener, Commander-in-Chief in India and the Empire's leading soldier, to thwart his grip on the army's bureaucracy, they gratefully accepted his over-hasty resignation. But it was not so much a change of Viceroy (in 1905) as a change of government in London that imposed a rough political truce between the Civilians and the Congress.

With the new Liberal government in London came a new Indian Secretary. John Morley had been an ardent Gladstonian, a radical and a Home Ruler. He lost no time in warning Lord Minto, Curzon's successor as Viceroy, that a large radical phalanx in the House of Commons was watching India closely.[76] Here was a clear signal, like that in the 1880s, that the Civilians' system must not become a 'factory of grievances' and that some move must be made towards 'reform'. Morley himself began with a strong prejudice against Civilian rule. But his real target was Curzon's inadmissible claim to Indian influence in British policy and the 'jingo' mentality of the Civilian regime. What he cared about most, he told his closest adviser, was to 'depose the Government of India from their usurped position of an independent power'.[77] He himself was a fervent supporter of the entente with Russia reached eventually in 1907. 'Forward policy' was out of date, and with it the whole Curzonian ethos. In June 1906, six months into office, he was keen to announce reforms 'in the popular direction'.[78] He may have reasoned that a larger 'popular' element in Indian government would curb its jingoistic excesses and forestall its obstruction of a Russian entente.

Morley's enthusiasm had been heightened by the prospect of a tacit partnership with the Congress. The Congress leadership had despaired of Curzon. Even Tilak agreed that nothing could be gained by agitation in India: London was the only hope.[79] With Curzon's fall and a new Liberal government, Gladstonian in sympathy, they hoped to turn the triangle of Anglo-Indian politics to their advantage. G. K. Gokhale, now the pre-eminent Congressman, hastened to London. In the classic language of Congress loyalism, he denounced Civilian rule and affirmed the bond of empire. Gokhale was a figure of impregnable rectitude, a 'moderate' who repudiated the 'extremism' of Tilak, and an appointed member of the Viceroy's legislative council, the legislature of the central government. He had made a good impression, Morley told Minto.[80] To Gokhale he stressed the importance of Congress support; its opposition would endanger reform.[81]

The Viceroy and the Civilians could see the writing on the wall but they were anything but cowed. Minto rejected the reversal of partition. The Civilians turned their hand to 'reform'. They were already disillusioned with the Councils Act of 1892: here was the chance to revise it. In the scheme they drafted, pride of place was given to a new Chamber of Princes (to influence opinion in Britain and India) and a 'native member' of the Viceroy's government (to prove the Indianness of the Raj). The 'natural leaders' of Indian society, they argued, were the chiefs, landholders, merchants and bankers. They had little sympathy for Congress-type reform. But the legislative councils of 1892 had distorted the image of Indian opinion. Thirty-six per cent of council members had been lawyers, only 23 per cent landowners. Reform should reverse this trend. It should also give Muslims their own seats in the councils.[82]

The thinking behind these proposals was amplified in the Reforms Despatch sent off to London in March 1907. It was a remarkable manifesto of Civilian politics, perhaps the last great statement of Civilian ideology. It acknowledged that the Congress had done much to implant a sense of nationality across India, but insisted that most of the 'educated class' had little sympathy with its programme. It saw in Civilian rule the convergence of two great sources of authority: its inheritance from the Mughal past and its role as the trustee of 'British principles'. The object of reform, it claimed, was to fuse them both in a 'constitutional autocracy': the Civilian Raj would 'govern by rule', merely reserving 'the predominant and absolute power which it can only abdicate at the risk of bringing back the chaos to which our rule put an end'.[83] If the legislative councils were enlarged to represent 'all the interests that are capable of being represented', and if the electorate were refashioned to prevent its falling 'into the hands of wire-pullers', a great common interest could be built up between the Raj and the 'conservative classes'. 'We are not without hope', Minto's government concluded,

> that in the course of a few years the constitution which we propose to establish will come to be regarded as a precious possession round which conservative sentiment will crystallise and will offer substantial opposition to any further change. We anticipate that the aristocratic elements in society and the moderate men, for whom there is at present little place in Indian politics, will range themselves by the side of government, and will oppose any further shifting in the balance of power and any attempt to democratise Indian institutions.[84]

The repudiation of the Congress demand for swifter progress towards self-government, and the admission to power of the anglo-literate class, could not have been blunter.

Morley's response to this provocative document was curiously tepid. He welcomed it, pressed the case for advisory councils in the provinces and remarked on the need for greater representation of *European* interests if the councils were enlarged. His caution was

understandable. Being *seen* to impose reform on the Indian government
was risky. He was nervous of Anglo-India-at-Home and its furious cor-
respondents. He knew that any constitutional scheme would have to
navigate the parliamentary rapids in the House of Lords with its phalanx of former Viceroys. There Curzon lay in wait, and without the
support of Lord Lansdowne (Viceroy 1888–92) Morley had little hope
of winning over its Conservative majority. To make matters worse,
his Indian ally, the Congress, was in disarray and threatened him with
embarrassment.

The Congress faced a syndrome all too familiar to colonial
nationalists in the twentieth century. Their leverage on colonial rulers
was usually increased by signs of general unrest. The official world
became uneasy and more open to modest concession. But, if unrest
challenged colonial power too openly, 'Home' opinion was quickly
hardened against 'agitators' or 'troublemakers'. Colonial officials made
up lost ground by stigmatising their critics as rebels-in-the-making.
Without *organised* mass support, nationalist leaders then faced the
choice between promoting chaos or accepting impotence. After 1906,
the Congress lurched dangerously towards this political impasse. The
swadeshi agitation in Bengal radicalised *bhadralok* opinion and the
local Congress supporters. It gave a chance to Congressmen from other
provinces who favoured more ruthless tactics against the Civilian Raj:
now they might swing the Congress behind them. In January 1907,
B. G. Tilak launched his 'New Party' and attacked the policy of relying
on British goodwill and Morley's reformism. The remedy, he declared,
'is not petitioning but boycott'.[85] Boycott was the way to shatter the
illusion of British power, resting as it did on 'our assistance'. For
'every Englishman knows that you are weak and they are strong . . . We
have been deceived by such a policy so long.'[86] After the Congress
annual meeting in Calcutta in December 1906, it looked as if Tilak's
programme – boycotting military service, revenue collection and the
administration of justice – would carry all before it.[87] In 1907, there
was serious unrest in the Punjab over land rights. In Bengal, young
bhadralok activists turned to assassination and bomb-throwing.[88] This
was hardly the right climate for Morley to force more reform on the government of India than it had proposed itself. The established Congress
leaders, for their part, were desperate to avoid the tag of extremism.[89]
The next annual meeting at Surat broke up in disorder. The leadership withdrew, and drafted its own manifesto, insisting on its loyalty
and rejecting unconstitutional action. The following year at Allahabad,

a new Congress constitution was drawn up to repudiate the Tilakite heresy and declare that 'colonial *swaraj*' – self-government within the Empire on the 'white dominion' model – was the grand objective. The British helped by arresting Tilak for sedition and exiling him to Burma. His 'party' in the Congress broke up. The Punjab unrest was appeased. The Bengal bombing died down. The moderates regained control of the Congress and imposed their new 'creed'.[90]

In this easier atmosphere, Morley, whose enthusiasm for reform had been ebbing, was able to insist on two crucial principles which the Civilians had hoped to bury. The new enlarged councils in the provinces would have 'unofficial majorities': a predominance of members who were not required (as were official members) to vote with the government as a condition of their place. Secondly, Morley insisted, against the Civilians' prejudice, that a substantial proportion of the unofficials would be chosen by electorates, not selected by interest groups. This, together with the provision that Indians could be appointed to the Viceroy's executive council, was the heart of the 'Morley-Minto' reforms. A new political order seemed in the making. The Congress received the prospect with enthusiasm. Morley, said Surendranath Banerjea, was the 'Simon de Montfort of India'.[91] The Congressmen looked forward to filling the lion's share of seats in the new provincial councils. With more liberal rules on debate and interpellation in the council chambers, they hoped for gradual progress towards a quasi-parliamentary constitution. At the very least, Morley had blocked the Civilians' project for a 'constitutional autocracy' based on the partnership of princes and landowners. But it soon became clear that the triumph of 'British Indian nationalism' was far from complete.

The stalemate

The struggle over the reforms had been fought on two levels and between several parties. At the imperial level, it had been a trial of strength between London and Simla, between Morley and the Viceroy's Civilian government. Morley had been determined to bring the Civilians to heel. 'It is not you or I who are responsible for [Indian] unrest', he told the Viceroy irritably in June 1908, 'but the over-confident, over-worked Tchinovniks who have had India in their hands for fifty years past.'[92] Morley had insisted on a Royal Commission to decentralise the Indian government and chose as Minto's successor the diplomat Lord

Hardinge (closely involved in negotiating the Anglo-Russian entente) to underline that the days of Curzonism were over. The Viceroy's government, remarked Morley's under-secretary, and perhaps at his suggestion, had acted as his 'agent' in making the reforms (a description received badly in Simla).[93] Implicit in Morley's whole policy was not so much the graceful acceptance of Indian claims as the deliberate extension of London's control. It was entirely in keeping with this that, while he pressed for unofficial majorities in the provincial councils, he bluntly rejected one at the Indian centre (on the Viceroy's legislative council) where India's budget and its military spending were settled. In the strange constitutional minuet it danced to keep London at bay, it had been the Viceroy's government that had proposed this seemingly radical innovation.[94]

In the Indian arena the contest was much more confused. The old struggle between the Civilians and Congress had widened out. The partition of Bengal had shown the potential of mobilising support on a larger scale and with a more emotive programme. Much of Tilak's 'new party' plan was soon to be revived by Gandhi. For the moment, this tendency had been checked by a tacit alliance between the British and the Congress moderates. There was one significant exception. The Congress attack on partition had infuriated its main beneficiaries, the Muslims of East Bengal. In 1906, their sympathisers in North India formed the All-India Muslim League. Since Muslim loyalty was vital to British rule across much of Northern India (especially in the United Provinces and Punjab), the embattled Civilians looked kindly on these likely allies. At a time of rising tension between Britain and Ottoman Turkey, Morley had extra reasons for conceding the Muslim demand for separate seats on the councils. 'The Mahomedans', he told Parliament, 'have a special and overwhelming claim upon us.'[95] But, overall, the surge of political unrest unleashed in 1905 produced a curiously indecisive result in which none of the interested parties – London, the Civilians, the Congress 'moderates', the 'extremists' or the Muslims (partition was reversed in 1911) – gained a clear advantage.

But, for the time being, it was the Civilians who carried off most of the spoils. As in 1892, London had been obliged to delegate the 'small print' of reform to the local officials. But, since the small print included choosing electors and electorates, and deciding the membership of the provincial councils, its importance was very large. The Civilians once more took full advantage. Minto and his advisers had disliked the idea of elections, but there was another string to their bow. 'We shall have to trust to a careful creation of electorates', said the Viceroy coolly.[96] And so they did. This creativity ensured that, in Bengal, out of twenty-six elective 'constituencies', perhaps only four could have been won by Congress and (in 1912–13) only three *were* won.[97] The same tactic brought disillusion in the United Provinces. 'They ... are just the opposite of reforms', Motilal Nehru reported angrily. 'The avowed object of the so-called reforms is to destroy the influence of the educated classes.'[98] The effects were soon seen. The provincial budget debate in 1910 was 'a farce', as a crowd of unofficial members stood up not to challenge the government but to praise it.[99] Nor were the Civilians content with new allies in the councils. They armed themselves with fresh weapons against attack in the press. Provincial governments were given wide powers to close down papers on grounds of sedition[100] and were encouraged to subsidise 'selected loyal vernacular newspapers'.[101] The new Department of Criminal Intelligence stepped up the scale of political surveillance.[102] There was little to choose between 'extremists' and 'moderates', said the Civilian in charge.[103] It was little wonder that a senior official could say in 1910, after five years of upheaval, that, in his province at least, 'the executive has never been stronger'.[104]

Nor was this all. The Civilians had been put on the defensive by Morley's alliance with the Congress moderates. But they were determined to recast Indian politics along lines of their own choosing. One symptom was Minto's appeasement of the Indian princes whom he promised to free from the strict supervision imposed by Curzon.[105] The next step was more daring. It was decided to reverse the partition of Bengal to which the whole Hindu elite remained bitterly hostile. But the *quid pro quo* would be the removal of the Indian capital from the 'disloyal' city of Calcutta to Delhi. Here was a partial if belated fulfilment of Curzon's vision. The centre of Indian politics would be shifted from the hectic lowlands of Bengal to the loyal heartlands of Upper India. From Delhi, the Raj would assert its link to the Indian past, its legacy from the Mughals, and the permanence of its rule.[106] A new imperial city was planned, to echo the Mughal foundations at Fatehpur Sikri and Shahjahanbad. At the grandiose Delhi Durbar in 1911, attended by the new King-Emperor George V, the public fealty of the Indian princes formed the climax of the ceremony. What better riposte to the pretensions of '*babu*' politics?

This new 'Delhi Raj' had still wider implications. In 1908, the Civilians smothered the inquiry that Morley had launched into administrative decentralisation. The Financial Secretary dismissed financial devolution as a dream.[107] The commission accepted his view. Three years later, as the new political landscape took form, decentralisation began to look more attractive. In the famous 'Delhi Despatch' of 1911, the new Viceroy, Lord Hardinge, sketched out a novel constitutional framework. Power was to be devolved increasingly to provincial governments and, indirectly, to the provincial councils and their carefully constructed 'electorates'.[108] But none of this was meant to upset the ability of the central government to meet its imperial obligations, pay the imperial dividend and impose, if necessary, the ultimate sanction of coercive power. In its new imperial enclave in Delhi, magnificently free from provincial distractions, buoyed up by feudal loyalty, confidently manipulating the levers and limits of provincial politics, the Civilian Raj would remain: indispensable and irremovable.

In the last years of peace, there was little time to test the new model Raj. Morley's successor in London, Lord Crewe, brusquely ruled out the parliamentary future on which the Congress moderates had pinned their hopes. 'Fancy a Liberal Secretary of State ... proclaiming the impossibility of Self-Government for the Indian people on the ground of their race', said Srinavasa Sastri sadly.[109] The Congress leaders grumbled but made the best of it. The reforms had reversed the growing estrangement between British and Indians; they were beneficial for all their defects; they had revived the 'drooping spirits' of the constitutional party.[110] The Delhi Despatch held out hope for provincial autonomy.[111] Perhaps fiscal autonomy might be granted.[112] The Congress goal remained 'an autonomous Government ... under the suzerainty of the most powerful and progressive of modern nations'.[113] It was only the onset of war that changed the mood. 'In Europe the war of nations, now in progress, will knock off the last weights of mediaeval domination of one man over many, of one race over another', declared the Congress president hopefully in December 1914.[114] A new phase of the political struggle was about to begin.

The idea of India

Behind the slogans, schemes and manoeuvres of these decades lay a deeper issue: the idea of India. In an age of such furious change – in communications technology, geopolitical assumptions, social mobility, cultural hierarchy, religious allegiance, economic structure, political order – in India and beyond, it was hardly surprising that the subcontinent evoked widely different and sharply contested visions of its political and cultural future. The idea of India was being made and remade with exceptional urgency. New formulas were concocted. New audiences were sought. The stakes were rising.

In London, the official and semi-official idea of India was predictably instrumental. As India grew more valuable, the costs of instability went up, and imperial supervision became more rigorous. If India's *relative* economic importance had slipped with the huge growth of British trade and investment in the Americas after 1900, it was still the largest export market for Britain's largest export. London's oversight (rather than Civilian rule) was Lancashire's guarantee of an open door for its cotton products. The continuing expansion of Indian trade and the ever-growing frequency of its communications with Britain suggested that India's place in the British pattern of trade, investment and payments was as important as ever. On the geostrategic front, the trend seemed even stronger. London's view of India had always been refracted through the prism of its military assets. India was the strategic reserve for the British system east (and sometimes west) of Suez. In 1899, (British) troops rushed from India (not distant Britain) had stopped the Boer dash for the sea and staved off disaster in the early phase of the South African War. As the division of the world into spheres and colonies speeded up, and the geopolitics of partition spread across Asia, geostrategic control over India came to seem more and more critical to the British world-system. This was the point of Curzon's address on 'India's place in the Empire'. This was the point made by *The Times* in 1911, when it drew the connection between command of India and command of the sea. 'India stands right across the greatest highway in the world', it proclaimed (with some hyperbole). 'It is the centre of the East ... The Power which holds India must of necessity command the sea. Supreme sea-power would be as difficult to maintain without control of India, as control of India without command of the sea. It is ... the centre of Imperial defence.'[115]

Of course, the view from London was heavily coloured by the vision of oriental backwardness so skilfully promoted in the literature of Anglo-India. But implicit in London's 'idea' was an unsentimental regard for India's utility and an indifference to those intra-Indian affairs that had no imperial significance. The Civilians would be backed to the hilt if India's imperial 'duty' was threatened by its politicians. But

London might be willing to cooperate with 'loyal' Indian 'moderates', especially at the provincial level where *its* interests were not at risk. There was always the *claque* of Anglo-India's friends at home to face. But, if the Civilian regime seemed a bar to modernising India *imperially*, or to the partnership of its native elites in some larger imperial purpose, it might yet find its privileges cut down by the London government. Before 1914, for all the sound and fury of Morley's reforms, there was little sign of this. The Civilians could not be replaced as the guardians of the imperial stake while its strategic component was growing so remorselessly in value.

Hence, perhaps, the continuing vigour and confidence with which the Civilians' idea of India was propagated. The Civilians had had to come to terms since the 1880s with the growth of an educated class and with a vociferous press, both of which challenged the dogmas of its rule. Their reaction had been to emphasise, by 'scientific' inquiry and with wider publicity, their vision of India as a cultural and political mosaic, a riot of castes, communities, religions and races, teetering on the brink of violent disorder. More pragmatically, they modified their bureaucratic despotism by limited devolution at local level and by the careful definition of interest groups with privileged access to authority and (after 1892) with seats on provincial councils. Under pressure from Congress and London, this idea had expanded into something more grandiose: India as a confederacy knit together by Civilian rule and the neo-feudal loyalty of its landed classes. With provincial devolution, 'conservative' (rather than 'Congress') India would be brought to the fore. The educated class would be revealed as one community among many, special perhaps in its claims, but not dominant in its influence. The horizontal and vertical links in this emergent India would remain under Civilian control. An untrammelled authority at the Indian centre would ensure that the Civilian Raj could pay the imperial dividend, the secret of its lease of power from London. In the meantime, it made sense for the Raj to identify itself more openly with Indian interests, where the 'dividend' was not involved. In 1913, the Viceroy, Lord Hardinge, expressed his government's sympathy for the Ottoman Empire (reeling from its Balkan defeats) as a fellow 'Muhammadan power'.[116] He promised to take up the grievances of Indian communities in settler Africa.[117] 'Anglo-India' and 'Indian-India' would be reconciled.

On the Congress politicians the travails of political struggle since the 1880s had also left their mark. But to a remarkable extent the

core of their programme survived unchanged. Like European nationalists, the Congress leaders saw in the educated class a proxy for the
nation. They saw themselves as trustees of the Indian idea. Their
vision of India was (politically at least) to remake it along Gladstonian lines. The object of the Congress, declared its president in 1912,
was 'to create a nation' whose citizens would be 'members of a worldwide empire'. 'Our great aim is to make the British Government the
National Government of the British Indian people.'[118] India was to
be a British Indian nation, inspired by the ideals of British-style Liberalism. The apparatus of the Raj would be the scaffolding of Indian
nationhood, just as the adoption of British values would be the secret
of self-rule. Pressing the old case for easier Indian entry into the ranks
of the Civilians, Motilal Nehru insisted that, even if Indian candidates
were locally chosen, they should still be sent to Britain to complete
their education: 'to acquire those characteristics which are essentially
British and ... absolutely necessary in the interests of good government
in India'.[119] It was 'axiomatic', he went on, that the administration in
India 'must have a pronounced British tone and character and too much
stress cannot be laid on Indians acquiring that character as a habit'.[120]
It was no accident that Motilal sent his son (Jawaharlal) to Harrow and
Cambridge: he was meant for the Civil Service, not Congress.

In retrospect, we can see that each of these ideas of India
received in this period a decisive check. By 1914 they were all at stalemate. A new cadre of imperially minded Indians, ready and willing
to do India's imperial duty, was the white hope of advanced opinion
in Britain. If the British world-system was not to weaken or stagnate,
India's contribution must grow greater, its role more dynamic, its leaders more receptive to their imperial task. In reality, there was not the
smallest sign that the most moderate of the Indian moderates would
agree to India's *existing* imperial burdens once self-government was
granted. Like it or not, London would find itself bound to the Civilian
Raj. The unofficial ties of sympathy between the Imperial centre and its
Indian friends would be fretted by this dilemma. As for the Civilians,
their hope of embedding their rule in Indian sympathies, fusing their
autocracy with Indian conservatism, had (as it turned out) little chance
of success. It depended too heavily upon stifling the appeal of Indian
nationalism in the educated class and on rallying new groups and interests to provincial institutions without the means to satisfy their wants.
For the 'British Indian nationalists' of the Congress, the future was just

as gloomy. Indeed, they were trapped in a paradox. Without mobilising a larger following (the course rejected in 1907) they had little hope of a breakthrough at the provincial (let alone the All-India) level. Without wresting more power and patronage from the Civilians, they had few means of widening the appeal of the 'manly liberalism' they espoused. When the dust had settled on the Morley-Minto reforms, that much was clear.

To an extent only dimly glimpsed before 1914, the political ground was heaving beneath them all. A fourth idea of India was in the making. It was less the dream of an Indian state than the anxious search for Indian community. Its prophet was Gandhi, whose *Hind Swaraj* (1909) brusquely rejected Western civilisation and Congress ideology in favour of a spiritual India of self-sufficient villages. Outside the formal world of Civilian rule and Congress politics, a host of new interests was emerging. Hindu *sabhas*,[121] Muslims,[122] caste associations, leagues of peasants,[123] even groups of workers, sought a new solidarity or defended an old. In Bengal[124] and Madras,[125] new social ambitions were afoot in the countryside. Congress's 'British India' meant little to such men. Regional interests and communal identities were much more pressing. Whom they would follow and to what effect were as yet unknown. The answers would come much sooner than anyone expected.

6 THE WEAKEST LINK: BRITAIN IN SOUTH AFRICA

In South Africa, the bond of empire was weaker and the strains on it much greater than in other colonies of settlement. The European whites were predominantly non-British; the indigenous blacks more numerous and resilient. The frontier wars of conquest lasted longer, were fought with greater ferocity and spread out over a whole sub-continent. For much of the nineteenth century, South Africa was viewed in London as a hybrid region: a composite of settler and 'native' states. Imperial policy veered unpredictably between a 'Canadian' solution of settler self-government and the 'Indian' solution of direct control – at least over the large zones where autonomous black communities survived. Partly as a result, on the white side certainly, the 'Imperial Factor' was regarded with profound mistrust.

South Africa was likely to be an awkward element in the imperial system at the best of times. The sub-continent was stuck in its own version of Catch-22. As long as the struggle between whites and blacks continued there could be no hope of devolving imperial authority to a settler government on the model of Canada, the Australian colonies or (most relevantly) New Zealand. The whites were too divided; and the blacks were too strong to be contained without the help of imperial troops. But every imperial effort to promote settler unity and impose a common policy towards black peoples and rulers roused fresh white animosity against London's 'dictation' – especially among the Afrikaner (or Boer) majority. Suspicion of the Imperial Factor was the main cause of South Africa's peculiar fragmented state structure, with its division between two colonies, two Boer republics and a scattering of black territories, some in direct relations with London through the High

Map 8 South Africa in the nineteenth century

Commissioner in Cape Town, who doubled as the Cape Colony's governor. But, in the late nineteenth century, South Africa turned into something more than a tiresome frontier province of the Empire. It became the arena where the political and strategic cohesion of the British world-system was tested to its limit.

There were several reasons for this. In the 1880s, South African politics were transformed by the new wealth from diamonds and gold. The rapid growth of the mineral economy sucked in foreign capital and sharpened the competition for trade between the South African states. But its most disturbing effect was to create uncertainty about the geopolitical orientation of the whole region. With its gold revenues and commercial leverage as the great inland market, the autonomous Boer republic in the Transvaal now had the means to strike free from British paramountcy, dragging the rest of Southern Africa with it. But it also ran the risk of being inundated by foreign (mainly British) immigrants attracted by its new prosperity. If that were to happen, the Transvaal would become British by default, pulling the Afrikaners of the interior back into Britain's orbit, and making South Africa another Canada. The stakes were high. By the 1890s, the grand problem of South African politics seemed about to be settled. But no one could be sure what the outcome would be.

What made this regional issue into an imperial question was the intersection of South Africa's economic revolution with two wider political forces. The fate of the Transvaal, and of South Africa, turned (or so it seemed) upon the treatment of the immigrant British, or Uitlanders. The Transvaal was the high water mark of British migration, the demographic imperialism that had served so well to extend British influence, power and wealth. Kruger's republic fiercely resisted the habitual demand of British communities overseas for political and cultural predominance as the self-appointed standard-bearers of progress. But, in doing so, it set itself against a tide of British ethnic nationalism then approaching its peak. As a result, the Transvaal's relations with Britain and the rest of South Africa became entangled in the bitter ethnic rivalry of Afrikaners and 'English' (the usual term for British settlers in South Africa) in the prelude to war in 1899. Worse still, at the very moment when economic change was maximising political uncertainty, South Africa became the focus of imperial rivalry. As the new geopolitics of partition extended ever more widely across the Afro-Asian world, Britain's claim to regional supremacy in Southern Africa, languidly asserted since 1815, became critical to her strategic interests and world power status. This sudden conjuncture of ethnic, economic and geopolitical tensions turned South Africa, almost overnight, from a colonial backwater into the most volatile quarter of the Victorian empire.

This was the setting for the prolonged struggle over the political control of Southern Africa which reached its crisis between 1895 and 1909. To all the main protagonists, cabinet ministers, proconsuls, British settlers, blacks and Boers, interests of fundamental importance seemed at stake: imperial safety, economic progress, personal liberty, political freedom, cultural survival. In the longer view, the outcome of the struggle, the unification of South Africa as a self-governing, British dominion rather than its secession, or balkanisation into competing states, created a vital adjunct of British world power in the century of global wars. But the more immediate question, as Southern Africa entered its time of troubles, was whether imperial power could reshape the sub-continent to its own design even at the point of the bayonet. The lessons of the South African past were not encouraging.

Supremacy or stalemate

The British seized the Cape from the Dutch in 1795, returned it, and took it again for good in 1806. The halfway house to India could not be left in the hands of an enfeebled client of France, which the Netherlands had become. For the British, what mattered was Table Bay and the naval base at Simonstown on the Indian Ocean side of Cape Point. But this southern Gibraltar had a straggling hinterland. Beyond the mountains around Cape Town lay a sprawling, thinly populated pastoral colony that stretched away for seven hundred miles to the north. Wandering trekboers lived by transhumance and practised slavery.[1] On the Cape's eastern frontier they had clashed since the 1770s with Nguni (or Xhosa) peoples moving south in search of pastures. Even before British rule began, friction between Boer frontiersmen and the colonial authorities in Cape Town had sparked a local rebellion.[2] After 1806, British efforts to pacify the frontier, reduce their military costs and outlaw slavery compounded Boer resentment at alien rule and its anglicising tendency.

Already there were early signs of the imperial dilemma. Should the British push forward and take control of the turbulent zone where whites and blacks raided and counter-raided? Could they impose a real separation between the quarrelsome frontier communities? Were Boer and black misdeeds to be punished with an even hand? Should the colonial government in Cape Town seek treaty partners among the Xhosa chiefs and extend protection to its African allies? Behind all this was the question of whether control of the South African Cape required command of the South African interior. But, after 1836, it was no longer just a matter of the Eastern Cape and its border wars. The British had to define their imperial interest across the whole sub-continent.

For by that time a double revolution was transforming the nature of the imperial problem. The drastic consolidation of the Zulu state under Shaka (c.1787–1828) had released a huge wave of demographic turmoil affecting much of modern South Africa and beyond:

the *mfecane* or 'crushing'.[3] Communities and tribes were disrupted, defeated and displaced. As Shaka's victims sought safety beyond his reach, they invaded new neighbourhoods and provoked fresh conflicts. Over a vast swathe of the interior highveld, the *mfecane* unleashed a chaotic process of forced migration and ethnic conflict. As old communities fragmented, rival leaders competed to build a following, claim land and assert their rule. The effects were felt all along the porous frontier of the Cape. As a result, white traders, trekkers and missionaries, as well as runaway slaves and servants, moved easily into the masterless realm beyond the Orange. Then, in the later 1830s, a large movement of Cape farmers from the embattled Eastern Province – some 15,000 between 1834 and 1840 – trekked north and east to found a Boer republic in Natal. Between them, the *mfecane* and the Great Trek sucked the Colony's human frontier deep into the interior. In a few short years, the zone of imperial concern had been driven north from the Orange to the Limpopo, and was on its way to the Zambezi.

To a succession of governors in Cape Town, the case for extending their imperial mandate over the whole sub-continent seemed unanswerable. The Cape's strategic value would be lost if any harbour in the region was controlled by independent whites: sooner or later they would solicit the presence of a foreign power. On this argument, Natal, with its magnificent port, was annexed in 1844, persuading the disgruntled trekkers to seek republican freedom on the interior highveld. Maritime supremacy was easy enough. But there was also a case for dogging the steps of the emigrant Boers wherever they went. For it soon became clear that the wars of expansion between the trekkers and rival statebuilders in the *mfecane* aftermath – like the Sotho ruler Moshesh or the Griqua captains Kok and Waterboer[4] – destabilised the whole frontier. Endless border wars forced up the imperial garrison but held back the Cape Colony's commercial and political growth. Without an inland paramountcy to impose order on all its warring communities, the sub-continent would remain a costly colonial backwater, a constant embarrassment to the humanitarian conscience and an inconvenient, perhaps dangerous, drain on the scarce resource of military power.

The argument was persuasive but the means were lacking. Governor after governor claimed that peace and plenty would follow an extended paramountcy. One proposed an elaborate scheme of treaties, magistrates and police beyond the Orange.[5] Three years later, Sir Harry Smith swept aside chiefly rule in Xhosaland and annexed the whole northern frontier up to the Vaal, to bring the Boers back under British rule. 'My position', he declared in a revealing analogy,

> *has been analogous to that of every Governor General who has proceeded to India. All have been fully impressed with the weakness of that Policy which extended the Company's possessions . . . [F]ew . . . especially the men of more gifted talents, have ever resigned . . . without having done that, which . . . circumstances demanded and imperatively imposed upon them. Such has been my case.*[6]

The Colonial Secretary gave reluctant sanction: enlargement, he said, was inevitable.[7] But, in 1851, after spending millions, the Colonial Office called a halt. The Boers were in revolt. The Eighth Xhosa War, provoked by Smith's policy, had been a military shambles hastily abandoned by Smith's successor. Further north, the Zulu state still loomed over the tiny colony in Natal. With black resistance unbroken, further coercion of the independent Boers beyond the Orange was politically futile and militarily dangerous. London made the best of a bad job. In 1852–4, in the conventions of Sand River and Bloemfontein, it conceded the Boer republics practical autonomy and patched up peace on the Cape frontier. A further advance under Governor Grey aimed to incorporate the whole border zone between the Cape's eastern frontier and Natal. It was aborted by the outbreak of the Indian Mutiny, and the hasty removal of much of Grey's force, and then by the deepening crisis in New Zealand to where Grey himself was transferred – although not before the great Xhosa cattle-killing of 1857 (a despairing act of self-immolation) had allowed him to push the settler frontier forward to the river Kei.[8] But, for nearly twenty years, the Imperial Factor withdrew from the South African interior, on the argument that, with the coast (mostly) under British control, the inland republics were no threat to the strategic command that was the *ultima ratio* of the imperial presence.

The 'conventions policy' was a grudging recognition of the underlying weakness vitiating all attempts to make the sub-continent as 'British' as Canada or Australia, or to master it imperially as the British had mastered India. The Imperial government would not finance a vast campaign of territorial conquest in Southern Africa. There (as elsewhere) imperial expansion waited on local agents to create a framework of information, order and opportunity: without it, reinforcements of capital and manpower were hard to attract. Nor was British military power a decisive weapon without the follow-through of local force. But, in South Africa, the coastal colonies in the Cape and Natal were cripplingly weak. They had no great staples like timber, wheat or wool (though wool came closest), attracted few migrants and borrowed little capital. Overland transport was costly and slow. The interior yielded few commodities. The commercial energy that drove forward the settler frontier elsewhere was in short supply. As a settler society, South Africa was a pale shadow of Canada. Nor, despite Sir Harry Smith, could it be a second India. There was no peasant economy to tax, no sepoy army to recruit, and no means to pay for the 'hire' of imperial troops – the three conditions which had allowed Anglo-Indian sub-imperialism to flourish unchecked by London's veto. Far from being the dominant force in Southern Africa, the coastal colonies found themselves in frustrating equipoise with the interior states, white and black. Black societies could be harassed and threatened, but they were mobile, resilient and difficult to incorporate – partly because, in the primitive state of the colonial economy, that meant seizing their land by force and conscripting their labour. The Boer republics were an even harder nut to crack.

It was easy to mistake the crudity of the Boer states for weakness. But the Boers had developed a highly effective means of 'primitive accumulation' to complement their social and military system.[9] On the highveld grassland and around its margins, their horse-borne mobility and firepower allowed them to capture African cattle, land and labour far more easily than in the dense bush and deep valleys of the old Cape borderlands. The Boer states existed to seize this wealth and redistribute it among their citizen-warriors organised into the key unit of their social and political life, the commando. The Boer elite were the commandants who had first pick of the spoils and on whose military prowess their followers depended. Boer institutions may have been simple,[10] but their pastoral economy, drawing labour and foodcrops from black dependants, allowed a thinly spread but highly effective occupation of the highveld to be imposed in less than twenty years. Boer warfare was perfectly adapted to the open veld. Against it, the square and the infantry charge, the standard British tactics, were largely ineffective.

Stalemate was thus the rule in South African politics. When the British tried again to break it in the 1870s, the outcome was crushing failure. Once more, the reason for a forward move was the chorus of settler and official alarm at growing black resistance in the cockpit of peoples between the Cape, Natal and the Boer republics. Once more the blame was laid on disunity and competition among the whites. Federal union of the white settler states, British and Boer, favoured by Cape governors as the acceptable face of annexation, was endorsed by official opinion in London.[11] Cape Colony was given Responsible (self-) Government in 1872 in the hope that its leaders would take up the federal cause. They refused, fearing that the whole burden of frontier control would fall on them. The Colonial Secretary, Lord Carnarvon, turned instead to the junior colony, Natal, and to Sir Theophilus Shepstone.[12] Shepstone was the son of a British settler in the Eastern Cape. He became an official interpreter and, in the border warfare of the 1830s, rose quickly to be the government's spokesman among the Xhosa chiefs. By 1846, he was 'diplomatic agent' to the Africans in Natal and to the Zulu kingdom beyond the Tugela. A large, impassive, secretive man, Shepstone became the uncrowned king of Natal. He was an imperial official, but a colonial patriot: an unrelenting Natal sub-imperialist, a proto-Rhodes without the diamonds. His aim was to build a greater Natal: to find new 'locations' for its blacks; to free more land for its whites; to annex the northern coast; to control the northern trade to the Zambezi; to conquer Zululand. Carnarvon's rebuff at the Cape gave him his chance, for London was now willing to throw the Imperial Factor and its army into his puny settler bridgehead. Natal would be the springboard for colonial federation. Shepstone's local influence, his mastery of frontier politics, his command of 'native policy', made him the obvious choice as the new supremo of the northern interior. At first all went well. Worsted in its war against the Pedi, the Transvaal in 1876 was bankrupt, divided and demoralised. Shepstone talked its dejected president into surrendering independence and conjured up a petition for annexation which he declared in February 1877.[13] The Pedi were defeated with imperial help.[14] Then, in the second stage of Shepstone's grand design, the army Carnarvon had sent invaded Zululand, and (after the disaster at Isandhlwana) decisively broke its power. In a single forward movement, the British had broken the cycle of frustration and transformed the geopolitics of Southern Africa. Or so it seemed.

The moment of triumph was short. There was barely time to broach federation before the Transvaal Boers began to throw off their new colonial state with its courts and taxes. Paul Kruger's fame as a frontier fighter made him the natural leader of revolt. With the shattering of Zulu and Pedi power, caution was redundant. In 1880, colonial control in the Transvaal crumbled rapidly. At Majuba, in February 1881, Boer commandos destroyed the imperial force sent to uphold annexation, killing General Colley, the high commissioner for South East Africa. With this fiasco, the Gladstone government threw in the towel, intimidated by reports that to prolong the struggle would unite Afrikaners in the Cape and Orange Free State against them.[15] With the Convention of Pretoria they scrapped the Transvaal's annexation and threw away the federal plan. Shepstone and Natal had been broken reeds. The coalition of colonial and imperial power had never materialised. As in 1848–52, the Imperial Factor had come, failed and gone. The interior had kept its autonomy: London fell back on its old strategy of coastline control. But its hand in the sub-continent was now much weaker than before. A self-governing Cape Colony, with its (white) Afrikaner majority, was a sandy foundation for imperial influence. The final demolition of black independence (though not of all resistance) – the by-product of forward policy in 1878–80 – left the Boer republics much stronger by default.[16] And, by the mid-1880s, French and German influence had begun to arrive in the region.

Kruger versus Rhodes

The Convention of Pretoria in 1881 settled the terms on which the Transvaal was to regain its freedom. The British withdrew, but not unconditionally. The Transvalers were forced to acknowledge British 'suzerainty' – a detached oversight of their internal affairs – and imperial control of their foreign relations. They were encumbered with debts and, most galling of all, forbidden to encroach on remaining African territory inside or outside the Transvaal boundary. The mistreatment of Africans within the Transvaal could be reported to the British resident.[17] It was hardly surprising that, when Kruger became the Transvaal president in 1883, he was determined to cut down the scope for imperial meddling and regain the old republican freedom conferred in 1852. He had little choice. The social economy of the Transvaal Boers was inimical to fixed boundaries. The acquisition of fresh land for speculation was the chief means of accumulating wealth in an underdeveloped pastoral economy. 'Encroachment has been their very life', observed Lord Salisbury, the scion of an encroaching aristocracy.[18] Indeed, the Convention had hardly been signed before groups of burghers began to push their way on to African land to east and west, threatening a new round of frontier disturbance and missionary outrage.

As Kruger sensed, the British position was getting weaker and their grip on the interior more tenuous. They had no will to confront the Boer filibusters and by 1883 scarcely any means. By 1883, the imperial garrison in South Africa was a mere 2,100 men. Besieged by Egyptian anxieties, the Gladstone cabinet had no appetite for quixotic adventures on the highveld. Most of all, senior ministers in London were now convinced that a false move in Southern Africa would unite all Afrikaners against them, wrecking what remained of imperial paramountcy and putting the Cape's strategic function at risk.[19] They dared not coerce the Transvaal Boers and needed Kruger's help in settling the frontier disputes. So, when Kruger came to London in 1883, it seemed a foregone conclusion that he would get his way and regain the 'independence' conceded in 1852.

Indeed, the Transvaal president got much of what he wanted and might have got more. In the new Convention of 1884, British oversight of African interests disappeared. So did all reference to 'suzerainty', though the bar to diplomatic freedom (and thus full independence) remained. The Transvaal was allowed to resume the grandiloquent title of 'South African Republic'. But, in return, Kruger made a fateful concession. He agreed to leave a corridor of land between the Transvaal and the Kalahari desert under British protection. This green strip, with its forage for oxen, was the 'Road to the North', the vital link between Cape Colony and the great unopened hinterland of Zambezia beyond the Limpopo. At the last minute, the High Commissioner in Cape Town had persuaded the Cape ministers to share the costs of British rule, and tipped the balance against surrender to Kruger's territorial demands. When later the Cape reneged and the Transvaal Boers violated the new boundary, an embarrassed government in London had no choice but to expel them by force and to assume the administrative burden of a Bechuanaland protectorate it had refused to consider before the Convention.

Part of Kruger's logic in accepting the western frontier of 1884 had been the urgency of debt relief – London's carrot.[20] Even in the mid-1880s, the Transvaal had not thrown off the spectre of bankruptcy. Its annual revenues were puny: the Cape's were fifteen times as great.

On any reckoning, the new republic was an impoverished backwater, a threadbare ruffian on the fringe of empire. Its nuisance value was local, not imperial. Kruger had reasserted the old autonomy of the South African interior but its persistent economic weakness remained. Then, in 1886, the discovery of the great gold reef on the Witwatersrand signalled a drastic reversal of fortune. Within four years, the Transvaal's gold production was worth nearly £2 million a year. By 1892, its revenues had reached half the Cape figure.[21] Six years later they were almost equal. The danger of bankruptcy (and political implosion) vanished. Rising land values created a wealthy ruling class. With commercial concessions to distribute, Kruger could build a patronage state among the Transvaal whites and complete the subjugation of the Transvaal blacks. He could construct a railway to Delagoa Bay. With open access to the outside world and a gold economy, the half-promise of 1884 could become the whole-hog of republican freedom.

Historians have made much of the 'mineral revolution' which blew away the old assumptions of imperial strategy and made the rebellious Transvaal the strongest state on the sub-continent. In fact, Southern Africa had not one mineral revolution but two. The diamond rush at Kimberley came first (from 1867), and Kimberley became colonial not republican soil. But, for that other, earlier, revolution, Kruger might have carried his goldstate to independence and destroyed the remnants of British primacy in Southern Africa. Instead, he was confronted by a local rival whose ruthlessness matched his own and whose resources, leveraged with reckless lack of scruple, built a roadblock in his path. This rival was Cecil Rhodes.

Rhodes had come to South Africa in 1870.[22] By 1876, still only twenty-three, he had made a small fortune in the diamond fields. Within a few years more, he emerged as a commanding figure in this rough speculative mining world whose voracious demand for imports, capital, railways and black labour transformed the Southern African economy. For the rest of his life, Kimberley remained the real centre of Rhodes' business and political ventures, the capital of the 'Rhodesian' empire. It was here that his wealth was concentrated. It was here that he met many of those who became his partners, allies and agents. It was from here that Rhodes looked north towards Zambezia. This jerry-built outpost of colonial South Africa had become a commercial dynamo. It was a magnet for capital and enterprise and the natural springboard for the penetration of the northern interior by traders, prospectors, speculators and land-hungry settlers. It was the forward base-camp of sub-imperialism.

And it was here that Rhodes' idle fantasies of imperial aggrandisement took on a local shape. In 1877, the Transvaal's annexation promised a new field for Kimberley's influence. Kruger's triumph closed it off; but, six weeks after the battle of Majuba, Rhodes entered the Cape Parliament. At first, he was preoccupied with defending the interest of the diamond fields against taxation and state interference. But, by 1883, Rhodes had grasped the importance of the 'Road to the North', the 'Suez Canal of South Africa' as he called it, stretching away from Kimberley towards Mafeking, Tuli and Bulawayo, capital of Lobengula's Ndebele state. By controlling access to this untold hinterland, Kimberley's ultimate mastery of the north, including Kruger's obstreperous Ruritania, would be assured. Under new Kimberley management, Cape Colony would throw off its rustic myopia and become the head and centre of a unified British South Africa.

Like his Canadian counterpart, John A. Macdonald, Rhodes saw that success depended upon mobilising the colonial state behind the programme for expansion. In South Africa, geography and economics demanded state sponsorship for the railway-building without which the whole sub-imperial plan would be still-born. Once in the Cape Parliament, Rhodes also grasped the need to win over the Afrikaner members who, under the leadership of Jan Hendrik Hofmeyr, had made the Afrikaner Bond the strongest political force in the Colony. The task seemed difficult. The Bond had emerged from a farmers' protection movement in the Western Cape, opposed to free trade; and from the cultural nationalism of the Dutch-speaking clerical elite hostile to the anglicising secularising effects of commercial growth.[23] In fact, the Bond's antipathy to British influence was surprisingly ambivalent. Afrikaners were prominent in the Cape's legal and professional elite. They prospered with its new diamond wealth and warmed to its parliamentary rule. Like the colonial elites in Quebec (or Bengal), they found much to admire in an imperial system which promised self-government, liberal culture and material progress.

Rhodes played on this ambivalence with astonishing skill. By the mid-1880s, he had repositioned himself not as a British 'imperialist' nor as a Kimberley capitalist but as a Cape Colony patriot. His programme was Cape not British expansion. It was the Cape's claim to the north that he touted, a Cape sub-empire that he wanted to win, as a fair field for 'English' and Afrikaner alike. Nor were Rhodes' motives crudely tactical. In politics as in business his instinct was always fusion. The 'great amalgamator' preferred a merger to an open struggle: rivals should be 'squared' not left to fight a bitter rearguard action. By drawing the Cape Afrikaners into his expansionist project, he hoped to build a 'progressive alliance'. Rural interests and cultural prejudice would be carefully appeased. But new wealth would breed an Anglo-Afrikaner elite loyal to its own parliamentary institutions and to the Imperial crown. Proud of their Cape heritage and of the Colony's growing status, they would share Rhodes' vision of a unified sub-continent and dismiss the Kruger republic as an ethnic cul-de-sac. Kimberley and Stellenbosch (the seedbed of Afrikaner culture) would unite to build a 'Greater Cape'.

Between 1888 and 1890, the stalemate of South African politics began to break up. Rhodes was accumulating wealth and power with sensational rapidity. In 1888, with his close partner, the financial 'genius' Alfred Beit, he centralised diamond production in a single great combine, De Beers Consolidated. Rhodes did not have full control – especially over the London partners – but at the South African end his influence was supreme.[24] De Beers became the treasure-chest from which he could fund his political activity and his schemes of sub-imperial expansion.[25] It helped provide collateral for the new share issues, which Rhodes could turn to his own profit and from which he could reward patrons, friends and allies. In the same year, Rhodes and another partner, Charles Rudd, persuaded the Ndebele ruler Lobengula to grant the right to prospect for minerals in his kingdom. This was the notorious Rudd Concession, largely paid for in rifles. Rhodes now had a long lead over his competitors for the hinterland beyond the Limpopo and the goldfields it was thought to conceal. But, before he could invade Zambezia and build a private empire in the North – the first stage of the 'Greater Cape' – he needed an imperial licence to sanction political control by his agents on the spot. He also needed the promise of imperial support against any rival territorial claim by Portugal (which regarded modern Zimbabwe as the natural hinterland of Mozambique), Germany or the Transvaal republic. He needed a charter.

Rhodes came to England in 1889, a little-known colonial businessman. He departed (with his charter) as the great white hope of speculative investors and imperial enthusiasts. It was the turning point of his career. He had become a promethean figure in imperial politics:

the supreme sub-imperialist who combined local power with ready access to wealth and influence at home. Rhodes outmanoeuvred his doubters and critics (including the Colonial Office) and squared every interest. A merger was arranged with his most dangerous rivals.[26] The idea of a chartered company to prospect for gold excited the City. The 'South Africa Committee' of parliamentarians, philanthropists and missionary interests, chaired by Joseph Chamberlain, was expected to resist the charter as a colonial land-grab. But Rhodes captured two of its key members for his Company, including the ardent imperialist Albert Grey[27] and won it over by a promise to help the struggling missionaries on Lake Nyasa. One of his henchmen, Cawston, had the effrontery to claim that the charter was intended to benefit the Zambezian blacks.[28] With the eager support of the High Commissioner in Cape Town, Rhodes now carried all before him. To Alfred Milner, then private secretary to the Chancellor of the Exchequer, it seemed obvious that, like it or not, northern expansion would make Rhodes more amenable to imperial control.[29] To the prime minister, Lord Salisbury, his promise of a British sphere in Central Africa at no public cost was a strategic windfall in hard times.

It was an extraordinary coup. Rhodes had made his own luck. But he also deftly exploited a political climate without which he might have needed much more. Anxiety over Ireland, the vulnerability of Egypt, and the global pressure exerted by Britain's imperial rivals created a jittery mood, especially among Liberal Unionists (like Milner and Chamberlain) who were attracted to ideas of imperial federation with the settlement colonies. To these uneasy imperialists Rhodes offered a winning combination of imperial patriotism and colonial expansion, uninhibited by the financial and diplomatic fetters they found so galling. Garnished with speculative profit, it was a seductive version of the imperial idea. Indeed, Rhodes' campaign for the charter and the constituency of admirers he created formed the basis for the public sympathy in Britain on which he (and Milner) were to draw so heavily after 1897. In the meantime, Rhodes returned to South Africa to make his paper empire real. His 'Pioneer Column', paid for by De Beers, trekked into Mashonaland and founded 'Salisbury' – now Harare. In the Cape, Rhodes was now the undisputed supremo. 1890 was his *annus mirabilis*. He was already managing director of De Beers, the greatest fount of wealth in the Colony, and of the British South Africa Company, over whose domain in Zambezia (soon 'Rhodesia') his authority was absolute. Now he became Cape premier as well.

Over the next four years Rhodes used this remarkable portfolio of political, financial and territorial power to drive forward his aim of Cape supremacy and strangle the Transvaal's independence. His system seemed unstoppable. In the Cape, his alliance with the Bond was sealed by the artful distribution of his company shares at par. Rhodes made no secret of his dislike of Downing Street. This was the usual language of British settler politicians from New Zealand to British Columbia: but it was soothing syrup to Afrikaner opinion. Rhodes identified himself with the Cape Dutch origins of South Africa's 'manifest destiny' as a 'white man's country'. His enthusiasm for Cape Dutch architecture, his purchase and restoration of Groote Schuur, his interest in agriculture, and his Afrikaner associates were all a reflection of his half-formed project for an Anglo-Afrikaner 'middle nation' within a wider Britannic confederacy.[30] As Cape premier, Rhodes oversaw the extension of the Colony's railway to the Rand, the great inland market. As the uncrowned king of Rhodesia, he approved the Ndbele war of 1893 by which white rule was somewhat precariously extended from Mashonaland to Matabeleland. He pressed for the hand-over of Bechuanaland to the Chartered Company as the land bridge from the Cape to its new inland empire. He made an abortive attempt to buy Delagoa Bay and also the railway that Kruger was building to the last accessible harbour outside British territory.

But, by 1894, it was becoming clear that he had over-reached himself. There was a critical weakness in his grand geopolitical design. Seizing Rhodesia had been meant to give him a stranglehold on the Boer republics. A great gold reef in the Chartered territory would draw in a torrent of capital and migrants from Britain, boosting the trade and revenues of the Cape. It would drive home the lesson that it was futile to stand out against a Cape-led South Africa. Kimberley would revenge Majuba. This was Rhodes' gamble: but it did not come off. By 1894, he knew that there was no great reef to be found: Rhodesia would not eclipse the Rand.[31] Nor could Rhodes and his allies exert economic control over Kruger by their grip on the Rand.

The Rand in fact was Rhodes' nemesis. Preoccupied by the struggle for De Beers, Rhodes had failed to foresee the Rand's vast potential. His company, 'Goldfields', was only one among several large mining houses that emerged in the 1890s. Rhodes lacked the capital to attempt the great amalgamation he achieved at Kimberley. Nor did the Rand lend itself to the tactics that had worked well with diamonds. It was easy for his rivals to raise money in London. The violent fluctuations in the value of shares, and the scale of speculative activity, ruled out the 'squaring' of interests, Rhodes' favoured technique. Nor would Kruger allow the commercial free rein that Rhodes enjoyed in the Cape. Instead, his sale of concessions, like the dynamite monopoly, his control of the railways and the black labour supply, and his canny restriction of political rights, kept the gold-mining houses in a state of grudging dependence. Rhodes' best hope was to use his connections with the 'Corner House', the largest mining house on the Rand and controlled by two of his partners in De Beers, Wernher and Beit, to foment opposition to Kruger. The danger was that the mining interests and the immigrant population – the Uitlanders or foreigners – would prefer an independent republic to domination by Rhodes' Cape conglomerate. This was what made the defeat of Kruger so urgent; this was why his overthrow had to be staged by rebels loyal to Rhodes.[32]

The Jameson Raid in December 1895 was Rhodes' attempt to seize control of the anti-Kruger movement in Johannesburg and mastermind the transfer of power in the Transvaal. Rhodes hoped to exploit the tacit sympathy of the Imperial government in London for Uitlander grievances and its willingness to intervene once Kruger's authority had been successfully challenged.[33] Jameson, Rhodes' closest henchman, was meant to arrive in Johannesburg in a show of solidarity with the local rebellion, but really to stamp on it Rhodes' authority. A complicit High Commissioner at the Cape would rule in his favour. By a dazzling coup, rather than slow attrition, the grand design would be forged. Notoriously, everything went wrong. The Johannesburg conspirators were tardy and disorganised, so that Jameson's 'raid' was recklessly premature. Kruger was forewarned. Jameson's force was no match for the Boer commandos who caught up with him before he reached the city. The High Commissioner and Imperial government (both implicated in the original plan) disavowed Rhodes' crude filibuster. The Johannesburg conspirators were rounded up, tried and imprisoned (commuting their death sentences cost Rhodes £300,000).[34] Worst of all, Rhodes' Afrikaner allies in the Cape whom he had kept in ignorance (believing perhaps that they would favour the end while loathing the means), turned against him in rage. His premiership collapsed. The 'Colossus' had suffered a huge reversal of fortune. Far from succumbing to the Rhodesian juggernaut, Kruger now seemed stronger than ever. His internal position was secure. And, after Rhodes' treachery, he could be sure that the Cape Afrikaners would block any move to coerce him again. As the competition between rival imperialisms reached its climax in Afro-Asia, Kruger's chances of wriggling out of the British sphere seemed better than ever.

The decision for war, 1896–9

In his bid to pull Kruger down and absorb the Transvaal, Rhodes had wanted to keep the Imperial government at arm's length, while exploiting the authority of its agent (the High Commissioner) in his intended coup on the Rand. Rhodes intended to remake South Africa to his design not Downing Street's. To this aim the disastrous outcome of the Jameson Raid was a massive but not fatal setback. It forced Rhodes and his local allies into partnership with the Imperial Factor since London alone had the power to *coerce* Kruger. But whether London would be willing to do so was another matter entirely.

Indeed, it might have been expected that, after the Jameson Raid, the Imperial government would revert to the policy of disengagement adopted after 1881. Amid suspicion that it was implicated in the Jameson Raid, its influence was weaker than ever. An imperial initiative to promote federation was out of the question. In fact, whatever its inclinations, the Salisbury cabinet was drawn deeper and deeper into the thicket of South African politics. Chamberlain's own prestige was invested heavily in preventing Kruger from exploiting his triumph. Threatening language and a squadron in Delagoa Bay served notice that Britain's *claim* to regional primacy was undiminished. Chamberlain's deputy, Lord Selborne (the prime minister's son-in-law), was imbued with a 'Rhodesian' outlook. His memorandum of March 1896 warning against a secessionist 'United States of South Africa' forming around a cosmopolitan English-speaking Transvaal republic[35] was inspired by the High Commissioner, Sir Hercules Robinson, and derived almost certainly from Rhodes. Nor, for all its absurdity, had the Jameson Raid failed to leave its mark on British policy. The furore over the Parliamentary enquiry into the Raid and indignation over the

Kaiser's congratulatory telegram to Kruger helped to turn the Uitlander grievances into a political issue in Britain and a nagging index of imperial prestige. In South Africa, the ironic legacy of Rhodes' fall had been the deliberate mobilisation of 'English' sentiment in Cape Colony behind a demand for imperial self-assertion against the Transvaal. Cool British detachment from South African affairs was hardly an option.

For Chamberlain, the immediate need was a capable proconsul: to watch Kruger closely against any breach of the Convention, especially the ban on his diplomatic freedom; to press the Uitlanders' case; and to avoid the dependence on Rhodes to which Robinson had succumbed. His choice was Sir Alfred Milner, then chairman of the Board of Inland Revenue. This was not as eccentric as it seemed. Like Chamberlain, Milner was a Liberal Unionist who had rebelled against the Irish Home Rule bill in 1886. He was deeply sympathetic to the idea of closer union between the settlement colonies of 'Greater Britain' to which Chamberlain was privately committed. He shared Chamberlain's concern that a unified 'British South Africa' should form part of this larger imperial association. He had served under Cromer in Egypt (1889–92) and had published an influential defence of the imperial 'mission' there.[36] As a safe pair of hands with wide friendships in both political camps, he enjoyed the prestige to place the government's South African policy on a fresh footing. The question was: what could he do?

To Milner himself, the immediate answer seemed not very much. He would do his best to persuade the Transvaal government down the path of reform, but without drawing in the Imperial government.[37] But the Uitlander franchise was out of the question.[38] The best hope was that the irrepressible growth of Johannesburg would force a change. Part of the difficulty lay in Cape politics where Rhodes' sudden removal had brought confusion. 'At present they are all dwarfs', Milner told his old political mentor, George Goschen, 'except Rhodes who is a really big man but thoroughly untrustworthy.'[39] By this time, Milner had already begun to drift towards the alliance with Rhodes against which Chamberlain had warned him.[40] He had little choice. Rhodes was the 'real' head of the Cape government, and the premier, Sprigg, his mouthpiece. More to the point, for all the disaster of the Jameson Raid, only Rhodes had the means to push forward the grand project which Milner saw as the real purpose of his proconsulship: the unification of British South Africa and the re-absorption of the Transvaal.

The key was the north, Rhodes' private empire in Rhodesia. Foiled on the Rand and frustrated at the Cape, Rhodes' best hope was to speed up Rhodesia's development and build a grand new colony embracing the Bechuanaland Protectorate (then still under imperial control). The Protectorate would be Rhodesia's land bridge to the Cape. As part of 'Greater Rhodesia' it would help surround the Transvaal on two sides. The third stage of Rhodes' plan was to promote the federal union of the Cape, Natal and Greater Rhodesia. Then 'the three combined will bring *peaceful* pressure to bear upon the republics to drive them into a S[outh] African federation'.[41] Milner proposed to fasten imperial policy once more to Rhodes' chariot wheels. But, this time, the 'Colossus' was to be kept on a leash 'unless he is to make a shipwreck of his own ambitions and our permanent interests'. The persistent African risings against Rhodes' Company government cast doubt on his schemes – at least for the moment. It was vital to preserve some imperial control over Rhodesia and to make him wait for the eventual transfer of the Protectorate. 'His projected game is a good game but . . . he is desperately anxious to have another slap at old Kruger by "peaceful means".'[42] As Milner recognised, Rhodes 'was much too strong to be merely used'. His cooperation had to be bought. But his 'Northern' strategy was the only shot in the imperial locker. Milner settled in for the long haul, and a 'qualified success'. 'A united and loyal S[outh] Africa on the Canadian pattern if it ever comes about is a thing of the very distant future', he told one of his oldest and closest friends.[43] But Britain's strategic interests, thought this 'civilian soldier of the Empire' (Milner's self-description), were safe enough: 'I don't mean in the least that I despair of the maintenance of British supremacy.'[44]

Cautious pragmatism was the keynote of an imperial policy which waited on the maturing of Rhodes' schemes. The Transvaal was 'bound to topple', Milner told Asquith, the future prime minister.[45] There was little point taking up the mine-owners' main grievance, the dynamite monopoly imposed by Kruger's government. Scarcely three months later, Milner performed an astonishing u-turn. Now he urged an openly aggressive policy towards the Transvaal, and, in a notorious speech (at Graaff Reinet on 3 March 1898), questioned the loyalty of the Cape Afrikaners to the imperial connection. Milner may have been reacting to Kruger's unexpectedly resounding success in the Transvaal's presidential election in February. He may have been anxious about

Rhodes' grip on Rhodesia. But there was another reason for his harder line. Early in 1898, Rhodes too was switching tactics. With the Parliamentary inquiry into the Jameson Raid behind him, and the black revolt in Rhodesia broken, he was ready to re-enter Cape politics. His old alliance with the Bond was irreparable; but he had a new vehicle. He had become the darling of the 'English' in the towns. In the Cape's Eastern Province, the South African League had been formed to rally loyalty to the Empire and (by a deft association) to Rhodes. In 1897, the League created the 'Progressive' party to campaign for free trade, agrarian improvement and the redistribution of seats – causes carefully identified with imperial loyalty. Before the end of 1897, a private understanding had been reached between the Progressives and Rhodes' own followers.[46] Six days after Milner's speech, Rhodes announced his conversion to the Progressive programme and opened fire on the Bond for its hostility to northern expansion and its resistance to an imperial naval contribution.[47] Rhodes, sneered his bitterest enemy in the Cape, wanted a majority 'not to unify South Africa, but to purchase . . . the Bulawayo railway and . . . that very bad egg Rhodesia'.[48] But Rhodes was also determined to give urban (and 'English') voters a fairer share of seats. His new alliance would bring him the townsmen's vote. With firm control of the Cape Parliament he could tighten the knot round Kruger's neck. Milner had little choice but to follow him.

In fact, throughout 1898, Milner's dependence on Rhodes grew deeper. His own attempt to draw Chamberlain into the struggle for 'reform' in the Transvaal misfired badly. A sharp rebuke arrived from London. Chamberlain had other fish to fry and was preoccupied with the struggle for hinterlands in *West* Africa. At Rhodes' direct request,[49] Milner pleaded for his grandiose scheme to build a new railway beyond the Zambezi and open a vast new northern extension. Britain's strategy in South Africa, he urged, depended upon the gamble of Rhodesia's development. Capital would be attracted by the sheer scale of Rhodes' project; a great new railway empire, pivoted on Bulawayo, would kickstart the Rhodesian economy as a counterpoise to the Transvaal.[50] Two weeks earlier, Milner had warned Rhodes against 'worrying' Chamberlain with this scheme.[51] But in the course of the year the prospects of direct imperial action grew steadily fainter. The British press was distracted by other imperial excitements in the Sudan and China. In South Africa, everything turned upon Rhodes. Chamberlain was anxious to hear about his gold prospects in Rhodesia.[52] The Transvaal was 'in a twitter' about his plans.[53] Redistribution and electoral victory would make Rhodes master of the Cape. His reward might be Bechuanaland.[54] After two years in the wilderness, Rhodes seemed once more near the pinnacle of power.

Rhodes may have calculated that an election victory in the Cape and a third premiership would give him scope for some rapprochement with his erstwhile allies in the Bond. The Cape Afrikaners were as anxious as he to promote South African unity (though not at imperial command) and just as fearful of Kruger's dabblings in great power diplomacy – a vice attributed to his 'Hollander' advisers. With their help, Kruger might yet be overcome. The triumph and the spoils would be his, not Downing Street's. It was perhaps not so much Rhodes' failure as the circumstances of his defeat that made conflict unavoidable. In the Cape elections of 1898, Rhodes had denounced 'Krugerism' and demanded 'equal rights for every white man south of the Zambezi'.[55] But, contrary to most prediction, and despite lavish spending, Rhodes' Progressives were narrowly defeated although winning a majority of votes cast. A Bond ministry took office. Rapprochement went out of the window: a fresh round of 'racial' politics came in at the door. English 'race-sentiment', the stock-in-trade of the South African League, was turned up to whip in the remaining 'English' politicians who had stood out against Rhodes. Rhodes harried the Bond ministry in parliament and out.[56] He pressed for redistribution, northern expansion and federal union. He erected a statue to Van Riebeek, the Dutch founder of Cape Town. Rhodes appealed squarely to Afrikaner misgivings and 'English' resentment at Kruger's refusal of white equality on the Rand.[57] Then, in January 1899, he set off for Britain to rally support, raise fresh capital for his Zambezian railway and negotiate the passage of his telegraph to Cairo through German East Africa.

As he did so, the pan-British rhetoric of loyalty and grievance that he and Milner had unleashed in March 1898 and which had reached a crescendo in October 1898 at last bore fruit on the Rand. Throughout 1898, the quiescence of the Uitlanders had been a source of frustration to Milner. He had made contact with Percy Fitzpatrick, the leading Uitlander politician; but, with the 'old reformers' of 1895 still under ban, political organisation was minimal. The mining companies, who had hopes of economic reform, were reluctant to antagonise the regime on whose goodwill they depended. They had no reason to manipulate Milner: still less to be used by him. But, in December

1898, two events combined to transform Rand politics. The forthcoming expiry of the dynamite monopoly reopened the central issue between the mining houses and the government in Pretoria. Smouldering resentment over the arbitrariness of Boer administration on the Rand came to a head with the murder of an Uitlander, Edgar, by an Afrikaner policeman. The main Uitlander movement, a branch of the South African League, barred from local demonstration, stumbled upon an alternative tactic. It framed a petition to the Crown. The means to link the political struggle on the Rand with imperial sentiment at home and in the Cape – the trick that had eluded Milner – had at last been found. It was a turning point.

In fact, the first Uitlander petition was turned away (to Milner's consternation) by his *locum tenens* in Cape Town. But the Transvaal government now showed open signs of anxiety. In February 1899, it attempted to divide its opponents by negotiating the 'Great Deal' with the mining houses, offering certain commercial concessions and a modest extension of political rights in exchange for a public disavowal by the houses of 'political agitation'.[58] With Milner's encouragement, Fitzpatrick, the vital linkman between the mining houses and the political movement, sabotaged the agreement by premature publicity.[59] Both men calculated that imperial intervention – evident in Chamberlain's renewed protest over the dynamite monopoly and his private warnings to the mining houses against the 'Great Deal' – could be mobilised. In March, the second Uitlander petition (with more than 20,000 signatures) was forwarded to London. Chamberlain had little choice but to accept it, since rebuffing it would have meant repudiating the 'suzerainty' which he had asserted in principle but avoided in practice. By early May it was clear that a new round of imperial pressure would supercharge the complaints of the mining houses and the Uitlanders. Milner's famous despatch likening their treatment to that of a servile class of 'helots'[60] was artfully designed to raise ethnic feeling at home and in South Africa to fever pitch. Behind Milner's populist rhetoric rallied the followers of Rhodes and the League. In Britain, he could rely on a chorus of journalists and lobbies, and here too Rhodes conducted a parallel campaign. Together with Alfred Beit, one of his closest allies, Rhodes heavily subsidised the (Imperial) South Africa Association, founded in 1896 to campaign for the Uitlander cause.[61] In the Transvaal, said *The Times*, was a 'vast number of British subjects whose grievances cannot be denied'. Could

Britain afford to let its protection be seen as 'inefficient against an insignificant Republic'.[62]

Kruger was too old a hand in imperial politics not to see the danger. Rhodes and Milner might 'bounce' the Imperial government into armed intervention before cooler judgment prevailed. By agreeing to meet Milner at Bloemfontein at the end of May 1899 to discuss Uitlander rights, he hoped to appease 'moderate' opinion in Britain and deflate the jingo mood. He probably calculated that a limited extension of the franchise would allow Chamberlain to draw back from confrontation. If so, it was a shrewd estimate. But at Bloemfontein Milner refused to negotiate, insisting upon the vote for Uitlanders of five years' residence and a fixed allocation of seats for the Rand. When Kruger refused, Milner broke off the talks. Chamberlain was furious. British opinion, Selborne (his deputy) warned Milner, was not ready for war. Milner's helot despatch had made less public impact than had been expected: 'we simply cannot force the pace.'[63] Milner was in despair. 'British South Africa had been tuned to concert pitch', he told Selborne. But now Chamberlain was playing for time. 'He seems to me *to wish a patch-up.*' But delay would erode the loyalty and resolution of the Uitlanders and their local supporters: the Transvaal would use it to prepare for war. Unless London was ready to stand firm and to send troop reinforcements to show it meant business, Milner concluded bluntly, he would ask to be removed.[64]

At the eleventh hour it seemed that Kruger was about to repeat his earlier triumphs in 1881 and 1884. Milner and Rhodes could huff and puff. 'English' opinion in the towns could seethe at Boer injustice. Editorials might rage. But, as Milner remarked candidly, Boer commandos with their rifles and horses, backed by the heavy guns that Kruger had been buying, were more than a match for the scattered British garrisons and the unarmed 'English' population. Unless London steeled itself to send an 'expedition' to coerce the Transvaal, Kruger's combination of military and economic strength would steadily tilt the regional balance in his favour. Why then did the Transvaal government not stand firm on Kruger's offer at Bloemfontein and test London's nerve in the way that Milner feared?

In reality, both principals, Kruger and the British cabinet, were more vulnerable than they appeared to the campaign that Rhodes and Milner had orchestrated. Chamberlain's instinct had been to settle. But he was faced with Uitlander hostility to any retreat from Milner's demands at Bloemfontein[65] and with signs of widespread feeling in Britain that the Uitlander cause could not be abandoned.[66] Chamberlain, whose own political ambition was far from sated, was reluctant to alienate his natural supporters. Both he and his cabinet colleagues now saw that anything short of Milner's demands on the franchise issue would count as a failure to assert the supremacy (and uphold the suzerainty) on which they had always insisted. For their part, Kruger and his agile lieutenant, the youthful J. C. Smuts, also realised that some agreement must be reached: to avert the danger of imperial intervention; to ease the threat that 'loyalist' ministries would take office in the Cape and Natal; and to stave off the slump brought by political uncertainty to the Rand. But, in seeking a way out of the franchise dispute, Smuts made a fatal misjudgment.

Smuts was the acceptable reformist face of the Kruger regime. A Cape Afrikaner, Cambridge educated, a passionate admirer of Rhodes before the Raid, Smuts regarded white unity as the most urgent political need in South Africa. 'We want a great South African nationality', he declared in 1895.[67] It was the deeper struggle of whites against blacks that mattered most. Left unplacated, Uitlander grievances would divide the whites and invite imperial meddling – the real threat to white supremacy. But Smuts was determined to secure a *quid pro quo* for conceding the Uitlander vote. Britain, he insisted, must give up its claim to influence the Transvaal's internal affairs: 'the suzerainty was pure nonsense' and should tacitly lapse.[68] Perhaps he believed that the Salisbury government, with so many commitments abroad, would shrink from war for a phrase, once the substance of Uitlander demands had been met. He may well have assumed that neither Kruger nor the Transvaal Raad (assembly) would accept a one-sided bargain. Whatever its motive, Smuts' move broke the iron rule that Kruger had carefully observed in his dealings with the British: not to challenge openly the provisions of the 1884 Convention in which Britain's diplomatic primacy was clearly stated. Smuts' condition was understood in London as a bid for diplomatic freedom.[69] It was confirmation that British supremacy was really at stake, not merely the detail of the Uitlander franchise: Kruger's real motive was at last laid bare. Negotiations collapsed. Early in September 1899, the cabinet authorised the troop reinforcements for which Milner had been begging and began to ponder an ultimatum. Before they could send it, Kruger despatched his own demanding the troops' recall. On 11 October, the war began.

The causes of the South African War have been endlessly debated. On one side were those who saw the policy of Milner and Chamberlain as a form of economic imperialism. There were several versions of this argument. One maintained that capitalism – the Rand-lords – had manipulated 'imperialism' – Milner and the Imperial government – into imposing their programme on Kruger to the point of war. Another that Kruger's 'pre-modern' republic was intolerable to British leaders and especially to Milner for whom capitalism was an indispensable part of modernity.[70] A third that British policy was driven most of all by the need to ensure the flow of Transvaal gold to London to support the gold reserves of the Bank of England. None of these arguments has withstood close scrutiny or mustered convincing documentary evidence. The Randlords, while bitterly opposed to aspects of Kruger's regime, showed no inclination to fish for trouble in London and preferred to settle their differences amicably with the Transvaal government. Kruger was much more amenable to the needs of the mining industry than was assumed by writers who saw the war as the clash between modern capitalism and a pre-modern state.[71] No evidence has been found that in the critical period before the war the supply of gold became an issue for British policy-makers. Milner himself, while contemptuous of Kruger's misgovernment and corruption, showed no desire, even in the most private correspondence, to annex the Transvaal for commercial reasons, let alone to go to war to replace Kruger with an oligarchy of Randlords.

The result has been to confirm the verdict pronounced more than forty years ago by the shrewdest analysts of late-Victorian imperialism. The British went to war, concluded Gallagher and Robinson, to defend their regional supremacy and its geopolitical corollary, control of the Cape and the sea route to India.[72] The sudden economic transformation of the Transvaal mattered not because it created new wealth to annex but because it gave Kruger the means to assert fuller independence and, sooner or later, to drag the rest of South Africa after him out of the British *imperium*. The stalemate between the coastal colonies and the highveld interior (the reason for the persistent failure of confederation) was about to be resolved in favour of Kruger's all-powerful gold-state. In the struggle to contain the secondary effects of the Transvaal's economic revolution, Milner had rehearsed every grievance, inflamed every issue and recruited every ally – until his relentless alarmism eventually drove home the threat Kruger posed to British supremacy. But what weighed most with British ministers, and especially with Lord Salisbury, the master of *Realpolitik*, was neither the economic stake British interests had amassed nor the rights of the Uitlanders – those 'people whom we despise'. It was the necessity of preserving, in more arduous conditions and by more vigorous methods, the old mid-Victorian supremacy in a vital strategic sphere.

This remains the most convincing account of the *ultimate* objective of British intervention in September 1899. But it does not do justice to the wider causes of the war, nor to the pressures that beat upon an uncertain cabinet. What made South Africa the sternest test of late-Victorian imperialism was the collision of three political forces of exceptional intensity. The first was the enormous geopolitical investment the British had made in the exclusion of any rival great power south and east of the Zambezi. It was not only a question of safeguarding the Cape. The ink was scarcely dry on the diplomatic map of Africa and the partition of China and the Middle East was on the cards. The surrender of British primacy in a region where their interests were so important and of such long standing would have implied an astonishing loss of confidence. Salisbury's sovereign cure for geopolitical uncertainty – the careful demarcation of spheres – would have been jettisoned, with unforeseeable consequences. It was inevitable, once the argument over Uitlander rights turned into a dispute about paramountcy, that Salisbury would insist on Kruger's submission. The 'old' British interest in the Cape had become part of a 'new' British stake in the peaceful partition of the world.

Salisbury's misfortune was that the three-masted barque (Salisbury was fond of maritime metaphors) of his partition diplomacy was struck amidships by a state-building project of unusual strength. Until the 1880s the Transvaal had been a ramshackle frontier settlement, an African Costaguana. After Britain's failed annexation, Kruger's personal rule imposed the rudiments of statehood. The discovery and exploitation of gold after 1886 was widely expected to rot the foundations of what Milner was to call a 'mediaeval race oligarchy'. Immigrants would swamp the old burghers; civilised commerce would displace their predatory pastoralism; Cape liberalism would discredit their crude trekker republicanism. Like the Trojan horse, the Rand would conceal an invading army ready at the signal to capture the Boer citadel and open its gates to British influence. Instead, Kruger skilfully utilised the bonanza of gold to reinforce his Afrikaner state. The Afro-Asian world was littered with failures in the 'race against time' to modernise before conquest: Kruger meant to be a winner. He was helped by the distinctive political economy of the goldfields. The Rand swelled his revenues, but remained a geographical and social enclave. It was easily contained, as was shown by the Jameson Raid and its aftermath. It depended heavily upon the state for its (black) labour supply and for transport. Its white population – many of them transients[73] – could be treated as restless aliens or guest-workers. Mining revenues and commercial prosperity served not (in the short term) to liberalise Kruger's state but to enlarge the patronage at his disposal and consolidate a loyal burgher elite. They also paid for the arsenal of heavy weapons to supplement the citizen commando. Under these conditions, to be a landlocked state in the South African interior was no longer the handicap it had originally seemed. Guarded by geography and the passive sympathy of the Cape Afrikaners, Kruger's South African republic had fashioned an exceptionally favourable geopolitical niche in a world of imperialisms.

It is at best uncertain whether Salisbury's government would have had the will, the means or the opportunity to throttle Kruger's quiet bid for independence but for the intervention of a third force. It was also doubtful whether the Imperial Factor alone was a match for the Transvaal whites, any more than it had been in 1880. But, since the 1880s, the political landscape of the sub-continent had been transformed and not just by gold. Rhodes had outflanked the Transvaal and checked its expansion. By astute publicity and prodigal largesse he harnessed the speculative frenzy of the 1890s to the idea of British expansion in Southern Africa. His disaster in 1896 was a check, but by that time his efforts to strangle Kruger had begun to mobilise new and unexpected support. Jameson's fiasco had roused an ethnic 'British' movement in the Cape which soon spread to the Rand. Its leaders there, with little prospect of imperial deliverance, looked to the Cape for support. Building a local constituency was uphill work. Many miners were short-term migrants with little interest in local politics. Many suspected the League to be a front organisation for the mine-owners, a suspicion Kruger tried to encourage. But, by the middle of 1899, the Edgar case and the new tactic of petitioning the Crown, had given the League far greater credibility as the voice of the Uitlander.[74]

The League's success among British settlers in South Africa was symptomatic of a wider late-Victorian phenomenon. 'Britannic' nationalism was fiercest where the claim of British communities to social and cultural predominance was challenged: by Metis, East Europeans,

French Canadians, Catholic Irishmen, Chinese migrants or Transvaal Boers. It was fostered by the growing closeness of educational and sporting connections, the new swiftness of communication, the growth of the press, the convergence between the urban society of the overseas British and their counterparts at home. It was no coincidence that the Wanderers club in Johannesburg, with its fierce assertion of British sporting values, was closely identified with the League and the venue for its meetings when permitted.[75] The League's appeal was to an injured sense of ethnic and cultural superiority. At a meeting in June 1899, wrote one Uitlander, the League's Transvaal secretary, Thomas Dodds, 'was cheered as . . . I have never heard any man cheered before, particularly at his words "we appeal to Caesar". He knows well the pride of race – of which thank God I still have a small portion left in me.'[76] Dodds' message was as obvious as it was popular: the Uitlanders were Roman citizens whose emperor would come to chastise the barbarians. Fitzpatrick's account of Uitlander suffering *The Transvaal From Within*, circulated at the same time in Britain, embodied a similar appeal.[77]

The Transvaal government was bound to suspect that the League was not only the voice of British 'race patriotism' but the tool of Rhodes' ambition. Despite his electoral defeat in 1898, Rhodes' hand was seen everywhere. To the Transvaal League he was its ultimate leader.[78] Rhodes' formula of 'equal rights for all white men' inspired the League's campaign for the franchise and spearheaded its appeal in Britain.[79] Rhodes kept in close touch with the campaign waged at home (and with his help) by the South Africa Association's campaign.[80] To the Transvaal Boers, the 'great amalgamator' had become the great manipulator. 'Rhodes presses the button and the figure works' was how Fitzpatrick described their fear.[81] As a result, the Transvaal leaders were anxious to forestall imperial intervention but also to break the alliance between the Uitlanders and Rhodes symbolised by the League. In his negotiations with Fitzpatrick, the Uitlander spokesman in March 1899, Smuts pressed him to repudiate the connection with the League in the Cape. Fitzpatrick's reply was uncompromising. The League, he told Smuts (or so he claimed in a speech), 'represent[s] a very large section in South Africa which section has been very friendly to us'. To his Uitlander audience he added: 'They [i.e. the Cape 'English'] are my people and I (for one) shall not turn my back on them . . . They are our people and we will stick to them.'[82]

The conclusion seemed obvious. The Uitlander leadership would use the franchise to widen the scope for Imperial influence. The League would take its orders from Kimberley. Kruger's dilemma was acute. As we have seen, he needed to defuse the feverish mood Milner and Rhodes had created and head off an Imperial coup. But he had to avoid a concession that would expose him to the 'salami tactics' of which Chamberlain, Milner and Rhodes were suspected. Smuts and Kruger may both have believed that the inherent strength of their strategic niche would deter Imperial aggression as long as they avoided the outright provocation of British opinion. Smuts' offer was designed to remove the excuse for Imperial intervention now and its warrant in future. The end of suzerainty would block future petitions to the Crown and erode the sense of common identity on which Milner and Rhodes had played so successfully. But this attempt to outflank the Britannic nationalism he distrusted roused the deepest fear of all in British leaders. A cabinet cynical of Uitlander grievances united round the threat to British supremacy that Smuts had let slip.

Imperial supremacy, Transvaal state-building and Britannic nationalism were a volatile mixture. What made them explosive was the extreme uncertainty created by the speed of South Africa's economic transformation. It was widely assumed that the pace of change would increase. The Transvaal would be richer and stronger. But it could also be swamped by a flood-tide of migrants. The Afrikaner state might dominate the region – or be drowned in the attempt. Yet it was only in the last months before the war that the issue seemed so stark. For all the efforts of Milner, the great impresario of imperial politics, there is little sign before July 1899 that British ministers were impressed by his apocalyptic vision of a united Afrikanerdom and a vanished supremacy. Chamberlain may have shared Milner's hopes for a new dominion of 'British South Africa'. But he had no idea how to achieve it. Instead, it was the insurgent force of Britannic nationalism on the Rand and in the Cape which exposed the race for power and brought Kruger and Smuts at last to their desperate remedy.

A British South Africa?

The decision by Kruger and Steyn, the Orange Free State president, to launch a pre-emptive attack upon the British may have smacked of desperation, but it was not uncalculated. Smuts had made much of Britain's strategic weaknesses: her multiple commitments; the chance of interference by her imperial rivals; the restlessness of colonial populations everywhere.[83] Military intervention in South Africa would come at a high price for a far-flung empire. Kruger's reputation had been made by his skilful adaptation of South Africa's peculiar geopolitics in 1880–1. For both men, it was tempting to believe that the same combination of geographical remoteness and the political sympathy of Cape Afrikanerdom would stop the Imperial coercion of the republics in its tracks. In fact, the Boer leaders intended to make London's task even harder. By moving first, they aimed to capture Durban (the nearest port from which the Transvaal could be invaded) and Kimberley, the great inland centre of the Cape. With these in their hands, the Boers would hold the strategic initiative. Faced with a long war to battle their way into the South African interior, Salisbury and Chamberlain would begin to see reason. The result would be not the surrender that Milner demanded but a new convention.

They were too optimistic. The invasion of Natal was indecisive and Kimberley withstood their siege. The humiliating defeats they inflicted on British troops in the dreadful 'Black Week' of December 1899 created alarm and anger in Britain not indifference or resignation. Twenty years earlier, the interior could be abandoned after Majuba. But, in 1899, the fate of Kimberley, Rhodesia and the Rand itself all turned on victory; so did Britain's reputation as a military power. The response was a steady build-up of military strength and a crushing advance that gradually overwhelmed the Boer armies. By the end of 1900, the Boer capitals had been occupied, the Rand brought under Imperial rule, and the republics annexed to the British Crown.

The Boers' collapse in the face of British military power was a brilliant vindication of the hopes of Milner and Rhodes. But it was also a mirage. By early 1901, it was plain that the Boer commandos intended to fight a war much more to their taste than the sieges and set-pieces in which they had been worsted. In the new guerrilla conflict that stretched from the Transvaal to Cape Colony, mobility, veldcraft and local sympathy made them more than a match for the Imperial forces sent to hunt them down. Far from disintegrating with the departure of the 'Kruger gang' (Kruger had escaped to Europe), Afrikaner patriotism was strengthened by comradeship and the racial bitterness of a total war. As the guerrilla struggle intensified, the Boer War became a civil war.[84] Ten thousand Cape Afrikaners, subjects of the Crown, turned rebel and joined the commandos. More than 50,000 'loyalists' were mobilised against them.[85] Several thousand 'poor white' Afrikaners in the republics changed sides to fight for the British as 'National Scouts'.[86] Black communities seized the moment to recover lost lands.[87] Hundreds, perhaps thousands, of blacks and (mixed race) coloureds, serving as British auxiliaries, or suspected of British sympathies, were murdered by Boer commandos.[88] The rural economy of the highveld was devastated by British farm-burning, while the terrible mortality (both white and black) of the civilian prison 'concentration' camps sowed a tradition of ethnic martyrdom among Afrikaners.

On the British side, as the 'expedition' that Milner had first imagined turned into a long war, public sympathy began to flag. Marching to Pretoria was one thing. A messy, inconclusive war of attrition, punctuated by defeats and compromised by 'barbarism' was quite another. The eagerness of British leaders for peace was sharpened by the sense of strategic vulnerability on which Smuts had counted. With their army and reserves tied down in South Africa, and a long oceanic supply line to guard, ministers could only hope that no emergency arose in the defence of India or of British interests in the ethnic cauldron of the Near East. The crisis in China over the Boxer Rebellion of 1900 and the threat that a partition would follow was a brusque reminder that a long war in South Africa was a strategic luxury that London could ill afford. Kitchener, who had taken over as commander-in-chief in South Africa when Roberts went home, was willing to make peace with the Boers for little more than recognition of British sovereignty[89] – a condition they rejected at the Middelburg negotiations of March 1901. It was only after a further year of war, with no hope of victory or of help from abroad, and amid the rising fear that their rural society might be permanently damaged, that the Boer leaders agreed at Vereeniging in May 1902 to give up the struggle.[90]

The terms of what was called significantly a 'treaty' bore all the hallmarks of a truce, not an outright British victory. The Boers surrendered their claim to independence. But, in return, they were promised that self-government (under the Crown) would be quickly restored. They kept their weapons. A substantial sum was granted to make good the damage the war had caused. And, in deference to the political traditions of the Afrikaner republics, they were not required to adopt the 'colour-blind' franchise of the Cape. With an amiable cynicism the question of whether anyone but whites should be granted the vote was deferred until the return of (white) self-government.[91] This was the fragile constitutional platform on which Milner now tried to build a united dominion of 'British South Africa', and bury forever the remnants of 'Krugerism'. The political omens could hardly have been worse. War weariness in Britain made further coercion of the Boers unlikely. The Boers themselves had preserved their political solidarity and their leaders had avoided a discreditable surrender. It was clear from early on that a determined effort would be needed to force them into the political mould that Milner had in mind. Three years of war had adjusted the old sub-continental balance of power, but not overthrown it.

For Milner, the war was to be the crucible of a new British South Africa. His immediate aim was to hold the ring until a new British majority (among the whites) was ready to govern. Ideally, he thought, a new federal parliament should be created first, to prevent the return of self-rule from reviving the old divisions. He was also determined to suspend the Cape Parliament, with its large Bond contingent, until his federal scheme was well under way.[92] Secondly, he planned a large influx of British settlement, much of it meant for the land. The settlers would dilute the rural Afrikaners, and open up the fastnesses that were as impenetrable to British influence, as Milner later told Selborne, as Kamchatka, the darkest corner of Russia's Asian empire.[93] Thirdly, to create the right conditions for immigration and federation, he was eager to revive the economy as quickly as possible, especially the gold mines. The Rand was the engine-room of the new South Africa: without its rapid recovery, Milner's own plans would be so much waste paper.

Milner realised from the beginning that his programme depended upon the support of the 'English' whose race patriotism he and Rhodes had worked to arouse before the war. To suspend the Cape constitution, he counted on Rhodes' support and that of his allies in the Progressive party and the South African League.[94] He looked to Rhodes and his Randlord friends to prime the pump of land settlement. They were to buy land discreetly in the ex-republics ready for sale to British settlers – a plan of which Rhodes himself was an ardent supporter[95] and on which a significant part of his estate would be spent.[96] Milner's real hope was that the war had transformed the English into a united community of 'British South Africans', the dominant element in his imagined dominion, 'a united self-governing South

Africa wh[ich] shall be British in its political complexion'.[97] It was the loyalists, he told Chamberlain, who best understood the point of the war. 'They are among the most devoted adherents of the Imperial cause', and were convinced that 'British supremacy and . . . one political system from Cape Town to the Zambezi is . . . the only salvation for men of their own race as well as for others'.[98] It was they who had grasped, far better than opinion at home, that there should be no compromise peace that permitted the recovery of Afrikaner national feeling. In the new state that Milner envisaged, the Uitlander meek would inherit the earth. With its British institutions, British civil service, British settlers on the land, British ownership of the mines, a British majority among whites,[99] and English as the language of education and government, the Afrikaners would be faced with a stark choice. They could choose to assimilate to the new South Africa, or retreat into impoverished rural isolation on the *platteland* as the stranded relics of a failed culture. Milner even planned a local colonial army, mainly English in manpower, to neutralise the joker in South African politics: the threat of an armed Afrikaner rebellion.[100] Thus the South African English would make up for the flabbiness of opinion at home. The South African League would become a 'national' movement, gluing the 'English together behind a single programme'.[101] Even if the Cape remained stubbornly Afrikaner in sympathy, mining and commerce would make the Transvaal British. 'A great Johannesburg . . . means a British Transvaal', said Milner.[102] The new Transvaal would be the 'stronghold' that British influence had always lacked in South Africa.[103]

The Milnerite vision was an imperial fantasy. The local triumph of Britannic nationalism, on which he had counted, was postponed indefinitely. For all his energy, Milner could not transcend the racial dynamic of white South African society and the limits it placed (as so often before) on the imperial initiative and proconsular power. The core of Milner's plan was a tide of British migration to reverse its old deficit. In a decade when emigration from Britain reached its secular peak, Milner's needs were modest. But his hopes were crushed, in part by the depth of the post-war depression (which discouraged immigrants with capital) but most of all by the great fact of a black majority – a low-wage workforce whose exploitation had already turned thousands of unskilled 'Europeans' (the South African term for whites) into the 'poor white problem' that haunted South African politics for a generation or more. It was this black majority that (by a cruel irony) guarded Afrikanerdom against an influx of British. Worse still, the more that Milner struggled to impose his programme, the more he united the Afrikaners and (bitter twist) divided the English. The first sign of this was the hostility of some English politicians in the Cape (including Sprigg, the prime minister) to suspending the constitution. With Rhodes' death in March 1902, before the war ended, the Cape Progressives were rudderless[104] and disunited. 'The party is rotten to the core', wrote its chief organiser.[105] No English Cape politician could fill Rhodes' shoes. In the Transvaal, Milner's 'stronghold', the situation was no better. There the Progressive leaders, George Farrar and Percy Fitzpatrick, were closely identified with the Randlords, whose prime aim was to drive down the cost of mine labour. Their alliance with Milner to delay self-government and 'solve' the labour problem affronted the tenets of Britannic nationalism. For, at the Randlords' behest, Milner proposed to bring in indentured labour from China to kick-start recovery. 'Lord Milner is our salvation', wrote Lionel Phillips, head of the largest mining house on the Rand.[106] The result was uproar. 'Chinese slavery' offended humanitarian feeling in Britain. Much more dangerously, it roused the fear of English labour on the Rand that it would be displaced by 'Asiatics' – the same kind of fear that lay behind 'White Australia'. It now suspected Milner's motives for delaying self-government and found common cause with the Afrikaner campaign to end direct rule. The racial bond uniting whites against blacks, Indians or Chinese was much too strong for the Imperial loyalism or British race patriotism on which Milner had counted so heavily.

By 1905, Milner's time was running out. Against the discontent of both English and Afrikaners, he needed strong backing from London. But Balfour's government was falling apart. Chamberlain had resigned in 1903 (over tariff reform) and war had broken out in the Unionist party. With the Liberals reunited behind the defence of free trade and against 'Chinese slavery' – Milner's gift to the opposition – their return to office seemed certain. When they did, guessed Milner, they would tear up his policy root and branch.[107] Liberal dislike of the Randlords, their sympathy for white labour, and their ear to English as well as Afrikaner demands for self-rule would sweep away what remained of Milnerite state-building. Before that could happen, Milner himself had resigned, and the emergence of the new Afrikaner party, Het Volk, under Louis Botha and Jan Smuts signalled the end of his hope that a British Transvaal would make a 'British South Africa'. Instead, the prompt concession of responsible government by the incoming Liberals brought Boer governments to power in the Orange Free State and (with the help of English voters) Transvaal by 1907. With the prospect of tension between the mining industry and its new political masters over non-white labour,[108] the discord between the South African states over their share of railway and customs revenue, and the furious row over Natal's repression of a black uprising in 1906,[109] the familiar cycle of South African politics seemed once more in full swing. After a brief frenzy of activity (as in 1878–81), Imperial influence had shrivelled in a winter of colonial discontent.

This prognosis proved too gloomy. It was easy to see the Transvaal movement under the two 'bitter-ender' generals as a portent of a revived 'Krugerism'. There was, Fitzpatrick had warned in 1904, a 'very powerful, silent, solid, organised party against us... [T]he Boers are politically irreconcilable... and will remain so until we completely and permanently outnumber them.'[110] In reality, Botha and Smuts were convinced that only by an alliance with the 'moderate English sections' could they hope to defeat the 'money power' of the Progressive leaders.[111] They were determined to prevent the 'race' card being used to rally the English vote, as Rhodes and Milner had used it before the war. Despite the Randlords' fears, they were much too cautious to risk the mining economy by imposing the all-white labour policy urged by labour leaders.[112] Far from adopting the linguistic and cultural nationalism of the Afrikaner leaders in the Cape and Free State, or championing the rural *platteland* against the Rand, the Het Volk government was careful to conciliate both English capital and English labour, in case their reunion let loose the power that had brought down Kruger's republic.

More to the point, both Botha and Smuts were in favour of South African union. Not the united British South Africa under English control that Milner had wanted, but a union nonetheless. Botha had deduced from the war that there was no room for two peoples and two flags in the sub-continent: 'let us... have one government... let us now leave the past', he had told Fitzpatrick in 1902.[113] Botha may have reasoned that, after the war, the Transvaal Afrikaners would not be able to hold their own. Even with self-government, they would face a surge of English numbers and influence brought by the growth of the Rand. For Smuts, the case for union was even more urgent. He was, after all, a Cape Afrikaner and an early supporter of Rhodes. After 1902, he was as convinced as ever that white unity was imperative in the face of the 'native problem'.[114] The fragility of white power on the African continent obsessed Smuts all his life. But, like other Afrikaners, Smuts had a second, complementary, purpose. For him, the gravest threat to white unity and supremacy came from imperial interference: dividing the whites with its siren call of race and imperial loyalty; imposing the prejudices of missionaries and humanitarians. Union would squeeze out the influence that the Imperial government exerted through the High Commissioner, end the Imperial claim to be the trustee of the black majority, and install a 'national' government with the status and prestige of the Canadian, Australian and New Zealand dominions.

It was far from clear that early union along these lines would get London's support. In Milner's terms, it was premature. But Milner's successor took a different view. Selborne had been Milner's old ally at the Colonial Office in the prelude to war. But he arrived in South Africa (in 1905) after five years at the Admiralty. He knew at first hand the strategic anxieties behind the Anglo-Japanese alliance of 1902, and the entente made with France in 1904. His view of Boer politics was also much more optimistic than Milner's. Krugerism was finished, he insisted. Commerce and education were dispelling the stagnation on which it depended.[115] Botha was a 'Tory' whose ideas were 'big' and who depended on English votes.[116] His views on education, railways and agriculture were really like Milner's.[117] Far from seeing the Transvaal under Botha as a threat to British interests, Selborne saw it as the engine of progress for the whole of South Africa. Union was vital to economic development (by breaking down differences over tariffs and railways). Economic development would draw more British migrants. More British migrants would speed the advance of modernity, dilute Afrikaner solidity and encourage Botha's non-racial politics. By an indirect route, Milner's great goal of 'British South Africa' would be reached after all.[118]

Selborne had a second reason to press union forward. The real danger to Britain's influence, so he began to argue, was the gulf between white opinion in South Africa and radicalism at home. With the Liberal triumph at the 1906 election, the radical phalanx in the House of Commons was pressing for change in India and Egypt as well as South Africa, where Liberal attacks on Natal (over its treatment of the Zulu rising in 1906) were fiercely resented.[119] The radicals would soon alienate the South African English as well as the Afrikaners.[120] But closer union would keep the radicals' trouble-making out of South Africa, and pave the way towards the grander aim of Imperial Federation, to which Selborne, like Milner and Chamberlain, was deeply committed. The 'Selborne Memorandum', issued ostensibly at the request of the Cape prime minister (the rehabilitated Jameson, Rhodes' political heir), was a coded call to arms for white unity against an overbearing metropole.[121] Selborne's 'kindergarten' promoted the federal idea in a propaganda campaign. Selborne's own contribution was to push the divided and leaderless English (Jameson was no Rhodes)[122] towards a union which (to some Transvaal Progressives) exchanged the distant hope of a 'British' Transvaal for the immediate certainty of an Afrikaner South Africa.[123] With the local consensus on union (not federation) at the Durban convention in 1908, Selborne's colonial bandwagon overcame all resistance in London. The South Africa Act of 1909 removed Imperial control over internal affairs, including 'native' rights. Its only concession to Liberal unease was the exclusion (temporary, so it was thought) of the 'High Commission territories' of Basutoland (Lesotho), Bechuanaland (Botswana) and Swaziland from the new dominion. In 1910, a (mainly) Afrikaner ministry took office in Pretoria. Imperial policy became 'trust Botha'.

It was a strange inconclusive finale to the greatest crisis of late-Victorian imperialism. But it was also a sign that the British connection was bound to depend on the scale and vigour of its local bridgehead. For much of the nineteenth century, the undecided struggle between whites and blacks for the South African interior had given significant leverage to the Imperial Factor and strengthened its grip on the coastal colonies. After the setback of 1881, the expanding influence of the Anglo-commercial elite had been the best hope of keeping the whole sub-continent within the British orbit. In 1898, Rhodes and Milner had fallen back on race loyalty and Britannic nationalism. After 1902, Milner had hoped to build his British South Africa on the surer foundation of a British majority. By 1908, even his staunchest friend among the South African English, Percy Fitzpatrick, acknowledged that, in the short term at least, there was no choice but to work with the 'moderate' Boers, Botha and Smuts, to prevent the revival of full-blooded republicanism – a view shared by Jameson. It is tempting to conclude that British blood and treasure had been spent in vain: that Britain's hold on South Africa was more dependent than ever upon Afrikaner goodwill. That would be mistaken.

In fact, Botha and Smuts understood how limited and conditional was their tenure of power. In theory, they could disavow their allegiance to the Imperial crown and secede from the Empire. In practice, loyalty was the only option. This was not because rebellion would be punished by a British invasion – though imperial intervention could not be ruled out. Nor because it would freeze the mineral economy with its close ties to London – though financial disruption would have followed. The real check on republican nationalism was more brutal. What Botha and Smuts feared most of all was a return to the 'racial politics' of 1899, and an English party united against them under Randlord leadership, under the banner of 'the Empire in danger'. If that were to happen, then 'Krugerism' would also revive: and *their* centre would not hold. They could hardly doubt the results of repudiating the British connection: at best the break-up of the Union; at worst a civil war, pitting loyalist veterans against Boer commandos. This was the real legacy of the South African War: not the failure of Milner or the breaking of Kruger, but the entrenchment of the South African English, forged by the war and its prelude into a self-conscious 'Britannic' community within a brittle, gimcrack, settler state. Divided as they were by class and region and personal antagonisms, they were strong enough to exclude Afrikaner republicanism from practical politics. It was not what Milner and Rhodes had intended; but it proved curiously durable all the same.

7 THE EDWARDIAN TRANSITION

The last long decade before the outbreak of the First World War was a proving ground. It tested the extent to which the British had been able to adapt their superstructure of power and influence to the more strenuous global conditions that set in during the 1880s and 1890s and reached a further peak of intensity after 1900. The judgment of historians has been variable. The Edwardian decade has sometimes been seen as the 'high noon' of empire, the last hurrah of a self-confident imperialism. But, usually, the view has been sterner. Indeed, the more closely the Edwardians have been scrutinised, the more they seem prone to well-merited anxieties. Far from delivering a new security, their abandonment of 'splendid isolation' brought the uncertain liabilities of the Triple Entente and an uneasy dependence on Japan in East Asia. The cost of defending their naval supremacy was a furious arms race with Germany, and ended in a strategic withdrawal from the Mediterranean Sea. The Edwardian economy lost ground on productivity, and real incomes stagnated – one cause of large-scale industrial unrest in the last years of peace. The scale of mass poverty revealed by contemporary inquiry was an indictment of both 'national efficiency' and social justice. Domestic stability was threatened by fierce divisions over tariffs, taxation and the constitution. The revival of the Irish Question after 1910 highlighted the failure of parliamentary government to resolve the future of Ulster and raised the spectre of civil war in the British Isles.

On this view, it is easy to see why the last years before the First World War are often contrasted unfavourably with the mid-Victorian era. Late-Victorian Britain was a 'declining hegemon'; Edwardian Britain a 'weary titan'. But the reasoning here is faulty. Britain's 'hegemonic' status in the mid-nineteenth century is often invoked but rarely described. It is a plausible myth. British power in mid-century had little purchase over much of continental Europe where allies were vital to intervention or leverage. Much of the non-European world lay beyond the reach of either the Royal Navy or the Indian Army. The sphere of mid-Victorian Britain's economic primacy was wide (though far from global) but it was also shallow – since much of it was barely exploited. The late Victorians' empire was richer as well as bigger. Too much can be made of their 'relative decline', especially when the measures for it are vague. Too little has been made of the rising wealth of the Edwardians' empire and the growing mass of assets they were piling up abroad. Indeed, for Edwardian Britain, the real question was not the retention or loss of a nebulous 'hegemony', but whether, as the British system expanded in a more intensely competitive world, its parts could be made to cohere.

Imperial grand strategy and the South African War

Before 1899, the grand strategy of empire had seemed obvious. British foreign policy was the policy of a sea-power, *the* sea-power. The Royal Navy was assumed to be capable of defeating any naval force that challenged it in a general war. Command of the sea would be secured by a decisive victory and the destruction of the enemy fleet – as had happened at Trafalgar. Thereafter, the great archipelago of British interests and possessions spread across the globe would be invulnerable to invasion – with the signal exceptions of India and Canada. British sea-power would apply the brutal tourniquet of blockade to bring the enemy to terms. The Navy was thus the great defensive and offensive weapon of British world power. By contrast, the functions of the Army were of almost secondary importance. It existed to support the civil power at home, not least in Ireland; to supply men for the large contingent maintained in India; to garrison the bases and coaling stations scattered round the world; to provide for home defence in the unlikely event of an invasion undetected by the Navy; and to supply, if need be, an expeditionary force of up to 70,000 men for service overseas.[1] In the Stanhope memorandum of 1891 that set out the Army's role in this order, the likelihood of such an expeditionary force being sent to Europe was treated as of almost fantastic improbability.

These strategic preconceptions dictated the distribution of British forces around the world and influenced their formations and tactics. The Navy was deployed on nine stations, each embracing a vast area of sea. On the Home Station were eighteen battleships and sixteen cruisers as well as a mass of smaller craft: this was the front line against invasion and the reserve against emergency elsewhere. In the Mediterranean, where the British had the greatest reason to fear a combined assault by France and Russia and much to lose, they kept a large force of twelve battleships and thirteen cruisers in a fleet of more than forty ships. On other stations, with the exception of China, they relied upon cruisers to maintain their seaborne primacy: ten in the Western Atlantic (the North America and West Indies station), two off the east coast of South America; four in the Eastern Pacific; seven to patrol the Cape of Good Hope and the West African coast; four on the East Indies station; and eight on the Australian.[2] On extra-European stations, the most visible sign of British sea-power was often the gunboat, a small, lightly armed ship of some 600 tons with a crew of between 60 and 100.[3] But the workhorse of British sea-power beyond European waters was the faster, well-armed, long-range cruiser, patrolling the sea-lanes and paying the courtesy calls that served as a none too subtle reminder that coastal states without navies and who depended upon the revenues from trade were wise to avoid the sea-power's displeasure.

By contrast with the Navy, the Army was somewhat more heavily concentrated. On the eve of the South African War it disposed of 31 cavalry regiments and 142 infantry battalions grouped in pairs to form the county regiments created by the Cardwell reforms.[4] The infantry battalions were maids-of-all-work. In 1896, eighteen were scattered in pockets around the world from Bermuda to Hong Kong, three were in Egypt, three in South Africa, and fifty-two were in India. The remainder were at home, not so much as a striking force as a reservoir from which the overseas units were filled up. Indeed, it was easy to imagine that the Army at home existed chiefly to service the great garrison kept in India since the Mutiny: this was the manpower problem that obsessed its chiefs. Where the Army had seen action since the Crimean War it had fought small wars with small formations against Asian or African foes, usually lacking modern weapons.[5] On colonial battlefields, individual resource and the brute courage of a professional army substituted for the staff skills and modern tactics prized by continental generals. Against an uncivilised foe military doctrine was straightforward. 'Dash at the first fellows that make their appearance', said Wellington, the greatest of the 'sepoy generals', 'and the campaign will be ours.'[6]

Of course, the late-Victorian system had been far from perfect. The generals fretted constantly over the shortage of manpower. 'We live from hand to mouth, like the insolvent debtor who meets his daily liabilities by shifts invented on the spur of the moment', complained Lord Wolseley in 1896. 'Is this a real military system, or is it a system of make-believe?'[7] The demand for more battleships on overseas stations rose inexorably: in the Mediterranean after the Franco-Russian alliance, and also in China. To cover the gaps, it had sometimes been necessary to make guarded promises of joint defensive action, as Salisbury had done with the Mediterranean agreements of 1887. Such precautions were needed, he told Queen Victoria, against the danger of the continental powers treating 'the English Empire as divisible booty by which their differences might be adjusted'.[8] But it was the South African War that was cause and occasion for the most drastic review of grand strategy since the 1860s.

There were several reasons for this. The defeats of 'Black Week' in December 1899 shattered any remaining complacency about the likely performance of the Army in a war against a first-class opponent. The humiliation of military failure bred a mood of recrimination that surfaced during the war and afterwards at the Elgin Commission's enquiry into its conduct. 'For frank, not to say malicious criticism of one another', remarked Milner sardonically in January 1900, 'I know of no set of men equal to our *haute armée*.'[9] To the Royal Commission, Kitchener and other senior officers presented a catalogue of defects: the poverty of intelligence; the shortage of staff skills; the age and infirmity of battalion commanders; the absence of professionalism among officers; above all the lack of any means to control the movements of an army far larger than the usual colonial expedition. One regimental adjutant had been reduced to advertising in a Cape Town newspaper for information on the whereabouts of his unit.[10] 'Regarded as an institution or society', remarked Leopold Amery crushingly in *The Times History of the War in South Africa*, 'the British army of 1899 was undoubtedly a success...As a fighting machine it was largely a sham.'[11] During the war, the concentration of so much military manpower in South Africa made the defence of India (the first object of imperial grand strategy) look increasingly precarious. With Russia's military frontier grinding towards the Himalayas, the Indian Viceroy Lord Curzon insisted that in the event of war 70,000 men would have to be sent immediately to India – a calculation the War Office was forced to accept in 1901.[12] Even if the men were available, South African experience was bound to raise doubts about the Army's ability to face an Armageddon in the Hindu Kush.

But it was sea-power not the defence of India that touched the rawest nerve and galvanised the British cabinet. When Lord Selborne became First Lord of the Admiralty in November 1900, he quickly sounded the alarm to his colleagues.[13] Britain faced a revival of French sea-power in the Mediterranean, making Admiral Fisher's call for more battleships there irresistible. Simultaneously, the Boxer Rebellion in China and the intervention by the Western Powers and Japan made the risk of a forced partition far greater, and with it the chance of conflict between the Powers. Britain had to match the rapid growth of Russia's eastern sea strength. 'We could not afford', wrote Selborne urgently, 'to see our Chinese trade disappear, or to see Hong Kong and Singapore fall, particularly not at a moment when a military struggle with Russia might be in progress on the confines of India.'[14] For Selborne, the emergency in East Asia on top of his Mediterranean difficulties was the last straw. A new course was essential. The cabinet toyed uneasily with a scheme to ally with Germany, but flinched at the prospect of military commitments in Europe. All the while, fear of Russia, that power to whom 'defeat, diplomatic, naval or military matters less ... than to any other power',[15] grew steadily stronger. 'A quarrel with Russia anywhere, about anything, means the invasion of India', groaned Balfour, Salisbury's nephew and heir-apparent, in December 1901.[16] Without allies, Britain would be fair game if France joined in. The short-term solution was a naval alliance with Japan in East Asia, concluded not without misgivings in January 1902. The end of the South African War in May 1902 did nothing to ease the naval strain. 'We must have a force which is reasonably calculated to beat France and Russia', wrote Selborne in January 1903, 'and we must have something in hand against Germany.'[17] Meanwhile, London struggled inconclusively with army reform to provide its share of the huge force of three or four hundred thousand men that Kitchener (now Commander-in-Chief in India) declared essential to repel an invasion brought closer by Russia's new strategic railways in Central Asia.[18] But the government's real decision was to endorse Selborne's demand for a large rise in naval spending (50 per cent greater by 1905 than in 1899) and the revolution in naval deployment that Fisher had planned.

Fisher became First Sea Lord and the Navy's professional head in October 1904.[19] He was determined to match the French and Russians in the Mediterranean, where Britain's imperial communications were most vulnerable, and was passionately committed to equipping the Navy with the fast, armoured 'all big gun' warships made possible by technical advance. The price, as Fisher saw with brutal realism, was the scrapping of large numbers of older, less powerful ships – 'too weak to fight, too slow to run away' – and the concentration of resources and manpower in a modern battle-fleet in European waters. In December 1904, Selborne announced a drastic redeployment. The South Atlantic station was wound up, the China, East Indies and Australian stations effectively merged. In place of the scattering of cruisers around the world, four cruiser squadrons, kept mainly in Europe, would be ready 'to show the flag in imposing force, wherever it may be deemed to be politically or strategically advisable'.[20] In the following year, the five battleships on the China station were brought home. Large numbers of gunboats, Fisher's 'bugtraps', were swept away. The dreadnought age had dawned.

The naval policies initiated by Selborne and Fisher were a response to the weakness revealed by Britain's isolation during the South African War and the growth in German, French and Russian sea-power. By 1907, the strategic situation had markedly improved, or so it seemed. The threat of a Franco-Russian attack had all but disappeared; the danger of a combined assault by the three great European powers had vanished. The reason lay in diplomatic success and vicarious military good fortune. In April 1904, Salisbury's successor as foreign secretary, Lord Lansdowne, at last succeeded where Salisbury had failed in persuading France to agree to a comprehensive settlement of outstanding disputes in the imperial sphere. At the heart of the 'Entente Cordiale' was the mutual recognition of each other's primacy in two zones of great diplomatic sensitivity: Egypt, where the British 'temporary occupation' had been an open sore in Anglo-French relations since 1882; and Morocco, whose proximity to French Algeria made its external connections a matter of intense concern to governments in Paris. The British hoped that the Anglo-French entente would open the way to an agreement with Russia, the real threat to their position in India and East Asia. The prospect looked bleak, and when Russia and Japan (Britain's regional partner in East Asia) went to war in 1904 over the future of Korea and Manchuria, the danger of an Anglo-Russian clash briefly seemed acute. But, in a dramatic reversal of expectations (Fisher expected Russia to beat Japan),[21] Russian naval power was shattered at the battle of Tsushima – Japan's Trafalgar – in May 1905.

The British regained a clear margin of naval superiority over Germany, France and Russia combined. In 1907, the Tsarist government, weakened by defeat and revolution, accepted a diplomatic compromise in Persia and Central Asia – where friction with Britain had been greatest – that left southern Persia and Afghanistan, the 'gates to India', firmly in the British sphere.[22] The Anglo-Russian entente completed the rapprochement between London and its long-standing rivals in the Outer World. Meanwhile, in the diplomatic crisis of 1905–6, when Germany had tried to disrupt the Anglo-French agreement over Morocco and revive British isolation, the new alignment had held firm – just.

The promise of a new international equilibrium did not last long. By the end of 1908, there was growing alarm in Britain at the open challenge now posed by the ship-building programme of the German navy. While fears about the German plans were somewhat exaggerated, the schedule for dreadnought construction by Germany's Mediterranean allies, Italy and Austria-Hungary, meant that a new round of the arms race had begun. In February 1909, the Asquith cabinet agreed to build eight new dreadnoughts, four more than their original estimate, on the assumption that proof would be forthcoming of German plans. By March, a full-blown 'scare' was under way, rapidly reaching Canada, Australia and New Zealand.[23] An agitation sprang up in Australia to give a dreadnought to the Royal Navy.[24] The New Zealand government offered two dreadnoughts. The Canadian government under Laurier compromised with a scheme for a Canadian Naval Service.[25] At a special imperial conference on defence held in July, the British Admiralty urged the formation of dominion 'fleet units', recognising that, in the Pacific dominions, public opinion would demand some local control over the ships for which it had paid – even if they came under Imperial command in time of war. But the centrepiece of British policy was the remorseless drift towards a single-minded concentration on the naval race with Germany. Already in 1909, the Admiralty had quietly accepted that it could no longer match the two next strongest naval powers combined (the 'two power standard') and must settle instead for a margin of 60 per cent over Germany. By 1912, even this looked ambitious as a new German naval law was broached. When the Haldane Mission failed to reach agreement with Berlin on a standstill, the need to preserve superiority in the decisive battleground of any Anglo-German naval war – the North Sea – forced the Asquith government into a strategic revolution.

The revolution was a naval withdrawal from the Mediterranean announced in July 1912 by Winston Churchill, the First Lord of the Admiralty. The most powerful ships of the Mediterranean fleet were to be redeployed to the North Sea: the rest would be no match for the Austrian or Italian dreadnoughts of Germany's allies. To protect her vast Mediterranean interests, her marine highway to the East and the naval approaches to Egypt, Britain would rely instead on the good-will of France, whose Atlantic squadron was transferred from Brest to Toulon in September. The clear implication was a deepening commit-ment to the support of France in any European conflict – the subject of secret 'military conversations' between the two general staffs since the Moroccan crisis of 1905–6. Britain's army, like her navy, now seemed to be focused not on the defence of a far-flung empire, but on deterring a German bid for primacy in Europe.

On the face of it, the change in Britain's strategic fortunes since the outbreak of the South African War in October 1899 had been dra-matic. Indeed, the new pattern of world politics suggested that between 1900 and 1914 Britain and its world-system had experienced a sharp phase of relative decline. The symptoms seem obvious. In regions once thought vital to British interests, their protection had been left to others or to luck. Once, governments in London had cut a lordly dash, treat-ing European diplomacy with insouciance and basing British power on seaborne self-reliance. Now they had been dragged into the European maelstrom as reluctant players in a volatile game of competing alliances. The Army had been remodelled for convenient deployment on the Euro-pean mainland, almost unthinkable before 1900. The old priorities of global power had shrunk to a continental commitment. Britain could no longer afford the luxury of 'splendid isolation' because British opinion would no longer pay for it. Indeed, as great power competition hotted up, British industrial power had slipped back. In a period of relative eco-nomic decline, the strain of upholding a worldwide pre-eminence and safeguarding the regional security of the British Isles had become too great. Over-extension abroad and under-performance at home forced a strategic change. The question was: if Britain gave up its role as the strategic guardian of the British system, how long would it be before its cohesion began to falter, its subject peoples became restless and its enemies closed in?

Plausible in its own terms, this description is too apocalyptic. 'Splendid isolation' was a romantic fiction. An active diplomacy in

Europe had always been vital to imperial interests: nowhere more so than in Egypt and the Near East. It was certainly true that there had been a fundamental shift in the theory and practice of British grand strategy. There was a new strategic setting. Britain's world interests were less secure. The margin of safety was narrower. The brittle alignments and fractious diplomacy of pre-1914 Europe can be seen with hindsight to foreshadow a catastrophic war. But the scale of pre-war change should not be exaggerated. The real question was not whether there had been a relative decline from some imaginary benchmark of mid-Victorian 'primacy', but whether the British were still strong enough to protect their system against rival powers – by whatever means. To answer this properly, and to take a more realistic view of Edwardian strategy, requires some account of the wider geopolitical scene.

Britain in world politics

The new shape of world politics after 1900 affected all the great powers competing to be 'world states'. To none of them did it offer unequivocal advantage, or a clear road to primacy and hegemonic status. Each faced political risks at home and abroad that drastically reduced the scope for forceful action on the international stage. This applied to Germany, Russia and the United States, the powers that were best placed to take the initiative. Germany was the strongest. A sustained programme of naval expansion had made it the principal threat to British sea-power. Germany's foreign trade had expanded rapidly and its new merchant fleet, like its navy, was second only to Britain's. German investment had begun to penetrate regions like Latin America, long the preserve of British capital.[26] Not surprisingly, in some naval, shipping and colonial circles, as well as among conservatives hostile to the liberal capitalism with which London was so closely identified, antagonism to Britain was commonplace. But, while German policy was committed to the Tirpitz plan, and a high seas fleet strong enough to enforce neutrality on Britain in the event of continental war, there was little enthusiasm in Berlin for a frontal assault on the British system. German diplomacy shifted uneasily between Bismarckism and the *Weltpolitik* favoured by the Kaiser. The Bismarckian tradition looked coolly on imperial self-assertion and the German nationalism with which it was associated. For Bismarck, the gravest threat to the new German Empire

had been the growth of national feeling among the subject peoples of
Eastern and Central Europe: Poles, Czechs, Slovaks, Ukrainians and
South Slavs.[27] Hence German security required good relations between
the three great imperial monarchies ruling over this vast multi-ethnic
Mitteleuropa: the Hohenzollerns, Hapsburgs and Romanovs. British
goodwill should be cultivated as a counterpoise to France whose hope
of *revanche* and the restoration of Alsace-Lorraine made it the joker of
European diplomacy. This more conservative view of German interests
grew stronger in the last years before 1914. After 1909, there was no
question of outbuilding Britain in dreadnoughts, not least because the
revenue base of the German central government was much more limited
than that of its British counterpart.[28] As the means to imperial expansion, the high seas fleet became a broken reed. Meanwhile, the fate of
Mitteleuropa had become more pressing – and Austro-Russian antipathy more dangerous. By the time of the First Balkan War (1912–
13), Berlin was anxious to mend its fences with London and came
to terms over the future disposal of Portugal's colonies (should Lis-
bon's bankruptcy bring them on the 'market') and the railway line to
the Persian Gulf (the *Bagdadbahn*). But one crucial element of *Weltpolitik* remained embedded in German policy. The Kaiser's government
refused to abandon its naval programme without the promise of British
neutrality in a European conflict. It was exactly the concession which
(as we shall see) the logic of Edwardian diplomacy was bound to reject.

The novelty and seriousness of Germany's naval challenge –
and the reason why it aroused so fierce a reaction in Britain – was
that it threatened to nullify the British claim to be a great power in
Europe, a claim founded ultimately on the possession of sea-power.
But for more than a century it had been the insidious threat of
Russian expansion that had haunted British thinking on imperial
defence. What made Russia so dangerous, thought the policy-makers,
was its ability to exert pressure on four different regions of great strategic or commercial importance to Britain: the maritime corridor between
the Black Sea and the Mediterranean (the 'Straits'); Persia and the
Persian Gulf; Afghanistan and the inner Asian frontiers of India; and
North China and Peking. In British eyes, the danger was compounded
by the brute scale of Russia's resources, especially in manpower, and
the erratic, inscrutable processes of Russian policy. In a secretive
hothouse atmosphere, periodically scorched by the gusts of pan-Slav
emotion, rival court camarillas competed for the Tsar's capricious

sympathy. Careerist soldiers, unscrupulous concessionaires and religious mystics touted their reckless projects amid grandiloquent talk of the Romanov mission. With so insatiable and unpredictable a power, the partition diplomacy that was Salisbury's forte stood little chance of success. This was a gloomy and misleading view of the Russian polity. But it reflected the feeling of impotence in the face of the northern leviathan: the 'invulnerable power' of Selborne's warning, the 'inland tyranny' immune to naval chastisement in Lord Salisbury's regretful phrase. It was fuelled by the paranoid fear that a Russian attack on the Indian frontier would spark a second Mutiny and bring down the Raj from within. It was grudging acknowledgment that Russian empire-building was on a scale as vast as Britain's and that the colonising drive, celebrated by Russian historians as much as by British, had accelerated in the late nineteenth century. As its railways reached further, tightening its grip on its vast peripheries, Russia's domination of North Asia seemed certain to grow.[29]

Instead, it received a violent check. Defeat by Japan in 1905 revealed the latent weakness of the Russian system and the fragile foundations on which Tsardom had erected so imposing a superstructure.[30] Economic backwardness was the root of the problem. Low agricultural productivity, a narrow industrial base, a stunted rail network and dependence upon foreign capital were the real index of Russian power and a massive brake on strategic freedom. Economic weakness reinforced (and was aggravated by) demographic inadequacy. Ethnic Russians were too few (forming 45 per cent of the Empire's population) and much too immobile to dominate the minorities that Tsardom had conquered. The frontiers of empire could not be closed: they were too porous to seal off the external connections that made the loyalty of frontier peoples so doubtful in time of crisis. In fact, the Empire remained a multi-ethnic construct to its very core since Tsardom had advanced not by building up a Russian state but by collaboration with non-Russian elites – in the Ukraine, the Baltic, Poland, Finland, Georgia, Armenia and elsewhere. Nor was Russian culture a substitute for political weakness since it lacked the absorptive quality or universal appeal to attract the European and Islamic minorities under Tsardom's sway.[31] The result was an imperial power whose size and spasmodic aggression masked weaknesses laid bare in the military catastrophe of 1905, and the near implosion of the whole regime. Thereafter, it was clear that for some time to come a forward movement in North Persia or towards the Straits would require the support of either Germany or Britain. Without one or the other, the outcome would be humiliation – a lesson confirmed in the Bosnian crisis of 1908.[32] In official circles, the need for caution was well understood.[33] To a realist as brutal as Peter Durnovo, the saviour of Tsardom in 1906, internal cohesion could hardly survive the effects of a European war. The age of expansion was over, he thought. The age of crisis was about to begin.[34]

Britain's greatest rival, judged by population and output, lay not in the Old World but in the New. Anglo-American antagonism was much older than Anglo-German. Relations had improved in the later nineteenth century. But, in the Caribbean and Central America, there had been persistent friction between the old colonial power and the new commercial prodigy. Canadian mistrust of American expansionism was a further complication. Then, with the Spanish-American War of 1898, the United States became an imperial power. It annexed Hawaii and tightened its grip on the Central Pacific. As ruler of the Philippines, it could claim new influence in maritime China. As master of Cuba, it dominated the Caribbean. But the most significant change, from the British point of view, was the new commitment to naval power in the presidency of Theodore Roosevelt (1901–9). By 1907, he had persuaded the Congress to fund the building of a fleet second only to Britain's. For the embattled Royal Navy, a new sea challenge to its rear joined the new sea challenge to its front.

If Tirpitz had been right, the rise of American sea-power would have sealed Britain's global fate. For Tirpitz believed that common antagonism to British supremacy was the natural policy of all sea states.[35] The reality was very different. The British were certainly at pains to conciliate American opinion. Soon after 1900, they had tacitly acknowledged that a war with the United States was militarily unwinnable and politically unthinkable. America's new status in the Caribbean was recognised in the Hay-Pauncefote treaty of 1901 when Britain disclaimed any interest in the Isthmus of Panama. Britain was no enemy of the Monroe Doctrine, declared Arthur Balfour in the House of Commons.[36] When the puppet state of Panama was carved out of Colombia with American help in 1903, and a canal zone leased in perpetuity to Washington, the way was open for an American-owned 'path between the seas'.[37] The balance of power had shifted abruptly in the Western Atlantic – or so it seemed.[38] Meanwhile, the inexorable rise of the American economy was a source of commercial unease in London.

But none of this meant that America now threatened the British world-system.

There were several reasons for this. American opinion was still too 'continentalist' in outlook to be converted to the 'navalist' views of Roosevelt or his successor Taft. After 1908, their ambitions were reined in by a sceptical Congress.[39] Secondly, American sea-power was hobbled by the need to guard two oceans, separated before 1914 by the voyage round Cape Horn. Thirdly, as Roosevelt gradually saw, American interests in China had been exposed by Russian defeat to the pressure of Japan, an ally of Britain since 1902. The Philippines looked less like a salient in Asia than a hostage to naval fortune. Fourthly, the onset of revolution in Mexico in 1910 renewed the old American nightmare: European (or even Japanese) intervention to check the assertion of Washington's influence in its own 'backyard'.[40] The timing here was crucial. For, as completion of the Panama Canal crept nearer, strategic control of the Caribbean and its approaches loomed larger and larger in American concerns.[41]

As a result, the social and cultural rapprochement between Britain and America, and the racial appeal of 'Anglo-Saxonism' on both sides of the Atlantic, had its counterpart in diplomacy. If British leaders repudiated all thought of Anglo-American conflict, it was no more thinkable in Washington. British naval supremacy, remarked Theodore Roosevelt, was 'the great guaranty for the peace of the world'.[42] For Roosevelt, a large and efficient United States Navy would be 'the junior member of an informal two-power alliance' tilting the international balance towards Anglo-American interests.[43] The cold calculations of naval planners were based on the same assumption. Japan ('War Plan Orange') and Germany ('War Plan Black') were the likely enemies.[44] A German attack was only possible in the 'highly improbable' event of British acquiescence. To American opinion, concludes a recent study, the real guarantor of its Atlantic security was British not American sea-power.[45] On this calculation, the United States looked less like an imperial rival and more like a forceful, determined 'super-dominion'.

These checks and balances in the scope of great power ambition help to explain why the theoretical vulnerability of Britain's vast and straggling empire, sprawled across the globe, as one official remarked, like 'a gouty giant', was not translated into territorial loss. By the yardstick of relative power, the British system was surprisingly strong. It could not be encircled. Its rivals were at odds. Its lines of communication were secure – unless naval catastrophe occurred in Europe. These were the assets that Edwardian strategy was designed to exploit. But, as the policy-makers came to realise, they could not be turned to account without a more or less drastic revision of the old assumptions of Salisbury's *Realpolitik*.

The South African War had been the forcing-house of change. International isolation and the unrealised threat of a great power combination against them left a lasting impression on British leaders. Postwar tension with Russia and Germany drove home the lesson that their imperial ambitions could not be contained by sea-power alone. In the Foreign Office, a diplomacy of studied caution seemed the only cure for Britain's exposed position. 'A maritime state', remarked a leading official, 'is, in the literal sense of the word, the neighbour of every country accessible by sea.' To avoid falling foul of a hostile coalition, it must aim to 'harmonize with the general ideals common to all mankind', paying careful attention to 'the primary and vital interests of a majority . . . of the other nations'.[46] Britain could not hope to frustrate the ambitions of all its rivals, was Crowe's implication. A new realism was necessary. This mood was shared even by the most ebullient of Edwardian politicians. 'We are not a young people with an innocent record and a scanty inheritance', Winston Churchill told his cabinet colleagues in January 1914. 'We have engrossed to ourselves an altogether disproportionate share of the wealth and traffic of the world. We have got all we want in territory, and our claim to be left in the unmolested enjoyment of vast and splendid possessions, mainly acquired by violence, largely maintained by force, often seems less reasonable to others than to us.'[47]

The spirit of Edwardian diplomacy was pragmatic acceptance that Britain now had to compete with 'world states' of broadly equal capabilities and appetites. A second insight followed. More than ever before, retreat into blue water isolation was impossible. The gradual integration of world politics since the 1880s was now complete. The fate of distant regions could not be localised: faraway rivalries led back ineluctably to the balance of power in Europe. The future of China, the Arab Middle East, Portuguese Africa or the Belgian Congo would be settled by the European great powers with the United States and Japan as their junior partners. Alarming from one point of view, this vision of a Eurocentric globe offered some consolation. It seemed to rule out the danger that Britain's rivals could make dramatic territorial gains by a military or diplomatic coup. The existing distribution of global influence and the colonial 'share-out' it embodied could only be changed by diplomatic agreement. Unless, that is, it was upset by a major breakdown of the European balance and the sudden emergence of a dominant superstate. The logic of this was that the British system could best be protected by the strenuous exercise of Britain's influence in European politics, with the right to be consulted, and the capacity to intervene, if the continental balance were at risk. To many late Victorians, the prospect of alliances and alignments with the continental powers had been unwelcome, even dangerous, and the threat of a European combination against them a real one. To their Edwardian successors, it seemed that the latent conflicts between the European powers now ran so deep that only by incompetence or abdication could Britain be isolated. This was the lesson of the ententes with France and Russia. An active, flexible diplomacy in Europe was thus the best guarantee of imperial safety. The 'balance of power' was not just an ideal: to the assumptions on which Edwardian diplomacy was based it had become a necessity.

These elements of Edwardian grand strategy crystallised in 1912 as the naval competition with Germany intensified. London rejected the German demand for its neutrality in a future war as the price of a naval 'holiday'. The whole point of naval primacy was to ensure Britain's capacity to intervene against disturbance of the continental equilibrium. Indeed, maritime power was her principal claim to great power status. The cost, as we have seen, was an even greater concentration of naval strength in the North Sea to deter aggression by Germany. The consequence was a naval withdrawal from the Mediterranean, the sacrifice, on a superficial view, of imperial to domestic safety. But the senior ministers of the Asquith cabinet vehemently rejected this implication. Churchill (First Lord of the Admiralty), Haldane (Secretary of State for War), Lloyd George (Chancellor of the Exchequer) and Grey (Foreign Secretary) all agreed that Britain's Mediterranean interests would only be in danger if she had first been defeated in the North Sea. Whatever setbacks she might suffer in the region would quickly be reversed once command of the sea had been gained in the decisive northern theatre.[48] And, anyway, Churchill insisted, by 1915 the Royal Navy would be strong enough to return in force.[49] Meanwhile, overwhelming strength where it mattered most, and the purchase that gave in European diplomacy (above all in securing the friendship of

France), were the real foundation of British world power. They were the vital source of leverage against the aggressive designs of rival powers; the best guarantee that, short of an earthquake in world affairs, any redivision of the global spoils could only be slow and partial. And, while British claims to new territory or wider spheres were sure to be contested, there was no reason to think that holding what she had (no mean inheritance) was now beyond her means.

The credibility of these assumptions would soon be tested in the First World War. But, in the meantime, the combination of entente diplomacy and naval concentration had achieved a striking recovery from the isolation and vulnerability that British leaders had feared during and after the South African War. More to the point, it had done so without driving a wedge between the different elements of the imperial system. Of course, the British taxpayer bore the overwhelming brunt of the financial burden. In that sense, a revolt at home was always the greatest threat to imperial cohesion. There were acrimonious struggles in cabinet over the naval estimates in 1908–9 and again in 1914. But, despite the demands of welfare reform and a fierce parliamentary lobby against the surging costs of the naval programme, domestic opinion accepted the dramatic rise in naval spending (from £31 millions a year in 1904 to £51 millions in 1914). It did so in part because the invasion of Britain seemed as great a danger as the loss of empire – exactly the premise on which both foreign and naval policy depended. Indeed, naval and diplomatic doctrine rendered meaningless the distinction between domestic and imperial interests. In the white dominions, this formula was less readily accepted. Dominion public opinion had been roused by the fear that Britain's naval decline would expose the Empire to external attack. If the Empire were broken up, remarked the (New Zealand) Nelson *Evening Mail*, 'in ten years the Asiatic population of New Zealand would exceed the European'.[50] In Canada, however, the dominion's response was caught up in a bitter party quarrel between those who favoured a local 'tin-pot' navy and those who preferred a direct contribution to the cost of new dreadnoughts – the policy of the premier Borden after 1911 but blocked by his opponents in the Senate. In the Pacific dominions, where the results of Churchill's concentration policy were felt most acutely amid growing mistrust of Japan, there was marked reluctance to see the battleships built by local money deployed far away in northern Europe. 'As a Briton', remarked the New Zealand defence minister, '[I] would like to see a consolidated

Empire strong enough to stand without the *Entente cordiale*.'[51] In practice, Australian and New Zealand leaders had little option but to accept Churchill's insistence that their security lay not in little local flotillas but in the Royal Navy's ability to face down the threat to its maritime primacy. 'The situation in the Pacific', he told them in April 1913, 'will be absolutely regulated by the decisions in the North Sea'.[52] After all, whatever its shortcomings, this version of imperial defence was plausible. The alternative, a more far-reaching coordination of military resources, might restrict the autonomy of dominion governments without giving them more influence on British grand strategy. Indeed, the great success of Liberal policy after 1905 had been a credible defence of British world power without recourse to Chamberlainite schemes of imperial unity and tariff reform. More remarkably still, at a time of rising international tension, it avoided the necessity of levying heavier costs on India, so long the milch-cow of imperial defence. A heavier load on the Indian taxpayer would have aggravated the resentments that Morley's reform was meant to soothe. Instead, from 1904 to 1914 (while Britain's defence spending was doubled), the Indian military budget rose barely at all.[53]

In the decade before the outbreak of war, British leaders exploited the errors and weaknesses of their imperial rivals and the new opportunities of global politics. They reinforced Britain's role as the strategic guardian of her worldwide system and in doing so shored up her imperial authority. But they had not of course devised a final solution to the problem of imperial security. Nor could they rule out extending the territorial burdens over whose vast scope official opinion was always fretting. In the partitioned world, re-partition was likely sooner or later. Portuguese Africa and the Belgian Congo might change hands if their owners went bankrupt or their commercial life became dominated by foreign interests – an outcome that Grey regarded as all but inevitable.[54] Indeed, Britain and Germany reached agreement in principle on the division of Portugal's colonies in 1913.[55] In the unpartitioned world, the difficulties of an amicable share-out and the risks of collision were considerably greater. In China, the revolution of 1911 had installed an unstable republican regime. The breakdown of central authority and the rise of regional warlords seemed likely to test the cooperation of the outside powers – Britain, Russia, Germany, France, the United States and Japan – even more than the Boxer Rebellion of 1900. Defending Britain's large slice of the Chinese commercial cake was unlikely to grow easier or its diplomatic and military costs less burdensome.[56] Most dangerous of all was the political flux in the Near and Middle East. In Persia, it seemed more than likely that the insistent pressure of Russian influence in the north and the gradual detachment of whole provinces like Azerbaijan (where there were 10,000 Russian troops by 1913) from Persian control would be mirrored in a British quasi-protectorate in the south and southwest of the shah's dominions – a tendency that the British oil concession there was bound to accentuate.[57] In the Persian Gulf and in the Hedjaz – the seat of the Muslim Holy Places – the British watched uneasily as the new 'Young Turk' regime in Constantinople cut down the freedoms of local notables – like the Sherif of Mecca, hereditary guardian of the Holy Places – and drove its railways and garrisons deeper into Arabia. An Ottoman 'forward policy' would push up the cost of British influence.[58] Worse still, after its catastrophic losses in 1912–13 (Libya, the Dodecanese, Crete and the rest of Ottoman Europe save Eastern Thrace), the Ottoman Empire might become the catspaw of Germany. In the Baghdad Railway agreement of 1914, the British insisted that no German-owned railway be allowed to reach the Gulf and challenge their political and commercial influence there. But here, as in North Persia, the British were well aware that the mutual antagonism of their European rivals was the key to the economical defence of their regional interests.

British leaders had made the best of the new geopolitical universe. They had squared the circle of domestic reform, imperial unity and great power rivalry. Buoyant revenues and diplomatic fortune had come to their rescue. But a real equilibrium had eluded them. Ultimately, their 'system' depended upon the stability of great power relations in Europe and the conservative ethos of 'old diplomacy'. It assumed that general war was improbable and that, if it broke out, neither side could gain decisive victory. It rested upon the accidents of dynastic politics in Central Europe, and the fate of Europe's semi-colonial periphery in the Balkans. But Europe was not the still calm centre of a restless world. And its stresses were soon to erupt with volcanic force.

The political economy of Edwardian Empire

The cohesion of the British world-system depended in the last resort upon Britain's independence and the guarantee of strategic protection offered by her naval and military power. But it was unlikely to last long if the British economy began to lose speed. Yet, by some measures, economic decline seemed to have set in by 1914. The era when Britain had been the unchallenged workshop of the world was over. In Germany and the United States, new industrial economies had grown up. In both iron and steel production (the basic index of industrial power), they had outstripped the first industrial nation. American output was three times as great; German production of crude steel was twice that of Britain by 1910.[59] As they industrialised, both Germany and the United States closed their doors to many British-manufactured imports, driving them towards other markets. Worse still, they began to compete strongly in export markets favoured by British manufacturers, especially in Europe, and invaded the home market as well. Not surprisingly, Britain's share of world trade fell steadily. Manufactures began to make up a larger share of British imports, rising to some 25 per cent by 1913. And, while Germany and the United States moved rapidly into the second generation of industrial products – electrical goods, chemicals, motor vehicles – Britain seemed to lag behind. Technological conservatism and excessive dependence upon 'old-fashioned' industries like cotton textiles, signalled an apparent loss of managerial dynamism, the onset of commercial sclerosis, and the triumph of a complacent upper-class amateurism over the scientific management demanded by the scale and scope of modern industry.

The implications of failure to compete with the most advanced and successful industrial economies were dire. If the British economy grew less swiftly than its main competitors, British consumers would become (relatively) poorer, and their demand for the commodities of Britain's trading partners in the extra-European world would slacken. If British technology stagnated, then new industries would be slow to emerge when old products like textiles could no longer compete with lower-cost rivals in the industrialising world. If neither exports nor imports kept pace with those of rival powers, Britain would gradually lose its claim to be the marketplace of the world, and the natural terminus of the world's merchant shipping. And, as the profits of trade and industry declined, it might be harder to find the capital for the investment overseas whose proceeds had buoyed up the buying power of the British consumer. Britain's trading partners within and without the Empire would turn instead to new sources of capital, to new and more vigorous markets, and to more up-to-date suppliers of the technologies and manufactures they needed. As the vicious circle tightened, the means to sustain the costly apparatus of world power – the expense of which was subject to constant inflation – would begin to dry up. The allies and associates of the British system would drift at best towards centrifugal autonomy, at worst towards a new constellation of imperial power. The British would enter the well-filled graveyard of empires.

But it is easy to exaggerate the symptoms of commercial decline and misleading to assume that the British economy was competing head on with its American and German counterparts. In trade as in strategy, the interests and capacities of Britain's main rivals limited the sphere of outright confrontation. The peculiar trajectory of British economic development meant that it complemented the growth of new industrial powers as much as competing with them. It was the viability of this 'economics of coexistence', rather than a Darwinian struggle for industrial supremacy, that would determine the fate of the British system.

In 1913, the four largest industrial economies in the world were the United States, Britain, Germany and France. The American economy had the largest output (at around £8 billion a year in current prices). Britain and Germany had smaller economies of roughly equal size (different estimates place Britain's GDP at between £2.2 and £2.5 billion, Germany's at £2.8 billion). France trailed some way behind; Russia was an industrial minnow. But this crude ranking conceals important differences. The British had little in common with the other industrial powers. They were still the world's greatest trader. Though their share of world trade had fallen with the huge increase of commercial traffic, they still exported and imported far more than any other state: 40 per cent more than Germany in 1913, nearly 60 per cent more than America. Their share of the world's manufactured exports at 30 per cent was comfortably ahead of both. With commercial primacy went a commanding superiority in shipping and business services. In 1907, they earned from these some £107 million, nine times the American figure. Britain's steam-powered mercantile fleet of over 10 million tons was four times the size of Germany's. British overseas banks were ubiquitous and their financial services indispensable to international business outside Europe and North America.[60] Their strength and importance owed much to London's unrivalled status as an international money market. At more than £4 billion, British overseas investment made up some 44 per cent of the world's total of foreign-owned capital in 1913. It was more than twice the size of France's, more than three times

Germany's, and six times that of America. And, unlike the investments of the French and Germans, it was to be found not in Europe but spread across the world, in the Americas, India, Africa and the Pacific. Taken together, the income from the export of services and from overseas investments contributed one-third of Britain's external earnings (the rest came from merchandise exports). Net export of services contributed over 5 per cent and net overseas income over 8 per cent of gross domestic product in 1913 – a greater proportion than that of any other major power.[61]

Thus Britain was quite unlike its main economic rivals. It was not just an industrial state, but an agency state (providing commercial services) and a rentier state as well, drawing a huge proportion of its wealth from these latter functions where the growth of international competition was much less acute. This distinctive pattern reflected Britain's comparative advantage as an economic power. In a seaborne age, its location between Europe and America and its excellent maritime communications made Britain a natural entrepot. A compact landmass and a dense rail network had encouraged simultaneously the growth of specialised industrial districts (like Lancashire, West Yorkshire, the Potteries, the Black Country, Clydeside, Tyneside and South Wales) and a centralised machinery of commerce and finance with its headquarters in London – a winning combination. With the second largest reserves of hard coal (thermally the most efficient) in the developed world, energy for industry and transport was abundant. With a large population, rapid population growth but an agricultural sector that employed proportionately far fewer workers than its German, French and American counterparts, Britain had relocated much of its agricultural production to overseas countries. In the 'white dominions' especially, this helped to turn its emigrant demographic surplus into suppliers, customers and borrowers on a grand scale. But it was the enormous growth of world trade and the world economy (to which the British had contributed heavily) that yielded a vital dividend of wealth in the last decade before the First World War.

The value of international trade is usually thought to have increased tenfold between 1850 and 1913. Between 1860 and 1880 it doubled from about £1.5 billion to £3.0 billion. The pace slackened between 1880 and 1900, by which date it had reached nearly £4 billion. Then, between 1900 and 1913, it doubled again to nearly £8 billion.[62] This phenomenal commercial growth was driven by the urbanisation and industrialisation of Europe (which accelerated sharply after 1870) and the opening up of new agrarian regions to supply the food and raw materials it needed. The key was the ever-falling cost of transport by sea and rail, the effect of which was initially to drive down the price of many agricultural commodities. But, after 1896, when wheat reached its lowest price for a century, commodity prices recovered, setting off the long boom in world trade up to 1913. As rural producers around the world reaped richer rewards, they bought more imports and borrowed more money. Vast new tracts of land in Argentina and the Canadian West were cultivated. Wheat was exported from India to Europe. West African farmers took up cocoa. The demand for rubber and oil began to soar.

Not surprisingly, in such dynamic conditions, the demand for capital became intense. It was needed above all to finance the transport infrastructure without which development would be retarded, curtailing the profits of speculation in land, mines and urban property. Commodity-producing regions competed furiously to bring their goods to market and capture the largest share. They needed the services of shipping lines, shipping agents, insurers, banks and brokers. They needed the fast accurate commercial information provided by the telegraph. In turn, they spent much of the proceeds of their newfound wealth on consumer goods, especially clothes and cotton goods which, in non-industrial countries, typically made up between 15 and 30 per cent of imports.[63] And, as the traffic in trade, capital and commercial information grew in scale and velocity, they experienced its 'globalising' effects. Their port-cities, the hinge between hinterland and world market, swelled in size and importance, especially those on the great trunk routes of maritime trade across the North Atlantic, to the River Plate and eastward via Colombo to Singapore, Hong Kong and Yokohama. Commercial elites waxed richer and their views more influential. Diasporas expanded and prospered as their networks became more valuable. Information, fashion, opinion and news were more widely, swiftly and sometimes accurately disseminated.

The principal great power beneficiary of these trends was Britain. The growth of world trade after 1900 was a huge opportunity. British steamship tonnage rose from 7.2 million in 1900 to 11.2 million in 1913.[64] The 'invisible' income from commercial services shot up from £109 million to over £168 million.[65] The value of British exports rose from £291 million to £525 million,[66] forming by 1913 some

25 per cent of GDP.[67] The total of British investment overseas all but doubled, and so did the income that it yielded – from £103 million to £199 million. Returns on investment abroad was now twice the figure for 1873, and four times that of the 1850s.[68] The overall surplus on the balance of payments (current account) climbed like a rocket from £37 million in 1900 to £224 million in 1913,[69] creating a huge new fund for investment overseas. And, as if to reflect the broadening stream of trade and capital, the number of emigrants from the British Isles to extra-European countries now reached its highest level in the last three years of peace, with Canada, Australia and New Zealand as the most popular destinations.[70]

This dramatic acceleration in global economic activity, and the active part played in it by Britain and the countries of the British world-system had important consequences for their stability and cohesion. For Britain's own role, the timing had been crucial. The fact that the great rise in industrial competition had occurred in a period of such exceptionally rapid growth in world trade sheltered British industry from its worst effects. Two other circumstances eased Britain's passage into a global economy in which competition was now 'multipolar'. First, although the neatness of the boundaries should not be exaggerated, the three great industrial powers tended to concentrate in different markets and (to a lesser extent) to specialise in different exports. American exports to Europe were chiefly food and raw materials, like cotton. American competition with British manufactures was strongest in Canada, taking by far the largest share of that country's imports (Canada's total imports in 1913 were $692 million: $441 million from the United States, $139 million from Britain, and $14 million from Germany),[71] and in Central America. In 1913, Germany's most important customers were in Europe, to which over three-quarters of her exports were consigned. Sixteen per cent went to the Americas, but only 8 per cent to Asia, Africa and Oceania combined.[72] By contrast, two-thirds of British trade lay outside Europe. The Americas took 21 per cent of British exports; Asia, Africa and Oceania 43 per cent.[73] Of course, in a hugely increased volume of trade, British exports no longer claimed the same overwhelming predominance even in old-established markets. But this had not prevented (as we have seen) a large increase in British exports. And, while Britain imported a growing proportion of manufactured goods, it was notable that German exports achieved a lower penetration there than in any other industrial country.[74]

Secondly, Britain retained, and perhaps even enhanced, her astonishing pre-eminence as the supplier of capital and commercial services. Here, too, we should not underestimate the importance of commercial rivalry. But no single grand challenger had emerged. The United States had barely begun to export capital, and except in Canada and Central America was of minor significance as a foreign investor. In Argentina, Brazil and Uruguay, where South American growth was strongest, American investment was negligible.[75] The sole exception in the 'Southern Cone' was Chile. France, second to Britain in foreign investment, was far behind in industrial output and French capital was concentrated overwhelmingly in Southern and Eastern Europe and in Russia.[76] There was little prospect of Britain's spheres being sucked into a French commercial *imperium*. German investment was much smaller in scale and, like France's, mainly found in Europe. Outside Europe, its infrastructure was underdeveloped. In Latin America, for example, German business found it easier to raise money through London.[77] Where German capital competed most aggressively in the extra-European world, it was usually where government pressure had been exerted on German banks and the objects were as much political as commercial.[78] In fact, the normal instinct of banks and investors in continental Europe was to cooperate with London and use its services. This was hardly surprising. So long as so much of world trade was financed by sterling bills (the medium for transactions between different national currencies) – and two-thirds of sterling bills in 1913 served trade between third parties – the City would be the natural magnet for short-term funds and foreign exchange.[79] These in turn would draw the foreign banks and their deposits to London, swelling still further the mass of capital and credit located there.

In the long decade before the First World War, the impact of commercial change on the British economy had been to alleviate industrial competition and perhaps even to prop up industries – like cotton and coal – that were labour- not capital-intensive. Far from weakening London's grip on its commercial empire, it helped the City to 'annex' new provinces (like Argentina), to consolidate old ones (like India, South Africa, Australia and New Zealand), and to advance new tropical bridgeheads into West Africa and Southeast Asia. In the process, vast new assets were acquired and further claims piled up on the productive capacity of new regions. All this signalled a deeper and closer integration between Britain and the varied parts of the British world-system.

For Britain's associates, clients and subjects in that system, the common experience had been the enormous growth of their foreign trade and the inflow of new investment, much of it directed to the improvement of their transport and communications. The weight in their economies shifted further towards the international sector, oriented if not always on Britain as a market then on London as the hub of their trade and finance. In independent countries like Argentina and Brazil, the City's power was felt as keenly as in any colony. They had adopted the gold standard (with its guarantee of convertibility) to attract the foreign (usually London-based) investor. Having done so, they were forced to accept its ruthless discipline. When their imports outran their exports (as happened in the economic cycle), and their foreign credits dwindled, they had either to borrow more abroad or to rein in their home economies by monetary contraction, perhaps both. They dare not offend the money power in London: the consequences of an investment famine were too dire. Without capital imports, their export production would stagnate; without foreign credits (and access to sterling bills), trade would dry up; without foreign trade, public revenues would collapse.[80] But the result was to transmit the fluctuations of export performance in exaggerated form into the internal economy: booms were wilder and contractions sharper. Moreover, gold standard countries on the 'periphery' soon felt the effects, if a correction was needed in the British economy, to check an adverse movement in foreign exchange. By raising interest rates, the Bank of England could swiftly draw gold and foreign credits into London at the expense of peripheral economies – a technique at which it grew very adept in the years before 1914. The City's pivotal role in world trade (with all its benefits) thus went hand in hand with its tightening grip on the economic life of extra-European states without money-markets of their own and dependent on foreign capital.

The dominions, India and Africa

The white dominions also saw large increases in their foreign trade and (with some variation) in their imports of capital between 1900 and 1913. Here, too, the result was to strengthen the pull of London and (in different ways) to reinforce their attachment to the British system. The most obvious case was Canada where 'continental' integration with the American economy had been the main competitor. But the creation of a wheat economy in the Prairie West after 1900 using largely British capital checked this continental drift. The transatlantic route, and its western extension to Winnipeg and beyond, grew busier. The great transport empire of the Canadian Pacific Railway (largely owned in Britain) prospered. Montreal, local metropole of the wheat economy, boomed. When reciprocity (free trade in natural products with the United States) was proposed in 1911 by Laurier's Liberal government, it drew furious opposition not just from Montreal and the Canadian Pacific Railway, but (fatally) from Laurier's Liberal allies in Ontario. For Toronto interests, as much as Montreal, now saw continentalism as a deadly threat to their vision of a national economy. The commercial tie with Britain was the best guarantee of Canadian autonomy, the continuing flow of British funds and the regional primacy of Central Canada in the confederation.[81]

In South Africa, finally unified in 1910, the London connection was no less critical to the dream of a 'national' future. Far more than wheat or wool in the other dominions, gold was the foundation of the South African economy, and the indispensable means of recovery from the catastrophe of 1899–1902. In the years up to 1914, production and employment on the Rand grew rapidly. Gold output rose from £16 million in 1898 (the last year before the War) to £38 million in 1912.[82] The workforce followed suit.[83] An authoritative estimate in 1914 claimed that gold mining contributed nearly half of government's public and railway revenue. It may already have given half the population its livelihood in what was otherwise (barring diamonds) an impoverished agrarian economy. It was gold that attracted foreign capital; gold that paid for the railway system; gold that made possible the Union of 1910 and the uneasy partnership of Boer and British. But the bonanza had strings. In the age of the gold standard, the international price of gold was fixed and invariable. Yet the cost of recovering the low-grade ores of the Rand rose remorselessly as the mines dug deeper. Profit depended upon driving costs lower, especially the cost of labour. Partly as a result, ownership of the mines was concentrated in the hands of a few large groups, of which the largest, the 'Corner House' group (Wernher, Beit, later the Central Mining Investment Corporation) controlled 50 per cent of production.[84] Corner House was managed from London – the world centre of mining finance – to which its principals had retired. On its fortunes depended much of South Africa's commercial credit, and hence the experiment in white self-government embarked on in 1910.

Powerful as it seemed, mining capital depended upon the Afrikaner-led government of Botha and Smuts for political support. It faced an increasingly embittered white working class in Johannesburg furiously opposed to 'dilution' of the workforce by black or Chinese labour.[85] Production, profits and share price were dangerously vulnerable to strikes and sabotage. White opinion (and almost all voters were white) was susceptible to *swaartgevaar* ('black peril'): the fear of black competition for jobs and a black presence in the towns. Afrikaner opinion (and the majority of whites were Afrikaners) disliked and mistrusted 'foreign' capital and the 'Randlords'. With their backs to this white wall, Smuts and Botha drove a hard bargain. They insisted on the expulsion of Chinese indentured labour – the red rag to the white bull – and encouraged the Randlords to replace foreign-born (largely British) mineworkers with local-born Afrikaners.[86] In the Mines and Works Act of 1911, they imposed an industrial colour-bar on the Rand. But, in return, they outlawed strike action, crushed white labour militancy spectacularly in 1914 and sanctioned the huge increase in black migrant workers. Behind this compromise, we can see an anxious attempt to mitigate the political risks of exposure to external economic forces. But in no other dominion did the political and social structure (with all its racial conflicts and inequities) rest so completely on an industry bound so inflexibly to the London market. Nor on one so perilously close (or so it seemed until the mid-1930s) to commercial failure and terminal decline.

Australia and New Zealand had suffered badly in the 1890s when falling export prices, over-borrowing, a banking crisis (as overseas deposits were withdrawn and their London assets shrank) and monetary contraction plunged them into depression. The steady rise in commodity prices in the new century brought relief and recovery. Australian exports reached £80 million by 1913[87] and an official commission rejoiced at the world's insatiable appetite for Australian products.[88] Yet Australia failed to attract new British capital. In London, disillusionment after the crash of 1893 was reinforced by mistrust of the new Commonwealth's blend of economic nationalism and home-grown socialism. The widening sphere of wage arbitration, state enterprise and protective tariffs caused irritation in the City.[89] Instead, Australians financed their capital needs and overseas debts from their rising export income. But none of this meant secession from the commercial world centred on London. Australian 'socialism' was not a reversion to autarky but (like the insistence on all-white immigration) a tactic to reduce the dominion's exposure to the external shocks felt so sharply in the 1890s.

Economic realities dictated reliance on the British market for half of Australia's rising exports, and on the City for the short-term funds that lubricated trade. As growth picked up, so did the need for British capital. Whatever their 'socialist' leanings, Australian leaders showed faultless conservatism when it came to banking. The Commonwealth Bank, set up in 1912 to meet the need for a central bank, carefully followed the fiduciary practice of the Bank of England.[90] Not coincidentally, perhaps, there was a sharp rise in British investment thereafter. In New Zealand, where the 1890s had been less painful, the British connection was even more important. Nearly 80 per cent of New Zealand exports were destined for Britain and perhaps 90 per cent of public debt was held there.[91] Tariffs were moderate, compensating (if that) for the fall in ocean freights and import costs.[92] Banking practice was cautious to an extreme lest the London investor be frightened again.[93] Above all, New Zealand farming was adapted to meet the surging demand in Britain for frozen meat and dairy products. The reward was an astonishing burst of economic growth. Between 1896 and 1911, production rose by 60 per cent, the area under white occupation by 50 per cent and population by 40 per cent. The fruit of this closer integration was a virtual remaking of New Zealand society, forging a political economy that would last for more than fifty years.

For all the overseas dominions, the boom in global trade had been a chance to strengthen their economies and stabilise their politics. But it had not brought greater freedom from London's commercial influence. In economic terms, as well as political, 'nation-building' in the white dominions meant greater dependence not less on the British market and the financial machinery of the City of London. In a global marketplace, access to capital, information and expertise from the commercial centre was more essential than ever to dominion producers whose fortunes depended upon good connections with London, perhaps even a base there. In India, which lacked self-government, the pattern was more complicated. In commercial terms, India's pattern of foreign trade was exceptionally valuable to London. India ran a trade surplus with Europe, the United States and Southeast Asia but a deficit with Britain, whose best customer it was. India's remittances of foreign exchange helped London meet Britain's trade deficits in America and Europe, lubricating the international payments system without which world trade would have expanded much more slowly. But India was also required to meet an annual bill for the interest

payments on borrowed British capital, for the pensions of British officials and for the 'hire' of some 70,000 British troops normally stationed
on the sub-continent. Since long-term borrowing was very difficult in
India, and its own revenues were inelastic, the government of India
relied on British lenders to supply the capital it needed for spending on
public works like railways and irrigation.

In the 1880s and 1890s, this economic relationship with Britain
had been strained. India had a silver-based currency and silver's value
fell sharply against gold. The government of India had to find more and
more silver rupees to pay its sterling debts. It faced a dangerous spiral
of rising taxation (increasing discontent), heavier borrowing (to cover
the deficit), ever-heavier debt service and the spectre of a default –
a political and financial catastrophe of unimaginable proportions.
India's double function – in Britain's payments balance and military
'economy' – was at risk. In practice, after 1900, this danger quickly
receded. At London's insistence, the Indian government adopted a 'gold
exchange standard'. The rupee–sterling exchange rate was fixed, and a
fund of gold and sterling assets established in London to maintain the
value of the rupee and cover any shortfall in Indian remittances.[94] The
experiment was a success, but chiefly perhaps because it was launched
at a time when India's foreign trade and payments surplus were also
rising rapidly. India's surplus on commodity trade was about Rs 200
million in 1900 and Rs 700 million in 1910 and Rs 570 million in
1913.[95] It was true that India continued to run an overall deficit with
London that arose in part from British loans and the service charges that
London imposed. This had to be met by further borrowing.[96] But the
scale was comparatively modest (perhaps £6 million per year) and part
of it was due to new investment in railways and irrigation in a period
of commercial expansion. It was also true that the domestic impact of
India's deepening involvement in international trade was muffled by
the vast scale of the rural economy much of it close to subsistence and
threatened by periodic famine – although export-producing regions
did experience rising living standards.[97] The bar on tariffs imposed
by London made diversification into industry more difficult. Overall,
however, the pre-war years saw the closer integration of India into the
British world-system. India remained Britain's largest single market. Its
export surpluses were larger. Its payments to Britain were met without
strain. Most important of all, perhaps, financial stability and economic
growth underwrote the political system of the Civilian Raj. Relieved

by prosperity from the pressure to tax more heavily or intervene more deeply in the agrarian economy, the Raj had no need to seek wider cooperation from its Indian subjects or pay the price in concessions.[98] It could balance its imperial obligations and the Indian books. This was the vital condition if it was to keep its freedom as much from its overlords in London as its subjects in India.

But perhaps nowhere were the effects of trade so striking as in Britain's new tropical dependencies in Afro-Asia. The commodity boom galvanised their economies after 1900. The rapid growth of production and export sales attracted larger British-based companies with better access to credit and capital than indigenous traders. In colonial Malaya they took the lead in rubber and tin.[99] In British West Africa, rocketing exports of cocoa and palm products transformed the prospects of the 'Coaster' firms.[100] The colonial states could push railways into their vast new hinterlands as their credit rose with their (customs-based) revenues. As the interior opened up, the scale of British business was transformed. Large British firms crowded out their local African rivals. The rush for Nigerian tin excited the City.[101] Shipping and banking fell under the control of the self-made magnate Alfred Jones, chairman of Elder Dempster and the British Bank of West Africa. Liverpool had long been the real metropolis of the British West African coast. Now its commercial reach extended to the fringes of the Sahara.[102] By 1905, the Lagos Chamber of Commerce was exclusively white.

After 1900, then, the British exploited to the full their comparative advantage as traders, shippers and financiers and their dominance in cotton textiles – the universal consumption good in Afro-Asian markets. The demand for their capital and commercial services and the primacy of London as the clearing-house of trade and investment deepened the mutual dependence between the different elements of the British world-system: the British Isles; India; the white dominions; and the property, assets, concessions and installations that made up the City's commercial empire in non-British countries. By 1913, nearly one half of British net assets were located overseas. British capital moved freely between the informal empire, the white dominions and the tropical dependencies. New business empires in railways and shipping combined interests in all three. With its monetary controls now centralised in London, the Indian economy (and its vital functions) had been brought under closer imperial supervision. For the white dominions, not only were British markets and capital indispensable, but close contacts with London were needed for local businessmen who hoped to expand abroad, invest surplus funds or exploit their expertise in less developed economies. In the British system, all (or almost all) commercial roads led to London. They would do for so long as London could play its part in global commerce; so long as the British economy could produce, consume and invest on an imperial scale; so long as its chosen partners could maintain their hectic growth; and so long as Britain was the safest and strongest haven for foreign money. But, on all these scores, even in the boom years up to 1914, there was at least some room for doubt.

Some of the symptoms of later weakness were already visible. For an advanced economy, the British were much too dependent upon the comparatively simple and labour-intensive technology of textile-making. They depended too heavily on coal, as an export and as a fuel. Their rate of saving was low and the failure to invest at home was reflected in stagnating industrial productivity. As many social critics complained, too much of the population was paid too little, a consequence of widespread under-employment. This limited consumption and promoted the migration that remained so marked a feature of British life. Among Britain's most dynamic trading partners, there were signs that the furious expansion of their agrarian economies was levelling off: in New Zealand, Canada and Argentina. Nor was the City's great role as banker to the world without risk. The American crisis of 1907 had shown that funds that rushed in could also rush out. The large volume of short-term funds that London attracted were potentially destabilising. Just holding them there might mean interest rates too high for domestic growth. Above all, perhaps, by relying so much on the proceeds of global trade, the British had staked their future on a world without war, or, at least, on a world without world-war. Some of these anxieties lay behind the campaign for tariff reform in Britain. Protection was meant to reduce Britain's over-exposure to external economic forces. Protectionists like Milner insisted that, in the age of world-states, cosmopolitanism was dead and its champions deluded. At the time prosperity helped deflate the protectionist cause. The imperialism of free trade still ruled. Its theory and practice had been the secret of both Victorian expansion and its Edwardian climax. The implications of its breakdown were massive. Acceptance of its logic and recognition of its benefits had held together the disparate elements of the British world-system. It weathered the Edwardian squalls. But its real test was to come.

The politics of cohesion

Like any worldwide empire, the British system was a prey to centrifugal forces. Resentment, recalcitrance, resistance and rebellion came naturally to those who felt (in different ways) the weight of British political and financial power. Political independence, economic self-sufficiency, or cultural autonomy promised obvious gains to at least some colonial (and semi-colonial) elites. But only if the conditions were right, the costs were low and the benefits clear.

In the long Edwardian decade, the economic and geopolitical conditions we have examined were, in general, *imperially* benign. They favoured not the break-up of empire but its cohesion and closer integration. In terms of grand strategy, the danger to imperial solidarity had been twofold. If British power was insufficient to exclude rival influence from its spheres, or promised inadequate protection against external attack, colonial leaders would drift towards home-grown policies in defence and diplomacy. In dependencies, the prestige of British rule would fall, forcing a choice between coercion and concession. The second danger was that the costs of defence would spiral uncontrollably. In the British system, they would fall most heavily on taxpayers at home and in India. The likely consequence would be a domestic revolt against imperial commitments and an Indian revolt against a grasping Raj.

In the event, both dangers were contained with surprising ease. Great power competition after 1900 was largely turned to Britain's advantage. Crucially, the main burden of defence was naval, and the main focus of fear was home not colonial – in Britain itself. Hence British opinion was easily rallied and the Indian taxpayer left unscathed. As an added bonus, the self-governing dominions were readily persuaded of the threat to British sea-power and of the urgency of offering (some) help. Though friction persisted (within the dominions and between their governments and London), it was smoothed by the credibility of British power, the aggressive demeanour of German diplomacy and the global scale of great power rivalry: isolation was not an option. Economic trends were similarly favourable. In the race for growth, colonial politicians and businessmen looked more than ever to Britain for money, markets or migrants. In a world of dynamic commerce, autarky was a cul-de-sac. Profits came from large combines and wide connections. In Britain, commercial buoyancy was especially timely. Naval spending floated on a high tide of revenue. Lloyd George's new taxes, controversial as they were, easily paid for the increase in naval and social expenditure.[103] The economic burden of rearmament was easily carried by the enormous surplus in the balance of payments. The sense of general prosperity checked the appeal of tariffs and helped smother the campaign for imperial preference. Since tariff reform and its political rider 'imperial unity' (between Britain and the white dominions) were at odds with the free trade basis of commercial empire and excluded India, their disruptive potential for the British system would have been considerable. Of course, the Edwardians were not free from economic anxiety. In *The Nation's Wealth* (1914), the radical MP Leo Chiozza Money gloomily compared Britain's natural resources with those of Germany and the United States. But even he conceded that Britain was still at the mid-point of her greatness: decline lay more than a century away.

In Britain, then, the political climate was sympathetic to empire but unpropitious for schemes of imperial 'reform'. Public alarm over defence shone a fitful spotlight on the white dominions as sources of loyal manpower. Their commercial prospects and migrant appeal were touted more aggressively in the British press.[104] Imperial news was more widely and professionally reported. An influential section of the political elite (on both sides of the party line) was attracted to the idea of 'closer union' with the sister nations of 'Greater Britain'. But wide differences existed on timing and method even among the enthusiasts. A broader consensus prevailed that, while imperial unity was desirable, perhaps even inevitable, imperial federation was at best premature, at worst unworkable.[105] Towards India and the tropical dependencies, British opinion was complacent. The Morley–Minto reforms had taken India off the political agenda. The commercial promise of tropical territories bought off half the critics of imperial aggrandisement. The new gospel of imperial duty, artfully diffused (not least in *The Times*), disarmed most of the rest. The radical critique of empire, fanned into flame by the South African War, burned low by the decade's end. In the age of diplomatic detente, constitutional devolution (in South Africa and India) and social reform, 'imperialism' was less easily damned as the road to national ruin.[106]

The dominions

The dominions' counterpart to this imperial attitude in Britain was the 'Britannic nationalism' of their English-speaking populations. Britannic nationalism was both more and less than an affirmation of empire loyalism. It asserted that Canada (or Australia or New Zealand) was (or must soon become) 'nations' – the highest stage of political and cultural development. Only as nations could the white dominions escape the dependent, parochial quarrelsomeness of their colonial origins. Only as nations could they offer their citizens security, opportunity and the promise of progress, cultural as well as material. But they must be 'British nations', because it was British (or British-derived) institutions, culture, ethnic origins and allegiance (to the British Crown) that held them together. It was being 'British' that endowed them with their 'progressive' qualities and their sense of a manifest, expansionist destiny. This was a far cry from colonial cringe. Nor was it always a recipe for imperial harmony. Britannic nationalism demanded partnership between Britain and the settler countries not central direction. It meant a dominion commitment to imperial defence but a dominion voice in imperial policy. It viewed empire as a cooperative and 'Britishness' as a common inheritance – not the private property of the 'old country'.

There were good reasons why Britannic nationalism and its message of political community among the British nations should have been influential (though not uncontested) in the pre-war years. The upsurge in trade, migration and investment showed that British expansion, far from being over, was more vigorous than ever. Whatever metropolitan doubters might say, there was little dispute on the imperial frontier that the future belonged to 'white men's countries'. So long, that was, as they took pains to defend their 'inheritance'. It was significant that alarm in Britain over Germany's threat to the naval shield coincided with dominion fears of the 'Yellow Peril' and of Japanese hegemony in the Pacific. These common sources of fear and hope took on added colour in each dominion. In Canada, it was resentment at the French Canadians' 'disloyalty' and their obstruction of the nation-making programme of the English Canadians. In Australia, the defence of 'White Australia' against an imaginary Asian invasion became the central purpose of the federation achieved in 1900 and the guarantee of its social cohesion. In New Zealand, racial purity as a 'British' country was part of the message of social reform in the Liberal era after 1890. Here, too, external defence and internal peace made a double case for Britannic sentiment. Relations between the dominions and Downing Street may have been tetchy. The scale of contribution to imperial defence was bound to be controversial – bitterly so in Canada. The cause was not so much doubt about the imperial association as division over how its burdens should be shared.

In South Africa, Britannic nationalism played a different part. The white 'nation' was predominantly Afrikaner not British. The grant of self-government to the former Boer republics had brought Afrikaner not British politicians to power. Union in 1910 gave them control over a unitary (not federal) dominion. To the ex-proconsul Lord Milner, conceding self-government before the British could form a majority among whites had been disastrous. 'I absolutely decline', he wrote in 1908, 'to take any further account of South Africa in drawing up the balance sheet of empire.'[107] But, he conceded, there was a saving grace. Because South Africa was 'technically a British country', British emigrants could exert their improving influence without losing their nationality. 'It may be', he concluded, 'that it is the destiny of the Englishman in South Africa to turn the scale in South Africa to save the better native [i.e. Afrikaner] element from being submerged by the worse.'[108] The leading 'English' politicians in South Africa adopted this view. Their Progressive (Unionist after 1910) party embraced the classic programme of Britannic nationalism: support for immigration, the 'Imperial Navy' and imperial preference in a 'united . . . nation, forming an integral part of the Empire and cooperating harmoniously with Imperial authority'.[109] But the party's leaders saw that, with an 'English' minority, opposition to the Afrikaners on purely racial lines was futile. Instead, their object must be to divide the 'extreme racial backveld' section from the 'progressive' elements under Botha and Smuts.[110] It was vital to prevent the Free State politicians, Hertzog and Steyn, and their 'cultural nationalist' allies in the Cape's Afrikaner Bond, from dominating the government.

Botha was too shrewd to wear his heart on his sleeve. He was an adept of the ambiguous phrase. His regime, grumbled Milner's South African confidant Percy Fitzpatrick, was 'dishonest and unclean'.[111]

But he made a reassuring figure. 'Ties with the Mother Country must be strengthened', he declared in 1910. He wanted a 'South African nationality... able to take an honourable place in the ranks of sister states'.[112] 'Botha really wants to do what is best for the British Empire', wrote Walter Long, a senior British Conservative who met him at the Imperial Conference in 1911. It would be disastrous to alienate him.[113] Even Milner agreed he was better than any alternative.[114] Both urged in favour of Jameson's policy of conditional cooperation. Botha's own motives are hard to reconstruct. Fitzpatrick believed that both he and Smuts had realised that they could not rule through the 'Dutch' (i.e. Afrikaner) party alone.[115] This analysis seems plausible. Certainly, they showed little inclination towards the cultural nationalism of their Cape and Free State allies, though they were wary of its ethnic appeal. They preferred to feel their way towards a more inclusive 'South Africanism' acceptable to 'moderate' Afrikaners and English – the old programme of Rhodes before 1895. So in the fluid aftermath of Union the local Britannic nationalism operated in low key. But its role was crucial nonetheless. For it served as a warning to Botha and Smuts that repudiation of the spirit of empire membership (never mind the letter of British sovereignty) would drive the English into all-out opposition and force them into the arms of those who wished to reverse the verdict of 1902.

India

Among the dominions, adhesion to the British system was a matter of sentiment and calculation. It was nourished by the feeling of 'British-ness', the benefits of 'British connection' and the promise of influence over British policy. Neither sentiment nor calculation had so much scope in India. Indians, after all, had almost no share of executive power in British-ruled (not princely) India. Their direct influence on imperial policy was negligible. And, as Indian nationalists regularly complained, India paid a tribute to Britain in money and men – burdens that London dared not impose on the dominions.

The British 'Civilians' (the name was gradually slipping out of use) were eager to cultivate Indian loyalty but uncertain how to do it. By 1900, the dominant strain in their policy was an appeal to 'feudal' attitudes they thought typically Indian: a sense of fealty; a respect for authority and the glamour of power. If India's natural leaders were princes and aristocrats, their instincts were conservative and royalist.

Hence British rule should clothe itself in imperial purple and assume the dignity of the Mughal empire. The corollary was indifference approaching hostility towards those Indians who had responded most enthusiastically to the modernising, liberal and 'scientific' face of British rule: the 'microscopic minority' organised in the Congress. Yet, in reality, this group could not be ignored. The Civilians might have *liked* a feudal polity: they certainly *needed* a profitable colony. They had to foster the modern India they came to dislike. They had to tolerate the Indians who helped to make it work. And they had to accept that the microscopic minority had the political means to embarrass their rule and upset their faraway masters in London.

As we have seen, the Congress did this to some effect in the years after 1905. But, in a larger view, political conditions in the pre-war Raj did not favour a serious assault on India's subordinate place in the British world-system. The British had been able to stabilise their military spending, a prime grievance of nationalist politics. Good times in trade took the heat out of *swadeshi* agitation in Bengal. The princes were appeased with the promise of non-interference. Muslims were conciliated by separate electorates. The Congress moderates received their schedule of constitutional reform: disappointment was buried in the small print. Unappeased were the followers of Tilak whose 'new party' principles bore the stamp of 'cultural nationalism': the repudiation of British rule, not a plea to share in it. But Tilak was rejected by the moderate majority: without their protection he was crushed by the British.

For all their impatience with the Civilian Raj and its parsimonious concessions, the Congress leaders were boxed in. In theory, they could have widened their popular appeal. They could have taken the Tilak road. But this was the low road to power through the cultivation of 'sub-national' feeling in India's linguistic provinces: playing on religion, caste or ethnic prejudice. It was a road the Civilians were determined to block. But the Congress leaders rejected it anyway, favouring instead the 'high' road: entering on merit the ranks of the Civilians and widening the scope of representative politics. In practice, their 'national' programme needed the British to abdicate voluntarily, allowing the Congress, once installed in power, to 'make a nation' from above. The only principle on which this nation could be made was the 'British' principle: a people unified not by religion or language, but by institutions and allegiance. It was not surprising then that the Congress leaders defined their goal as a status equivalent to that of the white dominions; that they protested their loyalty and proclaimed their attachment to British values. Less confidently than their dominion counterparts, these Indian politicians also asserted a claim to be British, in ethos, attitude and allegiance if not by 'race'. They felt all the more keenly the 'racial' antagonism their aspirations aroused. Hence perhaps the heartfelt plea of Surendranath Banerjea, long the most dynamic figure in Indian politics. 'May I be permitted to make an appeal...to...the Government of India', he told the Indian legislative council in 1913,

> That they may so discharge their exalted duties that this sentiment may be deepened...that we may all feel and realize, no matter whether we are Englishmen or Scotchmen or Irishmen or Indians, that we are Britishers: fellow-citizens, participating in the privileges and also in the obligations of of a common Empire.[116]

This was scarcely the promise of unconditional obedience to London's wishes. It was more a demand to be treated with respect. But it also suggested how far the pre-war Congress was from contemplating a future outside the Empire. As with the dominions, it was the terms not the fact of membership it was determined to challenge.

The new empire in Africa

In the old empire, the central question of imperial politics was how far the dominion peoples and Indian elites would identify their interests with the British world-system. In the 'new' empire, the issue was more fundamental. The buffer zones annexed to defend the mid-Victorian *imperium* were a jigsaw legacy of partition. It was hard to imagine their future as loyal imperial communities. Colonial states had to be made before colonial societies could form inside them. In West Africa, British rule before the Scramble had been confined to coastal enclaves. In the partition era after 1884, each enclave acquired an enormous hinterland (the exception was Gambia). Sovereignty was one thing, authority another. Imposing British control on these vast interiors required considerable force: against the Hut Tax revolt in Sierra Leone; against the Ashanti in 1901; against the Yoruba states and Ibo peoples of Southern Nigeria and the Muslim emirates of the North. With the defeat of this inland resistance (Kano and Sokoto submitted to Lugard in 1902) came the moment of political decision.

It might have been expected that the British would carry upcountry the political system they had devised for the Coast. This was far from democratic. But it provided for legislative bodies with nominated African members;[117] an English legal system with juries, a bar and a separate judiciary; and the beginnings of municipal government. A 'creole' elite spreading east from Freetown (the metropole of Creoledom) had grown up along the Coast, fervently conscious of its progressive, Christian and civilised credentials, and eager to share in the imperial advance.[118] But it soon became clear that the British had other ideas.

The dominant factor was the need to impose a colonial *pax* as quickly as possible and at minimum cost. With few sources of revenue and heavy military outgoings, the British in the interior were eager to settle with the emirs and chiefs they had defeated or overawed. There was no time to replace them or to reconstruct their conquered polities in the image of the Coast. It was easier and cheaper to restore the old regimes on condition of loyalty, and exert British paramountcy directly through a cadre of 'Residents' backed up by the threat of force. This was the system devised for Northern Nigeria, variations of which were applied in the Gold Coast and Sierra Leone. It left no room for legislatures, municipalities or English law. When Northern and Southern Nigeria were unified in 1914 to relieve the British Treasury of the burden of the impecunious North (annual revenues £210,000 per annum)[119] at the expense of the South (annual revenue £2 million),[119] Lugard, the architect of 'amalgamation' was careful to restrict coastal institutions to the old colony of Lagos. He was determined to spread his favoured system of 'indirect rule' as widely as possible. 'Fixing' the population geographically and socially became the overriding principle of British policy. It meant shoring up, or even inventing, 'traditional' rulers, and excluding the 'interference' of creole lawyers and 'speculators'[120] from the interior. Not surprisingly, the creole elite became increasingly restive, protesting its loyalty but denouncing the drift towards racial exclusion and arbitrary rule.[121] But its influence beyond the coastal towns was limited. The conservative bias of British over-rule was congenial to its 'traditional' allies. The cash-crop revolution, bringing rising incomes to an emergent peasantry, eased the strains of conquest. And, with the growth of its customs revenues, the colonial state in British West Africa could afford to govern and tax with a very light hand. Politically, then, the West African colonies were set to become not nations-in-the-making but so many tribal confederacies united only in subjection to their British overlord.[122]

In East Africa, the onset of colonial rule had been even more abrupt. There were no old enclaves of European rule on the coast. The interior had been a dangerous region, ravaged by the Arab slave trade and endemic warlordism. Once partition began, the British annexed Uganda in 1894 as the white hope of East African trade and a strategic wedge against French advance across the continent.[123] Uganda could be ruled in alliance with Buganda, largest and strongest of the Great Lakes kingdoms.[124] But the East African Protectorate ('Kenya' from 1920) was a different story. With no natural rulers, except the Arab sheikhs along the Swahili coast, no revenues, a railway (to Uganda) to maintain and interior populations fiercely resistant to external control, the East African Protectorate was a financial incubus inside an administrative nightmare. The colonial remedy – white farmers to develop the temperate highlands of central Kenya and Indians to help build the railway – had obvious dangers. The settlers were quick to adopt the programme of their brothers to the south: self-government (only for whites); the throwing open of land to white purchase; a white citizen militia (like the Boer commando) for security; and the exclusion of Indians from political life and the ownership of land.[125] The settlers extracted the 'Elgin pledge' effectively if not formally reserving the Kenya highlands for whites. But they were far too few in number to impose a South African 'solution'. Well before 1914, East African Indians were mobilising against the threat of settler hegemony.[126] African grievances were beginning to be voiced.[127] Yet, in this racially segmented society, no group was strong enough to seize control from below. The colonial state was too weak to build its 'nation' from above.

In West and East Africa alike, colonial rule had created 'shallow states' without roots in local society. Freed from the burden of external defence by partition diplomacy, the British had no need to dig deep. Colonial government became an over-rule concerned mainly to keep the peace between its fractious subjects. The political future of so protean an empire was at best opaque. To many enlightened imperialists (as well as liberal opinion more generally), the greed and brutality of unofficial whites was far more alarming than the political aspirations of (as yet) unorganised blacks. Hence segregation, not integration, seemed the best solution for the medium term. The threat of racial conflict was not ignored by contemporary observers of the imperial system. But they tended to be fatalistic about settler domination and thought African advance would be slow.

Islam

Rather less attention was paid (outside official circles) to the other great fissure that ran through the British world-system. By 1914, the British system depended upon the loyalty and cooperation of a vast array of Muslim rulers and notables: in Zanzibar, Nigeria, Egypt, the Sudan, the Persian Gulf, Princely India and British India, and the Malay States. British relations with the Ottoman Empire and Persia (the largest independent Muslim states) were also exceptionally delicate: both were buffer states whose hostility or collapse would threaten the strategic corridor connecting Britain and India. British attitudes to Islam were contradictory, and there was no tradition of studying the contemporary Islamic world as there was for example in the Netherlands.[128] Evangelicals and humanitarians, reared on tales of David Livingstone and the Arab slave trade, were deeply unsympathetic. Romantics were attracted by the 'timeless' pre-industrial East and the warrior ethos of desert society. But the most powerful influence on British policy was a wary respect for Islamic 'fanaticism': the supposed ability of Muslim rulers or preachers to arouse intense popular feeling against 'infidel' imperialists. The Indian Mutiny of 1857, Gordon's fate at Khartoum, and bloody disasters in Afghanistan had ingrained this deeply in the 'official mind'.

But how dangerous was Islam to the political cohesion of the British system? The Islamic world stretched from Morocco to the Philippines. Islam, remarked the intellectual traveller Gertrude Bell, 'is the electric current by which the transmission of sentiment is effected, and its potency is increased by the fact that there is little or no sense of territorial nationality to counterbalance it'.[129] The government of India harped constantly on the danger of a 'pan-Islamic' movement transmitting the grievances of Middle East Muslims to India and beyond. With its chronic anxiety about a second Mutiny, its turbulent borderlands on the Northwest Frontier, and its diplomatic interests in the Persian Gulf, the Indian government's fears were understandable. Its real purpose was to restrain the 'Gladstonian' enthusiasm for liberating the Ottoman Sultan's Christian subjects to which opinion at home seemed all too prone. As the 'great Muhammadan Power', the Civilians insisted, Britain could not be seen to act against the interests of Islam. But few British observers thought pan-Islamism counted for much. 'As a factor in British policy', recalled Ronald Storrs of his time in pre-1914 Egypt, 'the doctrine of the caliphate – of pan-Islamic theocracy – was mainly the creation of the India Office.'[130] It 'can never become a movement of importance', judged Arnold Wilson, then a young consul in Southwest Persia.[131] Lord Cromer was equally sceptical.[132] In a survey of India published shortly before 1914, Bampfylde Fuller, a former Lieutenant-Governor of Bengal (a Muslim majority province), contrasted the political and educational backwardness of Muslims with the progress of Hindus – the real source of any challenge to the Raj.[133]

In fact, British opinion, whether sympathetic or not, tended to regard Islam as a culture in decline. It commanded enormous popular piety but had failed intellectually. It was the 'speculative' and 'dogmatic' nature of Islam, argued Fuller, that made Muslims resistant to modern knowledge. 'Swathed in the bands of the Koran', remarked Sir William Muir, the leading academic expert on Islam, 'the Moslem faith, unlike the Christian, is powerless to adapt itself to varying time and place, keep pace with the march of humanity, direct and purify the social life or elevate mankind.'[134] Hence the British assumption that, so long as care was taken not to offend popular religiosity, or the vested interests of the *ulama*, the interpreters of Islamic law, a *modus vivendi* was perfectly possible. British authority should be decently veiled behind Muslim notables: this was the ruling principle of the Cromerian and Lugardian systems. If provocation was avoided, and prestige maintained, there was little danger of Muslim piety turning into nationalist passion.

Whatever its premises, this sanguine view of Anglo-Muslim relations looked plausible enough before 1914. In India, where most of Britain's Muslim subjects could be found, Muslim political attitudes were coloured by the fact of competition with Hindus and fear of Hindu predominance. In Northern Nigeria, the colonial *pax* had helped the emirs against their over-mighty subjects and permitted the extension of Islamic influence over long-resistant 'pagan' peoples.[135] In Egypt, where the Khedive was usually at odds with the *ulama* of the al-Azhar – the greatest centre of learning in the Muslim world – an independent Egyptian state held little appeal for the doctors of law and theology.

Islamic feeling ran athwart the ideas of nationalism and its religious guardians were suspicious of secular rule. Only in extreme conditions, where secular authority was unusually weak or social disruption exceptionally acute, did Islamic politics seem likely to thrive – or pose a real threat to British power.

Ireland and Empire

Ironically, in the last few years before 1914, the main threat to imperial unity lay closest to home – in Ireland. There was nothing new in this. Much the same had been true in the 1590s, the 1640s, the 1680s, the 1770s, 1780s and 1790s, the 1820s and the 1880s. But, after 1900, Home Rule 'nationalism' was supposed to have been killed by British 'kindness'.[136] The sale and redistribution of land had been expected to create a contented peasantry, immune to the violent rhetoric of the 'land war' that had raged since the 1870s, and shrewdly aware of the economic benefits brought by the Union of Britain and Ireland. Municipal and parliamentary politics, not agrarian terror, would be the political vehicle of this farmer class and its allies among the small-town tradesmen. In this prosaic new world, 'romantic Ireland' would be dead and gone, 'with O'Leary in the grave'.

It failed to happen, at least not on the decisive scale that the architects of 'kindness' had hoped for. Part of the reason was the success of the Irish National Party, once led by Charles Stewart Parnell, in entrenching itself over much of Catholic Ireland outside Ulster and the City of Dublin. The Irish party was a formidable machine. When elected local government was extended to Ireland in 1898 in the form of county councils, the party gained a virtual monopoly of the powers and patronage it gave – as Unionist landowners bitterly complained. Its local bosses played a prominent role in the machinery for land sales, the process that was rearing a new breed of wealth in the countryside. The rapid growth of a provincial press gave the party's leaders and their newspaper allies an efficient means of mobilising opinion and exerting pressure. The one thing the party could not do was to force the British government to concede Home Rule. Until 1905, it faced a massive Conservative majority at Westminster. After 1906, as one Anglo-Irish landlord remarked, the scale of the Liberal landslide meant that the new government had no reason to risk introducing a third Home Rule bill.[137] After all, Home Rule had twice before been the rock on which Liberal governments had been wrecked.

The Irish party leader, John Redmond, understood this. Redmond was from a Catholic landowning family. His strategy was subtle and perhaps – given the divisions among his followers – deliberately opaque. Raising money in America he spoke of an Irish nation as if complete independence was the plan. But his real aim was to win Ireland the equivalent of dominion autonomy, the same status as Canada, Australia, New Zealand and South Africa. He liked to compare himself to Louis Botha, who had reconciled Afrikanerdom to self-government under the British Crown. 'Our stake in the Empire', he told a Liberal journalist in 1908, 'is too large for us to be detached from it ... [T]he Irish people peopled the waste places of Greater Britain. Our roots are in the Imperial as well as the national.'[138] 'Once we receive home rule', he told the *Daily Express* in 1910, 'we shall demonstrate our imperial loyalty beyond question.'[139] In *The Framework of Home Rule* (1911), Erskine Childers appealed to the Unionist opponents of Home Rule in similar terms. Ireland had nothing to gain by separation (i.e. complete independence), he claimed. 'Ireland has taken her full share in winning and populating the Empire. The result is hers as much as Britain's.' Indeed, giving Ireland Home Rule was part of the project of imperial unity, 'the indispensable preliminary to the close union of all the English-speaking races'.[140] Redmond hoped to reassure the enemies of Home Rule in both Britain and Ireland, to portray the Irish party as sober and responsible, and to appeal to a sense of All-Irish national identity, Northern and Protestant as well as Southern and Catholic.

In fact, Redmond's analogy between Ireland and South Africa was misplaced and his chances of success were thin. More than half his parliamentary party were 'agrarians' for whom the land struggle was still a political talisman. The party's popular movement, the United Irish League, was implicated in harrying landowners into forced sales and in 'cattle-driving'.[141] A vocal part of his following were 'cultural' nationalists, dismayed by the suddenness and intensity with which a Gaelic-speaking and non-literate society had been overwhelmed by anglicisation.[142] Limited opportunities for the new Catholic middle class (the comparison with the Bengal *bhadralok* is suggestive) bred fierce impatience with 'Dublin Castle', the seat of British rule in Ireland. By 1913, the Gaelic Athletic Association, the seedbed of this revolutionary and culturalist nationalism, had more than 100,000 members.[143]

When Redmond declared (in October 1910) that he was in favour of a federal solution, making Ireland part of a 'Federal Empire', he was forced to retract and repudiate by the pressure of party opinion.[144] But, if the room for manoeuvre on the nationalist side was limited, the scope for concession by their Unionist opponents seemed even less.

If Ireland had been a thousand miles away, Joseph Chamberlain is supposed to have remarked in 1893,[145] it would long since have been granted self-government. Inescapable proximity and ineradicable difference were the Irish condition. To British critics of Home Rule, Ireland was too close to be entrusted with self-government: it was part of the Empire's 'central power', not an outlying province.[146] If Irish autonomy was abused, argued Balfour, there would be little that London could do: yet the strategic stakes – if Ireland was disloyal – were much too high for the risk to be taken. The champions of tariff reform and imperial federation, like Milner, saw Home Rule as a retrograde step that would delay not encourage imperial unity. But the greatest obstacle to Redmond's programme (and the real difference from South Africa) lay in the extent to which Ireland's affairs were entangled in the party politics of the British mainland. One symptom of this was the fact that perhaps a quarter of Conservative MPs after 1906 were either Irish Unionists, Southern Irish gentry sitting for mainland constituencies, or married into Southern Unionist families.[147] The second, and more serious, was the intensity of 'Britannic' sentiment in Northeast Ireland where religious and cultural antipathy to the Catholic South was rapidly mutating into an 'Ulster' identity with 'Britishness' at its core.[148] But, unlike the British minority in South Africa, which was forced to settle with the Afrikaner majority, Ulster (like the rest of Ireland) was represented in the British Parliament. It could rely on powerful allies in mainland politics to obstruct the progress of Home Rule. And, if the worst came to the worst, it could threaten civil war in the heart of the Empire.

From these rigidities sprang the crisis of 1910–14. Its origins, and Redmond's opportunity, lay in the travails of the Liberal government. By 1909, its social programme (and electoral credibility) were at risk from blocking tactics in the House of Lords and the scale of its spending on the Navy. Its counter-stroke, the budget of 1909 and the consequential bill to limit the powers of the House of Lords, brought a constitutional crisis and a general election. The levelling up of Liberal and Unionist (or Conservative) strength in the House of Commons forced the Liberal cabinet into the arms of the Irish party while the passage of the Parliament Act (removing the veto of the House of Lords) erased their excuse for not honouring the long-standing commitment to Irish autonomy. A third Home Rule bill was drafted. In January 1913 it passed its last stage in the Commons with a majority of 110.[149] While offering Redmond much less than he wanted, especially in Irish control over revenue and spending, it included Ulster in the Home Rule scheme. The result was an explosion. Predictably, the bill was rejected in the House of Lords. The Unionists demanded a general election, or a referendum, before the bill could be turned into law. In Ulster, preparations went ahead for armed resistance to a Home Rule government with the open encouragement of Unionist leaders like Milner. Elsewhere in Ireland, the resort to force began to be seen as inevitable: gun-running followed drilling. Compromise was elusive since all sides glimpsed the chance of triumph and feared the divisions that concession might bring. Even the belated acceptance by the Liberal government (at the instigation of Churchill and Lloyd George) of Ulster's exclusion from Home Rule brought further insoluble differences over the boundaries of the excluded area and the question of temporary or permanent exemption from the operation of the bill. At the moment when the shootings at Sarajevo and the prospect of a far more terrible crisis in Europe suspended domestic hostilities over Ireland, a descent into civil war in Ireland and (at best) constitutional impasse in Britain seemed all too likely.

The astonishing case of Irish Home Rule mocks the argument that the British world-system owed its strength and cohesion to the shrewd pragmatism and liberal instincts of the governing elite in London. Confronted by the twofold challenge of Irish nationalism and Ulster Unionism, that elite was at sixes and sevens. Both Liberals and Conservatives hoped to exploit Home Rule to win the party battle in mainland Britain. Neither dared alienate the Irish factions with whom they were allied. The Irish crisis throws into relief the chronic weakness to which the imperial centre was often subject. For London was only rarely capable of decisive intervention in local politics. Its usual role was to adjust the balance between the local parties: to regulate, encourage or obstruct. Its freedom of action was often constrained by the numerous and vocal colonial lobbies active in Britain though these also were usually too weak to impose their will. Where (as in the Irish case) the local parties were finely balanced, could exert almost equal pull inside

British politics and came to symbolise rival notions of imperial power, the strain became almost unbearable.

In the last resort, then, the cohesion of the British system was less a matter of British *policy* than of the complex workings of imperial politics. The theoretical paramountcy of the Imperial government was exercised under demanding conditions. It was hemmed in by the free trade convictions of the British working class, unmoved by the argument for tariff reform.[150] It was checked by the strength of the two old-established 'garrisons' in Ireland and India and of their allies and supporters in British opinion. It was wary of the militant appeal of Britannic nationalism that Milner had invoked so successfully in 1899. It dared not coerce the self-governing colonies. A determined proconsul with the press in his pocket, like Lord Lugard in Nigeria, was hard to restrain. It was the incoherence and improvisation to which all this gave rise that fuelled the ambition of the self-styled imperialists in Edwardian politics. To free 'imperial' questions from the messy entanglement in domestic politics, and to discipline the lobbies and factions whose influence loomed large, they wanted to create an Empire-wide public opinion and an Empire-wide parliament. Before 1914, they made little headway. But with the crash of the old order they thought they saw their chance.

Part II

'The great liner is sinking': the British world-system in the age of war

8 THE WAR FOR EMPIRE, 1914–1919

The longer war

1914 was the watershed between two ages of empire. In the long nine-teenth century after 1815, the British world-system had developed as if there were no danger of a general war in Europe or across the world. Despite the Crimean War, the wars of Italian and German unification and the Franco-Prussian War, this had proved a reasonable assump-tion. The results can be seen from a glance at the map. Britain's set-tlements, possessions, spheres and commercial property were scattered broadcast across the globe. Whatever the constitutional niceties, in the 'formal' empire colonial rule was highly devolved: to settler politicians in the white dominions; to imperial officials in the rest. Devolution assumed that their defence would fall to the Royal Navy, or be made redundant by its global reach. The exception was India which paid for its own standing army and much more beside (two-thirds, in fact, of the Empire's regular army). Imperial rivalry was real, and posed a threat to Britain's interests. But the threat was usually more regional (and Near Eastern) than general. Much of its force was deflected by the partition diplomacy of the 1880s and 1890s. As a consequence, across large parts of the world, British influence could be maintained by the 'soft power' of commerce and culture. This had made possible the coexistence of imperialism and liberalism in Britain, in the settler colonies and even, more fitfully, in India. For all its hard coercive face, colonial rule retained the power to engage local sympathy by its lib-eral promise – however sparingly fulfilled – of individual freedom and material progress. The imperialism of free trade, variously interpreted, frequently modified, often abused, remained the *Leitmotif* of a system whose protean ideology was a cocktail: global and cosmopolitan as much as racial and territorial.

The geopolitical foundations of the Victorian and Edwardian world-system rested in the last resort upon two sets of equations at the opposite ends of the Old World. In East Asia where a local great power might have challenged British influence, there had seemed little to fear before the mid-1890s. Thereafter, disintegration not self-assertion was the most likely prognosis for China. Japan was a different story. After 1895, when it seized Taiwan, it became a cadet imperialist. Ten years later, it became the strongest military power in East Asia, defeating the Russians. But Japan was still a 'country power': fearful of a European combination against it. Up to 1914, its local strength seemed to work to Britain's advantage. The Anglo-Japanese alliance, twice renewed, held the ring in East Asia while British efforts were concentrated on the deterrence of Germany.

In Europe, the geopolitical equation was very different. Europe was active, not passive. In Churchill's expressive phrase, it was 'where the weather came from'. Commercially, territorially and demographically, nineteenth-century Europe was in a phase of hyper-expansion. Towards the end of the century, the pace and scale of this European 'enlargement' rose sharply on a tide of trade and capital. International tensions – stoked by private interests – grew more acute. But only to a certain point. Dynamic though the continent had become in its social and economic character, politically it remained in the grip of the long conservative reaction that set in generally after 1815. The old regime persisted. No great power government dared contemplate kicking over the European chessboard – with the possible exception of Napoleon III in 1859. All had too much to lose, or were too uncertain of ultimate victory. Nor were they driven into general war by the threat to their survival. Nationalism exerted a potent appeal as the instrument of state-building ('official nationalism') and as an equal and opposite claim for the liberation of 'submerged nationalities' from the chains of dynastic Europe. Both versions could have volatile consequences. But, until the end of the century, great power governments seemed more than capable of restraining their disruptive potential.

For the British, this pattern of continental politics was highly convenient. They could not hope to prevent the overflow of European trade, influence and territorial ambition into the wider world. But there were good grounds to think that the distribution of power in continental

Europe between four and a half great powers (the half being Italy) would persist indefinitely. No single power, nor any likely combination of powers, could hope for a durable hegemony over all the rest. The mutual antipathy of the continental states neutralised their resentment at Britain's vast share of imperial booty. Fearing that they would be dragged into war by the antics of their frontiersmen in Afro-Asia (or the furore of their admirers at home), continental statesmen accepted the partition diplomacy through which Salisbury and his successors hoped to stabilise (and maximise) the British share. Thus, for all the intensity of Europe's engagement with the wider world after 1870, there were few signs before 1914 of a coming revolution in world politics. In a 'closed system' in which the global 'commons' had been all but shared out, international politics were bound to be stressful. Zones of insecurity would wax and wane. But, while the East remained passive, and the West was locked in the defensive diplomacy of the 'balance of power', the British world-system – strung out between the two – could guard its networks at bearable cost.

In retrospect, of course, we can see that the pre-war decade contained the omens of catastrophic change. German economic power was growing rapidly. Nationalism in East and Central Europe was becoming more violent. Urbanisation and agrarian hardship screwed up the social tensions. Most dangerous of all, as it turned out, were the volcanic nationalisms of Southeastern Europe. The Balkan Wars of 1912–13 and 1913–14, and the struggle of Serbian nationalists against Austrian over-rule in Bosnia, were symptomatic of a region where the writ of the great powers hardly ran, but where their rivalries were fuelled by the ethnic conflict of would-be clients. In July 1914, the Habsburg government tried to use the Sarajevo murders to crush Serbian nationalism, and humiliate Russia, Serbia's great power sponsor. It was a colossal blunder. Southeastern Europe was not a remote colonial region where the stakes were low and compromise easy. Its fate was thought crucial to the balance of Russian, Austrian and German power. So the statesmen who had partitioned half the world fell out over the most backward corner of their own continent.

The First World War was the violent rupture of the nineteenth-century world in which the vast scale of British expansion had been possible. It was the murderous first act of a conflict that was to last until the 1950s, or (by some criteria) until 1990. It helped blow apart the world economy and reversed the first 'globalisation' in a wave of economic nationalism. The collapse of the old imperial order in East and Central Europe wrecked the pre-war basis of great power diplomacy and sanctified the nation-state as the ideal form of territorial polity. In post-imperial Europe, ethnic conflict became even more bitter and much more wide-ranging. It was soon entangled in the ideological warfare between communism and its enemies, with drastic consequences for regional stability. Nor in the closed system the world had become could the war's effects be confined to Europe. By its end, almost every state had become a belligerent or been drawn willy-nilly into the fighting. In East Asia the consequences were especially dramatic. In this unpartitioned corner of the semi-colonial world, the wartime abdication of the European powers had been a golden opportunity for local ambition. 'Passive' East Asia entered its revolutionary phase in the triangular struggle of nationalists, communists and Japanese imperialists. Western interests could no longer be protected by a gunboat and a corporal's guard. By the mid-1930s, it seemed increasingly likely that the turbulence in East Asia would spill over into the 'colonial' lands of the South Pacific, Southeast Asia and even India.

The impact of these vast changes on the British system was profound and ultimately devastating. It is tempting in hindsight to see the First World War as the first and longest step towards its eventual disintegration. But that may be too simple a judgment. The war imposed huge strains on the British system. It permanently altered the external setting. It badly damaged the international economy with which British power had grown symbiotically. But the British were also the principal victors in this war of empires. They lost less and gained more than all the other original combatants. In the post-war world, with its corrosive frictions and shattered finances, this 'victory' won them a crucial breathing-space. It bought strategic gains and political time: to entrench their empire militarily and reform it constitutionally. It was a vital respite before the long war of the twentieth century resumed its course.

The Imperial Armageddon

Before the war, British leaders (and their strategic advisers) had assumed that the Royal Navy would be Britain's principal weapon in any Great Power conflict in Europe. The pre-war scheme for a small expeditionary force (the 'BEF') to fight on the continent alongside France had not altered this view: there were no plans to increase the size of the army even after a war had begun.[1] The reasoning behind this 'navalist' strategy was simple. The British expected that, in a war fought to maintain the European balance of power against German aggression, the great conscript armies of France and Russia would bear the brunt of the fighting on land. The BEF would be a useful reinforcement in the critical opening phase – and a gesture of solidarity. But Britain's real contribution would be maritime and economic. The navy would sweep the seas clear of enemy warships (and safeguard vital lanes of supply), gobble up the German colonies and impose the blockade that would steadily strangle the German economy. Meanwhile, British finance, industrial output and inexhaustible coal would sustain the war effort of the Entente. A war fought on these terms until the Germans gave in would have a minor impact on British interests around the world. It would leave the pre-war shape of the British world-system largely unchanged.

Within a few weeks of the outbreak of war in August 1914 it was clear that this grand strategy was quite unreal. It was true that Germany's surface navy was soon driven from the high seas. In Southwest Africa and the South Pacific (though not in German East Africa where Von Lettow Vorbeck held out to the bitter end), German colonies were quickly seized. But British sea-power was not the great offensive weapon on which navy traditionalists had counted. The attempt to break through the Dardanelles in 1915 was an embarrassing failure. The British Grand Fleet spent the war in the Orkneys waiting for the Germans to venture into the North Sea. When they did so in 1916, there was no Trafalgar but only the inconclusive battle of Jutland. The role of the Royal Navy was vital but *defensive*, though it was ill-equipped to counter the submarine menace especially after February 1917 when the Germans turned to unrestricted submarine warfare. Tied down in the North Sea, it watched the rise of American sea-power in the North Atlantic, and its Japanese counterpart in the Western Pacific. Blockade was its primary means of attack: the slow remorseless pressure on the morale and physique of the German army and people.[2] But, even in 1918, it was uncertain whether it could work fast enough to stop Germany winning the war.

Instead, for the British, like their continental allies, the 'real' war was on land. Although the Germans were denied a *Blitzkrieg* victory in 1914, by the end of the year they controlled most of Belgium, including part of its coastline, and a large area of Northern France to within fifty miles of Paris. Far from intervening to restore the balance of power, the British now found themselves in a dangerous position. If France were defeated outright, or gave up an unwinnable struggle to evict the Germans, Britain would have suffered a catastrophic setback. German control of Belgium and its ports would destroy the benefits of British insularity. French defeat would end the cooperation that allowed naval concentration against Germany. It might mean German control over France's fleet. At best, the security of Britain – the imperial centre – would have been compromised in ways that weakened British influence around the world. At worst, the Germans would have taken a long step towards uniting the European continent against Britain's global pretensions. In either case, the implications for the stability and cohesion of the British world-system were stark.

It followed that, from the end of 1914 until the armistice of November 1918, the British war effort was dominated by the increasingly desperate struggle to reverse the early verdict of the fighting and escape the geopolitical nightmare threatened by failure to liberate Belgium and Northern France. Lord Kitchener, who had been brought into the Liberal government to take charge of the army, quickly realised that a vast new volunteer force must be raised for the continental war. He intended to hold it back for a decisive blow, perhaps in 1917, when the continental powers had fought themselves to a standstill. This would ensure a loud British voice in the subsequent peace, an echo of the Vienna treaty in 1815. He was too optimistic. The scale of German success against the Entente powers forced a premature offensive in 1915. In 1916, the disasters on the Eastern Front,[3] and the attrition of France's manpower at Verdun, forced the British into a reluctant offensive on the Somme that was abandoned after 400,000 casualties. After two years of war on the Western Front, and a quarter of a million British dead, there had been no progress on the most vital of British war aims.

Indeed, by the end of 1916, the military problem seemed all but insoluble – except to the generals. To win on the Western Front, the British and the French had to drive the Germans from positions they had seized and fortified in the opening phase of the war. They had to achieve this against an enemy enjoying all the advantages of interior lines. As an attack developed, the Germans could shuttle their reinforcements across the battle zone by rail: the attackers had to walk through mud and barbed wire. Moving into the open exposed the attacking force not just to rifle and machine gun fire, but to the deadly barrage of heavy artillery, which inflicted three-quarters of all casualties. With little chance of a decisive breakthrough, the only means of breaking the enemy's will was through 'attrition': forcing German troops to fight, at whatever cost, in the hope of eventually wearing down their reserves of manpower and morale. With so desperate a strategy, and so few signs of success, it was hardly surprising that by November 1916 a mood of pessimism engulfed most of those responsible for the war effort of the British Empire.[4]

These were the circumstances in which the coalition government that Asquith had formed in May 1915 was overthrown by a political coup in December 1916. The new coalition led by Lloyd George, with some Liberal but more Tory support, signalled the determination to win and to mobilise every resource for victory. But Lloyd George, who grasped better than anyone the political and technical difficulties of a total war, and Lord Milner, who became his chief lieutenant, were both keenly aware of how the drain of blood on the Western Front would affect the deeper sources of British power. Even with conscription to filter the call-up of skilled men, the huge losses of attrition warfare would weaken the British economy, limit its war production and cut down the exports that helped pay the inflated bill of vital imports. Economic exhaustion would accelerate war-weariness, starve Britain's allies of the material they needed and might break both the will and the means of victory. Despite these misgivings, no alternative plan was possible in 1917.[5] Instead, the pressure grew for even greater sacrifice on the Western Front. The gradual collapse of the Russian army, the threatened collapse of the French – whose losses had been far higher than the British – made a new offensive against the German line a grand strategic necessity. This was Passchendaele: a battle in the mud from July to November 1917 that cost the BEF over 220,000 dead. Yet, by the end of 1917, as the Bolshevik revolution dragged Russia out of war, the prospects for victory in the West looked darker than ever. Triumph in the East would give the German High Command just the reinforcements it needed to break the Allied line, seize the Belgian coast and capture Paris. If it moved fast enough it could pre-empt the arrival of American troops and smother the impact of the United States' decision

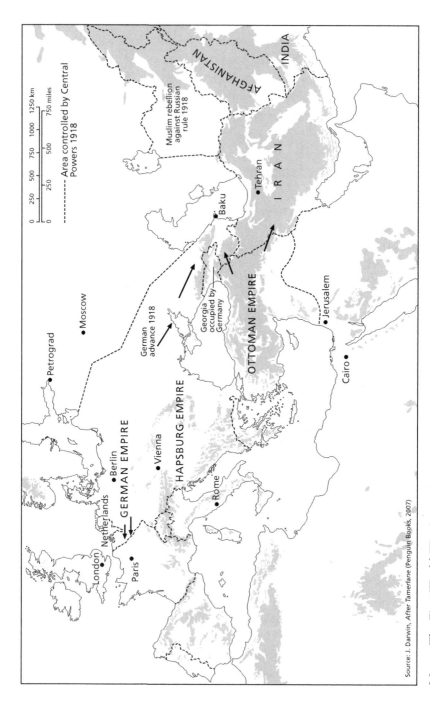

Map 9 The First World War in 1918

Source: J. Darwin, *After Tamerlane* (Penguin Books, 2007)

to enter the war (a result of Berlin's unrestricted submarine warfare) in April 1917. It could win the battle for Europe.

The spring and summer of 1918 thus turned out to be the climax of the war, the moment at which for the British and their allies defeat came closest. This was the 'new war' against which Milner warned Lloyd George in March 1918. With the signature of the treaty of Brest-Litovsk (6 March), the Germans had won the war against Russia 'which used to cover our whole Asian flank'. With the Germans poised to swing round the Black Sea and enter the Caucasus, and the Turks now freed from Russian pressure, 'we have a new campaign which really extends from the Mediterranean shore of Palestine to the frontier of India . . . [W]hether or not Japan takes on North Asia – I doubt her doing it – we alone have got to keep Southern Asia.'[6] The next day, the expected German blow fell in the West, but with unexpected force. Within days it had shattered the British Fifth Army in its path. 'We are very near a crash', wrote the government's chief military adviser, Sir Henry Wilson, on 24 March.[7] A week's fighting cost the BEF 114,000 men. 'You must fight with your backs to the wall', Haig, their commander, told his troops (the irreverent reply was: 'where's the wall?'). As the Germans pressed forward, the British faced the dilemma of abandoning the Channel ports or losing touch with the French armies to the south. 'No readjustment of our forces can save the situation', said Milner (now Secretary of State for War) until the British and French divisions began to hold their ground against the Germans.[8] 'We are a fast dwindling army', wrote Wilson on 12 April. 'This is desperately serious.'[9] By early June, with the Germans at the Marne, and shells falling in central Paris, British leaders began to ponder how they would fight on if France and Italy (where a new German-Austrian offensive was expected) gave up the struggle. 'The United States too late, too late, too late: what if it should turn out to be so?', groaned the American ambassador to his diary.[10]

Milner was in no doubt that the supreme crisis of the war had arrived. 'We must be prepared for France and Italy being beaten to their knees', he told Lloyd George. 'In that case, it is clear that the German-Austro-Turko-Bulgar bloc will be master of all Europe and Northern and Central Asia up to the point where Japan steps in to bar the way.'[11] Milner predicted a global war in which Britain and her allies would be forced to defend the maritime periphery against a 'heartland' dominated by German power. 'It is clear', he argued,

> *[t]hat unless the only remaining free peoples of the world, America, this country and the Dominions, are knit together in the closest conceivable alliance and prepared for the maximum sacrifice, the Central bloc under the hegemony of Germany will control not only Europe and most of Asia but the whole world . . . If all these things happen, the whole aspect of the war changes. These islands become an exposed outpost of the Allied positions encircling the world – a very disadvantageous position for the brain-centre of such a combination.*

The fight, he concluded, 'will now be for Southern Asia and above all for Africa (the Palestine bridgehead is of immense importance)'.[12] Here was a terrifying prospectus of Britain's imperial future from the most ardent of imperialists. The old balance of power had vanished like a dream. Britain's eastern empire now lay open to an attack far more dangerous than anything threatened by Russia in the days of the 'great game'. Japan's domination of East Asia, foreshadowed in its '21 demands' to China in 1915, would be the price of its support. American financial and military help would be more indispensable than ever, strengthening when peace came the American demand for the 'freedom of the seas' and the international settlement of colonial claims: key elements in Woodrow Wilson's 'Fourteen Points' published in January 1918. The 'new world' taking shape by the middle of 1918 bore a frightening resemblance to the warnings of Halford Mackinder, the geographer and imperialist, some fourteen years before: a vast 'heartland' (ruled by Germany) controlling the 'world island' (continental Europe, Asia and Africa) leaving only an outer fringe where sea-power could contest its claims. With Britain and India under siege, and London's commercial empire in ruins, the rump of the British world-system would have little choice but to look to the United States as its saviour.

We know in hindsight that Milner was too pessimistic. Within a month, the tide in the West had begun to turn. But his grim prognosis left a fateful imperial legacy. Failure on the Western Front, perhaps a 'Dunkirk' in which the British army abandoned the continent, made the Middle East the new fulcrum of imperial defence. It was there that the road must be barred to the Central Powers whose victory in the region would cut the British system in two and roll it up in detail. In the first part of the war this had hardly seemed likely. British ambitions had been correspondingly modest. But in 1918 they aspired to dominate the whole vast tract between Greece and Afghanistan, obliterating the Ottoman Empire in the process. Their moment in the Middle East began in earnest.

This great forward movement was a startling reversal of pre-war policy. Before 1914, the British had been favourable to the expulsion of the Ottomans from Europe, but opposed to the break-up of their empire in Asia. Long-standing fears of Russian or German attempts to disrupt the route to India and penetrate the Persian Gulf – the maritime frontier of India – made Turkish control over the Straits and the Arab lands the least worst solution. But, in October 1914, the Turkish military triumvirate that ruled the empire threw in its lot with the Central Powers, perhaps in fear that an Entente victory would bring Russian annexation of Constantinople and the Straits, the oldest and dearest of Tsarist war aims. The British now had to defend their 'veiled protectorate' in Egypt and their 'virtual' protectorate in the Persian Gulf, whose Arab statelets were superintended by the government of India, against Ottoman attack. They had to protect the oil concession at the head of the Gulf (in Persian territory but close to the Ottoman border) half-owned by the British government and intended to supply the Royal Navy. Above all, they had to blast open the Straits so that supplies could reach their vast but almost landlocked Russian ally and turn its huge manpower to account. At the same time, they had to think how to minimise the effects of Turkish defeat upon the 'post-war' security of their imperial system, when both France and Russia (it had to be assumed) would be victor powers and (soon) new rivals. Their instincts were cautious. Their first preference was to keep the Ottoman Empire in being but force it to decentralise into zones of interest shared out between the victors. In May 1915, with the attack on the Dardanelles, the Russians were promised Constantinople and the Straits, while the British were to take in compensation the large 'neutral' zone between the Russian and British spheres of influence in Persia. In May 1916, in a further effort to pre-empt any post-war dispute, the Sykes–Picot (or 'Tripartite') agreement proposed a comprehensive partition of the Ottoman lands. Russia was to receive (as well as the Straits) a large sphere of interest in Armenia, or eastern Anatolia. Much of central Anatolia, and the coastal lands of the Levant went to France. The British share was to be the provinces of Baghdad and Basra, in the southern part of modern Iraq. The remainder of Turkey's Arab territories (most of modern Syria, northern and western Iraq, Jordan and southern Israel) was divided into two zones, in each of which the British and French would enjoy an exclusive influence over autonomous states 'under the suzerainty of an Arab chief'.[13] Palestine was to be internationalised.

The logic of British policy was to limit the scale of their future commitments and place a swathe of French influence between the approaches to the Gulf and the rival they really feared – Russia. By the latter part of 1917, this grand scheme was in tatters. The Middle East war had gone disastrously wrong. The Dardanelles expedition to capture the Straits had been a humiliating failure: Turkey had not been knocked out. Turkish armies fought hard in Mesopotamia, surrounding and defeating the British Indian army at Kut in April 1916. It took another year before Baghdad was captured. The British army in Egypt struggled slowly into Palestine: but it took until December 1917 to capture Jerusalem. The Arab uprising promised by the Sherif of Mecca, with whom the British had made an alliance, proved of little military value. All this was bad enough: it did little for British prestige. The lack of progress on the Western Front made it much more serious. After January 1917, British leaders could not rule out the possibility of a peace on terms that left Germany unbeaten and poised to resume the struggle at a time of its choosing. That made it all the more important to secure the outer defences of Egypt (in Palestine) and Southern Mesopotamia. It was largely this thinking – 'strategic Zionism' – that converted the British War Cabinet to the Balfour Declaration in November 1917 promising a Jewish 'national home' in Palestine: a colony of Jewish settlers, fiercely anti-Turk in outlook, would help guard the approaches to Egypt.[14] As Russia tottered towards collapse at the end of 1917, the urgency of safeguarding the Canal and the Gulf against a new Turko-German offensive seemed greater than ever. As the Russian armies fell back from the Caucasus, they opened the road to German and Turkish advance into Northern Persia and even Central Asia outflanking Britain's defence of the route to India.

Thus, even before the catastrophic events of March and April 1918 on the Western Front, the British had been forced to rethink their Middle East war aims in drastic fashion. They were desperate to block the route through the Caucasus along which German armies might march from the Ukraine. They wanted control of North Persia and a client government in Teheran. That meant advancing north from

Baghdad towards Mosul and Kurdistan. With little prospect of defeating Germany and Austria-Hungary in Europe, it was all the more necessary to drive the Ottomans out of the Arab lands and hold them come what might in the West. Lloyd George and Milner had little faith in victory on the Western Front until American troops arrived en masse in 1919. At the beginning of February 1918, after a fierce argument with the other Entente leaders, they won agreement to their plan for a British offensive in Palestine, while standing their ground in Europe.[15] In March, the 'Eastern Committee' of the War Cabinet was set up under Curzon's chairmanship to coordinate British policy between Greece and Afghanistan, to preside, in effect, over the forward movement in the Middle East. In the event, the hope of a swift offensive was aborted by the scale of the crisis in the West. Far from advancing deeper into Ottoman Syria, General Allenby was forced to repatriate British units in the Egyptian Expeditionary Force to meet Haig's desperate need for reinforcement, and wait instead for the arrival of more Indian troops, who were to make up nearly half his fighting strength.[16] Not until September could the advance begin in earnest. When it did, the battle of Megiddo and the occupation of Damascus (1 October 1918) marked the virtual end of Ottoman resistance. On 2 October, the British and Indian army in Mesopotamia (which was two-thirds Indian) began its advance on Mosul. By 20 October, the Ottoman government had opened negotiations for an armistice, which was signed on the island of Mudros on 31 October.

As the scale of their victory began to unfold, the ministers of the Eastern Committee seized their chance to build a permanent barrier between their old European rivals and the approaches to what Milner's protégé, Leo Amery (a keen student of geopolitics), had called the 'Southern British World' in India, Africa and Oceania. The French were brutally told that their claims under the Sykes–Picot agreement were no longer valid. The ministers invoked instead the new ideals of self-determination, set out in Woodrow Wilson's Fourteen Points in January 1918, to propose a wide degree of self-government in the Arab provinces (with the significant exception of Palestine), on the understanding that Britain would enjoy a complete monopoly of external influence.[17] 'We will have a Protectorate but not declare it', remarked the Foreign Secretary, Arthur Balfour.[18] Further east, they sanctioned Curzon's project of turning Persia – where 'the British stake is a greater and not a less one in consequence of the war' – into a virtual protectorate, with British command of the army, a financial adviser and a treaty.[19] Only over Curzon's scheme for British occupation of the Caucasus and Trans-Caspia did his colleagues begin to cavil at the colossal scale of the commitments envisaged. But, by December 1918, a new British empire had been planned across much of the modern Middle East (the future of Armenia, the Straits and Constantinople was left undecided).

In the months that followed, this grandiose vision was gradually whittled down. The furious French refusal to give up their promised gains under Sykes–Picot forced a u-turn, and Syria, along with Lebanon, eventually became a League of Nations mandate under French trusteeship. The British foray into the Caucasus and Central Asia could not last. When demobilisation shrank the British army, the attempt to aid the successor states of the Tsarist empire against its Bolshevik successor was soon abandoned. Turkey revolted against the crushing terms of peace and the occupation of Asia Minor by the Greeks, willing allies in Britain's regional *imperium*. Even Persia resisted the quasi-protectorate that Curzon tried to force upon it in 1919. Across Egypt and the Arab lands in 1919–20, the British were caught up in a vast wave of political turbulence, much of it hostile to external control. Bitter arguments raged inside the British government over the cost of Iraq, the risks of confronting Turkey and the safety of the shoestring empire of 'hot air, aeroplanes and Arabs' (the characteristically acerbic phrase was Sir Henry Wilson's) that Churchill began to fashion in 1921. But, despite all this, the belief that defending the British world-system required a regional primacy across the whole Middle East, not fortified enclaves around the Gulf and the Canal, proved astonishingly durable. The strategic geography of imperial defence had been permanently recast. From now on until the end of empire, guarding this great salient in the middle of the world as the grand counterpoise to British weakness in Europe became the ultimate test of imperial power.

Of course, the imperial triumph in the Middle East was magnified by the victory over Germany and Austria-Hungary that had seemed so elusive for so long. As the Germans retreated, and then asked for an armistice, the British War Cabinet seized the chance to stop the war before the exhaustion of their manpower (and the shrinking size of their armies on the Western Front) began to tilt the balance of Allied power in favour of Wilson and Washington. They preferred the ambiguities of an armistice to the cost and delays that imposing unconditional surrender on Germany might entail. They hoped at the peace to limit the influence of American diplomacy and use it to restrain the demands of France. They had good reason to expect that, if the world had not been made safe for democracy, it had at least been made safe for the British Empire. The German navy – the great pre-war menace – was captured, and then scuttled by its own crews. The German colonies had been conquered. The Ottoman Empire had been demolished. The Russian empire had disintegrated in revolution. The peace conference would determine not the fact but the scale and permanence of British victory. The great unknown was American policy and the extent to which President Wilson would go to enforce the programme of the Fourteen Points.[20] Would British sea-power regain the easy primacy it had lost after 1890? Or would American naval rivalry and bitter dislike of the British claim to control neutral shipping in time of war (Point Two of Wilson's Fourteen Points) trigger a new and unwinnable arms race – as Colonel House threatened Lloyd George in October 1918?[21] Would the Americans insist upon the internationalising of wartime colonial conquests, and, if so, on what terms? Would the rise of Japanese power in East Asia, Chinese demands for an end to the unequal treaties, and the growing influence of the United States in the Western Pacific mean the attrition of British commercial and diplomatic influence in China? Above all, could victory on the Western Front be converted into a lasting reconstruction of the balance of power in Europe – and a guarantee that Britain would not again be faced with a continent united or dominated against her interests? On these, and on the economic aftermath of the war, the shape of the 'new world' would depend.

The price of victory

The war was bound to disrupt the global economy that had grown up after 1880 and depended upon the free movement of trade, capital and (with rather more restriction) people around the world. As the greatest beneficiary of this 'globalisation', Britain was bound to be affected, with uncertain consequences for the political and economic cohesion of the British world-system. But, at the outset of the war, once the turmoil of the financial markets had calmed down, it was widely assumed that the struggle would reveal Britain's latent strength as the pivot of the world economy. The British would use the huge credits built up over decades to draw in the produce needed from non-European countries.

British industry would supply the weapons for the Entente's war effort. The Germans by contrast would find their foreign trade strangled by the British blockade, and the gross inflation set off by the expansion of paper money would undermine their will to fight.[22] In a long war, the British were bound to win.

These were the views of John Maynard Keynes, the young Cambridge economist recruited to the British Treasury in August 1914. His technical knowledge and analytical brilliance quickly won him influence at the highest level. The essence of Keynes' thinking was that Britain should fight the war in the same way as it had been fought against Napoleon, but with the added advantage conferred by huge claims on overseas production (by the capital and income from foreign investments) and Germany's dependence on foreign trade – the result of rapid industrialisation before 1914. After a year of war, it was clear that this optimistic calculation was badly flawed. The Germans had won a position from which they could only be driven by frontal assault. They controlled much of the coal, iron and steel production of the French and Belgian economies. The huge mobilisation of French and (later) Italian manpower drastically reduced their production of food. With the Dardanelles closed, Russian wheat could not reach the West, nor could Russia pay for the munitions she needed. As the war went on, Britain's allies needed more and more shipping, food and equipment and had less and less means to pay for them. To make matters worse, there was no question of keeping British manpower at home in factory and farm while the fighting was done by their continental allies. If Germany was to be driven out of France and Belgium, it would need a huge British army as well.

By August 1915, Keynes (who was now responsible for British purchases in the United States) was well aware of the dilemma. Britain could not raise Kitchener's armies, he argued, as well as supporting her allies economically.[23] 'It is certain', he wrote in September, 'that the limitations of our resources are in sight.'[24] The nub of the problem was foreign exchange. London had to find dollars to pay for the American goods the war effort demanded. In ordinary times, Britain earned dollars by exports, from foreign investment, and from exchanging goods with countries (like India) that had a surplus of dollars. But the war had disrupted international trade and payments. It sharply reduced Britain's dollar earnings from exports, since much of British industry was supplying munitions to the Allies, paid for by British loans not foreign payments. The longer the war lasted, the greater the need of the Allied countries for American products, for which only Britain could pay in dollars. The pressure became relentless. To pay for British and Allied purchases, the Treasury bought up British-owned dollar securities (with sterling) and sold or pledged them in New York. It exported some of the precious reserve of gold. And it borrowed from American bankers, using the great firm of J. P. Morgan to raise dollar loans on its behalf. At all costs, it had to prevent a collapse in the value of sterling against the dollar. For, if American sellers and lenders lost confidence, American goods would become impossibly expensive and bring the Allied war effort to a standstill.

For Keynes, therefore, the economic pivot of the war was Britain's credit in New York. If it failed, the Allies were finished. 'We have one ally', Keynes told the Admiralty board in March 1916, 'the rest are mercenaries.'[25] There was no certainty that American lenders would continue to buy British bonds when their own economy was booming. If American opinion was alienated by some transatlantic quarrel, the effect might be devastating. For the rest of 1916, however, disaster was postponed. The British dribbled their gold (and that of their Allies) into the New York market. They spent heavily to hold up the value of sterling. The American investor, despite Keynes' pessimism, remained a willing buyer of Allied loans. But, by the end of 1916, the huge reserves of British financial power had reached the limits that Keynes predicted. In November 1916, the American authorities, disturbed by the rapid growth of so much debt, advised their banks to curtail foreign loans. At the same time, as the gold reserve in London reached a critical level, and dollar securities began to run out, British dependence on American lending became greater than ever. At the moment when the Asquith cabinet fell in early December, the Treasury privately calculated that it was scarcely a week away from exhausting its dollars. The immediate danger of a sterling collapse receded. But, in the spring of 1917, as Germany's unrestricted submarine warfare brought the United States closer and closer to intervention, there was barely a month's reserve in hand before a drastic reduction of British purchases would have been necessary.[26] Even after American entry in April 1917, the strain and uncertainty were intense. A hold-up on American credits in June brought the British to the point of default.[27] On 29 July 1917, Bonar Law, now Chancellor of the Exchequer, told his American counterpart, William Gibbs McAdoo, that, without urgent help, the 'whole financial fabric' of the Alliance would collapse within days.[28] Keynes pondered how to safeguard Britain's 'final reserve' of gold – implying the curtailment of British purchases or going off gold. At the time of Passchendaele, the French army mutinies, the break-up of the Russian armies and the holocaust of their shipping in the submarine war, the British faced a financial 'Dunkirk'. The implications were colossal. Financial breakdown would shatter the Alliance and force an early peace. A British default on their dollar loans, or a refusal to pay gold on demand to foreign holders of sterling balances kept in London, would ruin for the foreseeable future the City's reputation as a financial centre – together with sea-power, the principal source of Britain's world power.

The British were rescued from this dilemma by the willingness of the American government to take on the burden of lending to the Entente powers until the end of the war. Financial disaster was averted. The threat of a famine in food and munitions disappeared, especially with the fall in Atlantic sinkings by the end of 1917. But, as Keynes insisted, Britain's dependence on American goods, the burden of American loans and the diversion of industrial manpower into the war of attrition in Flanders, was bound to debilitate her commercial power. 'In another year', he wrote at the end of 1917 (when the war was expected to continue into 1919 or 1920), 'we shall have forfeited the claim we had staked out in the New World and . . . the country will be mortgaged to America.'[29] Indeed, Britain's displacement by America as the commercial and financial superpower seemed all but inevitable. As the British rushed to sell their dollar portfolio and borrowed to their limit from American lenders, the United States was transformed almost overnight from a debtor to a creditor.[30] Its foreign lending raced upwards towards the majestic level that the British had accumulated in 1913. With British exports sinking to 60 per cent of their pre-war value,[31] and America's rising to unprecedented heights, the dollar replaced sterling as the most coveted currency. American banks began to emerge from isolation to set up branches abroad. American exports filled the gap left by the British shortfall. In Latin America, where Anglo-American competition was sharpest, the fall-off of British trade to long-valued markets was particularly steep.[32] Nor was the Americans' challenge confined to trade, investment and commercial transactions. In 1916 began the vast expansion of their merchant marine through government subsidy. By the end of the war, this commercial fleet was 40 per cent as large as the British.[33] Behind this great American progress lurked the suggestion of a world reordered to America's design. 'When the war is over', Woodrow Wilson told his main foreign policy adviser, Colonel House, 'we can force them [the British] to our way of thinking, because by that time they will . . . be financially in our hands.' But, he added, 'we cannot force them now'.[34]

The scale of British debts at the end of the war was certainly huge. By November 1918, nearly £1 billion was owed to the American government and private lenders.[35] The backlog of payments made it considerably more by 1920,[36] equivalent perhaps to some 20 per cent of overseas assets in 1913. Around 15 per cent of Britain's overseas wealth had also been spent on vital dollar goods in the first years of the war. Britain would have to pay back its American loans at £100 million a year, Keynes calculated gloomily in March 1919. 'Such a burden will cripple our foreign development in other parts of the world.'[37] To make matters worse, much of this debt had been incurred on behalf of Britain's wartime allies, mainly Russia, from whom it was unlikely to be recovered. Added to that, the huge domestic borrowing that had financed much of the war effort[38] was likely to mean high interest rates and taxation, and a consequent burden on industry, for a long time to come. But the picture might have been worse.

Brutal though the strain had been, the British had defended the value of the pound in the vital arena of the New York market. By doing so, they kept much of their commercial empire in being. The sterling balances of their main trading partners remained in London. Battered though it was by submarine warfare, their vast merchant marine carried the great bulk of British goods and earned vital dollars in the Atlantic trade. When American troops were sent to the European war, more than half crossed the Atlantic in British ships. For that and other British supplies and services, Washington paid – nearly $2 billion (£400m) in 1918–19.[39] British investments overseas continued to earn a substantial income. The returns for 1920 show overseas investment earnings at £200 million and other invisible exports at £395 million – a grand total of nearly £600 million, compared with £369 million in 1913.[40] Against that must be set the huge rise in prices: by 1920, domestic wholesale prices were at three times their pre-war level,[41] and the price of raw cotton – one of Britain's largest imports – showed a similar rise.[42] 1920 was also the high point of the post-war boom, before the huge backlog of deferred purchases gave way to the depressed conditions (in Britain) of the early 1920s. Nevertheless, the scale of their overseas commerce and the arduous defence of sterling had enabled the British to offset considerably the external effects of their war economy.

An important element in the safeguarding of the commercial empire had been the resources drawn from the dominions and India. The dominions (South Africa in part) paid for the forces they sent to the imperial war effort. To buy the supplies they needed, they borrowed from London. To help balance this borrowing, the British government bought much of their produce at generous prices: the entire Australian wool-clip in 1916–17. Except in the case of Canada, which was part of the North American dollar zone, no payments in gold were made to Empire countries which had to be content with sterling balances piled up in London.[43] Gold was hoarded for the more vital task of propping sterling's value against the dollar. South African gold was exported to London, and the Treasury resisted the plaintive requests of South African banks for shipments to boost the supply of coin. 'We keep sending away our vast gold production and yet cannot get enough sovereigns to carry on the business of the country', complained one 'English' politician.[44] As a non-sterling country, Canada's role was especially vital. It had the most industrialised economy of any Empire country. As well as sending the largest contingent of dominion manpower (over 400,000 men) in the Canadian Expeditionary Force, it supplied by the second half of the war a large fraction of the munitions Britain needed. By 1917, between a quarter and a third of Britain's artillery ammunition was being produced in Canada.[45] An Imperial Munitions Board, staffed by 'some of the ablest men of business in Canada'[46] was set up in December 1915 to coordinate production among some 400 firms and 300,000 workers. Canada became a western extension of Britain's war production economy. In the quarter ending on 30 December 1916, the British ministry of munitions spent £66 million in the UK, £33 million in the US and £20 million in Canada.[47] With the pressure on Britain's hard currency reserves by the end of 1916, it became something more: a source of dollars for British war purchases. Much of the cost of the munitions produced in Canada was met with advances from the Canadian government and the loans it raised at home. Britain borrowed in all $1 billion in Canada: an amount equal to the value of the dollar securities sold in the United States, and to a quarter of London's borrowing from the American government.[48] It was heavily offset by the sterling expenses that Canada incurred in fighting the war (some

C\$714 million). In manpower, industrial production and dollars, the oldest dominion had been an indispensable ally.

India's case was different, though no less important. India was rich in manpower but poor in industry. Even more than in the dominions, whose money-markets were under-developed by comparison with Britain's, it was difficult to mobilise capital there. Under rules laid down before 1914, London bore the cost of sending troops out of India – both Indians and the British garrison – to a theatre of war. But, in September 1914, the Indian government agreed to meet the 'normal' cost of such forces as if they were in India.[49] This included Indian soldiers serving in France. By the end of the war, more than one million Indians had served overseas, and the Indian government had recruited over 800,000 volunteers to the army.[50] The economic price was considerable. While India piled up credits abroad with the sale of exports and London's payments for the army, little of this could be remitted in earnings, still less in gold. Strict exchange controls prevented trade in non-essential goods, and an embargo on grain exports reinforced the effects of a shortage of shipping (heavily concentrated in the short-haul Atlantic) to the detriment of grain producers. After 1916, the burden of war became steadily heavier. In 1917, the Viceroy's government made a gift of £100 million to Britain, equivalent to India's annual revenue. It meant, remarked an Indian member of the legislative council (which was not consulted), that 'for a lifetime of a generation internal improvements of even the most necessary kind will be considerably hampered'.[51] Inflation accelerated. The tax burden per head of population rose by 65 per cent between 1914–15 and 1918–19.[52] Public debt grew by half. In the last year of the war, as London faced the terrible wastage of British manpower, Indian resources were pressed more and more heavily. The Viceroy promised to raise a further half a million men in April 1918[53] and to meet the ordinary costs of a much larger part of the Indian forces overseas. The military budget rocketed upwards, doubling government spending by the end of the war. Like the dominions, though without their freedom of choice, India made a critical contribution to the economic cost of defending the British world-system.

Imperial aid reduced British dependence upon the United States and eased the strain upon sterling. It helped blunt the danger that financial and naval primacy – the woolsack and the trident – would both cross the Atlantic at the end of the war. In fact, for a number of reasons, the American challenge proved curiously muted. The economic muscle on which Woodrow Wilson had hoped to rely was not strong enough. The war had ended too soon. 'We cannot afford to enter into a competitive fight [with British shipping] for some time to come', warned his Shipping Commissioner in late 1918.[54] With two million Americans marooned in Europe, a shipping war with the British was out of the question. Nor were the British in need of American dollars once the shooting stopped. When the American treasury cut off its dollar loans, European countries ceased to buy American goods. Wilson's government also proved surprisingly reluctant to discuss economic cooperation with its European associates so that the universal free trade that was meant to accompany the League of Nations (and foster American industrial power) remained still-born. Indeed, the economic role of the American government shrank swiftly at the end of the war and there was little love lost between the Wilson administration and the money barons in New York, whom his finance minister (and also his son-in-law) described as 'reactionary, sinister, unscrupulous, mercenary and sordid'.[55] Nor did the war mark the prelude to the global triumph of American trade. In Latin America, there was a permanent shift in America's favour, although in Argentina particularly, British exporters staged a strong recovery.[56] But the overall picture was much less positive. By the mid-1920s, the real value of American exports was hardly above its pre-war level.[57] The United States had broken free from the commercial *imperium* once wielded from London. But it still lacked the means, and perhaps the motive, to build one of its own.

Rumours that the British had lost their premier place in the world economy by the end of the war were thus somewhat exaggerated. They remained the economic superpower with the largest foreign trade, the largest foreign income, the largest share of international services and the largest merchant fleet. Nevertheless, the war did bring a critical change, though it took time for the effects to become obvious. The place occupied by the City and its commercial empire in the British world-system was sharply modified. Before the war the City had enjoyed remarkable freedom from governmental control. It had been a commercial republic with its own *imperium*: cosmopolitan, self-interested and self-regulated. During the war it was brought brusquely to heel and its liberties cut down. Treasury control became stronger and stronger. By January 1917, it had the power to requisition all foreign securities.[58] Its view, not that of the Bank of England, was now decisive on interest rates and the gold reserve.[59] The Treasury decided where capital could be exported and for what purpose. After the war, 'informal' controls persisted, to channel investment into sterling countries, partly to protect the exchange rate.[60] Secondly, there was no doubt that the City's place in international finance had been seriously weakened by the massive wartime sell-off of dollar securities, the most mobile and therefore the most valuable of assets.[61] To have disposed of so much of its holding in the world's largest and strongest economy was bound to reduce the City's capacity to invest abroad and to aggravate Britain's dollar deficit, a marked feature even in pre-war times. Thirdly, the war had meant a huge rise in domestic borrowing in Britain: government debt rose tenfold from £700 million in 1914 to £7.5 billion in 1919.[62] Financing this home-grown debt became a major preoccupation of both government and City, driving up interest rates and redirecting capital from export overseas. The war made the City poorer, more inward-looking and more vulnerable to external shocks.

These changes in the City's position were the most obvious sign that the powerful symbiosis between economics and politics represented by the 'imperialism of free trade' had been seriously weakened. The unrestricted flow of trade into, through and out of Britain had made London the entrepot of the world. It had maximised Britain's income from shipping and services as well as her earnings from overseas property. It had spun two virtuous circles of wealth and power. The entrepot function, free trade, ready supplies of capital and credit and sterling–gold convertibility had made the City the reserve bank of most secondary states. They in turn were obliged to accept the commercial and financial disciplines expected by the London market. To retreat from the gold standard into a paper currency, or to default on their obligations, meant a stoppage in the stream of capital and credit on which their hopes of material progress (in an expanding world economy) depended. A developing economy like Canada, remarked the banker Robert Brand in 1913, 'had as much interest in maintaining unchecked the flow of capital from England as a city has in preventing the supply of water being cut off.'[63] The benefits accruing to Britain were not only profitable investment. British financial, commercial and even engineering practice was diffused more widely. British-based merchant houses managed much of world trade. Information and market expertise flowed increasingly to London. The huge British investment in telecommunications tightened the grip of the British news media on the information that passed to the 'Outer World'. In more subtle ways, the circulation of news, information and ideas, the prestige and volume of cultural (as well as material) imports, and the freer movement of pilgrims, tourists and migrants reduced the influence of local or regional identity. The scope for imperial or 'pan-British' loyalties (among others) was widened. It was not fantastic before 1914 to imagine a 'liberal empire' attached to Britain by cultural and ideological as well as commercial attraction.

But the commercial engine-room of this free-trade empire had been damaged by the war, and its machinery dislocated. With its resources straitened, its integrating function in the British world-system was throttled back. Without the carrot of credit, the stick of discipline was much harder to wield. The new technologies of transport and communications, the vital circuits of imperial power, were more difficult to fund. The full modernisation of military power – the top priority of pre-war governments – was too costly to contemplate. The expansive energies symbolised by the huge outpouring of capital and migrants before 1914 were checked, though post-war emigration revived for a while. But, when the world economy collapsed into depression after 1929, the imperialism of free trade would beat a final retreat in the face of a new world order.

The politics of solidarity

The war was bound to strain the political relations between Britain and its most important partners in the imperial association. The contributions in men or money made by the dominions, India and Ireland to the imperial war effort became a central issue in their local politics. The question was even more sharply posed in those other countries where British rule (or its virtual equivalent – as in Egypt) had commandeered the resources to fight or imposed stringent controls on grounds of security. In East and West Africa, for example, the 'sideshow' wars for German colonies meant labour conscription and social disruption on a major scale. Death, separation, disease and famine for Africans followed in the wake of the imperialists' grand quarrel. During the war, but mostly at its end (since wartime regulation restrained public debate), the political cost of 'British connection', the hope of reward for imperial loyalty and the demand for compensation for sufferings borne, reopened long-standing questions about the ordering of the imperial system.

War politics in Britain

Britain was no exception to this general rule, although the debate about empire was more muted than elsewhere. British leaders had always been wary of the complaint that empire had become too costly. They were uneasy with the claim that imperial expenditure benefited the few and cost the many. 'The more the empire expands, the more the Chamberlains contract' had been the radical gibe against Joseph Chamberlain's expansionist enthusiasm – a reference to the family's manufacturing interests. Before 1914, however, when the most visible charge of empire had been the soaring budget of the Royal Navy, radical criticism was aimed not at the intolerable burden of defending the empire but at the unproven need to defend Britain with such costly armaments. With the navy concentrated in the North Sea, it would have been hard to argue that it was imperial commitments that were costing Britain dear. So, unlike the mid- or late-Victorian radicals, who denounced feckless empire-building in India and Egypt as the enemy of domestic peace, Edwardian radicals were bound to take a different tack. But the argument that battleship-building was the needless provocation of a peaceable Germany,[64] or that colonial concessions would appease a disgruntled Berlin, had limited purchase on public opinion. It was the dispute over how much naval power was needed to defend Britain itself that was the real threat to the admirals' plans.

The immediate *casus belli* (the integrity of Belgium) and the shock of the German advance reinforced the pre-war consensus that the target of German aggression was British independence and great power status in Europe. From first to last, the Western Front consumed by far the largest proportion of British resources and the largest toll of British dead. It preoccupied British opinion to the exclusion of almost every other theatre. In this titanic struggle, the role of Britain's imperial partners and dependants became assistance in the common cause. With Canadian, Australian, New Zealand, South African and Indian troops on the Western Front, it would have been strange to complain that the Empire was a drain on British power.

Yet its converse, the idea that 'closer union' with the Empire countries (especially the white dominions) was now essential to British

survival, peddled by self-styled 'imperialists' before the war, made limited headway. For the first eighteen months of the war, it was blocked by
the survival of the Asquithian consensus, remodelled as a coalition ministry in May 1915. Asquith's fiercest critics had been Milner's band of
followers.[65] They denounced the refusal of the Asquithian regime (and
its coalition Tory allies) to accept the logic of total war and cast off the
mentality of *laissez-faire*. They looked forward to cleansing the Augean
stable of party politics with its 'old gang'. They hoped for a new alignment in which 'imperialism' – offering social reform, a more pro-active
state and 'closer unity' with the white dominions – would confront
'socialism' – the disruptive forces of class warfare, anti-imperialism and
anti-capitalism. A modernised imperial state, mobilising British and
imperial resources, and commanding the 'race-patriotism' of British
peoples at home and abroad, was needed if Britain was to survive
the struggle of 'world states' that the war represented. Had the war
ended in 1915 or 1916, they would have remained voices crying in the
wilderness. But, by the latter part of 1916, the Milnerites had found
powerful new allies. Lord Northcliffe, proprietor of *The Times* and the
Daily Mail, had joined the chorus against Asquith. So had Sir Edward
Carson, the uncrowned king of Ulster and darling of the Tory ultras
against Home Rule. But it was Lloyd George's revolt against Asquith
that was decisive.

From the early months of the war, Lloyd George had been the
Liberal minister most identified with the building of a war economy. As
minister of munitions and then Secretary of State for War (after Kitchener's death), his political influence (perhaps survival) depended upon
military success. By late 1916, he was as radically discontented with
Asquithian complacency as the Milnerites, with whom he had secret
contacts. When Asquith reneged in early December upon an agreement to hand over daily management of the war to a small committee
under his presidency, Lloyd George resigned. But to the chagrin of the
Asquithians, it was he who won over their Tory allies, and a critical following among Liberal MPs, to form a new government whose mandate
was victory at (almost) any price. In this new regime, the Milnerites
were strongly represented – a sign of Lloyd George's openness to new
ideas and his need for a network that would help break the grip of
the Asquithian 'establishment'. Milner himself became a member of the
small 'war cabinet' of five and Lloyd George's first lieutenant in the
running of the war. Bonar Law, the Tory leader, was the indispensable

guarantor of a Commons majority. And Arthur Henderson was the vital link with the trade unions and Labour. But Milner, with his knowledge of finance, his military and dominion connections and (as an Old Egyptian Hand) his Middle East expertise, became the workhorse of the war effort. In Lloyd George's eyes, he had other virtues as well. 'Milner and I stand for very much the same things', he told his confidant, the newspaper proprietor George Riddell, in February 1917. 'He is a poor man and so am I. He does not represent the landed and capitalist classes any more than I do. He is keen on social reform and so am I.'[66] To an embattled prime minister dependent on the support of his bitterest pre-war enemies, trust was a luxury. But Milner, he told Riddell a year later, 'is a man of first class courage'.[67]

The question was whether Milner and his followers would be able to turn Britain's domestic politics in the imperial direction for which they longed. Many omens were favourable. The party system against which Milner had railed was to all intents suspended. Public opinion was shaped more by the press than by parliament, and the Milnerites had plenty of friends in the press: it was their natural element. *The Times* was practically their house journal, its editor, Geoffrey Dawson, one of Milner's protégés. On the economic front, the food crisis of 1917–18 and the dollar shortage drove home their pre-war arguments for domestic and imperial self-sufficiency. Milner's Corn Production Act (1917) was designed to renovate Britain's dilapidated agrarian economy by incentives and controls.[68] The report of the Dominions Royal Commission urged the creation of an imperial development board to channel investment into Empire resources. Another committee urged tariff protection for strategic industries. Milner himself played an active role in making a new Ministry of Health to spearhead social reform and post-war 'reconstruction'. The siege economy would be reborn in peacetime as the engine of a new imperialism. *Laissez-faire* and 'cosmopolitanism' would be swept away.

In fact, the Milnerites' ambition outran their influence. In September 1918, Milner pressed on Lloyd George the importance of not returning to the 'old ways'. The key question was now 'national development'. 'The business nation should deal on specially favourable terms with its friends among the nations, and, first and foremost, with its own kith, the nations of its own civilisation and ideals, who can be reckoned on to be *always* friendly.'[69] Lloyd George ignored him.

There was little support for Milnerite reconstruction at the end of the war: quite the contrary. From business interests there were vehement demands to dismantle the apparatus of wartime controls on profit and production, reducing the scale and scope of government intervention as nearly as possible to its pre-war proportions. The call for a return to 'normality' was powerfully seconded in the City, which hoped for an early return to its old financial freedom. Secondly, it turned out that the war had suspended the party system but not destroyed it. A new 'imperial' constitution to smash the parties' grip was as far away as ever. Proportional representation, which Milner favoured for similar reasons,[70] was not adopted, and, though the coalition was renewed in December 1918, the huge Conservative majority in the post-war Commons soon proved as stultifyingly parochial as its pre-war counterpart. Thirdly, and chiefly, the war had mobilised a powerful new enemy to the Milnerite vision of tariff reform and imperial unity: organised labour.

The outbreak of the war had split the Labour party. The party leader, Ramsay MacDonald, opposed entry. The trade union leaders, who supplied the party with its funds and membership, supported the government. As the party's *de facto* chief, Arthur Henderson joined the Asquith coalition and then the Lloyd George war cabinet. But trade union patriotism was not without strings. 'Dilution' (the replacement of skilled by unskilled labour for the duration) was unpopular: any form of industrial conscription was anathema. The system of 'leaving certificates' (to permit a change of employment) was a constant source of friction. Price rises evoked fierce complaints about profiteering. There was a widespread suspicion that employers would exploit wartime flexibility in the workplace to drive down wages once peace had come. As inflation accelerated, shortages increased, and the struggle for manpower intensified, 'unofficial' militancy grew and strikes proliferated. Trade union membership swelled from 3.4 million in 1913 to 5.4 million five years later. In the Labour movement as a whole, early support for the war modulated into a more questioning attitude. American intervention and revolution in Russia heightened anticipations of a new world order. By the end of 1917, party differences over the conflict had been largely reconciled. The anti-war faction now commanded general approval for a 'peace of democratisation', with a limit on armaments, no annexations, and 'the abandonment of any form of imperialism'.[71] When the Labour party adopted a new constitution in January 1918, with individual party membership and a country-wide electoral organisation, a formidable new opposition was in the making.

What made it all the more significant was the vast extension of the franchise for which the wartime mobilisation of men and women had made an unanswerable case. Under the third reform Act of 1918, universal male suffrage and votes for women over thirty tripled the pre-war electorate. Little was known of the new voters' opinions, though much might be guessed. Lloyd George had made haste in January 1918 to declare his democratic war aims.[72] The Conservative party leadership feared a radical tide rolling westward from Russia. When the prospects of a Liberal reunion were shattered in the acrimony of the Maurice debate in May 1918, they embraced coalition with Lloyd George's followers as the best defence against the 'impact of labour'. Among Conservatives, a spirit of caution, defensiveness and introversion was even more deeply ingrained by the economic turbulence of the aftermath and the fear of a labour 'revolt'. The war had transformed British politics, but not in the direction for which Milner had hoped.

The dominions: Canada, Australia, New Zealand

The five self-governing states of the Empire (we must not forget Newfoundland) had no choice about entering the conflict. When their head of state, King George V, declared war on the advice of his British ministers, they were in the fight whether they liked it or not. But their contribution to the war effort was another matter entirely. In principle, the dominion governments were free to cheer from the sidelines, or to make only token gestures of support. In practice, their response was astonishing. In Australia, the Commonwealth prime minister promised help 'to the last man and the last shilling'. In Canada and New Zealand, the sentiment was the same (South Africa was a special case). By the end of the war, over a million men from the dominions had served on its battlefields, the vast majority in the terrible charnel-house of the Western Front. In the two largest, Canada and Australia, over 13 per cent of adult males had served overseas; in New Zealand, the figure exceeded 19 per cent. The proportion who were killed or wounded was appallingly high: nearly 50 per cent of the Canadians, 59 per cent of New Zealanders and 65 per cent of Australians. Over 60,000 Canadians were killed, 59,000 Australians and 16,000 New Zealanders.[73] The cost of raising and equipping armies for the imperial war was met (in these three cases) by the dominion governments themselves who incurred, like Britain, a heavy burden of war debt.

Cooperation on this scale and under such stressful conditions was bound to be difficult. As the war went on interminably, and the losses mounted up, the differences between London and the dominion governments grew sharper. In the first two years of the struggle, three factors had mitigated these tensions. The dominion leaders were content (perhaps surprisingly so) to leave the daily conduct of the war to British ministers in London, perhaps on the argument that their own expertise was so limited as to rule out assuming any responsibility for the deployment of their forces. Indeed, it was not until the summer of 1918 that the dominion governments mounted a sustained attack on the deficiencies of the British high command after the disastrous setbacks of the spring. Secondly, for Australia, New Zealand and South Africa, where anxiety about local security was greatest, the outbreak of war promised immediate territorial gains in their own backyard: in German New Guinea, Samoa and South West Africa. Thirdly, the economic burdens of war were eased by the large and growing scale of British purchases, and by the general prosperity that came with the booming demand for the commodities the dominions produced. Loyalty and self-interest marched in the same direction. Even so, there was friction. The dominions were infuriated by the British government's initial reluctance to let them borrow in London, fearing that such a stoppage would capsize their credit-based economies. They were determined to keep their volunteer armies together as 'national' units and not to see them dispersed among other British troops. And, by 1916, dominion leaders were becoming increasingly anxious to have, and to be seen to have, greater influence over the purposes for which the war was being fought. W. M. Hughes, the Australian premier, spent much of 1916 in London, partly to negotiate the sale of the wool-clip, but also to stake a claim for influence at the imperial centre. The Canadian premier, Robert Borden, an outspoken advocate of dominion influence over British foreign policy before 1914, was enraged by the frigid response of the Colonial Secretary, Bonar Law, to his request for greater participation in imperial policy. Canada had sent 101,000 men overseas, he told his London representative in October 1915, and had just authorised an increase to 250,000. 'We deem ourselves entitled to fuller information and consultation respecting general policy in war operations.'[74] By January 1916, when the Canadian commitment was doubled again, his mood was explosive. Canada could not be expected to put four to five hundred thousand men in the field and be treated like 'toy automata', he burst out to Perley. 'Is the war being waged by the UK alone, or is it a war waged by the whole Empire?'[75] Hughes' opinion 'as to the future necessity of the Overseas nations having an adequate voice in the Empire's foreign policy', he told Perley, 'coincides entirely with my own'.[76]

Borden and Hughes were determined that the dominions' contribution to the war should be rewarded by the unequivocal abolition of their 'colonial' status in matters of external policy. Unlike Joseph Ward, joint leader of the New Zealand coalition government, they were not interested in imperial federation. Their chance came with the arrival of Lloyd George in Downing Street, and the Milnerites in government. Milnerite enthusiasm for 'closer unity' coincided with the grim acceptance that dominion help in the unending war would be increasingly important, and the even grimmer recognition that dominion leaders had to be consulted about the minimum terms of peace acceptable. In late December 1916, the invitations went out to an 'Imperial War Conference' that ran from March until May 1917. In the event, Hughes remained in Australia to fight for conscription, and Louis Botha sent his deputy, General Smuts. The dominion delegates were convened with British ministers as the 'Imperial War Cabinet'. War aims were discussed. London made ambiguous promises about imperial preference after the war. But the main outcome of the meetings was agreement that relations with the dominion governments would have to be adjusted after the war to respect their status as 'autonomous nations of an Imperial Commonwealth', with arrangements for 'continuous consultation' and an 'adequate voice in foreign policy and . . . foreign relations'.[77] Smuts, who put the case against imperial federation with crushing force, remained behind as a member of the War Cabinet, but not in any representative capacity. Borden rushed home to deal with the crisis over conscription.

In fact, there was little agreement among the dominion leaders about the direction of constitutional change beyond the demand for autonomy. Nor was there much sign (apart from the presence of Smuts) that dominion views had more influence over the strategy of the war after May 1917 than before. When the Imperial War Conference reassembled in the summer of 1918, it was against the terrible backdrop of impending disaster: the crisis in Flanders; the risk that Italy and even

France might be forced into peace before American help could arrive; the desperate need, as British manpower sagged, for more men from the dominions; the prospect of Milner's 'new war' with Germany in control of the Eurasian heartland. Borden, Massey and Hughes raged against the incompetence of the British generals on the Western Front.[78] Lloyd George smoothly 'deduced . . . the lesson that they should share with the British Government the responsibility for the control of military operations in the future'.[79] New arrangements were agreed to allow the dominion premiers to communicate direct with their British counterpart. But the sudden change in the course of the war checked any further experiment. When it came to negotiating an armistice in October, Lloyd George simply ignored his dominion colleagues. It took a fierce protest from Borden, backed by Hughes, to ensure dominion representation in what became the British Empire delegation to the peace conference.[80]

Why did opinion in the dominions tolerate so unequal a partnership in a war that cost them so dear? Much of the answer lies in the complex emotions of Britannic nationalism. In Canada, the tidal wave of pre-war migration made the sentimental bond with Britain especially close. 'I am afraid of the element known as the British-born', confided the Liberal ex-premier Wilfrid Laurier, who saw the magnetic pull of imperial loyalism as the biggest threat to Canadian stability before the war.[81] Indeed, some 70 per cent of the first contingent of the Canadian Expeditionary Force were British-born, and, even in 1918, they made up around half of its manpower.[82] But the eager response of recent immigrants was only part of the explanation for Canada's commitment to the war. The Conservative premier, Robert Borden, had long been convinced that Armageddon was coming, that Canada should play its part at Britain's side, and that sharing the burden would clinch her case for an 'imperial nationhood' alongside the mother country.[83] In much of English-speaking Canada, support for the war and the manpower sacrifice it demanded became the test of Canadian status as a 'British nation' rather than a colonial dependency. 'Canada should do her whole duty', declared Clifford Sifton who had led the Liberal revolt against the reciprocity bill in 1911.[84] Volunteer recruitment became an affirmation of British identity and Protestant conscience, especially in Quebec among the 'Anglo-Protestant' elite[85] and on the prairies where Europeans and Americans, rather than settlers of British birth or origins, made up much of the population. It was heavily promoted by Protestant clergymen and the Orange Lodges.[86] It was no coincidence that the heightened emotion of wartime soon found expression in the attack on bilingualism in Ontario and Manitoba where there were French-medium schools. Abolishing bilingual schools was necessary if Manitoba was not to be a 'middle-Europe ... filled with warring races', claimed John Dafoe, editor of the *Manitoba Free Press*, the most influential Liberal paper in the West.[87]

English-speaking Canadians had watched with increasing resentment the apparent indifference of French Canadians to the call of national duty. Proportionately, 150,000 French Canadians should have joined up, not the 15,000 who had done so, said Dafoe, adding for good measure that they were 'the only known race of white men to quit'.[88] Dafoe's savagery was a measure of the chasm between French and English attitudes by the middle of the war. Even Oscar Skelton, an admirer (and later biographer) of Laurier, was critical of the 'provincialism' of the French Canadian outlook.[89] In Quebec, the reaction was incomprehension and growing bitterness. Henri Bourassa, the tribune of French Canadian opinion, dismissed the conflict as one between 'Anglo-Saxon mercantilism and love of gold' and 'German autocracy and militarism'. They were as bad as each other.[90] The war was an affair of 'agglomerations', not 'small nations'.[91] Bourassa had been violently opposed to sending a Canadian contingent to the Boer War. In 1910, he had denounced Laurier's naval scheme as a step towards the conscription of French Canadians in Britain's imperial wars and had helped to drive him from office on a tide of French Canadian suspicion. For Laurier, the course of the war threatened deep and lasting damage to his hopes of political recovery, based as they were upon a reconciliation between provincial nationalism in Quebec and the Liberals of English Canada. The closer Borden came to his object of participating in the planning of imperial defence, he feared, the more deeply Canada would be committed to 'all the wars of the Empire'[92] – and the more dangerously French Canadians would be alienated from the rest of Canada. But there was no mistaking the enthusiasm of English Canadian Liberals for Canada's part in the war.

These deep divisions reached a crisis in 1917. With the terrible losses on the Western Front, voluntary enlistments were no longer enough to fill and refill the ranks of the Canadian Expeditionary Force. The fairness and efficiency of 'voluntary' recruitment aroused misgiving. Even Bourassa conceded that conscription might be better than 'enlistment by intimidation, threat and blackmail'.[93] On his return from the Imperial War Conference in May 1917, Borden opened the campaign for compulsion. He pressed Laurier to join a coalition government to carry it through. Laurier refused, and argued instead for a referendum, mindful, no doubt, that in Australia (as we shall see) conscription had failed this test of opinion. But in English Canada his Liberal colleagues abandoned him for a 'Unionist' coalition formed under Borden's leadership in October 1917. For them, conscription became the test of Britannic nationhood. The fate of conscription, said Sifton, would show whether or not Canada was '[just] a helpless aggregation of sectional communities held together by time-serving interests'.[94] When the election came, however, the Unionist government took no chances. The year before, Arthur Meighen, Borden's fixer, had argued that 'to shift the franchise from the doubtful British and anti-British of the male sex and to extend it . . . to our patriotic women would be . . . a splendid stroke'.[95] In the Military Voters Act and the Wartime Elections Act, he had his way. Naturalised aliens (i.e. not of British birth) resident for less than fifteen years lost the vote. Every soldier, of whatever age or pre-war residence, gained it, as did nurses and the wives, widows, mothers and sisters of soldiers. With the help of the 'gag', whose effects were felt mainly in the prairie provinces, the election was a triumph for the Unionist coalition which took 153 seats against the 82 held by the Laurier Liberals, all but 20 in Quebec. The Conscription Act followed in 1918.

The passing of conscription was the highwater mark of Britannic nationalism in Canada. It marked the readiness of English Canadians to identify their contribution to the imperial war effort as the acid test of nationhood at whatever cost in racial friction. For the result was to divide Canadian politics along racial lines. 'The government have won', said Laurier, 'but the peace of the country is certainly in danger.'[96] Quebec no longer held the balance of political power, one of Borden's supporters told him, but the result might be to make 'an irreconcilable Ireland in this country'.[97] It would take a generation to repair 'what the fanatics have destroyed in a few months', groaned Skelton.[98] Once the war was over, however, the momentum behind Borden's grand alliance was quickly lost. Economic difficulties and sectional differences between the prairies and the East fractured the wartime unity of Britannic sentiment. The coalition fell apart and, by 1921, the Liberals, under Mackenzie King, had returned to power. And, in the meantime,

Borden's pre-war dream of a seat at the table when foreign policy was made for the Empire had dissolved in the cold clear air of the aftermath.

In Australia, recent British immigration was also a factor in the readiness with which public opinion responded to the outbreak of a faraway war. The flow of British migrants had picked up strongly in the last years before 1914, though not on the same scale as in Canada.[99] To a much greater extent than in Canada, the British-born minority were prominent in political life: both wartime premiers had been born in Britain.[100] But the eagerness with which Australians greeted the call of imperial duty was not just a result of nostalgia. Long before the war, anxiety about the 'Yellow Peril' of Asian migration and the rising power of Japan had made defence an important issue in Australian politics and bred two different but complementary reactions. The sense of remoteness from Britain placed a premium on self-help. The defence Act of 1903 authorised conscription for home defence, and from 1911 military training was compulsory for young men. Australian governments pressed hard for control over their own 'fleet unit' contribution to the Royal Navy. But they were just as anxious for a louder voice in British policy since the imperial umbrella rather than local defence was the real guarantee of White Australia's survival in an empty continent. That may have been why a secret promise was made in 1911 to send an expeditionary force to Britain's aid in time of war, and why the Australian government was determined that any troops it sent should fight together and not be split up amongst British units.[101] Their influence in London, so the Australian leaders believed, depended not just on what they contributed to empire defence, but also on what they were seen to contribute.

Official enthusiasm helped to ensure the rapid formation of an all-volunteer Australian Imperial Force (AIF), and the enlistment of over 50,000 men by the end of 1914. At the local level, recruiting was promoted through the existing system for military training, and by the 'patriotic leagues' who arranged the enlistment meetings where men 'joined up' in an emotional atmosphere of patriotic sacrifice. As in Canada, Protestant clergymen were vociferous recruiters. 'We are British first and Australians second', said the Anglican minister in one country district in Victoria.[102] A sense of adventure and fear of unemployment at the beginning of the war (when trade was disrupted) were reinforced by a happy naivety about life at the front. Nevertheless, once Australian troops were committed at Gallipoli, and the scale of the war became gradually clearer, the federal government hastened to boost the volunteer impulse. 'Eligible' men from eighteen to forty-five had to fill in a card to say whether they were willing to enlist, and, if not, why. Recruitment was reorganised to give a larger role to 'recruiting sergeants' and intensify the moral pressure to volunteer.[103] It was not enough. Once much of the AIF had been transferred to the Western Front after the evacuation of Gallipoli, and its losses began to mount (six times as many Australians were eventually killed there as at Gallipoli), the struggle to refill its ranks began to haunt the Australian ministers. If the AIF was not just to waste away, and with it Australia's reputation and influence in London, something had to be done. That something was compulsion.

The most ardent champion of this view was William Morris Hughes, who had become premier in 1915. Hughes exemplified the 'White Australia' outlook of the Labour party, and its Asian paranoia. He had been a strong supporter of military service before the war. He mistrusted British ministers, but had no doubt that the fate of the four million Australians turned on their claim to British support as partners in the imperial enterprise. He spent much of 1916 in London partly to negotiate terms for the Australian wool-clip, partly to publicise Australia's contribution to the war. On his return, he threw himself into a furious campaign for conscription, since compulsory service in Australia applied only to home defence. To dramatise his appeal and maximise cross-party support, Hughes chose to test opinion through a referendum, not a general election. The wide public support for recruitment (even among those who opposed conscription) suggested that he would win an overwhelming victory. But, at the referendum of 28 October 1916, he lost by over 90,000 votes.[104] When he tried again in December 1917, in what seemed even more desperate circumstances, the margin was even bigger.[105]

Conscription proved bitterly divisive in wartime Australia, and the divisions long outlasted the war. In country districts especially, they separated friends and even families. Opponents of conscription bore the taint of disloyalty. In the eyes of Protestant and middle-class opinion, the 'shirkers' who resisted compulsion were identified with the Catholic and Irish communities and with organised labour. The ruling Labour party split over the issue. Hughes led his followers into a new coalition and formed the Nationalist party in 1917. The rest of the Labour party drifted gradually to the left. By the middle of

1918, the New South Wales party had declared in favour of an immediate peace. At the party's federal conference, the resolutions of the Imperial War Conference were rejected in favour of full Australian self-government, an end to all legal appeals to London, and the abolition of the honours system. Labour leaders also gradually withdrew from the recruiting effort which relied heavily on the publicity of speeches and meetings.

What lay behind the double failure of conscription? How far did it reflect opposition to the 'misuse' of Australian manpower in a 'British' war? How far did it spring from mistrust of British strategy and alarm at British methods? How far did it signal the growth of a new Australian identity that was determined not to be taken for granted by an overweening mother-country? The answer must be: not very much. It was true, for example, that some of the fiercest opponents of conscription were both Irish and Catholic. Amongst the large Irish Catholic community in Australia, there was wide support for Irish Home Rule and (after Easter 1916) furious anger at London's brutal treatment of the leaders of the Dublin rising. Hughes himself had warned that Home Rule was an imperial, not just a British, question. It was natural that many Irish Australians should resist the Britannic rhetoric with which Australia's contribution to the war was justified. But the wider argument against conscription had little to do with the repudiation of Britishness or empire. In a voluntaristic society, it was an attack on individual rights. Some opponents complained that conscription would mean the permanent weakening of trade unionism, as the champion of working-class interests in the wage arbitration system. It would be the prelude to the industrial conscription of labour. Others insisted that Australia was doing as much as it could. In rural districts, and among farmers, conscription was feared as a remorseless drain on agricultural labour and the family farm. But the most widely vented, and probably most influential, arguments were those that portrayed conscription not as an attack on Australia's autonomy, but as a deadly threat to its white, Britannic identity.

The logic was not hard to follow. It appealed to the old, half-submerged tradition of isolationism in Australia: resentment at the costly involvement in European wars at the expense of more immediate concerns. Germany posed no danger, claimed the rising young Labour politician, John Curtin: Japan was the real menace.[106] And, while sending off Australia's manpower to Europe would make no difference

342 / 'The great liner is sinking'

against Germany, it would make all the difference in resisting Japan. This argument was especially powerful in Queensland, the 'invasion colony' most exposed (it was believed) to attack from the north.[107] But defence was not the only issue. The more insidious danger was the infiltration of non-white labour: the old bogey of the Labour party and the trade unions. 'Vote against conscription and Colonial Coloured labour' urged anti-conscriptionists in Victoria. 'The Coloured Ocean... will swamp us if we do not stop the forcible deportation of our men, who are the white walls of Australia', howled a Queensland pamphlet. 'Vote no and keep Australia for future Australians – pure, free, unfettered and peopled with our own race and blood', roared another.[108] Hughes was guilty of treason against White Australia, said Curtin.[109] The pro-conscription rhetoric of defence and democracy was neutralised by the claim that draining off white manpower would open the door not just to non-white labour but the erosion of hard-won political rights. One anti-conscription cartoon portrayed a dark-skinned, turbanned figure bringing down an axe labelled 'yes' on the neck of 'democracy's' crouching (white) form. 'Goodbye democracy' was its byline.

The vote against conscription was thus not a repudiation of empire, let alone of Britishness. It was a vote against an open-ended commitment to the war on the Western Front. It expressed a fear that the deeper purpose of empire – conceived as the expansion of 'White Australia' in its South Pacific homeland – would be jeopardised by the reckless expenditure of its most precious resource: white men. But it was far from reflecting any wider disenchantment with the war. Hughes' defeat in the first referendum was followed by the crushing victory of his Nationalist government in the general election of May 1917. The Labour government in Queensland, the only state ministry to oppose conscription (the Labour governments in South Australia and New South Wales had supported it), was at pains to reassure British opinion that its commitment to victory was unimpaired.[110] Other Labour leaders, perhaps fearful of the 'lose-the-war' label that Hughes tried to hang round their neck, insisted on their support for the war and enlistment. Nor was the 'digger' myth that emerged in the second half of the war to celebrate ANZAC heroism at Gallipoli at odds with the 'Britannic' tradition of White Australia as the British vanguard in the Southern Seas. The tough, independent-minded digger colonising the 'bush' fitted perfectly with a 'conservative imperial nationalism' in which Australia played the part of the 'imperial farm'.[111]

In the other Pacific dominion, contributing to the war aroused much less controversy. In New Zealand, there was the same eagerness as in Australia to be seen at Britain's side. During the war, over 40 per cent of eligible males enlisted for service, the vast majority of them volunteers. Press, public and government united behind the vision of empire unity. 'A great step forward is being made in the work of Imperial unification', declared *The Dominion* newspaper in September 1914.[112] In the race to send an imperial contingent, boasted Sir James Allen, the defence minister, in April 1915, 'we are a long way ahead of any one of the Dominions'.[113] The *quid pro quo* was a voice in foreign policy;[114] the *sine qua non*, a voice in London. The joint leaders of the government coalition, Massey and Sir Joseph Ward, spent much of the war in London, the real centre (as James Belich observes) of the New Zealand war effort.[115] In May–June 1916, conscription for overseas service was enacted by an overwhelming parliamentary majority.[116] There was no great feeling against it, Allen reported to Massey in London.[117] Of course, this remarkable commitment to a far-off conflict was not unqualified. By the end of 1916, there was growing nervousness about the commercial predominance of the United States and Japan in the Pacific, and industrial unrest welled up in the last year of the war. But the fierce divisions of Australian politics were largely avoided. War prosperity allowed the government to conciliate the most powerful trade unions. New Zealand's longer history of social intervention by central government may have made conscription more palatable. And the isolationist tradition was weaker: a reflection partly of demographic and strategic realities, and partly perhaps of the differences in ethnic composition (New Zealand's Irish Catholic community was smaller, less radical and less influential than Australia's) and immigrant tradition on the different shores of the Tasman Sea.

The spectre of revolt: South Africa, India, Ireland

South Africa

In Canada, Australia and New Zealand, ethnic majorities of British descent, urged on by a London-looking press, their Protestant clergies and the loyalism of recent immigrants, responded to the call of the Empire in danger. In all three dominions, the political elite insisted that the survival and solidarity of the Empire was a vital national interest, and that their future as 'British nations' (the only national future then imaginable) depended upon the fullest possible commitment to the imperial enterprise. But, in South Africa, India and Ireland, the politics of imperial war were very different. South Africa was a dominion too, but a dominion with a difference. Among whites, to whom political power was all but completely reserved, Dutch-speaking Afrikaners formed a clear majority. While the 'English' reacted to the outbreak of war with martial ardour – 'Johannesburg is full of patriotic emotion', reported the Unionist politician, Patrick Duncan[118] – Afrikaner feelings were much more ambivalent. There was little sense of obligation to the imperial power whose conquest of the Boer republics was such a recent and painful memory. Among those Afrikaners in whom the republican faith still burned fiercely, the old adage 'England's danger, Ireland's opportunity' bore an obvious South African meaning. The prime minister, Louis Botha, faced a dilemma. He was acutely sensitive to the charge of dividing the Afrikaner *volk*. But he was also aware that refusal to contribute to the war would enrage the South African English and expose him to the full force of London's displeasure. 'Racial' conflict between Afrikaners and English was likely to arise whether he participated too much or too little. Shrewdly, Botha sought a middle course. At London's request, he mounted a campaign to capture German South West Africa (modern Namibia). It was an obvious target and one that might have been expected to appeal to Afrikaner feeling as much as English. But politically it was a disaster. To many Afrikaners, the attack on Germany's colony was unjustified, and also counter-productive: it destroyed their best lever against the imperious British. Two of Botha's most senior commanders, and a number of commandos – the militia units that embodied Boer society at the local level – rejected the order to serve and rose in revolt. Perhaps 11,000 rebels took up arms against the government. From October 1914 until January 1915, the issue hung in the balance. 'People in Johannesburg do not realise how critical the situation in the country is', said Duncan, 'and how much depends on Botha's being able to keep his people in hand.'[119] Without Botha, 'anything might happen'.[120]

Botha's personal authority among Afrikaners and the loyalty he enjoyed from the majority of commandos enabled him to bring the revolt to an end. But bitterness and republican sympathy remained strong, especially in the countryside. Even in the towns, young Afrikaners were 'very disaffected'. 'The Empire means nothing to them or inspires them with revulsion.'[121] For the English politicians, fear of another revolt and dependence upon Botha to prevent it happening, were deeply frustrating.[122] They were furious at the terms on which South Africa's contribution to the larger war was made. In August 1915, Botha arranged for a volunteer contingent of brigade strength to be raised for overseas service. (In all, over 70,000 whites, overwhelmingly drawn from the English community, and 44,000 blacks served in Europe.[123]) But he insisted that they be paid for by London and incorporated in the British army – a decision which meant that their pay at 'imperial' rates was one-third of the 'Union' pay received by those who fought in South West Africa or by the (mainly Afrikaner) contingent that fought under Smuts in German East Africa. The Unionist party leaders raged privately at Botha's refusal to bring his South African party into a 'loyal' coalition to fight the war. But they dared not attack him openly, despite the strong feeling among their supporters, for fear he would resign or drift into alliance with the covert republicans in the National party.

Indeed, Botha became more not less indispensable the longer the war went on. Military failure in Europe and the Near East, the stimulus of the Dublin rising, and agrarian discontent among rural Afrikaners, helped to revive the republican cause in the second half of the war. In 1918, controversy over the Union government's payments to London (to meet some of the costs of the South African contingent), rumours that conscription would be introduced to meet the manpower crisis on the Western Front and mounting labour unrest (among whites and blacks) as shortage and inflation took their toll, heightened the political tension. Nationalists talked openly of demanding 'complete independence' (code for a republic) when the war ended. In January 1919, they agreed on a delegation to Paris to reverse the verdict of 1902 and restore republican status to the Transvaal and Orange Free State. English politicians looked on fearfully. 'The war . . . has opened up much of the old racial consciousness', said Duncan gloomily. 'It has also accentuated the sense of dependence involved in the subordination of our South African politics to the exigencies of a desperate war.'[124] But, if the Afrikaner majority united behind a republic and secession from the Empire, the result would be disastrous. 'The English would fight', and 'it would be impossible for the British Government and the rest of the Empire to keep out of it.' Something had to be done to appease the Afrikaner sense of racial subjection and build a real South

346 / 'The great liner is sinking'

African citizenship. If the Empire cannot provide adequately for South Africa in these respects, it will not keep South Africa as a member.'

In fact, the war had starkly revealed the peculiar terms on which South Africa was attached to the British system. Isolationism was a much more powerful factor there than in any of the other dominions. This was partly a matter of Afrikaner resistance to imperial 'service': the same feeling could be found in Quebec. But it sprang just as much from the unspoken fear that a holocaust of white men in a far-off war would imperil the physical base of white supremacy in a sub-continent where it was recent, hard-won and fragile. Though blacks had almost no political power, the *zwaartgevaar* ('black danger') was here, as in much else, the real governor of South African politics. For Unionist politicians, the war was a great disappointment. They had failed to force Botha into an Anglo-Afrikaner coalition avowedly 'loyal' to the imperial connection. Instead, the war had seemed to strengthen the old 'Krugerist' republican strand of Afrikaner nationalism. The English were divided by the politics of class. The standard-bearers of Britannic sentiment in South Africa resigned themselves to the role of an imperial garrison, ready to block the road to secession by whatever means. But, before the full impact of post-war unrest and instability could be felt, Botha died prematurely in August 1919.

India

In South Africa, the political compact of 1910 had been preserved by carefully limiting its contribution to the war. No such option existed for India. South Africa was a vital strategic outpost whose gold output was mobilised for London's war economy. But India was a main base, the second centre of British military power. Once the war spread to the Near and Middle East, India was expected to bear much of the burden: to counter the Turkish threat in the Persian Gulf (and to the British-controlled oilfield in Southwest Persia) and then to invade the Ottoman provinces of modern Iraq. In the dark days of 1918, when the 'new war' threatened imperial disaster, India was pressed even harder for men and resources to meet the shortfall elsewhere. All this was bound to be a source of heavy strain. India's modern infrastructure was only very partially developed. There was little reserve capacity for the sudden increase in the transport of persons and products. In an overwhelmingly agrarian economy, much of it near the margin of subsistence, there was little scope for the increase of revenue or for the vast domestic borrowing through which London had financed much of its war expenditure at home. Above all, a government in which all executive power was wielded by British officials faced the Himalayan task of winning Indian loyalty to an imperial war. If the war was to mean the recruitment (of volunteers), an increased burden of taxation, the economic hardships of inflation, shortage, bottlenecks, and the restriction of personal liberty, for what higher purpose were Indians being asked to make such sacrifice?

Symptoms of discontent were not lacking in India. Almost from the beginning of the war, the government in Delhi had been alarmed by the threat of armed conspiracy by Sikh militants based in the United States and the revival of terrorism in Bengal. But the war against the Ottoman Empire raised a much more worrying prospect. Many educated Muslims in India had been agitated before 1914 by the fear that Turkey as the largest independent Muslim state and guardian of the Holy Places in Mecca and Jerusalem was about to collapse. Defeat by Italy and the Balkan states in 1912–13 tolled the Turkish knell. Associations had been formed to express Muslim solidarity and send material help. Muslim politics in India became increasingly responsive to this sense of a wider Islamic identity. In May 1915, the government of India interned the most prominent of the younger and more radical Muslim politicians, the brothers Mohamed and Shaukat Ali, on the grounds that they had made contact with Turkish agents, were promoting pro-Turkish sympathies in their newspapers, and were active champions of 'pan-Islamism'.[125] The result was to pave the way for a much closer alignment between the leaders of the Muslim League and the Indian National Congress than had seemed possible before 1914. By early 1916, the Viceroy was becoming anxious to pre-empt the call for some political reward for Indian loyalty by a constitutional initiative of his own – though one that fell far short of the 'colonial *swaraj*' (dominion-style self-government) to which Congress was committed.[126] The appearance of the 'Home Rule Leagues' in 1916 showed that open discontent was spreading among Hindus as well as Muslims. But, before New Delhi could extract a decision from its embattled masters in London, the Indian politicians pulled off a stunning coup. In December 1916, the Congress and the Muslim League reached agreement upon a set of constitutional demands whose studied moderation concealed a far-reaching challenge to British authority. Far from being the handiwork of 'extremists', it had been endorsed by the elected members of the Viceroy's legislative council – a group of unimpeachable respectability.

Delhi and London were now galvanised into activity. The Viceroy pressed not for the promise of a post-war declaration, but a declaration now. Without it, he warned, it would be difficult 'to arrest the further defection of moderate opinion' to the campaign for 'immediate Home Rule'.[127] In London, the Secretary of State, Austen Chamberlain, was sympathetic. Like the Viceroy's, his reforming instincts were cautious. But, in the summer of 1917, Chamberlain was swept away by the damning report of the Mesopotamia Commission which blamed the India Office and the government of India for mismanaging the disastrous advance on Baghdad. He was replaced by a Liberal, a protégé of Asquith, but now a follower of Lloyd George, Edwin Montagu. Montagu had known the India Office as a junior minister. As a Jew, he was alert to the racial arrogance of British officialdom of which educated Indians so often complained. Most of all, he was fiercely critical of the bureaucratic mentality of the Civilian Raj. The government of India was 'too wooden, too iron, too inelastic, too antediluvian', he told the House of Commons shortly before his appointment. It had to become political, to argue its case, to win over opinion. With his abrasive manner and radical ideas, Montagu was an unlikely appointment to the India Office. But the accident of war had given him a doctor's mandate to shake up the lethargic Indian government and head off the danger of Indian unrest – at the very moment when the receding hope of victory in Europe made help from the empire countries all the more vital. In August 1917, Montagu extracted from the War Cabinet permission to announce a new departure in Indian politics. In his famous announcement on 20 August 1917, India was promised 'the gradual development of self-governing institutions' and 'the progressive realization of responsible government...as an integral part of the British Empire'.[128] What this coded language seemed to mean was that the Viceroy's opposition to 'colonial *swaraj*' had been overcome. The days of 'constitutional despotism' were numbered. India's political future lay in the promotion to dominion-type self-government that the Congress had so long been demanding.

The Congress–League scheme had been careful to disavow interference with India's imperial burdens, the likely cause of objections from London. External affairs, the princely states and the army budget were all excluded from the purview of the new elected councils it called for at provincial and All-India level.[129] But over internal affairs the control of elected Indians was to be very wide. Resolutions passed by the councils could be carried against the veto of the executive at the second attempt. The old adversary, the Indian Civil Service, was to be removed altogether from the new executive bodies in the provinces and in the government of India in Delhi, to be replaced by a mixture of appointed Indians and British from 'home', free (it was assumed) from the taint of the Civilian ethos. Montagu's plan was to extend devolution at the provincial level and push India firmly down the road to federation, the only 'thinkable' policy, he told Lloyd George.[130] In the autumn of 1917, he set out for India to persuade the Viceroy and the Civilians to adopt a much more drastic form of provincial self-government than they had intended, to reduce central control over provincial revenues and leave much of the provinces' affairs to elected Indian ministers. These ideas were badly received. When Montagu met the Viceroy and the provincial governors – the barons of the Civilian Raj – in Delhi, he was dismayed by the governors' hostility to real reform.[131] But, in 1918, the Civilian Raj was in low water. Its reputation for competence had been destroyed by the Mesopotamia Commission. Under this cloud, it had little hope of appealing over Montagu's head to opinion at home. If they did not heed his advice, Montagu bluntly told the governors, 'I would resign and they must get somebody else'.[132] Moreover, the need for a radical overhaul was voiced as much by 'imperialists' as by radicals in Britain. Lionel Curtis, the 'prophet' of the 'Round Table' (the influential pressure group for imperial federation), who was reputed to have the ear of Lords Milner and Curzon, as well as that of *The Times* (or so Montagu believed), had mobilised opinion in India and Britain behind an even more radical scheme of provincial devolution, breaking up the provinces into 'provincial states'.[133] The senior Civilians also knew that the demands of the war effort were bound to grow even more voracious, and with them the need for Indian cooperation. In the triangle of Indian politics, both London and local opinion were against them. They could not obstruct simultaneously a reforming minister and the grand coalition of Indian politicians.

With his doctrine of winning over the Indian 'moderates', Montagu eventually gained the grudging acquiescence of Chelmsford and his colleagues to what (the term was Curtis') came to be called 'dyarchy'. In the provinces, government business was to be divided into 'transferred' and 'reserved' subjects: with the first category coming under the control of Indian ministers 'responsible' to elected legislatures. At the centre, the old legislative council was to be enlarged and have an elected majority. But it would have no control over any part of the central government; it could not prevent the passing of the budget; nor would any member of the Viceroy's government be responsible to it. To meet the long-standing Congress complaint, one-third of the Indian Civil Service would henceforth be recruited in India. For all its compromises, this was strong medicine for the Civilians, and even the civil servant charged with drafting the report could hardly conceal his distaste for its recommendations.[134] Montagu went home to publish what was to be called the 'Montagu–Chelmsford Report' believing that he had headed off the impending crisis in Indian politics that he, like Curtis, had feared: the inevitable result (they thought) if Indian politicians were denied some responsibility for government and driven into demagogy or agitation. But, if Montagu had hoped that his reward for reforms that went far beyond what Morley had considered only nine years earlier would be the grateful thanks of 'political India', and the triumph of the 'moderates', he was to be sorely disappointed. In reality, India was on the brink of a political earthquake.

The first sign of this was the Congress' furious rejection of the reform scheme. At a special session to debate the reforms, speakers queued up to denounce the leisurely timetable for Indian self-government, the miserly allocation of civil service posts to Indians, and the failure to concede any measure of responsible government at the Indian centre.[135] The delegates still spoke the language of loyalty. 'We want to save the Empire', said one, 'we want to keep up the British connection . . . we see the far-ahead danger of an isolated India.'[136] But they were outraged by the government of India's plans for new laws to deal with the threat of sedition (an omnibus term that covered terrorism, conspiracy and political unrest) once the wartime legislation ran out. The Rowlatt Report (it took its name from the judge who wrote it) was roundly condemned. Montagu had also been uneasy at the draconian powers the report recommended. He had pressed Chelmsford to reform the Criminal Intelligence department, which routinely spied on Indian politicians. 'It is convenient but very dangerous to govern by means of your police', he lectured the Viceroy.[137] It was wrong to exaggerate the threat of violence by a 'handful of deluded fanatics'.[138] But he dared not press his opposition too far: the Rowlatt Act was the Viceroy's *quid pro quo* for reform. Whatever its justification, this was to be a staggering political blunder. For the Rowlatt Act was the catalyst for mass politics in India.

It was opposition to Rowlatt that brought Gandhi to the forefront of Indian nationalism. Gandhi had returned to India in 1915 after nearly twenty years in South Africa. He brought with him a new political creed of personal liberation through 'truth-force' or *satyagraha*. Gandhi professed indifference to the mechanics of constitutional reform and stressed instead a spiritual struggle against the mental domination of the British Raj. His ideal was not the unitary Indian state imagined by the Congress leadership but a myriad of self-sufficient villages, purged of the superstitions, inequalities and insanitariness that disfigured rural life, and an India freed from the tyranny of its overbearing foreign bureaucracy. By the middle of 1918, he had demonstrated in an electrifying way the potential of his social and political teaching for mobilising support far beyond the educated and literate. At Ahmedabad and Kaira in Western India, and at Champaran in Bihar, he championed local grievances and inspired local disciples. Skilful use of the press, and meticulous organisation allowed him to keep control over local activists, the *satyagrahis*; while mastery of paperwork and his willingness to act as an intermediary won him credibility with the government. He preserved a careful ambiguity over the constitutional issue, welcoming the Montagu–Chelmsford reforms but as the basis for transforming a 'top-heavy and ruinously expensive' regime.[139] More controversially, he gave enthusiastic backing to the recruitment drive for the Indian army in the summer of 1918, arguing that only if Indians showed their martial qualities would they win British respect. 'We want the same rights as an Englishman enjoys', but Indians could never be treated as equals if they depended on British protection.[140] But the Rowlatt Act seemed a throwback to the brutal dogmas of race supremacy. It was a moral outrage against which the whole force of Indian opinion could be rallied peacefully through *satyagraha* and *hartal*, the mass boycott or shutdown to show public discontent. It was the perfect issue with which to connect the local networks of Gandhian activism to the grander question of Indian freedom.

Part of Gandhi's motive was to throw a bridge to Muslim discontent. Indeed, Muslim irritation was just as dangerous to the Civilian Raj as Gandhi's experiments in local activism. Islamic consciousness had been growing before 1914 stimulated by the spread of newspapers, the diffusion of Islamic literature and more regular contact with the

Islamic heartland in Southwest Asia. During the war, an alliance grew up between the educated 'Young Muslim' politicians and the *ulama*, the religious elite.[141] The gaoling of the leading Young Muslim politicians showed how seriously the threat of pan-Islamic agitation was taken. Their continued incarceration after the war was over meant that Indian Muslims were especially sensitive to the repressive implications of the Rowlatt Act: they had felt the main weight of its wartime equivalent. This was bad enough. But, at the same moment, Muslim opinion was becoming more and more alarmed over the fate of the Ottoman Empire, defeated in war and now destined, so it seemed, to be partitioned between the victorious (Christian) powers. To Muslim leaders who had escaped internment, the Rowlatt Act and the subjugation of what remained of the free Muslim world (including its Holy Places) were inextricably linked.

By early 1919, then, the old slogans of the Congress politicians had been taken up by an army of new activists. Into this cocktail of discontent was stirred a long list of material grievances: wartime shortage and inflation; rising taxation; the terrible scourge of influenza that carried off millions in 1918. In March 1919, Gandhi launched the Rowlatt *satyagraha*. *Hartals*, demonstrations and riots followed in many North Indian cities, including Delhi, a centre of pan-Islamic feeling. But, in the Punjab towns, the violence was far worse. News of Gandhi's arrest lit the fuze for widespread disorder. It reached a bloody climax at Amritsar. After three Europeans had been killed, troops under General Dyer were rushed to the city. Political meetings were forbidden, but enforcement was patchy. Then, on the afternoon of 13 April, nearly 400 demonstrators were shot dead at the Jallianwala Bagh, an enclosed space not far from the Golden Temple.

The 'new politics' had arrived with a vengeance. The result was not a downward spiral into violent confrontation (from which both sides drew back) but a profound remaking of the political world. The pattern was not immediately clear, but two great trends had been set in motion. The first was the growth of a novel form of cultural politics, radically distinct from the liberal programme of the pre-war Congress. It was rooted above all in religious identity, Muslim and Hindu, the appeal of which had been growing rapidly. It gave huge new impetus to the 'communal' tendency visible before the war in the separatist claims of the Muslim League, and ratified in the electoral arrangements of the Congress–League scheme. It would fuel the great

Non-Cooperation movement of 1920–2, but cut short Gandhi's bold experiment in Hindu–Muslim unity, and give a lever to the embattled Civilians as they struggled to manage the new constitution. It would shape fundamentally the last phase of British rule. The second trend was its inevitable counterpart. As Indian politics became more 'religious', more populist and more introverted, the old identification of the educated elite with the Empire and 'British connection' became increasingly strained. They were harassed by new social and religious appeals, and betrayed by the meanness of the Montford reforms. They had expected (with British help) to make a British Indian nation from above. Now they had to reckon with the demand for new freedoms that welled up from below. In 1919, how it would all end was anyone's guess.

Ireland

In no part of the Empire, however, were the effects of war more drastic than in Ireland. Unless the British recovered the 'courage and sureness of touch which rendered us famous as Empire builders', Montagu had mused in June 1917, 'we shall simply make a series of Irelands in different parts of the world'[142] – a fate he meant to avoid in India. What Montagu had in mind, no doubt, was the unappeasable hostility with which a part at least of Irish nationalist opinion viewed the British connection; the vicious circle of forcible repression and violent resistance; the obstruction of Home Rule by Ulster and the Unionists. In fact, by the middle of 1917, much of Ireland outside Ulster was in the early stages of a political revolution that went far beyond anything seen before 1914. In the post-war election of December 1918, Sinn Fein swept the board with a programme of republican independence. In January 1919, it declared the new republic in being and began to create a parallel government. As London struggled to reassert its authority, the spasmodic violence between the republican 'army' and the Royal Irish Constabulary turned into full-scale guerrilla war.

What had made the Irish revolt against empire so much more extreme than that of Afrikaners or Indians? Of course, it was true that, in the last months before the outbreak of the war in 1914, the threat of armed Ulster resistance to Home Rule and the failure to find a political compromise had created a mood of violent confrontation between nationalists and unionists, and brought Ireland to the brink of civil war. But the emotions roused by the European war had brought an astonishing change of mood. The leaders of the Irish National party had declared their commitment to the imperial war effort. The 'Irish Volunteers', formed to counter the Ulster Volunteer Force, became the 'National Volunteers', the kernel, it was hoped, of an Irish Army Corps on the dominion model. John Redmond, the Irish Party leader, accepted the wartime deferment of Home Rule. Like Australian or New Zealand politicians (and like his Ulster rivals), Redmond intended this demonstration of imperial loyalty to reap a post-war reward. For the time being, the road to imperial influence lay through the drill-hall and recruitment meeting. The Irish dominion-to-be (Redmond's real objective) would be funded from London's wartime debt of honour.

The unsolved problem of Ulster's exclusion was bound to make this a risky and uncertain strategy. Many of Redmond's followers were bitterly opposed to anything that smacked of partition and deeply mistrustful of the London government. Redmond's best hope was that the wartime comradeship of Irish unionists and nationalists, and their common sacrifice, would soften their pre-war antagonism and win Ulster's agreement to Home Rule on a flood-tide of All-Irish patriotism. Any prospect of this was badly damaged by the Dublin Easter Rising in April 1916. The Irish Republican Brotherhood, which controlled the Volunteer units opposed to Redmond, had planned an armed insurrection in September 1915. It was delayed into 1916 for the sake of German help with the weapons needed for a general revolt. Even when these failed to arrive (they were intercepted by the Royal Navy), the conspirators under the charismatic leadership of Patrick Pearse went ahead with the Dublin rising. Their motives have been much debated, but a desperate determination to shock Irish opinion out of wartime loyalty, perhaps by a 'blood sacrifice', may have been uppermost. Whatever the aim, the effect was seismic. In six days of fighting, the city centre was wrecked and 450 people (mostly civilians) were killed. The initial revulsion against the reckless violence of the conspirators was disarmed by their subsequent fate: ninety were sentenced to death, sixteen were to die.[143] Republicanism had found its martyrs. More immediately, the Dublin rising convinced the London government (which wrongly attributed it to the influence of Sinn Fein) that some new gesture was needed to isolate the 'extremists' in Irish politics and bolster the loyalty of Redmond's followers. Home Rule returned to the political agenda but in circumstances no more favourable than in 1914.

The result was a stalemate. Lloyd George won the shadow of consent but only by telling the Ulster Unionists that their exclusion from a Home Rule Ireland would be permanent, and the Redmondites that it would be temporary. When the truth was revealed, the 'agreement' fell apart. Redmond angrily rejected the offer of immediate Home Rule for the twenty-six counties outside Ulster, knowing that much of his following would reject a compromise that left many Catholic nationalists in a separate North. In the House of Commons in March 1917, the Redmondites complained bitterly of British betrayal. 'What is it that stands in the way of Ireland's taking her place as a self-governing part of the Empire?', asked the leader's brother, William Redmond.[144] Ireland wanted to be like Canada, Australia and New Zealand, 'side by side in the common cause'. John Redmond himself offered a sombre and prophetic warning. The 'revolutionary party', almost banished before the war, was now reviving. His own position had been made untenable. In a savage peroration, Redmond blamed his political bankruptcy on the treachery of British leaders. 'Any British statesman who... once again teaches the Irish people the lesson that any National leader who, taking his political life in his hands, endeavours to combine local and Imperial patriotism, endeavours to combine loyalty to Ireland's rights with loyalty to the Empire – anyone who again teaches the lesson that such a man is certain to be let down and betrayed by this course, is guilty of treason not merely to the liberties of Ireland but to the unity, strength and best interests of this Empire.'[145] Lloyd George replied merely that Ulster could not be forced into Home Rule.

There was to be one last throw of the political dice. Too much was at stake to abandon all effort at settlement. For London, an unreconciled Ireland would embarrass Britain's relations with the United States (now a 'co-belligerent'), threaten Irish recruitment and alarm the Unionist majority in Parliament on which the Lloyd George ministry depended. For Redmond and the Irish National party it would ensure the oblivion that Redmond feared. The Irish Convention of 1917–18 was a desperate attempt to find a bargain acceptable to the nationalists, and both the Northern and the Southern Unionists (who had most to lose from partition).[146] It failed, but its real failure was to have been irrelevant. It was boycotted by Sinn Fein, and Sinn Fein was already by 1917 the most powerful force in Irish politics. While Redmond pursued a constitutional will-o'-the-wisp, Sinn Fein urged mass support for outright separation. It crushed the Redmondites in the by-elections. In May 1917, it won the open endorsement of the Catholic hierarchy. But the real secret of its remarkable rise was the Irish fear of conscription.

Ireland had been carefully exempted from the Military Service Act of 1916. But its shadow loomed large in Irish society. As the war dragged on, it seemed only a matter of time before conscription crossed the Irish Sea. There were many reasons why Irish attitudes were so different from those in mainland Britain. Even the Redmondites insisted that without Home Rule conscription was illegitimate. Like Afrikaners or French Canadians, the Catholic majority denied an *obligation* to fight for the Empire, even if many were willing to do so. Ireland had the highest rate of emigration in pre-war Europe:[147] even without conscription, the haemorrhage of young men (and women) was the cruellest fact in Irish life. In rural Ireland especially, conscription threatened (or was thought to) the survival of small farms dependent on family labour. Scares proliferated about the moral and physical pollution that army service would bring. Conscription would debauch as well as impoverish, a notion not discouraged by the clergy. Politically and culturally, it meant anglicisation, the fraying of local loyalty and Catholic identity.

The fear of conscription was thus the cause that turned the republican separatism of Sinn Fein into a popular movement, and Irish politics into its revolutionary phase. As the Convention floundered towards collapse, the slide towards open revolt gathered speed. For, by April 1918, the threat of conscription had become dangerously real. As the crisis of British manpower grew with the huge new losses on the Western Front, the call-up in Britain was extended to men as old as fifty-one. After a bitter internal row, the Lloyd George government shelved its application to Ireland – for the moment. The effect on Ireland was like a call to arms. The Volunteer brigades recruited and trained more actively than ever.[148] For many young men, armed resistance as a Volunteer seemed the only defence against compulsory service in the British army. Raiding and counter-raiding between Volunteers and police intensified. De Valera, now leader of Sinn Fein, drew up a national pledge against conscription that was signed by tens of thousands at the church door on 21 April 1918 and endorsed by a general strike two days later. Amid these signs of violent upheaval (and with deepening gloom on the Western Front), London turned once more to repression. The Sinn Fein leadership (some 150 persons) was gaoled and its meetings proscribed – a step widely seen as the prelude to conscription. But it was now too late to break the grip of the movement and its military wing on the Irish countryside. For the rest of the war, an armed truce prevailed. When peace came, Sinn Fein's electoral triumph (outside Ulster) and the opening shots of its military struggle showed how far and how quickly the war had transformed the old landscape of Anglo-Irish relations.

It was at first sight surprising that the revolt against empire had gone furthest so near the centre of the British system. The paradox is superficial. Though the demands of war had been felt across the whole imperial world, the alienation they caused had been deepest in Ireland. In pre-war Ireland, political expectations had been higher and the edge of violence closer than anywhere else – with the consequences seen in 1916. As in India, the imperial government could not promise enough to save its would-be allies from defeat by 'extremists'. As in India, its agents enraged their opponents by the threat of coercion. But the real catalyst of Irish nationalism in its republican and separatist mode was fear that the imperial state was about to drive its control deeper than ever before into the localities – through conscription and its enforcement – and thus *reverse* the pre-war trend to devolution. It was in Ireland, then, that the cloven hoof of war imperialism was most clearly visible, and in Ireland that the reaction was most deadly.

War and empire

The effects of the war on the British system were disturbing but also contradictory. Its extraordinary conclusion in Europe – unimaginable in 1914 – had wrecked, for the time being at least, the old balance of power, which had exerted so much influence on the extra-European diplomacy of the European states. Devising a stable successor regime that would restrain the jealousies of the European powers within Europe and beyond was one of the most pressing concerns of the 'peacemakers' who gathered in Paris in January 1919. Secondly, the war had set in motion a geopolitical revolution in East Asia. The weakness of a Russia engulfed in civil war (the disintegration of Russian colonial power in Northeast Asia seemed highly likely in 1919), the (relative) strength of Japan, and the rise of xenophobic nationalism in China (that was to burst out in May 1919) threatened a general onslaught against Western interests on this furthest frontier of the British world. Thirdly, the war had destabilised the world economy and checked the globalising trends from which Britain had profited so much before 1914. It loaded Britain with debts both internal and external. At the same time, the sacrifice of men and wealth and the terrible uncertainties that persisted almost until the end of the conflict had strained the old basis of cooperation between Britain and the empire countries, goading into life the secessionist strand of local nationalism in Ireland, India and even South Africa. By way of compensation, the war had crushed for the moment the great power rivalry of Germany and Russia, whose competitive expansion British leaders had feared most before 1914. As a result, the British had been able to occupy much of the Eurasian 'cockpit' in the Near and Middle East, the region where geopolitical uncertainty had seemed most dangerous to the imperial system – but at what cost, and for how long?

This was what one of Woodrow Wilson's advisers was to call 'the new world'.[149] How far British leaders could reconstruct their pre-war system, and adapt it to the shape of the new international order, and how far they could carry with them their partners, agents, allies and collaborators in India, the dominions and the 'outer empire', will be seen in the chapters that follow.

9   MAKING IMPERIAL PEACE, 1919–1926

In 1918, the British won an astonishing, almost fortuitous, victory, snatching an imperial triumph from what seemed, as late as June, the jaws of continental defeat. Their greatest imperial rivals had been broken, one (Russia) by the other (Germany). In the Armageddon of empires, British credit, domestic unity and imperial cohesion had been tested to the limit, but had survived. Of the three principal victor powers, the United States, France and Britain, the British seemed best placed to turn the making of peace to their advantage. They had made the largest territorial gains, in the Middle East, Africa and the Pacific and had most to bargain with. They had incurred heavy debts to the United States, but London's influence on post-war reconstruction was bound to be large, since it was from London that the European victor states had borrowed most. With their pre-war rivals in disarray, there seemed little danger that British authority would be challenged by colonial politicians – whose leverage had been cut down by peace – or client states, no longer able to play off two sides in the great game of imperial influence. Above all, perhaps, with the gravest threat to the balance of power in Europe extinguished by the defeat of the Central Powers, the British could hope to lower their naval guard (after the strain of the Anglo-German arms race) and ease the pre-war tensions over imperial defence created by their single-minded concentration on the North Sea. European peace would leave them free to remake their partnerships with dominion, Indian and colonial politicians. Devolution – promised to the dominions and India in 1918 – would earn a dividend of loyalty. The British world-system would enter an Antonine Age of peace and prosperity.

But it did not turn out like that. Inevitably, the violent disruption of the pre-war order could not be repaired overnight. Nor was it likely that a new blueprint for world politics would command ready assent among the victorious allies, let alone in the ranks of the defeated or disenfranchised. Everywhere the prospect of a post-war settlement that might last for decades raised the stakes of political and social struggle: between states, peoples, races, religions, clans and classes. Success – whether dominance, freedom or security – was vital before the new moulds hardened, before new rulers could climb into the saddle, before cynicism or despair set in among the rank and file on whose backing leaders at all levels depended. For all these reasons, the formal diplomacy of peacemaking was sure to be staged against the disorderly backdrop of political or armed struggle wherever there was the chance of a *fait accompli*, or the hope of winning the national status that the peacemakers seemed so willing to dispense.

The British system was bound to be especially vulnerable to this post-war turbulence. Sprawled across the globe, it faced nation-making movements at every point: Irish, Greek, Turkish, Arab, Egyptian, Persian, Afghan, Indian, Chinese and West African. Its open societies were easily permeable by new ideologies of class, nation, race or religion. Without a draconian apparatus of control (unimaginable in most places if only for reasons of cost), its colonial and semi-colonial regions could not be closed to external influence or new ideas. Its commercial prosperity depended upon an open trading economy and multilateral flows of goods and money. The prolonged dislocation of this fine-spun web threatened to wreck the mutual self-interest underpinning the politics of empire, and drain the wealth that paid for its costly superstructure. Peacemaking in its broadest sense – settling territorial boundaries and sovereignty, reopening the channels of trade, adjusting the spheres of great power interest – would need to be early and complete. The risk otherwise was that discontent and uncertainty would subvert the collaborative base of British rule and erode the loyalty of its self-governing partners to the idea of a British system. But peacemaking was anything but swift and far from complete. It was an intricate puzzle requiring dozens of pieces to be fitted together. Cooperation in one field required agreement in another and harmony in a third. Territorial settlement, strategic security and economic reconstruction were all entangled in a maddening knot of conflicting interests. Consequently, peacemaking in Europe dragged on until the Dawes Plan (1924) and Locarno (1925) and ignored Russia's place in the post-war order. In the Middle East, a territorial settlement was delayed until the treaty of Lausanne (1923) and final agreement over the northern border of Iraq until 1926. In East Asia, the Washington treaties of 1921–2 checked great power rivalries but not the determination of Chinese nationalists to attack the foreign privileges embodied in treaty-ports and concessions.

As a result, the claims of the dominion governments, as well as Irish, Indian, Egyptian, Arab and (some) African nationalists for wider influence and greater autonomy in the British system were caught up in the larger instabilities of the post-war world. Mistrustful of London's intentions, fearful of new British claims upon them, resentful of the apparent disregard for their ethnic, religious or constitutional aspirations, they had little sympathy for the mood of chronic anxiety that hung over the cabinets of Lloyd George and his prime ministerial successors. Among British ministers and their advisers, the avalanche of international and imperial demands bred a siege mentality that verged at times on paranoia. Die-hards and visionaries pondered loudly whether the end of empire was at hand. But, by the mid-1920s, the worst seemed over. The danger that internal stresses and external pressures would together set off a general crisis of the British system receded. Its strategic security and financial solvency did not break down. The centre held. As nationalism fell back from the high tide of 1919–20, its leaders made their peace – for the moment – with the British world-system.

'New World' geopolitics

The first priority of British ministers in London was to secure a peace that would avert a future commitment to European security on the terrible scale of the War. The logic of Britain's global interests, as they well understood, was to protect the imperial centre but not at such cost as to imperil the defence and development of the rest of their world-system. The stringent terms imposed in the treaty of Versailles (28 June 1919) were designed to disarm the terrifying power of German 'militarism'. Germany's navy was seized (but scuttled by its crews) and its rebuilding forbidden; her colonies were confiscated; and her army capped at 100,000 – one-third the peacetime size of the combined British and Indian armies, one-eighth the size of France's. But the larger problem remained: how to prevent the (eventual) resurgence of German power and enforce (in the meantime) the punitive terms of peace.

For an important group of British opinion, the answer lay in forging an Atlantic partnership with the United States.[1] There were many attractions. An Anglo-American alliance would rule the waves and the exchanges. It would be the decisive counter-weight to any power that aspired to dominate the European continent. It appealed to the vague emotion of pan-Anglo-Saxon racial unity to which politicians of all parties were susceptible. It would avert the risk of naval and financial rivalry, whose impact on Britain was bound to be adverse. It was favoured by Canadian leaders, and by Smuts, the heir-apparent in South African politics. It was the best guarantee against the continental entanglements upon which all the dominions looked with anxiety and disfavour as a dangerous distraction from imperial purposes. It would draw Britain away from the 'old diplomacy' of secret commitments and (as the war had shown) unlimited liabilities towards open covenants and defined obligations: and thus stabilise her claims on dominion loyalty.[2] Above all, it would make bearable the otherwise open-ended burdens of the League of Nations Covenant as the instrument for post-war collective security.

But in Europe such an Anglo-American partnership proved impossible. On the British side, even those keenest on Atlantic amity would not give up the claim to naval superiority and its vital instrument, the right of blockade.[3] The 'freedom of the seas' – on which Woodrow Wilson insisted – remained a bone of contention. For Wilson, naval parity with Britain was the only basis on which the United States could enter the new world order envisaged in the League of Nations Covenant.[4] But, before the naval issue could be resolved, as it was in part at the Washington conference in 1921–2, American membership of the League of Nations was bluntly rejected by the United States Senate. This reaction against further involvement in the rancorous quarrels of the Old World had a second vital consequence. It aborted the three-way security pact through which Britain and the United States were together to guarantee France against unprovoked attack by Germany. When ratification failed in Washington, the Anglo-French pact lapsed as well.[5]

From July 1919, therefore, the British were thrown back on less attractive solutions to the most pressing of their strategic concerns. They could not wash their hands of Europe for fear that the dangers that had forced their intervention in 1914 would quickly recur, and because a European settlement was economically vital. They might have been tempted to hark back to 'Edwardian' solutions: to rebuild a European 'balance of power' so that no state could dominate the continent against them. But the balance of power was now discredited by its failure in 1914, and by public suspicion of the 'old diplomacy' of alliance treaties and secret clauses. Instead, London was pledged to collective security and the League of Nations. In principle, this shared the burden of keeping the peace and enforcing the treaty system of post-war Europe among the great continental states. In practice, the Bolshevik revolution in Russia and the fragmentation of Eastern Europe threw the task of containing Germany and policing the treaties back upon Britain and France. Worse still, the communist 'contagion' from Russia threatened to spread through a Europe that was economically devastated and socially disoriented. What was needed was a Concert of Liberal Europe, to preside over the new era of national self-determination, to promote material recovery and to repel the Bolshevik menace. That meant the reconciliation and cooperation of Britain, France and Germany.

This was the object, often muddled and obscure, of Lloyd George's coalition government and those of his successors after his fall in October 1922. What made it Herculean, or worse, were the interlocking differences blocking a European settlement along the lines laid down in the peace treaties of 1919. Thus the peace treaties looked forward to the creation of new nation states in Poland, Czechoslovakia, Hungary and the 'South Slav state' (later Yugoslavia), and the ethnic 'rectification' of other pre-war boundaries. Such an ambitious programme depended heavily upon the cooperation of Germany. At the same time, the treaties prescribed reparations payments through which Germany would compensate France and Belgium (mainly) for the damage of the war. But, neither reparations on the scale demanded, nor the peaceful reconstruction of Central and Eastern Europe, were possible without a wider programme of economic recovery, and the provision of new capital to help rebuild Europe's war-shattered finances. Here was a further maddening complication. New capital meant American money. Fresh American loans were unlikely without agreement on repaying the wartime advances made mainly to Britain. The British were unwilling to promise payment unless the huge loans they had made to their European allies were part of the financial settlement. (Indeed, loud voices in Britain, including Keynes and a former Chancellor of the Exchequer, urged mutual cancellation of all war debts.) But, of their wartime allies, one (Russia) was a bankrupt outlaw; and the other (France) insisted upon large German reparations as the condition of any reckoning. And so the problem came full circle.

By the end of 1922, after three years of tortured diplomacy, periodic confrontation and a full-scale war between Poland and Russia, Europe's post-war instability approached a crisis. Anglo-French relations were embittered by growing differences over their approach to Germany (whose economic recovery was more urgent in British eyes than the enforcement of reparations) and by rivalry in the Near East. German resistance to French demands and resentment against the territorial losses imposed by the treaties were fanned by internal discontent and economic hardship. In January 1923, the Conservative government led by Bonar Law, who had emerged from retirement to break up the Lloyd George coalition, watched impotently as France occupied the Ruhr to extract German reparations. It faced the demand from the United States for repayment of its war loans on terms that Bonar Law rejected as intolerable. It fretted about the military consequences as the Foreign Secretary, Lord Curzon, struggled (at the Lausanne conference) to defend the draconian terms imposed on Turkey in the treaty of Sèvres (1920) against an insurgent regime led by Kemal Ataturk, the treachery (as Curzon saw it) of the French and the hostility of the Russians, posing now as Turkey's friend against the British ogre. 'I have realised from the first', Bonar Law had told Curzon in December 1922, 'the utmost importance of trying to get the Lausanne business settled before we came to grips with Poincaré over reparations.'[6] But, as the Turkish conference turned sour, and the German crisis deepened, he began to press the case for withdrawal from Britain's mandate in Iraq for whose northern third (the old *vilayet* of Mosul) the Turks were expected to wage an armed struggle.[7] The travails of the imperial centre were leaving their mark on imperial defence. The need for drastic economies at home (partly to meet the American bill), and the receding prospect of European peace and reconstruction seemed to be turning Britain's main strategic prize in the Middle East into an untenable liability.

1923 was a crisis year. But matters gradually improved. The nightmare of a Turkish, French and Russian combination against Britain in the Near and Middle East soon passed. In the treaty that was signed in July 1923, the Turks accepted the loss of their Arab provinces, and the demilitarisation of the Straits but regained full sovereignty in Anatolia and part of Thrace. Mosul was deferred for arbitration. Bonar Law's Cabinet colleagues insisted upon accepting the American terms over his bitter opposition and even his threat to resign (Bonar Law went so far as to write to *The Times* under the soubriquet of 'Colonial' to denounce his colleagues' views).[8] In doing so, they paved the way for American credits to flow to Europe as the severity of the crisis, highlighted by the Ruhr occupation, sounded the alarm across the Atlantic. With the Dawes Plan (1924), it at last seemed possible to cut the Gordian knot of debts and reparations, and begin to normalise the economic relations of the European states. In a more hopeful atmosphere, the idea of a Liberal Concert revived.

For the British, the question was how large a continental commitment they would have to make to ward off the danger of a new European conflagration. Relations with France would not improve, argued Austen Chamberlain (Foreign Secretary 1924–9), unless Britain guaranteed her safety against Germany. Nor would the Germans 'settle down' so long as they hoped to divide the wartime allies. Sooner or later, a 'new catastrophe' would occur, into which Britain would be dragged. 'We cannot afford to see France crushed, to have Germany, or an eventual Russo-German combination, supreme on the continent, or to allow any great military power to dominate the Low Countries.'[9] There were imperial arguments as well. If Britain was at loggerheads with France, said Maurice Hankey, who, as secretary to both the Cabinet and its Committee of Imperial Defence, exerted a powerful influence on ministerial thinking, 'our imperial communications [through the Channel and the Mediterranean] would be jeopardised' and London in 'extreme danger' from France's powerful fleet of bombers. It was an 'almost essential Imperial interest' to be on good terms with France – which meant a pact or guarantee.[10] Imperial defence, noted a Foreign Office memorandum, was 'closely related to a policy of European security'. The government should say publicly that the defence of the Empire entailed a guarantee of France and Belgium.[11] But the arguments against were formidable. Opinion at home was dead against a French pact. It would be denounced by both Liberals and Labour. It would shackle Britain to the Franco-Polish alliance and to the murky state-system of Eastern Europe. It would be anathema to the dominions and disliked in India. It would mean an intolerable strain on a post-war army barely sufficient for its imperial role.[12] In the event, Chamberlain achieved a triumph of limited liability. In the Locarno Pacts of October 1925, he avoided an outright guarantee of French security. Instead, France and Germany exchanged pledges to uphold their post-war borders, with Britain and

Italy as joint guarantors of their mutual promises. The significance of this implausible formula was largely symbolic. It marked Germany's acceptance of the new European order (in the West), signalled by her joining the League of Nations, not a new continental commitment for Britain. By the same token, it revealed how dependent Britain's *imperial* position had become upon a Liberal Concert in Europe – as a substitute for military power or a continental balance. The fragility of that concert was soon to be seen.

European security was a precondition of imperial safety; but it was not the only one. In his Locarno conversations, Chamberlain bluntly told the French and German leaders that, whatever happened, Britain could never be a party to economic sanctions that brought her into conflict with the United States. 'It is a fundamental condition of British policy', he insisted, 'I might almost say a condition of the continued existence of the British Empire, that we should not be involved in a quarrel with the United States.'[13] It was true, of course, that America had drawn back from the role that Woodrow Wilson had imagined for her in the post-war world, a role that promised friction with Britain as well as partnership. To Isaiah Bowman, one of Wilson's closest advisers in Paris, the failure came to seem inevitable. America's multi-ethnic politics, democratic government and commercial self-sufficiency made a definite foreign policy impossible. 'Whatever degree of participation we may finally come to have in world affairs', he wrote, 'it will be conditional in many respects and limited in all.'[14] But this did not make the US a negligible factor, least of all for the British. They treated American oil companies and their Middle East claims with wary respect. They needed the cooperation of American bankers for the financial reconstruction of Europe. They were conscious that Wilsonian ideals held a powerful attraction for British opinion in the centre and on the left: a fact of some weight in the fluid politics of the 1920s. Above all, they were anxious not to goad American leaders into an arms race at sea.

Britain had ended the war with a colossal navy: 70 battleships and battle-cruisers, 120 cruisers, 463 destroyers and 147 submarines. Once the German fleet was confiscated or scuttled, the American navy, with some 40 battleships, 35 cruisers and 131 destroyers, was the second most powerful. But these flattering figures were not the whole story. The British fleet was far too large to be maintained in peacetime: the naval budget crashed from £334 million in 1918–19 to £54 million in 1923–4. Secondly, many of its most powerful units would soon need replacing by more modern versions. Thirdly, it faced a post-war strategic revolution as far-reaching as that of 1912. For now, its main rivals were the American and Japanese navies: two potential enemies at opposite ends of the globe. The strategy of concentration used to bottle up Germany was obsolete. Worse still, American hostility to a continental blockade – Britain's key weapon in another war – meant that British sea-power in the Atlantic could not be weakened to reinforce the East except in a great emergency. At the very least, the Royal Navy needed parity with the Americans, whose Pacific commitments would then serve to balance its own obligations in the eastern seas.

In the aftermath of the war, this looked improbable. The Wilsonians were committed to a big navy. Their programme for 1918 had added 20 'super-dreadnoughts', 12 large battle-cruisers and 300 other ships.[15] The naval budget rocketed upwards from $37 million in 1914 to $433 million in 1921. As these new battleships came into service, even a numerically smaller American navy would outgun its Atlantic rival. At the end of 1920, British ministers anxiously debated how to contain the American challenge. Lloyd George argued for the pre-war view that America should be discounted as a possible enemy. But other ministers insisted that naval supremacy could not be surrendered.[16] It was agreed to seek negotiations, but from the Washington embassy came warnings of growing antagonism to Britain even amongst the incoming Republicans, exacerbated by friction over war debts and the war in Ireland.[17] This analysis proved excessively bleak. In fact, much American opinion regarded enmity towards Britain as unthinkable: talk of British aggression, said the *New York Times* was 'grotesque'.[18] The reaction against Wilsonian involvement in international politics had its counterpart in the revolt against 'navalism'. A big navy would drag America into overseas conflicts as surely as the League. Naval limitation attracted growing support. This new mood gave the British some much-needed leverage. They could hope to bargain their limited programme of March 1921 for American concessions. More to the point, by giving up their twenty-year-old alliance with Japan, whose renewal was disliked by both the Foreign Office and the Admiralty, they could neutralise the strongest card of the 'big navy' school in Washington: the fear that Britain would abet Japanese expansion in the Western Pacific. After a fierce debate, into which both Canada and Australia were drawn (on different sides), and amid much unease about the fate of British interests in China, the alliance was abandoned.

The balance was swung. At the Washington conference in
1921–2, the British and Americans settled their naval differences by
agreeing to parity in capital ships, and a ten-year 'holiday' in construction. The new rapprochement had a further consequence. Hesitation
over giving up the alliance derived partly from British alarm at the
semi-colonial expansion of Japan into China and especially her reluctance to give up the large Shantung concession seized from Germany.[19]
Without the alliance, argued its champions, restraining Japan would
become even harder. In fact, the show of Anglo-American unity helped
to push Japanese policy towards economic rather than military expansion in China, in financial partnership with American business.[20] The
Japanese agreed to attend the conference which framed a post-war settlement for East Asia. They gave up Shantung and agreed to limit their
battleship strength to 60 per cent of the British and American figure (the
5:5:3 ratio). They also signed the Four Power treaty alongside Britain,
France and America, guaranteeing the independence and integrity of
China, and the Nine Power treaty, promising no expansion of existing
foreign rights and concessions in the country.

The 'Washington system' was a promise of stability in East
Asia. But its strategic implications were only gradually clarified. To
British naval planners, the Washington logic was straightforward. To
conciliate Japan, the treaty had forbidden new fortifications across a
vast area of the Western Pacific. Henceforth, if a British fleet were sent
to East Asia, it must use Singapore as its base, not vulnerable, under-
fortified Hong Kong. Indeed, the need for a great new naval base at
Singapore had already been agreed by British ministers in 1921. Secondly, the post-war navy should be built and trained for a war against
its likeliest enemy, now Japan. Yet, as financial stringency bit deeper,
governments in London scaled down or postponed the Singapore base
and questioned the need for an East Asian strategy. Matters came to
a head in 1925 when Winston Churchill, as Chancellor of the Exchequer, dismissed the navy's spending plans as ruinously expensive. They
would infuriate taxpayers, he told Baldwin, the Conservative prime
minister, and unite Liberals and Labour in a campaign for economy.[21]
The Japanese threat was chimerical. 'Why', he asked, 'should there be a
war with Japan? I do not believe there is the slightest chance of it in my
lifetime.' No Japanese government would risk a war against the united
strength of the Anglo-Saxon sea-powers. The Cabinet agreed. Churchill

had his way. Navy spending was cut down and the Admiralty forbidden to prepare war plans against the Japanese navy.

In the seven years that followed the end of the war, the strains and tensions of imperial politics had been magnified by persistent geopolitical uncertainty. For the British, the defeat or exhaustion of their international rivals had been the main guarantee that the simultaneous emergencies they faced in Ireland, Egypt, China, India and the Middle East would not escalate into a general crisis of their global system. By 1925, they could be more hopeful. The settlements at Locarno and Washington (as Churchill had interpreted its meaning) revealed an emerging world order whose imperial consequences seemed reassuringly benign. International tranquillity at both ends of Eurasia dispelled the nightmare of war on fronts 12,000 miles apart. With Germany tied to the Liberal Concert (underwritten financially by American capital), and Japan constrained by Anglo-American friendship, only Russia could threaten the defences of empire – though more by ideological subversion than by military challenge. The gates of the British world would be guarded by the self-interested caution of its most likely predators: an agreeably cheap solution. The revolutionary excitement of 1919 had passed. The siren call of Wilsonian self-determination had modulated into the League of Nations mandate system, under the watchful eye of the two main colonial powers.[22] With little risk of external attack, the internal enemies of the British system could be dealt with in detail by an army freed from its old strategic burdens. The defence costs of empire could be axed to pay for its debts and fund social reform. As escape from the British system seemed less likely, colonial resistance would grow less fervent. The politics of empire could pass from the maelstrom of the aftermath to the calmer waters of the post-war world.

Rebuilding commercial empire

The necessary counterpart to international tranquillity was the revival of London's commercial *imperium*. Churchill's furious opposition to naval rearmament sprang from the fear that its costs would unhinge his financial strategy. Stringency, especially in defence, was necessary partly to pay for social spending – the price of political survival in the age of universal suffrage – but even more to fund the return to a gold-based currency. In the City, at the Bank of England and in the Treasury, it was axiomatic that London's reputation as a financial centre depended upon the restoration of the gold standard.[23] 'Gold', said Montagu Norman, the Governor of the Bank, 'is the guarantee of good faith.'[24] But there was a catch. If sterling was once more to be based upon a fixed value in gold, bullion had to be attracted to London. It would only come if London offered the safest haven or the highest rates. On both counts it was vital to reduce government spending and borrowing (hugely inflated by the war) to the minimum. Foreign depositors would be reassured by the strict management of public finance, and the interest rate needed to attract them would fall back gradually to a level that domestic industry could afford. Britain's return to gold in October 1925 was intended to signal the end of post-war economic turbulence, and London's resumption of its pre-war status. As we shall see, however, its old commercial empire was not so easily revived.

Before 1914, London's pre-eminence had been based upon the vast scale of its commercial and financial transactions. A huge proportion of the world's international business was conducted in or through the City. The City exerted its influence on the financial and commercial practice of states inside and outside the Empire to protect or enhance Britain's overseas wealth – perhaps one-third of her total by 1914. As the centre of the world's information network (all cables led to London), it was the principal engine of Britain's 'soft power': transmitting news, ideas and intellectual fashion to audiences abroad. Above all, perhaps, its claims on overseas production (the real meaning of its foreign investment) and its portfolio of foreign property formed a grand 'war-chest' to be drawn on in times of imperial emergency.

This commercial empire had survived the war. Its prospects in peacetime were much less certain. The rupture of the pre-war commercial and financial system was prolonged by the struggle over debts and reparations, the violent fluctuations in currency values, the proliferation of new states and frontiers and the revolution in Russia. To restart the flow of trade, from which the City drew its profits, required a massive injection of loans and credits. But the City lacked the ready cash. With a large dollar debt to service, small hope of recovering its wartime advances (especially to Russia), and so much British saving tied up in government borrowing at home, capital for once was in short supply. To make matters worse, the end of the war cut off the flow of American credits just as government spending was reaching its peak. The result was a wave of inflation and an outflow of gold. The gold standard was suspended, deterring short-term lenders from depositing their funds in London and further weakening the City against its great rival, New York. Orthodox remedies merely enfeebled the patient. Interest rates were raised and expenditure slashed. As dear money at home drove up its costs and dried up demand, British industry struggled to compete in foreign markets. Its failings were reflected in the balance of payments, the value of sterling and the credit of the City. Here was a vicious circle of decline from which no escape seemed easy.

Indeed, the post-war turbulence seemed to have drastically worsened the structural problems of the British economy, some of which had been visible before the war. The heavy dependence upon exports of cotton textiles and coal became an increasing liability. Cotton exports fell back heavily from £125 million in 1913 to £85 million in 1925 and £72 million by 1929.[25] Under the pressure of Japanese and local competition, the Indian market, Lancashire's great stand-by, began its inter-war collapse. Coal was damaged by cheap competition and the increasing use of oil as fuel. The index of all exports by volume declined from 173 (1913) to 119 (1922) and recovered only to 134 (1927).[26] But imports rose from 81 (1913) to 86 (1924) to 96 (1927) (1939 = 100). The result was ever-growing pressure on the balance of payments. As imports surged and exports faltered, the strain was taken up (as it had been before the war) by the income from invisibles. Before the war, however, the merchandise gap was narrower and invisible income far more buoyant. In the five years from 1922 to 1926, the income from both overseas investments and other invisibles fell well below their equivalent pre-war values.[27] Shipping, a huge source of pre-war earnings, was particularly hard-hit. One-fifth of the British merchant fleet was laid up in the 1920s.[28] Competition from the United States, Japan and the Scandinavian countries drove down the British share of world trade carried from 52% in 1913 to 40% in 1936,[29] and Britain's share of world tonnage began its long descent from 40% (in 1913) to 30% (in 1930), to 26% (1939).[30] The shipping giants of the pre-war years fell on hard times.[31] British shipping was slow to modernise by adopting oil instead of coal, and its share of the booming trade in oil transport was soon only half its pre-war level.

The full significance of these economic difficulties emerged only gradually after 1918. For seven years after the armistice, the British economy seemed on a roller-coaster: boom, followed by slump, followed by signs of recovery, a further setback and then cautious optimism as the Dawes Plan in 1924 promised to settle the problem of reparations and stabilise the European economy, to which one-third of British exports were normally sent. To the City, it was vital to rebuild the pre-war world, if need be by an active financial diplomacy. This was the role assumed by Montagu Norman, the Governor of the Bank of England, an idiosyncratic, highly strung and emotional figure of remarkable tenacity. Norman's recipe was the close cooperation of the main central banks, with London as the intermediary between New York and Europe. The severity of the depression after 1920 encouraged others to propose more radical solutions. The grudging nod by the wartime British government towards imperial preference, 'imperial development' and subsidised empire settlement was converted by post-war tariff reformers like Leo Amery into a full-scale programme to relieve unemployment and reorient the economy. Budgetary cuts and Treasury opposition meant that little came of this.[32] But it was desperation at the prospect of deepening economic crisis at the end of 1923 that led Baldwin, the Conservative prime minister, to declare a sudden conversion to protective tariffs. The occupation of the Ruhr, he told the House of Commons, meant that 'the restoration of Europe had been postponed for years . . . [W]e are . . . in a position of emergency that we have never had to meet before.' 'Radical and drastic measures' were needed.[33] Tariffs were rejected by the electorate. The 1924 Labour government and the second Baldwin ministry (1924–9), with the free-trader Churchill as Chancellor of the Exchequer, turned back to the orthodoxies of the gold standard as their escape from the economic labyrinth.

With the return to gold, the City might have hoped that the worst of its post-war uncertainties were over, and that it could begin to profit from the revival of the world economy. In reality, the economic damage revealed by the recovery period proved much more lasting. The gold standard was meant to restore confidence in London as the financial centre of the world economy. But the strain was felt by domestic industry struggling to compete abroad while an over-priced pound and high interest rates drove up its costs. Nor was going back on gold a cure for the most serious weakness of the City's commercial empire after 1918: the shrinkage of its foreign investment and the shortage of capital with which to rebuild its pre-war holdings. Indeed, in the effort to keep sterling high against the dollar and prevent interest rates at home (driven up by the enormous scale of government debt) from rising further, the Treasury and Bank of England had actively discouraged investment overseas except to sterling countries.[34] When the Bradbury Committee recommended ending the embargo on foreign issues in 1925, it remarked that Britain could not afford to lend abroad more than £100 or £120 million a year, far below the pre-war figure.[35] British investors seemed to heed this advice. Where British foreign investment in 1911–13 had taken some 8 per cent of national income, after 1925 the figure was 2.5 per cent.[36] By 1929, the nominal level of British capital abroad was the same as in 1913, but its real value had fallen by perhaps 40 per cent. High interest rates at home and uncompetitive exports reduced both the incentive and the means to invest or reinvest abroad. Well before the great depression, the old pattern of commercial empire practised since the 1870s was in retreat.

The shortage of British capital was not the only culprit. The operating conditions for British commerce and capital were also changing. In Latin America as a whole, American capital and trade competed much more heavily than before the war. The British position was strongest in Argentina. In 1914, Argentina had been the third largest destination for British capital after the United States and Canada.[37] British investment had boomed on the back of its exceptionally dynamic growth as a producer of meat and grain. In the 1920s, it still seemed of huge importance to British wealth. 'Argentina must be regarded as an essential part of the British Empire', remarked the British ambassador in 1929.[38] There were 40,000 British passport-holders in the country (substantially more than in the Rhodesias). It paid some £36 million a year to Britain in dividends and interest, perhaps 10 per cent of Britain's foreign property income. Its credit-rating was on a par with Canada and Australia.[39] Its British-owned railways were 'the backbone of our whole position out here',[40] not least because they bought most of their supplies, including coal, from Britain. But Argentina's growth was slowing down as the supply of new land dried up. British exports were declining. British-owned railways and utilities faced growing local resentment over rates and charges. Little British capital was forthcoming. Indeed, the Anglo-Argentine connection was becoming increasingly politicised, just as London began to press hard for import concessions to bring its visible trade into balance. It was only Argentina's extreme dependence on the British market after 1929 that checked for the time being the more vigorous expression of economic nationalism. In China, by contrast, political conditions in the 1920s were already having a direct impact upon British commerce. The lure of the China market (as opposed to its existing value) was strong, but London's apparent reluctance to abrogate the 'unequal treaties' and give up the extra-territorial privileges of the treaty-ports made British interests the prime target of Chinese nationalism after 1919. From Canton, where the nationalist movement (or Kuomintang) was concentrated, anti-British activism was aimed at nearby Hong Kong. In 1925, after the '30 May incident' in Shanghai, when several Chinese were killed by the municipal police of the Anglo-American (but mainly British) settlement, the Canton nationalists organised a highly effective sixteen-month boycott of British trade along the coast and a general strike in Hong Kong itself.[41] By the end of 1926, the damage was bad enough to push London (under pressure from the large British firms in China) towards the appeasement of Chinese nationalism. Official policy was now to move towards the surrender of extra-territorial rights and the concession of tariff autonomy – China's power to set import duties independently, taken away from Peking in 1842. British enterprise would now have to make the transition (welcomed by the larger firms) towards fending for themselves in their dealings with customers, politicians and warlords.

In the mid-1920s, however, economic nationalism in London's commercial empire had yet to pose a major threat to its financial and commercial interests. The great edifice of commercial primacy inherited from 1914 still *seemed* largely intact. In some sectors, like oil, telecommunications and international banking, British firms seemed well positioned to exploit the new opportunities of the post-war world. But a subtle shift was taking place whose full significance only became visible after 1930. The shortage of capital, uncompetitive industry and (in certain cases) outdated technology meant that overall the British were poorly placed to profit from the great expansion of international trade in the later 1920s.[42] In both trade and finance they were drifting steadily away from the cosmopolitan traditions of the pre-war City. Much more of the City's financial business was now devoted to domestic loans. Most of British industry was now protectionist in sympathy.[43] Banking and investment in Empire (rather than foreign) countries assumed an ever-growing importance. British capital now flowed predominantly into the development funds of Empire governments – Indian, dominion and colonial.[44] The City's foreign income, and ultimately its solvency, were becoming more and more dependent upon its ties with dominion governments and especially India. Most important of all was the fact that not even the return to gold could reverse the great shift of financial power towards New York. America had become, like Britain, a great creditor nation. London could no longer control interest rates across the world as it had before 1914, nor draw in the gold it needed by an upward shift in its own bank rate.[45] And, by the 1920s, the City's prime international asset, the collateral for any future crisis, was leaking rapidly away. In 1931, of the great treasure trove of dollar securities built up before 1914, scarcely one-tenth remained.[46] The war-chest of the British system was almost empty.

West of India: the British in the Middle East

The logic of Britain's position after 1918 was to maintain its world-system but cut down its cost. Its Middle East policy seemed to throw this in reverse. There the British acquired a huge new commitment. The original impulse sprang from the need to defeat the Ottoman Empire, once it became Germany's ally. It was supercharged by the panic (in 1918) that followed Russia's collapse and the great German offensive in the West. In retrospect we can see that the strategic imperative that drove the British into the Middle East was symptomatic of the fundamental instability of their whole system. Ever since the 1870s (arguably since the 1840s), protecting their most valuable spheres and preserving the cohesion of their global empire had forced them periodically into new and heavy liabilities. Whatever ultimate benefits they promised, these new zones of imperial control increased the risk of collision with a rival power. They raised the costs of imperial defence. And, partly as a result, they threatened to upset the political balance of the British world-system by loading new burdens on its taxpayers and rousing new fears among its disparate communities.

Before 1914, British leaders had been acutely aware of this danger even if they had few means of mitigating it. The furious arguments over the occupation of Egypt that lasted at cabinet level into the mid-1890s sprang from the fear that in so exposed a salient Britain would face (sooner or later) a hostile European combination or be driven willy-nilly into a costly alliance. To sprawl across the globe like a gouty giant, warned a philosophical diplomat, courted a united onslaught by resentful rivals. But as it turned out, neither the occupation of Egypt nor

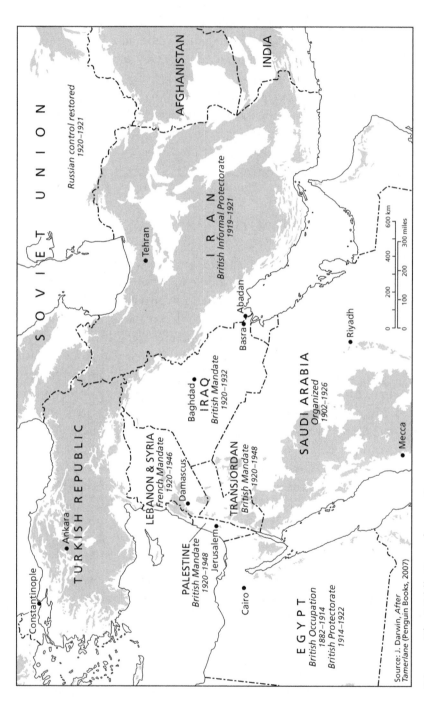

Map 10 The Middle East after 1918

SOVIET UNION

Russian control restored 1920–1921

AFGHANISTAN

INDIA

TURKISH REPUBLIC

Constantinople

Ankara

IRAN
British Informal Protectorate 1919–1921

Tehran

Abadan

Basra

LEBANON & SYRIA
French Mandate 1920–1946

Damascus

IRAQ
British Mandate 1920–1932

Baghdad

TRANSJORDAN
British Mandate 1920–1948

PALESTINE
British Mandate 1920–1948

Jerusalem

SAUDI ARABIA
Organized 1902–1926

Riyadh

Mecca

EGYPT
British Occupation 1882–1914
British Protectorate 1914–1922

Cairo

600 km

300 miles

400

200

300

200

100

0

0

Source: J. Darwin, *After Tamerlane* (Penguin Books, 2007)

the colossal share that Britain took in the partition of Africa brought on the confrontation the critics had feared. European statesmen, mindful of the tensions of continental diplomacy, were disinclined to risk much for 'light soil' in Africa, and only France was willing to challenge the British over Egypt – a challenge that ended in the humiliation of Fashoda in 1898. The mutual self-interest of the European powers in tranquillising (contemporaries would have said 'pacifying') their African possessions at the lowest cost had all but sterilised the African continent diplomatically by 1904, the year of the Anglo-French entente. But the Middle East was a different story.

If Egypt was a salient, the Middle East was a vast arena in the middle of the world that would have to be held against all comers. Since antiquity it had been a cockpit of rival imperialisms vying for its trade and agrarian wealth. It lay open to invasion over land from the north and east, and by sea from the west and south. There were wide internal frontiers of desert, marsh and mountain that waged a constant war of attrition against settled authority in the cultivation zones. Strategically, it was a quadrilateral. Mastery of the region meant keeping control of its four great gateways: at the Straits, in North Persia, on the Isthmus of Suez and round the shores of the Gulf – a task that defeated almost every conqueror except the Ottomans at the height of their power. Culturally, it was a mosaic of overlapping but impermeable communities, the residue of successive waves of conquest, conversion and migration and a reminder of the region's past as the commercial and intellectual crossroads of the Old World. In this heartland of Islam, no ruler could ignore the scribal elite (the *ulama*) who enjoyed wide popular loyalty, nor discount the traditions of religious militancy as fierce as any to be found in Europe. The guardianship of its Holy Places aroused intense concern among Islamic populations as far away as Senegal and Java. Economically, it was a region that had once been the junction of global trade, but had drifted into the relative poverty that intensified the isolation of its remoter hinterlands. Vulnerable and volatile, it was tempting to enter but hard to keep. It was small wonder that, while they had agonised over its strategic fate, no British government since 1800 toyed more than briefly with the idea of empire in the Middle East.

It was a measure of how far they had been driven from the old assumptions of imperial defence that British leaders could agree by mid-1918 that without Middle Eastern supremacy their world-system would collapse. In the year that followed, British policy was inspired by a grand design of which Lord Curzon was the principal architect. A former Viceroy, Curzon was chairman of the War Cabinet's Eastern Committee. His knowledge of the region was unmatched (but not unchallenged) by his ministerial colleagues. He was determined to exploit the twist of fate that had delivered the Middle East into British hands, for (or so he thought) it was the region in whose turbulent politics lay the most important key to imperial safety. 'You ask', he lectured the Eastern Committee, 'why should England do this? Why should Great Britain push herself out in these directions? Of course the answer is obvious – India.'[47] Protecting India required the exclusion of any other great power from Southwest Asia. But it did not mean the wholesale extension of colonial rule. Curzon's preference was for 'native states': local autonomy for Arabs (and Kurds) modelled on the princely states in India.[48] What mattered most was a proper settlement for Turkey and Persia. Curzon was convinced that Ottoman Turkey must be cut down to size, to demolish its pre-war status in the Islamic world and destroy forever the power it had used with such deadly effect against Britain: its control of the Straits. Denied their old leverage in European diplomacy (command of the Straits), and restricted to their Anatolian homeland, the Turks could do little harm. In the case of Persia, against whose domination by Russia he had warned so vociferously before 1914, Curzon's plan was to bind the shah's government in a treaty that exchanged aid for influence. Teheran's grip would be tightened on its unruly provinces with British help. The shah's ministers would defer to British 'advice'. The deal would be sweetened by a British loan. To insure against disruption from the north, a military presence would be maintained in the Caucasus and Trans-Caspia where post-imperial states were emerging from the wreck of Tsarism. And, needless to say, the whole vast scope of Curzon's plan assumed implicitly that the citadel of Britain's Middle Eastern power, her primacy in Egypt, would be even safer and stronger than before the war.

But Curzon's grand design was flawed from the outset. It assumed that the French could be denied what they had been promised in 1916: control of 'Syria' – a loosely defined region extending from the Lebanon coast to the Persian border. Clemenceau made it plain that British bad faith in the Middle East would cost it dearly in Europe, where French cooperation in treaty-making was vital: in September 1919, the British gave way. Curzon had assumed that the collapse of Tsarism would prevent, or postpone indefinitely, the revival of Russian influence in the Caucasus and Central Asia. By the middle of 1920, the Red Army had shown that this was a pipe-dream with immediate repercussions on the Anglo-Persian treaty, as yet unratified.[49] The easy monopoly of great power influence on which Curzon had counted thus rapidly dissolved. Even in the spheres under British control, his native state formula ran into the ground. There was no question of reversing the Balfour Declaration (its author was a senior member of the Lloyd George government) with its promise of a Jewish 'home'. That meant that in 'Palestine' – another ill-defined zone – Arab autonomy would have to be curtailed to protect the experiment in Jewish colonisation. Meanwhile, in Mesopotamia (modern Iraq), military occupation by an Anglo-Indian army was mutating into a form of government loosely modelled on an Indian province (not a native state), in which a cadre of British officials began to rule local communities much as they might have done in the Punjab. Indirect command of the Eurasian crossroads, cheap, flexible, cooperative, began to vanish like a mirage. But, on the other hand, there was no question of building a Middle East Raj in the way that the British had made an Indian empire: with its own army, administration, ideology and political tradition. Quite apart from the promise of accountability to an incipient League of Nations – under the mandate system – any such evolution was completely blocked by the harsh realities of financial control. In the Middle East, the main cost of such Raj-making would have fallen not on the locals as had happened in India, but on London and the taxpayers at home. But, there, the demand for demobilisation and retrenchment grew stronger every week.

In these conditions, local resistance to foreign rule spread rapidly across the region. In the Arab lands it was centred on Damascus, where a pre-war movement had sprung up among the notables against the growing assertiveness of the Turkish authorities.[50] Here, the notables looked forward to an independent 'Greater Syria', uniting much of the Fertile Crescent (including Palestine) in an Arab state of which the Hashemite prince Feisal would be the nominal head.[51] French over-rule and a 'Jewish commonwealth' in Palestine were fiercely rejected. As the hope of freedom receded, and the French mandate grew more certain, the Syrian leaders issued a despairing proclamation of Arab independence in Syria, Lebanon, Palestine and Iraq. Four months later, the French army scattered a Syrian militia and occupied Damascus. In Palestine, where late Ottoman rule had strengthened the position of the Arab notables in Jerusalem and extended their influence on the countryside,[52] the prospect of colonial-style rule and sharing power with a Jewish settlement was even less welcome. A 'Palestine Arab Congress' voted in favour of joining Syria in 1919, there were rumours of armed resistance and in the spring of 1920 protests against the Balfour Declaration spilled over into violence against Jews. Worst of all (from the British point of view) was Iraq. By mid-1920, the occupation regime was surrounded by enemies. In the Kurdish north, its authority was fragile. In Baghdad, the Sunni notables, encouraged from Damascus, plotted against rulers who excluded them from power even more than the Ottomans.[53] In the tribal zones of the centre and south, where much of the war had been fought, the British were resented as the gatherers of tax and the breakers of custom. In July, the revolt broke out in earnest. At the end of the month, Arnold Wilson, the Civil Commissioner, told London that 'our military weakness is so extreme' that the Euphrates valley might have to be abandoned. 'An Arab state...may yet come to pass but it will be by revolution not by evolution.'[54] The British garrison of 35,000 (its bayonet strength) was pinned down, unable to move beyond the railheads except in a force too small to be safe.[55] As their losses rose and costs soared, ministers in London began a furious debate on whether to pull back to Basra in the south or withdraw from the country altogether.

For the British, 1920 was a year of crises. With an army that had shrunk dramatically to its pre-war size of around 200,000 men, they faced a whole clutch of emergencies: in India, where Gandhi's non-cooperation movement was in full swing; in Ireland, against the IRA; and at home, where the sudden end of the post-war boom brought a wave of industrial unrest. Nor were their troubles in the Middle East confined to the Arabs. With its garrisons, camps and aerodromes, and the Canal, Egypt was the castle-keep of British power, the 'Clapham Junction' (as the cliché had it) of imperial communications, more important than ever with the post-war rise of Japanese sea-power. But, in March 1919, it too had burst out in revolt. The spark was lit by the refusal of the British to allow a delegation of Egyptian politicians (organised into the Wafd or 'delegation' party) to appeal for independence at the peace conference in Paris and by the arrest of the Wafd leader, Sa'ad Zaghlul. The revolt of the notables had been triggered by fear that the British were planning a constitutional 'reform' in which local influence would be cut down in favour of foreign interests, and was almost certainly encouraged by the Egyptian ruler, the Sultan.[56] Much more alarming was the revolt of the *fellahin*, embittered by the burdens and depredations of a war economy, and the violent unrest in the towns, where the Wafd made common cause with students and organised labour. In the spring of 1919, the British briefly faced an insurrection that cut off their communications (sixty-seven rail stations were destroyed, lines blocked, telegraph wires cut), made travel perilous and brought to mind hideous images of the Indian Mutiny. But, even when the rural dust had settled, they found themselves baffled by a political boycott. No Egyptian minister would (or dared) take office without insisting on the promise of independence. The British could stay on but they would face all the risks of violent confrontation (orchestrated at will by local politicians) and all the costs of an inflated garrison. A fruitless series of negotiations dragged on through 1920 and 1921. As if that were not enough, the early months of 1919 brought warning that the keystone of Curzon's geostrategic plan – the careful containment of post-war Turkey – was far from secure. On 19 May 1919, Mustapha Kemal (Ataturk) landed at Samsun on the Black Sea coast to rally Turkish national resistance against the Greeks and Armenians and their Great Power backers. In little more than a year, the danger of a great Turkish recovery drove London into a reluctant, and ultimately disastrous, alliance with the Greeks to destroy Ataturk before he could pull down the flimsy structure of its post-war *imperium*.

The scale of resistance was impressive, and at times it induced something near panic among British leaders. They found themselves trapped between an inglorious scuttle (throwing away all the gains of their eastern triumph) and the escalating cost of military occupation – at a moment when the reduction of their post-war spending had become extremely urgent. By the end of 1920, their naïve confidence in a cheap and convenient regional primacy had given way to anxiety, impatience and uncertainty. They were saved in part by the divisions and weaknesses of the nationalisms they feared. Significantly, the toughest was Mustapha Kemal's, forged in the sufferings of wartime Anatolia and infused with the bitterness between the Muslim 'Turks' and the Christian 'Greeks', with whom they fought for control over Asia Minor.[57] In the Arab lands it was a different story. The notables in Damascus, Baghdad and Jerusalem had no common programme. In Baghdad and Jerusalem they wanted their own state, not one ruled from Damascus.

As provincial elites of the Ottoman Empire, they knew little of international politics and depended upon the Hashemite princes, Feisal and
Abdullah, as their intermediaries with the imperial powers. Socially,
they were deeply conservative and recoiled from the risks of popular
politics. They were hobbled by religious and ethnic divisions: there was
little chance of the Sunni notables of Baghdad making common cause
with the Shia rebels along the Euphrates, still less with the Kurds in
the north. In Egypt, the same theme of division was played out in different ways. There too the Wafdist leaders (drawn largely from the
landowning class) refrained from encouraging a further round of the
rural violence that had shocked the British in 1919. But the real check
to a unified movement was the power of the court and the dynasty.
The sultan (soon to be the king) was as keen as the Wafd to reduce
the overweening power the British had assumed over Egypt. But he
was equally keen that the beneficiaries of a British retreat should not
be the Wafd, whose open purpose was to reduce the monarchy to
a constitutional figurehead. His influence was mobilised to frustrate
the unity that might have forced the British into the concessions that
Zaghlul had demanded from them: full diplomatic freedom abroad and
the withdrawal of the British garrison from Cairo and Alexandria to a
cantonment near the Canal. Factional politics in Egypt between court
and country and within the Wafd itself produced a stalemate. No group
would or could sign a treaty with the British. But nor would the British
give up their control of Egypt's external relations, their role as 'trustee'
of foreign interests in the country, or their political grip on Egypt's own
colony, the Sudan.[58]

From mid-1921 onwards, the British traced a tortuous path
towards compromise. In Iraq, Churchill (who as Colonial Secretary had
assumed responsibility for Britain's two Arab mandates) found in Feisal
a ruler-in-waiting (he had been driven out of Syria) who was acceptable
to the Sunni notables in Baghdad, and a seemingly reliable ally against
the threatened reflux of Turkish influence. After an 'election' in which
official influence was thrown openly on his side and his main local rival
was unceremoniously deported, he was declared the choice of the Iraqi
people. But, when it came to the treaty by which the new Iraq government was to accept the mandate, Britain's diplomatic supervision and a
military presence (in the form of bases), Feisal proved alarmingly obdu-
rate. It took a Kurdish revolt in the north, new signs of Shia unrest, and
Feisal's own temporary retirement with political appendicitis (a local

variant of the diplomatic cold) before the anti-treaty party in Baghdad
was repressed and an agreement endorsing the mandate and Britain's
supervisory rights was eventually signed in October 1922. In Palestine, Arab resentment was partially appeased by amputating its eastern
zone as a separate mandate of Trans-Jordan and installing Abdullah,
Feisal's elder brother, there as king; and by conceding, through the
creation of the Supreme Muslim Council, that Palestine proper would
be ruled on a communal, not a unitary, basis. The Council became
the instrument through which the Jerusalem notables would exert their
influence over the Arab population. In Egypt, the logjam was eventually
broken by the British High Commissioner, Lord Allenby, the victor of
Megiddo. Allenby scrapped the treaty that London had demanded from
the Egyptian politicians, and declared unilaterally that Egypt was now
'independent'. The protectorate of 1914 was terminated. British supervision would be confined henceforth to Egyptian diplomacy (it would
have to 'conform' to Britain's), the safety of foreign nationals (some
250,000, mainly Greeks, who enjoyed extra-territorial privileges) and
the Sudan. With the ambiguous, and perhaps disingenuous, promise
that the Residency would no longer interfere in local politics, an uneasy
calm descended upon Anglo-Egyptian relations.

These compromises were necessary for regional tranquillity
(and a reduction of Britain's military burden), but they were not sufficient. British influence in the Middle East (if it was not to be at prohibitive cost) still turned on a settlement of the Turkish question. A
resurgent and nationalist Turkey, in control of the Straits, bent on
recovering its old Arab provinces, and enjoying the open support of
Russia and the covert sympathy of France: this was the nightmare scenario that had led Curzon and Lloyd George to back the onslaught
of the Greeks on the Kemalist forces in Anatolia. In September 1922,
when the Greeks were routed, the nightmare seemed close to reality.
At Chanak, on the Straits, a shooting war between British and Turks
was only averted by the promise of a conference. When it convened
at Lausanne, Curzon (who had survived the fall of the Lloyd George
coalition in October after the Conservative rebellion occasioned in part
by the costs and risks of its eastern policy) faced the Turkish demand
for the restoration of the Straits, Istanbul and Thrace, and the return
of the Mosul *vilayet*, the northern and predominantly Kurdish third of
Iraq. Worse still, while Turkish claims were backed by Russia, Curzon
gained little help from France. It was a critical moment. To give up

Mosul, warned the Colonial Office, would mean the collapse of Iraq.[59] But, without peace with the Turks, the cost of its defence would be unacceptably high. To give back control over the Straits would hand Turkey the lever for the demolition of any Middle East settlement. Yet Curzon's hand was stronger than it looked. The Turks were reluctant to fight their way into Gallipoli and Thrace, and nervous of embracing the old enemy to the north. After seven months of diplomacy, prolonged by the deafness, sometimes feigned, of the Turkish delegate, the treaty of Lausanne was signed. The Turks regained Eastern Thrace, and full control over Istanbul and Asia Minor. In return, they agreed that the Straits should be permanently open and their shores demilitarised, a concession that turned the Black Sea (in the bitter phrase of a Russian delegate) into 'an English lake'.[60] But their real concession was to agree to reserve the dispute over Mosul for arbitration, a vital breathing space for the fragile mandate. It was a turning point.

In the end, geopolitics had been the decisive factor in the Middle East peace. By 1921, Russian power had revived enough to make coercing Turkey impossible and to ruin Curzon's hopes of imposing his semi-protectorate in Persia. But not enough to dissuade the two 'strong men' who came to power there from seeking an accommodation with Britain. Reza Pasha in Persia, like Kemal in Turkey, could exploit the new balance of power to restore the independence that had seemed all but lost in 1919. But he was not strong enough to exclude British influence or expel British interests, whether strategic or economic (like the Anglo-Persian Oil Company's concession in southwest Persia).[61] Both Turkey and Persia became buffer states, poised uneasily between Russian power to the north and British to the south.[62] But it was enough for British purposes. On the British side, their Middle East policy was governed by three powerful assumptions. First, that local leaders, Egyptian or Arab, were too realistic to expect a 'real' freedom and that, shrewdly managed, the *amour propre* of local nationalisms would not conflict with their imperial interests. It is quite possible, remarked Lord Milner hopefully, during his abortive attempt at an Egyptian settlement, 'that what we mean by "Protectorate" is not really incompatible with what they mean by "Independence"'.[63] Secondly, that British objects were best obtained by indirect methods and informal control. 'These Eastern peoples with whom we have to ride pillion', said Curzon with viceregal condescension, 'have different seats from Europeans, and it does not seem to me to matter very much whether we put them on the saddle in front of us or whether they cling on behind and hold us round the waist. The great thing is that the firm seat in the saddle should be ours.'[64] The alternative was a troublesome 'entanglement' in parochial concerns of no imperial value. Thirdly, that even the cut-down primacy they retained after the dust had settled in 1923 was of vital importance to their imperial system. Indeed, for all the setbacks they had suffered by 1922, the British had gained a real prize. The buffer zone protecting Suez and the Gulf was far wider and deeper than ever before. The costs of guarding it after 1923 were low. Its value as compensation for British weakness in Europe would soon enough be shown.

What is surprising in retrospect is how little interest the British seemed to take (beyond the 'official mind') in the new treaty empire they had founded in the Middle East, an empire that now included not only the mandates in Iraq, Trans-Jordan and Palestine, the 'veiled protectorate' in Egypt, the real protectorates in the Persian Gulf, and a colony in Aden (still under the Bombay government) but also two new client states in the Nejd and Hedjaz (soon to be forcibly united as Saudi Arabia by Ibn Saud). Part of the reason may lie in the absence of the causes that endeared tropical Africa to press and public: the crusade against slavery and the struggle for souls. Partly it may have been due to the ignorance or antagonism that shaped British views of the Islamic world, only partially (and later) offset by the romantic imagery of T. E. Lawrence.[65] But, most of all, the explanation may lie in the hour of its acquisition, a time of introversion and exhaustion when the relief of burdens was the first priority of domestic politics. With no energy to invest and no capital to send, the British connection remained narrow and shallow, the preserve for the most part of diplomats and pashas. There was almost no sympathetic engagement with the nation-building aspirations of the Arab *literati* – the constructive ambivalence that lubricated politics in India and the colonial world – a failure with a long and bitter legacy. In that sense, Britain's 'moment in the Middle East'[66] remained cast in the mould of its first imagining.

The politics of Gandhi

The vast new liability that Britain assumed in the Middle East after 1918 was bound to affect the internal balance of the British world-system. It was fiercely criticised in Britain on grounds of expense. It was a source of anxiety and irritation (as we will see) among Canadian leaders who feared its military implications. But the biggest repercussions were inevitably in India. After all, it was widely assumed that the main burden of defending the new 'imperial' interest in the Middle East would fall on India. The Indian taxpayer would foot the bill. Even more controversially, India would have become an accessory to the final liquidation of the Ottoman Empire, the humiliation of the Sultan-Caliph, and the imposition of Christian rule over the Muslim Arabs – a role that many millions of Indian Muslims might be expected to resent. As we have seen, nervousness about Muslim criticism of India's war effort in the Middle East had already led the government of India into the repression against which Gandhi had mobilised so effectively in the Rowlatt *satyagraha* of 1919.

These difficulties were compounded by the new political status towards which India was supposed to be moving. The August Declaration of 1917 had promised progress towards 'responsible government', the constitutional equivalent, it was widely assumed, of the self-government enjoyed by the dominions. The Imperial Conference in 1918 reinforced the impression that India would be treated in the meantime as an honorary dominion. India became, somewhat bizarrely, a non-self-governing member of the League of Nations and the Indian government campaigned actively (but abortively) to be given a mandate in East Africa as a reward for war service. These concessions implied that Indian views would be listened to more carefully than before the war in matters of foreign policy. The second complication was that both London and New Delhi were committed to implementing the 'Mont-ford' reforms, to win Congress support for the gradual devolution of British rule – but on British terms, with safeguards for British interests and to a British timetable. Political calm – or at least the absence of violent controversy – was a precondition for their successful launch, even more so after the Rowlatt Act and Amritsar. Thirdly, while the emergency of war had passed, the urgency, in London's view, of the close coordination of Indian and British policy was as great as ever. For, if India was to play its (large) part in the new imperial burden in the Middle East, its army would have to be managed much more closely from London than in pre-war times. Its trade, revenues and currency would also need more direct supervision if they were going to contribute positively to the revival of British economic power.

The omens were unfavourable even without the additional friction that the Middle East threatened in Indian politics. The aftermath of war brought economic turbulence: a steep price rise followed by a slump in 1920. Resentment at the tax increases of wartime, and the coercive methods of recruitment practised by the Punjab government, were now reinforced by additional grievances. As prices fell, tenants and cultivators paying rent to landlords and land revenue to government came under heavy pressure. In many places, the light, benevolent hand of government now seemed more grasping and, where it upheld the claims of landlords, less just. In the towns, the see-saw of prices created labour unrest, symptomatic, the British thought, of socialist or communist infiltration. From all these came the risk of widespread disturbance. But what made them really dangerous was the chance that they would fuse with two more political movements whose object was mass mobilisation round a single issue.

The first of these was the 'culturalist' revolt that Gandhi had been organising since his return to India in 1915. At the heart of Gandhi's message (spelt out in his 1909 manifesto, *Hind Swaraj*, or Indian self-rule) was the call for isolation from the West and cultural renewal from within. This was not unique to India (a similar programme was advanced by social critics in contemporary Japan) but Gandhi's appeal was exceptionally wide and his powers of persuasion extraordinary. From his newspapers *Navajivan* (in Gujerati) and *Young India* (in English) poured a stream of political direction, tactical advice and moral instruction. It was aimed at the disparate constituencies he was intent on forging into a grand coalition. Among the most important of these were the cultural activists for whom the propagation of India's vernacular languages (as print and literature) was the vital medium of social improvement; social reformers who wanted to restore traditional morality and social cohesion (for example, through restraint of liquor-selling); religious reformers anxious to purify and invigorate Hinduism by an attack on superstition and greater emphasis on its spiritual content; and other groups for whom the status of women, or the treatment of untouchables was the most pressing concern. To all these interests and many others, the institutional politics fashioned by the British and adopted by the Congress offered little. All of them wanted their public concerns forced on to the political agenda. All of them were susceptible to the 'culturalist' programme that Gandhi urged and to his claim that

India faced a parting of the ways between a genuine *swaraj* and the empty promise of British 'reform'.

Gandhi's was not the only movement that reached out beyond the anglo-literate elite. Even before the war, social and religious reformism among Muslims had been attracted by the appeal of pan-Islamic feeling. The Ottoman Empire, guardian of the Holy Places, was in danger from Christian imperialism. During the war, the Indian government had been nervous enough to throw the Ali brothers in gaol for fear that they would canalise Indian Muslim unease and undermine discipline in the disproportionately Muslim Indian army. Mahomed Ali had been kept in gaol until late 1919. But on his release he soon began to call for Indian Muslim support against the victor powers' treatment of the Ottoman Empire. The subjection of Muslim Arabs to Christian rule, the Greek invasion of Anatolian Turkey, the loss of Jerusalem – a Muslim Holy Place as much as a Christian – showed Western (and especially British) contempt for Muslim opinion. But it was the threat to the Ottoman Sultan, the Khalifa or 'Commander of the Faithful', that became the rallying cry for local Muslim elites who were keen to promote the cause of religious and social reform, and to assert their Islamic credentials. Through the *ulama* (scholars and scribes), and the sheikhs and mullahs who preached in the mosques, the downward transmission of this single-issue campaign to restore the Khilafat was likely to be more rapid and intense than any comparable movement among Hindus.

Gandhi grasped the urgency of uniting the Khilafat movement with his diffuse coalition of oppositional groups. The collapse of the Rowlatt *satyagraha* in the bloody aftermath of Amritsar had damaged his influence. The Congress leaders were rowing back hard from the confrontationist tactics of the spring. If the Muslims were left to go it alone, and the Congress endorsed the Montford constitution, his 'culturalist' programme would have failed and the reforms 'could be used to deprive us of our freedom'.[67] The Congress decision in December 1919 (meeting ironically in Amritsar) to accept the new constitution but press for its improvement showed the danger. Gandhi's response was immediate. In January 1920, he appeared at the Khilafat conference to call for Hindu–Muslim unity and urge non-cooperation with government. In March, the Congress inquiry into the Punjab disturbances – drafted mainly by Gandhi – was published. It was a brilliant polemic designed to convert the most respectable of Congress constitutionalists to the cause of the Khilafat and non-cooperation. Its main target was the Punjab government and the Lieutenant-Governor, Sir Michael O'Dwyer. His speeches were quoted to show his contemptuous attitude to Congress and the educated class – the 'grasshoppers' – reminiscent of Curzon's in 1905. The Punjab government was denounced as terroristic and corrupt. The moral was clear. By failing to repudiate O'Dwyer, the Raj had broken the concordat in which its respect for the law and the educated class was exchanged for Congress moderation. To right the 'Punjab wrong', and force British rule back to legality, Congress must unite with the Muslims and take up the 'Khilafat wrong' as its own. By the middle of 1920, Gandhi was winning the argument. The Turkish peace terms showed the scale of the Muslim grievance. The Indian members of the government's enquiry into the Punjab troubles (the Hunter Commission) refused to sign the report. The 'small print' of the Montford constitution showing that Civilian influence would still be entrenched in provincial politics was published in June.[68] With few urban seats to contest, electoral victory would depend on the support of Muslims in almost every province.[69] The Congress leaders risked being left behind by Gandhi's appeal for Hindu–Muslim unity and rejected by their disappointed provincial supporters. So, at the special Calcutta Congress in September, to which Gandhi brought large numbers of Muslim delegates, the Amritsar vote was reversed, and non-cooperation endorsed to bring 'swaraj in one year'.

The decision for non-cooperation, reaffirmed at the main Congress meeting at Nagpur at the end of the year, marked a crucial shift in the politics of the post-Mutiny Raj. Non-cooperation meant boycotting elections to the new provincial councils, refusing or returning the award of honours, rejecting government in favour of 'national' schools, avoiding the courts in favour of unofficial tribunals and practising swadeshi, the choice of local over imported products. It was to be enforced by volunteers who would engage in satyagraha – non-violent civil disobedience. Gandhi reconstructed the Congress as a vehicle for his supporters and an organisation to challenge government at every level. Most dramatic of all was his repudiation of Congress' loyalty to the 'British connection', and its hope of inheriting the British Indian state. The Raj, insisted Gandhi, was an evil empire, guilty of 'terrorism'[70] and 'Satanism'.[71] Hindu–Muslim unity was more important than preserving the British connection. What India needed was a 'separate existence without the presence of the English' and the right to secede from the Empire. Unless Indians were acknowledged as equals, only complete separation would bring 'Swaraj, equality, manliness'.[72] Non-cooperation was a programme for self-sufficiency and isolation, a rejection of the imperial duties whose discharge was burdensome to all and loathsome to Muslims. It redefined Indian nationalism as the search for community rooted in local values and vernacular culture, committed above all to Hindu–Muslim unity. It was an astonishing turn in Indian politics. Yet, Gandhi's success would have been inconceivable without Britain's advance into the Middle East, the furious reaction of India's Muslim politicians, and the skill he displayed in harnessing Congress and its 'constitutional' grievances to the Muslim cause and his own.

The campaign got under way in earnest in 1921. At the local level, it was often a struggle of wills between the Congress district committees and their volunteers and the British district officer, backed up by the police and local notables who were reluctant to alienate the official machine. The Viceroy's government thought that non-cooperation would fizzle out, and urged its officials not to make 'prison martyrs' of its leaders. But, by July 1921, the confrontation was becoming increasingly sharp. The Khilafat leadership veered towards more violent tactics. In September, the Ali brothers were arrested for sedition. In November, the visit by the Prince of Wales led to widespread rioting in Bombay in which several Europeans were killed. As the fear grew of more general violence, the Viceroy, Lord Reading, came under heavy pressure from London to arrest Gandhi and the Congress 'high command'. Then at the end of January 1922, at Bardoli in Bombay, the Congress leadership called for mass civil disobedience, including non-payment of taxes. Non-cooperation had reached its climax.

At first sight, Gandhi's decision seems strange, and it turned out to be reckless. There were already signs that the anger of Muslims and peasants was being turned not only on government but against other Indians, Hindus and landlords. The Congress politicians, always doubtful of Gandhi's tactics, looked on with misgiving. But there were also signs that the government might give way. Lord Reading had been looking for a way out. He was pressing for a change of heart towards Turkey. He had offered a round table conference. His masters in London had come to terms with Sinn Fein (in December 1921) and were about to concede the 'independence' of Egypt. One more push might break the British will, before the Hindu–Muslim alliance fell apart and non-cooperation collapsed. But Gandhi miscalculated. When Reading tried publicly to force London into concessions to Turkey (mainly to show the Indian government's sympathy for Muslim feelings), Montagu (who had published his telegram) was sacked. Then, at Chauri Chaura in the United Provinces, twenty-two policemen were killed by a mob. Gandhi called off mass civil disobedience. Soon afterwards he was gaoled. Within weeks, non-cooperation began to subside. By 1923, the return to constitutional politics had become irresistible. Had Gandhian politics been merely an episode?

The British certainly hoped so. The scale of non-cooperation had been a profound shock to the Civilians of the Indian Civil Service. They now had to work out new tactics for a constitution in which Indian ministers would control part of every provincial government, and elected politicians or 'MLCs' (Members of the Legislative Councils) would become much more important as intermediaries between provincial governments and the localities. The old 'Anglo-India' was dead, but the goal of the new polity seemed uncertain, even to the most senior Civilians. 'Today I walked with Hailey for an hour and a half before dinner', wrote Sir Frederick Whyte, who presided over the Central Legislative Assembly. 'We tried to answer the question "Where are we going?".'[73] In fact, Hailey, who was soon to be governor of the Punjab, became the arch-exponent of the new Civilian policy. It was based on the assumption that there were two Indias: Congress India in the towns and districts, where Congress influence was strong, and Traditional India, where it was not. The object of Civilian policy was to contain the one and mobilise the other. At the provincial level, that meant careful attention to the franchise and the distribution of seats, and the deft encouragement of politicians and parties that would 'play the game' of constitutional politics rather than resorting to boycott or agitation. If shrewdly done, it meant that, even when the Congress returned to the electoral fray, its 'assault on the Legislative Council can be awaited with interest and without alarm'.[74] At the district level, it meant the vigorous use of patronage, influence and reward (like the grant of pensions, honours, or gun licences) to counter the influence of Congress politicians and build up a 'loyal' party of 'Government men'.[75] It also meant guarding the princely states against pressure or criticism from Congress. India might be pledged to eventual self-government, but there was no reason to think that it had to be self-government in the Congress (let alone the Gandhi) style.

At the same time, the Civilians were determined (as so often in the past) to win more freedom from their masters in London. They had gained a major victory with the grant of 'fiscal autonomy' in 1919: a historic concession in which the old prohibition on Indian tariffs and import duties was lifted, in recognition of the urgent need to raise more revenue. They wanted a convention that London would not interfere in matters of purely Indian (as opposed to imperial) interest.[76] They wanted more latitude to deal with Indian politicians without coming under the kind of pressure to gaol or coerce felt by the Viceroy at the time of non-cooperation. London could scarcely dispense with their services. In its straitened financial circumstances after 1918, it had all the more need to keep up the old army system in India, in which one-third of the British army was barracked in India at Indian expense, and the Indian army was an imperial reserve. Against the furious protest of Montagu and the Indian government, tightening London's control over the Indian army (the main theme of the Esher Committee in 1920[77] had had to be shelved, but guarding the army budget against Indian politicians was a top priority after 1920. No less urgent was the need to control the value of the rupee and the monetary policy of the government of India. If the rupee fell too low, then India might default on its charges to Britain, and damage further the fragile balance of payments. All this was good reason why the Civilians were still the indispensable allies of the imperial interest in India, the guarantee that it would play its part in the British world-system. If nothing else, non-cooperation had shown that London still needed the 'steel frame' (Lloyd George's term) of the Indian Civil Service (ICS).

But had India's 'new politics' made their task hopeless? In the mid-1920s, the signs were ambiguous. Congress formally abandoned non-cooperation in 1924, in belated recognition that many of its members had already given up the boycott of the councils. By 1924 also, the Khilafat movement was dead: the office of *khalifa* had been abolished by the Turks themselves. The residue of non-cooperation seemed to be the rising antagonism of Hindus and Muslims and the deepening appeal of both Hindu and Muslim revivalism. The All-India nationalism that Gandhi had urged was less in evidence than the 'sub-nationalisms' of region, language, community (like the untouchables) and religion. For the Congress politicians, like Motilal Nehru and Chittaranjan Das, the uncrowned king of Bengal, who had followed Gandhi into agitational politics, the dilemma was obvious. Neither Gandhian populism nor the provincialism that the Civilians were eagerly promoting had much in common with the British Indian state they still wanted to make: both threatened in different ways to abort its birth. They hankered for an Indian dominion (inside the Empire), and an Indian ICS, to build the nation from above. Their instrument was the Swarajya party, formed in December 1922. But, if they were to extract new concessions from the Civilians, and force the pace towards full dominion status, they needed the resources that Gandhi had made: the mobilising potential of his new-style Congress; the inclusive ideology that drew a vast range of communities and classes to the Congress banner and out of the web of Civilian influence. It was vital to capture the Congress machine for constitutional politics[78] and to keep at bay the rising tide of Hindu communalism, whose leader Malaviya urged 'responsive cooperation' to defend Hindu interests.[79] The real enemy, insisted Das, was still 'the bureaucracy' – the ICS.[80] By 1926, however, the Swarajists seemed on the ropes as their provincial support was eroded by the communal appeal of 'Hindu' and 'Muslim' parties.[81] Squeezed between the Civilians and provincial communalism, their main hope lay now in alliance with Gandhi. After all, what non-cooperation had shown was that, with skilful leadership, Gandhian mass politics could turn the tables on government and push it towards the concessions that it had seemed in 1921 to be on the verge of making. What was far less certain in 1926 was when the chance to do so would come again.

Imperial nations?

The importance of the white dominions to British world power had been dramatically vindicated in the First World War. Their manpower and resources had made a crucial contribution to imperial victory. They had strengthened Britain's claim to be the leader of free states against autocracy and militarism. They had been a vital prop – perhaps the strongest proof – for the idea that empire was a central element of British life. The existence of self-governing 'British' states on three continents outside Europe gave substance to the notion – implicit in British attitudes after c.1880 – that the British were a 'world people' uniquely adapted to the task of creating new nations in temperate climes. But the place of the dominions in the British system after 1918 was as problematic as India's – and for similar reasons. There was the unfinished business of 1917, when the new conception of dominion statehood and equality with Britain had been mooted. There was the legacy of the war and the impact of its disturbing aftermath. In all four overseas dominions, the instability of trade, war debts and the downward pressure on wartime wages and prices created social unrest, political division and (in two) the danger of ethnic strife. Most worrying of all was the geopolitical turbulence that lasted into the mid-1920s, bringing with it the threat of unwanted commitments, unlimited liabilities and new insecurities, perhaps even of war. The question of mandates (1919), the renewal or not of the Anglo-Japanese alliance (1921), a possible war over Chanak (1922), the new British commitments in Europe foreshadowed in the Ruhr crisis of 1923 and the Locarno pact of 1925, and the military obligations to the League of Nations set out in the Geneva protocol of 1924, raised in the starkest form the meaning of dominion autonomy and imperial unity. Then there was the question of Ireland.

The result was a political argument in two dominions (muted in Canada, fierce in South Africa) over the form and substance of the 'British connection' and an armed struggle in Ireland which turned into civil war after the treaty of December 1921 conceded 'Canadian' status to the twenty-six counties of the new 'Irish Free State'. In Australia and New Zealand, as we will see, there was ample scope for friction with Britain, but much less interest in constitutional change or formulaic autonomy. Indeed, since each of the dominions had its own interests, political traditions and ethnic composition, it seemed highly unlikely that a common formula could evoke its particular place in the British system. This was the fundamental question at issue between 1918 and 1926. Would the five dominions (including Ireland after 1921)[82] divide between the three that still regarded themselves as 'British nations' (a less than unanimous view in Canada), and the two where republicanism was a powerful, perhaps dominant force? Would the idea of a common dominion status dissolve into a set of bilateral ties between Britain and the several self-governing states, some acknowledging the bonds of kinship, others only the terms of a treaty? Or could all the dominions agree upon a form of words that recognised their ties to each other, to the imperial association and to the British Crown? This was not merely a question of constitutional pedantry. To a wide circle of informed opinion in all the overseas dominions, some statement of common concerns was crucial. This was not to bend the knee to Downing Street but to resist the isolationism that was a latent force in dominion politics.

Without some vehicle through which to play an active part in the 'New World' created by the war, they argued, the dominions would see their most vital interests going by default.

Canada

As the largest and oldest of the dominions, Canada's attitude was of key importance. Before the war, the Canadian premier, Sir Robert Borden, had been an ardent advocate of a common imperial foreign policy, over which Canada should exert a significant influence. Canada had made the largest contribution in manpower to the imperial war effort. Borden's 'Unionist' coalition had driven through conscription against the passionate protest of the French Canadians in a bruising demonstration of Britannic loyalty. In 1918, Borden had been instrumental in gaining dominion representation at the peace conference in Paris as part of the 'British Empire Delegation'. But, after 1921, under the Liberal prime minister, Mackenzie King, the Canadian government repudiated much of the approach for which Borden had stood, insisted upon the right to negotiate and sign a separate treaty (the 'halibut' treaty with the United States in 1923) and supported (in 1926) the demand from Ireland and South Africa that dominion equality with Britain, including the right to their own foreign policy, should be formally recognised in a public statement.[83] King's apparent hostility to the claims of empire, his almost paranoid suspicion of the 'centralising' aims of the London government, and his determination that the Canadian government should have the first and last word on any external commitment were easily converted by a later mythology into a programme for independence. But King's objectives were much less spectacular. They are better understood as a defensive reaction to the fluid state of Canadian politics than as a novel vision of Canadian nationhood.

The end of the war in Canada saw a rapid deflation of the Britannic sentiment that had helped to carry the Unionist coalition and conscription to victory in 1917. The end of a booming war economy exacted an immediate toll. The gross domestic output per person, having risen by some 8 per cent between 1913 and 1917, fell back by an astonishing 27 per cent in the four years that followed, causing a slump in living standards.[84] The worst effects were felt on the Prairies among wheat farmers and the service industries they supported, and in rural Ontario. For the Unionist government, which struggled vainly to prop up grain prices, the political backlash was catastrophic. It had alienated Quebec by conscription. Now the west and the rural east were in revolt as well. In the cold post-war climate, the Unionist slogans of conscription, the flag and the tariff were redundant or worse. When they eventually went to the polls under Borden's tough and uncompromising successor, Arthur Meighen, the Unionists suffered a shattering defeat. A rejuvenated Liberal party under Mackenzie King won most seats (116). The farmer's protest party, newly formed in the west, carried 65. Meighen, who lost his own constituency, was reduced to 50. But the 1921 election did not bring about a settled regime like those that Macdonald, Laurier and Borden had been able to fashion. King had no overall majority. Three-party politics made for prolonged uncertainty in a period of great international turbulence. They placed a premium on excluding so far as possible the influence of unpredictable external factors. The greatest danger by far was a call to arms from London in a European or Near Eastern war and the fervent response it would evoke in Canada. Four times in twenty years the appeal to Britannic loyalty had struck the dominion's brittle politics with the force of an earthquake: in 1899, in 1911 (over reciprocity and a Canadian navy), in 1914 and (most destructively) over conscription in 1917. The short-lived Chanak crisis in September 1922 was a timely reminder that the threat was still there. 'The minute there is any war or threat of war in Europe in which Great Britain might be involved', remarked an Anglophone Quebec politician, 'the Jingoes will so stir up the Country that in a Plebiscite or Referendum 75% of the people would immediately vote for war.'[85]

Mackenzie King was an Ontario Presbyterian, the son of a Toronto barrister turned academic.[86] But his position as Liberal leader was crucially dependent on his support in Quebec – where Ernest Lapointe, the provincial leader, was his vital ally until his death in 1941[87] – and the avoidance of any damaging rupture between his followers there and in English Canada. A jingo storm would tear his government apart. This was why King waged his relentless bureaucratic war against any form of words that bound Canada to the chariot of British foreign policy, that made Canada party to the treaty obligations that London assumed in Europe and elsewhere, or which implied that the dominion prime ministers at the Imperial Conference formed an imperial 'cabinet' empowered to take decisions that were binding on their own dominions. King's fears ran deeper. A secretive, reclusive man, whose private views were carefully veiled, he was deeply suspicious (and not without reason) of British politicians and the British press. At the Imperial Conference in 1923, he expected a press attack in London on his 'disloyalty' to the Empire that would be loudly echoed in the Canadian papers.[88] He suspected British ministers of 'briefing' against him, and angrily complained to L. S. Amery of London's habit of appealing over Ottawa's head to public opinion in Canada.[89] King was determined to warn London off from such public appeals for Canadian support and to insist upon Ottawa's right to decide its external obligations. But he was equally determined not to be cast as an enemy of 'British connection' or as lukewarm about Canada's imperial ties. Neither (it seems likely) accorded with his private opinions; both would have been fatal to his public reputation. He did not want to redefine Canada's place in the world, and he showed little interest in the constitutional debate over dominion status until Irish and South African pressure made some declaration unavoidable in 1926. The Canadian delegation did not want a definition, King's senior official, Oscar Skelton, told a favoured journalist.[90] His real aim was to stabilise Canadian politics (and his own lease on power) by moving as close to an isolationist position within the British system as he dared. It was a solution very similar to Laurier's. It fell far short of nationalism.

There were nationalists in Canada after 1918, but King showed no sympathy for them, and they all but despaired of him. In Quebec, *nationaliste* feeling was moving gradually away from the outlook once championed by Henri Bourassa, towards a more hostile view of 'British connection' and (under the influence of the Abbé Groulx) towards the dream of peaceful separation from the rest of Canada.[91] In English Canada, post-war nationalism formed a polar opposite. It was built on the pre-war claim to full equality with Britain in the management of the Empire and on an angry repudiation of the 'isolationist' and 'abjectly colonial' mentality attributed to the French Canadians.[92] Its most articulate proponents after 1918 were Sifton and Dafoe, proprietor and editor of the Winnipeg-based *Manitoba Free Press*. Both had been ardent conscriptionists in 1917. But, by the early 1920s, both were convinced that the Britannic patriotism to which they were loyal was being abused by the reckless expansionism of the Lloyd George government, especially in the Middle East, and by its assumption of European liabilities that had little to do with the common concerns of the white dominions. They backed King's efforts to disentangle Canada from these 'false' imperial burdens, but they wanted to go further and gain formal recognition of Canadian sovereignty. They were in no doubt that Canada was and should be a 'British nation', and wanted the (white) Empire to become a 'league of British states', free and equal but bound together by racial sympathy and mutual interest. This sectional view of Canadian identity was anathema in Quebec (as Bourassa pointed out to Dafoe),[93] and, as Dafoe himself acknowledged, this 'national' idea had yet to supplant the imperial sentiment of which King was so nervous. Indeed, for all its ambivalence, King's careful formula proved surprisingly durable. His Conservative opponent, Arthur Meighen, had already asserted Canada's particular interests and her special ties with the United States in the argument over renewing the Anglo-Japanese alliance in 1921. Borden's closest adviser, the diplomat-lawyer Loring Christie, abandoned in the early 1920s the old Borden policy of a common foreign policy. Like Dafoe and Sifton, he was alarmed by the signs that Britain had turned away from her imperial destiny to plunge into the quagmire of European diplomacy.[94] To be true to the Empire was not to follow the same route. Meighen himself, in despair at reviving his electoral fortunes without support in Quebec, had conceded by 1925 that no Canadian government should follow Britain into war without holding and winning a general election. An uneasy consensus had been reached.

Australia

In Australia and New Zealand, by contrast, there was little enthusiasm for greater detachment in imperial relations: quite the reverse. Radical opinion in the Pacific dominions disliked the expansion of 'tropical empire' over non-white peoples and distrusted the motives that lay behind it – for similar reasons to radicals in Britain. It resented the influence of the City of London and its power to frustrate the political aims of Labour in the state governments. But, despite widespread industrial unrest at the end of the war, radicalism and the Labour party made little headway in the post-war decade.[95] The commemoration of the war was conservative and imperial-minded: Gallipoli as Britain's blunder and Australia's sacrifice was a much later mythology.[96] Australian leaders were more sympathetic than Canadian leaders to Britain's Middle Eastern travails: Australia's interest in the Suez Canal was second to none. Where differences arose between Australia and Britain, it was over Australia's claim to the German ex-colonies in the South Pacific and the thorny issue of the Anglo-Japanese alliance. Here there was a passionate Australian (and New Zealand) belief that renewing the alliance was the vital means of restraining Japan from imperial aggression. But, against Canadian opposition, and (more cogently) the urgency of reaching an Anglo-American accord, the Pacific dominions protested in vain.

Australian and New Zealand dissatisfaction arose not from a fear of imperial commitments but from what they saw as London's indifference to imperial interests. King saw a plot to make Canada party to a common imperial policy. Hughes and Massey (more realistically) resented their exclusion from the imperial decisions that mattered. At the peace conference in Paris, Hughes fought a stubborn battle to annex Germany's conquered colonies in the South Pacific not hold them as mandates under the League of Nations – a struggle that brought him into conflict with both the British government and President Wilson.[97] The 'class C' mandate (envisaging permanent trusteeship) was the compromise outcome. In the furious arguments over the Japanese alliance and at the Washington Conference in 1921-2, the Australian government saw further proof that its vital interests received little attention in British diplomacy. For Hughes, the last straw was the crisis at Chanak in September 1922 and the conference that followed at Lausanne. Unlike Canada and South Africa, he reminded London, Australia and New Zealand had answered Churchill's call for help and promised troops if they were needed to defend the Dardanelles against the resurgent Turks. But neither dominion was represented at the conference. Hughes' rage knew no bounds. 'The habit of asking Australia to agree to things when they are done and cannot be undone', he told the Bonar Law cabinet,

> is one which will wreck the Empire if persisted in. You have already seen Canada and South Africa standing aloof on the plea that they had not been consulted. I have pointed out . . . many times that what is wanted, and what we are entitled to, is a real share in moulding foreign and Imperial policy. In foreign affairs the Empire must speak with one voice.[98]

Hughes' frustration was the greater because, as he readily admitted, 'there is only one course open to us in practice and that is to follow Britain'.[99] Unless Australia spoke as part of the Empire, he told the Australian parliament in September 1921, its voice 'would be lost across the waste of waters'. 'But when Australia speaks as part of the British Empire

> [w]ith its 500,000,000 of people, its mighty navy, its flag
> on every sea, its strongholds on every continent, its power
> and glory shining and splendid, then she speaks in . . . tones
> that are heard and heeded . . . With our hands on the lever
> of Empire, we move the world, but casting this aside we are
> shorn of our strength and count for little or nothing.[100]

The uncompromising intensity of Hughes' Britannic nationalism was a measure of this brutal realism about Australia's prospects in isolated independence.

Hughes' language was characteristically blunt. But his suave successor as prime minister, Stanley Bruce, was just as unequivocal. 'It is useless for anyone to maintain that if we were an independent nation, with no connection with the British Empire, we should be in a position to protect ourselves', was his message in 1924.[101] The reason was simple. 'We have the most wonderful unprotected white man's country in the world': defending it relied on British help. The fierce rhetoric of Hughes and Bruce, and the similar attitude in New Zealand, showed that the war had quite different effects in the South Pacific from those it had set off in Canada and (as we shall see) in South Africa. In Australia, the issue of conscription had been deeply divisive. But neither there nor in New Zealand did it result in an ethnic fissure. Instead, it strongly reinforced the pre-war sense of racial and strategic vulnerability. The signs of China's resurgence in the 'May the Fourth' movement, and the visible evidence of Japanese sea-power and imperial ambition, were easily converted into the racial nightmare of 'teeming millions' of Asian immigrants that an Australia without British support might be forced to admit. It was this anxiety, and the fear that the post-war recession might drive Australia back to the dark days of the 1890s, that led post-war governments to call for even closer economic ties with Britain. What Australia needed, said Bruce, was 'men, money and markets': Britain must supply them. The limitless possibilities of Australian development became an article of faith. When the geographer Griffith Taylor sought to puncture inflated claims by pointing out that Australia could support at best 20 million people at an American standard, he found it wiser to pursue his career in another dominion.[102]

The population (a mere six million in 1925) must be boosted; the interior colonised. The same impulse was felt among writers and artists.[103] Coming to terms with Australia's landscape, love and fear of the Australian 'bush', and adaptation to the Australian environment became the hallmarks of 'Australianness': a creole identity not in conflict with 'Britishness' but a supercharged, perhaps superior, version of the north European original.

Indeed, Hughes and Bruce reasserted the British character of the Australian Commonwealth in terms inconceivable to a Canadian premier – at least one who wanted some votes in Quebec. 'We are all of the same race and speak the same tongue in the same way', said Hughes, 'we are more British than the people of Great Britain ... [O]ur great destiny is to hold this continent in trust for those of our race who come after.'[104] 'It is ... essential to remember', insisted Bruce, 'that the British Empire is one great nation ... the British people represent one nation and not many nations as some have endeavoured to suggest.'[105] Of course, not all Australian opinion was convinced by this heavy stress on imperial ties. Too much deference to Britain ran athwart the claim that Australian society was stronger, fairer, more democratic and more manly than the parent stock. Self-reliance and the cultivation of 'Australian sentiment' was how Labour preferred to lay the emphasis. It wanted to cut away some of the outward signs of subordinate status: the judicial appeal to London and the appointment of state governors by the Crown. But these were superficial. The defence of 'White Australia' remained the foremost plank on the party platform. Labour was as committed as Bruce's government to the urgent need for economic development, and accepted that large-scale immigration was the necessary price.[106] But, when immigrants flocked in from Southern Europe, it was quick to denounce them for taking jobs 'from British workmen'[107] and forced a government ban on employing 'foreigners'. For Hughes and Bruce, then, there was little to fear at home from a close association with imperial policy, as long as it reflected their views and protected their interests. Their real concern was not that the London government would impose its wishes, but that those wishes were becoming too selfishly narrow. Like Christie, and other old followers of Borden, they were alarmed by the European turn in British policy. The air defence of Britain (against a putative threat from France) might consume the resources needed for a stronger presence in the Pacific and at Singapore, Bruce warned in 1924. If post-war Britain with its straitened finances chose to protect the Home Islands at the expense of 'outlying parts', Australia would be in peril.[108] It was not declarations of dominion freedom that were needed (or so he might have said), but a clear reminder to opinion in Britain of the global scope of imperial interests.

South Africa

South Africa was not a 'British nation'. Nor was there a common feeling of South Africanness, even among its white minority. Of the four main overseas dominions, it had been the last to receive the full measure of self-government. Among the whites (a more fluid category than it became under *apartheid* after 1948) there was an Afrikaner majority but more than half a million 'English' – English speakers mostly of British origin. Afrikaans (a patois of Dutch) was still only a language in the making, and well-educated Afrikaners were as likely to use English as Dutch in business or professional life.[109] Indeed, there were many Afrikaners in the propertied and professional classes for whom the parliamentary government introduced to the Cape in the 1870s was the optimal combination of order and liberty. There a property-based franchise and the wide degree of local autonomy made symbolic allegiance to the British monarch at worst unobjectionable, at best a buttress of social stability and the racial order. When 'responsible government' was extended to the rest of the country after the South African War of 1899–1902 (but with manhood suffrage for whites and no votes for blacks), this pragmatic loyalty was adopted by many Afrikaners in the old republics. It was futile to break up the Union of 1910 to revive the pre-war states. To drag the whole country into secession from the Empire as the 'South African Republic' would mean imperial intervention and a third Boer War. Worse still, it would set off a civil war among the whites. In a sub-continent, where blacks outnumbered whites by nearly four to one, and where memories of war's catastrophic impact were all too recent, this was a desperate option.

Nevertheless, the First World War had placed a major strain on the pragmatic compromise that Botha embodied. Although the 1914–15 rebellion had collapsed, Afrikaner support for the National party established by General Barry Hertzog in 1913 was markedly stronger by the end of the war. Much Afrikaner opinion was bitterly resentful of South Africa's involvement in an 'English' war and regarded a British imperial triumph with foreboding. The rise of republicanism – which stood for an Afrikaner state outside the Empire – alarmed the

English politicians in South Africa. When Smuts returned from Europe
on Botha's death to take up the premiership, he found it hard to bend
the older man's bow. He lacked Botha's canny sense of Afrikaner feeling or the charm (some alleged more material inducements) through
which he kept his followers loyal. In the first post-war election in 1920,
Smuts' South Africa Party emerged neck and neck with the Nationalists, driving him towards fusion with the Unionists (the old party of
Rhodes, and led by his political and financial legatees) to keep his hold
on power.

Had politics in South Africa been solely a matter of the antagonism between the white communities, they would at least have been simple. The republican option repelled the English but also many Afrikaners who feared the turbulence it threatened. So long as that was true, the
British connection was safe. But, after 1918, Afrikaner opinion became
more susceptible to the appeal of nationalism not less, as the irritations
of wartime were replaced by new sources of grievance. The main reason lay in the rising fear of the educated class – clerics (*predikants*),
teachers, (a handful of) academics, lawyers and journalists – that the
deepening poverty among rural whites (almost all Afrikaners) would
destroy the cohesion of the Afrikaner people. By 1921, the numbers of
'poor whites' (the term was coined in 1906 for those neither skilled nor
semi-skilled) was estimated at over 150,000 – perhaps one-fifth of the
Afrikaner community.[110] Over much of South Africa, the land was too
poor or too dry to support much more than subsistence farming, and
after 1920 the problem was made worse by the huge fall in agricultural prices from the artificial heights of the First World War.[111] To the
Afrikaner elite, three outcomes of almost equal horror seemed all too
likely. The poor whites might be seduced by the appeal of socialism or
communism and exchange their ethnic loyalty for one based on class.
If they drifted to the towns, they might be absorbed by the English
culture that was dominant there. Or they might lapse into 'barbarism'
by adopting the living standards of the blacks and intermarrying with
them. It was this double crisis – the threatened loss of both Afrikaner
and white identity in so large a fraction of the Afrikaner people –
that gave Afrikaner nationalism its urgency and sharpened the edge of
its racial message: explicitly against imperialism and its *Doppelganger*
capitalism; implicitly against the silent threat of the black majority.

Social rather than ethnic antagonism was also a problem for
those English politicians who counted on Britannic solidarity to keep

Afrikaner republicanism at bay and force Afrikaner 'moderates' to
accept the permanence of the British connection. Class conflict between
English (often British immigrant) mineworkers and the mining interest
whose influence was strong in the Unionist party had been a feature
of pre-war politics and had led to the rise of the Labour party on the
Rand. After 1918, these intra-English class tensions erupted spectacularly. Post-war depression was the immediate cause. South African gold
producers were trapped between the fixed price of gold and the rising
costs of drilling ever deeper into the gold-bearing reef beneath Johannesburg. They longed to cut their costs by substituting cheap black labour
for the costlier white men they were forced to employ by the strength
of (white) organised labour on the Rand. The surge in prices during
wartime (when gold's price was still fixed) made matters worse, and
when the temporary relief that came with the fall in the post-war value
of the pound against gold was reversed by early 1922, and depression
led to declining production, the crisis could not be postponed. When
the mineowners suspended the old ratio of white to black workers, a
strike broke out. In early March 1922, it became a general strike on the
Rand, and then an armed insurrection as some of the strikers declared
a socialist republic. Smuts' reaction was uncompromising. Troops were
sent in, and in several days of fighting over 200 people were killed. The
strike was crushed. The number of white miners was cut by over 3,000
and real wages fell. The gold industry returned to profit.[112] But Smuts'
identification with the mining interest was to cost him dear. Three revolutions in a few short years, sighed one English politician, was 'too
much for any country'.[113]

Smuts was committed wholeheartedly to empire membership.
He had commanded the imperial force in the East African campaign.
He had represented South Africa at the Imperial Conferences of 1917
and 1918. By the last year of the war, he had become one of the most
powerful figures in Lloyd George's government. He played a leading
part in the planning for a league of nations and in the diplomacy of
peacemaking at Paris in 1919. In a secret mission in 1921, he had
pressed on the leaders of Sinn Fein the argument for accepting dominion status and not holding out for secession and an Irish republic.[114] Yet
Smuts had also been one of the loudest voices demanding British recognition of the dominions' equality: in constitutional status and external policy. And, like other dominion leaders, he thought that Britain's
involvement in post-war Europe would weaken her claims on dominion

support. It was vital, he urged, that Britain renounce secret diplomacy for open covenants. Then the dominions would know what commitments they faced.[115] Smuts knew very well that, whatever the guise, South African involvement with Britain's global interests was deeply unpopular with many Afrikaners. The 'bulk' of the Dutch people, he told a friend in Britain, were republicans.[116] But he was convinced that a united British Empire within the League of Nations was the key to world order in an age of great uncertainty; and that survival as a 'white man's country' (itself far from certain in the 1920s) made empire membership essential for South Africa. In a conscious echo of Rhodes' programme, Smuts looked forward to a chain of white states stretching north to Kenya – 'A great white Africa along the eastern backbone, with railway and road communications connecting north and south' – under South African influence and sooner or later as part of the South African Union. Here was the promise of South Africa's greatness, and her commercial prosperity (as the sub-metropole of this settler Africa) and the best guarantee against a colonial policy that favoured Indian traders or native (i.e. African) chiefs.[117] But this long game of South Africa's future made it all the more vital to have influence in London, to be a partner in African empire, and to keep the loyalty of the South African English and the British settlers to the north of the Limpopo.

In 1921, Smuts had turned the tables on his nationalist opponents. Post-war prosperity and the reaction of English voters against republicanism gave him and his ex-Unionist allies a clear election victory over both Hertzog and the Labour party. The electorate had given a 'decisive answer' on the question of secession, said Smuts.[118] After that, almost everything went wrong. Depression, the bloodshed on the Rand and the continuing fear of a crisis in Europe damaged Smuts' reputation. In 1923, to Smuts' great chagrin, the white settlers in Southern Rhodesia (where rule by the British South Africa Company was about to end) voted for a separate future as a self-governing colony rather than join the South African Union. In the general election of June 1924, although its popular vote held up well, the South Africa party lost badly to the National and Labour parties united in a pact.[119] Smuts was hated by Afrikaners and many British, Fitzpatrick told Lord Milner.[120] 'Intense unreasoning racialism (i.e. towards the English) and class hatred and communism', was how he explained the defeat to Amery.[121] But the 1924 election was not the prelude to South African secession.

Hertzog and his able lieutenant, Daniel François Malan (a *predikant* turned newspaper editor), had been the champions of republicanism. But, with the defeat of 1921 and the social crisis within the Afrikaner community, their priorities shifted. To tackle the problem of 'poor whites', if need be by a 'colour bar' in employment, to safeguard the cultural unity of the Afrikaner people and to promote Afrikaans as a national language (the 1910 constitution provided for English and Dutch) laid a premium on power not principled opposition. Hertzog knew that without Labour party support he had little hope of defeating Smuts, and that many of Labour's English voters would desert it if it allied with him on a republican ticket. Instead, he was able to trade on the widespread fear of white unemployment and the 'ignorant panic'[122] over black competition. His greatest fear was that Smuts would beat him by an appeal to the Britannic sentiments of the English minority. 'Smuts het net een kans', he told Malan in November 1923, 'en dit is nogmaals 'n khaki electie' – Smuts had one last chance, a khaki election.[123] What Hertzog wanted, when once in power, was the same formal status for which Smuts had pressed: constitutional equality within the Empire, as the substance (or so he claimed) if not the form of republican independence. By an ironic twist, the need to safeguard a white South Africa – the same ultimate goal as Smuts – had led him to accept, for the time being at least, the same constraints and the same solution.

The dominions and Ireland

Hertzog's opportunity came with the Imperial Conference in 1926. At the previous post-war conferences in 1921 and 1923, the dominion premiers showed no appetite for the constitutional debate envisaged in 1918. Hertzog gave warning of his intention, and the British government planned its tactics carefully. A. J. (now Lord) Balfour, who chaired the committee of British and dominion ministers set up at the conference to report on 'inter-imperial relations', had already signalled his willingness to concede the principle of equal status to the white dominions.[124] When Hertzog presented his draft, in which the dominions were described as 'independent states',[125] it was not the principle to which the British ministers objected but the wording. They were ready to concede the dominions' right to exercise external as much as internal autonomy – the right to conduct their own foreign policy – but resisted 'independence' as implying the lapse of their Empire membership. (Mackenzie King also opposed 'independence' as an American usage that would be badly received in English Canada.) After a blizzard of drafts, Balfour produced a formula of almost theological intricacy in which the central concession of the dominions' equal constitutional status (and their implicit right of secession) was carefully balanced against their free and willing recognition of empire membership. In a sunburst of good will it was accepted by all.

The effect of this pronouncement was twofold. It gave a meaning to dominionhood that was flexible enough to embrace all the dominions' varied relationships with Britain. The risk of a division between the dominions themselves was averted. Secondly (and consequentially), it reinvented the bilateral connection between Britain and the different dominions as an intimate form of international association whose terms of membership ('free association') were very attractive to small states in an age of collective insecurity. 'The British Empire', said Balfour's version, 'depends essentially . . . on positive ideals. Free institutions are its lifeblood. Free cooperation is its instrument. Peace, security, and progress are among its ideals.' This appealed to a wide segment of opinion in all the dominions for whom the dangers of isolation and diplomatic 'weightlessness' were as important as Britannic loyalty, if not more so. Balfour's formula acknowledged that the real ties that would hold the dominions to Britain were the informal ties of sentiment or self-interest. Its acceptance by the least Britannic of the dominions, South Africa and the Irish Free State, showed that for one reason or the other exit from the British world-system had as yet little appeal.

Balfour's motive is clear enough. He wanted to discredit the 'small but obstinate minority who . . . persistently advocate the break-up of the Empire'.[126] Free association would pull the rug out from beneath the secessionists. Austen Chamberlain, the Foreign Secretary, may have hoped that he would gain his reward in the dominions' diplomatic sympathy: indeed, in the defence discussions that followed, all except the Irish Free State said that they would come to Britain's aid if ever necessary.[127] Balfour, Chamberlain and Lord Birkenhead (the Secretary of State for India) bundled Amery, the Dominions Secretary, along with them. He was a political lightweight. But the three senior ministers may have had another reason for wanting an amicable settlement. All three, especially Birkenhead and Chamberlain, had been deeply involved in the Anglo-Irish treaty of December 1921. They had the strongest motive for avoiding confrontation with the Irish Free State government and rousing 'die-hardism' from its slumbers on the Tory backbenches. Nor could they be sure that too little flexibility at the conference might not damage the pro-Treaty government in Dublin and pave a path to power for its republican and secessionist enemies.

Indeed, of all the dominions, the Irish Free State was the one that British ministers watched most nervously.[128] Its assimilation to the dominion 'model' was more a hope than an expectation. Its 'Britannic garrison' after partition was far smaller than South Africa's. For all the practical limits to linguistic independence, its cultural revolt against Englishness was more vehement than anything seen in the other dominions. Alone of the dominions, it had won self-government in a violent insurrection against British rule. Alone among the dominions, its right to self-rule was limited by treaty. In the war of independence (1919–21), Sinn Fein declared an Irish Republic, and its candidates who were successful in the United Kingdom general election of December 1918 (but refused to take their seats at Westminster) met as a separate Irish parliament, the Dail Eireann. After eighteen months of guerrilla warfare, terrorism and reprisal had produced a stalemate truce in July 1921, and a treaty settlement was hammered out in London between the Lloyd George government and a Sinn Fein delegation. It gave the twenty-six counties of southern Ireland 'Canadian' status as a self-governing dominion, but rejected the demand for an Irish republic outside the Empire and insisted on an oath of allegiance to the King by those taking office or sitting in the Dail. The possibility of a united Ireland – if Northern Ireland agreed – or of repartition on terms more generous to the South was held open. By a narrow majority, the Dail upheld the treaty proposals. But the Sinn Fein government split. De Valera, president of the 1919 republic, denounced the oath of allegiance (though he was willing to recognise the King as the head of the Empire). Much of the Irish Republican Army in the south and west rebelled against a civilian regime whose treaty-based constitution was at odds with the claim that the citizen in arms was the true embodiment of the Irish nation – and which threatened to end the free rein that the 'flying columns' enjoyed.[129] It took a bloody civil war, with a death-toll heavier than in the Anglo-Irish struggle, to impose the authority of the 'treatyites' and the Free State government.

The fate of the treaty was watched in London with great anxiety. The risk of embroiling the North – where Catholic nationalists were harassed by Protestant paramilitaries – seemed high. Michael

Collins, the charismatic leader of the IRA, who led the Free State army in the civil war, was suspected of duplicity: few tears were shed in London when he was ambushed and murdered by the anti-treaty forces in August 1922.[130] For British leaders, the success of the Free State government was critical if Ireland was to escape a further round of turmoil and then a further round of imperial crisis. Partly for that reason, they acquiesced in a quasi-republican constitution in which authority was derived from 'the people of Ireland' (not the king-in-parliament).[131] When the North rejected a united Ireland and the boundary settlement left the frontier unchanged, they sweetened the pill for the Dublin government by financial concessions. The Free State government won a popular mandate, but the balance seemed fine. The army mutiny of 1924, the continued threat of IRA violence and the return of the anti-treatyites (as Fianna Fail) to the Dail, made its tenure seem fragile. The danger that it would repudiate the treaty and declare a republic could not be ruled out.[132]

British leaders may have exaggerated the risk. Despite the hangover of republican violence, the Free State government represented a powerful body of Irish opinion that preferred free trade (with Britain) to isolation and autarky,[133] and accepted that, without the association with Britain, the Irish voice in international affairs would be embarrassingly faint.[134] To the larger farmers and local businessmen who formed the backbone of the old Irish party before 1914, and supported the treatyite Cumann na nGaedheal, overthrowing the constitution was a menace to order. For the champions of Catholic conservatism, the most influential ideology in the new state,[135] republicanism was suspect for its atheism and socialism. Cosgrave and O'Higgins, his dynamic deputy, were determined to restore an ordered society of strong institutions, lawful authority and firm discipline.[136] Their aim was not to break the treaty, but to free themselves from the surviving relics of Ireland's subordination to Britain – in part to disarm their Fianna Fail opponents. This was why at the Imperial Conference they were quick to follow Hertzog with a list of detailed 'anomalies' in dominion status, and why O'Higgins insisted that Ireland's separate status should be formally marked in the royal title. When the 'O'Higgins comma' was inserted, the king was no longer 'King of Great Britain and Ireland' and the overseas dominions, but 'King of Great Britain, Ireland, and the British Dominions'. To Birkenhead, one of the signatories of the Anglo-Irish treaty, the need to meet the Irish leaders over their 'tiresome points'[137] and protect a settlement that is 'working better than our most extravagant hopes' was unarguable. In Ireland, more than anywhere else, what mattered most was to make cooperation a habit and ingrain the constitutionalist outlook that was its greatest ally.

Like Hertzog (who returned in triumph to South Africa), the Irish leaders found merit in the constitutional experiment codified by the conference. They had equal status and external autonomy. In return, they accepted the Crown (with some ambiguity) as their head of state and the symbol of their membership of the 'Empire-Commonwealth' – a term just creeping into use. Like the other dominions, they recognised the British system as the magnetic pole of their external relations. Like them, they had much to lose from an open break. For the moment, it seemed that Ireland might be shaped to the mould of an 'imperial nation', to become another Canada in substance as well as form. The stresses of the next decade would settle the question.

The Empire at home

After 1918, there was good reason to doubt whether the vast world-system the late Victorians had assembled would command the support of British society at home. A positive view of its costs and risks sprang from the distinctive complex of ideology and politics in late-Victorian Britain. The late Victorians had been loyal to *laissez-faire* economics. They accepted the logic of free trade and the gold standard and regarded with equanimity their ever-growing dependence on foreign food, foreign trade and a foreign income from investments. They acknowledged the force of the geopolitical corollary. That Britain must be a global power to defend the sphere of free commerce and guard its long lines of maritime transport was argued over in detail but rarely disputed in principle. The electorate that sanctioned this globe-wide imperialism excluded all women and more than one-third of adult men. No party dedicated to the ideas of socialism or the sectional interests of the working class could win a majority in parliament. The electorate's antipathy to Irish nationalism, partly on sectarian grounds, made it amenable to arguments for coercion elsewhere: unionism at home helped underwrite imperialism abroad. And, although some of its articles had come under attack in Edwardian politics – in the struggle over tariff reform and

Irish Home Rule – the prime assumptions of this 'liberal imperialism' went largely unchallenged until the First World War.

In the new landscape of post-war economics and politics, this late-Victorian consensus looked less secure. Economic discontent was real enough in late-Victorian society and industrial militancy had been a striking feature of the pre-war decade. But their political impact had been blunted by the general prosperity of skilled workers and by a franchise that excluded many of those most vulnerable to economic misfortune – the army of unskilled and casual labour. By the end of 1920, these pre-war conditions no longer held good. The post-war depression brought high unemployment to skilled workers as well as unskilled. It affected those organised in trade unions (a much larger number than before the war) as well as those who were not. But the most important change was that all men affected by the slump in trade now had the vote since adult males over twenty-one, as well as some women, had been enfranchised in the reform Act of 1918. The result politically was profoundly unsettling. A prolonged depression would mean an alienated class, excluded by poverty, but included by politics. It would be empowered by the franchise against a social system from which it had nothing to gain. Not surprisingly, fear of a 'socialism' (a vaguely defined creed) that would be swept into power by a working-class electorate, haunted the politicians of the older parties.[138] For there seemed no doubt about who would be the beneficiary of the two new facts of British politics: the great pool of working-class discontent and the huge new electorate (three times as big as the old) with no tradition of loyalty to either Liberals or Conservatives. In the excitable climate bred by the Russian revolution and industrial confrontation in Britain – at its tensest in 1921 – it was easy to credit the Labour party with the extremist views from which its leaders recoiled. Pacifism, 'bolshevik' sympathies, and antipathy to colonial rule, especially in India, seemed synonymous with socialism.

These fears (in some quarters, hopes) turned out to be exaggerated. It was industrial labour, not political Labour, that proved the real threat to the British world-system. It rejected the sacrifices on which the revival of London's commercial empire was supposed to depend. At the end of the war, it was widely agreed by expert opinion that British prosperity meant restoring the commercial conditions that had ruled in 1914. London must resume its place as the world's greatest

banker, lender and market-place. The gold standard must be revived
as a self-regulating mechanism of monetary control and the guarantee
of sterling's worth as *the* global currency. British debts must be repaid.
British exports must recover lost markets and win new ones to ease the
strain on the balance of payments and help renew the flow of outward
investment. At government level, this programme meant the stringent
control of public expenditure. But its social and industrial meaning was
much more drastic. If British exports were to be competitive, British
costs had to fall. The large gains in real income conceded in the war
and its inflationary aftermath would have to be clawed back. By Keynes'
estimate, while the cost of living had risen by 60 per cent, the combined
effect of higher wages and shorter hours had more than doubled real
wages.[139]

The fierce deflation of 1920–1 was aimed in part at this objective. But its results were not what its authors intended. The numbers of
unemployed rose rapidly from 700,000 at the end of 1920 to over two
million by mid-1921 and remained above 1.2 million for the rest of the
decade. But it proved impossible to push down the wages of those in
work. Instead, the sharp fall in prices that deflation produced boosted
their real incomes still further, by some 13 per cent between 1919 and
1922, on top of the wartime rise.[140] In the climate of industrial militancy
and electoral uncertainty that dominated the early 1920s, imposing a
wholesale reduction of wages was out of the question. It would have
meant economic controls as draconian as in wartime, repellent alike to
capital and labour, and hastily scrapped in 1919. In a tacit social and
political bargain, those in work kept the real income gains of 1914–22
(the exception were the miners).[141] The unintended victims were the
unemployed.

Worker resistance to cuts in real wages had a real significance
for the part Britain played in her imperial system. It made the price of
the return to gold in 1925 – the *sine qua non* of commercial empire –
uncomfortably high, and cut down the benefits it was supposed to bring.
High interest rates, a fragile pound and a restricted stream of investment
abroad were the penalty for setting the gold value of sterling at a level
designed to compete with the dollar, but without the fall in industrial
costs that was needed to make British exports competitive. In the crucial
phase of economic adjustment, industrial labour had refused to give up
what it had gained since 1914, and could not be coerced into doing so.
It could not be bent to the purpose of a revived commercial empire.

Its resistance to the 'logic' of bankers and businessmen could be seen, indeed, as an instinctive form of metropolitan 'isolationism', a refusal to bow to the harsh demands of the international economy. It set the limits to the post-war promise of the British world-system.

This was the most potent (if least conscious) act of worker 'anti-imperialism'. At the same time, the rapid growth of a mass constituency for the Labour party (Labour vote, 1910: 371,722; 1918: 2,385,472; 1922: 4,241,383; 1923: 4,438,508; 1924: 5,489,077) lent added weight to radical opinion in imperial matters. Before 1914, critics of empire had attacked the cost of imperial wars, the threat to peace of imperial rivalry, the authoritarian trend of colonial rule and the commercial exploitation of indigenous peoples. But their voice had been muffled by political concession in India and South Africa, the diplomatic settlement of colonial disputes (especially with France) and the domestic (rather than imperial) threat posed by the new German navy. Even J. A. Hobson, the critic-in-chief of British imperialism, had come to concede the beneficent effects of international trade.[142] But, as the war dragged on, he revived (in *Democracy after the War* (1917)) the old claim that imperial antagonism was the real cause of conflict. With militarism enthroned at the heart of government, and imperialism (in the person of Milner) at its elbow, an Allied victory would mean the triumph of reaction. The 'imperialist' project, checked since 1906, would resume its course. An imperial tariff, territorial expansion and the economic exploitation of Afro-Asian peoples would destroy free trade at home, cut down living standards and corrode the tradition of political liberty. The best defence was a league of nations, 'international government' and the careful protection of indigenous cultures against the social damage of enforced industrialism. In the last year of the war, this radical programme received a powerful boost. Official endorsement of the idea of a league, the publication of Woodrow Wilson's Fourteen Points and the emergence of Labour (which Hobson joined in 1918) as a mass-based party, strengthened its claim on public attention.

Hobson's warnings were echoed by the band of writers who made up Labour's 'intelligence branch' in imperial policy: Leonard Woolf, whose *Empire and Commerce in Africa* (1920) denounced colonial rule as a licence to rob; Sydney Olivier, whose *The League of Nations and Primitive Peoples* (1918) pressed the case for international trusteeship; and E. D. Morel, veteran of the Congo campaign, who published *The Black Man's Burden* in 1920. Their critical view

of the pre-war world (Olivier believed that the humanitarian traditions of colonial rule had been corrupted by business after 1890)[143]
chimed with a larger body of 'middle opinion' disillusioned by political, diplomatic and economic failure in the aftermath of the war. A
new commitment to the reconstruction of Europe was urged by Alfred
Zimmern in *Europe in Convalescence* (1922). The destructive impact
of the reparations demand was condemned by J. M. Keynes in *The
Economic Consequences of the Peace* (1920). The hidden commitments and secret promises that had sheltered 'old diplomacy' from
public opinion were denounced in Lowes Dickinson's *The International Anarchy* in 1926. Such polemics by themselves meant little. But
the electoral support for the Liberals and Labour (in 1923, they commanded together nearly nine million votes to the Conservatives' five
and a half) suggested that a large body of public opinion took a similar
'neo-Gladstonian' view of Britain's overseas interests. The pre-war version of imperial diplomacy (if not already discredited) had been made
redundant by victory. Peaceful cooperation through an international
concert, not an empire in arms, was the need of the moment. The
predatory instincts of colonial settlers and businessmen should be carefully restrained before they whipped up revolt, or provoked a fresh clash
between colonial powers. A new bond of sympathy must be forged with
the aspirations of colonial peoples, when they embraced the values of
the Liberal state.

Of course, none of this implied the repudiation of power. The
Labour leadership had refused any truck with Gandhian agitation in
1920, and insisted in its first (minority) government in 1924 on strict
adherence to the Montford constitution.[144] The champions of trusteeship insisted that African self-government lay far in the future. The
effect was more subtle. The liberal mood of the early 1920s inspired
a more thoughtful defence of colonial rule and a more critical view
of its actual practice. The ex-proconsul, Lord Lugard, whose sense of
publicity was unusually sharp (his wife had been on the staff of *The
Times*) urged a 'dual mandate' in tropical Africa. Economic development brought reciprocal benefits to Europeans and Africans. The task
of government was to balance the interests of international trade and its
indigenous subjects.[145] Amid the new stress on enlightened trusteeship
and non-interference with 'primitive' peoples, 'indirect rule' acquired
additional merit. A neo-traditional regime based on customary law and
chiefly rule became the settled dogma of African policy. In the new

wave of paternalism, humanitarian causes, including education and anti-slavery, attracted fresh attention if not more resources. Extending self-government (however gradually) to the non-white colonies meant that cultural sympathy across racial lines had become more urgent. In E. M. Forster's *A Passage to India* (1924), the stilted parochialism of 'Anglo-India' and its cold rejection of educated Indians was held up to ridicule and proclaimed as a warning.

The strongest emotion in this age of flux was the fear of commitments and the urge to save. This was hard to square with the leftover business of the First World War. The political turbulence of the post-war years arose from this conflict. The Lloyd George government faced a huge agenda: in Europe, at home, and in Ireland as well as in the imperial sphere in India, Egypt and the Middle East. On almost every issue it faced fierce dissent, some of the bitterest from its backbench supporters in the House of Commons. Over Ireland particularly, Lloyd George's readiness to negotiate with Sinn Fein (from July 1921) enraged the 'die-hards' in the Conservative party. Signs of compromise in the treatment of 'extremists' in India and Egypt (like the failure to arrest Gandhi) strengthened die-hard claims of the 'empire in danger'. It was Lloyd George's misfortune that some of the credit he gained from the Irish treaty in December 1921 was devalued by the civil war between the Irish 'treatyites' and 'anti-treatyites'. But the real cause of his downfall in October 1922 was the lack of economic recovery at home and the sense of over-commitment abroad. Working-class discontent over unemployment and pay was matched by middle-class anger at the high rate of taxation (income tax had risen to five shillings (25 per cent) in the pound in 1917, and was at six shillings (30 per cent) throughout 1919-22). Government 'waste' became the target of a public campaign and had to be appeased by a formal enquiry (the 'Geddes axe'). The military cost of British control in Iraq (partly perhaps because Winston Churchill, a coalition Liberal, was the minister responsible) drew especially bitter complaint from the Conservative backbenches, on whose support the coalition cabinet was overwhelmingly dependent. It was the lightning rod for unease over a Middle East policy whose aims seemed obscure and whose outcome uncertain. When the British force at Chanak in the Dardanelles faced the Turkish army advancing north from Izmir in September 1922, and military conflict seemed likely, two streams of discontent were united. Whatever the merits of its case – the strategic argument for preventing the Turks from recovering the

Straits – the coalition government had risked a new war in the Middle East for which public opinion was quite unprepared.[146] When Bonar Law (who had favoured coalition in 1918 and been Lloyd George's loyal lieutenant until 1921) came out of retirement to lead the Conservative revolt against continued partnership with the Lloyd George Liberals, he could draw on multiple sources of Tory resentment. But it was the over-extension of British power that he chose to emphasise. Britain, he said in a famous phrase, 'cannot alone act as the policeman of the world'.[147]

The fall of Lloyd George opened two more years of party manoeuvre, induced in the main by economic uncertainty. The Conservative ministry of Bonar Law (until May 1923) and Baldwin was dominated by the setback to European recovery, by the need to cut spending and by the fear that Lloyd George would build a new coalition against its economic failure. Baldwin's sudden leap to protection was intended to offer a definite programme and unite his party round the cause to which much of it was already loyal. It was an electoral disaster. In December 1923, the Conservative vote held up well (at 38.1 per cent compared with 38.2 per cent in November 1922), but Baldwin was swept away by the Free Trade opposition. But the result was inconclusive. A minority Labour government took power with Liberal support in January 1924. Neither circumstance, inclination, nor, perhaps, talent, could make Ramsay MacDonald a second Gladstone.[148] No great centre-left party emerged in a grand realignment of political forces. When MacDonald was pulled down by the petty scandal of the 'Campbell case', and by public suspicion of his party's communist ties (the Zinoviev letter), it was Baldwinite Conservatism that won the high ground electorally. In October 1924, it gained a decisive victory. With the long-awaited revival of European prosperity, and the return in Britain of a 'social peace',[149] the domestic instability of the post-war years seemed a thing of the past.

Yet it had left its mark on the British role in their imperial system. Baldwin's aim was a broad-based party that would annex the centre in British politics. He renounced protection and installed a free trade Chancellor (Winston Churchill). He embraced 'economy' in defence, partly to fund the rising cost of welfare expenditure. He had learnt from Chanak to fear confrontation abroad as a hostage to fortune. He and other leading Conservatives accepted much of the 'liberal' outlook on international affairs, as a rough approximation to informed opinion

and as a useful guide to the post-war world. As a result, the imperial attitudes of the post-war years seem curiously tepid. At another time, high
unemployment, a vast new electorate and the nationalist revolts against
imperial rule might have prompted the embrace of a jingo populism.
Indeed, tariff reform at home, 'splendid isolation' abroad, opening up
the 'undeveloped estates', and a firm way with 'agitators', all had their
advocates in Conservative ranks. But the overwhelming need was to
bind the new political nation to an economic order (capitalism) it had
no reason to like. An attack on free trade (as Baldwin discovered) would
be deeply resented by the new constituency. Pre-war-style thinking on
imperial defence – as if Britain were still surrounded by rival world
empires – was (or seemed) obsolete at a time when the reconciliation of
Europe was the most immediate need and competing imperialisms at an
unusually low ebb. Coercive tactics against colonial (or semi-colonial)
dissidents in the Empire, Egypt, Iraq or China could not be ruled out.
But their likely cost, and the fear that they would lead to political
extremism and guerrilla war (the 'Irish syndrome' frequently invoked
after 1921) gave an added premium to emollient policies. To a much
greater extent than before 1914, the demands of empire on society at
home were to be monitored closely and reduced to the minimum. What
sort of empire that made in the age of depression the following chapter
will try to explain.

10 HOLDING THE CENTRE, 1927–1937

Until the mid-1920s, it had seemed as if the profound dislocation of economic and political life unleashed by the war would defeat all attempts to devise a new equilibrium. After 1925, the outlook improved. A new economic order took shape in Europe, underwritten by the flow of American investment. Franco-German reconciliation lifted the threat of a new European struggle. The impetus behind anti-colonial nationalism slackened off. The world economy recovered the vigour of its pre-war decade. The volume of trade surpassed the levels of 1913. As the age of extremes receded, liberalism and 'moderation' seemed in the ascendant. But it proved a false dawn. In October 1929, the Wall Street 'crash' signalled the return of economic uncertainty, followed soon after by the huge fall in commodity prices, the sharp contraction of trade, deep rural impoverishment and mass unemployment. The crisis of capitalism became the crisis of liberalism. The survival of nations and their internal stability demanded illiberal solutions: protection, autarky, or aggressive imperialism (to those with the means); a retreat to the land, exiguous self-sufficiency, or desperate rural rebellion to those without power. In culture, as in trade, free exchange was devalued in so hostile a climate. Utopianism, despair and nostalgia were its more typical products.

This massive upheaval in global conditions held huge implications for the British world-system. In the late 1920s, its liberal apologists had talked of a 'third British Empire', based not on rule but on the growth of cooperation and partnership in a world-spanning 'Commonwealth'.[1] Less liberal politicians looked forward to a period of political calm in which 'nationalist' demands in India, the dominions and elsewhere would be soothed by the concession of greater autonomy, and disarmed by the knowledge that secession or exit from the imperial embrace was self-defeating at best. The geopolitical scene was benign. The risks of devolution declined and the costs of defence fell as the threat of armed conflict receded. Despite the heavy burden of war debt, the great revival of trade promised the gradual return of Britain's old role as the merchant, shipper, insurer and banker to much of the world, and the entrepot of its commerce. Britain remained the one great free trading power, just as it had been before 1914. Even British migration (now almost entirely to Empire destinations) picked up to the levels of the 1890s, if not to the great rush of 1900–14.[2] But all this was the prelude to a great reversal of fortune.

From 1929 onwards, the British system was caught up in the world's economic and geopolitical earthquake. Almost all the conditions on which its wealth and safety depended now looked much more uncertain. The threat of a great power assault on British interests or territory, a remote possibility before 1930, became increasingly real and imperial defence a more arduous task. The contraction of world trade, the ever-higher walls of protection, and the renewed war between currencies, wrecked the hopes of British exporters and shrank the 'invisible income' which made up the deficit on the balance of trade. Britain's wealth and prosperity, the core of its power, seemed to be dwindling away. As economic catastrophe loomed over much of the world, the virus of nationalism (as opinion in Britain was inclined to see it) spread wider and deeper. It infected the great powers on whose mutual restraint the British system relied – if the costs of defence were to be kept within bounds. It encouraged the attack on foreign property and trade which the British (with more of both to lose than anyone else) had good reason to dread. Nationalist ideology corroded the 'steel frame' of colonial rule, challenged its systems of political influence and drove it willy-nilly into costly coercion. As geopolitics, economics and nationalism converged, Britain's loose-knit empire, far-flung, ill-defended and so reliant on trade, looked like a hostage to fate. Secure in its 'Antonine Age' only twenty years earlier, by the mid-1930s the British system seemed plunged (to some observers at least) in a terminal crisis. 'The storm clouds are gathering', Churchill told the Conservative party in December 1934, 'others are ready and waiting to take our place in the world.'[3]

There were plenty of those who for partisan reasons foretold the early demise of British world power. Expectant Marxists, frustrated nationalists and embittered imperialists all wrote its obituary. Even sympathetic observers, peering in from outside, were deeply alarmed. 'England is beset by manifold dangers', wrote the German jurist, Herman Kantorowicz, in a book first published (in German) in November 1929. 'The economic foundation of her greatness grows narrower from day to day.'[4] The Americans were richer, the Germans better trained, even the Russians more numerous. Britain's industries were outdated, its workforce overpaid, the recourse to tariffs a delusion. In the age of the aeroplane, it was no longer an island, and was too small geographically to be an effective air power. The British were also the main object of Muslim and Asian resentment, and the 'colonial epoch' was on its last legs. 'In this age of nationalism, it will be impossible to hold India'; Iraq and Egypt were already slipping the leash. Deprived of its empire, Britain would decline 'into a second Holland'. Much of Kantorowicz's warning was echoed by André Siegfried, a French political scientist of unrivalled prestige. In *England's Crisis* (1931), he emphasised industrial obsolescence, an unsustainable standard of living and the falling away of British foreign investment as the seeds of economic decline. The British depended upon international trade: they had no choice in the matter. Protection would do them no good. But economic nationalism posed a deadly threat. 'Caught between a "Fordised" America and a "cartelised" Europe, [Britain] will eventually have to enter an international economic alliance.'[5] It was not strong enough to preserve a worldwide influence and 'stand alone as before'.

For much of the decade after 1929, British leaders struggled to contain the effects of geopolitical change, economic depression and nationalist politics. For much of the time, they saw themselves as confronting the centrifugal forces that were pulling their system apart. Their aim, so far as consistent purpose can be seen, was to hold the centre: against the threat of strategic defeat, economic implosion or social upheaval. They wanted Britain to remain, so far as it could, at the centre of world trade. They were determined to keep it in its central position in its own world-system, by hook or by crook. They were also anxious to soften the social conflict at home that high unemployment might bring. But there was a limit to what they could achieve on their own. In the self-governing dominions, preserving the 'British connection' in more straitened conditions required the support of local political leaders acutely aware of their own public opinion. In India it was caught up in the four-cornered struggle between the Raj's 'steel frame' of British officials, the Congress politicians, the Muslims and the princes. London's survival as a centre of world trade would turn on how well it adapted to the new global economy of blocs, tariffs and barter. But what mattered most was beyond British control. The fate of their system, British leaders were beginning to learn by the late 1930s, might really depend on the unsated ambitions of the 'have-not' powers – Germany, Italy and Japan – and their inscrutable leaders.

Imperial defence

Before 1930, there had been good grounds for thinking that the British world-system had entered a phase of exceptional freedom from external assault. In no previous period since the 1880s, when the age of 'world politics' began, had British interests (or those of the dominions) appeared less exposed to the threat of a great power attack. Of course, it was true that mutual suspicion still governed the conduct of great power relations. There was much British resentment at the gratuitous expansion of the American navy (as it seemed in London) and the symbolic dethronement of the Royal Navy's supremacy that they had been forced to concede. Periodic tensions with France evoked the reminder that, in European terms (and especially in air power), the French would be a formidable enemy. The Italians were an irritant when they jostled and threatened on the frontiers of Egypt, and cast covetous eyes on Ethiopia and Yemen. The subversive activity of the Soviet Union, whose red hand was seen in the growth of working-class militancy in both Europe and Asia, attracted much official attention. Russian agents were credited with anti-British activity in the Middle East (in Iran) as well as in China. The old imperial bogey of the Russian menace to India via the Northwest Frontier took on a new ideological meaning. The growth of Japanese power, bluntly restrained by Anglo-American pressure in 1921–2, required a watchful presence if Britain's large interests in East Asia were not to be squeezed. Indeed, the British suspected that Japan and the Americans were both happy to see British interests bear the brunt of the Chinese nationalist attack on foreign privilege that was growing in virulence after 1925.

Yet this pattern of friction was actually quite reassuring. For what it revealed was that the most dangerous connections in pre-war international diplomacy had fallen apart. Before 1914, the British had seen their main danger in the German domination of Europe. They relied by default on the alliance of Russia and France, and on winning the arms race against German naval expansion. Maintaining the European balance of power had been the main pillar of empire defence. But its far-reaching demands had been increasingly felt in every vicinity where European interests competed, in the Middle East and East Asia especially. Almost no local matter could be settled without reference to its effect on the European balance: and great power relations in Europe, with its high-voltage circuits of rumour and fear, quivered with the shock of remote detonations and consular outbursts on faraway bunds. The ghastly outcome of this 'old diplomacy' had revealed the fine thread upon which Britain's security (and imperial defence) had really been hung. But, once European peace had been assured at Locarno by the Franco-German reconciliation, Europe's balance of power was no longer the key to the peace of the world. Soviet Russia was isolated and geostrategically weak. Japan was much stronger in its own sphere in East Asia, but had almost no prospect of finding a friend among the other great powers. The result was a 'de-linking' of the regional conflicts so dangerously linked up before 1914 – to Britain's great strategic advantage. With a navy that was more than equal under the Washington terms to those of France and Italy combined, and much stronger than Japan's, the British had little to fear from a Mediterranean dispute, or a Japanese attack on their interests in Asia, and no reason to fear that they might coincide. There was no likely combination of powers to prevent them from holding their own in Europe, the Middle East, the Indian Ocean or East Asia, nor from applying their power in the theatre they wanted and at the time of their choosing. It was not simply that the British were the one global power: no coalition against them had any chance of cohering.

This highly favourable turn owed a great deal to the path of American power. The British approached this leviathan with a volatile mixture of admiration, mistrust and judicious appeasement. Britain is faced, remarked a senior Foreign Office official (with an American wife) in late 1928,

> *with a phenomenon for which there is no parallel in our modern history – a State twenty-five times as large, five times as wealthy, three times as populous, twice as ambitious, almost invulnerable, and at least our equal in*

prosperity, vital energy, technical equipment and industrial science. This State has risen to its present stage of development at a time when Great Britain is still staggering from the effects of the superhuman effort made during the War, is loaded with a great burden of debt and is crippled by the evil of unemployment.[6]

As Craigie's memorandum suggested, the American challenge to Britain's commercial and industrial power was just as potent as that to its maritime primacy. But, if yielding naval supremacy still stuck in the admirals' craw, and if the American 'style' in diplomatic exchange seemed designed to annoy, the transatlantic 'phenomenon' had done little real damage to British world interests. Perhaps the reverse. It was American capital (as we saw in the last chapter) that had smoothed the path of European peace, but without exacting the price in diplomatic allegiance another great power might have sought. America's maritime might, scaled against Britain's, was in practice deployed against the power that was thought to threaten them both. From 1922 onwards, the bulk of the United States Navy was placed in the Pacific.[7] While 'War Plan Red' (for an Anglo-American war) gathered dust, 'War Plan Orange' (against Japan) was real. Anglo-American tensions remained. They were fuelled by the old quarrel over 'belligerent rights': whether a naval blockade (*the* British weapon in a European war) could be used to prevent the traffic of 'neutral' (in practice American) trade; and by American pressure for a further reduction of fleet strengths. In London, governments of both parties accepted the case for a new naval agreement. The London Naval Conference of 1930 preserved the existing distribution of maritime power (including that of Japan), extended the 'holiday' in battleship building until 1936, averted the threat of a race to build cruisers, and restored good relations across the Atlantic.[8]

As it turned out, the conference was the swan song of the short golden age of post-war security. The lowering background to the naval agreement had been the deepening crisis in the world economy. The storm broke in East Asia. The acute dependence of Japan on overseas trade, Japanese fears of exclusion from their markets in China (as Kuomintang rule was extended), and their long-standing suspicion of British and American commercial designs in East Asia, created an aggressive and panicky mood in Japanese politics.[9] When the full force

of depression was felt in early 1931, and with it the threat of violent social unrest, civilian politicians lost control of the army. China's
huge northern province of Manchuria had been a target of Japanese
economic penetration since before 1914. The 'South Manchurian Railway', its large 'railway zone', and the colonial army based on the Kwantung peninsula, were the means through which their regional power was
asserted. In September 1931, perhaps to pre-empt future resistance from
the migrant Chinese now flooding into Manchuria,[10] Japanese officers
exploited a trivial fracas to impose the 'Kwantung' army's control over
the whole of the province, to which their colleagues at home extracted
Tokyo's assent. It was a gross contravention of the Washington treaties
(the post-war charter of East Asian security), a massive infringement of
China's territorial integrity and (not least) an obvious breach of Japan's
obligations as a member of the League.

There was thus every reason for a fierce British reaction. The
restraint of Japan had been a key part of the post-war peace settlement.
It meant a great deal to the Pacific dominions, whose fear of Japan was
tightly bound up with their racial exclusiveness as white British societies. Among the Western powers with a stake in China's economy, the
British had the most to lose – with much more in investment and trade
than the United States. Of the great hub of their interests, the port-city
of Shanghai and its British-run enclave the 'International Settlement',
the Foreign Office had remarked that 'no Chinese government is as yet
fit to control the destinies of a city which . . . compares with London and
New York'. Indeed, 'whenever real danger threatens the city . . . British
interests . . . are so great that British troops must be sent to protect the
Settlement, just as though it were a British possession'.[11] Japan's economic imperialism was unlikely to stay far away in the north: Taiwan,
after all, was a Japanese colony, and the Japanese presence was already
strong in Shanghai. London, however, was very reluctant to take the
lead on Manchuria. 'Avoid at all costs an open breach with Japan'[12]
was the watchword of policy. This was partly because a possible armed
confrontation was extremely unwelcome at a time of enormous uncertainty in Britain's own politics in 1931–2. But it also reflected two
other constraints whose force was compelling. The first was the doubt
whether it was in Britain's real interests to oppose Japan on Manchuria.
The British had conceded (in 1926) that their extra-territorial privileges
in China (symbolised by their treaty-port rights, in Shanghai above all)
could not be maintained against the nationalist opposition in China.

They had begun their retreat from the beleaguered outposts of the old treaty-port system. But they regarded the Kuomintang national-ism of Chiang Kai-shek as xenophobic and unstable, and dreaded a wholesale assault on British persons and property. 'A strong China is not a necessity to us; indeed the preservation of Hong Kong, and, as long as possible, of our remaining special rights in China, suffices to suggest the contrary', was the cold comment in London on an enthusi-astic despatch from the Peking legation expressing the opposite view.[13] Attacking Japan on China's behalf thus had little appeal. The second factor at work was a well-merited caution. Coercing Japan meant send-ing a fleet to Northeastern Asia at a time when the nearest fully fledged naval base was no closer than Malta. Few naval strategists would have needed reminding that sending a navy from Europe into the Sea of Japan was an exceptionally hazardous business. For the Russians at Tshushima in May 1905 it had been a catastrophe.[14] Even courting a quarrel (by the imposing of sanctions on Japanese trade) might expose British interests to threats and reprisals that would be hard to fend off without a strong naval presence, and unsafe to embark on without large reinforcements to send if need be.

As a result, and with no hope of forging an Anglo-American front, the British response was carefully muted. Japan was condemned by the League, but took little notice. However, the need to strengthen Britain's East Asian presence was taken up by the Admiralty which began its campaign for naval expansion and a fleet large enough to fight *simultaneously* in Europe and the Far East. Hitler's accession to power in January 1933, and his open rejection of disarmament in October that year, hugely strengthened its case. Even those who believed that Japan would only be dangerous if Britain were already embroiled elsewhere, now had to consider the renewed possibility of a conflict with Germany, by far the strongest (if only potentially) of the European powers. It was no longer a matter of an (improbable) war with France or Italy. If Germany resumed its old place as a great military power, the Navy would need to be able to impose a blockade (its weapon of choice) or contain a new German fleet built along pre-1914 lines. The Chiefs of Staff had already denounced (in March 1932) Britain's 'defenceless' position in East Asia. In November 1933, in the wake of Hitler's pro-nouncement, the Cabinet approved the creation of a 'Defence Require-ments Sub-Committee' to consider what extra spending was needed.[15] Its proceedings record the drastic alteration of the geopolitical scene since the halcyon days of 1926–31. But they also reveal the doubts and divisions over how best to respond to the (still dimly glimpsed) new patterns of power.

The argument turned on the relative dangers posed by German and Japanese aggression. In the Admiralty's view, Britain had to be able to deter and defeat an attack by Japan, which meant a strong Eastern fleet to match the Japanese navy. Japan, after all, was now a great island empire that stretched from the Kuriles to Taiwan and since 1918 into the Central and South Pacific; and a mainland power that ruled over Korea and the client state of Manchukuo (as Manchuria was renamed). The disarmament terms of the Washington treaties had barred new fortified bases in East Asian waters – a strategic boon to Japan which had little to fear from Hong Kong or American bases in Guam and the Philippines.[16] Even Singapore was poorly defended and lacked proper dry-docking facilities. Yet the Royal Navy had to defend Britain's interests in China (in an era when new markets had exceptional value), its commercial sea-lanes, its Southeast Asian possessions (and those of the Dutch, their strategic dependants), as well as two great provinces of the 'British world' in Australia and New Zealand. If it failed to do so, or suffered a setback in trying, the British world-system would suffer a staggering and perhaps irreversible blow. For, in a naval perspective, a defeat of this kind would quickly lead on to the loss of British control in the Indian Ocean, severing Britain's links with its most powerful possession of all, and opening the East and South African coasts to attack from the sea. The whole hinterland of British world power, that had helped Britain sustain the brutal struggle in Europe and the Middle East less than two decades earlier, would have been swept from its grasp. The rest would soon follow. This apocalyptic scenario was reinforced by the view that Japan had become a new 'Prussian' state: aggressive, militaristic and set on regional domination[17] – a suspicion that was strengthened by its further advance in North China. Japan was a real and immediate danger, so this argument ran: the Germans would follow in several years' time. But what was urgently necessary was the decision to build up the navy to be able to deal with them both simultaneously.[18]

But not everyone believed in the scale or immediacy of the Japanese challenge, let alone the wisdom of confronting it militarily. Britain could not fight two wars at once, said the Treasury flatly. Other expert opinion saw the Japanese threat as more economic than military, and hobbled by the resistance of Kuomintang China. Still others insisted that the Germans remained the 'ultimate' enemy – the phrase that crept into the Committee's report. If they were deterred, then the Japanese would not move. The fiercest attack on the navy's position came from Neville Chamberlain, now Chancellor of the Exchequer in the National Government. As Chancellor he was determined to keep defence spending within bounds, since the public finances were the bedrock of everything. But he was also (for a Chamberlain) surprisingly sceptical about the real threat from Japan and the fear it evoked in the Pacific dominions. His favoured solution was a friendly approach to Japan, perhaps even a pact.[19] The much more urgent priority in Chamberlain's eyes was the protection of Britain in Europe, and against attack from the air. This was best done not by expanding the navy but by deploying a 'deterrent' – a large force of bombers to cripple any potential assailant. When the Cabinet came to discuss the Committee's report, Chamberlain's campaign for an Anglo-Japanese understanding won little support. The objection was obvious – that it would wreck Anglo-American relations with far-reaching effects on Britain's general position – and also decisive. But there was no real agreement on how to proceed, perhaps because of the scale of the 'Eastern' commitment required. Instead, Chamberlain was allowed to draw up the final recommendations – a chance he seized with a vengeance. The result was to cut back the sum proposed for the navy by some 60 per cent and put it instead towards expanding the air force.[20]

The sometimes angry debate in Committee and Cabinet exposed the strategic dilemma of the whole British system. If the East was neglected the whole empire might fall. If the West was exposed, Britain itself was at risk. If both were defended to the level required, Britain would be bankrupt. It was not surprising, perhaps, that policymakers looked for less drastic solutions, and hoped to get by. The British and Americans both came to agree that the real restraint on Japan was the Soviet Union, which had much more to lose from Japan's East Asian imperialism, and had the military power to strike Japan where it mattered.[21] British officials worked hard to persuade the Americans that they shared the same view of Japan as a threat and would not jeopardise Anglo-American solidarity by an approach to Japan – whatever Chamberlain said. They largely succeeded. When the naval agreements came up for review in 1934–5, President Roosevelt conveyed by a nod and a wink that no objection would be made to Britain's

428 / 'The great liner is sinking'

naval expansion: Atlantic rivalry was suspended.[22] In Europe, meanwhile, the Admiralty won what it saw as a useful reprieve. Abandoning
the fiction that the Germans were bound by Versailles, it got Hitler's
agreement that a new German navy would be kept at just over one-
third of Britain's own strength – a concession that bought time for its
own naval programme.[23] When the Chiefs of Staff reviewed the state
of British defences at the start of 1935 (and before the agreement), they
made the grudging admission that there was enough naval strength to
fight Germany and Japan at the same time – as long as France was an
ally. 'With France as our Ally, the naval situation in Europe would wear
a different complexion, and the main British fleet would be available
to defend our Empire in the East.'[24] Six months later, their view was
much darker.

What had happened in between was a third great shock to the
geostrategic foundations of the British world-system. In late 1934, a
fierce dispute had blown up between Italy and Ethiopia on the border
between the Ethiopian Ogaden and Italian Somaliland. It soon became
clear that Mussolini had no intention of reaching a peaceful resolution and was set on the partial or total acquisition of Haile Selassie's
empire. The French government was concerned most of all to avoid
friction with Italy (its long-standing Mediterranean rival) which would
weaken its hand in dealing with Hitler. In January 1935, it agreed
that Rome should be free to deal with Ethiopia as it wished. This
confronted the British with an unpleasant dilemma. As the strongest
League power and champion of collective security, Britain could hardly
look on while one League member state set out to swallow another.
But taking the lead to thwart the aggressor was just as unwelcome.
Britain should not be manoeuvred 'into playing an isolated and futile
role of opposition', said Robert Vansittart, the permanent head of the
Foreign Office.[25] It was perfectly obvious, said a chorus of voices,
that the effort to do so would enrage Mussolini, and drive him out
of the League and into a compact with Hitler. Vansittart dreamed
hopelessly of an imperial deal: compensating an Ethiopian cession to
Italy with a tract of British Somaliland. The crisis, he said, was really
the fault of 'our hogging policy' in not giving the Italians one of the
German lost colonies. 'I have long thought the distribution of this limited globe quite untenable and quite unjustifiable. Like fools we made
it worse at Versailles... We are grossly overloaded.'[26] There was no
French support for such an exchange, and, by August 1935, the British

were contemplating the cost if the League imposed sanctions to restrain Mussolini.

Quite apart from the danger of playing into Germany's hands, the risk of an armed confrontation with Italy was regarded with horror in the Admiralty. Britain was quite unprepared for a conflict, the First Sea Lord warned.[27] The programme of replacements meant that the navy's strength would decline before it recovered at the end of the decade, so that even the loss of two or three large ships in a Mediterranean war would be calamitous.[28] Both he and Hankey, the powerful Secretary to the Committee of Imperial Defence, were determined that Britain should avoid being dragged into 'the miserable business of collective security' (Chatfield's phrase). What was needed was a two-power fleet to counter Germany and Japan, and good relations with Italy. As matters fell out, the British had the worst of both worlds. Under pressure, the Cabinet decided to apply certain sanctions to show disapproval. But, fearing to take the decisive step of imposing sanctions on oil, in December 1935 it despatched Samuel Hoare, the Foreign Secretary, to concert with the French on a new compromise offer that would give Mussolini effective control over much of Ethiopia: the infamous Hoare–Laval pact. Amid a huge public outcry (the government had just won re-election on a platform extolling its commitment to collective security), Hoare was disowned, the pact cast aside and 'light' sanctions maintained. Amid continuing high tension in the Mediterranean, the means and the will were lacking to challenge Hitler's forced remilitarisation of the Rhineland in March 1936. 'If we are seriously to consider the possibility of war with Germany', declared the Chiefs of Staff on 1 April, 'it is essential that the Services should be relieved of their Mediterranean responsibilities, otherwise our position is utterly unsafe.'[29] In May, Mussolini declared the war in Ethiopia won. In June, the British abandoned their sanctions. But the hope of restoring Anglo-Italian amity proved very far-fetched.

'There is now the possibility of a hostile Italy on our main line of imperial communications', reported the Defence Requirements Committee in November 1935.[30] By the following year, although there was some disagreement over Mussolini's objectives, Italy's hostility (and its alignment with Germany) had become a new fact of geopolitical life. The result was to force a drastic revision of imperial strategy. There could be no question of a war on three fronts: the Navy would have its hands full in the East and at home. The implication was brutal. Unless

French support was assured, the British could not hope to maintain their naval command in the Mediterranean if a crisis arose in the East. It was a tacit admission – despite public denials – that, faced with a war in the East, the route round the Cape and not the short route via Suez might have to be used. Britain's Middle East empire would have to fend for itself.[31] Of course, this was still just a grim calculation not an actual reality. But it hugely reinforced the sense of strain and anxiety that had begun to infuse British foreign policy as a whole.

It is important, however, not to exaggerate the scale of British difficulties as they appeared at this stage. In effect, what had happened was that, after the dream-like interval in which the peace of Europe had seemed safe, the British found themselves back in the world of competitive *Weltpolitik* they had known before 1914. The need to withdraw from the Mediterranean to meet the German threat had been accepted once before – in the great strategic rethink of 1912. The threat posed by Germany in 1936–7 was still modest indeed compared with that which had faced them in 1914. Of course, the real source of British, and especially naval, alarm was the new fact of dispersal. In 1914, the British could mass almost their whole fleet in the Orkneys, in the knowledge that the blockade of German sea-power would keep their Empire secure. Now they must divide their sea strength in two at opposite ends of the globe if their rivals coalesced. The most urgent requirement that followed from this was to ease the friction with Italy, while pressing on with the rearmament needed for a 'new standard' navy that could face down the Germans and the Japanese, simultaneously if need be. It was from this position of strength that British leaders hoped to restore 'discipline' to Europe's diplomacy, and persuade the Hitler regime that it would gain little by delaying a new general settlement. In the meantime, of course, they had to be cautious, and sometimes disingenuous – as when they reassured the Pacific dominions that they would guard the Mediterranean as well as sending the fleet to Singapore, come what may. 'Singapore', said Lord Chatfield, the First Sea Lord and professional head of the navy, 'was first class assurance for the security of Australia.'[32] It was vital not to provoke their three possible enemies into a real (as opposed to rhetorical) combination.[33] But, if they kept up their guard, and avoided a crisis, the long-run alignment of forces seemed set in their favour. 'Welfare states', remarked Alfred Zimmern (he meant the democratic states of Europe, the United States and the white dominions), 'enjoy an overwhelming preponderance of power, confirmed and increased by their command of the oceans, except for the time being the Western Pacific.'[34] Rejecting economic concessions to Germany, Neville Chamberlain expected the improvement in world trade (and the rise in world prices) to force an eventual retreat from Hitler's policy of arms and autarky.[35] Indeed, almost as much as before 1914, the British expected that their commerce power would have the last word in any global confrontation – as long as they played their cards well in the game of world politics.

The new economics of Empire

At first sight, such confidence seems strange. After all, the British economy lived in the shadow of depression as much as any other. There were also good grounds for thinking that the British had been the great losers from the economic catastrophe of 1929–31 and the huge contraction in world trade that had set in thereafter – just as they had prospered in the era of trade boom before 1914. Worse still, they had entered the depression from a position of weakness: burdened by debt; with their old staple industries of cotton and coal in decline; and with their exports held back by the high value of sterling. Because the collapse of world prices in 1930 was severest in commodities like grain, rice, rubber and minerals, it was primary producers that were hardest hit. As their incomes declined, so did their imports. For the British at home this meant a triple disaster. Much of their export trade was directed towards such primary producers, in their Empire especially. The great commodities traffic, and the reverse flow of manufactures, employed much British shipping – a critical source of invisible income. And a huge amount of British capital was still invested in the infrastructure needed to bring primary goods to market (railways, harbours, freezing works, warehousing etc.) as well as in their actual production on plantations and in mines. The slump in world trade threatened British wealth on almost all fronts.

Indeed, it is easy to see the 1930s as marking the great watershed in Britain's capacity to meet the economic demands of imperial power, or to sustain a world-system of which it was the leader. As many contemporaries observed, the engines that had driven the long age of expansion up to 1914 now seemed worn out. British manufactures lost their competitive edge and also a large part of their market. The failure was most glaring in the sad condition of the textile industry, especially Lancashire cottons. Before 1914, textiles made up around 40 per cent of British exports by value; and the British supplied two-thirds of the world trade in cotton goods. By 1938, that figure had fallen to around a quarter.[36] In India, by far Lancashire's best market in 1913, its sales had fallen by nearly 90 per cent by the end of the 1930s.[37] Overall, Britain's share of the world's manufactured exports fell from 25 per cent in 1913 to 19 per cent in 1937, partly reflecting the fact that its newer industries (like cars and pharmaceuticals) could not fill the gap left by the old and declining industries. Industrial weakness was bound to do damage to British trade and traders. Without competitive goods to sell, British trading companies that had played a large role in the organisation of commerce in Asia, Africa and Latin America found themselves under pressure from European, American and Japanese rivals. Some went to the wall and their misfortunes spilt over to affect London's place in world trade.[38] These difficulties in the export of goods were matched by the fall-off in the export of capital. Partly because of the effects of the slump in the traditional fields of British investment, partly because of public and private borrowing at home, the amounts raised in London for overseas issues fell to perhaps one tenth of their pre-1914 level[39] virtually all of it for sterling country destinations. In the harsh conditions of the 1930s, the British seemed to have abandoned the practice once regarded as vital to their commercial success: priming the pump of economic development in less-developed countries, and creating consumers for their export industries. Finally, as if all this was not enough, it looked as if the long surge of population growth in mainland Britain had finally petered out. The 'export surplus' of migrants would no longer pour out to the 'white dominions'. Perhaps even more serious was the clear implication that, as a market for foodstuffs (the staples of Canadian, Australian and New Zealand trade), Britain was now stagnant.[40] Perhaps the old mutual interest in markets, money and men between Britain and its 'invisible empire' of trade (inside and outside the 'visible' Empire) was just fading away.

The causes went deeper than the apparent shortcomings of the British economy. Much of Britain's prosperity before the First World War had been due to the relative openness of markets in Europe and Latin America, as well as in Asia, where free trade was imposed by rule (as in India) or by force (as in China). Free trading conditions encouraged the investment of capital, whose dividend could be paid from the proceeds of exports that reached the world market through London. They made it natural for many primary-product economies to rely on British shipping, insurance and banks to get their produce to market and manage its sale. But, after 1918, there was no real return to the age of free-ish trade. Instead, the disruptions of war, the burden of debt (requiring new revenue sources) and the break-up of empires in Europe and the Near East fostered economic nationalism: to safeguard domestic prosperity against external upheaval and (in new states especially) to reinforce weak political bonds with the glue of economic self-interest. Agrarian protection became almost universal in Europe.[41] With the onset of slump, things got far worse. Soviet Russia and Germany became closed autarkic economies. The United States withdrew behind massive walls of protection – the Smoot–Hawley tariff of 1930. Existing tariff barriers (as in the 'white dominions') rose higher. Exchange control became widespread, threatening the multilateral pattern of trade with bilateral bargains and barter. None of this boded well for British finance, trade and industry. Nor, at least in the short term, did another new feature of the global economy, the industrialisation of Asia. It was the intense competition of Japanese cottons, combined with the growth of textile manufacture in India, which destroyed so much of Lancashire's market. Even in China, where mechanised production had developed more slowly, it was a similar story. There, British cottons sold barely 1 per cent of their 1913 figure in 1936.[42]

Despite all these setbacks, the decade of depression in the world economy did not bring a collapse in British economic power. But it did lead to big changes in the way that it worked. The impact of the crash on the New York stock exchange in October 1929, and the trade contraction that followed, were soon felt in London. Unemployment rose steeply from 1.2 million in 1929 to 1.9 million the following year and 2.6 million in 1931. The balance of payments grew less healthy and then crashed into deficit. Public spending shot up to meet the new burdens of borrowing and benefits. As American lenders began to call in their loans to meet obligations at home, they sparked a banking crisis in Europe where too much had been lent 'long' on the back of American funds. Soon, those who held sterling in London (attracted in part by the high interest rates offered there) became anxious to sell it or exchange it for gold (the pound was freely convertible) for similar reasons. By August 1931, the loss of gold was acute, while the 'unbalanced' budget stoked fears of financial collapse, as the government borrowed more to meet

434 / 'The great liner is sinking'

its current outgoings. Governing without an overall majority, Ramsay MacDonald accepted the need for an all-party coalition, a 'national' government to meet the emergency. What began as a temporary measure, to last for a few weeks, became a coalition regime that endured for a decade. Likewise, its emergency actions to forestall the danger of sterling's collapse shaped an economic regime that lasted until it was overcome by disaster after June 1940.

The National Government took two crucial decisions. The first was to abandon the fixed price of sterling in gold, allowing the pound to 'float' against other currencies. In effect, the pound was devalued. Since sterling was still the most widely used currency in international trade (and thus a source of great profit to the City of London), such a move might have seemed exceptionally risky, to be reversed as quickly as conditions allowed. But that is not what happened. Instead, sterling was left to float for the rest of the decade, while remaining convertible. For much of that time, between 1933 and 1938, its value was stable, and the pound kept its status as the principal medium of international exchange. There were two reasons for this.

The first was London's success in forming a large 'sterling bloc', whose members pegged the value of their currency to sterling, and kept much if not all of their reserves of foreign exchange as sterling. This formed a huge trading zone – the largest in the world – whose currencies enjoyed a stable relationship. Parts of this zone had little choice in the matter. The monetary affairs of Britain's colonial territories were run by local 'currency boards'. A colony's money supply was directly controlled by the size and value of its sterling reserve in London. When London devalued, so did the colony. Much the same was true – although with considerably more argument – in the case of India. India suffered badly from the fall in commodity prices and the fragile state of its public finances (with their heavy dependence on customs receipts and agrarian revenues) threatened to damage the value of the rupee – a situation made worse by the protracted uncertainty over India's new constitution. A further large complication was India's sterling debt – the so-called 'Home Charges' – made up of pensions, loan interest and the annual bill for the large British garrison, all of whose costs fell on the Indian budget. London insisted that the Home Charges be paid, whatever the price. It demanded that the rupee remained pegged to sterling, and vetoed any idea of reducing its value in sterling terms. The reason it could do so was that, although the Viceroy and his government enjoyed some fiscal autonomy (and would have liked more), ultimate control over India's external finances was kept firmly in Whitehall, even after the promise of dominion self-government in the 1935 Act.[43]

With other users of sterling, London relied not on rule but self-interest. In three of the six white dominions, Australia, New Zealand and South Africa, the local pound was now pegged to sterling, not gold.[44] Here, the British market was all-important and commercial banking was too enmeshed with the City to make any alternative viable – although South Africa's gold and its nationalist politics kept it on the gold standard until 1933. Canada might have followed with its dollar except for the scale of its debts in New York: the fall of sterling against the American dollar had made this too much of a risk. Two 'semi-colonies' did follow: Egypt, which sold almost all its raw cotton to Britain (and sold little else), and Iraq (a British mandate until 1932). Lastly, there was a group of European states – the four Nordic countries and Portugal – for whom Britain's huge share of their exports and their dependence on sterling receipts, made pegging on sterling the key to financial stability.

Secondly, the attractions of sterling were greatly reinforced by the overall success of its management. This was jealously guarded in London and largely controlled not so much by the Bank as by the Treasury and the 'Exchange Equalisation Account' whose funds it supplied.[45] The object of the Account was partly to prevent sterling rising or falling too sharply. But it was also meant to ensure that sterling's value was kept at a level that allowed 'cheap money' – interest rates of around 2 per cent – to prevail in Britain. A cheap money policy helped Britain recover from depression more quickly than most other economies (the main exception was Japan) and much more quickly than the United States. Financially conservative governments (pursuing balanced budgets) reassured overseas holders of sterling. The result, so it seemed, was a virtuous circle. The willingness of sterling bloc countries to keep substantial balances in London helped to strengthen the pound. The balances allowed London to keep up sterling's value, despite the large deficit in Britain's balance of payments, without drawing down its investment overseas. Indeed, they even permitted some modest new issues to sterling countries abroad – as the tacit pay-off for their discretion and loyalty.[46]

In the depths of the crisis in 1931–2, the British government had taken a second decision no less far-reaching than 'going off gold'. At the

Imperial Conference in 1930, the Labour government and its Cobdenite chancellor, Philip Snowden, had dismissed the idea of a graded tariff on imports to give dominion producers a privileged share in the British market. But, as economic prospects grew bleaker, the appeal of protection in Britain, once confined to sections of the *industrial* economy, became almost irresistible. Even the City, where free trade sentiment had usually been strong, had now been won over.[47] Over the protests of its rump of free traders, the National Government (whose leaders had decided to seek an electoral mandate in October 1931) agreed to impose a new general tariff. The clinching argument was that action was needed to check the huge wave of imports and a further run on the pound.[48] However, Neville Chamberlain's import duties bill in February 1932[49] offered to delay tariffs against British Empire countries to allow time to arrange a system of mutual preferences. This was the purpose of the Ottawa Conference in 1932.

The Ottawa system marked the double departure of Britain from free trade. The British had adopted unilateral protection to save their balance of payments and the value of sterling, and to guard what remained of their agriculture against an impending disaster. With the Ottawa system they emerged as the leader of a large trading bloc, whose members favoured each other by discriminatory tariffs – the so-called 'imperial preference'. Needless to say, this did not mean that London imposed its commercial agenda – we shall see in a minute that the City's commercial empire had very mixed fortunes after 1930. If the British delegation had hoped for 'empire free trade' – giving their manufactures free entry to dominion markets, they were quickly disabused. Dominion leaders were determined to protect their own 'infant' industries, and would not have survived had they failed to do so. They were (as always) deeply suspicious of London's official 'machine' – the bureaucratic phrase-mongers who would tie them in knots – and its political masters. As Joseph Chamberlain's son, Neville Chamberlain might have expected a warm Canadian welcome, especially from Prime Minister Bennett, a Canadian tory. But Bennett, said Chamberlain (privately), 'lied like a trooper and . . . alternately blustered, bullied, sobbed, prevaricated, delayed and obstructed to the very last moment'.[50] The British delegates found themselves conceding preferential access to the British market. What they got in return was far from free entry: it was more like exemption from the still higher tariff rates that were piled on non-British imports. Hence the best estimate is that, while the Empire countries increased their share of Britain's imports by around 10 per cent, their share of British exports grew by only half that figure: the effects on British output were marginal.[51] The Empire market, despite much excitable rhetoric,[52] could not be the saviour of the British export economy.

Yet British leaders were not entirely dissatisfied. They wanted to protect Britain's own floundering agriculture, but could hardly have done so without some concession to dominion producers. They may have thought that offering imperial preference would help to silence demands for a general devaluation of dominion currencies against sterling, with dangerous consequences for its strength and stability. Ensuring the dominions' access to the market in Britain would make it less difficult for them to remit what they owed in interest and dividends. They had also checked the drift upwards of dominion tariffs against British goods. Most of all, perhaps, they hoped that the agreed lowering of tariffs among all Empire countries would create a zone of recovery that would encourage other states.[53] Meanwhile, they pressed on with the making of bilateral agreements with those non-Empire countries with whom their commercial relations were close. Denmark (which competed with Canada in supplying bacon to the British breakfast-table) was given a fixed share of the market in return for its promise to buy British coal.[54] Similar agreements were made with the other Scandinavian countries. In 1933, the so-called Roca–Runciman pact allowed Argentina, which sent 40 per cent of its exports to Britain, to keep almost all its pre-Ottawa share of the British market for chilled beef. The price the British attached for throwing this lifeline (no other market existed for Argentine beef) was that almost all the foreign exchange that Buenos Aires earned from Britain would be used to remit the interest and dividends from the large British investment in the country's railways and utilities. These had been blocked by Argentina's exchange control since the onset of depression.[55]

Imperial preference and the pacts London made with the 'agreement' countries helped to stave off the worst effects of depression and also the danger that other countries would retaliate against the British recourse to devaluation and protection.[56] They softened the blow of export weakness elsewhere – against Japanese and Indian competition, the closing of Germany, and universal high tariffs. But, by 1937, it was clear that they could not reverse the relative decline of British economic power since the First World War. In the ten years before 1914, the deficit on merchandise trade had usually been balanced by the income that poured in from investments overseas, so that when other invisible trade was added the result was a large current account surplus. In the 1930s, this ceased to be true, as imports surged up and invisibles fell back. This reflected in part the senescence of parts of London's commercial empire – its huge holdings in railways and shipping, now largely unprofitable – and the loss of income from commodity trades. Though the British kept their grip on telecommunications[57] in other new industries like civil aircraft and oil (on which global pre-eminence would come to depend) they were less well placed than the United States. Nor could the British deter even their closest trade partners from the quest for new markets (as Australia looked to Japan), and greater self-sufficiency in industrial goods. Neville Chamberlain admitted as much. The dominions, he noted in May 1936,

> have reached an important turning-point in their
> history . . . It must be brought home to them that their most
> important market, namely the United Kingdom, could no
> longer absorb their expanding production, and in years to
> come would take a diminishing rather than increasing share
> of their production . . . If the Dominions in future were to
> be able to find employment for an increasing population,
> they must develop their secondary industries.[58]

Yet, for the moment at least, the British held on. London remained the centre of a great commercial system commanding almost one-third of world trade.[59] It was no longer the 'Queen City' of its Edwardian heyday: the United States was too powerful. It frustrated the British attempt to devalue the pound against the American dollar – by devaluing the dollar. Its huge gold reserve, the new gold-backed dollar (revalued against gold in 1934) and its massive industrial power made its enmity dangerous in economic affairs. At moments of crisis, capital lodged in London might flee to New York. But it seems premature to assume that America had taken Britain's old place as the pivot of the world economy. The American commitment to free trade (under the Reciprocal Trade Agreement Act of 1934) made only limited progress.[60] America remained mired in depression and recovered much more slowly than Britain. And, while the Americans had invested abroad at a much higher rate than the British between

1924 and 1931, the roles were reversed thereafter when US investment slumped almost to nothing.[61] In a world economy without a single great centre, the British were still a great economic power, able to muster huge foreign resources and call up old debts. But the Achilles heel of their system – the lack of a war-chest in American dollars, and the frailty of the pound once Europe lurched towards war – would soon be revealed.

The Empire state

How did opinion in Britain react to the upheaval and stress that afflicted the British world-system after 1929? There was some reason to doubt whether an electorate now based on universal adult suffrage (women under thirty were enfranchised in 1928) would respond sympathetically to the calls for rearmament or approve the confrontation with Germany, Italy and Japan over the fate of 'far-off countries of which we know nothing'. Beset by economic misfortune at home, would the British electorate regard the furious parliamentary arguments over Indian self-rule that raged from 1930 until 1934 as an annoying distraction and India itself as an unprofitable burden better quickly laid down? Would a fully democratic electorate repudiate the coercive and authoritarian methods on which imperial rule still had to depend? Would the feeling of kinship towards 'overseas Britons' survive in an age when migration had ground to a halt? With the violent contraction of world trade, had the old argument of empire – that it helped to secure industrial employment at home – now gone by the board? Would the public see the Empire as an obsolete shell, a set of futile global commitments bringing neither profit nor honour? After all, the most striking effect of depression on the British economy was the apparent decline of its external dependence. Exports had absorbed one-quarter of output in 1914. Twenty years later, that proportion had halved. Had Britain turned inward?

There were certainly many Conservatives who feared the advance of 'socialist' sympathies in the new mass electorate, and the careless indifference of 'socialist' governments to the value of empire. They liked to contrast the tough-minded realism of Conservative attitudes, and their genuine devotion to the imperial 'ideal' (a nebulous relic to which many laid claim), with the naïve sentimentality of their

Labour opponents. In their nightmare scenario, an electorate enraged by economic disaster might return an 'extreme' socialist government that neglected the navy, alienated the dominions, succumbed to the blandishments of Gandhi in India, and abandoned Britain's claim to great power authority in Europe, the Middle East and East Asia. In reality, of course, the electorate showed little interest in such drastic solutions. The Labour ministry of 1929–31 was a minority government that had won fewer votes at the 1929 election than the Conservative party. When its leaders threw in the towel in August 1931 and agreed to an all-party coalition to meet the economic emergency, they split from the bulk of the Labour party which refused to cut unemployment benefit to balance the budget. The electorate endorsed the new 'national' government at the general election of October 1931, and did so again – although not quite so enthusiastically – in November 1935.[62] The result from 1931 onwards was governments (under Ramsay MacDonald, Baldwin and Chamberlain) that were Conservative-dominated and depended upon huge Conservative majorities in the House of Commons. Thus, while it was true that the economic, political and international crises of a 'low, dishonest decade' evoked an outpouring of radical, socialist and communist comment, and the 'decadence' of Western civilisation in general and parliamentary government in particular united extremists of Left and Right, this was barely reflected in the actual mobilisation of public opinion or its electoral expression.

Perhaps part of the reason was that economic misfortune was felt very unevenly across British society. Some regions – those where the old staples of textiles, shipbuilding and coal were still strongly entrenched – suffered acute unemployment and the deprivation that followed. South Wales, Lancashire, Northeast England and industrial Scotland were especially hard-hit. Here, political feeling displayed deep alienation from the Victorian ethos of liberal capitalism, including perhaps the Victorian conception of a free-trading empire. The sense of betrayal was sharpened by the irony that it was in these old staple regions that wages had been highest, labour unions strongest, and awareness of Britain's great place in the world most widely diffused. But the critical fact was that, despite all their visible hardship, the 'old' industrial regions were not representative of the British economy as a whole. The 1930s also saw the rapid expansion of the 'neotechnic' industries: electrical goods, chemicals, cars and (later) aircraft. Much of this new industry was built on greenfield sites in the Midlands and the South, and especially around London. It sucked in migrants from the depressed regions of mainland Britain and Ireland.[63] For those in *continuous* employment, the huge fall in prices after 1930 in many basic commodities meant a large real rise in their standard of living perhaps by as much as 30 per cent.[64] This new 'disposable' income fuelled the demand for a vast wave of housebuilding (and the transport systems that went with it) as well as for consumer products and leisure: cars, telephones, electric cookers, toys, hobbies, the cinema and holidays. One other key point should be noted. While depression had devastating effects on the skilled working class of the old industrial regions, it left the middle-class fifth of the population not only largely unscathed, but also (because of the price fall) generally better off.[65] Political stability after 1931 was at least partly built on this relative middle-class contentment.

At the time, of course, stability often seemed both elusive and fragile. The famous East Fulham by-election in October 1933 saw an anti-government swing of 29 per cent. In the Putney election in the following year, the swing was almost as large. Both raised the spectre (in Conservative minds) of a great Labour triumph in the next general election. They suggested the volatility of public opinion, and the political hazards of more economic misfortune or diplomatic embarrassment. They help to explain the efforts of Baldwin, the Conservative leader (1923–37), to strike a conciliatory, reassuring, even sentimental note in his public addresses, and lay claim to the centre-ground in British politics.[66] Baldwin was understandably nervous that public perception of disarray, uncertainty or precipitate action in economic policy, foreign policy or imperial questions would destroy the credibility of the National Government, before and after he succeeded MacDonald as prime minister in June 1935. But, as it turned out, there was no real danger that opinion at home would become disenchanted with the costs and burdens of the British world-system or with the sometimes machiavellian pragmatism that its upkeep required.

One reason for this was the broad public sympathy for the goal of rearmament. Despite the emphasis given in the official debate to the imperial threat posed by Japanese sea-power, it was the defence of Britain itself that took centre stage in public discussion. As Neville Chamberlain saw, reinforcing Britain's *air* power to deter an aggressor was the least controversial way of spending more on defence. There was no real public debate about the cost of *imperial* (as opposed to home)

defence, or about the load Britain carried of far-flung commitments. Perhaps paradoxically, public support for 'collective security' – joint action
to uphold the principles of the League of Nations Covenant – chimed
with the notion of Britain's great power obligations. The National Government wrapped itself carefully in this ideological cloak, so much so
that it was forced to disavow the attempt to reach an agreement with
Italy at the expense of Abyssinia's independence – the abortive Hoare –
Laval pact. It was helped by the incoherence of the Labour opposition,
torn between support for collective security, opposition to armaments
and the pacifism of its party leader, George Lansbury, until his displacement by Attlee in 1935. On the other hand, the public mood promised
little support for a bellicose reaction to Italian and German demands.
There was nothing to resemble the naval scare of 1909 and the jingo
outcry that followed. The military threat to Britain's overseas interests, the dominions, India or the colonies, remained conjectural and
speculative. Those who claimed otherwise risked being denounced as
scaremongers or worse. Thus the real constraint on the government's
defence programme was not public pressure for more arms or less,
but the need, as it seemed, to limit public expenditure (to protect the
value of sterling) and avoid a worsening trade deficit (if more export
production were switched over to weapons).

The economic pattern was similar. In the past, the part played
by the Empire in Britain's prosperity had been sometimes fiercely
debated. Even those who conceded that command of the seas and of
the Indian sub-continent were vital ingredients of economic success
balked at the idea of the Empire as an economic community. Because
British trade and investment were global in scale and not simply imperial (Britain's European trade and Latin American investments were
among the obvious cases), imperial self-sufficiency held little appeal to
the economically literate. By contrast, free trade had a talismanic attraction as the source of cheap food (and thus higher working-class living
standards) and of the City's pre-eminence in global finance. Those who
demanded an imperial tariff, offering preferential access to the British
market for the white dominions – the programme of Chamberlainism
before 1914 – met entrenched opposition. The claim that this would
bind the dominions more closely to their imperial mother-country cut
little ice. Then, and again in 1923, the electorate rejected protection. By
1930, however, the tide had turned almost completely. As the depression bit deeper, industry, agriculture, the trade unions and the City

all swung round in favour. As foreign markets grew tighter or closed altogether, the willingness of the dominions to offer reciprocal preference looked much more attractive. In a world of trade blocs, colonies acquired a new value – however inflated by economic illusion. The claim that Lancashire's battered cotton industry would suffer directly from more Indian self-government – because Indian politicians would increase the protection of their own cotton interests – threatened a backlash at home against London's scheme for reform. Indeed, it seems likely that the popular image of the Empire as the source for Britain's food and raw materials – Canadian wheat, Australian wool, New Zealand butter – like South Africa's revived reputation (for a much smaller band) as a fount of gold-mining profits, was really fixed in the 1930s, even if its roots were laid earlier. For investors, exporters and consumers alike, the sterling economy had become indispensable. It was left to *The Economist* and a few lonely voices to denounce the recourse to protection and preference as an economic blind alley.[67]

The turn to protection was not the only great change in Britain's relation to other parts of its world-system. At almost the same time as the Cabinet agreed to press ahead with the tariff, the Statute of Westminster was passing through Parliament. The Statute was meant to settle once and for all the constitutional link between Britain and the self-governing dominions. It renounced all claim by the British Parliament to legislate for the dominions (except with their explicit consent), effectively conferring full sovereignty upon them. In substance, the issue had been resolved at the Imperial Conference of 1926, when Balfour's subtle formula had acknowledged the equality of all the self-governing states – Canada, Australia, New Zealand, South Africa, the Irish Free State and Newfoundland – with Britain itself.[68] What remained to be done was to set the new rule in statutory stone, if only to guard against judicial perversity. The reason for this was that law still in force – the Colonial Laws Validity Act 1865 – explicitly licensed the Imperial Parliament to legislate if it chose for every part of the Empire and forbade the dominions from passing laws repugnant to an Imperial Act.[69] British ministers regarded the turgid report that emerged with little enthusiasm as 'an attempt to write by lawyers a very complicated constitution which had better never been written at all'.[70] 'Personally, I am rather sorry', wrote the Lord Chancellor Sankey when the Statute was passed, 'but after Balfour's declaration we had no choice.'[71] For British politicians and officials, the detailed spelling out of dominion equality was a tiresome obligation imposed by the need to appease the 'troublesome' (Sankey's description) South Africans and Irish. But they saw little cause for concern except on two points. The first was how the new statutory definition of dominion rights might affect the status of India (whose future dominionhood had been affirmed by the Viceroy in October 1929). The Cabinet was anxious that its right to declare India a dominion should not have to depend on the (uncertain) approval of the other dominions.[72] It was also uneasy that, under the draft statute, a dominion could repeal an Imperial Act. As its main legal adviser on India pointed out, once India was declared a dominion, the elaborate statutory 'safeguards' by which London proposed to limit the powers of its new responsible government could be cast off in a trice.[73] This proved a gift later to the opponents of their Indian reforms. The other source of anxiety was the likely effect of the Statute on the Anglo-Irish treaty of 1921, the constitutional basis of the Irish Free State's reluctant allegiance to the British Crown. Among Conservative MPs (an overwhelming Commons majority at the time of the Statute's passage through Parliament), mistrust of Irish intentions ran deep. Since the treaty took the form of an Imperial Act, it was certainly arguable that under the Statute the Free State parliament could repeal it at will.

As a result, when the draft statute was debated in November 1931, it made 'heavy weather'.[74] Churchill, the grand rebel, appealed to both strands of the Die Hard tradition, linking Ireland and India in a Cassandra-like warning of impending decay. Ominously for the government, he drew 'ministerial cheers' – support from the Conservative benches.[75] To ward off the danger of a deeply embarrassing retreat (and an open division among the Conservative followers of the National Government), all the stops were pulled out. Jimmy Thomas, the rough diamond Dominions Secretary, warned that any delay would enrage not just the Irish but the South Africans as well. The Attorney-General, Inskip, insisted (inaccurately) that the legal standing of the Anglo-Irish treaty was unaffected by the Statute (a view overturned by the House of Lords three years later). A letter from Cosgrave, the Free State prime minister, was read out in the Commons, denying any intent to alter the treaty except by agreement. Austen Chamberlain, the party's grandest elder statesman and (like Churchill) a signatory of the treaty, declared his faith in the Free State government. Baldwin, as party leader, warned his supporters that delaying the Statute would deeply offend the dominions 'even the most British of them', and shrewdly referred to the prize that most of them (though not Churchill) wanted most: the forthcoming conference on imperial economic unity.[76] It was enough to secure an overwhelming majority.

As Churchill had prophesied, Cosgrave soon dropped through the trap-door, to be replaced by De Valera. But, the Free State apart, most opinion in Britain observed little change in the dominion relationship. Jimmy Thomas' claim that the Statute was the 'cutting away of dead wood which will render possible new growth'[77] was largely accepted. Certainly, among ministers, scepticism about the honesty and even the intelligence of dominion politicians was deeply ingrained. Close encounter at Ottawa reinforced this impression: 'Bennett a cad and deceitful' (Baldwin); 'Bluff!! Mendacity!! Dishonest!! Liar!!' (Neville Chamberlain); 'Bennett a liar' (Thomas).[78] The financial instincts of Australian leaders were viewed with suspicion. When New Zealand's first Labour government declared its support for a 'planned economy', the reaction was bemused irritation at such doctrinaire folly. But, if most politicians in the overseas dominions were regarded in Britain as parochial in outlook and meagre in talent, they also seemed free of any 'nationalist' aspirations to 'real' independence. The 'British' identity of Canada, Australia and New Zealand was taken for granted. The exception was South Africa, whose 'native policy' had already attracted humanitarian disapproval in Britain.[79] But doubts over South African 'loyalty' were largely assuaged by the entry of Smuts into coalition with Hertzog in 1933. The most ardent British imperialists, including Leo Amery, Edward Grigg and Lionel Curtis who kept the Milnerite faith, were also among Smuts' warmest admirers. Appeasing Afrikaner demands for the symbols of sovereignty was the surest way, so they argued, of creating a loyal Anglo-Afrikaner dominion. They looked forward to the prospect of a union of two peoples (the blacks were invisible) that would 'follow the history of the Union of England and Scotland'.[80] The powerful Anglo-South African interest entrenched in the City, at *The Times*, and in academe as well, exerted its influence against any criticism that might offend Afrikaners and endanger the prospects of 'fusion' as the South African historian, W. M. Macmillan, found when coming to Britain in 1934.[81]

This complacent British view of their dominion relations did not extend to India. Between 1928 and 1935, three British governments wrestled with Indian 'reform': to frame a new constitution that would win Indian consent – or at least acquiescence. Part of their problem was the refusal of the Congress to accept anything short of full independence, with a 'strong' central government. But they were also hemmed in by the widespread unease in the Conservative party that extended well beyond the notorious Die Hards. Neither the minority Labour government of 1929–31 nor the National Government that followed it could hope to enact a new constitution unless its Conservative critics were kept to a minimum. The main difficulty lay in persuading Conservative party opinion that elective self-government should be granted not just to the provinces (as the 1930 Simon Report had proposed and to which even most Die Hards agreed), but to the centre as well, and that India should be promised a future as a self-governing dominion. A loud chorus of outrage, orchestrated by Churchill, denounced both these ideas. It drew on a mass of inherited prejudice about Indian incapacity (lovingly cultivated by generations of 'Old India Hands'), as well as more recent alarm about caste and communal violence. It castigated the betrayal of imperial duty, an ethos still loudly proclaimed in other parts of the Empire. It exploited the embarrassing absence of Indian leaders pledged to work the reforms in a loyal and cooperative spirit, and pointed instead to the Congress campaign of civil disobedience from mid-1930. It took up the cause of Lancashire cotton, whose waning market in India might decline even more if a self-governing India adopted local protection. It evoked an intangible sense that conceding self-rule to 'babu' politicians (so often the butt of official disparagement) would mark a shameful defeat, a blow to 'race-pride', and a public avowal that British 'decline' had become irreversible.

The pull of these powerful emotions was sometimes unnerving. To Conservative leaders, the danger of being painted as less than loyal to the Empire posed an obvious risk. A sudden upset in India might set off an earthquake in the mood of their followers. Their endorsement of the 1933 constitutional plan offering India responsible government at the centre, and future dominionhood as an 'All-India' federation, was shot through with unease. Yet, at the reform bill's second reading in February 1935, it was supported by more than three-quarters of Conservative MPs.[82] It seems very unlikely that (as has sometimes been claimed) this decisive result reflected a falling away in the British commitment to Empire. Its arduous passage suggests quite the reverse. The real explanation for the success of the bill was both the widespread belief that (in its eventual form) it would secure key British interests without a sterile (and costly) repression, and the backing it won from almost all senior politicians. To accuse this great phalanx of age and authority (what Lord Hugh Cecil called 'Front Benchdom'[83]) of being indifferent to the safety of British world power was too much even for Churchill.

But what lay behind this consensus, and how had it been built? Perhaps the critical stage was the conversion of Baldwin, the Conservative leader, to the need to make more than purely provincial concessions, and offer progress towards Indian self-government at the centre. Like Ramsay MacDonald, Baldwin accepted the view of Lord Irwin (whom he had appointed as Viceroy) that a way had to be found to reconcile Indian 'moderate' opinion to the British connection, and that to appear to renege on the promise of eventual self-government made in 1917 would be politically fatal. It chimed with his instinct that the art of good government was holding the centre against the extremes – in both Britain and India. On three vital occasions – in November 1929, in March 1931 and in December 1934 – Baldwin threw all his prestige behind the cause of reform. His message was shrewd. Again and again he insisted that the aim of concession was 'to keep India in the Empire';[84] that to fall back on repression 'would break up the Empire' (a silent reminder of Ireland);[85] that 'the Empire was organic and alive and in constant process of evolution'[86] and could not be governed by Victorian methods. 'The present proposals', he told his Cabinet colleagues in March 1933 when the reform scheme white paper was about to be published, 'might save India to the Empire, but if they were not introduced we should certainly lose it.'[87] Indeed, far from conceding that Britain's position in India had become a lost cause, or that its Empire was redundant, Baldwin argued the opposite, portraying his Die Hard opponents as defeatists and wreckers with obsolescent ideas. 'The Empire of today', he declared in a memorable phrase, 'is not the Empire of the first Jubilee.'[88]

Baldwin could count on two useful supports. First, some of the most ardent imperialists shared his view of India, including Geoffrey Dawson, the editor of *The Times*. They rejected Die Hard ideas as crude and old-fashioned, and Churchill himself as a political fossil. Secondly, the expert advice from the 'men on the spot' echoed the need for an advance at the centre to draw the sting of the Congress and force it back into 'constitutional' politics. Two recent ex-Viceroys, Lords Reading (1921–6) and Irwin (1926–31), pressed the same case.[89]

Retired Indian officials were quietly called up to preach the new gospel. The 'Union of Britain and India' society was formed in May 1933 to back the white paper policy: its chairman, steering committee and membership were almost entirely made up from former members of the Indian Civil Service.[90] Churchill could play on the fears of Conservative activists and enjoyed the support of two great press barons, Rothermere and Beaverbrook, both old foes of Baldwin. But some of his allies mistrusted his motives; his tactics in Parliament offended even some of his friends; and his knowledge of India was transparently shallow. The Die Hards' best hope was to stir up enough internal party division to frighten the leadership into dropping the bill. Their most dangerous claim was that under its rules the Congress would capture the vast bulk of the seats in any central assembly, and that an Indian dominion on the Statute of Westminster model could repeal any safeguards that London laid down. It was precisely these points that worried Austen Chamberlain, who exerted his influence over a large middle group otherwise sympathetic to the government scheme. But, once the Cabinet agreed to excise any reference to India's future 'Dominion Status' from the bill, and to adopt indirect election to the proposed federal assembly, it won over the last major figure with the power to obstruct it.[91] Of the seventy-nine Conservative MPs who rejected the bill in February 1935, only Churchill himself had held cabinet rank. 'Front benchdom' had triumphed.

The price of consensus had been a large helping of caution. The bill's supporters assumed that India's advance to self-government would be closely controlled by the Viceroy (armed with an arsenal of 'safeguards'); that London's grip on India's army and its external relations would remain absolute for a long time to come; that the Congress would be hobbled by the constitutional privileges conferred on the Muslims and Princes; and that India's dominionhood (the content of which was left carefully vague) would only begin at an unspecified time in the future. How far these conditions could be imposed in fact, and in constitutional theory, will be discussed later on. But, as an index of British ideas about their own place in the world, the Act is revealing. The sound and fury of the Die Hard campaign was a noisy distraction. What really stood out was the solid insistence of the most ardent reformers that India must remain part of the British world-system, and that, until its leaders accepted this 'imperial' fate, they would languish in the limbo of semi-self-government.

Of course, opinion in Britain on India and the Empire was not monolithic. On the Left, the reform scheme was derided as too little and too late to reconcile the nationalists in India. The turn to protection revived the old radical charge that economic imperialism was bound to bring war. Labour's election manifesto in 1935 urged 'equitable arrangements for access to markets, the international control of . . . raw materials and . . . the extension of the mandate system to colonial territories'.[92] It was the Cobdenite formula: more free trade meant more peace. But most of those who condemned the current practice of rule in the Empire imagined a future in which Britain was the centre of a loyal community of self-governing satellite states, bound together by common interests and values. There is little reason to think that this imperial world-view was unrepresentative of British opinion at large. 'The people of this country', remarked Neville Chamberlain, 'have a deep sentiment about the Empire, but it is remote from their ordinary thoughts'.[93] Perhaps this was true, although there was much to remind even the least politically minded of Britain's imperial ties – not least the stream of those travelling to the white dominions and back. Indeed, 'ordinary' opinion in Britain relied for its knowledge of much of the world on accounts that were shaped by settler, administrative, missionary or commercial interests, each in their way committed to empire. In the inter-war years, as much if not more than in previous eras, three grand propositions still framed British thinking: that they formed a distinct British 'race' among the world's peoples;[94] that their institutions and culture enjoyed both global pre-eminence and universal appeal; and that Britain was still the emporium of the world's trade and ideas. Set against these, the divisions and boundaries *within* their imperial system seemed of little importance. 'The British prefer to emphasize the unity of the Empire', remarked an acute foreign observer. 'To them England and the Empire are one, and no such thing exists as an England conceived separately.'[95]

In the 'Newer World': the dominions[96]

The arduous negotiations at Ottawa taught British ministers – if they needed reminding – that dominion politicians had as keen a sense of their own 'national' interest as the London government itself. With the formal conferment of the dominions' full sovereignty under the Statute of Westminster, the vigorous assertion of their economic self-interest, and their increasing alarm that Britain might be drawn into a conflict in Europe in which *they* had no stake, it has sometimes appeared as if this was the time when the dominions acquired a fully fledged sense of their national identity. A new 'nationalist' spirit had replaced colonial sub-servience. They were nation-states in the making, no longer stuck fast in uneasy 'dominionhood'. It would be hard to deny that the language of 'nation' became more widely used among dominion politicians in the inter-war years. But it would be wrong to assume that more than a handful of such 'nationalists' envisaged a future outside the British world-system or favoured an open rebellion against it. There were sev-eral reasons for this. First, among communities of mainly British ori-gin, affirming a Canadian or Australian identity was not meant to deny their continuing Britishness. They would still be 'British nations' as well, numbered among the 'British peoples'. Secondly, even European immigrants from outside the British Isles displayed a strong attachment to 'British' institutions (especially parliamentary government) and the Crown as a source of common allegiance. Thirdly, even where such attachments were weak or contested, as among some French Cana-dians, Afrikaners and Irish, the right to secede from the Empire and become a republic (to which the Statute of Westminster gave tacit con-sent) exerted at best an ambiguous appeal. The costs and risks in each case were dauntingly high, and full exit from the Empire was carefully assigned to the indefinite future.

The Pacific dominions

Among the five dominions, there was inevitably wide variation in the extent to which the 'British connection' impinged upon their local pol-itics in a period of considerable turmoil. Of the four overseas domin-ions, Australia and New Zealand were the most homogeneously British. Ethnic resentment against Britain, even in hard times, had little political scope. Both declined to enact the Statute of Westminster in their own legislatures, and showed little interest in the work of its drafting.[97] Both were keenly aware of how dependent they were on British sea-power for strategic protection and to safeguard the racial exclusiveness – 'White Australia' and 'White New Zealand' – that formed the bedrock of their social and cultural identity. In both, the political and business elite (and many farmers as well) acknowledged the umbilical link between their economic prosperity and their close relations with Britain, nowhere more than in Melbourne's Collins Street, Australia's 'City'. This was not just a matter of markets. In both Pacific dominions, the circulation of credit and cash was tied very closely to the size of the sterling reserves that their banks held in London. The London balances were 'the real regulative factor and the key to the whole banking system'.[98] A short-fall in earnings or the failure to raise a loan in the City threatened the drastic contraction of the local money supply and a savage depression of the kind both had suffered some forty years earlier.

In Australia particularly, the effects of the slump were extremely unsettling. The huge fall in world prices was part of the story. What made things much worse was the scale of the borrowing, public and private, in the boom decade that ended abruptly in October 1929. With public revenues falling, huge railway losses, and the drastic decline in overseas earnings, the risk of default on local and overseas debts loomed large. But the action required to avert this calamity was bound to be painful and to evoke fierce opposition, especially from the supporters of the government in power, the first Labour government since 1916. When the Scullin ministry accepted the advice of the Niemeyer mission (Sir Otto Niemeyer was deputy governor of the Bank of England) that cuts had to be made and wages reduced to balance the federal and state government budgets, the reaction was bitter. The Australian Council of Trade Unions denounced the Loans Councils (which managed public borrowing) for being 'in the hands of money sharks, loan-mongers and capitalists'.[99] As unemployment shot up towards 30 per cent, the Labour party executive called for the nationalisation of banks and insurance companies, and the renegotiation of Australia's war debt to Britain. While Scullin was away at the 1930 Imperial Conference (and promising that Australia would not consider default[100]), a civil war was being fought within his party and government. In New South Wales, the radical populist Jack Lang won the state election for Labour, and led the demand to 'nationalise credit'. 'Enthroned in our society', he later declared, 'is a hierarchy of financial anarchists playing with the world of men and women for sheer personal gain': the villains of the piece were the British banks in Australia and the leaders who had made Australia into a 'chattel nation'.[101] After twice defaulting on the New South Wales overseas debt, Lang was dismissed by the state's governor in May 1932, by which time Scullin's government had also collapsed. In December 1931, the United Australia party, a composite of the National party and Labour rebels like Joe Lyons, the new party's leader, came into power, promising, in Lyons' words, 'ruthlessly to eradicate all influences insidiously or openly weakening the ties of Empire'.[102]

Some historians have been tempted to see in the crisis a conflict between conservative middle-class loyalists, deferential to Britain and earnestly mimicking British upper-class rituals, and Labour's 'radical nationalists', bent on resisting Britain's 'imperial demands'.[103] It was certainly true that the professional and business elite (most visible in Melbourne, and closely connected to mining finance) regarded itself as the Australian embodiment of Britain's upper class, and subscribed to its political and educational ideals as well as its leisure habits. The young Robert Menzies (a Melbourne barrister) contrasted the refinement of the British 'establishment' with the crudeness and avarice of its American counterpart. 'They engage in a nauseating mixture of sentiment ("Mother's Day") and dollar-chasing, not palatable to the English mind', he wrote after a visit to the United States. 'They have no consciousness of responsibility for the well-being or security of the world; no sense of Imperial destiny.'[104] It was equally true that an acrid dislike for the British monied elite was voiced on the left of Australian politics. But it is much too crude to equate this with rejection of Britishness or Australia's British identity. One of the first steps of the Labour government when the depression arrived was to close the door to 'alien' (i.e. non-British) migration. In a speech criticising the Ottawa terms, Scullin (whose origins were Catholic and Irish) insisted that the point of imperial preference was the mutual advantage of 'British nations trading with one another and... keeping the maximum amount of business within the British family of nations'.[105] His successor as party leader, John Curtin (also Catholic and Irish), who had flirted with repudiating Australia's debts, was no less emphatic. Australians, he claimed, 'not only desire to be one people but that we shall be kindred from a common stock; that we shall... be a white people predominantly of British origin'.[106] As leader of the United Australia party, Joe Lyons (Catholic and Irish) played the 'Empire' card. His more conservative colleagues, like Menzies' mentor, J. G. Latham, might have disliked the Statute of Westminster, but they were also determined to extract the most favourable trade terms from Britain and be ready to look to the Japanese market.[107] Trade with the East was where Australia's economic destiny lay, was Latham's conclusion.[108] The notorious reluctance of Lyons' government to question the Royal Navy's ability to defend Australia may have owed most to its fear that this would weaken the Admiralty's case for a strong Eastern fleet and throw an intolerable burden back on Australia itself.

Nor was there much sign that the cultural ferment of the 1930s, that affected Australia like almost everywhere else, had brought a direct confrontation with Australia's peculiar Britishness. Quite the contrary in fact. In 1936, the writer P. K. Stephensen published an influential manifesto, *The Foundations of Culture in Australia*. Stephensen insisted that Australia must have its own national culture that would diverge 'from the purely local colour of the British Islands to the precise extent that our environment differs from that of Britain'. 'Is it sedition or blasphemy to the idea of the British Empire to suggest that each Dominion in this loose alliance will tend to become autonomous politically, commercially, and *culturally*?'[109] But the Australia that Stephensen wanted was a '*New Britannia* . . . cured of some of the vices . . . of the Old One', and avoiding 'Europe's brawls'. 'This Island, Australia Felix, effectively occupied by the British race, would be easily defensible against all-comers: which Britain to-day is not. This Island is waiting for the British people to *occupy it effectively* . . . . There is no other part of the British Empire so suited as the permanent domicile of the British Race . . . *the British people could find no better stronghold and focus than in the Island Continent of Australia*.'[110] The Australian accent was clear. But this was the cultural programme not of national separatism but of Britannic nationalism: the claim to be a distinct British people, equal at least and perhaps even superior to the original stock.

Canada

Scarred by his encounter with its prime minister, R. B. Bennett, at the Ottawa Conference, Neville Chamberlain took a sour view of Canada's part in the Empire. The United States, he said, 'controls capital and politics in Canada'.[111] Only ten years earlier he had been 'surprised and delighted' on a visit to Canada 'to find the most intense British feeling'.[112] Chamberlain resented what he saw as Bennett's bullying tactics, and not without reason. Even Canadian observers were embarrassed and uneasy. But Chamberlain's diagnosis was crude. Canada was bound to be influenced by its huge southern neighbour, at once the world's largest economy, the largest English-speaking country and Canada's largest market. The ease and convenience of cross-border traffic, the importance of New York in Canadian finance, and the influence of the American media – radio, film and the press – made this all-but-inevitable. But pragmatic acceptance of the American fact was combined with affirmation of Canada's British identity by English Canadians, and (with certain qualifications) by French Canadians as well. At the Conservative convention in 1927, the outgoing leader, Arthur Meighen, defended his argument that a Canadian government should consult Canadian opinion before joining Britain in a war by saying that this would reassure the people that Canada was a 'real British democracy' and thus strengthen 'British institutions and British fidelity'.[113] A Liberal party pamphlet of 1933 declared that the party 'stood for British principles of Free Speech and Free Association'.[114] A prairie Liberal like Crerar, who disliked 'Toronto imperialists' and the 'strange shore dwellers' whose first loyalty was to Britain,[115] could still think of Britain as 'the Old Country' and feel an affinity with its Liberal party and opinion.[116] The scale of non-British migration into the west after 1918 sharpened the mood of its bare British majority.[117] The Social Credit party, which ruled Alberta after 1935 (and whose leader, William Aberhart, was an 'intense Anglophile'), wrapped its electoral platforms in the Union Jack.[118] A well-regulated service, concluded the parliamentary committee on radio broadcasting, would be 'one of the most efficient mediums for developing a greater National and Empire consciousness'.[119]

Canadian nationalism was not an insignificant force, but, as in Australia, it was rarely defined in conflict with Britishness. Its urgency seemed greater after 1930 as the economic depression threatened to fracture the country. 'Never before had provinces, races, classes and parties been so divided', complained the Anglophone Montreal lawyer, Brooke Claxton, a former Rhodes Scholar who bought his suits in London.[120] What was needed was a strong central government to hold them together. Nationalism reflected the feeling that Canada was still little more than a grouping of regions and provinces.[121] But its strongest supporters were equally sure that the nation they wanted should be a 'British nation'. John W. Dafoe was the editor of the *Manitoba Free Press* in Winnipeg, the voice of prairie Liberalism, and the most influential Canadian journalist of his day.[122] Dafoe was an ardent nationalist. But he saw Canada's future as one of the 'British nations'. 'I have never believed', he told one correspondent in 1928, 'that one of a number of British nations having a common king could remain neutral in a war which threatened the existence of another British nation.'[123] Dafoe fiercely opposed the 'tory-imperialist' view that Canada had no choice but to follow Britain blindly into any war that it fought. But nor did he want their foreign policies to diverge. The best solution, he thought, would be 'agreement by the British nations, that . . . none of them, not even Great Britain, are 100 per cent international "persons"'.[124] They should not make war on their own, nor even make treaties that might involve them in wars without each other's consent.

Canadian nationalism of the Dafoe variety was highly articulate but had a limited following. It attracted suspicion. Dafoe himself acknowledged that 'the Canadian people do not want now any definite break in what we call the "British connection"'.[125] There was still a very powerful minority, 'holding the money, employing labour, owning the newspapers and controlling the parties', who 'are very British in sentiment' and who would answer 'Ready, aye ready' to an appeal from Britain, whatever the cause and however divided the rest of Canadian opinion.[126] It denounced the idea that Canada had interests that were different from Britain's. The headquarters of this feeling were found in Toronto, the 'Belfast of Canada', and the 'most assertively British of Canadian cities'.[127] But just as disheartening in the nationalist view was the indifference of the 'isolationists' to events elsewhere in the world as if Canadians could 'contract out of the universe'.[128] Isolationism seemed to be growing in strength after 1931 along with the fear of involvement in Europe's intractable conflicts. Its domestic parallel was endemic provincialism, and the rooted mistrust of the federal government. It was this that had led to the clause in the Statute of Westminster by which power to amend the Canadian constitution was carefully reserved to the Imperial Parliament (and denied to Canada's), at the explicit request of Canadian leaders. 'Provincial rights' remained a potent political cry, in Quebec above all, where Canadian 'nationalism' was readily seen as a 'British' conspiracy. Maintaining the 'British connection' in its unreformed shape, ill-defined, emotive and open (as some thought) to British abuse, was thus the great bulwark to unwanted constitutional change.

The boldest challenge to this political impasse came paradoxically from the Conservative government of R. B. Bennett between 1930 and 1935. Bennett had denounced the Liberals for failing to deal with the depression effectively. Bennett's own cry was 'Canada First', a sharp rise in tariffs to defend Canadian industry. This cut little ice on the prairies which had to pay more for home-made manufactures while grain prices fell steeply. Bennett had gone to the Imperial Conference in London to demand an imperial (and thus Canadian) preference in the British market for food. Labour rebuffed this attack on free trade. But the 1931 crisis in Britain, the new National Government and its swift turn to protection gave Bennett his chance. By inviting the British and other Empire governments to an economic conference at Ottawa, he aimed to reverse that defeat. The British would be forced to concede the ultimate prize, a protected home market for Empire food exports in return for a modest revision in Canadian tariffs. Bennett's plans were concerted (by his own tacit admission) with the Australian chief delegate, Stanley Bruce, the former prime minister, and now the *eminence grise* of Australia's economic diplomacy. He had the British 'completely encircled'.[129] Bennett may well have believed that the British delegation would not dare to resist. As a close friend of Lord Beaverbrook, he may have been swayed by his and Leo Amery's hopes of promoting a real protectionist government in Britain, much more fully committed to 'Empire Free Trade'. A hard line in Ottawa (where Amery was active) would help this to happen.[130] It may have been an inkling of this that enraged Baldwin and Chamberlain with Bennett's conference tactics. Certainly Bennett was playing for high stakes. He regarded himself as the saviour of Empire, who would drag the British kicking and screaming towards his own version of it. To have upheld 'Canada First', saved the prairie's grain market, and imposed a form of 'Empire Free Trade' on the recalcitrant British would have been a remarkable triumph for his vision of Empire. But Baldwin and Chamberlain were not so easily broken.

As a shrewd businessman, Bennett hedged his imperial bets. Access to American markets (closed up by Washington's emergency tariff) remained a vital concern. When President Roosevelt embraced freer trade, Bennett eagerly sought a commercial agreement to match that with Britain. But his domestic experiment in a strong central government and the Bennett 'New Deal' fell apart in the face of provincial resistance, internal party division and Bennett's ill-health. The 1935 election was a Conservative bloodbath. Although both parties agreed in opposing Canadian involvement in Britain's confrontation with Italy, the new Liberal government soon faced the old question: what would Canada do if Britain was drawn into a conflict in Europe. Mackenzie King may have thought privately that Canada neither could nor should stand apart.[131] But his public position was to say as little as possible and fall back on the formula 'parliament will decide'. The prime reason for this, as for many years past, was fear that Quebec would revolt against any prior commitment to Britain and bring down the Liberals, both party and government. 'British imperialism', said Henri Bourassa, still the great tribune of Quebec's *survivance*, 'must not be allowed to drag Canada into any more wars.'[132] Ernest Lapointe, the Quebec Liberal leader, said much the same thing. Both were fiercely opposed to the separatist nationalism of the 'Action française' and its clerical leader, the Abbé Lionel Groulx. Neither was anxious to give him a cause. Indeed, while this sleeping dog lay, *Canadien* separatism remained carefully vague about when and how a separate Quebec state might come into being. Its leaders denied any wish to break Canada up: 'Nous ne voulons rien détruire', said the Abbé Groulx piously.[133] Nor could they count on any support from the voters. The real political voice of French Canada's nationalism was the 'Union nationale' of Maurice Duplessis. Duplessis' government was a thorn in Ottawa's side. Its programme was not separation but the unremitting defence of provincial autonomy.[134] Canada's 'British connection' – by default or by choice – remained the pole of its politics.

South Africa

In the cruel trajectory of South African history, the inter-war years have often been seen as the prelude to the triumph of Afrikaner nationalism and its programme of *apartheid*. It was certainly true that an amalgam of paternalism, segregationist attitudes and overt racial discrimination (especially in the treatment of labour) prefigured much of the substance of post-war *apartheid* although without the ideological 'rigour', systematic enforcement (by classification and removal) and violent repression of the 1950s and after.[135] Africans (some 10,000 of whom had qualified for the vote under the property-based franchise that prevailed in the Cape) were removed from the voters' roll in 1936, but 'coloureds' (the South African term for those of mixed race) were not. *Zwaartgevaar* ('black peril') was invoked continually by white politicians in search of cheap votes. But the inter-war state lacked the means to impose real control over many black communities in town and country alike. In a similar way, the irresistible rise of Afrikaner nationalism to political dominance was much less apparent to contemporary eyes than hindsight suggests.

There were several reasons for this. The dominant personality in South African politics was General J. B. M. Hertzog, prime minister from 1924 until 1939. To his political critics, Hertzog's shortcomings were plain. He was the 'apostle of the short view' and shared 'that latent sense of racial grievance' that inspired many of his followers, wrote Patrick Duncan, Smuts' right-hand man in the South African party.[136] Hertzog was often accused of cloudy and imprecise language (as were Botha and Smuts), the means of survival in South African politics as almost everywhere else. But he was ready to claim that the Imperial Conferences of 1926 and 1930 had lifted the burden of British hegemony, and removed any doubt about South African sovereignty. With the hypothetical right of secession assured, pragmatic acceptance of the *Britse konneksie* had become politically possible. Hertzog lent his authority to *The King's Republics*, published by H. J. Schlosberg, a South African lawyer,[137] which claimed that, though the dominions now had the right to neutrality, it was inconceivable that they would exercise it if Britain were in danger.[138] Hertzog himself now veered towards the position that no issue of substance divided Afrikaners and 'English' (the local term for those of British descent). The task of the National party, he told its 1930 congress, was to build a *'gekonsolideerde Suid-Afrikaanse volk'*. The two streams of English and Afrikaans culture must eventually merge (*'saamvloei'*).[139] Here, perhaps, was a tacit admission that the struggle to define an Afrikaner identity by the systematic denial of 'English' influences and attitudes was futile and unwinnable, and could only prolong the sometimes bitter antipathy of the previous decade.

Hertzog may have also been hoping to undermine Smuts, his main political rival. Smuts' South African party enjoyed the support of many better-off Afrikaners who disliked the (white) populist style of the Nationalists, their pact with the Labour party and the secessionist republicanism favoured by a vociferous wing.[140] It also attracted most of the English vote, since Smuts' attachment to the *Britse konneksie* could hardly be doubted. 'Are we going to desert General Smuts, a Dutchman who is sacrificing health and leisure for the British cause?', asked the young Harry Lawrence in a speech at Kalk Bay near Cape Town in 1927.[141] Smuts seems to have regarded himself more and more as the bearer of Rhodes' old vision of a grander South Africa: fully self-governing, Anglo-Afrikaner in culture, but part of the Empire. He was keener than ever upon South Africa's northward expansion by a 'fair linking up with the two Rhodesias', as well as 'friendship and collaboration with the rest of British Africa' as 'junior members of the family'.[142] A federation of states from the Cape to the Equator[143] would form a great African dominion to rival Australia or Canada – a prospect his opponents denounced as a 'kaffir state' nightmare. Yet, for all Smuts' prestige, his party's survival could not be taken for granted. He had no obvious successor (Smuts was sixty in 1930) with the connections and skill to keep the party's Afrikaner support. His English lieutenants feared that the siren call of *hereniging* (reunion) would lure their Afrikaner allies away. And the party's cohesion was constantly strained by its English 'extremists' who opposed what they saw as the steady erosion of the link with the Empire. 'Politically they are like children', said Duncan contemptuously of a breakaway faction in Natal. 'I do not think the fits of imperial hysteria are good for us or the British connection.'[144] The suggestion by one of his English frontbenchers that the party should abandon the dual language provisions of the South Africa Act was dangerous enough to draw a savage rebuke from Smuts himself.[145]

Perhaps surprisingly, the politics of Depression allowed both Hertzog and Smuts to escape their extremists and construct a 'moderate' centre enjoying broad Afrikaner and English support. Hertzog had hoped to ride out the storm without leaving the gold standard, as the British had done. But signs of white unrest on the Rand[146] and the bruising effect on agricultural exporters brought a revolt in his party and pushed him towards a coalition with Smuts in February 1933. Both came under pressure from their Afrikaner supporters to press on towards 'fusion', a union of parties. The critical issue became South Africa's 'status' – the real extent of the freedom conferred by the Statute of Westminster. Within Hertzog's party a sizeable faction led by D. F. Malan was hostile to fusion, because it meant accepting dominionhood as a permanent condition and losing the hope of a republican future outside the Empire. For some of Smuts' English supporters, there was the opposite fear that their voice would be drowned by the Afrikaner majority, and that Malanite republicanism would enjoy too much influence. But, when the 'status' bill was debated (the bill enacted the terms of the Statute of Westminster in South African law), Smuts won over his doubters while those who favoured a future republic also drew back.[147] Only seven MPs opposed the bill. The way was now open to form the 'United' party: the status Act was its charter. However, much to

Duncan's relief, Malan and his followers chose in the end to stay out.
'It will consolidate our [new] party against a republic', was Duncan's
conclusion, while 'a small ultra-British group mainly in Durban and
East London' formed on the opposite wing.[148] The so-called 'Dominion' party won a sensational by-election in 1935 ('Are you a bulldog
or a handsupper?' was its cry),[149] but most English voters elsewhere
heeded the warning that 'the English-speaking must have the support
of the moderate Afrikaans-speaking. They alone cannot prevent the
country from seceding from the British Empire.'[150]

But what had fusion achieved? To its supporters it marked
the end of 'race' conflict between Briton and Boer and the creation
of a new 'South Africanism'. To ensure its success, they were willing, like Duncan, to remove the African franchise – on the grounds
that it might cause a dispute among whites. But fusion did not stop
the movement to build a distinct Afrikaner identity, which gathered
speed in the 1930s, with the promotion of the Afrikaans language (a
patois which replaced Dutch as the country's official second language
in 1924), the rapid growth in the number of Afrikaans-only schools
(by 1936, 55 per cent of white children were receiving instruction
only in Afrikaans[151]), and the systematic propagation of an 'Afrikaner'
account of South African history in which the Afrikaners were cast
as the innocent victims of black barbarity and British imperialism.[152]
The approaching centenary in 1938 of the Great Trek was perfectly
timed to advance the agreeable myth that the Afrikaners were a chosen, martyred but ultimately victorious people and the republic their
symbol of national 'liberation'. Against the power of this racial and
cultural appeal (which hindsight confirms), the United party's 'South
Africanism' now looks rather wan. But it would be wrong to assume
that success was assured to separatist nationalism before the Second
World War. For many Afrikaners, it was the weakness and poverty of
their language and culture that really stood out. The higher civil service was still overwhelmingly English, and few senior officials could or
would speak Afrikaans. English opinion was voiced by English-owned
newspapers in all the main cities. Almost the entire business world was
English and a large proportion of its most influential members were also
British by birth. The same was true of the main professions – medicine,
law, education, journalism, engineering and architecture.[153] Their ties
with Britain – family, business or professional – remained strong. The
towns into which many Afrikaners were moving were mainly English

in culture. It was hardly conceivable that a political movement that proposed to root out the *Britse konneksie* could escape the furious opposition of this English middle class to an Afrikaner republic outside the Empire. Few well-informed Afrikaners believed that it could be imposed on a hostile minority. Indeed, even republicans were forced to concede that it lay far in the future, while half of those teaching at Stellenbosch University, the seed-plot and seminary of Afrikaner nationalism, backed Hertzog and Smuts, not Malan's 'Purified Nationalists'. A true (*ware*) Afrikaner society might be the white hope of ages to come: in the world of practical politics, South Africa would remain a dominion.

It was true that dominionhood left undefined the terms of the British connection in several crucial respects and made the tacit concession that any dominion could secede from the Empire if it chose. The fact that no dominion did so after 1931 was not because there was a constitutional bar, but because in each case the balance of its politics was against such a move. New Zealand's Labour government, elected in 1935, might have had little ideological sympathy with the National Government in London. But its deep British attachment was strongly affirmed: 'New Zealand was bound to Britain by unbreakable ties of blood', declared the new prime minister.[154] Its planned economy rested on hopes of closer economic integration with Britain – the only real outlet for the increased production of primary products.[155] At the other end of the spectrum, the Irish Free State under De Valera's Fianna Fail government rejected the oath of allegiance, refused to pay the annuities owing under the 1921 treaty, and resisted the economic coercion with which London responded. In 1937, a new constitution recognised the Crown but only by virtue of Eire's 'external association' with the Commonwealth. But De Valera stopped short of declaring a republic or leaving the Commonwealth, partly because to have done so seemed likely to erase any hope of Ireland's reunification.[156] For all the dominions, the greatest source of concern was Britain's involvement in a new European conflict. For Australia and New Zealand, this arose from anxiety that London might overlook its real imperial duty in the Asia-Pacific. In South Africa and Canada, it sprang from the fear that, unless Britain itself was in obvious danger, the local response would foment a racial divide and destroy the fragile consensus on which dominionhood rested. As Europe slid towards war, both kinds of risk grew greater and greater.

Holding India: 'from power to influence'?[157]

Had India become the grand anomaly in the British world-system by the mid-1930s? Certainly some people thought so. 'India is a great historical accident and remains an incredible anomaly', opined John Dafoe. Hindus and Muslims, he thought, 'are not part of the moral unit . . . I might call the British Commonwealth of Nations'.[158] The link between Britain and the white dominions had now become voluntary. It was a matter of choice, however theoretical, whether or not to stay in the Empire. In much of the tropical empire, the demand for self-government barely existed as yet outside a very narrow elite. But India was different. There, since the end of the First World War, the British had faced a mass nationalist movement whose leaders had called if not for *purna swaraj* (complete independence) then for self-government as full as that of Australia or Canada. Under Gandhi's dynamic direction, the Indian National Congress had challenged British authority in a large-scale campaign of civil disobedience that was only abandoned (in 1922) for fear of a rising spiral of violence. But, as a tactical weapon, as well as a way of restoring momentum and extending support, it retained its appeal to the Congress' Gandhian wing. In 1930, it was turned to again to lever major concessions at a time when the British seemed at sixes and sevens.

The British for their part seemed less sure than they had been before 1914 about what their Raj was to do. The social problems of India had always seemed daunting, but now they were more conscious than ever that they had only makeshift solutions. The Royal Commission on Indian Agriculture (1928) was set up to inquire into the causes of low productivity. But it pointedly ignored the key issue of land tenure so as not to enrage the Raj's key allies among the landholding classes. As the Congress pushed deeper into rural society, the old British claim that they were the guardians of peasants and cultivators looked more and more threadbare. Indeed, the reforms of 1918–19 were meant to shift the burden of social questions towards the 'transferred' departments in provincial governments under the charge of elected Indian ministers. The Raj seemed to be asking, as Milner had asked of the British in Egypt in 1920: 'Are we trying to do too much for these people and getting ourselves disliked without materially benefiting them?'[159]

Yet (as we have seen) the British could hardly imagine an imperial life after India. The real issue for them was how they could reconcile the Indians' demand for self-government (which they accepted in principle) with their own irreducible interests. It was India's contribution to the strength and cohesion of the British world-system that really concerned them. Despite its savage contraction as a buyer of Lancashire cottons, India remained a key market for Britain's industrial products, all the more so in the age of the segmented global economy and closed trading blocs. Thus, although the overall value of British exports to India fell in the 1930s, India remained the largest single market for cotton piece-goods, machinery and chemicals, and the second or third market for electricals and iron and steel goods.[160] Nor was trade the only or most important economic consideration. Some £500 million (around 12 per cent of British overseas capital) was invested in India, three-quarters of it in government debt. India also contributed to the British balance of payments through its payment for services, pensions (for British officials), debt interest (mostly on railways) and the costs of the large British garrison 'borrowed' from home. Before 1931, and even more so after, any change that might affect India's ability to pay these 'Home Charges' rang loud alarm bells in London. An elected government in Delhi that sent the garrison home, repudiated its debts or devalued the rupee might wreck sterling's precarious stability.[161] It was hard enough sometimes to bully the Viceroy and his British officials: an independent government of India would be a different matter entirely. It was widely agreed in London that Britain's 'financial stake . . . in India remains, for all practical purposes, as a permanent obstacle to anything that could reasonably be termed financial self-government'.[162]

In the Depression decade, commerce and finance were an urgent concern. But even more rooted in British thinking about India was its strategic importance. This could be thought of as active and passive. By comparison with other parts of the British world-system, India's defence budget was huge: six times that of Australia, the next biggest spender. India still paid the ordinary costs of almost one-third of Britain's regular army, stationed in the sub-continent. By convention, India's own army of some 140,000 men, with its British officer corps, was also available for imperial duty, although London would pay the 'extraordinary' costs. After 1920, it was accepted that imperial use of this 'sepoy' army would be careful and sparing; but India remained the strategic reserve of the British Empire in Asia and its great supply base in war. Troops and supplies could be sent from its ports to a vast arc of targets from Cairo to Shanghai. Its vast pool of labour was a pioneer corps in waiting – as in 1914–18. But 'passively' also India was crucial. Together with

British-ruled Burma and Ceylon (Sri Lanka), its orientation was one key to the Asian balance of power, and thus that of the world as a whole. Its Muslim minority looked towards Persia and the Arab Middle East. The leaders of Congress admired Chiang Kai-shek's nationalist struggle in China, and some of them longed for a pan-Asian front against British imperialism. But, from the British perspective, a divided, neutral or hostile India, spread-eagled across their route to Southeast Asia, Australasia and China, would be an unimaginable disaster. So hard was it to think of 'imperial defence' in these terms that the 'loss' of India was almost literally unthinkable.

The constitutional tactics that the British pursued to safeguard their interests and sap Indian opposition were extraordinarily tortuous, although this was partly because of their own internal divisions. The first constitutional scheme was advanced by the Simon Commission, set up in 1927–8 to review the Montford reforms. The Commission (which was boycotted by most Indian leaders in protest against its 'all-white' complexion) proposed to give the Indian provinces almost complete control of their local affairs ('provincial autonomy' with ministerial or 'responsible' government on the Westminster model), with the distant prospect of eventual federation when and if they agreed upon it. In the central government, the Viceroy's executive power would remain unfettered by a toothless central assembly, while the Indian army would be placed even more clearly under London's control, with a guaranteed budget that Indian politicians could not even discuss.[163] Simon's object was clear. If the provinces became the arena where Indian politicians could exercise real power, provincial and not 'All-India' politics would attract most political energy. The Congress party as a 'national' movement would soon fall apart as its provincial divisions went their own separate ways and abandoned the chimaera of early British withdrawal. In political terms, the Raj would have rounded Cape Horn.

Simon's scheme was shot down not so much by its Indian critics as by the Viceroy, Lord Irwin, who saw the lack of any advance at the 'centre' as the cause around which Congress would unite to disrupt British rule. He had already insisted that the promise of India's future dominionhood should be clearly affirmed. What Irwin urged was a round table conference at which all interested parties – British and Indian – would draw up proposals for a new constitution. Three such conferences in London in 1930–2 failed to produce an agreed solution. But they did throw up a novel suggestion on which the British seized with alacrity. This was the idea of an 'All-India' federation of the Indian states (whose Princes acknowledged Britain's 'paramount' power) as well as the 'British Indian' provinces.[164] The seductive charm of this scheme was its promise of a large conservative bloc of Princes and Muslims (who would keep separate representation) in a new federal government, antipathetic to Congress and anxious to keep the 'British connection' as their political guardian for (at least) a long time to come. In the federal assembly that the British envisaged – and to which the Viceroy's government would gradually become more and more answerable as dominionhood arrived by instalments – one-third of the seats would be filled by Muslims and one-third by the delegates sent by the Princes. Even if Congress won all of the open seats that remained, the most vociferous opponents of the British connection could never command a majority.

But, leaving nothing to chance (and under the baleful eye of the Die Hards), London piled up further defences against any untoward weakening of the imperial interest in India. A mass of safeguards entrenched the executive powers of the Viceroy against interference in the army, in India's external relations, or in the rights of minorities. These were meant to continue even after India had become a dominion. The Viceroy also had powers to set the level of spending on the items of greatest interest in London: defence; the pension bill; and railway expenditure. One Congress leader commented acidly that scarcely one-fifth of federal spending would pass under the scrutiny of the federal assembly.[165] However, what British plans really relied on was the provincial dynamic towards which Simon had pointed. Giving provincial autonomy would draw Indian leaders away from rhetorical politics towards 'real' and 'responsible' political power, and make them far more responsive to the needs of their voters. Provincial politics would also come to reflect the wide variation in interests and attitudes in different parts of the sub-continent. Provincial government ministers, even those in the Congress, would resist the demands of 'All-India' nationalists and wriggle free from their grasp. All-India politics would be fraught with frustrations for those who aspired to drive out the British. Boxed in by the rules, and by the careful design of the federal assembly, they would find very little had left the Viceroy's control. Yet to struggle against him by mass agitation would get harder and harder against the indifference or hostility of provincial politicians, where control over the party machine would soon come to lie.

But how realistic was this machiavellian scheme? Did the British really have the power on the ground to make it work as they wished? Could they hold on long enough to bend Indian politics in the direction they wanted? There were certainly grounds for a positive view. One of them was the resilience of the old 'steel frame', the so-called 'Superior Services': the 800 or so members of the Indian Civil Service (ICS); the 150-strong Indian Political Service (still almost entirely British-born[166]) that dealt with the Princes, and the 500 British officers of the Indian Police. Under the 1935 Act, the pay and conditions of the Superior Services remained under London's control. The Indian Civil Service retained much of its cherished cohesion. It was, said the Viceroy (Lord Willingdon, 1931–6), 'the most powerful Trade Union that I know'.[167] In the late 1930s, despite uncertainties and under-recruitment, British-born officials still made up the majority of its ranks.[168] Nor was the loyalty of its Indian contingent yet in serious doubt.[169] Faced with the growth of Indian political activity, the ICS accepted the need to enlarge provincial self-government and increase the shift towards federalism originally envisaged before 1914. It learned from mass civil unrest and the bursts of terrorism in Bengal, the risks of exposing its minute administrative manpower, the need to employ more indirect methods, and the logic of retreat to the political centre both in the provinces and in India as a whole. The Indian politicians would have to be guided, not governed. In keeping with this was a new political mantra put about by its leaders. 'The civilian who used to serve by ruling must learn to rule by serving', said an Old India Hand, Sir Edward Blunt.[170]

In the provincial arena, the Indian politicians were bound to rely heavily upon the expertise and advice of the ICS men. They were also bound to observe the constitutional rules that the governors would enforce. The governor could dismiss ministers, dissolve the assemblies and call fresh elections. He could also insist on attending cabinet meetings.[171] Where party competition was fierce, party organisation fragile or factionalism rife, these were formidable powers – the reason why Congress tried but failed to secure a promise not to use them. They were deployed with the aim of weaning Congress leaders in the provinces away from their deference to the Congress 'high command' and encouraging 'local' initiative.[172] After 1935, of course, British and ICS power was concentrated at the centre, in the government of India. There, the Viceroy and his ICS staff exercised almost unchecked authority, and would continue to do so long after (and if) the federal assembly came into existence. Indeed, the Viceroy, not London, now held most of the reserved powers that were meant to slide slowly into the hands of responsible federal ministers. His control of the budget was almost absolute. More to the point, the centre had grabbed the lion's share of the most buoyant revenue sources, leaving the rind to the provinces: the rigid, costly and inflammatory land revenue.[173] Financially, at least, the centre was stronger than ever, and provincial politicians would need its goodwill. But, if all else failed politically, the Viceroy's ultimate weapon was his command of armed force, the police and the army. Here, too, it seemed, the British had little to fear. Apart from the British contingent (the 50,000 or more men from the British army at home), the Indian army appeared almost untouched by two decades of politics. Its British officer corps (around 20 British officers in each of the army's 120 regiments[174]) was scheduled for 'Indianisation' at the pace of the snail, and Indian applications for officer training (in contrast with the ICS) slumped badly in the 1930s.[175] The army's colonial structure, with its heavy reliance on 'martial races' and hill peoples, expressly excluded most of the elements that might have been drawn to the Congress. An army mutiny designed to bring Gandhi to power was absurdly improbable.

All this would have counted for less had the British in India faced a united nationalist movement that could grant or withhold its cooperation at will. But the reverse was the case. Since the glory days of the first non-cooperation movement in 1920–2, unity had collapsed. Although Muslims themselves were far from united (and some remained loyal to Congress), their provincial leaders were deeply opposed to the Congress desire for a strong central state which they saw as the instrument of the Hindu majority. In the Muslim majority provinces of Bengal, Sind and Punjab (the North West Frontier Province was a special case), they were determined to hold on to the widest autonomy, and to cling to the privilege of separate electorates. When Congress staged its second civil disobedience campaign in 1930–1, the Muslims took no part.[176] The Congress itself was prey to divisions. The moderate non-Gandhian wing, led by Motilal Nehru, Jawaharlal's father, would have settled for 'Dominion Status' within the Empire, parliamentary-style government at the Indian centre and an end to separate electorates.[177] But their chances were wrecked by Muslim opposition, the Gandhians' impatience and the tactics of the British. When civil disobedience was suspended (by the Gandhi–Irwin pact), Gandhi went as the Congress' sole representative to the (second) Round Table Conference convened by the British in late 1931 to consider the federal scheme. But Gandhi gained little. Civil disobedience had been noisy, but was a political failure. The Round Table Conference (attended by Muslims, Sikhs, Princes, untouchables and Eurasians, among others) belied his grand claim that the Congress alone represented India. The new constitution was drawn up in London while the stuttering attempt to restart civil disobedience was crushed by a vigilant Viceroy. When the India Act was passed, Congress faced a dilemma. Would it boycott the reforms that Jawaharlal Nehru called 'a charter of slavery'? Would it fight the elections, now to be fought on a far larger franchise including millions of women? Would it take office in the provinces where its supporters won a majority? Would it risk being trapped in the constitutional labyrinth the British had constructed around it?

Loud voices were raised against any compromise. Nehru (elected Congress president 1936–8) fiercely opposed the acceptance of office. The Congress should not share responsibility with 'the apparatus of imperialism', he told its meeting at Lucknow in April 1936.[178] If it did so, the 'narrowest provincialism [will] rear its ugly head'.[179] But, the following year, the vote went against him. This was partly because of the hunger for power after long years in the wilderness. But it was also inspired by the scale of the victory in the provincial elections. Congress had won a clear majority of seats in five of the eleven provinces and was the largest party in a sixth (Bombay). It had crushed the ICS hopes that provincially based parties would attract the voters' support. Its success was a tribute to organisational strength,[180] and its appeal to the peasants as the scourge of the landlords. The landlord party in the United Provinces (to the dismay of the governor) was roundly defeated. But what would Congress leaders do once in office? They proclaimed the intention of using their powers to smash the new constitution. But the British clung to the hope that, once its local leaders were engaged with 'the great mass of provincial interests', this would quickly slacken the grip of Congress' 'central organisation'.[181]

The early pattern of politics seemed inconclusive. The cohesion of the Congress was certainly strained and its inclusive appeal began to fray at the edges. Provincial leaders resented 'supervision' by the 'high command's' triumvirate.[182] Faced with peasant unrest in Bihar and labour unrest in Bombay, Congress ministers applied repression with vigour.[183] The Congress Socialist party had been formed in 1934.

Nehru himself proclaimed the virtues of socialism and admired Stalin's Russia. But Sardar Patel, Gandhi's 'enforcer', dismissed socialism as 'nonsense,'[184] and other voices were raised against Nehru's 'destructive and subversive' doctrine.[185] The 'high command' intervened in provincial affairs to defend Indian businessmen against radical or leftist opinion in Congress.[186] Subhas Chandra Bose, Nehru's main rival as the radical voice of the Congress, pressed for more recognition of regional and cultural autonomy (reflecting the Bengali Hindu dilemma) and urged Congress support for a federal republic, not a unitary state.[187] The Congress old guard engineered his removal. Amid so much division, it was perhaps hardly surprising that Nehru should have thought 'the sooner we are out of office the better'.[188] But, despite all the strain, the Congress did not fragment. Its three-man committee, with Gandhi behind them, imposed a tight central rein. There were also clear signs that the growing strength of the Congress would deter the Princely states from agreeing to join the federal system, and that federation itself might remain a dead letter.

But in the last year of peace it was too early to tell. The Congress had eluded the trap that the British had set. Whether it could stage an early advance to the All-India centre and expel the British from India in the foreseeable future was far more uncertain. The strict central control that the high command had maintained had saved the Congress from splits. But its veto on coalitions and monolithic authority had further antagonised both Muslims and Princes. For the moment at least, in the trial of strength, stalemate had set in, the prelude perhaps to a new round of adjustments. But, before that could happen, an external crisis of colossal intensity transformed the whole pattern of Indian politics.

Holding the centre

Despite their travails in India and East Asia, the growing tension in Europe and the sense of economic and financial strain after 1930, there was little to show that the British had abandoned their claim to be a world power. Nowhere, perhaps, was this clearer than in the Middle East, the cross-roads of Eurasia and of what Mackinder had called the 'world-island'. Across a vast arc of territories, including the Sudan, Egypt, Cyprus, Palestine, Trans-Jordan, Iraq, the Persian Gulf statelets, the Hadramaut and Aden (the 'southern gates of Arabia'), British influence *circa* 1930 was fiercely exerted through a wide range of regimes: a condominium, a crown colony, three mandates, several protectorates, and a 'veiled occupation' in Egypt, while Aden remained an outpost of Bombay until 1937.

To the casual eye, such administrative chaos had an improvised look, as if the British presence was temporary ('temporary' had been the notorious adjective applied to the British occupation of Egypt in 1882). In fact, in the inter-war years, far from becoming redundant, the Middle East countries assumed growing imperial value for two different reasons. One was the steady rise in their output of oil, mainly from Anglo-Persian's concession in Southwest Iran and its port-refinery at Abadan, but with the promise of new fields in Iraq and the Gulf. Although Middle East oil supplied only 5 per cent of world product as late as 1939, it reduced British dependence on American oil and was conveniently close to the imperial 'trunk route' to Suez and India. The second reason was strategy. The old threat from Russia was dormant, but the risk of a clash with Japan was much more immediate. That meant the rapid despatch of a naval task force from Europe to defend British interests in the Asia-Pacific from the Singapore base. Hence the vital importance of the Suez Canal as the wind-pipe of Empire was notched up still further. Nor was it only a matter of sea-power. The value of air routes to bind the Empire together, and of air-power as a means of internal control and external defence, were well understood. Half of Britain's air strength stationed overseas was in Egypt, Palestine and Iraq. Cairo had already become the hub of air transport, through which flights to Africa, India and the Pacific had to pass. With other bases and airports in Palestine and Iraq and along the Arab coast of the Gulf, the British had constructed an air route to India to which they attached great importance.[189] 'The Gulf is becoming', wrote a *Times* correspondent breathlessly, 'the Suez Canal of the air, an essential channel of communication with India, Singapore and Australia.'[190]

Since the early 1920s, the British had preferred to make their regional presence as unobtrusive as possible, for financial as much as for political reasons. They had come to terms with the two main state-builders, Kemal Ataturk in Turkey and Reza Pahlavi Shah in Iran. Having installed Feisal in Iraq as the strong-man who would hold its disparate parts together with his 'Sharifian' followers (the Sunni elite who formed the administrative caste and the officer corps), they were keen to exchange their Mandatory role for a treaty of alliance that gave Iraq independence – a change carried through between 1930 and 1932. With the air bases they wanted, and with Iraqi dependence on British support against the 'old enemy' Turkey (not to mention Iran), there was no conflict of interest between their imperial system and the ruling group in Baghdad.[191] London also looked kindly on the state-making ambitions of Ibn Saud in what became Saudi Arabia, and forced its Hashemite clients in Trans-Jordan and Iraq not to encourage his tribal opponents.[192] Thus the British *imperium* was intended to function by indirect means, through a form of hegemonic diplomacy, not old-fashioned rule. As the only great power in the region (for the French offered no challenge), they would be arbiters of its conflicts and quarrels, patrons – or not – of its rulers' ambitions, regulating the affairs of the region in its best interests and their own.

The heart and centre of British regional influence was, as it had been since 1882, to be found in Egypt. Egypt had the largest population of any Arab country, and the region's most developed economy. Cairo's Al-Azhar mosque was the greatest centre of learning in the Islamic world. With the Suez Canal, the port of Alexandria, its airports and railways, its agrarian resources and its large pool of labour, Egypt was a uniquely valuable asset to Britain's defence system: the 'swing door', as one minister put it, between East and West. Having rejected the prospect of direct control at the end of the War, the British would have liked to enshrine their special position in the form of a treaty. But, as they insisted that the terms should include the right to maintain troops there, to require Egyptian conformity with British foreign policy, to be the sole guardian of foreign interests and persons, and to keep effective control of the 'Anglo-Egyptian' Sudan (Egypt's great colony), no Egyptian politician who valued his name and his health could be persuaded to sign. After several abortive attempts, the British had all but decided by late 1934 that further effort was futile.[193] Their situation in Cairo was not so uncomfortable. Despite official insistence that the British Residency played no part in Egyptian political life, successive high commissioners interfered with a will. It was widely assumed that no Egyptian prime minister could survive their displeasure. Since 1930, in fact, the British had simplified matters by allowing the king to repress the Wafd, the main popular party, and rule by decree through his nominee minister. Their rationale was straightforward. If the British disowned him, said a Foreign Office official, the king's position would be precarious if not untenable.[194] When the High Commissioner Lampson went to bully King Fuad (r.1917–36) on an occasion in 1935, he told him that failure to comply would raise 'issues of the gravest kind ... including ... his continued capacity to rule and the whole future of his dynasty'.[195] 'J'accepte', said King Fuad. Since the Qasr el-Nil barracks, where the British garrison was stationed, was ten minutes' drive from the king's Abdin Palace (and ten minutes' drive from the Wafd party headquarters), and since the British had removed his predecessor but one, Fuad's discretion was wise.

Nevertheless, in the mid-1930s, the British ability to exploit the political rivalry between the Wafd and the Court was no longer enough to safeguard their interests. Part of the reason was their troubles in Palestine, the one Middle East state where their favoured retreat to indirect rule was thoroughly barred. Under the terms of their Mandate, the British had to provide a 'national home' for the immigrant Jews. But it had been obvious from the beginning that the Arab majority was deeply opposed to Jewish land settlement and still more resentful that it had denied them self-rule. Since a shared legislature was out of the question, the British practice had been to deal with Arabs and Jews separately through the Supreme Muslim Council and the Jewish Agency. But this had not prevented fierce communal tensions and recurrent outbreaks of violence. The violence was fuelled by rising rural unrest. By 1930, nearly one-third of Arab peasants were totally landless and more than three-quarters had less than the level of subsistence required.[196] The Palestine peasants, reported a British commission, were 'probably more politically minded than many of the peoples of Europe'.[197] Their resentment was probably aimed as much at the Arab notable class (who were selling the land) as at the Jewish intruders. The problem was compounded by the bitter divisions among the Arab elite, between 'Husseinis' (the Husseini family were the hereditary *muftis* of Jerusalem),[198] and 'Nashashibis', who were supported by larger landowners and businessmen. When rural violence burst out into the open with the murder of two Jews in the spring of 1936, bringing reprisals, a general strike and a state of emergency, armed peasant bands began to appear in the highlands. Amin al-Husseini called for the non-payment of taxes and denounced the police presence in Palestinian villages. The British were forced to deploy some 20,000 men (a tenth of their army) to try to restore their control.

This was not the only anxiety. From late 1935, and the break-down of the Anglo-French plan to surrender Ethiopia to Italy, the British had to court the risks of a Mediterranean war and suffer the propaganda bombardment from Italian radio. Almost at the same moment, the High Commissioner in Cairo, Sir Miles Lampson, detected an ominous shift in the political climate. All the main parties formed a 'United Front' to demand restoration of the 1923 (parliamentary) constitution, and treaty negotiations with London.[199] To stand in their way, argued the key British expert on internal security, might mean a return to the massive uprising of 1919. London accepted the case. By May 1936, the Cabinet was debating the prospective treaty in detail. The main attraction on offer was an Anglo-Egyptian alliance, to defend Egypt 'jointly'. The main stumbling block was the demand by Nahas, the Wafd leader, that the British renounce their claim to occupy the Canal Zone indefinitely, and accept League of Nations arbitration if the two sides disagreed over the treaty's renewal.[200] The thought of the backbench reaction to a fresh imperial 'scuttle' made some ministers quake. But, by the middle of June, that midsummer of madness, they had steeled themselves for it. A treaty was 'indispensable', said Neville Chamberlain, a previous critic, now a key convert. They should accept the twenty-year term on Britain's military rights in the Canal Zone.[201] Not to settle with Egypt, said Baldwin, would mean locking 30,000 men in the country 'during the very critical five or six years immediately in front of us'.[202] Nahas, too, was eager to win the great treaty prize. He offered a perpetual alliance (only its terms to be varied in future) and unlimited British reinforcements in an 'apprehended international emergency'.[203] It was enough. At a further Cabinet meeting on 23 June, Baldwin summed up the argument. 'The immediate reasons for the early conclusion of a treaty', he told his Cabinet colleagues,

> *were the reactions of failure on the Arab area. The situation in the Near East was one of considerable gravity. There was also danger of disturbance in Egypt... Failure to conclude a treaty would add a disorganized Near East to the existing disturbed state of Europe. It was essential therefore to obtain a treaty... [H]e hoped that in twenty years time... our position in the Eastern Mediterranean would be very much stronger than it was today, with troops near the Canal.*[204]

Baldwin's remarks were intended, no doubt, to quieten the critics. But it would be wrong to assume that even the treaty's most ardent
British supporters saw it as marking a real British retreat. The British
had agreed to withdraw their troops from Egypt's main cities. But (as
the map to accompany the treaty revealed) their Canal Zone 'training
grounds' conveniently extended to within a few miles of Cairo.[205] As
for Nahas, within twelve months of the treaty he had been driven from
office by the new king, Farouk. He 'relied too much on British influence
to keep him in power', said Lampson.[206] The old game was renewed.
'With tact and firmness', he reassured London, 'British influence should
remain the governing factor... under the new conditions of the post-
treaty regime.'[207] In Palestine, meanwhile, a Royal Commission had
come and gone, and its plan for partition considered and scrapped.
More British troops fought the Arab insurgents. Far away in the south,
the frontier of control in the Aden protectorate was pushed gradually
forward. By adjusting their tactics and searching for allies, the British
meant to hold their ground in the region they regarded as indispensable strategically, and imperially 'central'. What really mattered was
whether they could hold the ring. Whatever the treaty terms, Lampson
told London in May 1936, 'in twenty years time Egypt would be just
as dependent on us as now if we were still the power we now are'.[208]
The British meant to hold the centre, but would the centre hold?

Dog days of Empire

In 1937, the omens were unclear. With hindsight, of course, it is easy
to see the tensions and strains to which the British system was subject.
Economic resentments, nationalist fervour, racial antipathy, religious
antagonism and the appeal to class hatred: together they threatened
to pull the system apart at the seams. On this diagnosis, the chance
of survival was slim. Swift devolution might stave off a crisis but not
for too long. Crippled economically by the end of free trade, sapped
internally by the growth of separatist feeling in the dominions and
India, assaulted externally by new and more ruthless imperialisms, the
British world-system could only decline, and eventually fall. It was just
a matter of time.

Yet, as we have seen, to many contemporaries (both observers
and actors), that was not how it seemed. The economic upheaval was

deeply disturbing. The rise of India's mass politics had been a political shock. The surge of new ideologies on the Left and the Right had unsettled old loyalties. The aggressive ambitions of the 'revisionist' powers exposed the weakness and confusion of the guardians of world order. But (except to ideologues and visionaries) it was hard to determine the collective significance of these unwelcome developments. Indeed, it was only in the late 1930s, from 1937 onwards, that the pattern became clearer, and their meaning more ominous. Even then, as we will see, it took a strategic catastrophe to inflict irreversible damage.

In the meantime, even the most hard-headed of realists might have hesitated to write the British system's obituary. In the more 'British' dominions, there might be impatience with London's zigzag foreign policy, but the sense of British community remained deeply entrenched, with the common Crown as its focus. The coronation of King George VI in 1937 was covered in Canada by twenty-three hours of continuous broadcasting.[209] In India, the Congress had abandoned mass agitation and settled for the constitutional politics in which the British had been trying to entrap it for more than a decade. In much of the 'tropical' empire, the adoption of indirect rule had anaesthetised politics. Nor was it obvious that there was any escape from the grip of the City on its 'dominions of debt': the economic obligations that bound so many producers to the market in London and to dealing in sterling. British expansion might have come to an end, and a form of stalemate set in across the colonial dependencies. But in a fragmenting world it was not unrealistic to expect that the British 'bloc' might hold the balance of economic and geopolitical power for an indefinite time. If history was a guide, it would outlast its parvenu rivals. But history was not.

11 THE STRATEGIC ABYSS, 1937–1942

At the beginning of 1937, Britain was the only global power with interests in every continent and, in theory, the means to defend them. The British system was a close approximation to a world empire. Its prestige had been dented by recent events, and its wealth diminished by depression. But no other great power could match its combination of military (mainly naval) and economic strength or its latent ability to coerce its enemies. The intimidating scale of its territorial extent, including its self-governing member states and colonial possessions, made it hard to imagine the ultimate defeat of such a global leviathan. Indeed, life outside the limits of empire seemed scarcely conceivable to the sturdiest nationalist – at least as a realistic prospect in the foreseeable future. In what was still an imperial world across much of Afro-Asia, there were few free places on the map.

But empires can disintegrate with astonishing speed. The collapse of the Soviet empire at the end of the 1980s took almost everyone by surprise, not least the school who had proclaimed the imminent decline of American power. In the British case, the change was almost as sudden. By the middle of 1942, Britain, the imperial centre, was effectively bankrupt and dependent upon American aid. With the fall of Singapore in February, the invasion of Burma, and the German advance into Egypt (the battle of Alamein was fought scarcely 100 miles from Cairo), the British system looked set to collapse. Its precarious survival and the eventual victory of 1945 were a tribute to its residual strength, but not the sign of a full recovery. The post-war empire was a pale shadow of its former self. The cohesion of its constituent parts had been badly damaged. Much of its wealth had been lost or redistributed. By 1968, the last vestige of its world power status had vanished.

Revolution and Empire

It is commonplace to attribute this dramatic descent to the overextension of imperial power, the final cause in Gibbon's account of the decline of Rome. At best this is a truism, at worst a tautology. The British system was sustained not by the unique resources of Imperial Britain, but by a combination of elements not so much ruled as managed from London. It is the failure of the combination that needs to be explained. A more serious objection to the 'overstretch' explanation is its determinism – as if the downfall of the British system was an inevitable outcome which contemporaries were too blinkered to see for themselves. Of course, the British system broke up because it lacked the resources to overwhelm its enemies. But that is only half the story. No less important was the fact that the struggle to survive was waged in an age of revolution: a Eurasian revolution that cumulatively (but very quickly) destroyed almost all the global preconditions on which the British system had depended since the 1830s.

It is arguable that the roots of this revolution lay in the very changes from which the British had profited so much in the past: the gradual integration of the world's politics and economics into a universal system. As the world became a single market, and more and more of its regions came to depend upon international trade, commercial rivalry had become more intense. The strains of economic transformation were felt more deeply; the threat posed by commercial disruption to social stability became more obvious. At the same time, the 'globalising' climate in trade and diplomacy intensified the trend towards competitive state-building, since only well-organised states could secure social order, economic development and international sovereignty. Partly because of the easier diffusion of ideas and values across districts, countries and continents that technology made possible, socio-economic change and state-construction provoked rival forms of cultural mobilisation: to make states or break them; to build new communities, or refurbish old ones. Ethnic nationalism became the secret weapon of modernising states, and also a potent means of subverting them.

Before 1914, these sources of tension in world affairs had been eased by three countervailing influences. First, the rapid growth of international trade softened the impact of economic competition and enhanced the appeal of the open economy. Secondly, the political structures that had grown up since the 1870s survived the stresses of external rivalry and internal revolt. The European great powers who had partitioned so much of the world had settled their differences peacefully if grudgingly. Partly for ideological reasons (a shared conceit about their civilising mission), partly from self-interest, they showed little desire (though some) to stir up trouble in each others' empires. Despite alliance systems, war plans and mobilisation timetables, they preferred to rattle their sabres rather than use them. Thirdly, the conservative elites who retained their grip over the dynastic empires of East and Central Europe had kept in hand the ethnic nationalisms that threatened the stability of the European states-system. The result had been not a durable peace but an uneasy equilibrium whose fragility was eventually revealed in the July Crisis of 1914. In the four years that followed, much of Old Europe's political architecture was abandoned or destroyed. As the war reached its climax in 1917–18, it seemed as if the progressive collapse of political, social and economic order would spread a revolution across Europe and ignite a revolt of the subalterns in the colonial lands beyond. If this terrifying prospect had receded by the mid-1920s, as we saw in the last chapter, it did not vanish for long. The peace of the 1920s was the prelude to a revolutionary age, although it was not until the mid-1930s that its full global meaning had begun to emerge and the prospect of 'holding the centre' grew increasingly faint.

The revolution of the 1930s was the overthrow of the international regime so laboriously reconstructed between 1919 and 1925. Economic in origin, the revolution was systemic in scope, affecting almost every aspect of international order. Its most obvious dimension was in geopolitics. After 1930, the 'weak' powers became strong and the 'strong' powers weaker. Less than three years after Hitler's accession to power in January 1933, Germany had repudiated the terms of the Versailles treaty and began to create a great-power army, an air force and a modern navy one-third as large as Britain's. By reoccupying the Rhineland in 1936, and building the 'West Wall' (the 'Siegfried Line'), Hitler made Germany far less vulnerable to an attack from France, and much freer to pursue his designs in the East. The German revolt against Versailles had been closely followed by Italy's. Although Italy was the weakest of the three European victor powers of 1919, her strategic position bisecting the Mediterranean, fear of her air power, and the new alignment between Rome and Berlin (the 'axis' of November 1936) created a new military balance in the Mediterranean Sea. The third great change was the growing might of the Soviet Union. Amid the gross upheavals of collectivisation after 1928, rapid industrialisation, the Stalinist terror and the purges (which had led to the murder of some 40,000 officers in the Soviet army by 1938), the Soviet Union had become a great military and industrial power whose military spending ranked second only to that of Germany.[1] The rise of Stalin's state held a profound significance for the successor states of Eastern Europe, for East Asia, and above all for Nazi Germany.

The growth of Soviet power was the link that connected East Asia to Europe. It helped to provoke the Japanese conquest of Manchuria and the rapid dissolution of the Washington regime. After 1931, much of North China was caught up in the escalation of Soviet–Japanese rivalry.[2] Japan's military intervention in Shanghai (1932) and the attack on the Kuomintang government's authority in the northern provinces presaged the drastic remaking of East Asia's political geography. In 1935–6, Tokyo's search for allies against the Soviet Union led to closer relations with Germany, and then to the Anti-Comintern Pact of November 1936. When the Sino-Japanese War broke out in earnest in July 1937, and Japanese control extended remorselessly over China's coastal regions (Hankow and Canton were occupied in October 1938), the political revolution in East Asia was all but complete. There, as in Europe, the champions of the post-war settlement seemed weak and divided, reluctant to challenge the revisionist powers, let alone to match their military power. For all the fragility of its industrial base (carefully noted in London), Japan's military spending between 1933 and 1938 exceeded that of Britain or America.[3]

The revolt against the geopolitical order was also a revolt against liberal capitalism and its two great centres in London and New York.[4] By the mid-1930s, a new world economy had emerged, bringing a drastic reversal of the post-war 'normality' of the late 1920s. Commercial liberalism was replaced by economic nationalism. Almost every state had built a wall of controls to reduce its exposure to external pressures – trade competition, capital movements and currency fluctuations – and the domestic unrest that followed closely behind. Instead of the old multilateral pattern, which allowed export earnings from one country to be spent in another, and paid for in freely convertible gold-backed currencies, world trade was more and more segmented into blocs that discriminated against each other by tariffs or exchange controls: the sterling area, the dollar bloc, the gold bloc, the Soviet world, the German sphere,[5] the Japanese empire.[6] It was widely assumed that, as a proportion of output, international trade was bound to decrease and all economies become more and more self-sufficient.[7] In abstract principle, as one contemporary noted, the drift towards autarky might be expected to reduce economic friction. But only in theory, since autarky sharpened the difference in living standards between the less well endowed and their more fortunate neighbours, and increased the incentive to bring economic resources under political control.[8] Worse still, by trapping the producers of primary products within a single bloc, it lowered their prices, reduced their purchases, restricted their growth and dried up investment.[9] In the brave new world of declining trade, there would be less and less scope for the globe-wide trade in services, shipping and capital on which Britain had waxed fat in the recent past.

The third great mine to explode beneath the liberal order was the violent escalation of ideological warfare. The conflict of ideas was itself nothing new. What made the 1930s an ideological battleground was the widespread fear of catastrophic change. The political appeal of revolutionary Marxism, somewhat muted by the late 1920s, was hugely inflated by the visible signs of the collapse of capitalism. To anti-communist parties, interests and opinion, the massive scale of the social crisis required an urgent riposte to the Marxist challenge. The new mass media, their assumed domination over mass opinion, and the comparative novelty of democratic politics in Europe and East Asia (Japan adopted universal manhood suffrage in 1925) made the war of ideas (or slogans) the vital front in the political struggle. But there was no grand alliance against the communist threat. The striking feature of the European scene was the ferocity with which the anti-communist ideologues of fascism and Nazism attacked 'bourgeois' liberalism as decadent and corrupt, and parliamentary government as an obsolete sham.[10] On Europe's imperial periphery, the devastating impact of the economic crisis on agrarian communities, and similar fears of social catastrophe, exposed colonial and semi-colonial regimes to a rhetorical onslaught from both Marxists and nationalists.

Ideological warfare had a seismic effect on international politics. It turned diplomatic differences into wars of manoeuvre and territorial disputes into set-piece campaigns. To the ideological warriors of the 1930s, secret diplomacy and the squaring of interests in smoke-filled rooms were as repellent as they had been to the most idealistic Wilsonian. In the crowded cockpit of European diplomacy, the three-way split between fascist, liberal and Marxist governments made a firm coalition against aggressor powers impossibly difficult. Ideological 'programming' brought a widening gulf in the language and assumptions of national leaders and governments. As the tensions increased, the fog of incomprehension grew thicker. The familiar landscape of great-power diplomacy disappeared in the mist. Negotiation in the era of ideological war became a journey without maps.

The cumulative effect of this triple assault on the post-war order was the rapid erosion of its perceived legitimacy – perhaps the most insidious influence on the decade's diplomacy. After 1930, it seemed more obvious than ever that the humiliating treatment handed out to Germany in 1919, and the attempt to deny her a great-power status, were unjust and unwise. As the value of empires rose in a world of trading 'blocs', it became harder to deny the imperial claims of 'civilised' states like Germany, Italy and Japan. It became commonplace to speak of 'have-not powers' whose unequal share of international wealth was widely seen as the primary source of international tension. But it was one thing to acknowledge that legitimacy was lacking in international politics, quite another to find ways of repairing the deficit. Almost everything conspired against a new equilibrium. It was hardly surprising that the effort to agree on a revised post-war settlement in Europe and East Asia should have come to nothing. Instead, the pressures of geopolitical ambition, economic crisis and ideological struggle had created a revolution in the making in Europe and East Asia by the later 1930s. At opposite ends of the Old World, new imperialisms had emerged that were far more powerful than those of fifty years earlier and much more disruptive of the existing order. Far from being confined to a remote periphery, they concerned the fate of Eurasia's heartlands. Far from being restrained by the European balance of power, they rejected its claims and aimed to destroy it. Far from doubting the value of new colonial possessions, they treated territorial expansion as the key to survival. And, since the world was already partitioned between sovereign states and established empires, this new imperialism meant the forcible overthrow, by war or coercion, of the existing pattern of international property.

Dilemmas of containment

With the advantage of hindsight, we can see that the revolutionary crisis of the 1930s was dissolving the Eurasian preconditions of British imperialism. The peculiar evolution of the British system, and the secret of its viability, had depended upon two vital corollaries. First, that a strategic balance would prevail in Europe, precluding a single continental empire in West Eurasia. Secondly, that East Asia would remain 'passive', more acted upon than acting, confined within its regional bounds, with its sea communications under foreign control. It had been these conditions that had allowed the British to push their lightly defended bridgeheads of trade and settlement into the Asia-Pacific, to concede self-rule to their settler colonies without a levy for external defence, and to construct their extraordinary Indian Raj. Only under conditions of exceptional stability in Europe could they have dared to keep so much of their army so many weeks away in their Indian garrisons. It was those garrisons that (in the last resort) had secured their claim on India's resources to help build a secondary 'Anglo-Indian' empire in Afro-Asia.

British public attitudes towards the defence of empire and of Britain's world interests were complex and ambivalent. On the one hand, there was after 1930 a widespread revulsion against the thought of war. On the other, except among a very small minority, there was no sign of revolt against the imperial system or the commitments it imposed. The key assumptions of the late-Victorian outlook were still in place. Indeed, their persistence may help to explain why the imperial system was so rarely discussed as a dispensable burden, or as an entity separate from the British Isles. Despite the rise of American power, it was still widely thought that Britain held the 'central place' in the world economy. She remained after all the world's greatest trader and investor, with the most diverse portfolio and the largest business network. The economics of sea transport and the flow of communications still worked in her favour. In geopolitical terms, this centrality meant an intermediate position between Continental Eurasia and the Outer

World. In the early 1930s, the benefits of this had seemed more obvious than ever. In the Home Islands, the Middle East and India, the British held forward bases from which to intervene in the Continental world, but without becoming part of it. This was the crucial advantage. To be wholly in the Outer World (like the United States) without purchase in Eurasia, was to risk commercial exclusion from the wealthiest and most populated parts of the globe. Without any influence in Continental politics, an Outer power might find the Old World unified against it, driving it into defensive isolation, or threatening it with encirclement and attrition.[11] A purely Continental power, by contrast, was forced into constant territorial rivalry. Its frontiers were always at risk. The fixed costs of its defence were always high. Access to the Outer World was always in doubt. The scope for political and economic freedom was narrow, impeding its economic and social development. But the intermediate power – Britain – had the best of both worlds. It was less exposed to territorial friction. It was hard to isolate and even harder to encircle. It could draw on the products of the Outer World and deny them to the Continent. And, with a modicum of luck or skill, it could ensure that no Continental combination could be formed against it – or, if formed, last long.

These assumptions about Britain's special trajectory in world affairs – what we might call 'British exceptionalism' – meant that mainstream opinion had been remarkably sanguine that the progressive devolution of political power to the white dominions, India, the Middle Eastern states and, ultimately, perhaps, the other divisions of the British system, would not destroy its 'natural' cohesion. It assumed that, under almost all imaginable conditions, membership of Britain's imperial association would be far more attractive than the status of client to a Continental power or a notably indifferent United States. For small or weak states in the modern world, isolation was a mere delusion. Even in India, where anti-colonial nationalism was fiercest in the 1930s, the British expected a new generation of political leaders to turn its back on Gandhi's atavistic utopia once real self-government came into sight.[12] For India's self-interest, whether strategic or commercial, was bound to tie it to the maritime world that the British had made, not to Inner or East Asia. Autarkic self-sufficiency (as the sub-continent's whole history seemed to prove) was out of the question.[13] This passive imperialism of the *status quo* coexisted amicably with public attachment to the League of Nations as the guarantor of international peace, and with faith in 'collective security' as the most effective deterrent against a would-be aggressor. When the Baldwin government seemed on the verge of betraying the collective principle it had so recently endorsed (in the general election of 1935) by agreeing to the dismemberment of Ethiopia, public outcry forced it to repudiate the Hoare–Laval pact (the offer to Italy) and sacrifice Hoare as Foreign Secretary. Public fear of involvement in war (fuelled by scares over mass slaughter from bombing) made the rearmament programme a delicate issue. The British people, Churchill warned in April 1936, would reject rearmament 'except as part of the League policy'.[14] But, as the limitations of the League were brutally revealed by the fall of Ethiopia, and the threat from Germany became more explicit, this consensus broke down. An influential section remained fiercely opposed to the use of force. The veteran campaigner, Norman Angell, led those who urged a tougher response to international aggression in a reconstructed League modelled upon a devolved democratic British Empire–Commonwealth.[15] There remained a wide measure of public agreement that the Versailles settlement was unjust and unworkable, and must be revised by 'peaceful change'; and a corresponding antipathy to Britain's involvement in a continental war aimed at propping it up. Imperial isolationists (the target of Angell's criticism) sought to square the circle. Lord Lothian, Leo Amery and Edward Grigg (all former Milnerites), and *The Observer*'s editor, J. L. Garvin, wanted to bind the Empire together as a cohesive bloc and limit any continental commitment to the barest minimum for Britain's home defence.[16] They saw little objection to a German advance into Eastern Europe if it served to promote an Anglo-German détente. 'Realist' appeasement was even blunter. Its public champion was E. H. Carr, ex-diplomat, polemicist and a pioneering professor of international relations. Carr treated collective security as a utopian fantasy and turned a ruthless eye on Britain's international weakness. Restoring equilibrium to the international system required peaceful concession to the have-not powers – a view that led him to approve of the outcome of Munich.[17]

The most subtle exponent of British grand strategy in the 1930s was Basil Liddell Hart, the leading writer on the theory of war. His main achievement was to reconcile the contradictions in British public opinion: horror at the prospect of another 'great war'; confidence in Britain's 'manifest destiny' as a global power. He denounced the continental campaigns of the First World War as a disastrous departure from Britain's 'historic strategy'. The 'British way of warfare', he argued, was to combine all the elements where Britain was powerful to defeat the threats to her global system. A small professional army would use amphibious mobility to throw the enemy off balance – not engage in the brutal combat of the Western Front. Sea-power would throttle a landlocked aggressor. Economic warfare would demolish its civilian morale. 'Moral war' would subvert its self-belief and ideology. The aim was to avoid a new Armageddon, one decisive battle on which all would turn. The 'indirect approach' (Liddell Hart's key concept) was intended to dissuade an aggressor as much as defeat him. A cold war of diplomacy and suasion, on the Byzantine principle of 'watch and weaken', could be waged indefinitely at sustainable cost. Its central virtue in the political climate of the 1930s was to make the defence of empire compatible with mass democracy.[18] The unanswered question as war drew nearer was whether it would be enough to save Britain's system from catastrophic defeat.

The uncertain state of British public opinion was a major influence on policy. For a time, the political and practical limits to rearmament seemed to argue against a futile attempt to hold on to everything. Perhaps the profligate sweep of Britain's possessions and spheres (expanded still further after 1918) was too vast to defend. Perhaps some retrenchment was wise. It was widely acknowledged that seizing Germany's colonies after 1918 had been an act of injustice. Some colonial concession might pave the way for a European détente.[19] The same might have been said for the imperial ambitions of Italy and Japan. At a time of depression, Britain lacked both motive and means to finance the progress of her 'undeveloped estates'. A more equitable share-out of the colonial world might improve diplomatic relations and curb the costs of defence. But, for all their agonising over how to protect them, British leaders showed little desire to shrink their global commitments. Indeed, the whole logic of their policy – and of the resort to appeasement – was a tenacious defence of Britain's worldwide claims.

The paradox perhaps is more apparent than real. Returning Germany's lost colonies to a Nazi regime raised awkward questions about their status as mandates. The attempt to do so would have roused humanitarian outrage. Some of them, anyway, were not Britain's to return. Nor was it easier to practise partition diplomacy on the few sovereign states that survived in Afro-Asia – the obvious lesson of the Ethiopian debacle. Any acknowledgment of Japanese claims in China (as opposed to outlying provinces like Manchuria) would have faced similar protest and the intimidating prospect of American hostility. A further objection was the uncertain reward for such painful concessions. Hitler showed no disposition to trade a European settlement for colonial small change. There was no serious chance that Tokyo's army-dominated governments would agree a limit on their deepening involvement in mainland China. British leaders had to bear in mind that to acquiesce in more than modest adjustments to the post-war treaties would ruin their claim to represent legality and order in international affairs. This inhibition was closely connected to another constraint no less powerful for remaining implicit. Governments in London were all too aware that their imperial system was in a delicate stage of constitutional transition. The dominions' independence had been formally ceded in the Statute of Westminster. India's promotion to (qualified) dominion status was clearly foreshadowed in the 1935 Act. Imperial devolution made it harder to be sure of the dominions' support for British commitments in Europe, of which their governments had always been wary. But it also placed a premium on British prestige as the *primus inter pares* of the 'British nations'. Any public admission of Britain's military weakness, or of her reluctance to defend all her worldwide interests, might weaken her grip on dominion loyalty. Official doubts about the navy's ability to reinforce Singapore in a Far Eastern crisis were carefully concealed from the dominion premiers at the Imperial Conference in 1937. Similar arguments about imperial prestige applied with even greater force in India, Egypt and the Middle Eastern states.

With so few concessions to make, and no reliable clues as to where Germany's, Italy's and Japan's ambitions might lead, there was little alternative but to strengthen the base of British military power as quickly as possible. From 1936 onwards, the strategic debate became more and more fraught. The 'Anti-Comintern Pact' signed between Berlin and Tokyo in November 1936, despite its avowed purpose, warned that the two main 'revisionist' powers might combine their assault on the Eurasian peace settlement of 1919–22, and its main champion, Britain. Deterring Japan, insisted the Admiralty, meant sending the 'Main Fleet' to Singapore. But sending the Fleet east would leave the Mediterranean defenceless for an indefinite period, exposing Malta, Suez and Egypt. By May 1937, the planners were saying that the Fleet could only set out if Germany and Italy had declared their neutrality in an East Asia war – an unlikely scenario.[20] A 'new standard navy', matching the sea-power of Germany and Japan, would not be enough if

Italy entered the war. Nor could it defend Britain against what seemed the greatest danger of all, not a cross-Channel invasion but a 'knock-out' blow from the air. To counter the threat of such a German attack, the Defence Requirements Committee insisted on 'air parity' with Germany: a heavy bomber force; 2,000 planes with the vital reserves; and the industrial capacity to match Germany's effort. When the Treasury came to add up the bill, the figures were daunting. The maximum sum that could be spent safely over the following five years, Cabinet ministers were told, was barely enough for the navy and air force, let alone the army as well.[21]

Thus, by the time that Neville Chamberlain became prime minister in May 1937, the strategic outlook had become suddenly bleaker and was getting much worse. In July, full-scale war broke out between China and Japan. In August, there was fierce fighting in Shanghai, and, by September, a Japanese blockade of the China coast. Japan's invading army would soon be more than a million strong. In November 1937, Italy joined the Anti-Comintern Pact to affirm solidarity with Germany and Japan. Meanwhile, in what was Britain's most likely outside source of supply, the American Congress passed the Neutrality Act to bar the sale of munitions of war to any belligerent. The raising of loans there (a major recourse in the First World War) had already been blocked by the Johnson Act three years earlier. But Chamberlain was a strong and self-confident leader whose administrative ability and careful stewardship of public finance since the 1931 crash had earned him his name as a safe pair of hands. Like most mainstream opinion, he was strongly against a continental commitment for the British army, or an alliance with France that might drag Britain into an East European war. He also opposed too fierce a response to Japan's advance into China, preferring the 'indirect approach' of giving the Kuomintang government some financial assistance. On this, and on his eagerness to bury the hatchet with Italy, he was at odds with Anthony Eden, his Foreign Secretary.[22] Unlike Eden (and the Admiralty), Chamberlain saw little point in challenging Japan to win American goodwill,[23] and privately disparaged Washington's diplomacy as no more than words. In early 1938, he resisted Roosevelt's proposal of a peace initiative as untimely, pushing a discontented Eden into resignation.

Chamberlain took what he considered a realistic view. He favoured the build-up of naval strength, though not on the scale that the Admiralty wanted. But he regarded the deterrent of air power as a greater priority. With a heavy bomber force at Britain's disposal, there would be almost no danger of a German 'knock-out blow', since the RAF's retaliation would be swift and devastating. With the 'knock-out blow' ruled out, Hitler would have to reckon on a 'long war', if he aimed to fight a war at all. In a 'long war', almost all experts agreed, German chances were slender. There would be stalemate on the Western Front, where France was defended by the Maginot Line, and stalemate in the air. The longer war went on, the tighter would be the British blockade on a German economy that was already over-strained. And the more likely it would be that the United States would relax its prohibition on providing cash and supplies. With every month that passed, the Western Powers would grow stronger and Germany weaker. In light of this, it seemed very unlikely that Hitler would be rash enough to risk a second German defeat. The best he could hope for was some territorial gains, a colony or two and an informal hegemony in Southeastern Europe. So the centrepiece of Chamberlain's grand strategy was to inveigle Hitler into a European settlement. Once that was done, the 'brutal friendship' between Rome and Berlin would quickly fade. When Europe was restabilised would be the time to deal with Japan's opportunistic imperialism. There was a wide con-sensus (that included Churchill) that Japan would not dare to attack British interests directly unless Britain had already been defeated in Europe.

Chamberlain's design had a seductive coherence. His critics disliked his political tactics but they found it hard to gainsay his strategic assumptions – in public at least. It was widely assumed that the 'have-not' powers could not sustain their huge military budgets for much longer without drastic damage to their civilian economies. The chances that they could agree upon war aims and synchronise their strategies against a set of great-power enemies that might include the United States and the Soviet Union as well as Britain and France, seemed remote. It seemed more likely that, after huffing and puffing, a new equilibrium would emerge in Europe. In the short term, it was vital to avoid an 'accidental' conflict. Thereafter, the greatest danger that faced the British system was of bankrupting itself by overspending on defence and risking a new financial crisis on the scale it had faced in 1931. If that were to happen, the Chamberlainites might have argued, the British world-system would disintegrate anyway.

Chamberlain's ideas were soon to be put to the severest of tests. In March 1938, the German army marched into Austria to impose the *Anschluss* – Austro-German unification – to wild local enthusiasm. Two months later, Hitler opened the campaign for the separation of the German-speaking Sudetenland from the main body of Czechoslovakia, with the transparent intention (after the *Anschluss*) of absorbing it into Germany. The Chamberlain policy now came to its crisis. It seemed hard to oppose in principle the right of self-determination for the Sudeten Germans. It was even harder to see in practice how Britain could prevent the outcome Hitler wanted, without forming an alliance with France and the Soviet Union.[24] The danger to Chamberlain's policy was that, if Hitler imposed his will without regard to Britain and France (and then annexed the dismembered Czech state), their prestige would collapse, and with it the leverage they needed to make Hitler agree to a general settlement. This was the issue on which the crisis turned. Britain and France had already agreed to the Sudetenland's 'return' (in actuality it had never been part of Germany) when Hitler demanded (at the Godesberg meeting on 23–24 September) the immediate military occupation of the Sudeten areas to ensure 'stability'. Chamberlain's own inclination was to press the Czech government not to resist. But a Cabinet revolt on 27 September, led by Halifax and Simon, his two colleagues in the Inner Cabinet dealing with the crisis, brought matters to the brink. The next day, the Royal Navy was mobilised. But a further appeal to Hitler, and intervention by Mussolini, prepared the way for the Munich Conference. At the fateful meeting on 30 September, Hitler agreed to delay occupation and allow an international commission to supervise the sovereignty transfer. But, far more important, from Chamberlain's viewpoint, was his agreement that all future change in European affairs should be settled peacefully between Britain and Germany. Hitler, it seemed, had lost his nerve. It was this piece of paper that Chamberlain flourished to such huge acclaim on his return to London, and with which he all but demolished his domestic critics.

The euphoria was pardonable. All roads had led to Munich. The Admiralty view had been strongly against a premature confrontation with Germany before the new fleet was ready.[25] British intelligence about the bomber threat (badly flawed in practice) assumed that Germany enjoyed decisive air superiority[26] and that Britain was still in the danger zone of the 'knock-out blow'. Despite French belligerence, British leaders were highly sceptical of the French will to fight or their capacity to do so. It was widely doubted that British opinion would support a war to keep the Sudetenland Czech. A grand alliance with the Soviet Union and France, even had it been possible, would have courted the risk of a European war with an aftermath worse than after 1918. The fly in the ointment had been Hitler's last brutal demand and the angry reaction it evoked in Cabinet. The astonishing outcome had seemed the best of all worlds, the vital first step down the road to a settlement. Hitler had even reiterated the naval promises made in June 1935.[27] But, as even Chamberlain himself may have sensed, it was too good to be true. Hitler's negative intentions soon became clear. And less than six months after the Munich accords he occupied Prague and added the rest of Czechoslovakia to the German Reich.[28] The defence of empire had been based on the hope of a European peace: now it must be built on the virtual certainty of a European war.

With the final collapse of Chamberlain's grand strategy, British world policy fell apart in confusion. To salvage the shreds of his own credibility and shore up French confidence in British intentions, Chamberlain issued a guarantee to Poland: Britain would fight for Poland's 'integrity'.[29] As panic spread about German influence in Southeastern Europe and the Mediterranean, further guarantees (and financial aid) were extended to Turkey, Greece and oil-rich Romania. Now that resistance to Germany depended so heavily on France's will to fight, it was no longer possible to refuse a continental commitment. Introducing conscription was an early sign that sending a large army into Europe was no longer ruled out. The strategic implications went wider and wider. On the reasonable assumption that, when war came, Italy would join Germany in an attack on France, the old order of priorities was abruptly reversed. The Fleet would stay in the Mediterranean to protect vital interests (especially the Canal) and begin the assault on the 'soft underbelly' of the Axis powers. Whatever happened in East Asia, there would be no 'Main Fleet to Singapore', or anything like it, for an indefinite time. The Admiralty refused to abandon the Singapore strategy and insisted that a defensive force would be sent to cover any threat from Japan.[30] Their nerve was tested in June 1939 when the British concession area at Tientsin, a treaty-port near Peking, was blockaded by the Japanese army searching for Chinese 'terrorists'. The Chiefs of Staff decided that no more than two of the navy's eleven available battleships could be sent to the East if the confrontation turned violent: six had to be kept in Home waters, and three in the Eastern

Mediterranean.[31] At best, they could act as 'some deterrent' against a major Japanese move into 'the South China Seas or Australasian waters'. If the Japanese moved south 'in force', the China squadron would have to leave Singapore and 'retire westwards'.[32] To relieve the crisis, the British ate humble pie.[33] Meanwhile, home defence loomed larger and larger. As rearmament quickened and its cost raced ahead of the projected budget (hurriedly increased from £1,500 million to £2,100 million), purely defensive needs assumed an ever higher priority: fighters (to defend) not bombers (to attack); escort vessels (to guard convoys) not battleships. The Admiralty's request for a building programme to match the expected new level of German construction (Hitler had denounced the 35 per cent limit) was quietly shelved.[34] The 'new standard navy' would never be built.

Two further shocks lay in wait. Fighting the 'long war' had been the centrepiece of British grand strategy. Offensively, that meant blockade. Defensively, it meant Britain's using her financial muscle to outlast any enemy, to fund her allies and buy war materials from any part of the globe. In early July, the Treasury punctured this grand illusion. Britain's gold stock was larger than in 1914, it said, but much of it was 'fugitive money' escaping from Europe. A large fraction had gone (to the United States), and more would follow if and when the threat of war continued. In other respects, the situation was even worse. In 1914, short-term capital or 'hot money' had flowed back to London: in 1939, it was flowing away. In 1914, Britain had a foreign income stream of £200 million a year to help finance any overseas purchases and provide collateral on foreign loans. In 1939, £200 million was the total sum of Britain's saleable foreign securities. In the First World War, Britain had been able to borrow over £800 million from the American government. In 1939, such loans were banned by the Johnson Act against defaulting debtors. Even at pre-war levels of spending, the reserves in gold and foreign securities 'would barely last three years': in conditions of war, it would be very much shorter.[35] In Cabinet, the Chancellor drew the brutal lesson. The longer that war was delayed, the weaker would be Britain's financial position.[36] But the last shock was the worst. In the aftermath of Hitler's entry into Prague, British leaders had toyed with the idea of a Soviet alliance to restore the European balance of power. There were many doubts. Could the Red Army fight? Would the East European states desert to the Germans? Would the dominions disapprove (Canada and South Africa were said to)? Would Stalin embroil

Britain and France in an East European war? Chamberlain's fear was that an alliance would trigger not stop an all-out war and recreate the catastrophe of the First World War. Perhaps for this reason the negotiations were desultory. It soon turned out that they were also academic. On 23 August 1939, the Molotov–Ribbentrop pact was announced to the world. Germany and Russia were to be friends if not allies. Russia's vast resources (including its oil) would be open to Hitler. The blockade had been broken before it began. Britain was at war less than two weeks later.

By a series of steps the policy-makers in London had led the British world-system into a strategic impasse of almost catastrophic proportions. They had placed home defence first because Britain's safety in Europe was the ultimate surety for her imperial power. But when it came to a fight they found they had no means of winning a European war. They had abandoned one ally (Czechoslovakia) that had a modern army, and chosen another (however gallant) that did not. They had done so on a premise – that time was on their side – which turned out to be wrong. They could do almost nothing to help their chosen ally, Poland, nor bring pressure to bear on their enemy, Germany. They had hesitated over an alliance with Stalin, only to find that he had joined their enemies. The weapon of blockade was struck from their hands. Planning to crush Germany by their financial power, they found their own war-chest shrinking with every month that passed. Their last hope of forestalling Germany's continental supremacy rested almost entirely on resistance by France. But 'war to the last Frenchman' proved a dangerous motto for the British Empire.

In less than half a decade, British world power seemed to have shrunk to undignified impotence, exposing the British system to an international war it had little chance of winning. With all the wisdom of hindsight, historians have assembled a catalogue of errors. But the deeper question is much more interesting. What shaped the course that took British leaders into the strategic quagmire of September 1939? Five factors exerted a magnetic force upon their geopolitical reasoning. First, the system they managed was dispersed and devolved. This had its advantages, but its resources could not be assembled quickly, or used to meet a sudden emergency. Neither the dominions nor India nor her commercial empire could contribute anything to strengthen Britain's hand in the pre-war crises when the initiative was lost. Secondly, British leaders were acutely conscious of the peculiar openness of their global system. There was no *limes* behind which to retreat, no East Wall or South Wall to keep out the 'barbarians'. The British system was a marine archipelago: even India was to all intents a strategic 'island'. Its survival amidst the new imperialisms depended upon Britain's ability to shuffle military power between its various segments, refusing to commit more than the minimum needed in particular places at a particular time. They had no choice but to maintain their huge fixed investment in an all-purpose navy even at the expense of their offensive capacity, since sea-power alone permitted the strategy of 'shuffle'. Thirdly, almost no one believed that Britain should be an economic Sparta, with a controlled economy organised for war. On the contrary, 'overstraining' the civilian economy would be a self-inflicted and perhaps fatal wound. Germany, reasoned most British observers, was bound to 'blow up': the pressure of rearmament on its civilian sector would become unbearable. Britain's 'free' economy would win the day. And, if the worst came to the worst, its open structure and global connections would be the vital means of throttling Germany in the economic struggle. Hence what was needed was not an all-out drive but a skilful balance between immediate need and conserving strength for the longer war. Fourthly, for all their pragmatism and their inherited lore of imperial statecraft (a ruthless business), British leaders displayed a curious faith in the international system and its framework of law, perhaps because so much of it was their handiwork and it functioned *de facto* as an informal extension of their imperial system. They were loath to admit that, for other states, it offered little to ease their frustrations and grievances. They found it hard to conceive that 'civilised' governments would show contemptuous indifference for its rules and procedures. In their insular safety, they failed to grasp the cyclonic force of the ideological wars being fought in Eurasia. This was most tragically evident in Chamberlain's failure (and that of so many others) to grasp the unlimited scope of Hitler's ambitions, the savage nature of the Nazi regime, the tectonic scale of the coming conflict and the brutal imperatives behind the Nazi–Soviet pact. They were liberals at sea in a revolutionary age.

Finally, they were also the victims of a cognitive bias that had grown notably stronger in Britain's inter-war culture. The idea that Britain formed a world of its own was very old. Primacy at sea, the rewards of trade and the growth of 'new Britains' sharpened the Victorians' sense of British 'exceptionalism'. The assumptions behind it were tested to the limit in the First World War. Through a tortuous rationale, they were vindicated by victory. The horror of war on the Western Front and revulsion against what seemed a futile slaughter made it easy to claim a decisive role for economic blockade and what Liddell Hart would call 'the indirect approach'. The crucial lesson of 1918 was lost. Mackinder's insistence that, without decisive action to stop a 'heartland' empire being formed in Eurasia, the 'world-island' would soon come to rule the world, was almost forgotten. Its corollary, that British world power required the closest attention to the European balance, seemed alarmist, impracticable and unnecessary. Hence the cavalier presumption that French power would suffice in a German war, and that the most ambiguous promise of British aid was all that was needed to steel French opinion for a future fight. Hence the failure to see that a geostrategic earthquake at their own front door could tear up the foundations of their worldwide power.

The road to Singapore

The immediate question on the outbreak of war was whether the British world-system would hold together. A year before, there had been grounds for unease. In Canada, Australia and South Africa, the prospect of war in defence of Czech rule over the Sudeten Germans had aroused strong misgivings. But there, as in Britain, Hitler's brutal repudiation of the Munich agreement was a turning point. The European crisis could no longer be dismissed as a question of frontier adjustment in Eastern Europe. In March 1939, in the Canadian Parliament, the Prime Minister, Mackenzie King, who had made the dominion's autonomy in external affairs a constant refrain since the early 1920s, all but acknowledged that, if Britain went to war, Canada was bound to follow. He rehearsed the importance of Canada's ties with Britain, and the unaggressive nature of British world power. 'A world in which Britain was weak would be greatly worse for small countries than a world in which she was strong.'[37] As a member of the Commonwealth, Canada would not escape attack by an enemy of Britain. But the crucial speech was made by King's French Canadian deputy, Ernest Lapointe. Since the conscription crisis of 1917–18, French Canadian antipathy to involvement in a 'British' war had been the most dangerous theme in Canadian politics. For the Liberals especially, even debating the issue held enormous risks since almost any definition of the party's view was likely to drive a wedge between its supporters in Quebec and those elsewhere in Canada. This was why King had strenuously insisted that no decision could be made in advance. But, by March 1939, this carefully disingenuous position had become untenable. It was Lapointe who spelled out the compromise. He shrewdly reminded Quebec that to declare neutrality would mean seceding from the Commonwealth, and breaking with the Crown and Westminster, where the power to change the Canadian constitution was still deposited – largely because of French Canadian fears that its 'patriation' would be exploited by the non-French majority. But his central argument was one of brutal realism. Canadian neutrality would mean the internment of British soldiers and ships of war. 'I ask any one of my fellow countrymen whether they believe seriously that this could be done without a civil war in Canada.'[38] On neutrality, British Canadian sentiment was far too strong to be thwarted.[39] Quebec's price, said Lapointe, was a promise that there should be no conscription. King made the best of it. The idea of sending Canadian troops to Europe was out of date, he said. The defence of the Empire had been decentralised. The issue would not arise. The King–Lapointe formula was a political triumph. The huge popular success of the royal tour of Canada in the summer gave ample proof that Lapointe was right. When London declared war, the Canadian decision was the merest formality.[40]

For quite different reasons, the careful distinction made by Mackenzie King between entering the war and sending troops to Europe was forcefully echoed by Australian leaders. There was never any question of Australia's not following the British lead. 'Let me be clear on this', said the Prime Minister Robert Menzies in a broadcast at the end of April, 'I cannot have a defence of Australia that depends upon British sea-power as its first element . . . and at the same time refuse Britain Australian co-operation at a time of common danger. The British countries of the world must stand or fall together.'[41] But, in his speech on 6 September, Menzies carefully avoided spelling out the military implications of Australian entry; in fact, sending an expeditionary force to Europe along the lines of 1914 had been ruled out the previous day. Like the Labor leader John Curtin, Menzies and his cabinet regarded the first priority as the defence of Australia against the growing threat from the 'Near North'. Throwing their lot in with Britain was to express Britannic solidarity, assert a reciprocal claim on British naval protection and seek the best available guarantee of Australia's survival as a 'free white country'.[42] In the New Zealand Parliament, the government's affirmation of loyalty to King and Commonwealth was seconded by the opposition, and the House proceeded without further ado to sing the national anthem.[43] In South Africa, however, things were not so simple.

Since 1933, South Africa had been governed by a coalition between the National party led by General Hertzog, and the South Africa party of Smuts, supported by most 'English' voters. After 'fusion' in 1934, they came together as the United party. By agreeing upon South Africa's status as a fully self-governing dominion, with the King as head of state, fusion seemed to have buried the long-standing quarrel between 'republicans' and 'loyalists', and paved the way for a (white) South African identity common to both Afrikaners and English. With the return of prosperity, the United party trounced the Nationalist rump led by D. F. Malan in the general election in 1938. But Afrikaner opinion was volatile. 1938 saw a huge commemoration of the Afrikaner 'Great Trek' a century before, the crystallisation of the founding myth of the Afrikaner people, and its physical expression in the plans to construct a great Voortrekker monument. At precisely this moment, the crisis in Europe reopened the subject of South Africa's status: was Pretoria free to stay neutral in a 'British' war? For Hertzog, the price of fusion was a definite yes, and he held to this view when the theoretical war of 1938 became the actual war of 1939. To decide otherwise would split the Afrikaner people, wreck the fragile bark of racial good feeling ('racialism' in this period referred usually to English–Afrikaner antipathy) and smooth the path of Malanite republicanism.[44] The Governor-General, Patrick Duncan, Smuts' former lieutenant and an old protégé of Milner, raged privately against London's 'war for Danzig' and the damage it would do to fusion, the crowning achievement of South African politics since the making of Union.[45] But, when Hertzog put his views to the fusion Cabinet, it voted against him by seven to six.

As a result, the debate in parliament on South African entry was quite unlike those in the other dominions, where (whether for or against) they were largely formal. Hertzog rejected the argument that Hitler was set on world domination and proposed a convoluted 'neutrality' by which South Africa would meet its obligations to its Commonwealth associates and the defence of the Simonstown base while playing no part in the 'European' war. He was opposed by Smuts. Smuts had been critical of British policy in Europe and had agreed to neutrality in 1938. But he was also convinced that South Africa would be irrevocably damaged by breaking the British connection and by the isolation that would follow a declaration of neutrality. Unlike most of the Afrikaner politicians, Smuts was convinced that a 'white' South Africa would only be safe if it absorbed the colonial regions that lay to the north – a future that the break with Britain would instantly abort. Smuts did not lay bare this reasoning. He avoided any hint of a 'duty' to Britain – the red rag to the Afrikaner bull. He emphasised instead the danger to South Africa (especially South West Africa) of Hitler's drive for world domination, and her need for friends. But perhaps his shrewdest hit was to yoke together a threat and a promise. Smuts carefully quoted the speech by Lapointe in which he conceded that neutrality was impossible, except at the risk of a civil war in Canada. And he was at pains to insist that there was no question of South African troops being sent to the war. In the vote that followed, Smuts carried more than half of the United party with him, as well as the English in the small Dominion and Labour parties. Neutrality was rejected by sixty-seven to eighty.[46]

In all these four cases, 'Britannic' feeling was a powerful force for alignment with Britain, and an implicit threat that neutrality was unworkable. In the quasi-dominion of Southern Rhodesia, it ensured that 'automatic' entry was enthusiastically endorsed by white settler opinion. In the Irish Free State ('Eire' since 1937), where it did not exist, and where hostility to partition trumped any sense of shared strategic interest, a pragmatic neutrality (sometimes described as 'half in, half out') was the only option. The debate in the Dail on 2 September 1939 turned more on the emergency powers that the government would assume.[47] In most of the rest of the Empire, dependent status made participation involuntary. In India, however, the position was more complicated. Under the constitution of 1935, provincial self-government had been conceded to much of British (i.e. non-Princely) India, and, after the 1937 elections, most of the provinces were to be ruled by Congress ministers. Technically, since India had not yet attained its promised status as a federal dominion, it entered the war by the Viceroy's proclamation. But the real issue was whether the Indian ministers in the provincial governments would remain at their posts and serve a war effort directed by the Viceroy in Delhi.

It was an awkward dilemma. To abandon office after only two years might wreck the chance of entrenching Congress at the provincial level and reinforcing its leverage on the central government where the Viceroy was still supreme. On the other hand, well before the war, there had been a growing fear among many Congress leaders that the provincial ministries would prefer the fruits of power to a perhaps futile struggle against the federal constitution that Nehru had called 'a charter of slavery' (it balanced Congress' influence against that of the Muslims and the Princes). The approach of war gave the High Command an opportunity to reassert its control over the Congress ministries, reunify the movement and restore the priority of political advance at the Indian centre by forcing the British to scrap federation. It insisted that Indian support could only be given if the London government renounced imperialism and promised independence to India, with immediate effect so far as was possible.[48] At the provincial level, this ideological appeal was reinforced by more practical fears. Congress ministers were bound to be anxious that remaining in office, and aiding the war effort, would make them the target for public resentment when its costs were felt. So, when the Viceroy promised no more than a post-war review of the 1935 constitution, the Congress ministries in Bombay, Madras, the United Provinces, the Central Provinces, Bihar, Orissa and the North West Frontier Province followed the High Command's instructions and resigned in a body. What Congress could not do was to win the support of the Muslim League for its policy of pressure. Jinnah's price was predictably high: recognition of the League as the sole representative of all Indian Muslims. No agreement was possible.[49] So, while Jinnah too had a bone to pick with the British Raj, Muslim cooperation was not withdrawn, and in the Punjab and Bengal Muslim-dominated governments gave unconditional backing to the imperial war.

For many months it was war in slow motion and a war without strategy. Chamberlain's plans were opaque, but the apparent aim was to contain German expansion without recourse to unlimited war. The first priority was to strengthen the air force, the vital shield against the 'knock-out' blow. The timetable for sending a large army to France was much more leisurely. Instead of the fifty-five divisions that Churchill wanted to match France's effort, barely twenty were planned for the second year of war.[50] Far from rearming to the hilt with maximum speed, Chamberlain was determined to conserve British resources and avoid the sell-off of overseas assets. At the present rate of spending, calculated the American business magazine *Fortune* (a little wistfully) in the spring of 1940, it would be four years before Britain and France had to realise their direct investments abroad.[51] Meanwhile, the Western Powers stood on the defensive: even at sea the Royal Navy was fully stretched to contain the German attack using U-boats and cruisers. One German raider in the North Atlantic, grumbled Churchill (now First Lord of the Admiralty), required the efforts of half of Britain's battle fleet.[52] But, as the weeks of inaction stretched into months, the risk of disaster seemed more and more remote. The 'worst-case scenario' of the pre-war strategists had failed to materialise. Italy and Japan both remained neutral. Germany's failure to strike suggested a loss of self-confidence. On 4 April 1940, Chamberlain told a Conservative party meeting that 'Hitler had missed the bus'. Hitler might have replied: some miss, some bus. Five days later, he invaded Denmark. On 10 May (as Churchill became premier), the Germans attacked in the West. On 14 June, they occupied Paris, and, on 22 June, received the surrender of France.

The fall of France opened the decisive phase of Britain's imperial crisis. While the hiatus had lasted, the internal relations of the British system had seemed little affected by the strains of war. But the collapse of France was a catastrophic blow, whose full implications had been scarcely imaginable before it actually happened. The disaster that had loomed only briefly over the British world-system in mid-1918 now arrived in earnest. Britain itself was exposed to invasion. France's coastline became the springboard for the German onslaught in the North Atlantic. French defeat was the signal for Italian aggression in the Mediterranean and a direct attack on British control over Egypt and Suez. It was an open encouragement to a Japanese advance into French Indo-China, as the forward base for the invasion of British Malaya and the Dutch East Indies. It was the brutal demolition of almost all the assumptions on which confidence in the future of British world power had come to depend: the shield afforded by the European balance of power; the sufficiency of British naval strength once adequately modernised; the latent force of global economic power once properly mobilised. The Allied economic strategy, remarked a writer in *Fortune*, 'like their military, had a Maginot Line – their free and fruitful institutions against which no reluctant army of slaves could possibly prevail. Behind these, as behind the immobile bastions in France, they hopefully undertook to fight a war of position, "of limited risks", until they could laboriously convert their incredible wealth into goods of destruction. But the enemy, who was committed to a war of unlimited risk, did not wait.'[53] Amid the terrible urgencies of an ever-widening war, both the material resources and sustaining myths of the pre-war empire began to look dangerously frail.

Between June 1940 and October 1942 a disastrous defeat in one or more theatre of war threatened the rapid collapse of British world power. The most pressing danger was the invasion of Britain itself, thwarted in the hour of maximum danger by the desperate struggle for air supremacy over Southeast England and the English Channel in the Battle of Britain. But the extreme vulnerability of Britain during the long year of war without any great-power ally meant that Chamberlain's financial caution had to be cast to the wind in the race to buy arms before it was too late. The long-war illusion had become the short-war nightmare. Meanwhile, a vast effort was being put into the build-up of air power, the one weapon with which Britain could strike directly at Germany. The new war in the Middle East also created a voracious demand for manpower, supplies and the shipping to send them. As the Mediterranean route grew more dangerous (and was eventually closed), the importance of the Cape and of reinforcements from South Africa, Australia, New Zealand and India in the defence of Egypt became greater and greater. 'On no account', wrote Churchill in January 1941, 'must General Smuts be discouraged from his bold and sound policy or working South African Forces into the main theatre.'[54] By June 1941, Churchill intended Britain's Middle East forces to comprise some sixteen divisions: eight Indian, four Australian, two South African, one New Zealand and three British.[55] But the calamitous intervention in Greece (partly to forestall the German overawing of Turkey), and the dramatic impact of Rommel's Afrika Korps on the North African campaign, wrecked the early hopes of a decisive imperial victory. By June 1942, the defence of Egypt and Suez, and Britain's whole position in the Middle East, had reached its lowest ebb. To Churchill and his advisers it was obvious that, if Egypt fell, the British world-system would be cut in half. In the North Atlantic, they faced a struggle that was no less decisive for British prospects. A huge proportion of Britain's naval capacity, including some of the most powerful ships, was diverted to convoying and the hunt for U-boats and the even more dangerous German surface raiders. By June 1941, the losses of shipping had become so heavy that further announcement of them was abruptly halted. The intense strain felt in the North Atlantic and Mediterranean meant that any sizeable reinforcement of British sea-power in Southeast Asia was out of the question, despite the warning signs of a Japanese advance and the rising tension between Tokyo and Washington. It was the impossibility of assembling a larger force in time that led to the fateful decision in October 1941 to send *Prince of Wales*, one of the Navy's most up-to-date battleships, to deter any Japanese move – but without the air-cover or flotilla defence that was its vital complement. The sinking of *Prince of Wales* and *Repulse* within days of the outbreak of the Pacific War removed all chance of disrupting Japan's invasion of Malaya, and its epic climax, the fall of Singapore in the middle of February 1942.

The four-cornered assault on the British world-system did not bring about a catastrophic defeat, nor the total disintegration that haunted the strategists. But it did set in motion a rapid, cumulative and irreversible transformation of the pre-war structure of British world power. This was felt differently by the four dominions that had joined the war. In Canada, Mackenzie King's initial caution about sending troops to Europe had been quickly overcome.[56] King and his colleagues were uneasy that too slow a mobilisation would expose them to attack by the Conservative opposition for lack of loyalty to Britain.[57] But the fall of France in June 1940 was a turning point. It rammed home the danger that Canada itself might be exposed to attack if Britain were invaded or British sea-power disabled. In August 1940, joint planning for the defence of the North American continent was agreed by Roosevelt and King in their discussions at Ogdensburg. A long stride had been taken towards strategic integration between the United States and Canada. It passed almost unchallenged by King's Conservative critics[58] – although not by Churchill, to whom King retorted that Canada was sending Britain military aid.[59] It would be wrong to see the Ogdensburg agreement as the calculated transfer of Canadian security from one great-power patron to another, or as a deliberate switch from 'imperialism' to 'continentalism'. In the frantic summer of 1940, Canadian leaders contemplated the prospect of a British surrender – in which all their available military strength would be swallowed up – and its effects upon their trade-dependent economy and fragile sectional politics. Canada might have to assume the leadership of the Commonwealth much sooner than anyone expected, Mackenzie King told his colleagues.[60] Once the immediate crisis was past, ministers like Ralston (a First World War veteran) and Macdonald were determined that Canada should be fully committed to the military as well as the industrial struggle. But, at the moment of Britain's greatest weakness, Ottawa had been forced to agree that its continental alliance should henceforth be permanent.[61] The British connection was now to be limited by a third-party contract. Secondly, within a few months it was also clear that the Canadian supplies for which Britain was desperate could only be sent if Washington helped Canada to buy its American imports, and filled the foreign exchange gap left by Britain's inability to pay for Canadian goods in convertible funds (before 1939, Canada had met its deficit with the United States from its positive balance on British trade). The Hyde Park agreement of April 1941, said King, was the 'economic corollary' of Ogdensburg:[62] strategic partnership implied economic integration. Thirdly, the savage battle of the shipping lanes that raged deep into 1943, and the huge Canadian effort that was needed to guard North America's eastern approaches against U-boat attack, gave cruel proof that Britain had lost (for the time being at least) the 'empire of the North Atlantic'.[63] Whatever the strength of the sentimental tie, the material basis of Anglo-Canadian relations had been altered for good.

Much the same was true of the Pacific dominions. Australia had joined Britain at war without hesitation, but the Australian government pinned its hopes on an early peace.[64] Thereafter, it waged an unrelenting campaign for influence in London – through representation in an 'Imperial War Cabinet' (promptly rejected in London), through a personal visit by the Prime Minister, Menzies, in the spring of 1941, and by urging a meeting of dominion prime ministers.[65] Australian ministers were deeply uneasy over the concentration of British naval and military power in Europe, and the lack of any real deterrent to a Japanese attack. To make matters worse, the prompt offer by New Zealand to send a division to fight in Europe had forced them to make a matching offer.[66] By 1941, three Australian divisions were fighting in the Middle East, and the small Australian navy had been placed at Britain's disposal. As alarm about Japanese intentions grew, the Australian and New Zealand governments were forced to accept Churchill's reassurances that Japan would do nothing until Britain was defeated, and that, if they were attacked, the British would abandon the Mediterranean struggle and send army and navy to protect kith and kin. The military debacle of mid-1941, when the disastrous invasion of Greece and Crete wrecked an Australian and a New Zealand division, intensified Canberra's mistrust of Churchill. But the new Labor Prime Minister, John Curtin (who had originally opposed sending Australian troops abroad), was very reluctant to ask for the return of Australian troops. He accepted the argument that Singapore was the key to Australia's defence.[67] When Australian troops were sent back from the Middle East (at Churchill's suggestion) after Pearl Harbor, their destination was Java. It was only after the fall of Singapore on 15 February 1942 that Curtin insisted, after a furious exchange with Churchill, that the two divisions in transit – the dominion's sole trained fighting force – should be diverted not to Burma but home to Australia.

By that time, Curtin had already infuriated Churchill by his notorious New Year's message announcing that Australia 'looks to America, free of any pangs as to our traditional links or kinship with the United Kingdom'. What has often been seen as a symbolic repudiation of the old tradition of imperial loyalty was much more ambivalent. It is better seen as an anxious attempt to claim a full Australian place in strategic planning as America's main partner in the Pacific War (a claim badly received in Washington). In this role, Curtin was saying, Australia would not be Britain's poodle. Both Curtin and Fraser, the New Zealand Prime Minister, recognised that their own defence, as well as ultimate victory in the Pacific conflict, largely rested in American hands. But neither wanted to abandon the British connection or would have been allowed to do so by their public opinion. As the overweening scale of American power became more and more evident, they searched for better ways to influence Anglo-American policy and the post-war settlement. Closer Commonwealth unity (to secure British backing), local solidarity (as in the Australia–New Zealand agreement of January 1944) and the long-standing claim that the Pacific dominions should represent all Britain's interests in the South Pacific (as the 'trustees of British civilisation') were their preferred (and perhaps only) means to this urgent end. But there was no brooking the fact that, with the fall of Singapore (taking with it all hope of a British fleet being sent to Southeast Asia – Churchill had planned to send a battle squadron east in May 1942), the Pacific dominions had passed from the strategic sphere of the British system into that of the United States.

In all three dominions where there was a Britannic majority, the sense of being 'British' countries remained strong and there was a continued and intense commitment to the survival of Britain as an independent great power. The armies despatched by dominion governments told only half the story. Among RAF aircrews, where losses were highest and life expectancy shortest, dominion volunteers were out of all proportion to their population size.[68] 'England is the home of our race', said an Australian Labor MP in June 1940. 'We love England, and if England should go down, it would seem to me as if the sun went down.'[69] But all three had been forced to find ways of compensating for the British weaknesses so starkly revealed between 1940 and 1942. All three had been forced to recognise that the old reciprocity of the British system could no longer be counted on. The unstinting commitment of the dominions' manpower to an imperial war had been based on the assumption that British sea-power would keep their homelands safe. After 1940–2, that assumption could no longer be made: another great-power protector was needed whose claims might be greater. For the British system, the implications were profound. Since the late nineteenth century, the mutual and unconditional loyalty of the 'British' countries had lain at the core of British world power. Their relatively high levels of economic development (Canada's national income, calculated *The Economist* in 1941, was as large as Italy's[70]), their shared political values, and their astonishing capacity to mobilise their manpower for faraway wars, made them valued allies out of all proportion to their population size. Their oft-declared loyalty to King and Empire was an important source of psychological reassurance to the British at home that their global burdens would be shared in a crisis. Though it took some time before the pattern was clear, 1942 saw the end of this old imperial nexus. As they took stock of their interests in the worldwide war, it was to a new international order that they began to look to supplement, replace or incorporate the British connection.

It was ironic that this trend was weakest in the least Britannic of the overseas dominions. In South Africa, Smuts had won the support of enough Afrikaners to back South African entry. The volunteer army despatched to fight in East and North Africa was composed of Afrikaners as much as English South Africans.[71] Smuts waged a vigorous propaganda campaign to win over South African opinion and counter the calls for peace made by opposition politicians after the fall of France. But in South Africa's case there was no Singapore, although, with the crisis of the North African war in July 1942, Smuts was anxious enough to start thinking of how South African forces might be withdrawn to stage a fighting retreat up the Nile valley.[72] In 1943, after Alamein, Smuts was strong enough to win a decisive victory in a general election (another 'khaki electie' as his opponents complained). The pragmatic basis of Anglo-South African relations, helped by the specially favourable treatment in imports and shipping by which Churchill aimed to bolster

Smuts' popularity,[73] was undisturbed by the presence of an alternative great-power patron in the Southern African sub-continent. But there were warning signs that the greater warmth that Smuts had brought to the imperial link would only be temporary. Afrikaner nationalism, frustrated in parliament, mobilised furiously among teachers and journalists and denounced Smuts' government as a British lackey. The 1943 election was a formal triumph, but a closer analysis was less reassuring. The percentage of Afrikaners who voted for the United party fell from 40 per cent in 1938 to 32 per cent,[74] while the nationalist opposition was united firmly behind D. F. Malan and an independent republic outside the Empire.[75] The dream of fusion and Afrikaner reconciliation to the British system was fading away.

The second pillar of British world power was the Indian Raj. India had been the captive market for Britain's largest export, an important field for British investment and a vital contributor to Britain's balance of payments – though all three had suffered badly in the 1930s. But its greatest value after 1900 had been as the indispensable auxiliary to Britain's military power. The Indian budget had paid for two-thirds of the Empire's standing army. Its vast rural manpower formed an inexhaustible reserve against an imperial emergency. At the outbreak of war, however, India's military strength was in decline. The Indian army was unmechanised. Funds were short. The modernisation programme, for which London was paying, had hardly begun. Nor was it expected that Indian troops would play an important part in the European war. The main objective of the Army in India (a term used for the combined British garrison and the Indian army proper) was to defend the Northwest Frontier against Afghanistan. The Nazi–Soviet pact of August 1939 made it seem all the more important to keep watch on the Central Asian front against the 'old enemy'.

As a result, although the Viceroy would have liked to enlist Congress support and keep their ministries in office, there was no sense of urgency on the British side. After May 1940, the picture changed dramatically. Over the next six months, the Indian army was almost doubled in size. In the following two years, the total strength of its combat arms rose to over two million.[76] Recruitment, supply and the promotion of war industries became the central preoccupation of the Indian government. The cooperation of Indians (especially the educated) became more and more vital, and the wooing of opinion all the more necessary. Not surprisingly, then, the Viceroy, Lord Linlithgow, made another attempt to draw representatives of the Congress into the government. The 'August Offer' promised dominion status at the end of the war (no deadline had been offered previously), Congress seats in the Viceroy's 'cabinet', and an advisory council to bring a larger Indian voice into the war effort.[77] The Congress refused. Dominion status, said Jawaharlal Nehru, was 'as dead as a doornail'. India must be free to leave the Empire–Commonwealth.

The widening rift between the British and Congress was not just the result of nationalist mistrust of British intentions, or the pacifist inclinations of the large Gandhian wing. The real reason was the tacit but deepening commitment of the British to the claims advanced by the Muslim League. Since the Lahore resolution of March 1940, its leader Jinnah had insisted on a Muslim veto – in effect a League veto – on any constitutional settlement hammered out for India. An independent India must acknowledge 'Pakistan' – the whole community of Indian Muslims – as an equal partner in a confederal India.[78] The League would negotiate an equal footing with the Congress. Of course, successive Viceroys had long recognised the Muslim claim to separate representation, to protection against a 'Hindu Raj', and to the right to govern the Muslim majority provinces. The grand federal scheme of 1935 had been designed to prevent the concentration of power in Congress hands by devolving heavily to semi-autonomous provinces. But, from 1940 onwards, the politics of war gave a fierce twist to this established policy. The most vital zones of the Indian war effort were Muslim majority provinces: Bengal, which contained more than half of India's industrial capacity; and the Punjab, the main recruiting ground of the Indian army. In both, Muslim-dominated governments had co-operated willingly.[79] But their goodwill and stability could not be taken for granted – especially if talk of constitutional change raised the temperature of Hindu–Muslim rivalry. Nor would recruitment continue if communal tensions discouraged would-be sepoys from leaving their homes.[80]

The result politically was that, at the very moment when it was more important than ever to gain the cooperation of Congress, the British had less than ever (of what really mattered) to give away in return. The stalemate persisted until the end of 1941 and the early phase of the Pacific War. Then the rapid advance of the Japanese armies showed that India would soon be in the war's front-line and that its war effort would need to be cranked up to even higher levels. This was not the only worry. The dismal failure of Malaya's defence raised a disturbing question. What would happen if India were attacked or invaded? Would the internal administration fall apart as Indians refused to take orders or abandoned their posts? Would the Indian masses simply disown a colonial regime in which the largest party had no share of power? The prospect unnerved the government in London. The case for a new approach was strengthened by signs that the Congress 'moderates' might be more amenable, and even more perhaps by Churchill's grudging acceptance that some new initiative was needed to disarm American complaints against colonial rule.[81] Congress endorsement of the British war effort (then at its nadir) would be helpful evidence of the continued vitality of the British system. What was needed, urged Clement Attlee, in a burst of hyperbole, was someone who would save the British Empire in the East as Lord Durham had once saved Canada.[82] Singapore fell thirteen days later.

The fruit of this rethink at the war's worst moment was to be a new constitutional offer. As soon as the war ended, India's political future would be handed over to a 'constitution-making body', free to withdraw India from Empire membership and the British system. Meanwhile, Indian participation in the Viceroy's government would be increased significantly. It would even include a defence minister with control over almost everything except operational matters. At the Viceroy's insistence (he threatened to resign), the offer was not published. Instead, it was taken to India (and published there) by Sir Stafford Cripps, widely considered Churchill's likeliest successor. Cripps began with high hopes that his old friendships in Congress would win him a deal. But two insoluble differences wrecked his prospects. The first (and less serious) was the Congress insistence on a direct say in defence operations – a demand to which London, the Viceroy and Cripps himself were unanimously opposed. The second (and more fundamental) was the British insistence that, whatever the model of independence proposed after the war, the Muslim provinces and the princely states would be free to opt out and make their own arrangements in negotiation with Britain. It would be up to the Congress to find an acceptable formula. This was the recipe for 'Pakistan' or – worse still 'balkanisation' – that the Congress feared most and rejected completely. With an imperial war effort ever more deeply dependent upon Muslim goodwill, it was also the recipe that London could not surrender. By early April, all negotiation was over (Congress gave its final rejection on 10 April), and Cripps was on his way home.[83] Two months later, as the Japanese armies drove closer towards the Indian frontier, the Congress passed its 'Quit India' resolution, and set in motion a mass campaign to bring British rule to an immediate end.

The failure to agree with Congress did not prevent the British from using Indian resources and manpower to fight the rest of their imperial war. Nor did Quit India prevent the successful defence of the Indian frontier in the desperate battles of Imphal and Kohima. Nevertheless, the Cripps offer and its violent aftermath signalled the definite end of India's special place in the British system: the sentence of death was merely postponed. It was true, of course, that the federal scheme on which the British set such store had stalled politically before the war. It was also true that any further advance towards dominion status would have meant a progressive reduction in India's military contribution to imperial defence. The British garrison, for which India paid, would have had to go home. On the other hand, it was more than likely that, with the power to shape its successor regime (without a deadline, a 'constitution-making body', or a prior commitment that India could secede from the British system), the Viceroy's government would have secured special status for the Indian army, largely officered by British expatriates, and tied India closely (through a treaty or bases) into the global system of imperial defence. But for the Pacific War, India would still have been a financial debtor, a dependent part of London's sterling empire. But, in its desperate scramble for a constitutional settlement amid the political fall-out of the Singapore surrender, Churchill's Cabinet was forced to play almost all its trumps. Abdicating control over the constitutional process, let alone the timing of the constitutional convention, was a last-ditch effort to soothe away Congress outrage at the Muslim veto. Cripps' ultimate failure and the violent unrest of Quit India that followed left the Raj a political bankrupt. It could repress disorder and gaol the Congress leadership (Nehru went to gaol for the rest of the war[84]). But it had no means of containing the rising tide of communal tension, and nothing left to trade with India's political leaders. The promise to go had been published abroad. In two revolutionary years, the British had 'sold off' what remained of their Indian empire to meet the pressing demands of their last imperial crisis.

The third blow was perhaps the hardest: the collapse of London's commercial empire, the ultimate guarantee, alongside sea-power and the Home Islands' resources, of Britain's global status. By the outbreak of war, that commercial empire was very different from what it had been in 1913. Then London had been the undisputed centre of a global trading system, and sterling the indispensable medium for international transactions. British investment, like British trade, was as much international as imperial: nearly half was placed in Latin America or the United States. The huge stream of income from Britain's 'invisible exports' was reinvested abroad to build up still further the enormous claim on overseas resources. The First World War had cut this empire down to size. Its dollar assets were sold to buy munitions in the United States (by 1929, claimed *The Economist*, only 3 per cent of British investment was in the US[85]). A huge debt was contracted. And heavy borrowing at home reduced the capital available to lend overseas. After 1931, when Britain went off gold and adopted protection, the commercial empire had become more and more a sterling empire. Following the Ottawa agreements of 1932, the British Empire countries with Argentina (and some other non-empire states) formed a trading bloc. With the exception of Canada, they also acted as a currency bloc, the sterling area. By the late 1930s, a large proportion of British trade was conducted within the sterling area and the post-war tendency to concentrate British investment in empire countries became even more marked – reaching 62 per cent of the total at the end of 1936.[86] As the effects of depression bit deeper, Britain's portfolio of overseas assets slowly shrank. The marked shift towards investment at home, and a much less favourable balance of payments after 1930, made it hard to replenish the capital fund at the rate that was needed to maintain its value. Nevertheless, in a world divided into economic zones, London's commercial empire was second to none. London was still the banker to the largest group of trading countries. It had preserved the core of its old financial business, and its overseas clients (including the dominions and India) were among the soundest. Britain's overseas trade was as large as that of the United States – despite the huge disparity in national output. The invisible earnings from this great commercial network still paid for a quarter of her merchandise imports and supplied 5 per cent of the national income.[87]

The Achilles' heel of the British system was its need for dollars. Before the war this was a manageable problem: protection and sterling area cooperation had cut the demand for American goods. Predictions of America's commercial primacy had been decidedly premature. In fact, America's record of economic recovery from depression had been much worse than Britain's. Nor was it obvious that there could be any escape to a permanent level of greater prosperity. The American economy had been badly squeezed by the general collapse of agricultural prices, affecting up to one-third of its workforce. To prop them up and defend manufacturing against outside competition meant heavy protection and a growing burden of internal debt. As imports shrivelled, American exports also suffered – from retaliation abroad and the lack of dollars in foreign hands. There was no 'dollar empire' of complementary producers to soak up the surplus of American industry. American resentment at economic misfortune was partly aimed at London's sterling empire, and at what were seen as Britain's persistent attempts to devalue sterling against the dollar.[88] Although the late 1930s had seen somewhat better relations (the Anglo-American trade agreement of 1938 had made limited concessions to American exports), there could be little doubt that breaking up (or into) London's commercial empire was the most obvious way of expanding America's trade in a deeply segmented international economy.

Until 1940, there was little chance that they could do so. Chamberlain had been very protective of the sterling empire and part of the rationale of his slow-motion war had been to reduce to the minimum the financial strain of additional dollar purchases. Britain's dollar assets were carefully husbanded and London built up a large stockpile of gold, buying the entire production of South Africa's mines in return for sterling. But, after June 1940, this cautious strategy was blown to pieces. In the desperate rush to re-equip Britain's armies for a war of survival, every marketable asset was pressed into service. Paying cash on the nail, the British purchasing mission bought all the American supplies they could find. By December 1940, more than half of Britain's prewar stock of dollars and gold had been spent[89] and the haemorrhage was such that the rest would have been spent by March 1941. In the event, the threat of bankruptcy, default and economic defeat was lifted by lend–lease. Even so, by September 1941, gold and dollar assets had shrunk even further to $1,527 million (approximately £340 million), out of which pre-lend–lease contracts and non-lend–lease items had still to be met, a total of more than $1 billion.[90] Nor, of course, was lend–lease a gift without strings.

Roosevelt's eagerness to help Britain rearm was entirely genuine, and entirely self-interested. From his economic advisers, and the business interests represented in Congress, British pleas for financial aid drew a calculated response. They were determined not to ease London's shortfall in dollars and gold only to find that, when the war had ended, they were back where they started, facing a sterling empire. They were deeply suspicious that the British were hiding their fabled wealth. They demanded a visible sacrifice of British-owned enterprises in the United States.[91] And they made three stipulations in return for lend–lease. British reserves were to be run down to the lowest possible level (a demand later eased); British exports, especially to dollar markets, were to be pegged back sharply – to less than one-third of pre-war levels; and, at the end of the war, the British would have to agree to abandon any trade discrimination against American exports. The sterling empire would be blasted open. Its industrial engine-room and financial power-house would be drastically weakened. In unspecified ways, it would have to make good the largesse of lend–lease.[92] Its member states would look elsewhere. To J. M. Keynes, the 'Churchill' of the economic war, the negotiation with America was a gruelling struggle for what was left of Britain's commercial independence.[93]

This doomsday scenario was not entirely realised – for reasons to be explained in the following chapter. But there was little doubt that between 1940 and 1942 the pre-war balance of commercial power between London and Washington shifted for good and erased in the process Britain's century-old status as a (and, for much of the time, *the*) dominant force in the world's trading economy. This was not just a matter of exhausting Britain's assets in dollars and gold. In the sterling empire, too, the dramatic change in the scope of the war piled up new obligations overseas. 'The growth of balances in favour of other parts of the sterling area is becoming unmanageable', remarked Keynes in June 1942. 'The more the war moves to the East, the more we spend in the Middle East and India.'[94] By September 1942, Britain already owed India some £360 million for goods and services supplied to the war effort, wiping out the whole of India's pre-war debt to Britain. A year later, the figure was £655 million. Egypt was owed some £250 million. It would mean, said Keynes, 'great prospective embarrassment'.[95] What Keynes had in mind was obvious enough. The large sterling balances (i.e. the amounts Britain would have to pay sterling area countries at the end of the war) would mean much larger exports than before the war, to meet overseas debts and compensate for the loss of invisible income. Without the cushion of invisibles, it would be a constant struggle to avoid a deficit on the balance of payments. There would be no surplus to rebuild Britain's overseas investment, and the attractions of sterling as an international currency (a highly profitable status) would soon disappear. The vicious circle would close. Across the Atlantic, the new economic order had already been glimpsed. The Pax Britannica was dead, announced *Fortune* magazine in May 1942. Britain was 'broke, her empire shrivelled... her banking and insurance income will never come back and her merchant marine is sinking'.[96] 'Since the Pax Britannica can no longer be counted on to defend America, what kind of world-power system does America propose to put in its place?'

The fall of Singapore

Churchill had convinced himself, and sought to convince others, that Japan would not dare enter the war until Britain was defeated or disabled. Under the terrible strain of the invasion threat, the Atlantic struggle and the see-saw war in the Mediterranean and North Africa, it was hardly surprising that neither he nor his Chiefs of Staff found much time to ponder the risks of defeat if Japan attacked Singapore and Malaya. Even after Pearl Harbor, Churchill fell back on the comforting mantra that Singapore could hold out in a six-month siege.[97] Local army opinion took refuge in racial contempt for Japanese military prowess: the Japanese might beat Chinese armies; Europeans would be different. But, when the Japanese army invaded northern Malaya, its battle-hardened veterans were more than a match for its British, Indian and Australian defenders, many of them recently recruited, poorly trained or barely acclimatised. The catastrophic loss of *Prince of Wales* and *Repulse*, poor intelligence and the lack of air power combined with poor generalship to turn Singapore from an 'impregnable fortress' into the 'naked island'. Once the British forces had abandoned the mainland and fled onto Singapore island, their fate was sealed. On 15 February 1942, 130,000 British Empire troops surrendered to a numerically inferior attacking force.

The symbolic importance of such a shameful failure was bound to be large. In *The Times* despatch from nearby Batavia (modern Jakarta), the obvious lesson was drawn. '"Soft" troops, unenterprising commanders, an apathetic native population – these are not the signs of a gallant army betrayed only by bad luck; they sound uncomfortably like the dissolution of an empire.'[98] In his private diary, Churchill's most senior military adviser expressed a similar foreboding. 'We are paying very heavily now for failing to face the insurance premiums necessary for security of an Empire! This has usually been the main cause for the loss of Empires in the past.'[99] As defeat sank in at home, there were loud demands for a new approach to colonial rule, and a 'colonial charter' to win the hearts and minds of Britain's subject millions. Fresh impetus was given (as we saw earlier) to the search for an Indian settlement. A propaganda campaign was launched to make the imperial case in the United States, before opinion there hardened into an angry contempt for Britain's dysfunctional empire. But the meaning of Singapore was not just symbolic.

Singapore's fall was the brutal proof that the Eurasian Revolution of the 1930s and 1940s had reached its climax. The global preconditions in which a British world-system had been continuously viable since the 1830s and 1840s had all but disappeared in the storms of war. The European balance, precariously restored after 1918, had been comprehensively wrecked: indeed, German domination of Russia seemed more than likely in the early summer of 1942. 'Passive' East Asia had become an uncontrollable vortex of anti-Western imperialism. In this colossal emergency, the British system lacked the means to defend itself unaided and had not the faintest hope of restoring the *status quo ante*. The internal structure of Britain's pre-war system, as well as its ethos and assumptions, had been drastically destabilised by a geopolitical earthquake: the relentless consequence of Anglo-French strategic defeat in 1938–40. How much would survive in a modified form, were the Allies to emerge victorious, was, in 1942, anyone's guess.

12 THE PRICE OF SURVIVAL, 1943-1951

Amid the calamities that crashed over them in 1942, it was hardly surprising that British leaders, including Churchill, should have thought mainly in terms of survival. In the course of that year, they faced the prospect of defeat in the Middle East and the loss of Egypt and the Canal, a disaster which would have meant far greater losses than those incurred at Singapore. Without their main fighting force, their hope of keeping control over India – let alone of exploiting its resources and manpower – would have been fatally weakened. The Viceroy's ability to suppress the Quit India movement would not have been helped by the sight of the Germans in Cairo. At much the same time, they could only watch helplessly as the German advance into Russia threatened the collapse of the Soviet regime. A huge reordering of Eurasia seemed on the cards with the 'world-island' divided between the Nazi and Japanese empires. Preserving a maritime 'rimland' without the Middle East, India and Southeast Asia, and keeping Britain's connection with Australia and New Zealand, would have been all but impossible. The British world-system would have been a funeral pyre.

Of course, it was true that America's entry in December 1941 had brought massive relief and the assurance, perhaps, of survival in some form. In June 1942, the battle of Midway destroyed Japan's hopes of naval control of the Western Pacific. By the end of the year, victory at Alamein and the grim Russian defence of Stalingrad seemed to promise that the relentless expansion of Germany's power had at last been contained. But neither was remotely a guarantee of ultimate victory in Europe, which depended on the Red Army and the Anglo-Americans fighting their way into the European 'fortress' heavily defended by the Germans and their allies. The risk of defeat, or stalemate, was high, especially in the case of an amphibious attack, the Anglo-American route. If either were to happen, then Britain's 'survival' would resemble that of a patient on a life-support machine: dependent indefinitely on American aid to fend off invasion; incapable of defending, supplying, financing or controlling the component parts of the pre-war imperial system. Neither Churchill nor his advisers regarded such a fate as remotely acceptable. 'Our history and geography demand', said Anthony Eden, 'that we should remain a world power with worldwide interests.'[1] They imagined survival in imperial terms, as the full recovery of the British world-system. Deprived of its 'system', Britain would be desperately vulnerable to the will of whatever great powers had outlasted the conflict. Real survival meant the freedom to restore London's global network of trade and resuming Britain's function as a banker and investor. It meant regaining the footholds (in the Mediterranean especially) that underpinned Britain's status as a great *European* power. It meant reaffirming Britain's leadership over the white dominions on whose loyalty, manpower and resources British influence and interests already depended in part. It meant recovering sufficient power and prestige to negotiate authoritatively over the future of India, and resist the demand (largely from American voices) that Britain's colonial territories should be administered internationally and opened to American business. It meant – above all – recreating the geopolitical conditions that secured the European mainland from a single power's domination. British leaders suspected that the failure to achieve all – or almost all – of these war aims (most of them tacit) would unravel the links and connections on which Britain's place in the world was actually (if rather mysteriously) based. In the second half of the war, much of their energy was spent in the struggle to make a military victory that would meet this demanding wish-list.

Strategy and Empire, 1943–1945

1943 was the year in which the tide of battle turned. It was also the year in which the shape of a post-war world could begin to be glimpsed, if only in outline. For the British, the signs were not reassuring. Their victories in North Africa and the successful invasion of Italy did not strengthen their hand. At the level of strategy, 1943 was to be dominated by the furious Anglo-American arguments over the priority to be given to the Mediterranean attack on Germany and the planned cross-Channel invasion already named 'Overlord'. The British resented the scale of America's commitment to the war on Japan and suspected the motive behind American support for Kuomintang China in whose military potential they had little confidence. They were also deeply uneasy at what they regarded as the dangerous ignorance of the American planners about the risks and demands of an amphibious invasion against the full weight of German military power in the West. A premature onslaught quickly bogged down in a war of attrition (with a huge cost in life for every advance) or, worse still, a catastrophic defeat and a second Dunkirk, were bound to inflict disproportionate (and perhaps irrecoverable) damage on British resources and British prestige. On the American side, British devotion to a Mediterranean strategy, at the expense of postponing the decisive attack through Northern France to the Rhine, was cynically regarded as a means of shoring up British imperial interests and as evidence that the British lacked the stomach to fight in the theatre that mattered. Too great a delay in the onslaught on Germany would weaken the case of those in the Roosevelt administration who favoured the 'Europe first' strategy, against those who demanded priority for the war on Japan. In Washington's view, it would also worsen the friction with their Soviet ally and increase the danger that Stalin would make a separate peace (of which there were signs). Indeed, the British themselves were all too aware of how much their recovery depended upon Soviet success on the Eastern Front. A Soviet collapse would have released huge German reinforcements to regain the ground lost in the Mediterranean, and open the door into the Caucasus and Iran, hurling the British back into the terrible crisis of July 1942. Yet, by the same token, the Red Army's advance (it had driven the Wehrmacht out of the Caucasus and most of the Ukraine by the end of 1943) reinforced Stalin's claim to a very large voice in any eventual peace, and in the strategic decisions required to achieve it.

By late 1943, as planning began in earnest for the invasion of France the following summer, the growing reliance of the Anglo-American armies upon American manpower as well as materiel,[2] and the enormous scale of the Soviet military effort, drove home the lesson that the post-war world-order would be shaped to the wishes of these emerging 'superpowers' more than to Britain's. At the Teheran conference in November 1943, Stalin and Roosevelt, as Churchill later lamented, negotiated over his head. At almost the same time, a speech by Jan Smuts on 'Thoughts on the New World' (to the Empire

Parliamentary Association in London) spelt out the dangers of the new balance of power that would follow German defeat. 'We have moved into a strange new world . . . such as has not been seen for hundreds of years, perhaps not for a thousand years. Europe is completely changing . . . the map is being rolled up and a new map is unrolling before us.' Three of the continent's five great powers would have vanished. 'Germany will disappear . . . France has gone . . . Italy may never be a great power again.' Instead, Russia would be 'the new Colossus of Europe', all the stronger once the threat from Japan in the rear had been vanquished. Britain would have great prestige, but 'she will be a poor country . . . there is nothing left in the till'. The best hope for peace in the world, Smuts insisted, lay in a new world organisation, but one in which the 'trinity' of great powers exercised real leadership. But for the British to play their proper part in this required them not only to reorganise their overseas system, but also to strengthen their hand in Europe. That meant closer relations with the small democracies of Western Europe, who knew that 'their future is with Great Britain and the next world-wide British system'. Closer union with Britain would create a 'great European state . . . an equal partner with the other Colossi in the leadership of nations'.[3]

Smuts called for 'fundamental thinking' and admitted that his ideas were 'explosive stuff'. But his speech was a remarkable summary of the challenges facing the Churchill government in the last two years of the war. Indeed, his speculations about a British 'closer union' with Europe have a more than passing resemblance to the 'European union' for which Churchill himself was to call. Amid the press of day-to-day business before and after the landings in Normandy in June 1944, entailing the conduct of campaigns in France, Italy, Greece and Southeast Asia, and in the air over Germany, the looming shape of a Soviet-dominated Europe, from which the American armies would have quickly withdrawn at the end of the war, exerted more and more influence over British military planning. Its conclusions were deeply unwelcome. The defeat of Germany would result in a much heavier strategic burden on Britain than she had had to carry before the descent towards war after 1937. In June 1945, the Post Hostilities Planning Staff told the Chiefs of Staff Committee that even a united British Empire would be no match for Soviet aggression, and would need the help of the United States. To keep the Red Army at bay, Britain would have to be ready to give early help to her European allies, and hold a deep air defence belt in Northern Europe. To keep India safe and guard communications through the Indian Ocean would require new naval and air bases and a main base in Ceylon (Sri Lanka). To deter a Soviet advance in the Middle East, Britain's defence system there would have to be pushed further north, but with no guarantee that either the oilfields or the Suez Canal could be saved in a war. Even in peacetime, maintaining internal security in the Middle East 'will involve a formidable military commitment'.[4] It is not hard to see why close cooperation between the Great Power 'trinity', in the new 'world organisation', appeared so urgently necessary to the makers of policy in London. It was the best guarantee that the British could limit the liabilities that otherwise threatened to over-tax their strength.

For, as Smuts had said candidly, there was nothing left in the till. Strictly speaking, of course, this was an exaggeration. The British had sold off their assets in dollars and acquired a great burden of overseas debt. They had retained investments in the sterling area countries, but had also assumed huge sterling obligations by their purchases from them. Egypt and certain Middle East states, the colonial territories that supplied British needs, and above all India with its army of two million men and its industrial base, built up credits in London, the so-called 'sterling balances'. Britain's war effort was sustained in large measure by American aid, especially 'lend-lease'. When peace came, Britain's post-war economy would carry a mass of overseas debt considerably greater than in 1919 even though the vast bulk of lend-lease (perhaps $20 billions' worth) would be forgiven. This was one side of the ledger. But the sources of overseas income had also been damaged. This was partly a matter of the assets sold off in the war to the tune of £1.5 billion, more than one-third of the total. It was also a consequence of huge physical losses, including a large share of Britain's mercantile fleet, the largest in the world before 1939, and a valuable earner of invisible income. As part of the terms of lend-lease, the British were required to cut down their exports and withdraw from many overseas markets. By the middle of the war, their exports had fallen to well under one-third of their pre-war level.[5] All the main sources of overseas earnings – from exports, investments, shipping and services – had been drastically shrunk. The destruction of industrial plant at home, the conversion of much of the rest to the production of war goods, and the huge diversion of manpower into military service meant that rebuilding the civilian economy and Britain's export capacity would need a major investment as well as a period of grace. Yet the conditions laid down in return for America's wartime aid demanded the rapid return to peacetime 'normality' making sterling convertible (so that sterling countries could buy dollar goods freely) and ending imperial preference (to remove the tariffs imposed on dollar goods in British Empire countries since the early 1930s). On this scenario, before the British could catch their breath, or begin to scale down the vast military load of the war and its aftermath, their foreign markets would vanish and they would be bankrupt.

To avert this disaster, the British set out in the autumn of 1944 to persuade their American allies to help them revive much of their pre-war role in the world economy as soon as Germany was defeated. 'Stage II' – as the period between the defeat of Germany and the surrender of Japan was termed – was expected to last for a year or longer. During Stage II, the British were anxious to begin the process of civilianising their economy. More manpower would be moved into civilian production and much more effort put into the manufacture of exports. Britain would begin to start paying its way. With a nod from Roosevelt, agreements were framed to prolong wartime support and permit its application to the task of post-war recovery.[6] Had Stage II taken the time that the planners expected, the economic transition to peace might have been much less painful. In fact, it barely lasted three months. As soon as Japan was defeated, Roosevelt's successor, Harry S. Truman, abruptly halted lend-lease. To bail out their economy and keep it afloat, the British were forced to apply for an American loan, but without the leverage that their war effort had given them. In the graphic language of John Maynard Keynes, who had master-minded the management of Britain's external finances, the British were faced at the end of the war with a 'financial Dunkirk'.[7] Without a drastic reduction of their foreign commitments, and perhaps even with one, they would have to accept years of even greater austerity than they had already endured. The financial and commercial power on which they had always relied as the 'fourth arm' in warfare would have vanished completely.

The full extent of their economic fragility was thus partially hidden from British leaders until the very end of the conflict. But they were already aware of the enormous importance of close cooperation with the white dominions if they were to make good their claim to be one of the 'Big Three'. In the traumatic twelve months after June

1940, before Hitler's onslaught on Russia gave Britain a reluctant, suspicious and (as it seemed for some time) ill-fated ally, dominion support had been important materially and perhaps vital psychologically. The dominions' contribution to Britain's fighting strength, unlike that of India, cost London nothing. Canadian, South African, Australian and New Zealand troops fought in the Mediterranean and Northern European theatres, as well as closer to home (in the Australian case). Canadian enlistment exceeded the levels of 1914–18.[8] Dominion supplies could be purchased on tick. Canada's dollars and its industrial base (much larger than that of the other dominions) were mobilised for the war effort. The Royal Canadian Navy gradually took over the anti-submarine war in the Northwest Atlantic.[9] South Africa's value as the great redoubt guarding the only safe route to Egypt and India was greater than ever by 1941–2. The main base from which the British intended to launch their part in the defeat of Japan after 1944 was expected to be in Australia and to use Australian resources.

Perhaps as a consequence, British leaders began to talk enthusiastically about the need for imperial unity and a common foreign policy to which Britain, the dominions and the rest of the Empire, including India, would be tied. They may have been encouraged by the speech made by John Curtin, the Australian Prime Minister in August 1943. Curtin had enraged Churchill by his notorious statement (at the end of December 1941) that Australia 'looks to America, free of any pangs as to our links or kinship with the United Kingdom'.[10] Now, like the prodigal son, he had returned to the fold. His Adelaide speech (amplified some three weeks later) roundly declared that 'some imperial authority had to be evolved', and called for an 'Empire Council' and a permanent secretariat to give it effect.[11] His ideas were welcomed in *The Times*. The Empire, it said, could only keep peace in the future as one of the four great powers of the United Nations. But the dominions 'would fail in these duties if they accepted individual membership of the United Nations as a substitute for the Imperial bond'.[12] In July 1943, Sir Edward Grigg, a leading Round Tabler and soon to be Resident Minister in the Middle East, had published a manifesto calling for a 'Commonwealth, coherent, united and strong', able to stand beside the United States, Russia and China. Its disintegration, he claimed, 'would expose many parts of Asia, the Pacific, the Atlantic and Africa to open international rivalry'.[13] The book was reissued in December to catch the following wind that now seemed to be blowing. Then, in January 1944, Lord Halifax, the British Ambassador in Washington, and former Foreign Secretary, delivered a widely reported speech in Toronto (where the flame of Empire loyalty usually burned brightest). 'Not Great Britain only', he declared, 'but the British Commonwealth and Empire must be the fourth power in that group on which . . . the peace of the world will henceforth depend.'[14] When the dominion prime ministers met in London in May 1944, it was left to Mackenzie King, the Canadian premier, to challenge the formula that the British ministers present proposed to insert in the final communiqué. It would refer, said Eden, to the Empire's foreign *policy*. 'All agreed', said Attlee. There would be an 'Imperial Joint Board for Defence', said Cranborne, the Secretary of State for the Dominions. But King refused to agree. 'The more I think of the high pressure methods that have been used the more indignant I feel', he wrote in his diary that evening.[15]

The reality was that there was little agreement among the dominions or between them and the London government on what Commonwealth unity should actually mean. Curtin had emphasised Australia's British identity. His election campaign in 1943 had wrapped itself in the Union Jack: Australia should be a 'second Britannia in the Antipodes'.[16] When he came to London in May 1944, he told his Guildhall audience: 'Australia is a British people, Australia is a British land.'[17] But Curtin (and Fraser, the New Zealand Prime Minister, who supported Curtin's call for an Empire Council) did not intend the subordination of the Pacific dominions to the wishes of London. Far from it. In the long tradition of Australian statecraft, his aim was to commit more imperial resources to the South Pacific and to assert Australia's claim to manage all 'British' interests in the region. 'We are in the south what the motherland is in the north', he told a Sydney audience in May 1942.[18] His 'Empire Council' was meant to rotate between the dominion capitals and London because the Empire could not be run by a government sitting in Britain. In case there should be any doubt in the matter, the Australia–New Zealand Agreement in January 1944 had bluntly insisted that any settlement in their region would require the active assent of Canberra and Wellington – an assertion that was even more badly received in Roosevelt's Washington than in Churchill's London. Curtin and Fraser's 'imperial regionalism' was implicitly shared by Smuts in South Africa. The northward extension of South African influence and the gradual inclusion of Central and

East Africa in the South African sphere were long-cherished ambitions. They duly emerged in Smuts' 'explosive' speech in November 1943. The British system needed 'tightening up' but also decentralising if it were to match the 'Colossi'. That meant consolidating the colonial territories into larger units and tying them more closely to the neighbouring dominion – a delicate euphemism.[19] Smuts may also have hoped that this sub-imperial vision would strengthen his United party's appeal against its National party opponents. The 'old narrow little-Afrikanerdom had been defeated for good', he told Leo Amery in October 1943.[20] But Smuts (with an Afrikaner majority on the electoral roll) knew better than to call for new imperial machinery. The government-inspired *Cape Times* had rubbished Curtin's ideas.[21] Talk of imperial unity, Smuts confided to King, was just 'damn nonsense';[22] it 'was a thing of the past'.[23] And, for Smuts perhaps, as for Curtin and Fraser, the prospect of Britain's huge wartime commitments in the Mediterranean and Europe continuing on into the peace made it all the more urgent to wrest the direction of British power in their regions into dominion hands.

All this made less sense in the senior dominion. Mackenzie King was keenly aware of the strength of pan-British patriotism in Canada. One of his closest allies, the Montrealer Brooke Claxton, echoed Curtin's 'Britannic' sentiments in a speech made at much the same time. 'Canada', he said, 'is a British Nation in North America'.[24] King himself was irritated by the 'isolationist and autonomist position in intra-Imperial relations' adopted by his own officials in the External Affairs department. 'Of all countries', he noted, 'we are really the most vulnerable because of our extensive territory, resources and the like.' Canada 'will greatly need strength alike of British Commonwealth as a whole and of US in protecting her position' (he was thinking of the threat that the Soviet Union would pose).[25] But, since the conscription election in 1918, King had been obsessed by the danger of an irreconcilable rift between Quebec and 'English Canada' that would tear his party, as well as the country, in half. English Canada's loyalty to Britain, and to Canada's identity as a 'British nation', were facts of political life. They had forced King into the 1942 referendum that authorised the government to apply conscription 'if necessary'. Quebec's low rate of enlistment was observed with resentment. 'Quebec is hated in the rest of Canada', noted 'Chubby' Power, one of King's ministers, an English-speaking, Catholic Quebecker and a much decorated veteran of the First World War.[26] Power opposed conscription, arguing that it would turn Quebec into 'Ireland all over again',[27] but several of King's cabinet colleagues were determined to enforce conscription for overseas service once the losses from 'Overlord' began to be felt. To King these cross-pressures made it all the more critical that Ottawa should be visibly free from any last vestige of imperial control, most of all when it came to external commitments. At the prime ministers' meeting in May 1944, he threw his weight against any change in the way that dominion governments were consulted. When the premiers discussed the proposed 'World Organisation', King insisted that Canada would want its own representation 'as one of the medium powers', a position soon followed by Curtin, Fraser and Smuts.[28] For all four dominions, a separate voice at the United Nations offered better protection of their 'national' interest than collective membership of a Commonwealth bloc in which London would enjoy an inevitable lead.

The main imperial legacy of the second half of the War was the scale of the British commitment in the Mediterranean and Middle East. This was an echo (with certain key differences) of the 'Eastern' war in 1914–18. Then, as later, the British responded to a double imperative. They had to guard the road to India through Iraq and Iran, and defend Egypt, the 'Clapham Junction' (as the cliché had it) of their imperial communications and the northern gateway to the Indian Ocean. But the Middle East was also a huge bastion that was meant to make up for Britain's weakness in Europe. In 1918, it had been the grim prospect of outright defeat on the continent that drove the British forward in Palestine and Iraq and towards the Caucasus. The fall of France in June 1940 and the German advance into Russia the following year recreated the nightmare of 1918. For the British once again, the Middle East was the theatre where their fate would be settled. If they were to lose the Middle East war, their world-system would be cut in half, and Britain's dependence on American aid would become absolute. But, if they could hold on and secure their position, the Middle East was a springboard from which they might hope to reassert their position as a *Mediterranean* power and as a great power in Europe. The equation was not new. Britain's claim to be a great power in Europe had rested in part on her Mediterranean presence since the seventeenth century.

Of course, the pattern of conflict after June 1940 had followed a different trajectory. In 1914–18, the British had fought the Ottoman Empire at Gallipoli, in Palestine and in modern Iraq. After

June 1940, they fought the Italians and Germans in a war that was as much Mediterranean as Middle Eastern and became steadily more so with the invasion of Italy and the British intervention in Greece. The invasion of Normandy in June 1944 reduced the strategic importance of the Mediterranean theatre and also signalled the moment when the United States army became the indisputably dominant force in the Anglo-American alliance. The final struggle for Europe would be fought for the most part between German, Russian and American armies: two-thirds of the eighty-five divisions assembled for Eisenhower's advance into Germany in the spring of 1945 were American. In the Mediterranean, however, the British remained the senior partner, and a British general was the Supreme Commander. In the Italian campaign, there were as many British and Commonwealth troops as American.[29] 'Italy is a country which we can get at and in which we rather than Russia should naturally expect to exert predominant influence', remarked a senior British official.[30] The British were eager to 'reconstruct' Italy as a parliamentary state that would look towards Britain. They were just as determined that the liberation of Greece would produce a regime that was friendly to Britain, if not dependent upon her. Intervention in Greece, Eden told his War Cabinet colleagues in August 1944, was indispensable to Britain's strategy in the Balkans and the Eastern Mediterranean.[31] Churchill's notorious 'percentages' deal with Stalin in Moscow in October 1944 (Greece was to be '90 per cent' British) was designed to exclude Soviet influence from the Mediterranean. Whatever was to happen elsewhere in Europe, Churchill and Eden were determined to use Britain's large share in the Mediterranean victory to contain Soviet expansion and reinforce Britain's claims as one of the 'trinity' – what Smuts had seen as the post-war executive of the United Nations.

It was this grand ambition that made the Middle East so important. Historians have often been scornful of the British failure to rethink their Middle East interests at the end of the war. In fact, the course of the war had reinforced their belief in the region's exceptional value. Egypt was the base from which the British had fought their Mediterranean campaign. It was from Cairo, after all, that their war and diplomacy in the Eastern Mediterranean had been organised and directed. At the British Embassy there, in the elegant house of the British Resident Minister in the Garden City nearby, and at the Mena Palace Hotel beneath the Great Pyramid, diplomats, soldiers and politicians in transit had pondered British policy for the entire vast region from Greece to Iran. The Arab Middle East as a whole, but especially Egypt, had become a supply zone, partly filling the role that India had played in the First World War. By 1945, the British owed Egypt some £400 million for goods and services rendered.[32] With its barracks and bases, repair shops and storage, Egypt was the arsenal of British military power as well as the way-station through which it was shuttled en route to the East or back 'home' to Europe. The practical closure of the Mediterranean to shipping for much of the war had diminished the value of the Suez Canal, but its importance in peacetime was expected to rise sharply. Finally, the strategic importance of the Middle East region had been emphasised still further by technological change. Without the Abadan oil refinery at the head of the Gulf, the British war effort across a huge swathe of Eurasia would have ground to a halt: fear of its loss was so great that a separate command had been created to guard it. Middle East oil had supplied nearly one-quarter of Western Europe's needs in 1938, a figure expected to rise sharply at the end of the war.[33] No one could doubt the enormous advantage conferred by control of it. The same could be said of Egypt's importance as a hub of air transport. The gruelling air journeys undertaken in wartime by British civilians and soldiers to Moscow, Yalta, Teheran or New Delhi, or to confer with the men on the spot, invariably took them through Cairo. The need for air bases to link the scattered components of the British world-system, and for an overland 'trunk route' between Europe and India, had long been recognised. The colossal expansion of air power and air travel during the Second World War (and the general assumption that a new air age was dawning) only hammered it home.

The instinct to build on their established position was sharpened by opportunity and also by fear. There were numerous signs before the end of the war that Stalin would demand more control over the Straits, an old Russian ambition. It also seemed likely that Russia's military presence in Northern Iran (part of the Anglo-Russian occupation imposed in 1941) would be used as a lever to enlarge Russian influence. At the same time, the British were determined that Libya should not be restored to Italy, and that Russian claims to a share in its post-war control should be firmly resisted. Instead, it should form part of Britain's great arc of influence extending all round the Eastern Mediterranean, and stretching away to the Gulf and Iran. In the three-way division of global power that was widely predicted (China's great power capacity was somewhat discounted), the share of the British was bound to be large, indeed had to be large. But the readiness to contemplate a burden on this scale really depended on two unspoken assumptions. The first was that Britain would be able to bear the costs that would follow. As we have seen, an illusion persisted until the defeat of Japan in August 1945 that American aid would fund Britain's revival as a great trading economy. The second assumption proved even more fragile. It was that the British would be able to 'manage' the nationalisms of their Middle East client-states, and 'rally the moderates' by artful concessions. It was easy to think – especially while the war lasted – that uncooperative locals would be brought to their senses by the threat of coercion.[34] In so divided a region with such deep social differences, it was hard to imagine a common nationalist front strong enough to evict them.

There was one other assumption that should not be forgotten. Since their first invasion of Egypt in 1801, the British had counted on India for part of the military means to exert their power in the region. They had often been tempted to attribute their presence to the need to defend India or uphold the prestige of its (British) government. 'Why', asked Lord Curzon in 1918 (in one of those questions that only he answered), 'should Great Britain push herself out in these directions? Of course the answer is obvious – India.'[35] It was a short step from this to insist that what was in India's interests should be paid for by India, and guarded by its army. After the First World War, there had been imperative reasons to reduce the military burden on India, then in the throes of political upheaval and constitutional change. But, in the Second World War, India had become once again a huge reservoir of military manpower, and an army of two million men had been raised. Indian divisions fought in the Middle East, North Africa and Italy as well as in the Southeast Asia campaigns and the bloody defence of Imphal. India was the main base from which the reconquest of Burma, Malaya and the Dutch East Indies was launched. Yet its political future was deeply uncertain. The Cripps Mission had failed to win Congress support for the war. The Quit India movement that Gandhi unleashed as a mass insurrection was crushed by the British, and large numbers of Congress activists gaoled. Gandhi's prison fast was a 'flop' without the activists' backing.[36] The British ruled by decree or with Muslim support. 'Politically the position is very easy here at the moment', reported the Viceroy in mid-1943 to Leo Amery, the Secretary of State.[37] Only one thing was clear. The British had committed themselves irrevocably (in the Cripps Mission 'offer') to full Indian self-government at the end of the war. What that would mean for India's role in Britain's world-system was shrouded in mystery.

For Amery in London, this was the key issue. 'To keep India within the Commonwealth during the next ten years is much the biggest thing before us', he told Churchill in April 1943. 'If we can keep her for ten years I am convinced we can keep her for good.'[38] Amery was anxious to reform Indian politics while the Congress was banned. He was eager to give the Viceroy's Indian ministers more political influence and to make them more credible as the voice of Indian opinion. But his real objective was a drastic revision of India's constitutional future. Parliamentary-style government was completely unsuitable for the Indian centre, he told the House of Commons in March 1943, because it meant party government. The federal government should 'emanate' from the states and provinces. Like the Swiss executive, it should be non-party and enjoy independence from the federal assembly. Amery's scheme was transparently obvious: a non-party executive chosen by the units of a 'looser' federation much at odds with each other would have little will to sever the British connection completely. It would be much more likely to acknowledge India's need for British assistance, and much more willing to sign an Anglo-Indian treaty of the kind London wanted. The new Viceroy Lord Wavell (1943–47) shared Amery's zeal for a political move and his geostrategic perspective. 'The future of the Commonwealth, from the defence point of view, and also perhaps economically, will depend to a great extent on what happens in India in the next ten years or so', he pronounced in July 1944.[39] But he and his advisers thought Amery's scheme futile. The answer instead lay in drawing the Congress and the Muslim League into a coalition government for the phase of transition. But, as Wavell complained, the will was lacking in London to push matters forward: 'Winston had no intention of helping it on.'[40] Churchill's own view was characteristically blunt: 'Victory is the best foundation for great constitutional departures'.[41] So India's politics waited on victory: how triumphant a victory remained to be seen.

Imperial Labour

Of course, it was not to be Churchill or his Conservative colleagues who wrestled with the fate of the British world-system, or the independence of India, when the war finally ended in August 1945. In July 1945, a vast electoral wave swept the Labour party to power, giving it (for the first time) an absolute majority in the House of Commons. This political earthquake was widely understood to mean that British opinion was impatient for social reform. As a 'patriotic' party whose leaders had been central to the war effort at home, Labour was trusted to implement the wartime promises on social insurance, education and employment, as well as reorganising under public control the services and industries whose performance was vital to economic and social recovery: the mines, the railways and the provision of healthcare. The scale of the task and the need to preserve the apparatus of central control were visible in the damage suffered by almost every major city. The popular hope that the sacrifices of the war would bring a fairer, more equal and more secure society was combined with the fear that without a strong centralised system reconstruction would be slow, inefficient and unfair, destroying in the process (as after 1918) the promise of change.

Yet it was certainly not true that the new Labour leadership was preoccupied with domestic over external priorities, or indifferent to the requirements of British world power. The Prime Minister, Clement Attlee, had served on the Simon Commission in 1927–30, and was keenly concerned with the Anglo-Indian relationship. He had wanted the Cripps Mission in 1942 to save India as '[Lord] Durham had saved Canada.'[42] He was keen to enlist the dominions' post-war help especially in defence. Ernest Bevin, the new Foreign Secretary, had been a leading pre-war trade unionist and a stout defender of the need to protect British overseas markets. He quickly embodied an all-but-Churchillian view of Britain's place in the world and of the need to defend its claims and prerogatives. This did not mean a passive endorsement of the colonial *status quo*. Labour's leaders had sympathised with the vigorous attack on British colonial practice that had burst out in the open after the fall of Singapore in February 1942. The fierce critique launched by Margery Perham, the African expert and protégé of Lord Lugard, and published in *The Times*, lambasted the failure to meet the aspirations of colonial peoples, to develop their economies or to democratise their politics. Economically and socially, colonial rule had created 'tropical East Ends' and promoted the colour bar, 'an attitude of mind that, at its worst, regards other races of men almost as if they were other species'.[43] Perham's strictures chimed with the dislike of Labour's colonial experts – whose ties were closest with missionary and humanitarian interests – for white settler communities and the reactionary ethos (as they saw it) of indirect rule, which aligned the colonial power with chiefly authority against educated commoners.[44] A 'progressive' policy of social advancement and political partnership was as much a necessity in the colonies as at home. But this reformism coexisted with a reaffirmation of faith in the 'British system'. There was 'no fixed line between Dominions and dependencies', declared Herbert Morrison in his Newcastle speech of January 1943. India 'can have full self-government for the taking' at the end of the war. 'We are no greedy exploiters.' The real burden of his speech was to warn against the 'myth of a self-sufficient empire', and to insist on the need for international cooperation between all the great powers. The strongest claim of the 'British system' on other nations, he concluded, was that its long-term interests were the same as those of international society as a whole.[45] No Victorian could have phrased it better.

Indeed, at the end of the war, there was no obvious conflict between the needs of domestic reform and the task of upholding the substance of British world power. It was axiomatic that Britain's global trading economy should be restored as quickly as possible to its pre-war position (at least), and that domestic prosperity depended on overseas markets more acutely in Britain than anywhere else in the industrial world. The immediate need for food and raw materials could only be met by keeping in place the wartime version of the imperial economy with its bulk purchases from the dominions and official control over the price and supply of colonial produce. The demands of war and the stringent restrictions imposed under lend-lease had largely confined British trade to Empire and sterling area countries after 1940. The most practical reasons dictated the need to preserve these imperial connections as the platform on which economic recovery could be built. From that point of view, reforming the Empire (along the lines that Perham had urged) – to make it more dynamic, efficient and productive – seemed a perfect combination of profit and virtue. In an era of shortage, economic growth in the colonies would supply Britain's needs and fund their own modernisation. Secondly, it was quite easy to believe in the first months of peace that the costs of remaining a great power in the world would not be prohibitive. If the United Nations were to function (as British leaders intended) primarily as the instrument of Great Power cooperation between the United States, the Soviet Union and themselves, with tacit spheres of influence and sanctions against territorial aggression, the crippling burden of imperial defence would become far more bearable. It was precisely in this spirit that Attlee was to urge (in September 1945) Britain's military withdrawal from the Middle East.

In fact, the uncertainties soon began to pile up, and with them the costs. The British had harboured deep suspicion of Stalin well before the war ended. It quickly became clear that friendly recognition of Britain's spheres of influence was not on Moscow's agenda. Stalin demanded a role at the Straits (as the counterpart to British control of the Suez Canal); his army remained in northern Iran; and Moscow laid claim to a share in the trusteeship of the Italian colonies in Libya (the prize the British had reserved for themselves). The Soviet Union had all the old Tsarist ambitions in the Middle East, warned the British ambassador.[46] There was hardly any doubt, recorded another senior diplomat in February 1946, 'that Russia is intent on the destruction of the British Empire'.[47] Britain was being dragged willy-nilly into confrontation with a power of awesome military strength and possibly limitless ambitions. At the same time, it was also deeply uncertain (or so it seemed in London) what part the United States might play in resisting Soviet aggression. The rapid demobilisation of American forces, America's interest in exploiting erstwhile British markets and the security conferred by its nuclear weapons, might make its leaders indifferent at best to the survival of the British world-system, content perhaps to carry off the spoils if it collapsed under the strain of a confrontation with Russia. Thirdly, the failure to agree upon a peace treaty with Germany, and the strength of communist movements in both France and Italy (in part a reflection of economic distress), wrecked any hope that Europe's old powers would balance Soviet strength. On the contrary, it seemed that their divisions and weakness had opened the way for the Soviet penetration of the south and west of Europe as much as its east and centre.

These were worrying signs that the favourable geopolitical position that the British might have hoped would be theirs at the end of the war would turn into the nightmare envisaged by Smuts in 1943. A British world-system, poised between two continental 'superpowers' (the term was coined in 1943), might have hoped to exploit their rivalry and exact favourable terms, economically at least, from the United States. Instead, it was the British themselves who felt the pressure of Soviet expansion. Worse still, they did so at a time when they lacked the means to pay for the essential dollar goods needed to sustain their domestic economy and their overseas burdens, not to mention

the programme of industrial and commercial recovery. With the lapse
of lend-lease, this became in fact the most urgent priority. Nor could
British leaders assume that the 'internal' politics of their imperial system would remain passive while they grappled with its economic and
geostrategic crises. In India, the Middle East, and in the reoccupied
colonies in Southeast Asia, British authority was soon under strain.
Among the white dominions, as the wartime prime ministers meeting
had signalled, their ties with Britain were bound to be mediated by
the logic of self-interest in a world of such geopolitical uncertainty
and when Britain was no longer their ultimate geostrategic protector.
The solid British Commonwealth 'bloc' assumed in some visions of a
three-power world was no more than a pipe-dream.

Within a matter of weeks, then, the new Labour government
was confronted by a mass of problems so grave as to amount to a
general crisis – economic, geostrategic, political – of the British world-
system. The struggle for survival in war was succeeded by a struggle for
survival in peace. In the autumn of 1945, the immediate pressure was
eased by a dollar loan from the United States of $3.75 billion (some
£750 million). But the terms were arduous, and much more severe
than Keynes who had hoped for a gift of $5 billion (£1.2 billion) had
expected.[48] The British were required to dismantle the barriers that
favoured the trade between sterling area countries and to allow holders
of sterling to exchange it for dollars by mid-1947. Indeed, the United
States government saw the main purpose of the loan as being to allow
those countries who had built up large sterling credits in London to
exchange them for dollars if they wished to do so. The sterling economy
was to be blasted open to American exports. When the terms became
public, there was widespread unease (there had been much private
unease in the Bank of England and Treasury). The loan agreement
was an 'economic Munich', declared Robert Boothby, a Conservative
MP. However unpalatable, it could not be rejected. It was not just a
matter of averting an imminent crisis: rejecting the loan, said Dalton,
the Chancellor, 'would mean less food of every kind except bread and
potatoes'.[49] British hopes of reviving their pre-war commercial and
financial position also depended upon the breathing space that the loan
would give them. 'The way to remain an international banker', Keynes
told the House of Lords, 'is to allow cheques to be drawn upon you;
the way to destroy the sterling area is to prey on it and try to live on
it. The way to retain it is to restore its privileges and opportunities

as soon as possible to what they were before the war.'[50] Indeed, the early signs were hopeful: as millions of servicemen and women were demobilised, the task of reconverting the war economy got under way. 1946 was an *annus mirabilis*. Exports went up, the stock exchange rose. At the Lord Mayor's banquet in October, the traditional venue for an authoritative statement of the economic outlook, the Chancellor of the Exchequer, Hugh Dalton, gave a sunny account of Britain's progress and prospects. The fly in the ointment was the burden of overseas costs, the very delicate balance between dollar income and spending, and the huge size of the 'sterling balances', whose owners were impatient to release them for current consumption: including India (with some £1.3 billion) and Egypt (with £400 million).

Meanwhile, the Labour cabinet struggled on with the task of easing the pressures on Britain's world-system. There was little scope for reducing their commitments in Europe while Germany's fate remained unresolved. No agreement was reached between the Soviet Union and the Western Powers. That meant the continuing occupation of Germany and meeting the desperate shortage of food in the British zone: a 'colony' that was costing £100 million a year.[51] For similar reasons – the need to contain Soviet influence until a peace treaty was signed – aid had to be sent to Greece and Turkey who barred the way against a Soviet advance to the Mediterranean. In India, they hoped to forestall serious unrest by taking the political initiative. In January 1946, Attlee pressed the case for sending a Cabinet Mission (whose real leader was Cripps) to settle the terms on which independence would be given. It was already apparent that a constitution acceptable to both the Congress and the Muslim League would be very hard to contrive, and that the leaders of the Congress were deeply suspicious that the British would favour Muslim demands for a balkanised India. In London, by contrast, there was still a white hope that, by promising swift independence, a new Indian 'dominion' would emerge, willing if not eager to uphold its old British connection. Once hot heads had cooled, so the argument ran, the Indian leaders would see that their economic self-interest, strategic exposure (to Soviet aggression) and political ethos made alignment with Britain the inevitable choice. With British encouragement, India might even assume the role of a regional power, sharing with Britain diplomatic supervision of Southeast Asia. Hence it was the primary aim of the Cabinet Mission to find a constitutional formula that preserved Indian unity by hook or by crook. But their Heath Robinson scheme for a three-tier federation (combining Hindu and Muslim 'sub-federations') was also inspired by the fear that the division of India would suck Britain into a vortex of chaos. By mid-1946, it was accepted in London that there were no longer the means to crush an Indian mass movement: the arm of coercion on which British rule had relied as its last resort had withered at last.[52]

The British were also at pains to pre-empt the local resentment that was expected to boil up in Egypt, where their wartime occupation had grossly exceeded the limits permitted by the 1936 treaty. Here, too, they were hoping that a 'generous' offer would pave the way for an Anglo-Egyptian agreement that would tie Cairo in to a system of regional defence under British command. The key issue here was the right to reactivate the bases in the Suez Canal Zone if an external threat was detected. In May 1946, after much internal debate between the soldiers and diplomats, the British declared themselves willing to evacuate Egypt completely over the course of five years. There were further disputes over how much consultation should take place between London and Cairo before a 'threat' was acknowledged and the bases reopened, and over what undertakings should be formalised in a treaty. Then, towards the end of the year, Egypt's old claim to its Sudanese 'colony' (in theory an Anglo-Egyptian condominium, in practice ruled solely by Britain) became a fresh bone of contention. The minister, Sidky, with whom the British were dealing, was pushed out of office and the negotiations collapsed.

By the end of the year, the British had little to show for their efforts to adjust their world-system and reduce the costs it imposed – financial, strategic and political. It may have been this that fuelled the persistent critique directed by Attlee towards the retention of Britain's large Middle Eastern *imperium*. Attlee had expressed misgivings about the original plan to seek British trusteeship over Cyrenaica and Tripolitania, Italy's Libyan ex-colonies. He had warned (in February 1946) against the cost of defence, running at twice the level expected at the end of the war. He challenged the claim of the Foreign Office and the Chiefs of Staff that the Middle East was vital to Britain's world interests. He remained deeply committed to the idea of a 'world organisation', and opposed to 'old-fashioned' manoeuvres and policies that might prevent its fruition. Britain's entrenchment in the post-war Middle East, he repeatedly argued, would be regarded by Russia as a threatening move. It would discourage Moscow's commitment to a new international order centred upon the United Nations and might even provoke Soviet aggression in Europe. Nor had Britain the means to build up the weak Middle East states against a Soviet advance. Agreement with Russia, not confrontation, was the only safe course.

Attlee's ideas were those of an ardent internationalist who hoped that victory in the Second World War marked the end of the age of predatory imperialisms, the vale of tears through which the world had struggled since the early 1930s.[53] But they were not a rejection of British world power. Attlee acknowledged that the great new fact of world politics was American power, and that the independence of India would limit Britain's ability to exert influence in Asia. But he was far from writing off Britain's claims on the loyal partnership of the dominions or its colonial rights elsewhere in the world, especially in Africa. At the dominion prime ministers meeting in April 1946, he had hoped to commit them to a unified system of Commonwealth defence but had to accept a much more decentralised formula whereby each dominion took responsibility in its region 'to maintain conditions favourable to the British Commonwealth and to accept joint responsibility for their defence in war'.[54] Britain's vulnerability to external attack made it wise, so he thought, to relocate certain vital industries to the safety of Australia. And Britain's links with the two Pacific dominions could be maintained by a line that ran across Africa, not through the Mediterranean and Middle East. Embedded in Attlee's approach was an old not a new view of empire. Like Bonar Law, or Balfour or many Gladstonians, Attlee regarded the Middle East as a dangerous outpost, made even more dangerous in the era of air power. It would be far better to make it into a neutral zone – a 'wide glacis of desert and Arabs' was the phrase Dalton remembered – separating the spheres of British and Russian predominance, than to run the risks and bear the costs of an *imperium* still more extensive than that Britain had seized after 1918.[55]

Attlee was Prime Minister, and his comments were trenchant. But he never came close to winning the argument, and by February 1947 had abandoned the effort. He faced the combined opposition of the Foreign Office and Chiefs of Staff: indeed, it may have been the threat of the latter to resign en masse that forced him into retreat. The central weakness of Attlee's position was its optimistic view of Russian intentions, justified by faith, it had to be said, rather than by works. His proposal that the Middle East become a 'neutral zone' assumed

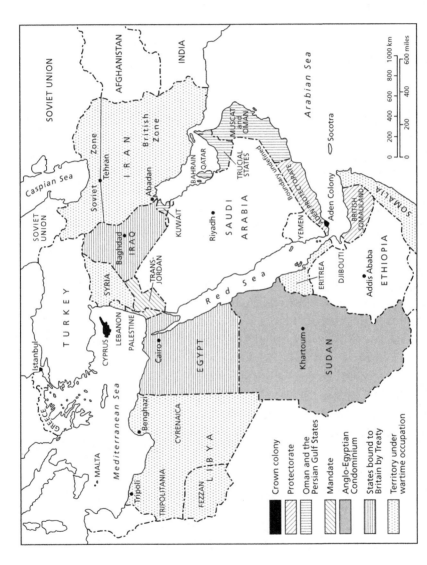

Map 11 The Middle East in 1945

SOVIET UNION

AFGHANISTAN

INDIA

Arabian Sea

Caspian Sea

Soviet Zone

British Zone

IRAN

MUSCAT and OMAN

Tehran

Abadan

BAHRAIN

QATAR

TRUCIAL STATES

SOVIET UNION

Baghdad

IRAQ

KUWAIT

Riyadh

SAUDI ARABIA

ADEN PROTECTORATE

Aden Colony

Socotra

YEMEN

Boundary undefined

TURKEY

SYRIA

TRANS-JORDAN

Istanbul

CYPRUS

LEBANON

PALESTINE

Red Sea

ERITREA

DJIBOUTI

BRITISH SOMALILAND

SOMALIA

GREECE

MALTA

Cairo

EGYPT

Addis Ababa

ETHIOPIA

Mediterranean Sea

Benghazi

CYRENAICA

Khartoum

SUDAN

Tripoli

TRIPOLITANIA

FEZZAN

LIBYA

0   200   400   600   800   1000 km
0   200   400   600 miles

Crown colony

Protectorate

Oman and the Persian Gulf States

Mandate

Anglo-Egyptian Condominium

States bound to Britain by Treaty

Territory under wartime occupation

that Stalin would not revive the designs on the Straits and North Persia, that he had already revealed, once British power was withdrawn. The Chiefs of Staff were incredulous at Attlee's 'naivety'; Bevin's answer was lapidary, almost Curzonian. He dismissed Attlee's suggestion that withdrawal from the Middle East would assuage Russian aggression: 'It would be Munich over again, only on a world scale, with Greece, Turkey and Persia as the victims in place of Czechoslovakia... Russia would certainly fill the gap we leave empty, whatever her promises.' It would wreck Britain's relations with the United States, on whose aid Britain depended, and whose leaders had just been persuaded that American interests, like those of Britain, required the Middle East to be held. 'If we now withdraw at this moment, I should expect them to write us off entirely.' Nor was the Middle East economically valueless: it was worth £100 million to Britain 'and possibly a great difference in our future dollar earnings'. Indeed, the Middle East might take India's place as an economic partner for Britain. If, instead, Britain left, hard on the heels of its departure from India, it 'would appear to the world as the abdication of our position as a world power'. India would move towards Russia; 'the effect on the Dominions would be incalculable.'[56] Here was the case, cast in oracular terms, that Britain's survival as a power in the world now hinged – in the geopolitical conditions that Soviet advance had created – on this dangerous salient in Middle Eurasia.

Ironically, Attlee's reluctant endorsement of the Middle East policy occurred on the eve of the *annus horribilis*, the year in which British world power seemed less real than the threat of financial and political bankruptcy. A terrible winter brought on a fuel crisis and damaged the export drive (to raise British earnings by 50 per cent above the pre-war level) on which hopes of recovery were pinned. The American loan was being quickly used up. In March 1947, Stafford Cripps, the avenging angel of socialism, forecast a long period of austerity. In July 1947, under the terms of the Anglo-American loan, holders of sterling could convert their pounds into dollars. The result was disastrous. Britain's dollar reserves, already depleted by the cost of American imports, sank like a stone. Faced with sterling's collapse, London abruptly suspended convertibility on 20 August. Rations of petrol and food were reduced, and potatoes joined the list of rationed supplies. The Cabinet agonised over how many men could be spared from the civilian economy, how large the army should be and how long those 'called up' should serve in the armed forces. At Dalton's insistence, the provision of aid to Turkey and Greece had already been scrapped: this was the burden that the United States now assumed under the 'Truman Doctrine' promising help to those states fearful of Soviet aggression. Against this background of deepening economic gloom, the government faced an impasse in its effort to ease India into an agreed independence. With no sign of a compromise between the Congress and the League, growing communal friction and rising anxiety that the British in India would be caught up in a storm of political violence, panic in London began to set in. The Cabinet Mission had failed. Attlee and his colleagues rejected the Viceroy, Lord Wavell's, 'breakdown plan' (a staged withdrawal to the Indian ports, handing power over province by province) as a recipe for turmoil, but had no plan of their own. The sacking of Wavell and the choice of Mountbatten were acts of inspired desperation. But Attlee was forced to give Mountbatten a virtual free hand to decide on the timing and settle the manner of Britain's departure. Mountbatten was lucky. His arrival in India in March 1947 coincided with the grudging recognition in the Congress that, without an early transfer of power, and agreement on partition, the spiral of communal violence would destroy their authority over the Indian masses as much as that of the British. This was the chink through which Mountbatten would drive with ruthless diplomacy to impose partitioned independence in August 1947.[57]

The late summer of 1947 erased any lingering hope that Britain would quickly regain the substance of its world position before the catastrophe of 1940. A further turn of the screw was the rapid deterioration of the situation in Palestine. Here the British had struggled to find a settlement acceptable to both Arabs and Jews whilst also reserving an enclave of their own – in the event of withdrawal from their Canal Zone bases. There was no question of stopping further Jewish immigration or preserving Palestine as an Arab-majority state – the 'solution' envisaged in 1939. That was ruled out by American disapproval, and the growing intensity of Zionist terrorism, against which the large British garrison seemed poorly equipped. Even after the bombing of the King David Hotel in July 1946 – aimed at the heart of the British mandate administration – the Cabinet rejected the repression of Jewish organisations for fear of American anger.[58] Instead, the British found themselves drifting into the worst of all worlds: as the unwilling executants of a territorial partition fashioned in New York by the United Nations, but whose real sponsor was the United States. The likely costs of this role for Britain's relations with the Arab states, at precisely the moment when the terms of their post-war alliances were being redefined, were regarded in London with horror. The only solution, it came to appear, was an ignominious departure, without even the fig leaf of an ordered transition, leaving the field to the local contestants and the war that followed.[59]

For an imperial system that laid so much stress on the prestige of its rule, and which depended so much on its claim to embody public order and justice, the events of 1947 were especially damaging. London's authority – among its 'subordinate' allies (like Egypt or Jordan), its dominion 'partners', as well as its colonial subjects (who enjoyed very varying degrees of local self-rule) – was a function in part of local opinion. The appearance of strength, the assertion of will, and the promise of rewards to bestow, were the often invisible strings with which the British had tied their ramshackle system together. The 'illusion of permanence' – that, in any future world order, British power would loom large – was a vital constraint on the colonial temptation to flout London's wishes too rudely. It did not require a Cassandra to wonder in late 1947 whether the spell had been broken. It seemed after all that the disasters that the British had suffered between 1940 and 1942 could not be repaired. They might have hoped that victory would restore the European balance, with the Soviet Union as the great guarantor against a new Hitler. But, without a European peace, their domestic security looked increasingly fraught. Their commercial empire was crippled by weakness and what seemed like hopeless mismanagement. India as an asset was finally gone. Their Middle East clients were in open revolt. The dominions resisted commitment to 'imperial defence', doubted London's dire warnings about Soviet intentions, and declined London's anxious request to write down their sterling claims by up to 50 per cent.[60] What remained of the Empire might yield windfall gains, but it was a patchwork of colonies, some undeveloped, some under-governed, and some (like Malaya) barely recovered from foreign occupation.

This was a gloomy prospectus, but, as it turned out, unrealistically gloomy. The British world-system did not implode. The politicians in London may have resented its costs but they could not imagine a post-imperial future. They were spared the need for a drastic rethink. Grim as they looked, the pressures they faced were not unremitting.

The geopolitical position did not become critical. In Europe and the Middle East, the Soviet Union was cautious. The British were not driven back – in the way that Attlee had feared – to the strategic periphery. Their uncertain defences were not seriously tested. Crucially, too, their default on the loan agreement was accepted without too much rancour in Washington.[61] The Truman administration acknowledged the need to keep Britain solvent, and ideally strong, as the best ally it had against Soviet expansion. The offer of help had already been mooted in the famous speech of George Marshall, the Secretary of State, on 5 June 1947 which sketched out what became the European Recovery Programme. So the British were allowed to seal off the sterling economy from American competition, to discriminate heavily against dollar goods, to keep 'imperial preference' and put off the day when the pound was exchanged freely for dollars – precisely those things that American leaders had been so determined to crush eighteen months earlier. Their departure from India had been swift and involuntary but not catastrophic. Both Nehru and Jinnah had been pragmatically willing to accept independence as dominions and not to demand a republic. The transfer of power was thus a constitutional pageant, performed in London through an Act of Parliament, the Indian Independence Act, as well as in India. It allowed Attlee to claim that the end of the Raj was the triumphant completion of a long-matured plan to give the Indians self-government, a pleasing if transparent fiction. It also held out some hope that the two new dominions would be Britain's partners across Southern Asia, balancing the new international weight that China (under Kuomintang rule) was expected to have. In the Middle East, for all the difficulties faced by the British in securing fresh treaties with their key Arab allies (a proposed treaty with Iraq collapsed in the face of a popular outburst, the so-called *Wathbah*), there was as yet little sign that nationalism was a strong enough glue to unify Britain's opponents and break down the suspicions that divided parties and factions. Among the dominions, Britain's staunchest allies in the Second World War, impatience with British imperial attitudes and the desire to assert their own regional claims modulated gradually into a growing unease at the scale of American power, and a stark realisation (among the sterling dominions) that their economic survival was closely tied up with Britain's recovery and the fate of the pound.

Much of the flexibility that British leaders had hoped to enjoy in the war's aftermath had faded away. But the crucial fact was that the scope for an empire had not disappeared. The seismic shift in American policy meant that Britain's importance as an *imperial* ally had been grasped in Washington, as well as the need to support its imperial claims, for the time being at least. In a war-shattered world, the sterling economies also accounted for around half of world trade. For all the irritation that London's breach of faith had caused on the other side of the Atlantic, this was too large an egg to think of killing the goose. The sterling area had to be given a last-minute reprieve. Nor so far had there been any great revulsion of sentiment in Britain itself against the burden of empire, felt most directly in the prolonging of conscription, abandoned precipitately after the First World War. 'One should not overlook the resurgence of nationalism which is characteristic of this country in its post-war mood', remarked one thoughtful observer.[62] It reflected not only the confidence that victory had brought but also acceptance that, for both better (social reform) and worse (austerity), there would be no return to a pre-war 'normality'. No major voice had called for a general withdrawal from overseas commitments – perhaps a measure of how far the Churchillian idea of Britain's place in the world (if not Churchill himself) ruled the political realm (a strong case could be made that it shaped public attitudes to Britain in the white dominions as well). Finally, the British had also begun to equip themselves for the next age of warfare. By early 1947, the decision had been taken to build an atomic weapon that would deter the most powerful assailant. When that was in place – a ten-year wait was envisaged – Britain's scientific prowess, hugely developed by the stress of war, could be mobilised fully behind her claim to world power.

In this brave new world of unforeseen fears, the Labour government shuffled uneasily, with American and dominion help, towards a new version of empire, with a new ideology, a new geostrategy, and an all-but-new economic system. This we might call the fourth (and last) British Empire.

The fourth British Empire

There was, of course, nothing that resembled an imperial programme, still less an announcement that Britain had embarked upon a new phase of empire-building. This was partly because, as in earlier times, no single department or source of authority ruled over all Britain's multiple external connections, or could grasp their full meaning. Labour's new empire emerged instead from piecemeal decisions, made in pursuit of a wide range of objectives. The result was an untidy, even ramshackle, system like all previous versions of British world power. It was shaped inevitably by the impress of forces largely outside the control of any government in London. Indeed, it was mainly the product of an economic and geopolitical crisis that was far more severe (from the British point of view) than that which they had faced after 1918. Its prospects were decided not only by the means that the British themselves could commit, but by the help they enlisted inside and outside their imperial system. Indeed, the scale of its dependence upon foreign assistance became one of its hallmarks, and perhaps the principal cause of its systemic instability. Indeed, as a 'solution' to the problem of restoring Britain's world position (as an independent great power co-equal with the United States and the Soviet Union), its shortcomings were obvious – or had become so by 1952 at the latest.

Labour's embrace of an imperial destiny may have derived in part from the innate conservatism of its leaders' world-view or their reluctance to challenge the passions and prejudices ascribed to public opinion – the loathing for 'scuttle' which the Cabinet had feared would discredit their Indian policy.[63] But, from mid-1947, their imperial thinking was driven by two more urgent concerns. The first was the danger that Stalin would repeat Hitler's success in uniting Europe against them, if by more indirect means, before American help could be brought to bear. In geopolitical terms, Britain's weakness in Europe was bound to make them lean more heavily on their extra-European resources. The second was the need, felt no less acutely, to secure their achievements at home, and safeguard Labour's position as the party of government. The priority here was economic recovery, or, as it seemed in the wake of the convertibility crisis, economic survival. But, for Attlee and his colleagues, there was little real choice in the road to recovery. The central plank in Labour's electoral platform, the glue that held the government, the party and its trade union supporters (the main source of its funds) together, was the promise of full employment, originally laid down in the wartime white paper in 1944. Full employment was the key guarantee that the sacrifices of wartime had not been in vain, and that victory had made possible a better, fairer, Britain. It could not be repudiated. It was also the essential condition without which Labour's whole social programme would quickly unravel. Extending social insurance, increasing state benefits for the jobless or sick, and funding a national health service, assumed a very high level of productive employment: mass unemployment on the scale of the 1930s would wreck their finances. The savage deflation through which governments in the 1920s had sought to rebalance Britain's trade deficit was no longer an option. Nor was the mechanism through which that deflation was imposed, the use of high interest rates to restrict the money supply. Instead, Labour was committed to a 'cheap money' policy (interest rates were kept at 2 per cent) partly to keep employment levels high, partly because the cost of nationalising Britain's mines and transport drove up government borrowing. Cheap money was as vital to Labour's public finances as to its social policy and electoral hopes.

These considerations ruled out defending Britain's solvency in the open international economy that the Bretton Woods agreements had envisaged. Cheap money at home required a closed sterling economy abroad, to guard sterling's value and protect the overseas (sterling area) markets to which much of her exports were sent. Nor was it just a matter of weathering the immediate threat of a sterling collapse. The convertibility disaster brought home to ministers and their advisers that the fundamental imbalance of the British economy required both immediate action and a longer-term remedy. They had to secure fresh supplies of food and fuel to improve living standards, ease the huge burden of food subsidies and improve distribution and output at home. But they had to obtain them from dollar-free sources. They were anxious if possible not just to save dollars by buying in sterling, but to earn dollars as well by re-exporting sterling imports to the voracious American economy. Foodstuffs (especially grain and fats), oil, gold (from South Africa) and high-value minerals like copper and tin, were among their key targets. The shortage of oil and the otherwise heavy dependence on American imports made Middle Eastern supplies from British-owned concessions there a glittering but vulnerable prize. 'Should Russia overrun this area', worried Hugh Gaitskell, then Minister of Fuel and Power, in January 1948,

> [t]here would not merely be insufficient oil for Britain but
> for a large part of the rest of the world ... God knows
> when we shall really get our expansion programme going
> there, and how precarious it will be even when the output is
> doubled.[64]

'It is hoped that by 1951 82 per cent of our oil supplies will be drawn from the Middle East (as compared with 23 per cent in 1938)', Bevin told his Cabinet colleagues in October 1949. 'This will present the largest single factor in balancing our overseas payments. If we failed to maintain our position in the Middle East, our plans for economic recovery... would fail.'[65] This was a game that other ministers could play. Malaya 'is by far the most important source of dollars in the Colonial Empire', warned the Colonial Secretary in July 1948. 'It would gravely worsen the whole dollar balance of the Sterling Area if there were serious interference with Malayan exports.'[66] Malayan security was not just a matter of local importance, or even a primarily strategic matter. It had become one of the crutches of a convalescent British economy.

For the foreseeable future, then, the Labour government pinned its hopes of economic revival to closer integration with the sterling Commonwealth countries (mainly Australia, New Zealand and South Africa), the rapid development of their most valuable dependencies (including Malaya, the Gold Coast and Northern Rhodesia) and the drastic expansion of output from Britain's oil concessions in the Middle East. Only in this way could they restore some equilibrium between Britain's dollar income and outgoings, build up the reserves required for sterling's eventual return to convertible status, and (above all) protect the British economy from a drastic slump in employment and living standards. Pressing arguments of geostrategy pushed them in the same outward direction. By the end of 1947, the failure of the Council of Foreign Ministers meeting in London in November–December, had convinced British leaders that a negotiated settlement with Stalin was more remote than ever. Deterring a Soviet advance into, or its subversion of, the Western European states meant a military build-up, and a firmer commitment by London to the defence of the half-continent. In the Western European Union in January 1948 and the Brussels Treaty a few months later, the British pledged themselves more deeply to their European partners than in any previous peacetime. But they were all too aware that the military means to make good this commitment were scanty at best. Without adequate means to defeat the Soviet Union on land, a 'Middle East' strategy to bomb Southern Russia (despite its manifold shortcomings[67]) remained the best option. The argument went wider. On 5 January 1948, Attlee had broadcast an attack on Soviet imperialism in Europe. A week later, he appealed for Australian and New Zealand support. Britain, he told prime ministers Chifley and Fraser, had proposed a 'Western European Regional Economic and Security Group'. Britain would provide the 'political and moral leadership', but would depend upon the material support of the United States and the Commonwealth.[68] Eager as they were to elicit American help, both Attlee and Bevin were determined to avoid mere dependence on Washington. 'If it is our aim', remarked the Cabinet Secretary, Sir Norman Brook, 'to achieve the leadership of a Western Union sufficiently powerful to be independent of both the Soviet and the American blocs, we must be at the heart of a Commonwealth of nations which is as large as and powerful as we can make it.'[69] Bevin was blunter. 'More stress should be laid', he told his ministerial colleagues, 'on the need to build up a Commonwealth defence system which together with Western Union, would result in a bloc equivalent in strength to the United States or the Soviet Union.'[70] Defending Britain-in-Europe and preserving British world power were imperial tasks.

At first sight, it seems strange that, at a time of such acute economic hardship, domestic opposition to the burdens of empire was not more vociferous. By late 1947, even potatoes were rationed (bread had been rationed since mid-1946) and the ration of petrol suspended altogether. Quite apart from Britain's overseas debts, there was also a mountain of borrowing at home increasing in size from some £13 billion at the end of the war to more than £15 billion by 1951.[71] Partly in consequence, the level of income tax remained at a far higher level than after the First World War. By 1951, six years into the peace, it had fallen only marginally from 10 shillings (50 per cent) in the pound to 9 shillings (45 per cent), twice the rate current in 1925. Nor was it simply a question of feeling the pinch. There was also the matter of public attitudes to empire. Britain's impoverishment had coincided with an ideological conversion to social democracy. After 1918, the blueprint for social reconstruction had been largely torn up when the government abandoned most of the levers of economic control at the onset of depression. This pattern was not repeated after 1945. Instead, the Labour government embarked upon a huge social programme to extend educational opportunity, widen access to healthcare and (most fundamental of all) secure full employment. It also took charge of two basic industries whose renovation was vital to economic recovery: transport (including railways, harbours and road haulage) and the mines. The result was high levels of public expenditure for domestic recovery and social reform. Yet, at exactly the same time, spending on defence remained obstinately high. In the late 1940s it stood at more than double the proportion of GDP spent in 1931–7, and at the end of the decade was to rise even higher. The fourth British empire was not a cheap option. It seems not a little surprising that opinion in Britain, having voted decisively for domestic reform, and facing a blizzard of taxation and rationing, failed to revolt against the deadweight of empire.

Perhaps a key part of the answer was that there was no obvious conflict between empire and social reform, between social democracy at home and imperialism abroad. The hostility to Britain's imperial commitments voiced after 1920 was largely directed against London's new empire in the Middle East, and the danger that this would provoke a Near Eastern war. Much of its force derived, however, from the angry belief that heavy spending abroad was preventing a return to economic normality and prolonging the post-war depression – a cry that appealed to the Left as well as the Right. Little of this applied in late 1947. Far from unemployment, the problem if anything was an acute shortage of manpower. The scale of Labour's domestic programme disposed of the argument that empire had delayed the renovation of British society. By mid-1948, the largest and most controversial of overseas military burdens – the garrisons in India and Palestine – had been given up. Dislike of conscription and military service abroad may have been widespread, but public resentment was probably muted by the fact that the 'call-up' was no longer a novelty. It had begun in peacetime on the eve of the war and had been part and parcel of the mobilisation of Britain's resources whose fairness and thoroughness were regarded as the talismans of survival and victory. Trade union antipathy to 'national service' and foreign military spending – a notable feature of the political climate in 1918–22 – was restrained by Bevin's massive prestige, as the principal champion of 'imperial' duty, and by the extent to which they could be seen as necessary for Britain's own protection against Soviet aggression. Indeed, the conflation of 'containment' (to safeguard Britain at home) and 'imperial defence' (to secure its overseas spheres) was one of the ways in which any residual opposition to imperial burdens could be readily neutralised. Finally, although there was room for doubt as to its application in practice, Labour – and particularly Bevin – had been at pains to promote a new social democratic ideology of empire. Pre-war anxiety about social crisis in the colonies (where depression had bitten deep), and growing belief in the urgency of 'colonial development' from above, fused with the wartime need to remake the image of empire, in the United States above all, and the chastened atmosphere of colonial failure brilliantly evoked by Margery Perham in 1942. The result was the rise of a new ideology of 'partnership', in which empire was the instrument of social, economic and political uplift, the imperial counterpart to the welfare state at home. Reassuring and flexible, it could easily cover a multitude of colonial sins and offered firm reassurance that what was good for Britain (the rapid expansion of colonial production) was also an act of imperial benevolence.

For these kinds of reasons, British leaders were largely able to discount the risk of opposition at home to their Churchillian ambitions. They also disposed of some vital resources to uphold Britain's influence. Despite the shortage of manpower in the civilian economy, they kept over 800,000 men in the armed services in 1948 (more than double the figure for 1938).[72] With a large navy and air force, and a great network of bases, the British were far from being a negligible military power. Meanwhile, Britain's connection with the white dominions was refreshed by the flow of post-war migration. Nearly 600,000 people left Britain between 1946 and 1949, mostly to settle there. A further 700,000 followed in 1950–4.[73] The commercial apparatus for investing abroad had survived the war, and enthusiasm for doing so remained deeply rooted in British economic behaviour. The hunger for capital in the sterling dominions still drew them to London. And, as the Cold War grew fiercer, Britain's great power position could be leveraged for the assistance that mattered. From 1948, Britain began to receive the Marshall Aid dollars. London had already obtained Washington's *de facto* approval for Britain's Middle East presence. In April 1949, with the North Atlantic alliance, it secured the guarantee of American support in the event of Soviet aggression in Europe. The threat of a second Dunkirk now looked less likely. If empires depend upon the exchange of reciprocal benefits, the British had something to offer their imperial partners.

The engine-room of Labour's fourth British empire was the sterling area economy. Its performance was critical to the reconstruction and modernisation of the domestic economy, and to the wider revival of British world influence. Between 1947 and 1950, the results were mixed, but far from discouraging. 1948 was a year of recovery from the convertibility crisis. The other sterling area countries may have disliked London's determination to manage their non-sterling purchases through a centrally administered 'dollar-pool', but they had little real choice but to comply. They dared not risk a collapse in sterling's value, which would wipe out their holdings in London. For Australia and New Zealand especially, Britain remained their most important customer: its economic devastation would ruin them too. Indeed, for the overseas sterling area as a whole, for some four-fifths of their total exports the British market was 50 per cent greater than the American (the main exceptions were cocoa, rubber and wool).[74] There was also the issue of borrowing in London. Despite the huge growth of American foreign investment, it still remained difficult for the sterling dominions to borrow much there – partly because there was little demand for their produce from the American consumer. Access to London's capital market was a valuable lever. The South African government was reluctant to accept the 'dollar-pool' rules, even more so when Smuts was displaced as prime minister by D. F. Malan in 1948. But Malan had to eat humble pie. Fear that his government would declare a republic led to capital flight, just at the moment when new investment was needed to expand gold production. Pretoria caved in and agreed to the exchange of its gold for sterling.[75] In the colonial economies, London could set the price that was paid for their commodity exports, and restrict the manufactures they were sent in return. This was a way of exporting Britain's austerity, and reducing colonial consumption to hoard 'British' dollars. In the Treasury's view, selling on colonial produce was a far more promising way of increasing London's dollar income than closer relations with the Western European countries.[76] Meanwhile, in a world starved of industrial goods, and with most of their pre-war competitors in disarray, the British could sell abroad all they could make. There were also promising signs that London was resuming its classical role as a supplier of capital. Some £1,500 million was sent to sterling area borrowers in 1947-9.[77] To a suspicious American expert, it seemed that the British were still doing surprisingly well from their investment in empire.[78]

Yet Britain's position remained fundamentally fragile and with it the hope of restoring the pound sterling to equal status with the dollar in international transactions. Equality mattered because only then would London be able to recover the profitable business in banking, insurance and services that had made it so rich before 1914, and which depended upon the confidence of its overseas clients. Buoyed up by the injection of Marshall Aid dollars (some $1.2 billion), 1948 turned out well. But, in 1949, sterling was once more on the ropes. An American slowdown, the cessation of stockpiling, and (so some observers suggested) the high cost of British exports, slashed dollar earnings. The dollar deficit soared. With encouragement from Washington (where there was growing anxiety that the dollar famine in Europe would create a permanent division between the two halves of the West's trading world), London devalued the pound from $4.03 to $2.80, followed by the other sterling area countries. The following year saw a striking recovery in the British balance of payments, and a new burst of optimism. But, as we shall see, disillusion soon followed.

'The Commonwealth nations are our closest friends', Attlee proclaimed in the Commons foreign affairs debate in May 1948.[79] Even more perhaps than before 1939, British ministers saw the white dominions as the indispensable elements of British world power. It was they that would serve as the 'Main Support Areas' in the event of another world war, or so the defence planners hoped. But of course Anglo-dominion relations were not so straightforward. Britain's crushing defeat in Europe and Asia in 1940–2 had broken the spell. Never again could dominion leaders blithely confide their strategic defence to the imperial centre. As we have seen, Canadian, Australian and New Zealand reactions had passed through two phases. They recognised the necessity of American aid against a great power aggressor. But they were anxious as well that the new 'World Organisation' would protect their 'middle power' status and limit the scope of American predominance. Both in Wellington and in Canberra, there had been a marked reluctance to accept London's dire warnings about Soviet intentions, and the need to form a solid anti-Soviet bloc. 'I find myself equally opposed to the extremes of both sides', wrote the New Zealand prime minister, Peter Fraser.[80] Both in New Zealand and in Australia, mistrust of the United States was mixed with resentment at what was seen as its ungenerous treatment of Britain, and the desire to see London adopt a more independent line. As so often before, Australian leaders were irritated by London's obtuseness: its refusal to see that Australia was doing its British and imperial duty. 'Australia today', said the prime minister, Ben Chifley, 'has become the great bastion of the British-speaking race south of the Equator. Strategically and economically this country has assumed a position in the Pacific on behalf of the British Commonwealth.'[81] British calls for help in Europe and the Middle East would confuse and distract Australian public opinion. So Chifley bluntly rejected Attlee's urgent appeal in January 1948. 'The Australian people . . . are not convinced of the desirability of . . . a Western alliance directed against the Soviet', he wrote.[82] Anyway, Australia would have its hands full in the Pacific if another war broke out: there would be nothing to spare. There was less consultation from the Labour government, complained his foreign minister Evatt, than there had been from Churchill – an indictment indeed![83] The view from New Zealand (as in previous times) was not so assertive. Fraser acknowledged the Soviet threat, sought London's advice on how New Zealand could help, and agreed that New Zealand should have a division to send to the Middle East on the outbreak of war.[84] The following year, he pressed ahead with a scheme for compulsory military training, on which a successful referendum was held in August 1949.[85]

1949 was a year of political change in both Australia and New Zealand. The new New Zealand prime minister, Sidney Holland, was an ardent imperial patriot. 'I love the British Empire with all my heart', had been his response to the great sterling crisis of August 1947.[86] The Australian election restored Robert Menzies to power after a gap of eight years. Menzies, like Holland, was a vocal exponent of the British connection and (in his case) of a British Australia. As a wealthy lawyer from Melbourne (Australia's financial capital with close ties to the City), he was deeply attached to the strength and stability of British institutions ('the quietness, the tolerance, the sense of values, the ordered justice, the security of England').[87] But Menzies was far from being Downing Street's doormat. There was too little awareness of empire in Britain, he thought on a visit in 1948.[88] Yet Menzies saw Australia's future as more reliant than ever on its closeness to Britain. The Australian economy would be a 'food arsenal' for Europe: its growth was tied up with Britain's recovery and the survival of sterling.[89] He was also keenly aware of Australia's deep isolation and clutched at the hope that it could be a member of NATO. He seized the great chance given by London's nuclear ambitions to offer Australia as Britain's partner and test-ground.[90] He was not in a hurry to promise Australian troops to the Middle East theatre. But, after the outbreak of war in Korea in June 1950 (which intensified fears of an imminent world war), he reversed Chifley's stance and (some eighteen months later) committed Australia to a Middle East role.[91] The timing was not accidental. By that time, the Australia–New Zealand–United States security pact (ANZUS) was settled, the 'Near North' was now guarded by American sea-power and

the British were committed to the defence of Malaya. With the back
door now bolted, Menzies was ready to do his imperial duty.[92]

Economic and strategic self-interest fused with their sense of a
British identity to make the Southern dominions the most reliable partners in the fourth British empire. With the senior dominion (the term
itself was slipping out of use), Britain's post-war relations were somewhat more complex. There were plenty of voices still raised to assert
that Canada was, in Brooke Claxton's phrase, 'a British nation in North
America', or to argue, like George Grant, that 'if we have no link with
the British Commonwealth we shall soon cease to be a nation.'[93] 'Newfoundland' (whose adhesion to Canada was then under discussion) 'is
ultra-loyal to the British Crown', remarked an Ontario newspaper. 'We
can stand some of that too.'[94] Canada's Britishness was regarded by
most English Canadians as an uncontroversial fact.[95] Mackenzie King,
then the outgoing prime minister, warned his successor, St Laurent, that
the Conservative opposition would exploit 'British' sentiment to press
for a stronger commitment to imperial defence – a call bound to inflame
French Canadian feeling and threaten the cohesion of the Liberal party.
'You will probably have to fight all Sir Wilfrid's [Laurier's] battles over
again.'[96] Yet King himself was deeply uneasy about showing too much
preference for Canada's ties with America over those with Britain.

The Canadian problem lay in striking the balance. It was perfectly clear, a senior military officer had remarked in August 1945, that
Canada was 'not going to participate in a war... over the frontiers of
Iraq or to preserve the Indian Ocean as a British lake'. But, as two
great wars had shown, 'the Canadian people have, on the occasion of a
great emergency arising, quickly realised that the security of the United
Kingdom is a vital interest'.[97] Mackenzie King's instinct (a habitual
reflex) was to avoid any forward commitment, but a greater theoretical
risk was that Canada's integration into America's continental defence
system would constrain its ability to lend Britain its aid. NATO averted
this danger. From the Canadian angle, the North Atlantic Treaty signed
in April 1949 was the perfect solution: Canada would contribute to
North Atlantic defence alongside its two great partners: pragmatism,
sentiment and self-interest were reconciled. But, in commercial relations, such compromise was elusive. This was not for want of Canadian
efforts. The British market was hugely important to Canada, taking
40 per cent of Canadian exports before the war.[98] The sterling they
earned helped to offset Canada's large deficit with the United States.

During the war, Britain's shortage of dollars had been met by allowing American aid to be spent in Canada. After the war, Canadian eagerness to restore the old pattern had been part of the motive for the large dollar loan they advanced to Britain. But nothing went right. The Canadians had banked on a swift British revival. The convertibility crisis was a shattering blow. As Britain's dollar purchases were cut to the bone, Canada's balance of payments also lurched into crisis. Marshall Aid dollars eased things for a while, and allowed London to pay for Canadian wheat. But the second sterling crisis in 1949 marked a parting of ways. The British tried to persuade the Canadians to accept inconvertible sterling, and to help British exports by restricting their purchase of American goods. To the Canadians it seemed like a transparent manoeuvre, to suck them willy-nilly into the sterling area[99] and give a great boost to its dollar reserve. It was also bound to infuriate Washington.[100] Ottawa drew back. But its export dilemma was not fully resolved until the Korean war boom widened the American market for Canadian manufactures and foodstuffs. By the early 1950s, 54 per cent of Canadian exports (40 per cent in 1937) were sent there, and 17 per cent to Britain. A mere 9 per cent of Canadian imports (half the pre-war percentage) were now drawn from Britain. Canada's economic and strategic integration into the imperial system of its great southern neighbour looked almost irreversible.

With the fourth dominion, relations had never been easy and seemed likely to worsen. In South African politics, the dominant fact was that Afrikaners formed a majority of the white population who alone (except for a handful of 'coloured' or mixed-race voters) had the franchise. The extent of republican or nationalist feeling among the Afrikaner electorate was thus a critical issue and a vociferous minority of Afrikaner politicians had long demanded a republic and secession from the Empire (one was assumed to lead to the other). Yet South Africa had entered the Second World War freely and its soldiers and airmen – including many Afrikaners – fought beside British and other Empire troops. This seemed to suggest that for a significant fraction of Afrikaner opinion the republican path was divisive and dangerous, alienating the 'English' minority and isolating South Africa. General Smuts was regarded – in Britain especially – as the indispensable leader. His global prestige, local charisma and political skill ('Slim Jannie' was a nickname with somewhat mixed connotations) made him the ideal (Afrikaner) champion of Anglo-Afrikaner amity and South Africa's

Commonwealth membership. It was his intervention that had tipped the balance in the vote to enter the war. As the wartime prime minister, he had faced down the furious outcry of the anti-war faction and the paramilitary violence of the Ossewa Brandwag (the name was meant to invoke the Voortrekker tradition), while the Allied victory in Africa had helped his supporters to electoral victory in 1943. After the war, despite the strains of economic transition, and the fiasco of Smuts' attempt to get United Nations approval to incorporate South West Africa (still a League mandate) into the Union, defeat by the Nationalists seemed highly unlikely so long as Smuts was leader of the United party.[101] But, at the general election in 1948, Smuts was defeated – despite winning a majority of the popular vote – and the Nationalists came to power under D. F. Malan.

This was bound to set the alarm bells ringing in London. On any view of Britain's post-war system, South Africa was a large and important component. In the Second World War, as a semi-industrial economy, a supplier of gold, and a great naval and air base in the South Atlantic and Indian Ocean, its cooperation had been vital to the imperial war effort. In a future war against the Soviet Union, it was expected to become perhaps even more valuable. Declaring a republic and leaving the Commonwealth would create a huge crisis in Anglo-South African relations at a critical moment. There was already the danger that a Nationalist government would demand the return of the Simonstown base and renew the old pressure for the 'High Commission Territories' (Basutoland, Bechuanaland and Swaziland – today's Lesotho, Botswana and Swaziland) to be incorporated as part of the Union. Nor was it likely that a government so explicitly committed to *baaskap* (white supremacy) and *apartheid* (racial separation) would fit very willingly into a Commonwealth group that had just been enlarged by three Asian dominions. But, as it turned out, Malan was pragmatic and his hand was weak. The capital flight that greeted his victory threatened economic disaster. Malan was forced to place his dollar income in the sterling area pool in return for access to the London capital market – a major concession that Smuts had escaped, with considerable benefit to the white standard of living.[102] The referendum on a republic was put off *sine die*. And, since fear of communism was even more of a bogey in the National than in the United party, a retreat into the *laager* away from European complications (that had had great appeal in the inter-war years) now looked less wise.

Malan's dilemma was neatly exposed in the wider debate set off over the Commonwealth's future in 1948–9. It was triggered by the question of India's status. Nehru and the Congress had accepted 'dominion status' in 1947 as an expedient to quicken the transfer of power *before* a new Indian constitution was framed. It soon became obvious that the new constitution would take a republican form. Within the Congress there were also those who disliked any formal connection, whether material or symbolic, with the imperial past and who were deeply suspicious that the British intended to drag India back into their imperialist toils. A Congress party resolution in December 1948 proclaimed its commitment to the 'ending of Imperialism and Colonialism' and declared that Indian foreign policy should 'avoid entanglement in military or similar alliances which tend to divide up the world in rival groups'. India's 'complete independence' meant that 'her present association with the United Kingdom and the Commonwealth of Nations will necessarily have to change'.[103] The difficulty lay in the strong supposition that allegiance to the Crown was the essential element in Commonwealth membership: a dominion that rejected the king as its head of state automatically left the Commonwealth. In 1948, this had led to the departure of both Burma and Eire (the former Irish Free State). 'There can be no doubt', reported a British official committee, 'that the king has been the symbol and expression of that community of feeling which has been the mainspring of cooperation particularly at times of crisis ... Some South African politicians ... recommend the severance of allegiance to the Crown on the very ground that some South Africans are influenced ... by the emotional pull of the Commonwealth connection and that South Africa's decision to declare war in 1939 would not have been taken but for this sense of "obligation".'[104] The dilemma was whether to loosen the monarchical bond, risk the erosion of the Crown's 'emotional pull' and weaken the solidarity of the Commonwealth's 'central countries' (defined as Britain, Canada, Australia and New Zealand)[105] or to maintain the old 'rule' and exclude a republican India.

It was India's geostrategic importance that weighed most with London. If India's request for a new kind of membership was rejected, what would the consequences be? In the climate of 1948–9, it was hard to be insouciant. For all their eagerness to win American backing, Attlee and Bevin saw themselves at that moment as the heroic builders of a grand coalition against the Soviet threat, now being extended – with the

advance of Mao's armies in China – into Asia as well. Western European
Union and Commonwealth backing were its vital components. Whether
India contributed to 'Commonwealth defence' or not, 'her exclusion
from the Commonwealth against her own wishes would encourage her
to concentrate her attention on the creation of an Asiatic bloc, isolated
from and possibly hostile to the Western Powers.'[106] If India left, it
might be followed by Pakistan and Ceylon (Sri Lanka), and by Britain's
other Asian colonies as they became independent. It was 'a matter of
major importance', the Cabinet were told, 'that the leading power in
South East Asia should remain a member of the Commonwealth'.[107] In
the Chiefs of Staff's view, keeping India in offered the best chance for
the common defence of South Asia, and for Britain's getting access in
wartime to India's manpower and industry. But a formula acceptable
to the 'old dominions' was not easy to find. New Zealand did not want
a 'flabby Commonwealth with no guiding principle': it might be better
if India stayed out.[108] Even at this late stage, Attlee himself tried rather
desperately to dissuade Nehru. 'Does a republic really appeal to the
masses in India? . . . [R]epublicanism is an alien import from Europe',
he urged.[109] But, in the end, all the dominion governments accepted
that keeping India in was of vital importance, and in this 'can-do'
atmosphere a compromise formula was hammered out at the Commonwealth prime ministers meeting in April 1949. India accepted the
king 'as the symbol of free association' of the Commonwealth's independent member nations and 'as such the Head of the Commonwealth'.
The remaining dominions declared their position unchanged. The real
surprise of the meeting was what Malan had to say. Malan had been
worried by the phrase 'head of the Commonwealth', fearing its 'superstate' overtones – an old phobia in South Africa and of the Liberals in
Canada. But he affirmed South African loyalty to the Commonwealth.
'South Africa cannot stand isolated, but must have friends and must
find them generally among the like-minded nations . . . but more especially . . . in the inner circle of the free and independent nations of the
Commonwealth.'[110] It was a remarkable u-turn, and opinion in South
Africa was divided on Malan's real intentions. But Baring (the British
representative there) was convinced that Malan actually meant what he
said.[111]

The successful inclusion of republican India and Malan's public
confession of Commonwealth faith were promising signs that the will
was there to preserve the British connection and to acknowledge the

Commonwealth as an informal alliance against the communist threat. Even Nehru agreed that 'Commonwealth countries must be prepared to resist military and political aggression by the Soviet government'.[112] It vindicated Attlee's willingness to reinvent the Commonwealth, recognising that 'dominion' was no longer favoured as a title (it was being discarded even in New Zealand[113]), and that the name 'British Commonwealth' should sometimes give way to 'Commonwealth of Nations' as the best designation.[114] The modified Commonwealth had become a key part of Labour's new world-system. But even more striking was the extent to which Britain's own role as its head and centre had come to depend upon an ever deeper commitment in two large spheres, in each of which British influence and authority suffered from potentially crippling sources of weakness.

The first of these was the Middle East. As we have seen, in post-war conditions the Middle East's value had risen sharply for Britain. As the base from which to attack Russian oilfields and industry in the event of world war, and as the source for 'dollar-free' oil extracted from British 'concessions', the Middle East had become much more than a bastion of the old Anglo-Indian nexus. It was no longer an adjunct to the British world-system but an integral part of it. This was the meaning of Bevin's victory over Attlee in 1946–7. Britain's ability to promote Western Union, to hold the Commonwealth together, to stage an economic recovery, or to deter Soviet aggression required a regional presence that was at least as commanding as before 1939, and much more intrusive. It was really made up of a four-cornered connection: with Iraq and Jordan, where the British relied on the local 'strong men', Nuri al-Said and the ageing King Abdullah; with Iran and the special position enjoyed by the Anglo-Iranian Oil Company; and above all with Egypt and the Suez Canal Zone. Indeed, for the British, Egypt remained the irreplaceable centrepiece of their Middle East *imperium*. It was not just a matter of their huge complex of bases in the Suez Canal Zone. There was also the vast depot at Tel el-Kebir (the Plassey of Egypt). Egyptian labour and Egypt's ports and railways were equally vital if the Canal Zone bases were to serve their purpose efficiently. This meant, in effect, that the British must enlist the cooperation, however grudging or reluctant, of the government in Cairo and its local officials. It was this realisation that had pushed Bevin and the Foreign Office into offering a large-scale withdrawal of the British military presence in return for the right to return in a Middle Eastern 'emergency'. Those talks had failed (largely over Cairo's demand for a much larger say in the affairs of the Sudan). Meanwhile, their abrupt departure from Palestine had deprived the British of the alternative base where their troops could be kept and hardened their view about the value of Egypt. With the onset of the Berlin crisis in mid-1948, and the increased possibility of a war with Russia, the idea of any real withdrawal from Egypt disappeared almost completely. It was now essential, declared the Chiefs of Staff in September 1948, to keep at least 20,000 troops in Egypt, and to go on using the Tel el-Kebir depot.[115]

The reality was, as the British admitted to themselves, that not only was evacuation now inconceivable but that 'our military requirements go beyond those of the present [1936] treaty'.[116] There was no chance of finding any Egyptian regime that would agree to such terms.[117] The embassy in Cairo was left, as so often before, to square the circle. Its tactics were well tried: every proconsul from Cromer to Lampson had played much the same hand. The aim was to tempt King Farouk with the promise of a treaty, or to bully him into allowing a government of the main popular party, the Wafd, who might also be tempted (as in 1936). The difficulty was that London had little or nothing to give. Worse still, there were growing signs of upheaval as the Arab defeat in Palestine, the effects of inflation and the Islamist influence of the Muslim Brotherhood undermined 'pashadom' and the king's prestige. They were facing 1919 all over again, thought some British observers. If violence broke out, it would be necessary to send three major military units 'and dominate the European quarter of Cairo'.[118] Nor could the British allow Egypt to fall into political chaos. But how could they stop it, or prevent a populist government from disrupting overtly or covertly the transport links and labour supply on which they depended? It might happen at a moment of great international tension, and 'Egypt is the only country in the Middle East', so the Chiefs of Staff declared, 'possessing the facilities and resources for the conduct of a major war'.[119] 'All interpretations of Middle East strategy require the location of a Middle East base in Egypt in war.'[120] By hook or by crook some agreement must be made. 1950 was a year of desultory talks with the new Wafd government and the prime minister, Nahas Pasha, 'an old, stubborn and enfeebled man' in *The Times*' dismissive phrase.[121] At the end of the year, Nahas raised the stakes. Egypt would end its treaty with Britain unilaterally if necessary. In October 1951, he made good his threat, and the real confrontation began.

By that time the British had suffered a highly damaging blow to their pride and pocket from Iranian nationalism. They had placed heavy reliance upon the British-owned Anglo-Iranian Oil Company (later British Petroleum) and its refinery at Abadan (then the largest in the world) to produce 'sterling oil', and reduce the dollar deficit (to which the cost of oil imported from the United States, much the world's largest producer, made the biggest contribution).[122] To palliate Iranian discontent with its oil royalties, a 'supplemental' agreement had been negotiated. But, from Teheran's point of view, this did little to redress the *growing* imbalance between its share of oil revenues and those accruing to London. In 1950, the company made net profits of £33 million, paid more than £50 million in taxes to the British government (five times as much as in 1946) but barely £16 million in royalties to Teheran. New dividend rules applicable in London also depressed the income that the Iranians received.[123] To make matters worse, at the end of 1950 it became known that, in Saudi Arabia, the region's second-largest producer, the Arab-American Oil Company (Aramco) had agreed on a fifty–fifty sharing of profits with the government in Riyadh. It was hardly surprising that the Iranians cavilled at a much less generous deal. Too late in the day, the British proposed the 'Aramco' terms. But, by early 1951, Iranian politics were being convulsed by the fierce nationalist rhetoric of Mohamed Mussadiq and the struggle for power between the youthful shah and his opponents, including the Tudeh, a mass radical party suspected of communist leanings.[124] In this stormy climate, British interference and Anglo-Iranian's greed became irresistible targets. At the end of April 1951, the Iranian Parliament nationalised the company, and on 10 June the Iranian flag was raised over its main office in Abadan.

The British were nonplussed. They considered and rejected a familiar strategy: the occupation of Southwest Iran where Teheran's authority had always been weak. Without the Indian army, said the Chiefs of Staff sorrowfully, Britain lacked the military means to carry this out.[125] They thought about occupying Abadan Island, where the refinery stood. But this Attlee vetoed, knowing that Washington was fiercely opposed to military action against which the Soviet Union might riposte in the north of Iran. 'We could not afford a break with the United States on an issue of this kind', recorded the Cabinet minutes.[126] So the grand British concession closed down with a whimper. On 4 October 1951, the remaining British staff embarked on a cruiser and sailed away.

In Egypt and Iran, the British were thus caught in a vice. The logic of their economic and geopolitical position had deepened their dependence upon their Middle East 'assets'. Far from slackening their ties with this turbulent region, they were determined to integrate its strategic and commercial resources much more closely into their post-war world-system, even while they acknowledged that Britain's own strength was, at least temporarily, in relative decline. The British largely hid from themselves the inconvenient truth that the burden they imposed upon Middle East polities was actually growing at a time when those polities were under intense social and political strain. Hence the unpredictable force of local nationalist feeling, as well as the growing American presence and the looming shadow of Soviet military power, heightened the risks and anxieties of this half-concealed 'forward movement'. By October 1951, visibly in Iran, not much less so in Egypt, it had been stopped in its tracks.

The second great sphere was in Britain's tropical empire, for long the poor relation of the imperial system. Shoe-string budgets and skeletal government had been the lot of most tropical colonies, especially during the depression years when their economies shrank. The war and its aftermath transformed their place in the imperial structure. Their potential value to the imperial centre now began to be recognised. And the war had driven home the lesson (robustly pointed out by Margery Perham in 1942) that, without a more pro-active approach by their rulers, many colonial territories would become tropical 'East Ends' with impoverished, disaffected populations, troublesome to govern and an economic liability. An energetic expansion of the colonial state was thus on the cards.[127] What made it more urgent was the dawning realisation that tropical produce (cocoa, groundnuts, coffee, rubber) and minerals (tin and copper especially) from the 'crown colony' empire could provide a large dollar income and contribute significantly to the urgent recovery of the sterling economy. By 1948, it was estimated that the colonies were earning $600 million a year, with a net surplus of $200 million for the sterling area dollar-pool. Since this was enough to cover the dollar deficit of the self-governing countries of the overseas sterling area (i.e. excluding Britain), its contribution to the smoothness and cohesion of the sterling area's working relations was highly significant. But there were bound to be costs. To raise local production, the colonial state had to become (compared with its past) almost hyperactive. It would need to discard the allies that had served it in the age of immobility and seek new friends who would grasp the advantage of rapid development, not least to themselves. Local administration would need reforming to give them a voice. Advisers and experts would descend on the countryside: imposing new rules (against overstocking or deforestation); attacking diseases (like cocoa 'swollen shoot' where the trees were cut down); or commandeering labour (for anti-erosion activity). And, because colonial incomes could not be allowed to grow quickly (to prevent inflation and conserve the dollars), the colonial state would become an economic leviathan, setting prices and wages wherever it could. The tropical colonies were to be integrated forcibly into the sterling economy on terms not of their choosing, but, it was claimed, to their considerable benefit. What has aptly been called the 'second colonial occupation' was the most self-confident face of the fourth British empire.

But, almost immediately, there were signs that the colonial governments were badly under-engined for their demanding new role. They lacked the intelligence, the financial incentives and above all the manpower to assert their power over what had hitherto been very lightly ruled hinterlands. In the Gold Coast (modern Ghana), this opened the space for a mass movement of protest, when a breakaway group of coast politicians, led by Kwame Nkrumah, began to mobilise growing discontent against the government's rural reforms. In February 1951, under the slogan of 'Self-Government Now', Nkrumah's Convention People's Party made 'practically a clean sweep' in the elections to the new local legislature created to conciliate 'moderate opinion'.[128] In Kenya, where the colonial government relied on its old chiefly allies to force through a programme for better land husbandry, the result was a spiral of increasingly violent social conflict among the Kikuyu, the main ethnic group in the central highlands. What became known as Mau Mau – the spread of 'oathing', urban militancy and agrarian terror – was already well established long before London agreed to a state of emergency in October 1952.[129] The crisis came earlier in Malaya, where British rule had been demolished by the Japanese conquest. Here the colonial state had to be rebuilt, so London insisted, on more robust lines. Singapore would remain the great centre of British power in the East, Malaya its outwork and economic annexe. A Malayan *Union* giving more power to the colonial centre would unite the ramshackle 'Federated' and 'Unfederated' states of the pre-war era with the old 'Straits Settlements', the four crown colony enclaves of which Singapore was the largest. The revived colonial state would extend its control into the forested hinterland, and over the labour force of the mines and plantations whose 'discipline' had broken down in the occupation period. In fact, 'Union' was abandoned in the face of the angry reaction of the Malay elite, who feared that including Singapore would give the Chinese a predominant voice in the new Malaya. Singapore stayed separate and Malay feelings were soothed. But, in the Chinese community (in both Singapore and Malaya), the effects of occupation and of civil war in China deepened social divisions, and the appeal of communism. When the colonial government entered the fray to check rural squatting and labour militancy, violence soon spread.[130] In June 1948, the British declared a state of emergency, to protect the white planters and safeguard the dollar earnings from rubber and tin which London valued so highly. It was to take more than five years before they broke the back of the communist-led insurrection. In Malaya, the British were willing to make a huge effort to protect what they saw as an economic resource and a prime strategic asset. But, here, as in the Gold Coast and Kenya, it soon became clear that the colonial state had become much more dependent on the local indigenous elite. The imperial initiative had run out of steam.

Test of Empire, 1951–1952

In its six years of office from July 1945 until October 1951, the Labour government had followed a remarkably consistent external policy. Its aim had been to protect British independence in Europe, where it seemed to be threatened by Soviet expansion, as well as British power in the world. It was no less committed to regaining Britain's old place in world trade as the best guarantee of domestic prosperity and restored living standards. It pursued these objectives by what seemed the logical means. It sought to engage the United States as fully as possible in the defence of Western Europe, recognising that Britain, even with its Empire and Commonwealth behind it, could not hope to hold out against a Soviet onslaught in another world war. It hoped to deter a further Soviet advance partly by alliance diplomacy in Europe ('Western European Union') and partly by digging in on the Soviet flank in the Middle East. After the dramatic upset of the convertibility crisis in July–August 1947, it vowed to defend the sterling economy by exchange control and commercial restriction until London's reserves of dollars and gold were sufficient to meet the pound's post-war liabilities and restore the City to its premier place in global finance. It was committed, in short, to building a new British world-system, not as grand perhaps as its pre-war model, but more *dirigiste*, more development-minded and, up to a point, more democratic.

In retrospect, this might be seen as a quixotic endeavour to turn back a tide that had set irrevocably against European empires in general and Britain's in particular. In fact, the Labour leaders behaved with what they clearly regarded as tough-minded pragmatism. They accepted the need to let India go quickly lest it drag them into a vast communal conflict. They abandoned Burma as ungovernable and made almost no effort to dissuade its new rulers from leaving the Commonwealth. They acknowledged the claim of Ceylon's Sinhalese elite to swift independence and endorsed the claim of the Commonwealth Secretary that 'if we treat them strictly as a[n] [independent] dominion, they will behave very like a loyal colony.'[131] They made little fuss when the Irish Free State became the Irish Republic, preferring a bilateral agreement to the tattered remains of the crown connection to protect British interests. They threw up the Palestine mandate and simply withdrew rather than enforce a partition that would further damage their relations with the Arab states. On the other hand, they were also determined to hold the Commonwealth together and get the help of the self-governing dominions in the defence of sterling – by forceful methods if necessary. They were ready to modify what was widely regarded as its main source of cohesion to mitigate the effects of the end of the Raj and retain the friendship of India. After their initial attempt to win Egyptian agreement to a new defence treaty by the drastic reduction of their military presence, they showed a stubborn refusal to give up British rights to use Egypt as a vast military base in the event of a new war. And, across the wide expanse of their tropical empire, they demanded economic and political change on a scale and at a speed that seemed likely to test the colonial state to the point of destruction.

After April 1949 and the signing of the North Atlantic treaty, with its promise of American help in the defence of Western Europe, Attlee and Bevin could have been forgiven for thinking that they had turned the main corner. Their aim, after all, was to preserve British power as a 'third force' in world affairs, in alliance with America to contain Soviet aggression, but not subordinate to it. Just as they hoped to restore sterling to something like parity with the dollar as a trading currency, they thought that a modified British world-system, with its treaty relations, Commonwealth links, informal connections and far-flung network of bases, would secure Britain's status as America's all but co-equal in the Western alliance. They looked forward to the easing of Cold War tensions and the demands they had made on the British economy. What remained of these hopes was largely demolished in the course of 1951–2 by the seismic consequences of the Korean War and the delayed after-shocks of the Palestine conflict.

1950 had been a good year for the British economy and the sterling area. With the balance of payments back in surplus and the easing of the dollar deficit, Marshall Aid was suspended. The sterling area, the Chancellor of the Exchequer told his Australian counterpart, was stronger than at any time since the war.[132] But, he warned, it was a 'darkening picture'. The darkest cloud was the huge increase in Britain's defence spending, the price Britain must pay, so the Attlee government argued, to maintain the American commitment to Europe's defence at a time when East Asia had become Washington's most urgent priority. The defence budget was raised to the enormous figure of £4.7 billion over three years, doubling the level of 1948–9, and threatening to consume more than 10 per cent – perhaps even 14 per cent – of output. Almost at once a vicious circle set in. The price of dollar goods rose just as rearmament made them more necessary. British production was diverted from overseas exports and dollar-earning activity. Britain's dollar reserves, the key to sterling's revival as a convertible currency, began to dwindle rapidly. Even in March 1951, before the crisis really set in, they stood at only one-third of the 1938 figure.[133] Between June 1951 and March 1952, they fell by half. By October, the incoming Conservative government was engulfed in a full-blown sterling crisis, the third in six years. At an emergency meeting of Commonwealth finance ministers in January 1952, an urgent programme of dollar-saving was agreed.

Sterling recovered and staggered on to achieve convertible status in the (briefly) easier conditions of 1958. But the 1951 crisis was a real turning point. It offered stark evidence that the closed sterling economy could not be the springboard to the pound's full recovery as a world 'master-currency' or London's revival in global finance. The pound's credibility was badly damaged in Europe. Nor was it possible to prevent the leakage of sterling as dollars were bought by indirect methods. We have reached a 'dead end', concluded a secret report in the Bank of England.[134] The draft communiqué of the Commonwealth finance ministers in January 1952 acknowledged the core of the problem.[135] Sterling could only rebuild its old status and be safely convertible if London's reserves were restored to pre-war levels. That would require an enormous effort to increase trade and earn more dollars. But this could only be done if more investment was raised and if the sterling countries gained better access to the goods and capital of the dollar economies. Britain alone could not provide the development capital that was needed to improve the productiveness of its sterling area partners. Indeed, much of what it did send abroad was not the result of domestic saving but capital brought back from non-sterling countries (like Argentina).[136] As a result, investment (in Australia) was 'incredibly and worryingly low'.[137] The finance ministers agreed that capital had to be sought from outside the sterling area, but, as the Australian ministers gloomily noted, it was hard to attract while sterling remained a 'soft' currency. And so the circle was closed. It was hard to escape the conclusion that its long convalescence had prepared Britain's commercial empire – the central pillar of British strength in the world – not for rejuvenation but for premature senility.

At almost exactly the same moment, the same wasting disease became painfully visible at the heart of Britain's Middle Eastern *imperium*. As we have seen, quite apart from the value of the Suez Canal Zone as the main base from which Britain's regional presence could be supplied and reinforced in time of war, and the need to use Egyptian resources and assets outside the Canal Zone, the Anglo-Egyptian relationship remained the centrepiece of Britain's Middle East influence. It was hard to imagine how that could survive the defection of Egypt from the British connection. That was why the British were so anxious to reconcile Cairo to their military claims. But they remained surprisingly confident that they could sit out the storm in the short term at least. In the last resort, or so they assumed, they could seal off the Canal Zone and send troops into Cairo and Alexandria to protect their citizens and enforce a change of government. But, between October 1951 and January 1952, a revolution took place in Anglo-Egyptian relations.

It was triggered by the treaty abrogation that Nahas had announced. At first, the British were tempted to dismiss it as simply 'hot air'. But it soon became clear that something much more than an empty gesture had happened. Egyptian labour disappeared from the Canal Zone. The police became hostile.[138] British soldiers began to be murdered. The Canal Zone, remarked the Middle East Office in Cairo, 'can no longer be considered a base for the defence of the Middle East, having lost its wider operational potential'.[139] The British cast around for remedial measures. Reinforcements were sent out to Cyprus, but, since the strategic reserve in Britain was already exhausted, flooding the Canal Zone with troops was not a viable option. Financial sanctions against Egypt were considered and rejected.[140] Sealing off the Canal Zone under a military government would impose administrative complications that were 'almost intolerable', said the Chiefs of Staff.[141] Instead, the local commander-in-chief was empowered to disarm the troublesome Egyptian police. Then came disaster. At Ismailia on the Canal, on 25 January 1952, the British stormed the police station, killing more than forty Egyptians. The next day, in Cairo, there were violent anti-British disturbances in which British civilians were killed and British property wrecked including the famous Shepheard's Hotel. The British had long had a plan in case of such an event. Operation 'Rodeo' would bring British troops from the Canal Zone to the city. But now the generals held back. They could not be sure to keep the Canal Zone secure and have an adequate force to make 'Rodeo' work. For two things had changed. The first was the rise of a popular nationalism, a form of mass opposition that the British had not faced since 1919. The second was the risk of a clash with the Egyptian army, on whose tacit acquiescence the British had always previously counted. The immediate crisis blew over; Nahas was dismissed by Farouk; the desultory talks were resumed. But, almost unnoticed, the armed strength that had underlain British influence in Egypt since 1882, and which had given the Residency its 'whisper behind the throne', was melting away. The decolonisation of Egypt that Nasser completed was now under way.

'Thinking over our difficulties in Egypt', remarked a senior Foreign Office official, 'it seems to me that the essential difficulty arises from the very obvious fact that we lack power. The Egyptians know this, and that accounts for their intransigence.'[142] The 'basic and fundamental aim of British policy', he went on, 'is to build up our lost power. Once we despair of doing so, we shall never attain this aim.' It was a lapidary comment on the British dilemma: 'We are not strong enough to carry out the policies needed if we are to retain our position in the world; if we show weakness, our position in the world diminishes.'[143] Until the double crisis over Egypt and sterling, it had been possible to think that, by subtle diplomacy, Spartan economics, and the vigorous deployment of Britain's imperial 'assets', Britain would regain its old position as an independent centre of world power. But the crippling weakness at the core of their post-war system had now been revealed, with little hope of relief. Without a strong sterling economy or the great power leverage conferred by their Middle Eastern *imperium*, the British claim to world power would look threadbare indeed. The huge expansion of the Cold War conflict that Korea had signalled sealed their geopolitical fate. It marked the final arrival of the bipolar world that had advanced in stages since 1943. It meant that British dependence on American power would not lessen but grow. It forced British policy into a stance both defensive and brittle, and driven more and more by the search for prestige. After 1951, the best they could hope for was to be the third world power: within a few years, they had become something different – a power in the third world.

13 THE THIRD WORLD POWER, 1951-1959

An empire of influence

As the economic crisis unleashed by the Korean War and the strain of rearmament began to intensify, a new government came to power in London. It was headed by the indomitable Churchill, now seeking to crown his career by a summit conference with Stalin to end the Cold War – a plan regarded coldly in Washington and by his own Foreign Office. The Conservative party had won the election under a populist banner – 'Set the people free!' – that decried the bureaucratic austerity of the Labour regime. Rationing was indeed abandoned in 1954, and Labour's late nationalisation of the steel industry reversed. But there was no major departure from the domestic priorities of the previous government. Full employment remained at the centre of economic policy. The welfare state, its social corollary, was politically sacrosanct: indeed, one of its main Conservative architects, R. A. Butler, was Chancellor of the Exchequer from 1951 to 1955. The tax system was left much as it was.[1] No great ideological shift separated the two phases of British post-war politics between 1945 and 1963, even if over particular issues (like the Suez crisis or entry into the Common Market) there was sometimes a wide gap between the two major parties.

In their approach to the management of British world power and what remained of Britain's world-system, Churchill and his colleagues displayed what might be called a limited pragmatism. The senior ministers – Churchill himself, Anthony Eden (the new Foreign Secretary), Lord Salisbury, Lord Swinton (who became Secretary of State for Commonwealth Relations in 1952), Oliver Lyttelton (Colonial

Secretary) – had direct experience of the crushing burden of war on British prestige and resources. They knew at first hand how the astonishing scale of American wealth had tipped the balance of power in Anglo-American relations. Lyttelton had been Minister of Production in the second half of the war; as Minister of Civil Aviation, Swinton had struggled to defend Britain's imperial air routes against American demands for the 'open skies'. Coming to power amid the third great crisis of the British economy in six years of peace, they had good reason to think that Britain's commitments must be brought more into balance with its available strength. They were also bombarded with their officials' advice: a litany of warnings about the ever-growing constraints of economic weakness, 'Asiatic' nationalism, and the demands of Cold War. Churchill himself played an ambivalent role. His impulsiveness and unpredictability alternately enraged and intimidated his cabinet colleagues and drove Eden, his 'crown prince', to ineffectual despair. 'The fact is', said Lord Salisbury, 'the PM is much tougher than Anthony.'[2] Churchill's instincts were to conserve British energy (by ending the Cold War) but also maintain British imperial claims by outright force if need be (his view about Egypt). The question of when he would go (or die) hung over his government like a fog. His extraordinary position and the intrigues of the Churchillian 'court' made the task of decision in any area that attracted his interest one of exceptional difficulty.

It would be a mistake to suppose that Churchill's 'die hardism' frustrated every new policy, and wrong to assume that Churchillian reaction was the primary obstacle to more radical thinking about Britain's place in the world. His colleagues believed that better management was the key to reducing the strain on a hard-pressed economy. They did not draw too dramatic a conclusion from the crisis conditions in which they had come into office. They still thought in terms of a British world-system, necessarily modified in methods and scope, but still recognisably global in reach. Behind this 'conservative' outlook lay three connected assumptions. First, in common with most 'informed' opinion across the whole Western world, they still drew a distinction between the political capacities of whites and non-whites. The independence of India, Burma and Ceylon (Sri Lanka), the resurgence of China under Kuomintang and then Communist rule, and the popular appeal of Arab nationalist movements wrung a grudging acceptance that 'Asiatic nationalism' was a force to be reckoned with. They accepted that confrontation with it was counter-productive and futile. But they were instinctively sceptical about how far such nationalism (or its communist variant) could build a modern nation-state. They thought that the challenge facing Asia's nationalist leaders was how to shrug off obsolete anti-colonial attitudes and acknowledge their dependence upon Western know-how and cash as the means to transform their backward economies. The danger they feared was that by bad luck or bad judgment the West might alienate the new Asian states, delay their transition to 'moderation' and 'realism', or even drive them like China into the communist bloc. British imperial power, on this view of the world, still had a large role to play in the transformation of Asia – in the Middle East and Southeast Asia especially. In Africa, where nationalism lagged far behind Asia in its mobilising potential, that role seemed likely to loom a lot larger. Here, the nationalist leaders (or so it was hoped) could be kept at a safe distance from the virus of Marxism, and coached in the arts of modern state management before being allowed to drive on their own. In its African version, the empire of influence would last a lot longer and compromise a lot less.

Their second assumption also seemed to be vindicated by the course of events since the end of the war. It was that the world would remain divided between great rival blocs and between international groupings that were actually empires or closely resembled them. Survival outside them would be short-lived and risky. The successor-states of empire in the Middle East and Asia would be targets of subversion, and would be forced to choose between rival great power protectors sooner or later. It was in this context that British leaders found Indian criticism of their colonial policies particularly irritating, although it seemed to be driven in part by New Delhi's special concern for the rights of Indian communities in African and other colonial territories.[3] Nehru's public support for the Mau Mau rebellion in Kenya brought a strong private protest. It was only gradually that the defects of this geopolitical outlook began to be seen. In 1955, at the Bandung 'Asian-African' conference (to which colonial leaders were invited), Nehru and Sukarno, the Indonesian prime minister, urged 'non-alignment' for Afro-Asian states, rejecting association with either the West or the Soviet bloc, and calling for the swift end of colonial rule.[4] By the mid-1950s, the United Nations was becoming the forum where post-colonial states could make common cause, and mount a propaganda offensive against the remaining colonial powers. This trend was dramatically strengthened by the Suez crisis in 1956 after which Britain became for many ex-colonial states 'Public Enemy Number One'.[5]

Their third assumption was also subject to rapid erosion as the decade proceeded. But, in 1951–2, it was still possible for senior ministers to take satisfaction in the moral reputation of British colonial rule and of British foreign policy generally. This strengthened their resistance to calls for a more rapid contraction of Britain's imperial role and deepened their confidence that ex-colonial states would want a special relationship with their former imperial master. Indeed, Britain's adherence to a broadly liberal ideology, newly infused with post-war social democracy, seemed likely to make it a more 'attractive' great power in certain respects than the United States, the seat of red-blooded capitalism and race segregation. British policy-makers liked to contrast their tactful handling of the new Asian states (especially India) with what they saw as Washington's ham-handed treatment of post-colonial sensitivities. Where hubris led, nemesis followed.

There was, even so, a considerable sense of urgency in the crisis conditions of 1951. There was little disagreement in principle that Britain must cut its overseas costs, and find a new equilibrium in those countries and regions where its power and influence had come under challenge. Economic and technological change had transformed the conditions in which British world power had been made. 'I believe', the new Colonial Secretary told his Cabinet colleagues on his return from Malaya,

> *that the ever-improving communications of our century –
> Singapore will soon be less than twenty-four hours by
> Comet from London – the rapidity with which news and
> propaganda can now be spread, and above all the
> increasing education and literacy of all people make it
> impossible to hold any other policy than the creation
> of new Dominions, self-governing but part of the
> Commonwealth owing allegiance to the Crown . . . Fifty
> million islanders shorn of so much of their economic power
> can no longer by themselves expect to hold dominion over
> palm and pine on the nineteenth century model of power
> and paternalism which made us the greatest nation in the
> world. We may regain our pinnacle of fame and power by
> the pursuit of this new policy.*[6]

In much the same spirit, he pressed ahead with the rapid development of self-government in the Gold Coast (modern Ghana) under way since 1948, and persuaded the Cabinet in February 1952 that Nkrumah, the 'leader of government business' in its legislative assembly, should be allowed the title of 'prime minister'.[7] To his ministerial colleagues, Lyttelton sometimes struck a pose of reluctant consent to the *force majeure* of events. But, in both the Gold Coast and Nigeria, he endorsed expectations of a steady advance to independence. 'It has been the expressed intention of successive . . . governments', he declared in September 1953,

> to help the Colonies to attain self-government within the Commonwealth. The timing and method of attaining this objective must vary from one territory to another; but the Gold Coast, with no racial problem, considerable natural wealth and a popular African Government . . . is offering . . . enough evidence of ability to manage its own affairs to deprive [us] of any justification for refusing this request.[8]

What mattered was to devise a political system robust enough to survive the strains of independence and to manoeuvre the local politicians into accepting it. This approach was even more obvious in the case of Nigeria where the 1951 constitution, designed to promote the gradual emergence of a unified state out of the political fragments of the inter-war regime of indirect rule, broke down almost immediately. There was no question of falling back on coercion. Here, too, Lyttelton licensed a major concession. The three regional governments – North, East and West – were to get self-government by 1956, with the implicit suggestion that independence for a federal Nigeria would follow soon after.[9] The main concern in British policy was to prevent the Muslim North, where popular nationalism was far less in evidence than it was in the South, from going its own way. As in the Gold Coast (and in Malaya), Lyttelton's aim was the creation of 'new Dominions', independent and sovereign, but bound in reality to follow the lead of the 'Mother-Country'.

Of course, there were plenty of colonies where promoting self-government raised many more difficulties. In East Africa, British policy-makers were attracted to the idea of federating Kenya, Tanganyika (a United Nations trust territory) and Uganda, partly because they thought that a federation would hasten economic development, partly because they hoped it would diffuse settler anxieties in Kenya (where settler opinion was vocal and organised) and Tanganyika. They certainly expected that political progress in East Africa would be much more leisurely than it was in the West African colonies, and the outbreak of Kenya's Mau Mau rebellion in 1952 seemed to confirm this. Yet, even in Kenya, which, said its governor, 'is and will remain an exceptionally explosive country',[10] Lyttelton supported the move towards greater local self-rule and the sharing of power between settlers and Asians, to be extended in time to Africans as well. It was the only way, the governor argued, to break down the 'opposition mentality' from which the whites seemed to suffer and make government work better. In the British Caribbean, London had long favoured federation as the only practicable framework through which a group of small and impoverished territories could achieve greater self-rule and increased prosperity. In the early 1950s, it was anxious to 'manage' the constitutional progress of the larger islands like Jamaica, Trinidad and Barbados in ways that would not foreclose the larger objective of a West Indies Federation – a difficult and ultimately futile endeavour. In Malaya, where the worst of the communist insurrection was over by 1953, British policy was similarly dominated by two interlocking objectives. In Malaya itself, they were eager to encourage the formation of multiracial parties and break down the communal antagonism of Malays and Chinese. The promise of staged self-government was the carrot they offered. But they were also determined that Malaya should be part of a larger federal dominion embracing Singapore and the Borneo territories (Sarawak and British North Borneo), as a durable vehicle for British influence and interests in the post-colonial era.[11]

The larger issue was how that influence could be maintained in ex-colonial territories. Lyttelton had talked of retaining their allegiance to the Crown. The notion that Commonwealth membership would act as the key source of solidarity between Britain and the post-colonial states had already been aired during the Labour government. But, after 1951, it assumed much greater importance as the prospect of self-government in West Africa, the Caribbean and Southeast Asia loomed larger. In the Churchill government there was more than a little unease about the effects of 'admitting' new African and Asian members into what was still mainly a white dominions' club, in which India, Pakistan and Ceylon still formed a minority. Lord Swinton especially worried that the intimacy between Britain and the 'old dominions', already under pressure from the new Asian members, would fray to breaking point once the Commonwealth became an association mainly composed of Afro-Asian ex-colonies.[12] Yet it was really on the support of the 'old' members that Britain would have to rely in the event (still not improbable) of a third world war. One solution proposed was to create two grades of members: in effect an 'old' and a 'new' Commonwealth. The arguments rattled through Whitehall in 1953 and 1954. The clinching objection was that a two-tier Commonwealth would fail to achieve the primary purpose of the whole Commonwealth system. It would anger and alienate the ex-colonial territories where pro-British feeling was weakest, and where the prestige of 'full' Commonwealth membership was the most promising way of maintaining the British connection. To this, Swinton bowed.[13] In reality, of course, a pragmatic distinction was made between those Commonwealth countries with whom Britain worked closely in defence and intelligence, and those outside the magic circle of old friends. Meanwhile, the Commonwealth idea became more and more central to British hopes of upholding their status as the third *world* power, comparable to – if certainly weaker than – the two superpowers, but clearly different in stature from any other great power. 'Were the United Kingdom to stand by herself', remarked a departmental memorandum in June 1956, 'her importance would still be great, but immensely less than it is while she remains the centre of the Commonwealth'.[14] Britain's 'authority and influence will continue, in an increasing degree as its rivals grow in strength and power, to derive from its headship of, or association with, the world-wide group of States that compose the Commonwealth'.[15]

It could be objected, of course, that this was so much pie in the sky if Britain itself were to be drastically weakened by economic exhaustion or geopolitical crisis, or if the pace of change in the colonial world got out of control. Churchill's obsession with promoting a summit conference with Stalin and (after his death in 1953) his successors worried his colleagues, unnerved the Foreign Office and annoyed the Americans.[16] It was rooted in Churchill's belief that his personal influence could achieve the breakthrough to a real European peace and end the Cold War. But it also reflected his deep sense of foreboding at the effects on Britain and British world power of a prolonged 'armed peace'. As much as, if not more than, his Cabinet colleagues, Churchill was conscious of the limits of Britain's material strength and the vital importance of economic recovery, on which the huge burden of defence spending (around 8 per cent of GDP in 1952) hung like an albatross. Continued Cold War would drive Britain deeper into dependence on

America. Even more worrying was the risk that the American will to confront communist power would set off a crisis that could not be stopped. There could be no illusion that either British world power, or even Britain itself, could survive a third world war in the twentieth century.

In fact, the failure of summitry did not prevent an easing of the tensions that had made Attlee's rearmament programme seem so urgent in 1951. Meanwhile, British leaders drew comfort from the powerful advantages that Britain's geopolitical position still seemed to confer. Despite a niggling sense of American rivalry, they enjoyed Washington's general backing for their Middle East policies, and their effort to keep Britain's regional primacy there. American antipathy to European colonialism had already been modified by the fear that the over-hasty demolition of European rule would open the door not to West-leaning nationalism but an East-leaning Marxism. The growing intensity of Cold War competition by 1950 and ever heavier emphasis on the supply of strategic materials strengthened the case for keeping key colonial producers under politically reliable management. The Belgian Congo supplied more than 50 per cent of the 'free world's' uranium (all of it destined for the United States) and 75 per cent of its cobalt. Even *Fortune* magazine, mouthpiece of American big business, choked back its dislike of the Belgian cartels that controlled the Congo's economy in light of these facts.[17] Even the French, on whose colonial methods Franklin D. Roosevelt had once lavished his vitriol, enjoyed the support and extensive largesse of the American government in their Vietnamese war. There was good reason to think that Britain's contribution to global 'containment' would earn Washington's goodwill for as long as the Soviet threat lasted.

Thus London could hope for far greater leverage in Washington than any other Western country. It could also exploit its special position in Europe. This was not just a matter of being (for the moment) economically stronger than other European countries. It derived in great part from the deep rift of mistrust between France and West Germany, and French opposition to the rearming of Germany or the German admission to NATO. So long as this rift lasted, France was bound to look to Britain as its most reliable ally: after all, the Germans might be bribed into pro-Soviet neutrality; and American willingness to pay the full price of keeping France free could never be more than a matter of faith. But British self-interest bound them to France against both the Soviet threat and the danger of German aggrandisement. It was the

British undertaking (in the Paris agreement of 1954) to keep 50,000 men in West Germany (the 'British Army of the Rhine') that cleared the logjam and won French agreement to recruiting a West German army, the vital reinforcement of NATO that Washington wanted. The British were the key (or so it appeared) to the internal solidarity of the West European members of NATO. Their blessing was needed (or so it appeared) for any West European project. Their cooperation was vital if the United States was to manage its cumbrous European commitments alongside its burdens in Northeast and Southeast Asia and in Latin America.

Finally, the British could take some satisfaction, in the early 1950s at least, from the fact that their colonial empire was still little exposed to direct assault from outside. Hong Kong was perhaps the greatest exception. Elsewhere, for the most part, it was the risk of internal subversion that threatened colonial authority and the efforts to orchestrate colonial politics. Nor had their colonial power yet become the embarrassing archaism that it later appeared. The British could point to the French, the Portuguese and the Belgians as practitioners of colonialisms far less liberal than their own, and far less likely to lead to the self-governing nation-states, the ideal form of polity enshrined in the Charter of the United Nations. Much effort was expended in the reinvention of empire as the preparatory school for colonial adulthood, finally recognised with the key to the door – sovereign membership of the (British) Commonwealth.

These aims and plans belonged to the world of 'high' policy-making: they drew on the products of a *Realpolitik* calculus. But how far were they 'viable' in terms of public opinion? In Britain itself, the rough rule of thumb for working politicians remained much as it had been for decades. British opinion was largely indifferent to the detail of what happened in 'remote corners' of the Empire. But it could be quickly aroused by reports of the murder or mistreatment of other (white) Britons, and expected the smack of firm government to be felt by the miscreants. On the other hand, intervention that went wrong or produced heavy casualties for little return, would damage a government's prestige, perhaps very badly. It might be better in those cases to stage a rapid retreat from an untenable salient (like Palestine or Abadan) and hope that this would be seen as cool-headed restraint. As an index of attitudes the British newspaper market offered a very approximate guide. Of the daily papers, those leaning to the

Right (*Daily Express, Daily Mail, Daily Sketch* and *Daily Telegraph*) had a circulation (in 1956) of approximately 8.2 million; those to the Left (*Daily Mirror, Daily Herald* and *News Chronicle*) approximately 7.2 million.[18] Although it could not be assumed that this reflected the relative strength of opinion for or against the defence of empire, these figures gave some indication of the fine line to be trodden if it was to enjoy general backing at home. The more serious danger was that public opinion in general would become disillusioned by the cost (in lives and money) of fighting colonial insurrections; that the burden of world power on the domestic standard of living would grow unacceptably heavy; or that some shocking abuse of colonial rule would give the critics of empire (usually a vociferous but minority group[19]) a chance to derail official policy and encourage its local opponents – those politicians who were labelled 'extremists' by the colonial authorities. In general, however, a revolt by public opinion seemed unlikely, and the counter-insurgencies in Malaya, Kenya and (after 1954) Cyprus were successfully portrayed as a fight against communism, terrorism and barbarism.

British opinion was important, but so was opinion elsewhere in what was still meant to be Britain's sphere of influence. In Australia, the sense of being a 'British' country was still very strong. Intense rivalry in cricket, periodic bursts of resentment over trading arrangements, irritation at London's indifference to Australia's regional defence and the knowledge that Australia now depended more upon American power for its national security had not erased the close identification with Britain's fate and fortunes.[20] Britain's survival as a major world power and the centre of a global trading system still seemed emphatically in Australia's interests. To most Australians, the stability of their own society and its cultural cohesion still seemed to derive mainly from its British origins and continuing 'British' character. As a small community of European stock on the maritime margins of Asia, the cultural lifeline to Britain had always been important. The independence of India, Pakistan, Sri Lanka, Burma and Indonesia, and the political change impending elsewhere in Southeast Asia may have deepened the feeling of antipodean isolation, and increased the urgency of keeping the British connection. One measure of this continuing bond was the pattern of migration. Increasing Australia's *British-born* population was government policy, and (white) British immigrants (a large proportion of them 'assisted immigrants') made up half the intake of newcomers until the 1960s.[21] There was also a migration in the other direction as Australians came to Britain in substantial numbers to pursue education and seek career opportunities. The public stance of the Menzies government (Menzies was prime minister from 1949 to 1966) of loyalty to Britain and devotion to the Crown (the Queen's visit to Australia in 1954 – the year after her coronation – was received with great popular enthusiasm) thus largely reflected Australian feeling – and the expectation that the British should continue to behave like an imperial people.

Not surprisingly, perhaps, these attitudes were echoed with still greater vehemence across the Tasman Sea in New Zealand. There, the cool calculation of an expert committee at the end of the war that immigration from Britain was unnecessary[22] was overturned by 'the clamour of public opinion'.[23] The sense of dependence on the British market for New Zealand's foodstuffs and wool was almost overwhelming. Under the National party government of Sidney Holland, New Zealand's place in a Britain-centred world was announced unequivocally. 'Where Britain goes, we go', declared Holland's press statement after the Commonwealth Finance Ministers Conference in early 1952. 'If Britain sinks, we are sunk... but neither of us will sink', he added – perhaps a little hastily.[24] Like the Australians, New Zealanders expected the British to behave imperially, especially when it came to safeguarding the Suez route to the South Pacific. On the future of the Suez Canal, the New Zealand press was even more unbending than the Conservative diehards in Britain.[25] At the height of the Suez crisis in November 1956, Holland asked himself: 'Do we want to be in a position where Britain will say, or even think, we sought their help and it was not forthcoming...?'.[26] His answer was no. Of course, there was scope for friction and disagreement, not least over the role of British-owned shipping companies in New Zealand's trade.[27] But, in the Cold War climate, there were few parts of the 'British world' where London could hope for a more sympathetic hearing than in 1950s New Zealand.

In the other 'old dominions', public attitudes were less crystalline. Canada 'is no longer a British dominion trying to act like a nation', said *Fortune* magazine approvingly in August 1952.[28] Its population had risen by 20 per cent since 1940, its national product by 90 per cent while its foreign trade had tripled. The presumption remained deeply rooted that what made Canada Canada was its British inheritance, in institutions particularly. Canada also continued to be a major destination for migrants from Britain. But, in communications, business and cultural life, the dominant influences now came up from the south. After the Second World War, Canada was integrated much more fully into a 'continental' economy. A huge tide of investment poured in from the United States to develop Canada's natural resources: a huge stream of raw or semi-processed materials, especially minerals and wood-pulp, poured back in return. Canada's '"triangular trade" seems nearly done for', crowed *Fortune*: now Canada had to pay for its American imports by exporting not to Europe (as before the war) but to the United States. Defending Canada against the effects of American mass culture came to seem urgent enough to prompt a 'Royal Commission on Arts, Letters and Sciences in Canada' – a revealing designation. Perhaps the need to define a distinctively Canadian culture signalled the increasingly rapid decline of older British connections in the media, publishing and higher education. Canadian troops formed part of the 'Commonwealth' division that fought in Korea and Canadian ministers took a prominent part in Commonwealth meetings. But Canadian opinion had far less reason than Australian or New Zealand to interest itself in Britain's imperial problems in the Middle East or elsewhere, and was far less likely (as events were to prove) to give public support where that risked disagreement with the United States.[29]

South Africa was a paradox. After 1948, Afrikaner nationalism had strengthened its grip on the country. While the shift to republican status that had been a public goal of the National party for thirty years was quietly deferred, the right of 'coloureds' (i.e. persons of mixed race) to vote – a right confined to Cape Province and a relic of its 'colonial' parliamentary system – was swept away amidst a fierce constitutional crisis. As the elements of what became the *apartheid* policy (residential segregation, urban removals, formalised racial status, stricter labour controls, and prohibitions on political and social mixing) were gradually enforced, the volume of public disapproval from interested parties in Britain became far louder than before 1939. In their relations with London, however, the governments of Malan and Strijdom showed caution and pragmatism. The long-standing demand for the transfer of the 'High Commission Territories', Basutoland (now Lesotho), Bechuanaland (Botswana) and Swaziland, to South African control was kept in low key. In 1955, the Simonstown agreement ended British control over the naval base near Cape Town, but placed the

South African navy under the overall command of the Royal Navy in wartime.[30] Meanwhile, British investment in South African mining and industrial companies continued to grow rapidly. Among the South African 'English', still around 40 per cent of whites, attachment to Britain remained strong, reinforced by disdain for Afrikaans (a 'kitchen' language) and for most Afrikaners, stereotyped as the dim 'Van der Merwe' (a common Afrikaner surname) from the *platteland* or backblocks. By the mid-1950s, however, 'English' feeling was being cooled by resentment at the chorus of criticism from Britain aimed at *apartheid* and by the growing suspicion that British colonial policy elsewhere in Africa posed a threat to white supremacy.

Elsewhere in their 'system', the British could draw comfort from what still seemed the malleability of colonial opinion in their Asian and African empire. Even in Kenya, where they faced the Mau Mau uprising and resorted to drastic measures to 'rehabilitate' those suspected of Mau Mau sympathies, they could rely on a much larger group of anti-Mau Mau 'loyalists'.[31] In Northern Rhodesia (now Zambia) and Nyasaland (now Malawi), they dismissed African opposition to the making of a white-ruled federation as a temporary ebullition fomented by 'extremists' and insisted that it would die away once federation's material benefits were seen.[32] Nor by the mid-1950s had London given up hope of Anglo-Indian friendship as Eden's diplomacy at the 1954 Geneva conference revealed. Once the policy of colonial self-government was fully established, or so it was thought, much of the friction in Anglo-Indian relations would be soothed away. The one region of British influence where the prospects seemed gloomier (although not so gloomy as they later appeared) was the Middle East.

This formed the context in which British governments tried to set their course through the 1950s. They were eager for detente to ease the strain on their overloaded economy. They were also determined to uphold if they could their regional pre-eminence among the Western European powers and check any change there that threatened their interests. They expected to enjoy a privileged status as Washington's closest and most valuable ally in the evolving Cold War. They attached huge priority to rebuilding the strength of the sterling economy and restoring as much as they could of Britain's old commercial role in the world. They were anxious to retain Britain's Middle East *imperium* as much for the leverage it conferred geopolitically as for the access it promised to oil – rapidly replacing coal as the source of industrial energy. And they were keen to reinforce Britain's close relations with the 'old' dominions – especially Australia and New Zealand – and, where they could, to build new ones. We can trace the faint outlines (however opaque) of a grand design. Britain would remain at the centre of an empire of both influence and identity, the head of a civic association (the Commonwealth) and a 'British world' held together in part by ethnic and cultural ties. But, as British leaders half-acknowledged, and as their advisers insisted, the fate of this 'project' depended almost entirely on forces that lay beyond Britain's control. As the 1950s unfolded, these were to turn London's uphill struggle into a headlong descent.

The sterling economy

Any hope of restoring Britain's pre-war position as the centre of an independent world-system was bound to turn on its economic performance. This was not just a question of achieving a surplus on the balance of payments, and competing successfully in overseas markets, nor of attaining a steady improvement in the standard of living, depressed by the austerity of wartime and post-war conditions. Regaining the economic independence, commercial influence and relative wealth that Britain had enjoyed in 1938, let alone in 1913, was a much more demanding task. It required Britain to be free from external obligations and debts and the distorting effect these might have on its domestic economy. It meant reviving the capacity to be the prime source of overseas borrowing for established clients among the developing countries (like Australia and South Africa) as well as some new ones. It implied the steady (re-)acquisition of those overseas assets that had contributed so much to past British wealth and security. It needed Britain to serve as an expanding market for overseas produce, both for domestic consumption and for re-export to other 'end-users' – its old entrepot function. For this to work smoothly, it was vital to have a freely convertible currency that could be traded easily and which potential customers would be willing to hold. It also followed that Britain would have to supply in return a large portion of the manufactures wanted by its non-industrial partners if their commercial relations were not to become too unbalanced. And, of course, the efficient working of this commercial system would depend (as it had in the past) upon a vast network of services: shipping, insurance, banking and merchanting. Largely managed from

London, these had been one of the most profitable elements of the pre-war 'commercial empire'.

It was a daunting list. But British leaders in the 1950s were determined to restore Britain as an economic great power, and to use its economic strength to preserve a wide sphere of influence and a world-power status. They were acutely conscious of the enormous scale of the American economy, which produced almost two-thirds of the world's manufactured goods in the late 1940s. They expected the Soviet Union to become in time an advanced industrial power within its closed trading bloc. They were aware of how quickly Germany was emerging from the economic abyss of the end of the war to compete with Britain in industrial exports. They hoped nevertheless to exploit Britain's assets and its economic inheritance to construct a modified form of commercial empire to underpin the domestic economy and meet the overseas costs of a world-power role. It was a goal they pursued with gradually waning confidence until its futility overwhelmed them after 1960.

The economic crisis of 1951–2 could be blamed in part on the huge rearmament programme on which the Attlee government had embarked. It was eased quite quickly by imposing strict controls on imported dollar goods, and by restraining domestic demand through higher interest rates. But it was a painful reminder that, after six years of recovery, the British economy was still very vulnerable to sudden fluctuations in overseas trade. The reserve of dollars and gold to meet any emergency was still desperately slim. Despite the huge effort to raise British merchandise exports well above their pre-war level, building a margin of safety in the balance of payments proved very hard. A key reason for this was the drastic reduction in overseas income and the corresponding huge rise in foreign obligations since 1939. In 1913, Britain's net overseas assets (at £4 billion) had been nearly twice as large as its GDP.[33] In the depressed 1930s, they had fallen just below the figure for GDP. But, in 1951, after wartime disinvestment and large-scale borrowing from other sterling area countries (incurring the so-called 'sterling balances'), net overseas assets were actually negative: −0.05 per cent of GDP. In constant (1938) prices, they had declined from £7.3 billion in 1913, to £4.1 billion in 1937 to −£0.3 billion in 1951. Income from abroad as a proportion of national production was one-sixth of what it had been in 1913. The huge foreign earnings that had helped keep Britain solvent and fund ever more foreign investment had largely vanished. So had the means to restore the huge foreign portfolio sold off or mortgaged after 1940. In 1913, overseas assets accounted for over one-third of all British assets: in 1973, despite a wave of post-war investment, they stood at only 3 per cent.[34]

But the picture was not an entirely bleak one. The British may have lagged far behind the United States in industrial production but they remained at the centre of a far-flung system of trade. In the early 1950s, about half the world's trade was still transacted in sterling. Britain imported more foodstuffs and raw cotton than the United States. The Americans had built up their overseas assets to around $17 billion by 1950 – perhaps a total no larger than Britain had held before 1939.[35] But nearly 70 per cent was concentrated in Canada and Latin America and both regulation and practice made lending difficult to many of those countries that had traditionally looked to London. The Soviet Union was not a foreign investor and showed (at first) little sign of offering economic aid to countries in the British 'sphere'. The British hoped to restore the City's role as the banker and financier of the developing countries. They expected to profit from the surging demand for raw materials that had loomed so large in the post-war recovery. With much of the world's high-value minerals in their colonial empire or in 'sterling' countries, and with other raw materials like cocoa and tin under their economic control, they looked well placed to profit from the general expansion of trade. With a large part of the world's deep-sea shipping still British-owned, they could expect to earn a handsome dividend from supplying the services that kept commerce moving, just as they had before 1914. British merchant enterprise was still very active across much of the Afro-Asian world. Nor was it solely a matter of exploiting colonial windfalls or long-practised trades. Britain also seemed in the van of the new science-based economy. It had large investments in oil, the fuel of the future. Its large aerospace industry – partly the product of war – had built the world's first jet airliner (the ill-fated Comet) to transform long-distance air travel. The post-war commitment to building nuclear weapons promised economic advantages. With the opening of Calder Hall in 1956, the British pioneered the generation of electricity using nuclear power, an achievement revealed to an awed New Zealand prime minister.[36] And, right through the decade, the British spent heavily on research and development (both civil and military), more heavily than any other Western country except the United States.[37]

We shall see later on that few of these 'assets' yielded more than a modest return in the quest for economic revival. The immediate task, which commanded a wide consensus in both Whitehall and the City, was to maintain and enhance the strength of the pound, and restore its position as a 'top currency': that is, a 'top favourite for international monetary transactions, most often and most widely used for a great variety of monetary purposes...the choice of the world market'.[38] The strong pound would enable Britain to profit from the growth of world trade. It would attract the deposits of other currencies to London, swelling the funds at the City's disposal. It would boost the appeal of the commercial services that London could offer, since overseas confidence in insurance and other financial arrangements was bound to be greater if sterling's value was impregnable. It would help to stabilise the domestic economy and reduce the threat of inflation which had briefly reached 9 per cent in 1951–2. A strong pound was the key to a strong British economy. The weak post-war pound had to put on weight and gain muscles. The question that tormented bankers, officials and their ministerial masters through the 1950s was how to achieve this goal.

What was generally agreed was that the sterling area was the essential platform for sterling's revival as a top currency. Under its rules, the member countries held their dollar earnings in a common pool managed in London, pegged their currencies on sterling, and imposed strict control over their dollar purchases and the exchange of sterling into other currencies. The incentive for Britain's sterling partners to observe these rules sprang from their fear that the shortage of dollars worldwide (a result of the huge demand for American goods and the difficulty of selling into the American market) meant that the freedom to exchange sterling at will would result in a crash of its value (as in the near-disaster of 1947). If that were to happen, their claims on London (the sterling balances) would be worthless, and the economic dislocation in Britain would wipe out their most important market. For the British, the sterling area's existence offered a guarantee that the sums Britain owed to the other sterling countries (mainly debts arising from the war) could be paid off at an affordable rate and without jeopardising sterling's value against the dollar. It averted the risk that a country holding large sums in sterling might suddenly sell them for dollars and wreck the British balance of payments. It also allowed a gradual resumption of British overseas lending but without the danger of that foreign investment being exchanged into dollars. It propped up the system of trading preferences ('Commonwealth preference' also extended to Canada) to which British industry was still deeply attached. More than 50 per cent of British exports were being sent to 'British countries' throughout most of the 1950s.[39] As late as 1958, the sterling area's merits were still being trumpeted in the most influential quarters. It was well designed for its members' interests and also for world trade, declared Sir Oliver Franks, a former ambassador in Washington and chairman of Lloyds Bank. Member countries had no need to worry about bilateral balances, and using the pound kept down the demand for gold – any shortage of which would restrain world trade. The sterling area also allowed Britain to earn gold (by its trade with South Africa), and encouraged the City to use its financial machinery to help expand British exports.[40] It was not a system to be abandoned lightly.

But it was also acknowledged in the Bank of England, by Treasury officials and even by ministers, that preserving the sterling area as a closed currency zone was not a long-term solution to the problem of sterling. Sooner or later, the 'one world' economy envisaged in the Bretton Woods agreements at the close of the war would have to come into force. The alternative was return to the protectionist blocs of the inter-war years with all the consequences that might follow from that. Open disavowal of the Bretton Woods system would be hugely controversial. It might easily lead to an open breach with the United States, and perhaps the break-up of the Western Alliance. Washington had been patient with London's delays, but on the understanding that it intended to honour the promise of a convertible pound as soon as it could. There were other reasons as well. It was widely agreed that, before very long (the timescale was unclear), the dollar famine would end (as more countries recovered and were able to earn dollars). The case for restrictions would be harder to make. The sterling area countries were already eager to borrow American dollars for development purposes but were unlikely to entice the American investor if his dividend was paid in inconvertible pounds. Their interest lay in a looser system. And the British themselves knew perfectly well that, so long as the pound was 'soft' and the dollar was 'hard', they would lose the race to restore sterling's old status and win back for the City its central place in international trade. It was too much to hope for the long-lost pre-eminence of 1913. But, in the 1930s, as the head of the sterling bloc and with a convertible pound, Britain had been the world's largest trading economy.

The terms and timing of 'convertibility' became the central issue in economic policy. Within the Bank of England and the Treasury, there were those who were eager to get it done quickly, arguing that sterling's prospects would not improve with delay. The sterling crisis that broke over their heads at the end of 1951 pushed them into a radical plan. Under the acronym 'ROBOT', it proposed to make sterling convertible subject to two drastic conditions. First, it would be necessary to persuade those countries with large sterling balances that the bulk of them should be frozen, leaving only the amounts they needed for normal trading purposes. This was the *quid pro quo* for the end of exchange control. Secondly (and much more controversially), the plan proposed that sterling should 'float' (just as it had in the 1930s). The reason for this was that defending a fixed rate (sterling had been fixed at $2.80 to £1 in 1949) might quickly consume much of Britain's reserve of dollars and gold (just as it had in 1947) and wreck the experiment almost before it had started. Allowing sterling to find its own level in the period of sharp adjustment that would follow free exchange would also reduce the risk of British exports becoming uncompetitive with the end of import controls and dollar restriction in sterling area markets.[41] With the support of the Bank of England and his own expert advisers, the Chancellor of the Exchequer, R. A. Butler, presented ROBOT to his colleagues as the best solution to the financial crisis that the new Churchill government had inherited. The sequel was instructive.

For all its heavyweight backing, ROBOT soon attracted fierce opposition, not least from Lord Cherwell, Churchill's scientific adviser, known colloquially as the 'Prime Minister's Adder'. Cherwell was scornful of the flimsy statistical basis on which ROBOT was built, and argued persuasively that the pressure on sterling could be relieved by the use of much less drastic measures. It was, he said, 'a reckless leap in the dark involving appalling political and economic risks at home and abroad'.[42] The objection to ROBOT was not just that Butler's medicine was unnecessarily strong. Four arguments sank it. First, although there had been ambiguous signals from across the Atlantic, floating the pound would breach the first commandment of the Bretton Woods doctrine. It was hard to believe that the American response would not be severe. Secondly, it was far from certain that all the other countries in the sterling area would adopt a floating exchange rate. Far from forming a bloc of like-minded states, the sterling countries might break up in anger and acrimony. Thirdly, floating the pound might lead to the break-up of the European Payments Union (a currency pool along sterling area lines) if the pound was devalued against some European currencies. At a time when London was also trying to promote defence cooperation among the Western European states, and soothing French fears of future German aggrandisement, such a large spanner in the European works was unwelcome at best. The Foreign Office and Foreign Secretary were among ROBOT's fiercest critics.[43] Finally, since it was hard to predict how far sterling's value would fall under the ROBOT regime, it was hard to deny that, at least in the short run, the domestic effects might be very unsettling: rapid inflation if imports cost more; severe unemployment if other countries retaliated against a devaluing pound.

ROBOT was opposed by those who thought Britain's position too fragile to survive the shock treatment it promised and by those (like Cherwell) who argued that sticking to 'the long steady task of building up our reserves' was the best recipe for success. That it would be a long haul seemed amply confirmed in the next few years. In 1955, after two better years, inflationary pressure in the British economy and a sharp negative movement in the balance of payments led to credit restrictions to dampen home demand and strengthen sterling abroad. The following year was the year of Suez. The British invasion of Egypt triggered a flight from the pound; the cost of supporting its value from a fast dwindling reserve of dollars and gold was the critical factor in forcing the British withdrawal. In 1957, inflation in Britain and the devaluation of the French franc reopened doubts over whether sterling could hold its fixed dollar value. It took a fierce contraction of credit (the Bank rate rose to 7 per cent, its highest level since 1921) and an American loan to beat off the threat. It seems somewhat surprising after this ragged performance that the Macmillan government quietly made sterling convertible over the Christmas break in 1958. It was certainly true that the balance of trade had improved and inflation was down. But it was also true that its hand was being forced. Strict exchange control had already collapsed: it was the buying and selling of sterling in the market of currencies that now determined its value. Secondly, France had pre-empted the British in making the franc convertible (while devaluing again). At the moment when London was straining to persuade the new European Economic Community to include Britain in a 'free trade agreement', the pound had to look the *franc demi-fort* in the eye. But had the reserves that were needed to defend sterling's value been salted away? The Treasury's target for a payments surplus had still not been reached. Instead, reliance was now placed on being able to borrow from the International Monetary Fund if the going got hard.[44] Convertibility, remarked *The Economist* in a phrase that ought to have struck a ministerial chill, was an 'act of bravery'.[45]

British leaders knew of course that convertibility was not enough. To be an economic great power required a central position in the flows of world trade, and reasonable access to some of the world's richest markets. Before 1914, over one-third of British trade had been with Europe, and nearly one-quarter with the countries that became the European Economic Community (the 'EEC Six') in 1958. In the inter-war years, the share of British exports sent to the future 'EEC Six' fell to under 15%. After the Second World War, it fell even further, to less than 10% in 1948.[46] But, by the 1950s, these were the countries that were growing most rapidly. More generally, it was industrial countries that made the best markets. Here, too, Britain lagged behind its main competitors. Its principal rivals increased the share of their exports to other industrial countries from 58% in 1950-2 to 61% in 1957-9. The British share rose from 39% to 45%.[47] To keep up the momentum that had doubled British exports from their pre-war levels required a major effort in Europe.

For this reason alone, London kept a wary eye on the progress of European schemes for economic and political unity that were gathering pace in the early 1950s. Its negative attitude towards the plans that emerged for an Economic Community from the Messina Conference in 1955 has been much derided in hindsight. In fact, the British regarded the idea of forming an inner group (with discriminatory tariffs) within the larger collectivity of Western European states with considerable hostility. They thought it would damage the prospects for freer trade in general and for British trade in particular. They wanted it to fail, and thought that it would.[48] They saw no point in lending it any support. But this was far from an attitude of indifference or hostility towards closer cooperation with Europe, although there were plenty of those in the Conservative party who took a 'blue water' view of continental commitments. Instead, in the late summer of 1956, the Cabinet agreed on a plan that was intended deliberately to seize control of the movement towards a European customs union and drive it in the direction that British policy favoured. This was 'Plan G', which proposed to sink the EEC project within a larger 'Free Trade Area' within which there would be free trade in manufactured goods but no common agricultural policy. The obvious merit from a British point of view was that this would allow continued preferential arrangements both for British farmers (heavily protected since the Second World War) and for Commonwealth producers. It would give Britain the benefits of a large open European market with few of the drawbacks of being tied to an economic bloc.

The plan was put to the Cabinet by Harold Macmillan, then Chancellor of the Exchequer, as a series of rhetorical questions, designed to flush out its fiercest opponents. 'Is this a good plan for the British economy?', asked the Chancellor,

> *Will it bring us strength in the long run . . . ? Can the British economy survive alone, insulated and protected from European competition? Will it be able to maintain its exports to Europe . . . ? Equally important, can it maintain its exports to other countries against the competition of European countries, either individually, as now, or in a unified Europe largely under German domination? Can we enter into a new structure and at the same time maintain the advantages of the Commonwealth, our preferences and all the rest? Can we retain them even if we keep out?*[49]

Nor, of course, were the issues at stake of solely economic concern. Were the aims of Plan G 'politically sound'? 'Can we retain the leadership of the Commonwealth world

> *and at the same time seize the leadership of Europe? Would it help us to create a new period of British strength and power, or should we be foolishly throwing away what we have? Would it bring us promise for the future, or is it an abdication and betrayal of our past?*[50]

Macmillan also spelled out the risk of division within the Conservative party, the threat posed by free trade to maintaining full employment and the need to reassure both Commonwealth countries and the United States. But there was no doubt that he wanted his colleagues' approval for a plan which among other things, was intended to make London the centre for Europe's foreign investment. 'The economic unification of much of Western Europe', declared Peter Thorneycroft, President of the Board of Trade, 'would create a new source of investment capital for overseas development which might be expected to flow out to Commonwealth countries through London under our management'.[51] In the discussion that followed, there were predictable fears that the main Commonwealth countries would turn away from Britain towards the United States and 'the status of Britain as a world power depends on her position as head of the Commonwealth'.[52] But Macmillan insisted that, without a new basis for the British economy, it could not provide the market that the Commonwealth needed, nor secure the future of sterling. When Eden summed up, his view was decisive. There was little hope, he said, of an economic policy based on the Commonwealth: even Australia and New Zealand seemed to be turning towards the United States. The Asian Commonwealth could not be relied on. 'Unless we were capable, acting alone, of meeting formidable European competition in oversea markets, there seemed no alternative but to base our policy on the proposed plan for closer association with Europe'.[53] After further consultations, and some positive signals from the United States, Europe, the Commonwealth and domestic opinion, the decision was made in early November to press ahead and negotiate.

But, as it turned out, the British had badly mistaken the strength of their hand. They had coolly assumed that, if they took a firm line on the exclusion of foodstuffs from the free trade arrangements, they would get their way: 'We should expect this condition to be ultimately accepted', said Macmillan and Thorneycroft.[54] They also assumed that, once they had given a lead, the idea of a free trade area would trump the plan for an economic community drawn up by the Six. One key to their thinking was the belief that France shared Britain's fear of a 'German-dominated' Europe, to which Macmillan had referred, but felt it even more deeply. French paranoia would give the British the lever they needed to switch the points towards the free trade line, or derail the train. All this proved wrong. The European Six signed the Treaty of Rome in March 1957. When the British began to negotiate in October that year, they met a stubborn refusal on the foodstuffs question. And, far from France proving the weak link in the EEC chain, the reverse was the case. In June 1958, General De Gaulle returned to power, first as prime minister in the dying Fourth Republic, then as president in the Fifth. It was De Gaulle who firmly put an end to the free trade area diplomacy. It was an unmistakable omen. All the British could hope (with some justification from history) was that his tenure would be short and his retirement long.

It was a major defeat. London tried to make the best of things. The British had already committed themselves (at the Montreal Commonwealth Economic Conference) to stand by the system of Commonwealth preference and to make up the shortfall of private investment in their colonial and ex-colonial territories through government aid and loans.[55] All this was intended to hold the Commonwealth together as a system of trade and influence and provide reassurance of British aims and intentions. But it was starkly clear as the decade came to an end that what mattered most was the export competitiveness of the British economy. The 1959 Radcliffe Report on the British monetary system gave a ringing endorsement of 'the general harmony of interest between the United Kingdom economy and that of the rest of the sterling area',[56] and insisted that it was in Britain's interest to invest more and more in the economic development of the Commonwealth countries.[57] But it also warned that sterling's role as a reserve currency had been displaced by the dollar, and that the UK's reserves still formed only a fraction of sterling's liabilities. The only solution, as Cherwell had argued some seven years earlier, was to press on in the hope that export growth would build up the margin of safety to protect the domestic economy, make sterling secure and fund the export of capital to non-industrial countries.

But, on this battlefront, there were very mixed signals. The British economy had not performed badly. It had paid for a notable increase in living standards at home – the 'affluence' for which the Conservative government was keen to take credit. But it had not performed well enough to allow Britain to become (or remain) an economic great power. There were several reasons for this. It may have been partly the fault of an old or obsolete infrastructure whose renewal was too costly under post-war conditions. This was the burden of being an 'old' industrial power. A more immediate difficulty was the need to transform an industrial structure largely adapted to the highly diversified markets in non-industrial countries that had been Britain's main customers since the inter-war years and before. The move towards a production system based on higher volume and standardisation was technically difficult and very disruptive in labour relations.[58] As a result, the great shift from textiles to engineering as Britain's industrial staple was made too slowly.[59] Thirdly, British leaders shrank from the challenge to domestic opinion. In theory at least, they might have hoped to improve Britain's export performance and suppressed the inflationary trend that helped make sterling so fragile by enforcing a 'flexible' market in labour. An attack on restrictive practices, and the willingness to risk a short-term rise in unemployment, might have forced down real wages and secured productivity gains. Politically, there was no question of this. Full employment was part of the post-war compact: it was widely assumed that electoral suicide would follow its breach. Thus the sterling economy followed a zigzag path dictated by the aspiration to great-power status, the fear of abandoning its traditional base in the 'Commonwealth world', and mortal terror of an electorate enraged by an attack on job security and hard-won affluence. It would have needed an exceptionally benign outside world for this course to have brought British leaders the results that they craved.

Descent to Suez

As we saw in the last chapter, almost unobserved there had been a critical change in the position of Britain in Egypt. The means and the will to exert British military power directly in Cairo had quietly collapsed in January 1952. The political crowbar in the Residency's possession since the era of Cromer could no longer be used. Yet, in London, the value of Egypt and the Canal Zone base had never seemed higher. Reaching an agreement over the use of the base and for Egypt's cooperation in Middle East defence was as urgent a priority for Churchill's government as it had been for Attlee's. But, by the time it was signed in October 1954, it was an open question whether the hard-won agreement had any value at all, except to avoid a hugely embarrassing 'scuttle'. The arduous path to its making had signalled a shift in the balance of strength. The tragedy that followed sprang from a gross paradox. The importance that London attached to its regional primacy now had no counterpart in its regional power: the reverse was the case. The desperate remedy of Eden's Suez invasion was required to conceal this. The crushing failure that followed exposed its truth.

Why did London care so much about Egypt and the Canal Zone? Behind the logistical detail of stores and supply routes, the imaginary defence lines against a Soviet advance into the Middle East, and the plans to bomb Southern Russia in the event of world war, lay a (largely) unspoken assumption. Britain's ability to use the Canal Zone and its bases (as well as drawing more widely on Egyptian resources since the Zone was not self-sufficient) was its greatest surviving geostrategic asset outside the Home Islands. It served as the pivot from which British power could be projected north towards Russia, eastwards to the Gulf (and its oil), across the Indian Ocean to Australia and New Zealand, and south to East Africa. The Canal Zone depended upon Egyptian goodwill to function efficiently; but it was also the lever with which to extract cooperation from Cairo. Preserving Britain's claim to make use of the Zone was a standing affront to Egyptian nationalist feeling. But it was also the main guarantee that Egypt's leaders would take a 'realistic' view of their national interests and accept the reality of their 'satellite' status in the British world-system.

Egypt was important for itself. It was also the pre-eminent state of the Arab Middle East. It had the biggest population, the largest middle class and the oldest tradition of nationalist politics. Its writers, intellectuals and journalists exerted a pan-Arab influence. For most cultural purposes, Cairo was the capital of the Arab world. The Al-Azhar, half mosque, half university, was *the* great centre of Islamic learning. This gave Anglo-Egyptian relations a particular delicacy. A compliant, if not 'loyal', Egypt was the key component of Britain's Middle Eastern *imperium* as *the* regional power, regulating the relations of the Arab states with each other as well as with the outside world. An Egyptian 'revolt' against this 'system' would be a serious threat. As we have seen, under post-war conditions the Arab Middle East as a whole had become even more valuable from London's viewpoint than before 1939. This was partly a matter of strategic defence against Russia, partly a matter of oil. But, despite the prominence that both these assume in the archival record, the intensity with which British leaders regarded their Middle East interests, and the extent to which they became the index of Britain's world power status, hint at a larger assumption. It was sometimes expressed in terms of prestige, but its real meaning ran deeper.

Before 1939, it was a commonplace that the ultimate source of British power in the world, including its great-power status in Europe, was the Royal Navy. British sea-power had had to share global supremacy with that of America: but, in European waters and the Indian Ocean, it had remained pre-eminent in the inter-war years. Almost unheralded, the course and outcome of the Second World War struck the maritime sword from Britain's hand. Taken together, the growth of air warfare, the massive scale of Soviet land forces and the colossal expansion of the American navy removed any illusion that the strategic significance of Britain's sea-power was remotely comparable with what it had been just a decade before. We 'cannot afford the American technique of building up large naval forces to support continental land battles', remarked the Chiefs of Staff sorrowfully.[60] The Middle East *imperium* silently filled the gap. Strategic command of the region gave Britain a critical role in the defence of Europe. It secured its primacy among the West European states and (perhaps more important) conferred an exceptional leverage in London's often tetchy relations with Washington. More than anything else, it lifted Britain out of the category of a merely European power. And, although London sought material help from the Americans, it insisted on Britain's claim to be the *political* guardian of the West's regional interests. In the plans drawn up in mid-1953, it was British, Arab and Commonwealth forces that were to defend the Middle East against a Soviet invasion.[61] Among British leaders, no one was more sensitive than Anthony Eden to the grand geopolitics of Middle East power.

This was the setting in which the British tried to reopen the question of their right to use the Canal Zone bases after the expiry of the 1936 treaty due in 1956. Eden as Foreign Secretary was determined to do this, despite lurid warnings from Cairo where the British ambassador was convinced that Egypt was on the brink of chaos.[62] Against Churchill's scepticism and the ambassador's proposal that, rather than seek an agreement, British policy should aim 'to isolate Egypt as a potential enemy',[63] Eden insisted that the new set of ministers King Farouk had appointed (following the bloody riots in Cairo) offered the best chance for striking a bargain. Egypt, as part of a new 'Middle East Command', would take charge of the Canal Zone bases in peacetime. The British would keep on the spot only the minimum force needed to 'help' the Egyptians to maintain the bases. The alternative, Eden warned his Cabinet colleagues, was a long confrontation and the effective loss of the base. 'I am convinced', he told Churchill,

> that we shall not reach an agreement unless we are willing
> to agree to the principle of evacuation. The net result of the
> last five months has been to bring Egypt to the verge of
> anarchy. The present Egyptian government is the best we
> can hope for. Its position is precarious and its continuance

*in power depends on its ability to clip the wings of the
Wafd. To do this it needs some helpful move by us, and it
needs it soon . . . The plain fact is that we are no longer in
a position to impose our will on Egypt, regardless of the
cost in men, money, and international goodwill both
throughout the Middle East and in the rest of the world.*[64]

But progress was meagre. There was little incentive for the Egyptian
ministers to risk acceptance of Eden's terms, all too readily seen as a
transparent device for keeping Britain's grip on the Zone and its military
bases. Nor did they dare give up Egypt's claim to be sovereign in the
Sudan, whose political future remained deeply uncertain. The Egyptian
ambassador was convinced, reported a senior Foreign Office official,

*that the only chance of our inducing the Egyptians either to
accept our formula or to begin negotiations with us over
the Sudan . . . lay in our being able to make them believe
that the ultimate result of their refusal . . . would be the
reoccupation of Cairo by British forces. This was the only
thing they were really scared of.*[65]

While the British brooded over this latest rebuff and pondered Egypt's
place in their new global strategy, Cairo's politics lurched in an unexpected direction.[66] In July 1952, a military coup pushed aside the old
rivalry between the Court and the Wafd. The 'Revolutionary Command Council', led by Neguib and Nasser, became the real power. The
Egyptian army, hitherto a quiescent if discontented force, now had to
be squared.

By the end of the year, Eden was ready to try again. The same
set of pressures was still pushing him forward. Without Egyptian goodwill, the Canal Zone was useless as a great military base. Indeed, without an agreement, it might become the scene of a guerrilla war. Its
huge British garrison of 80,000 men was chiefly employed in defending
itself: 'It is their presence that creates the need for them to be there',
said a British official with mandarin irony.[67] But simply handing it
over would be a colossal defeat. It must be available in case of a war
against Russia, said the military planners. Egypt had to promise its help
if the Middle East were invaded. To let Cairo completely cut loose from
its British connection would weaken Britain's allies in the other Arab

states, and might provoke further demands for British withdrawal – including from the important air bases at Habbaniya and Shaiba in Iraq. It would signal a drastic decline in both the will and the means to enforce British interests. It would be bound to stir up fierce objection at home among those who disliked the 'appeasement' of nationalism or any retreat on the front line of empire – opinions well represented in the Conservative party. Eden's new formula was a cautious advance on the abortive proposal for a 'Middle East Command'. Now, with American backing, the Egyptians were urged to join a new organisation for the region's defence, the 'Middle East Defence Organisation' or MEDO. Loosely modelled on NATO, MEDO would include both the Arab states and their Western 'friends', principally Britain and the United States. On joining this club, Egypt would be entrusted with the Canal Zone and its bases, to be run with some British help. This time the prospects for settlement seemed brighter. In February 1953, London and Cairo reached an agreement on the future of the Sudan, so often the stumbling block to their friendly relations. Like all previous regimes, Egypt's military leaders were determined to regain what they saw as its rightful authority in the vast country it had colonised in the previous century but then lost to the Mahdist revolt and the British reconquest. All shades of opinion resented what was seen as a British conspiracy to encourage Sudan's separation and patronise Sudanese nationalism. The British, for their part, had briefly considered giving up the Sudan as the price for a new treaty with Cairo in 1946, but then had drawn back.[68] Neither Attlee nor Bevin had known the Sudan's peculiar history – unlike the veteran of Omdurman now at 10 Downing Street. The 1953 agreement was an interesting compromise. It promised Sudanese self-government by 1956, the same year that the Anglo-Egyptian treaty expired. The Sudanese people would choose through the ballot box whether they wished to become independent or seek a union with Egypt. For both the signatories it was a calculated risk. But Neguib (who had close ties with the Sudan) may have hoped that giving up Egypt's sovereignty claim would increase the backing for union in Sudanese politics against its Mahdist opponents and their nationalist rhetoric.[69]

But as the pessimists had predicted, the defence talks soon stalled. Neguib and his colleagues rejected an advance commitment to MEDO. Nasser knew about 'Rodeo', said an embassy official[70] and was deeply suspicious of British intentions. The Revolutionary Command

Council had one ambition – to get the British troops out and end any risk of British intervention in Cairo. The delicate balance of Egyptian politics, in which Revolutionary Command Council rule coexisted uneasily with the monarchy (only abolished in July 1953), the Wafd party and the Muslim Brotherhood, sharpened their fear of a British 'coup' on the one hand and popular outrage on the other. They dreaded being painted as pro-British puppets betraying the national cause. They were determined not to let any British military units, however disguised as 'technicians', remain in the Canal Zone. On the British side, when deadlock was reached in the middle of May, a new wave of violence was feared. 'Serious trouble may now be imminent', warned the Joint Intelligence Committee.[71] Despite Churchill's reluctance to make any further concessions, a new round of talks was begun, with the outgoing British commander-in-chief in Egypt, General Sir Brian Robertson, negotiating soldier to soldier. With MEDO now dead (the final rejection came in July), disagreement was centred on how the base would be managed once the British withdrew, and how large a force of technicians would be required to maintain it. The discussions struggled on. In September, the Egyptians raised a further objection: the British technicians must be in civilian clothes. In London, the Cabinet decided first to break off, but then to press on. But, as the year came to an end, they had little to show. The Egyptians were willing to let the Canal base be used if an Arab state was attacked, but not Turkey or Iran, the Soviet Union's Middle East neighbours. They wanted a swift British withdrawal and a minimal presence of non-uniformed technicians. They would only consider a seven-year agreement.

The reaction in London was frustration and rage. From the Cairo embassy came a bitter reflection on the futility of continuing the search for agreement. Even if one were made, wrote Robin Hankey, then in charge at the embassy, it was highly doubtful that the Egyptians would honour it. 'If after making the new defence agreement we are held in the same utter contempt as we seem to have been since the Sudan Agreement, no favourable outcome in the Canal Zone can conceivably be hoped for'.[72] The agreement, anyway, was most unlikely to be renewed and 'may well be turned into a farce before its expiry'. In Hankey's grim view, 'the effect...on our position in the other Arab countries and on our whole position in the Mediterranean, in the Persian Gulf and in the Indian Ocean would be incalculable... it would far surpass the effect of Abadan or Palestine'.[73] Churchill's impatience now boiled over. He had carefully distanced himself from Eden's diplomacy and what he called 'your treaty'. He was much more receptive than Eden had been to the flouts and jibes of the 'Suez Group', the forty-one Conservative MPs led by Charles Waterhouse and Julian Amery who opposed evacuation, and may even have hinted at his private approval. As the Queen's first minister, he did not wish to preside over the liquidation of the Suez Canal base, that great symbol of empire. Like Hankey, he feared that, once a withdrawal began, it would become a rout. Then 'many in our own party will be able to say "I told you so", and the others will mock'. Churchill's solution was to make a clean break but exact a revenge: to redeploy British troops to bases elsewhere in the region, but send reinforcements to Khartoum. Egypt would thus forfeit its Sudanese prize. Once this was done, 'all the Conservative troubles here would be quenched...There is no alternative except a prolonged humiliating scuttle before all the world'.[74]

Eden rejected this view completely. To leave the Canal Zone without an agreement would be 'less satisfactory from the point of view of our continuing authority in the Middle East'.[75] This was his real concern. He had told Churchill earlier that a unilateral withdrawal posed considerable risks. 'It could be very damaging to our whole reputation and position if it looked like running away...It could destroy all hope of maintaining our position in Iraq and the Persian Gulf.'[76] Nor would it help matters to arouse the suspicions of Sudanese nationalists that London meant to renege on the promises made in the Sudan agreement. Like his officials in Cairo, Eden was inclined to lay much of the blame for Egyptian intransigence on American disloyalty and their tacit subversion of British prestige. 'The American position over Egypt becomes increasingly unhelpful', he minuted bitterly. 'The Americans will have no friends left if they go on in this way.'[77] What was becoming uncomfortably obvious was that without American backing there was little that could drive the Egyptians to sign. Lord Salisbury, Eden's stand-in during his long illness in 1953, had made the point bluntly. 'If we reach an agreement with Egypt', he told the Cabinet in July 1953, 'it will...be essential that the Americans underwrite such an agreement if there is to be any prospect of the Egyptians keeping it.'[78] Churchill now pressed Eisenhower to refuse the Egyptians economic aid until they agreed on a treaty, but the reply was guarded. How far, Eisenhower asked, was Britain willing to go to support American efforts to isolate 'the bloody Chinese aggressor' and oppose its admission into the United Nations?[79]

Had not the British been happy to trade with China? The implication was obvious. Perhaps it was this that occasioned Eden's anti-American outburst.

He had little choice, however, but to rehearse to his colleagues the urgency of reaching some kind of agreement: 'If we do not succeed, we are in a bad position.'[80] Failure would mean the more or less rapid erosion of Britain's Arab prestige. It would reduce Britain's claim on the support of Australia, New Zealand and South Africa. And, if the Suez base were simply abandoned, it would be almost impossible to persuade British opinion to accept other commitments in the Middle East. When the Chiefs of Staff weighed in with a warning that a withdrawal agreement was of the 'utmost importance', a subtle change could be seen coming over the British approach. However useful the Canal base might be in a general war (now thought less likely), it was more important to get out – to save money, men and morale. Indeed, in the spring and summer of 1954, geostrategic change suggested that the base was now of secondary value at best. Its exposure to air attack was greatly enhanced – or so it was argued – by the advent of the hydrogen bomb. Secondly, the strategic defence of the Middle East was conceived more and more in terms of the 'Northern Tier' states – Turkey, Iraq, Iran and Pakistan – backed up by the use of tactical nuclear weapons and local air bases: the drift of American thinking since mid-1953. What mattered most to the British was a dignified exit from the Canal Zone and (increasingly) reassurance that their use of the Canal would not be affected by a military withdrawal. When the Americans promised to delay any aid until Egypt signed up, and Nasser let it be known that an attack on Turkey would permit reactivation of the base, a light seemed to glint at the end of the tunnel. But clinching the deal seemed as elusive as ever. In Cairo, General Neguib was first removed as the leader of the Revolutionary Command Council and then restored. The transfer of power to civilian rule and a return to party politics were promised and rescinded within a matter of days.[81] It was only during April that Nasser's authority seemed firmly established. The British still fretted over how to present the concessions they were now willing to make (the use of civilian labour to service the base) and how to ensure that, with no military presence, the Egyptians could be held to their promise to maintain the base and respect free transit through the Canal. Churchill and Eden now agreed (Eden with some show of reluctance) to seek more explicit American help. At the

Washington conference in June (mainly taken up with discussion of Churchill's scheme for a summit conference with the Russians), Dulles and Eisenhower gave the vital assurance: Nasser would be told that all American aid would depend on his keeping the promises made in a treaty.[82] The British agreed to give way on the uniforms question. Within three weeks, the 'heads of agreement' had been signed in Cairo. The British would pull out completely over the course of twenty months (by June 1956), leaving civilian contractors to look after the base. They could use the base to help defend either Turkey or an Arab state from attack. But the treaty would last (as Nasser insisted) not twenty years but seven.

It is an intriguing question as to what persuaded Churchill to give his reluctant assent to the retreat he disliked. In his public defence he stressed the impact of the new H-bomb as making the Canal base redundant. But, if that were the reason, as a Tory critic remarked later, why was so much of the treaty concerned with its future use?[83] In the Cabinet discussion, there is more than a hint that the H-bomb was a rabbit pulled out of the hat: it gave Churchill the escape route that he (and the government) needed, dousing (for the moment) the smouldering backbench rebellion. Churchill may also have wanted to clear the decks for his real ambition – the summit with Stalin's successors. The more interesting question is what the agreement meant for Britain's Middle Eastern position – the main justification that Eden advanced. Leaving the base was meant to give Britain's regional *imperium* a new lease of life, not to signal a general retreat. It did not turn out like that.

In fact, the Canal base agreement embodied a transfer of power as important as any that was made in the retreat from empire after 1945, with the single exception of the withdrawal from India. This was veiled at the time from the makers of policy (although not from their critics). They averted their eyes from the three critical factors that governed the course and outcome of their diplomatic ordeal. The first was the change in the nature of Egyptian politics. Disillusioned with the Wafd and the king, the British were not unsympathetic to the military rulers who replaced them. Nasser, they thought, was a 'realist' and honest. The political turmoil of 1952–4 made it harder to see that the chaos and corruption of 'liberal' Egypt was making way for an authoritarian regime driven restlessly forward by populist nationalism and geopolitical ambition. The Canal base agreement was its ticket to power. The British liked to think that Nasser would be a new Ataturk, the Turkish strong man with whom they had come to amicable terms after 1922. Nasser, they thought, would follow the Ataturk model, and devote his political energy to internal reform. It was a drastic misjudgment. The second great shift may have been easier to see but harder to acknowledge. Again and again the men on the spot had complained that their efforts to make the Egyptians see reason had been frustrated by the nods and winks of the American ambassador, Jefferson Caffery. At a much higher level, the British were dimly aware that Washington was pursuing a different agenda, that they could not match its promise of aid, and that without American backing the treaty they sought would be hard to achieve and worse to enforce. The Canal base agreement was a silent reminder that British authority now needed the weight of American power, and was unlikely to flourish without its support. The third was the change from Egypt to Iraq as the strategic pivot of the British position. The growing importance of the 'Northern Tier' states (Turkey, Iraq, Iran and Pakistan) as the main barrier to a Soviet advance had helped to devalue the Canal base and ease the pangs of the British withdrawal. It made the British now eager to build up Iraq as the main Arab component of a new Middle Eastern alliance, and to attach as many Arab states as they could to what became known as the 'Baghdad Pact'[84] of which they themselves would also be members. This would be the new platform of their Middle Eastern position: an Arab 'bloc' of which the 'Hashemite' kingdoms of Iraq and Jordan and the Syrian Republic (domination of Syria was an old Hashemite aim) would be the core members. But, between the Hashemite kings and the Iraq 'strong man' Nuri as-Said on the one hand, and Nasser on the other, there was little love lost. Both claimed the leadership of the Arab world. Thus the curious sequel to the British agreement with Nasser was their strategic partnership with his bitterest enemies.

In earlier times the British might have laughed at Cairo's annoyance. But now they could not afford to do so. An intelligence briefing in late 1954 spelt out their dilemma. The political threat from the Soviet Union, declared the Joint Intelligence Committee, could be intensified at any time and no Arab state had the means to resist it any more than it could beat off a military assault. British help was needed, but 'xenophobia is endemic in the Middle East as a whole', while the end of the Raj 'had undermined confidence' that British power would be used to restrain or protect the Middle East countries'.[85] Britain's position was not getting easier; it was now more precarious. But its stake in the region seemed greater than ever: the Western interest in excluding Soviet influence; the British need to be seen as the West's regional guardian; and Britain's share of the oil industry, much of it located in northern Iraq. In April 1955, Eden, now at last prime minister, committed Britain to the Baghdad Pact and to building a new Arab alliance. Nasser's riposte was not long in coming. By the following September he had arranged to buy arms from the Soviet bloc and break the embargo that the West had imposed. The Soviet entrée had begun in earnest. Nasser's prestige and Egypt's military power were now certain to grow. Nasser proclaimed himself champion of the pan-Arab cause and denounced Britain's friends as betrayers and toadies. The Baghdad Pact was a 'relic of colonialism'. Whether Iraq, Britain's main Arab ally, and its tight oligarchic regime under Nuri as-Said, would survive the political storm seemed uncertain at best. 'If we lose Egypt', minuted the British official in charge of Middle East policy, 'we shall lose the rest of the Arab World.'[86] This was the setting in which the British began their 'descent to Suez'.

The stages passed in rapid succession. By October, the British had begun to fret over their oil supplies if Soviet influence and Egyptian hostility continued to grow. 'Our interests', said Eden (in what proved to be a prophetic phrase),

> *were greater than those of the United States because of our*
> *dependence on Middle East oil, and our experience in the*
> *area was greater than theirs. We should not . . . allow*
> *ourselves to be restricted overmuch by reluctance to act*
> *without full American concurrence and support. We should*
> *frame our own policy in the light of our interests in the*
> *area.*[87]

In December, Nasser, with Saudi support, raised an outcry in Jordan and blocked the kingdom's accession to the Baghdad Pact. The British were furious. In March 1956, while the British Foreign Secretary was actually visiting Cairo, the British commander of the Jordanian army, General John Glubb, was dismissed – a move widely (but wrongly) attributed to Nasser's machinations. In the same month, Plan Alpha, the Anglo-American effort to draw Nasser into peace negotiations with Israel and lance the boil of anti-Western feeling, broke down completely. Today, recorded Evelyn Shuckburgh, head of the Foreign Office's Middle East department on 8 March, 'we and the Americans really gave up hope of Nasser and began to look round for means of destroying him'.[88] For Eden, especially, the destruction of Nasser had become a priority. 'It's either him or us, don't forget that', he said.[89] But, as the British pondered how to isolate Nasser, events in the region spun out of control. When the United States blocked the funds for the Aswan High Dam, Nasser's grand project, his response was even more daring than the Soviet arms deal. On 26 July, with all British troops safely out of the Canal Zone, he nationalised the Suez Canal Company, an Anglo-French enterprise with a substantial British government holding. It was an astonishing move. It seemed to prove beyond doubt that his ultimate aim was to drive Britain out of the Arab world bag and baggage.

It was now that the weaknesses of the British position, painfully exposed in the Canal Zone diplomacy, made themselves felt. The Cabinet agreed straightaway that Nasser should be made to back down, if need be by force and by Britain alone. But the coercion of Egypt was not going to be easy. It would mean a major invasion with repercussions elsewhere on British commitments. It might mean the occupation of Egypt until a compliant government was formed – if indeed one could be found. It would deeply embarrass Britain's closest Arab allies and vindicate Nasserite claims that they were colonialist toadies. Above all, perhaps, although there were signs that Nasser's removal would be welcomed in Washington, American backing for a British invasion was out of the question. Paratroop diplomacy, in Washington's view, would be a crime and a blunder, and wreck Western influence at a critical time. The British hoped for international action, but the legal case against Nasser was transparently weak (the Suez Canal Company was after all an Egyptian company). Once Dulles made clear that he did not favour action against Nasser to extract the Canal dues (reversing the effect of nationalisation), Eden's position was desperate. No British leader had been more deeply committed to upholding Britain's Middle Eastern *imperium* as an 'empire by treaty'. Now that Nasser had revealed it as a house of cards, his authority as prime minister could hardly survive.

Although Eden could not or would not admit it, his position was so difficult as to be almost impossible. Awareness of his own part in handing back the Canal Zone, and thus freeing Nasser to act, may have made matters worse. How far he acknowledged that the scheme to invade Egypt in concert with France, drawn up and agreed on by the middle of August, was based on very fragile assumptions is unclear. But it may explain his reluctance to consult more widely among his colleagues and officials. Indeed, it seems clear that, insofar as they grasped his intentions, these aroused doubt and uncertainty. The Foreign Secretary (Selwyn Lloyd), the Minister of Defence (Walter Monckton), the Lord Privy Seal (R. A. Butler), the First Lord of the Admiralty (Lord Hailsham) and the Chief of Naval Staff (the redoubtable Lord Mountbatten) were all of this number. But neither doubts nor doubters had any effect.

Part of the reason was that few outside a very small circle knew enough of the detail of what Eden intended or had enough status to voice their dissent. To challenge Eden's authority in a period of crisis would have been exceptionally dangerous, especially for one of his Conservative colleagues. As Churchill's successor, Eden had stepped into his shoes as the great anti-appeaser, and champion of British world power. Moreover, a very strong group in the Cabinet endorsed his decision to erase Nasser's influence, and to do so by force. They could not have ignored the risks that this ran. But the real question they faced was what else could be done. Any compromise deal (of the kind Selwyn Lloyd hoped for) that left Nasser in power would not meet their purpose – to uphold what Eden called Britain's 'Middle Eastern position'. They may have accepted, like Eden himself, that the jumble of treaties, alliances, protectorates, colonies, bases, gunboats and garrisons that made up this undeclared empire could not stand the challenge that Nasser's defiance would pose; and that without this undeclared empire Britain's world power could not survive long. For behind the dire warnings about the Canal and Nasser's hand on 'our windpipe', this was the real issue.

On one point at least, Eden knew he was vulnerable. He needed a pretext to launch an invasion or risk being denounced as an imperialist aggressor. This would have been deeply embarrassing both abroad and at home, where the cross-party support he had enjoyed at the outset could not have survived. To escape this dilemma he embarked on what came to be seen as the most reckless gamble of all. On 13 October, as the decision to launch the invasion grew nearer, he was urged by the French to make a secret arrangement with Israel, which was also eager to weaken Nasser, and willing to strike.

The sequel is infamous. On 22 October, the British and French (who had their own quarrel with Nasser) made their secret pact with Israel to occupy the Canal Zone in concert with an Israeli invasion of Sinai. The prize for all three was the elimination of Nasser. On 29 October, the Israeli attack began. On 1 November, when Nasser rejected their demand to stop fighting, the Anglo-French intervention began. Egyptian airfields were bombed, and on 5 November British and French troops landed in Egypt to seize the Canal. But, in a matter of days, intense pressure from Washington and the threat of sterling's collapse without dollar support forced first a ceasefire and then the withdrawal of the Anglo-French forces, to be replaced by a 'peace-keeping' contingent under United Nations authority. Eden's health now collapsed and so did his premiership. The confrontation with Nasser, on which he was set, consigned him to oblivion and raised Nasser to power as the pan-Arab hero.[90] In less than two years, the Iraqi regime on which Eden's policy was centred had been destroyed in a coup. The British fell back on Southern Arabia and the Gulf. The British 'moment' in the Middle East, when they had been the authors and arbiters of its regional politics, was over.

'Anthony, are you out of your mind?' was how Eisenhower put it to Eden when he learnt of the British invasion. There was certainly much about Eden's conduct of policy that was reckless and irregular. He chose to ignore the widespread misgivings among both his military and his diplomatic advisers over the use of force against Nasser: whether it was justified legally and morally; whether it was practicable militarily; whether it could work politically to produce a replacement for Nasser; whether it would wreck Britain's standing in the Arab Middle East more surely than compromise, however unpalatable. Eden's secretive style, the exclusion of almost all of his expert advisers, his highly strung manner, the rough edge of his tongue, and his over-vehement language, unnerved many who saw him as to his balance and judgment. If it had been known more widely that he had concealed his intentions from Washington's eyes, let alone colluded with France in an Israeli invasion, opposition to his policy inside and outside the government would have been much greater. Eden was unlucky that his Suez expedition coincided with the popular uprising in Hungary. This raised the temperature of East–West relations and fuelled Washington's fury at the ill-timed embarrassment to Western diplomacy that Eden inflicted. But his misjudgment of Eisenhower was a catastrophic mistake, and so was the assumption – on Macmillan's advice soon retracted in panic – that sterling was strong enough to ride the political storm.

But should Eden's actions be seen as the great aberration in Britain's last phase of imperial power? Only if we subscribe to the historical myth of 'managed decline'. In this fanciful tale, (most) British leaders responded pragmatically to the symptoms of weakness: pulling back here; devolving power there; carefully cutting their coat to the available cloth; steering their bark towards the safety of Europe. Eden stands out as the reactionary relic, impervious to reason. But the tortuous approach march to the crisis at Suez (and not just the crisis itself) gives little comfort to this sanctimonious legend. The assumption that Nasser could and should be removed extended far beyond Eden. Eden himself had been the apostle of pragmatism in the wearying struggle for an Anglo-Egyptian agreement. At the Geneva conference in 1954, his restraining influence on the United States, and his support for a compromise peace, played a key role in bringing the first Indochina war to an end. His metamorphosis into a war-mongering imperialist less than eighteen months later seems hard to explain. Invoking his health, or his need to appear 'strong' for party political reasons, may have some virtue but misses the main point. For Eden had always been clear that settling the Anglo-Egyptian dispute would mark a new phase in Britain's Middle Eastern diplomacy, but not a retreat. With the Canal base disposed of, and Egyptian resentment subsiding, the British would be in a far better position to 'manage' the region's affairs. He was acutely aware of how vital it was to make good Britain's claim to be the regional 'guardian'. Without it, the influence he was able to wield (not least at Geneva) was bound to decline sharply, while American power would rise in proportion. He was convinced from the outset (so his actions suggest) that the British position, already under siege from American, Soviet and Arab nationalist pressure, could not survive Nasser's challenge, and certainly not once he took the Canal. Eden's tragedy was that most of the means to bring Nasser to heel had already dissolved – the hidden lesson of 1954. The informal 'empire-by–treaty' which he had hoped to construct was already dying or dead. It was the frantic effort to revive it that led to the desperate measures, and even more desperate failure, of October–November 1956.

No end of a lesson?

'Let us admit it fairly as a business people should, We have had no end of a lesson: it will do us no end of good.' This was Rudyard Kipling's harsh comment on the failings and blunders that the Boer War had exposed.[91] Its key phrase was adopted by Anthony Nutting (Eden's junior minister at the Foreign Office, who had resigned in protest at his policy) as the title of his book published ten years after the crisis.[92] For Kipling, the point of the lesson was to waken British opinion to its imperial duty. 'We have had an Imperial lesson. It may make us an Empire yet.' For the 'Suez generation', perhaps the lesson was different: bleaker for those who were still deeply attached to an imperial destiny; salutary for those who were anxious to escape from the futile pursuit of imperial power, and the deadweight of tradition it laid (so they thought) on British society.

Suez has been seen very widely as the real turning point in Britain's post-war attempt to remain a great power. The crushing humiliation of the premature ceasefire; the enforced withdrawal of British and French troops; the public excoriation at the United Nations; the open breach with the United States; and Eden's fall as prime minister (even if masked by ill-health): these were misfortunes that befell lesser powers, not one of the Big Three that had won the Second World War. Suez on this count appears as the end of illusion: a brutal exposure of geopolitical realities in a 'superpower' world. Suez marked the pricking of the Churchillian bubble: the belief that Britain could intervene decisively in world affairs, when and if it chose. Yet it is doubtful how far British leaders drew such an apocalyptic conclusion or abandoned their great power mentality. It has also been argued that Britain's defeat over Suez was the trigger for the rapid withdrawal from colonial responsibilities that set in after 1960. That too may be too simple a view. Official opinion had long since accepted that maintaining colonial rule against mass opposition, or the resistance of local political leaders, was counter-productive at best. Independence for Ghana, Malaya and Nigeria, and increasing self-government in most other colonies, were agreed as objectives well before Suez. The conversion of 'empire' into a self-governing 'Commonwealth' had been loudly proclaimed as the keystone of policy. And, although the disaster of Suez might have made British governments more nervous about the risks of military action, it did not deter them from keeping their existing commitments in Aden, South Arabia and the Persian Gulf as well as in Southeast Asia after 1960, although the military burden these imposed began to rise steeply. Nor did it discourage the confident view that British power was sufficient to delay self-rule in East Africa until 'safe' successor regimes had emerged on the scene.

It may be more plausible to see the domestic divisions over Suez as heralding a more sceptical view of the value of Empire to Britain. The prestige and appeal of 'imperial attitudes' had suffered severely: to mock or attack them had become somewhat safer. Suez in that sense might almost be thought of as the domestic equivalent to the loss of Singapore in 1942. After Singapore's fall, recalled the novelist J. G. Ballard, then a youthful internee in Shanghai, 'Chinese shopkeepers, French dentists and Sikh school-bus drivers made disparaging remarks about British power'.[93] After Suez, an alternative view of Britain's place in the world, no longer 'great', no longer imperial, could not be lightly dismissed. Indeed, some six months before the Suez invasion was launched, the BBC had screened a series of programmes titled 'We the British: Are We in Decline?', a question to which the first (on colonial wars) had replied with a disconcertingly definite yes.[94] Yet it took considerably longer before it seemed wise to assume that the imperial idea (in however diluted a form) no longer commanded wide public loyalty.

From our vantage point some fifty years later, the 'logic' of Suez was to show how constrained British power had become. Eden had struggled to maintain at least the appearance of parity with the United States. Britain's Middle East role had been crucial to this. The defeat over Suez had a dual implication. It revealed the grim truth that to incur serious disapproval in Washington would place any British government in considerable danger, while the collapse of British influence in the Middle East region simultaneously shrivelled the leverage that London could exert on its superpower partner. Henceforth, Britain's place in great power diplomacy would depend even more on a rhetorical 'leadership', on a confident voice influencing global opinion, and on the reinvention of empire as a beneficent legacy, a school of stable democracy. It may have been this that made Harold Macmillan, an actor to his fingertips, a more attractive successor to Eden than his main

Conservative rival, R. A. Butler. Only very gradually did British leaders begin to accept that the adventure of Suez had made them 'Public
Enemy Number One' in the eyes of much of the world.[95]

Secondly, Suez revealed the continued fragility of the sterling
economy. 'Whatever longer term effects Suez may prove to have on the
economy', the Governor of the Bank of England told Harold Macmillan soon after, 'it has certainly had the immediate effect of laying bare
to the public eye, both at home and abroad, some of the weaknesses
of which we have long been conscious.'[96] It was a strident reminder
that diplomatic isolation could disrupt economic and financial stability, and thus hopes of recovery. London had always depended on flows
of 'hot money' – short-term deposits by overseas lenders, placed there
for convenience or to exploit higher interest rates. They made London
more 'liquid', and were a profitable adjunct to the City's other activities. Before 1914, fears of conflict or crisis would usually drive 'hot
money' towards London, not away. By 1939, the strength of the dollar
meant that New York was a haven, so the prospect of Britain's involvement in war drained money westwards. But the danger this posed was
reduced by the scale of Britain's overseas assets and it took defeat in
the European war of 1939–40 to make it acute. In 1956, however,
no 'cushion' of assets was there to protect sterling from anxious or
speculative selling – and the Chancellor of the Exchequer from his
descent into panic. In fact, it seems likely that Macmillan exaggerated
the loss of sterling reserves, through muddle or deliberately.[97] But fear
of falling short of the minimum floating balance for the sterling area
was undoubtedly real.[98] As long as sterling's fixed value was the centrepiece of their policy, British governments were desperately vulnerable to
the threat of a 'run', whether imagined or real. Eden's successors knew
how quickly sterling's weakness could disable a policy that offended
the White House.

Thirdly, Suez exposed the divisions that would make themselves
felt if London resorted to unilateral action internationally – the alliance
with France cut little ice with the critics of Suez. It might have been
true that Eden's opponents at home were more vocal than numerous,
and that he enjoyed the support of a silent majority. The protracted
delay before he took action may have amplified doubts and multiplied
doubters. But the torrent of criticism showed that 'liberal internation-
alism' – faith in collective action and the 'rule of law' – enjoyed wide
public support, not least among the elite. Ignoring its precepts risked

the corrosion of a government's moral authority, and made it more vulnerable to external pressures. Division at home was mirrored in the Commonwealth. Among the Commonwealth countries, only Australia and New Zealand gave Eden full backing. The Liberal government in Canada, mindful of Washington's views, and traditionally mistrustful of Britain's Middle Eastern adventures, expressed deep reservations. Nehru's opposition was vehement.[99] It could hardly be doubted that, if they wanted the Commonwealth to reflect British influence, British leaders would have to take care not to upset its new member states, henceforth mainly Asian and African. Old-fashioned imperialism (of the Suez variety) would be self-defeating at best.

Fourthly, Suez suggested the limits of British military power. In 1882, they had landed from the Canal, scattering the Egyptians at Tel el-Kebir before entering Cairo to install a puppet regime. In 1956, they occupied (most of) the Canal Zone alongside the French. But there would be no knock-out blow and no Egyptian collapse.[100] The British faced a tougher regime, an urban environment and a hostile population. Nor could they count on their regional allies where the popular mood was one of Arab nationalist outrage: their bases in Libya (perfect for use against Egypt) could not be used.[101] Their military action was then brusquely called off on Washington's orders. Suez seemed to show that the age of colonial 'expeditions' had passed. It was one thing to engage in counter-insurgency (as in Malaya, Kenya or Cyprus) or to defend a frontier against foreign incursions (as the British were to do in Kuwait, Borneo and Oman). But invading a recalcitrant state to defend British interests was now beyond British strength. Of course, this was a symptom not just of military weakness but of geopolitical change. 1956 marked a shift in superpower competition. The dual crisis set off by the Soviet invasion of Hungary and the Anglo-French intervention in Egypt signalled a new phase of Cold War. It confirmed the effective partition of Europe between two grand 'protectors'. But it was also the moment at which Soviet–American rivalry began to extend much more widely in the ex- (or nearly ex-) colonial world. The British had their part in this new global struggle, but they had to observe the new rules of the game. It was more important than ever to show that the West was the nationalists' friend. Independent Afro-Asia must not turn to the East. Colonialism's aim should be to wind itself up, as a finishing school for Afro-Asia's new nation-states. The other ground-rule was just as important. Deploying British troops against mass political movements had always been risky, and was rarely favoured in London. By the late 1950s, to be trapped in a struggle against any popular movement with no end in sight and no local allies seemed the worst possible option. We will see in the next chapter how London reacted to the threat of this happening.

It might be deduced from these objective conditions that a British world-system could survive in some form, at least for a while. But it could have no real independence while the Cold War persisted (as Churchill had seen) and could face no serious opposition. Its internal solidarity (as a grouping of Commonwealth countries) was bound to be fragile. The burden on Britain, economic and military, was bound to be large. Yet British leaders, however shrewd and pragmatic, saw little choice but to press on. Why they did so, and what happened, is the theme of what follows.

14 RELUCTANT RETREAT, 1959–1968

The most curious aspect of the British reaction to Suez, once the immediate drama had passed, was the mood of public indifference. There was no grand debate about Britain's place in the world, no official inquiry into what had gone wrong. Neither main party showed any desire to rake over the details, perhaps because even those most against Eden's policy realised how deeply the crisis had divided British public opinion. Instead, all sides seemed anxious to treat it as an unfortunate accident, or as Eden's personal tragedy, as if the whole episode could be laid at his door. A desire to avoid any further embarrassment, or perhaps some awareness of what an inquiry might reveal, may explain this response. But what seems even more curious is that, after such a defeat, British leaders still showed an extraordinary faith that, with its sails duly trimmed, Britain must remain a world power. For, despite the conventional view that they hastened to scuttle their remaining commitments and fall back upon Europe, the reverse was the case. The dream of a British world-system, updated and modernised, haunted Harold Macmillan, prime minister 1957–63. A less robust version, more anaemic and ethereal, bewitched Harold Wilson, who led the Labour government of 1964–70. The rapidity with which what remained of the Empire was wound up politically, far from being planned, was a painful surprise. Official opinion had intended a 'managed' withdrawal, with a 'transfer of power' to carefully chosen 'moderates'. Constitutional change would proceed on a schedule, and local politicians would have to 'earn' each incremental advance by displaying their fitness to govern. Respect for the institutions with which a benevolent Britain had endowed them, and a desire to maintain some form of 'British connection', would be the test of this. But, when these plans began to unravel, British policy fell into confusion. Behind the facade of memoranda and minutes, official anxiety sometimes bordered on panic. By the time that a general withdrawal from Britain's eastern commitments was eventually ordered in January 1968 (to take effect three years later), the familiar conception of a British world policy, inherited from the late Victorians, had almost completely dissolved. Amid a blizzard of vacuous reports into what Britain's interests now were, a future in Europe (as yet undefined) seemed the only fixed point on which (almost) all could agree.

Why was it possible to go on believing in a British world-system (however constrained) in the later 1950s? In fact, as is often the case, the logic of their situation appeared quite different to contemporaries who had no means of predicting the scale and speed of geopolitical change. Far from enforcing a drastic rethink, that logic encouraged their hopes of renewal and prolonged a Churchillian view of Britain's 'manifest destiny' for nearly a decade. The main source of hope was the rapid resumption of friendly relations across the Atlantic. Washington's fury at Suez was quickly assuaged. The growth of superpower competition and Khrushchev's global ambitions made the British too useful an ally to fall out with for long. Their curious attachment to an 'independent' nuclear deterrent could be safely indulged: indeed, it quickly led London to scrap its own missile programme for an American substitute. From the British viewpoint, this was a huge reassurance that, if they avoided the sort of catastrophic misjudgment of which Eden was guilty, they would enjoy the support – diplomatic and material – which they now knew was essential. It reinforced their belief that what remained of their empire, if properly managed, was an invaluable asset as the Cold War expanded. The process of transition from an empire of rule to an empire of influence was as yet incomplete. In plenty of places, a decade might be needed before a suitable class of political leaders could be trained up for the work of representative government. Nor was it obvious that colonial authority was bound to break down in the foreseeable future. Where it was still a 'going concern', it was hard to imagine its sudden displacement or who might push it aside. Constitutional change was essential. But it was easy to think that London held the initiative and could settle the timing.

In holding these views, British leaders were in tune with the main stream of public opinion. Another Suez adventure would have led to an outcry. But belief that Britain held a special place in the world was still deeply embedded in popular attitudes. This was only partly a residue of the imperial past. It also sprang from the feeling that Britain's parliamentary, industrial and cultural achievements embodied a wealth of experience and conferred a moral authority that no other country could match. No one could doubt (this was the premise) that British institutions were best, and that British motives for fostering them were altruistic and disinterested. A hasty withdrawal – as had happened in Palestine – might be forced by necessity. But it should not be a 'policy' or a deliberate plan. And, in the late 1950s, one other force was at work. Britain was still in the grip of its 'post-war' mood and mentality. A heroic conception of the British war against Hitler pervaded both popular culture and middle-class attitudes. It was purveyed by film, a huge war literature and an array of children's comics, then at the height of their influence before the full advent of television.[1] Settling instead for a secondary role in the world was not easy to square with the service and sacrifice of Dunkirk, the Battle of Britain, the Blitz, Alamein or the D-Day invasion. It was an historical irony that patriotic support for some version of empire had been nourished by the war that had destroyed its foundations.

White hopes in Black Africa

One of the main justifications for retaining Britain's presence in the Middle East after 1945 had been that it would help to protect Sub-Saharan Africa from Soviet intrusion and subversion. Even Attlee, who had opposed staying on there in 1946–7, had imagined a neutralised Middle East as a 'glacis of desert and Arabs', barring the way to the valuable – and defensible – British sphere in Africa. Far beyond Attlee, and far beyond Whitehall, Africa's importance was now on the rise. With the loss of India, and all that it had meant for British power and prestige, Africa became the main theatre for constructive imperial energy.

Three kinds of assumptions helped to entrench what appears in retrospect a romantic delusion, cherished as much on the Left as on the Right in British politics. The first was that Sub-Saharan Africa was still a safe geopolitical niche, sheltered from the storms of the post-war world. Without a bridgehead in the Middle East, the Soviet Union lacked the will or the means to exert any influence in the African colonies, British, French, Portuguese or Belgian. Geographical access from the Soviet bloc was very restricted. Colonial Africa lay well behind the front-line in the emerging Cold War. There was little need for the British to take much account of external pressures on a continent still largely frozen in diplomatic time. Secondly, Africa's politics remained on the face of it extraordinarily placid. The political legacy of the inter-war years in the British dependencies had been 'indirect rule'. The effect was to localise political life and marginalise those who wanted states and nations on the Western model. Colonial Africa thus lagged far behind Asia. There was nothing to compare with the vast popular movements that had revolutionised politics in India, China, Indonesia and Vietnam before and during the Second World War. Hence it was widely assumed that Africans were still in their political innocence. Their ideas and habits could be formed and moulded by the adept use of tutelage. Unlike Asians ('Asiatics' remained common usage in the 1950s), with their tenacious traditions, complex religiosity and hyper-sensitive cultures (to which the intensity of 'Asiatic nationalism' was usually attributed), Africans seemed likely to embrace Western modernity with much less ambivalence. So the colonial mission would be much easier, as well as more satisfying, than it had been in Asia.

Thirdly, there was Africa's place in the world economy. In the depressed 1930s, African resources had attracted little interest (with the exception of gold). But the Second World War and its turbulent aftermath transformed the prospects of its export commodities. In the era of shortage and Britain's 'dollar famine', they assumed a vast new importance. Colonial producers, after all, could be paid in inconvertible 'soft' sterling and at prices prescribed by official 'marketing boards'. Strategic minerals like uranium, copper and tin; foodstuffs like cocoa and vegetable oils; and tobacco (the one indispensable luxury in the age of austerity): all were urgently needed to speed Britain's recovery, ease the pangs of denial, earn dollars or save them. Modernising the colonial economies became an official priority. Partitioned in haste, ruled on a shoestring, colonial Africa had come into its own. And with the richest parts – if not the largest share – of Sub-Saharan Africa, the British could expect to profit the most from this reversal of fortune.

The easy assumption that political change would proceed at worst on a leisurely timetable, allowing plenty of time for a controlled experiment in social and economic reform, did not last long. Within fifteen years of the end of the war, British power in Africa was in a state of collapse. Between 1960 and 1965, it vanished altogether. But, although the symptoms of weakness can be detected much earlier, it was surprisingly late before the loss of British authority had become a political fact and not a fear, a hope or a rumour. It is sometimes supposed that the British withdrawal was a serial affair: marked by the orderly transfer of power to successor regimes by due constitutional process. And so it was on the surface, with one crucial exception. The reality was that British plans for transition were swept away by the crises that afflicted much of the continent from early 1959 onwards, so that in the event the British departure was at best hasty and improvised where it did not break down altogether (as over Southern Rhodesia). Yet, until the crises set in, it had seemed quite realistic to treat colonial Africa as a cluster of regions, with different demands, different solutions and different political clocks. Hence the British applied different rules and imposed different timetables in the three main divisions of their African empire: in 'British West Africa', where there were no white settlers or major strategic interests; in the East African territories, where the settler interest was vocal (in Kenya), absent (in Uganda) or muted (in Tanganyika, a United Nations trust territory); and in South Central Africa, where a self-governing settler colony (Southern Rhodesia) was yoked in 1953 to the two 'Northern' protectorates, in one of which (Northern Rhodesia) the settler population was rapidly growing with the boom on the Copperbelt. Looming over British interests (and also their thinking) was the fourth great component of Britain's African *imperium*. The Union of South Africa was a fully self-governing dominion, and a sovereign state (unlike Southern Rhodesia). After 1948, it had an Afrikaner nationalist government. But, in the long view from London, it was a quarrelsome, irritating, but exceptionally valuable partner in the defence of what remained of British world power. The hope that its British connections (including the 40 per cent of whites who were 'English', i.e. English-speaking) would help liberalise its politics was not given up until after 1960.

By the mid-1950s (as we saw earlier), the British had accepted the need to stage a more or less rapid transfer of power in their main West African colonies, the Gold Coast (now Ghana) and Nigeria. Failure to press on in this direction, the Colonial Secretary told his Cabinet colleagues in September 1953, 'would bring to an end settled government by consent and forfeit the goodwill towards the United Kingdom and the desire to retain the British connection which are common to all parties in the Gold Coast'.[2] Two years later, as the timing of independence was gradually finalised, it was the crudeness and immaturity of the Gold Coast leadership that worried British observers. It was highly likely, concluded one, that Nkrumah would want to assert his new freedom in 'embarrassing' ways.[3] But the die had been cast. The British forced Nkrumah to decentralise power to the regions (he faced strong opposition in the old Ashanti protectorate) before independence was granted. He also agreed to remain in the sterling area – perhaps in the hope of getting funds for development. British personnel were retained in the army and civil service. But the main British interest was that the Gold Coast should be a more or less respectable ex-colony, with a regime that would hold its disparate parts together – a task for which Nkrumah seemed better suited than any alternative leader. In Nigeria, meanwhile, the main British concern was to keep the southern regions in step with the northern. Here, too, they saw little future in denying the political leaders thrown up by the widening of electoral politics after 1945. As in the Gold Coast, they found that this new form of politics was far harder to manage than they had originally thought. Its practitioners proved to be surprisingly adept at exploiting resentment against the colonial state. Indeed, in its new role as agrarian reformer, productivity raiser and controller of prices, colonial rule was a much bigger target than in the inter-war years. The difficulty lay not in constructing a Gold Coast-type bargain with southern political leaders, but in preventing a huge gulf opening up between the forms of politics conceded to them and those preferred by the Muslim aristocracy who commanded the North. It hardly required the Indian case to show where that led.

These differences had come to a head when the Northern leaders (where more than half of the colony's population lived) opposed the Southern demand for full self-government by 1956. They feared the 'democratic' appeal that the Southern politicians might make in their own backyard and Southern domination of a new independent federation. British ingenuity was devoted, not to repressing the demand for self-rule (which was seen as impossible), but to solving the

> dilemma with which we are faced: Either to give
> independence too soon and risk disintegration and a
> breakdown of administration; or to hang on too long, risk
> ill-feeling and disturbances, and eventually to leave
> bitterness behind, with little hope thereafter of our being
> able to influence Nigerian thinking in world affairs on lines
> we would wish.[4]

Among British officials there was sharp disagreement on the wisdom of imposing strict constitutional rules to protect ethnic and religious minorities if the result was to weaken the central government's ability to hold independent Nigeria together. But, when all the main Nigerian parties agreed at the Constitutional Conference in 1958 that they wanted independence by 1960, the British quickly caved in. 'To continue to govern a discontented and possibly rebellious Nigeria', remarked the Colonial Secretary, 'would...present wellnigh insoluble administrative problems...It might even need substantial military forces.'[5] The threat was enough. Independence was timetabled for October 1960.

It is clear that the British saw no major interest was threatened by conceding Ghana and Nigeria their full independence. Indeed, the reverse was the case. Their real concern was to avoid a political breakdown and a backlash that damaged their post-colonial influence and trade (around half of Nigeria's trade was with Britain). They saw as yet little reason to fear the growth of rival influence in an old British sphere. They persuaded the Nigerians to sign a defence agreement giving them over-fly and staging rights. 'Nigeria', the Cabinet was told authoritatively in February 1960, 'will be a relatively large and stable community within the Commonwealth, likely to exercise increasing influence in our favour in the rest of Africa.'[6] With a 'loyal' Nigeria, the remaining West African colonies could be cheerfully shrugged off. Tiny Gambia should be merged with a neighbouring (francophone) state, perhaps Senegal.[7] Sierra Leone, where there were bitter divisions between the 'Creoles' of the old coastal 'colony' and the peoples of the interior 'protectorate', was at first considered too fractious to be allowed full independence. It 'will be a small weak state unless it is tied up with its neighbours'.[8] But only independence was politically practical and the promise was given in 1959. By mid-1960, the British seemed to have made (or be in the process of making) a largely successful transition from colonial master to post-colonial ally, from imperial rule to post-imperial influence.

Britain's African crisis

Preserving East Africa for British interests and influence was a quite different story. East Africa had much more strategic significance. It flanked the Indian Ocean where the British expected to remain the regional great power even after the debacle of Suez. It provided a way round the so-called 'Middle East air barrier' once military flights over Egypt and other Arab states were no longer an option. It might act as a support base for military operations in the Persian Gulf and beyond. In Kenya, a vocal British settler community, whose survival was threatened by a resurgence of 'barbarism' (for this was how Mau Mau was presented to opinion at home), could not be abandoned. Nowhere in the region was there a prospective successor regime to which the colonial state could be safely entrusted. In Uganda, where the British were eager to build a strong central government to press on with the task of economic development, they were frustrated by the resistance of the kingdom of Buganda (the largest and strongest of the 'Bantu' kingdoms in Uganda) which had enjoyed considerable autonomy from the earliest days of the British protectorate. The *kabaka* (ruler) was 'exiled' to Britain in 1953 and the British set out to make the Uganda Legislative Council the main focus of political life, partly to mobilise non-Bugandan opinion, partly to encourage Bugandan commoners to defy their chiefly elite. In Tanganyika, the aim had been to use constitutional change to keep a careful balance between the minority groups of Europeans and Asians and the African majority, which was fragmented into a large number of tribes. Insofar as the British had a 'master-plan' for East Africa, it was to promote an East African federation. This was the way, thought official opinion, to hasten economic development and to manage the conflicts between African, Asian and settler interests, especially in Kenya. It was fear of being merged into a 'Greater East Africa' that might give the settlers a voice in Buganda's affairs that pushed the *kabaka* into open defiance and temporarily cost him his freedom.

The British might have been cautious about change in East Africa, but they could not stand still. Against the Mau Mau revolt in Kenya, they deployed a huge machine of repression. They raised a loyalist 'home guard' among the Kikuyu and turned a blind eye to the atrocities that followed.[9] They hanged scores of suspects, sometimes on evidence that was threadbare at best. They interned hundreds of thousands in 'rehabilitation camps' to sift out those deemed irreconcilably Mau Mau in sympathy. To pacify the rural unrest from which Mau Mau had sprung (Mau Mau was at heart a revolt of the Kikuyu landless against their aggrandising chiefly class), they devised the 'Swynnerton Plan' to replace communal land rights with individual title, creating a class of peasant proprietors – peaceable, conservative and (it was hoped) loyal. But it was also necessary to reform the political centre, to show 'loyal' Africans that loyalty paid and to push the white settlers (still the loudest voice in the colony's politics) towards greater cooperation with African leaders. The Europeans, said Evelyn Baring, the governor, 'with the low whisky prices and high altitude pressures are both irresponsible and hysterical'.[10] It was vital, London thought, to bring Africans into the government and 'close ranks against Mau Mau'.[11] At the end of 1957, a new constitution provided for fourteen African elected members in the Kenya legislature (giving parity with the European elected members) with the balance being held by twelve 'specially elected members' (representing Africans, Asians and Europeans) chosen by the elected members. But, under the vigorous leadership of Tom Mboya, the African members demanded nothing less than majority rule, and, when this was rejected, boycotted the legislature. The threat of 'extremism' and a new round of civil unrest shook London's nerve. When the leading settler politician, Michael Blundell (the son of a London solicitor), resigned from the government and announced the formation of a new multiracial party, the 'New Kenya Group', it seized the opportunity to announce a new constitutional conference to be held in London in January 1960. In Uganda, too, the effort to persuade the *ancien régime* in Buganda to support the gradual move towards an elective government for the whole of Uganda had reached an impasse by 1959. Only in Tanganyika, where both settlers and Asians were 'of little account',[12] did there seem some chance of achieving London's ideal solution: an elective government, 'moderate', 'progressive' and 'realistic' in outlook, and willing to keep the British connection. Across the whole of East Africa, however, the pace of political change was still meant to be cautious. At the 'Chequers meeting', to which the East African governors came in January 1959, it was agreed that even internal self-government for Tanganyika and Uganda was at least a decade away. Kenya was a much more difficult case: here no definite timetable could be laid down at all.[13]

There was no mistaking the anxious tone of official discussion. 'The long term future of the African continent', remarked Harold Macmillan, 'presented a sombre picture.'[14] The British had found the drive to 'modernise' their African colonies more and more burdensome. They had wanted to make their colonial states more effective, improve the productivity of African agriculture, bring in new experts and impose new methods. They encountered, not surprisingly, intense local suspicion and the deep-seated fear that the real meaning of change was a larger white presence and more white control. Neither words nor deeds could prevent the growth of an African 'nationalism' which promised to block the loss of African rights by expelling white power. More worrying still was the fact that colonial governments, theoretically armed to the teeth with emergency powers, were poorly equipped to deal with large-scale unrest: the prospect of more Mau Maus aroused deep apprehension. A further cause for concern had appeared on the horizon. By the late 1950s, the advance of Soviet influence could no longer be ruled out and London needed to reassure Washington that its policies would not turn African opinion away from the West.[15] But, before the British could settle their next step in East Africa, the whole of their African policy was galvanised by a crisis.

It broke over Nyasaland (modern Malawi), one of the three territories of the Central African Federation. The Federation had been the centrepiece of the Conservative government's African plans since its establishment in 1953. It was a new 'dominion' in the making, to be set one day beside Canada, Australia, New Zealand and South Africa. It carried their hopes of a racial partnership between whites and blacks in a dynamic economy.[16] But the Federation was also an unfinished structure, whose constitutional future had been left unresolved. Southern Rhodesia was a self-governing, settler-ruled colony, with a 'colour-blind' franchise but hardly any black voters. But Northern Rhodesia and Nyasaland were protectorates, administered largely by British officials. Among the white politicians in the Federation, it was taken for granted that white political leadership would continue for the indefinite future. They were particularly anxious that the whites in Northern Rhodesia, mostly clustered on the Copperbelt, should acquire the same political rights as those in Southern Rhodesia and control in effect the protectorate's government. No one felt this more strongly than Roy Welensky, federal prime minister from 1956, and a Northern Rhodesian white.[17] Indeed, if both Rhodesias were self-governing colonies, albeit still under white domination, the case for federal independence would become irresistible, and the whites would be able to force its concession. Meanwhile, London was torn between two conflicting demands: to honour their 'promise' (by nods and winks) to grant the Federation its independence in 1960; and to achieve enough self-rule in the two northern protectorates to be able to claim that independence enjoyed popular (including African) backing. By the late 1950s, reconciling these aims required something more than the wisdom of Solomon.

Nyasaland was the storm centre because, with only a handful of whites, it was clear that any advance towards electoral politics would give black politicians a much greater say in its government. It had been the scene of greatest resistance to the federal scheme in 1953, and hostility to federation as a veil for white rule remained deeply felt. In Dr Hastings Banda, it had a political leader who enjoyed unchallenged command over its main popular movement, the Nyasaland African Congress (NAC). When London promised to discuss constitutional change in 1959, Banda returned from the Gold Coast (where he had been working as a doctor) to lead the NAC campaign for an African majority in the protectorate's legislature and (by clear implication) against federation. But, in March 1959, the Nyasaland governor, Sir Robert Armitage, who foresaw the collapse of his government's authority unless the NAC were checked, and who knew that his masters in London were still deeply committed to federation, declared an emergency. Crucially, Armitage sought to strengthen his case with intelligence reports of a 'murder plot' by the leaders of the NAC against government officials. The NAC was proscribed and its leaders (including Banda) thrown into gaol. With reinforcements from Northern and Southern Rhodesia, the government began to round up the NAC activists. But, to London's dismay, in the operations that followed some fifty-one Africans were killed, nearly half in a single incident at Nkata Bay.[18]

The scale of the violence made an inquiry inevitable. Both London and the federal ministers in Salisbury (modern Harare) seem to have expected a favourable verdict. The NAC's 'murder plot', with its sinister echo of Mau Mau, would vindicate the measures that the government had taken. Anti-federation 'nationalism' would be heavily tainted with extremism and violence. With the NAC broken, African 'moderates' would take the political lead. Then they could claim that the 'real' African view was no longer so hostile to a federal future. But London and Salisbury were utterly wrong. When the Devlin Report was published in July 1959 (Devlin was a leading British high court judge), it dismissed the murder plot as an implausible fiction, denounced the Nyasaland government as a 'police state' employing illegal and unnecessary force, and (worst of all) endorsed the opinion that the vast majority of Nyasaland Africans were bitterly opposed to federation. After desperate efforts to discredit Devlin's conclusions,[19] Macmillan and his colleagues won the ensuing parliamentary debate. But their panic was real. With the almost simultaneous revelations of atrocious maltreatment at the Hola prison camp in Kenya, they feared a wave of revulsion from 'middle opinion' at home. Colonial brutality was a political albatross which the Labour opposition showed every sign of exploiting. In July 1959, a general election was close. And, though Macmillan was to score an electoral triumph in October, the scars of the summer remained. 'No more Nyasalands' became the unspoken motto of his African policy.

The logic of this was that, by hook or by crook, colonial governments must avoid confrontation and enlist the cooperation of African leaders. Emergency rule was a hostage to fortune that London had no wish to redeem. This did not mean that Macmillan was set on a rapid transfer of power or the swift imposition of African majority rule in the Federation and East Africa. Quite the reverse. His immediate step was to appoint Iain Macleod as the new Colonial Secretary in October 1959, perhaps chiefly because Macleod (who had no colonial experience at all) was free from any sentimental attachment to the colonial 'cause'. Macleod was liberal-minded, courageous, intellectually tough, ruthless, brusque and not infrequently disingenuous (whites in Central Africa used a different word).[20] There is a pervasive myth (which Macleod himself fostered) that he grasped from the outset the need to withdraw quickly and hand over all power to African leaders. The archival record lends this little support. What is certainly true is that he saw the urgency from the British point of view of engaging African politicians in a constitutional process that would head off 'extremism' – the category in which he included Jomo Kenyatta[21] – and avert the recourse to coercion. What he came to see by the end of his tenure (Macmillan removed him in October 1961) was that, once the commitment was made to majority rule as a goal, and an instalment of power was conceded to African leaders, control was soon lost over the pace and direction of political change. The coercion needed to reimpose imperial authority increased geometrically with each increment of self-rule. And so did the odium of using it.

The first sign of this came in Tanganyika. Here Macleod had proposed (in November 1959) a schedule for gradual advance from partial self-government to reach full independence in 1968.[22] 'Having yielded to [Nyerere's] demand to have the major share of responsibility we should be on much firmer ground in resisting further premature changes', he told his colleagues blithely.[23] It might even be necessary to put off independence beyond 1968. Eight months later, when the strength of Nyerere's support was becoming more obvious, he told his advisers that July 1962 would be a 'reasonable' date for Tanganyika's independence.[24] When Nyerere came to London in November 1960, the Colonial Secretary insisted that Tanganyika's advance would have to keep step with progress towards an East African federation – still the grand object of Britain's regional policy. Tanganyika 'would only reach independence when the Federation became independent as a whole'.[25] Three months later, he abandoned this condition completely. Now the goodwill of Nyerere and the Tanganyika African National Union (TANU) had become indispensable. 'His continuance in power is vital to us in East Africa, and if independence by the end of December 1961 is essential to maintain his position, I am sure we should agree.'[26] It was, and they did.

Much of Nyerere's appeal to the British came from the careful 'moderation' of his public pronouncements and the unchallenged authority that he seemed to exert over a unified movement: good omens, they thought, for holding the territory together and keeping the British connection. In Uganda, the local material was a great deal less promising. The British stuck to their aim of making a strong central state and bringing the kingdoms – especially Buganda – to heel. Direct elections to a Uganda legislature would signal that this was where power now lay and encourage 'national' politicians to rally a following.[27] The bait was the promise of internal self-government, the prize that would go to the leader who did best in the new electoral game. If the *kabaka* resisted, Macleod told his colleagues, he might have to be replaced.[28] The old Buganda elite, said the Colonial Office sternly, would have to like it or lump it: it was the future.[29] But Buganda did neither. Instead, its *lukiko* (or parliament) resolved to secede from the Uganda protectorate by the end of the year, and there were ominous signs that violence would follow. Meanwhile, the promised elections produced a clear winner: Benedict Kiwanuka and the Democratic party which appealed particularly to Catholic Christians and especially to commoners in Buganda itself. But Kiwanuka was anathema to the Buganda elite, and the temperature rose. Another Nyasaland was perhaps in the making. So London reversed course. A breakneck inquiry unveiled a new scheme. Buganda was now to have 'federal' status, and the Buganda government, not the voters, would select its representatives in the national parliament. Despite growing doubts over Uganda's future cohesion under such a regime, London accepted this formula.[30] To sweeten the pill, Kiwanuka was promised internal self-government in early 1962. But he was now an embarrassment and was duly denounced by an incoming governor as a threat to stability.[31] His main political rival, Milton Obote and his Uganda People's Congress, seized the chance that was offered. By allying with the *kabaka*, he pushed Kiwanuka aside. The prize of self-rule was now to be his. London was eager to make its escape. Its last precondition was more 'federal' autonomy for the smaller kingdoms along Bugandan lines before it conceded the final transfer of power in October 1962.

The pace had been frantic. Despite much verbal camouflage, this was not a planned march towards granting Uganda its nationhood, but a series of zigzags and u-turns, failures and fixes. From late 1960 onwards, almost its sole rationale was to avert local violence and find an African leader with a plausible claim to hold Uganda together. The rising chaos in the Congo, Uganda's immediate neighbour, made this all the more urgent. London did not fear confrontation with Ugandan 'nationalism', for it scarcely existed. What it dreaded was being sucked into a morass of anarchy or, still worse, civil war, caused by (if anything) its own state-building policies. There was at least the advantage that Uganda's affairs attracted little outside attention. It was quite the opposite with Kenya. Here Macleod and Macmillan could expect the closest possible scrutiny for the dispositions they made: from those who championed the cause of the settlers; and those who denounced the appeasement of 'darkness and death', the Kikuyu 'extremism' of which Jomo Kenyatta was still seen as leader. Macleod's own approach mixed opportunism with caution. Some months before taking office, he had met Michael Blundell and was deeply attracted to the 'non-racial' message of his New Kenya Group (of which Macleod's own younger brother, a farmer in Kenya, had become an adherent).[32] At the Lancaster House Conference in January 1960 (promised eight months earlier by Macleod's predecessor), his aim was not to propel Kenya quickly towards independence (on which no promise was given), but to build a coalition between Blundell's supporters and 'moderate' Africans drawn in the main from outside the dominant Luo-Kikuyu grouping.[33] Once again, the bait was a larger dose of self-government (and the scope that would give to attract clients and followers). To lend the African 'moderates' some much needed credibility, there was a firm declaration that the goal in Kenya was no longer race parity but majority rule. There were encouraging signs, reported Macleod in May 1960, that there would be no 'monolithic' African party.[34] When elections were held in early 1961, two African parties emerged: the Kenya African National Union (KANU), led by Mboya and Oginga Odinga with mainly Luo and Kikuyu support; and the Kenya African Democratic Union (KADU), largely supported by minority tribes. 'I am delighted to read your excellent news showing firming up of support for a KADU based government', wrote Macleod to the governor in April. 'If this comes off it will be wholly consistent with all our constitutional hopes at Lancaster House.'[35] 'I want to emphasize', he went on, 'how much I welcome ... a Government based primarily on KADU and New Kenya Party, and very good chance there seems to be of leaving Kenyatta behind.'

The 'great prize' in Kenya was an African government that was ready to work with European interests, and soothe the fear of the settlers that they would be robbed of their farms by land-hungry Africans. What London hoped also was that a 'moderate' governing party would suck supporters away from the KANU majority (KANU had won more of the elective seats for Africans than KADU). The KADU ministers, said Macleod, must be 'backed to the hilt' and internal self-government (and by implication independence) brought forward.[36] This prospect soon crumbled. The KADU leader Ngala was desperate for more power than the governor would give him. To win over KANU supporters, he joined in the call for Kenyatta's release. But his ministers performed poorly[37] and his tribal coalition seemed more likely than KANU to pull apart at the seams. There hung over all the threat of more violence (there were 80,000 ex-detainees in Kenya, reported *The Times*[38]) if KANU were kept out of power. The governor's efforts to foster a coalition broke down. The British released Kenyatta in August, and by the end of October he had become leader of KANU. But both London and the British officials in Kenya remained deeply suspicious of his methods and motives and convinced of his guilt as a prime mover in Mau Mau. To escape from the deadlock (and avoid an emergency), there were fanciful schemes for a federal Kenya. London clung to the dream of an East African federation to dilute Kenya's ethnic and racial divisions. A new constitutional conference was to be convened in the spring. Before it met, a new Colonial Secretary, Reginald Maudling, confronted his colleagues with some unpalatable truths.

The object of the conference, he told them bluntly, was to pave the way for independence, strewn as it was with many difficulties and dangers. 'It is not possible for us, even if we wished, to secure the continuance of European political power in Kenya... Arithmetic and African nationalism are against this. The best we can hope to achieve

> is the orderly transfer of power so a securely-based and
> African-dominated Government which is genuinely anxious
> to see Kenya develop as a modern state to avoid chaos, civil
> war and a relapse into tribalism... Nor is it likely that we
> shall see in Kenya a Government which is actively
> pro-Western in its foreign policy. The most we can expect is
> one which is not committed to either side in the East–West
> struggle and one which... does not offer too many
> opportunities for exploitation and penetration by the
> Communist powers.[39]

'Over everything broods the threat of Mau Mau, the influence of the ex-detainees in [KANU] and the persistence of personal violence.'[40] London still schemed to engineer a split within KANU to isolate Kenyatta and the 'men of violence and communist contacts'.[41] But the hope was forlorn. A new constitution promised universal suffrage and internal self-government but without producing agreement between the Kenya politicians or assuaging the fears of minority tribes and European settlers. But as Maudling had hinted, the initiative now lay with the leaders of KANU, and in fact with Kenyatta. It was Kenyatta's command over his quarrelsome colleagues that procured at long last in October 1963 a settlement that satisfied the minority tribes and lifted the threat of a communal war. With a huge sigh of relief, London completed the transfer of power before the end of the year.

Just as they found in Tanganyika and Uganda, the British discovered in Kenya that the offer of internal self-government was a runaway train that refused to stop at the stations they built or to pick up the passengers they meant it to carry. What made Kenya so stressful was the threat of extreme violence and the vulnerable position of the European settlers whose fate was bound to arouse close attention at home. From late 1961 onwards (and perhaps even earlier), the British were no longer in power in Kenya. They had become brokers. They lacked the will to repress a fresh insurrection and dreaded an outbreak before they withdrew. The highest card in their hand was Kenyatta's reluctance to risk civil war, and his hope of attaining an agreed independence and the constitutional legitimacy that was in London's gift. It proved just enough.

It was, however, in Central and Southern Africa that the British had most to lose. This was where the bulk of their economic interests lay. Here, in the Rhodesias and South Africa, there were together perhaps some 1.5 million people of British stock and sympathies, as well as a long connection with African elites who (in varying degrees) admired British institutions and values. The British government's diplomatic representative in South Africa was also a proconsul who supervised the so-called 'High Commission Territories' (today's Botswana, Lesotho and Swaziland) that London refused to hand over to the white-ruled Union. Of the Central African Federation's three territorial units, two remained for most purposes (including law and order) under Whitehall's control and that of its men on the spot. Despite some reservations about how the Afrikaner Nationalist government in Pretoria might behave in a world crisis, it was assumed that both South Africa and the new Federation would be Britain's regional allies, and provide the critical link (both air and sea) between Britain itself and its partners and interests in Southeast Asia and the South Pacific. Like Australia and New Zealand, they would go on being part of what had once been called the 'Southern British World'. But, between the late 1950s and the mid-1960s, this quasi-imperial connection vanished almost completely. The long British 'moment' in South-Central Africa ended. Its post-imperial 'relic' – the rebel white colony of (Southern) Rhodesia – was a galling reminder of how far and how fast Britain's power in the region had fallen.

The onset of crisis had been signalled (as Macmillan and his ministers were already aware) by the Nyasaland Emergency. It drove home the lesson that rule by coercion had gone up sharply in price – locally, internationally and in domestic politics as well. But the strife in Nyasaland had another dimension. It turned the future of the Federation into an urgent and highly controversial matter. London was already committed to 'review' the question of the Federation's independence (the long-standing demand of its white settler leaders) in

1960: it was this that provoked the Nyasaland protest. Now it had to decide how to conduct that review in light of the findings of the Devlin Report: that African hostility to the Federation was total, and could only be stemmed by rule based on force. To make matters worse, any concession that was made to the Nyasaland Africans, perhaps a louder voice in the protectorate's affairs, could not be withheld (or not very easily) from the African majority in Northern Rhodesia, where anti-Federation feeling was almost as strong. But, if doubt were cast on the adherence of Northern Rhodesia – with its mineral wealth and substantial white population of some 70,000 – the Federation was as good as dead.

It is sometimes suggested that, by late 1959, Macmillan and Macleod had decided to ditch federation as a useless encumbrance and push ahead as fast as they could with majority rule in the two northern protectorates. Two schools of thought converge on this judgment: those who believe that the Federation was betrayed by these two Machiavellis; and those who admire their 'realistic' appraisal that African nationalism was an unstoppable force. But though the archive reveals much double-talk and evasion, it stops well short of supporting this view. Nor is this surprising. Between 1959 and 1961, the British had good reasons not to want its demise: by 1962, perhaps, they had given up hope. Whatever its defects as a parliamentary democracy, the Federation was a bulwark of Western interests and influence with its own air force and army. 'We should surely lean towards [Welensky] as far as is possible without compromising the discharge of our responsibilities towards the black peoples', wrote one of the prime minister's closest aides with this fact in mind towards the end of 1958.[42] The African leaders were an unknown quantity, and, when Macleod met Hastings Banda in April 1960, his account was derisive. 'He is a very vain and ignorant man', he told Macmillan.[43] Nyasaland was impoverished, but entrusting the Copperbelt to an untried African government was a different matter entirely. Thirdly, if the Federation were demolished, the commercial and political links between its three units might break up completely, setting back the whole region's economic development and its hopes of stability. Fourthly, there was a practical question: it had not been easy to make the Federation: to pull it apart meant crossing a legal, constitutional and political minefield, with the prospect of ambush by the well-organised lobby of the Federation's British supporters. Last, and by no means least, if London threw the Federation over the side, what remained of its influence with the whites in South Africa would likely go with it. There is much to suggest that Macmillan himself was deeply mindful of this.

Yet, if the Federation was to continue, a decision on its future could not be delayed. Amongst white settler opinion (which looked enviously south at white South African 'freedom') there was a furious impatience to achieve the full independence already given or promised to the West African colonies. Most whites regarded the colonial administrations in the two northern protectorates as archaic survivals, undermining the influence of the federal government and encouraging African hopes of its eventual destruction. Without swift independence from London, it might be too late to check what they thought of as 'extreme' African nationalism sweeping down from the north. In Southern Rhodesia, where the whites already enjoyed almost complete independence, a powerful body disliked federation as a ball and chain holding them back from gaining full sovereignty. In April 1959, at the same time as they set up the Devlin enquiry, the Macmillan government extracted the grudging agreement of Sir Roy Welensky, the federal prime minister, to an 'advisory commission' to make recommendations on the Federation's future and (implicitly) on its prospects of independence. It was the only way, Macmillan insisted, to remove the issue from the party arena at home, and dampen the furore set off by the Central African emergencies.[44] 'We are your staunch friends', he told Welensky, 'and are with you on convincing the world that your Federation is a splendid conception with a great and honourable future.'[45] When he met the Federal ministers during his African tour in January–February 1960, Macmillan repeated the argument that the commission would allow the Federation's virtues to be properly seen; its dissolution, he said, would be a disaster.[46] But it was during his visit that Macmillan revealed that London intended to release Hastings Banda, regarded in Salisbury as the evil genius behind all African opposition.

Even in hindsight, decoding British intentions is far from straightforward despite the abundance of documentation that is now available. This is partly because there were sharp divisions in Whitehall, inside the Conservative party and within the Cabinet. The Federation's future became a political battleground that briefly threatened to divide the Conservatives as much as the question of India had done in the 1930s. Macmillan was anxious not to enrage the party's powerful right wing, where sympathy for a white-ruled federation was still deeply entrenched. He was also afraid of the Federation's becoming a party political issue, exposing him to Labour and Liberal attack. Despite his warm words to Welensky, he wanted to keep a distance between them, to keep up the pressure for political change, and uphold Britain's claim to stand for the progressive extension of African political rights. To keep all these balls in the air, Macmillan deployed a highly flexible language, at once evasive and cloying. However, Banda's release was a critical moment. Macleod as Colonial Secretary insisted that Banda must be set free in time to give evidence to the Monckton Advisory Commission. After furious arguments with the Nyasaland government and the Federal ministers, as well as within Whitehall, Macleod's will prevailed (he had threatened resignation). But his motive was not simply to speed Nyasaland on its way to a separate independence. Macleod was convinced that he could separate Banda from his extremist lieutenants. 'The hard core does NOT include Banda', he told Macmillan.[47] Banda, he thought, would accept the need to keep Nyasaland calm. He might even be willing to give up his opposition to federation.[48] To help to persuade him, Macleod proposed a reform of the Nyasaland constitution that would give the appearance of an African majority in its legislature – a cautious reform that even Welensky was prepared to approve.[49] For Northern Rhodesia, he favoured a similar tactic, although here he ran foul of the settler politicians who already enjoyed considerable power and were fiercely opposed to even the shadow of majority rule. Macleod continued to regard federation as the best solution – the view he had held in December 1959.[50] 'If we were left to ourselves', he wrote to Macmillan, 'we could make a success of Federation as I am sure it will be re-defined by Walter Monckton...But I am very much afraid that [Welensky's] United Federal Party think of Federation and of their own Party as one and the same thing, and will in the end be too stubborn for our efforts.'[51]

So far as London had a coherent aim, it was to try to manoeuvre towards a 'reformed' federation that would command the assent of 'moderate' whites and blacks. This was what the Monckton Commission was meant to promote. Its report acknowledged the 'almost pathological' dislike of the African majority towards the Federation.[52] But it also insisted that the multiracial partnership it was meant to embody was too important to fail. The solution lay in devolving most powers except external affairs, defence, and general economic policy to three territorial governments; conceding black majority rule to the northern protectorates; and instigating a drastic liberalisation of Southern Rhodesia's discriminatory laws. But it was heavy political going. The Federal Review Conference in December 1960, attended by most of the main Central African parties, black and white, quickly broke down. The following year, London forced through a new constitution for Northern Rhodesia designed with intricate care to yield the appearance of a black majority but deny it real power except in alliance with moderate whites, in effect the 'officials' nominated by the governor.[53] Meanwhile, in Southern Rhodesia, the mainly white electorate agreed to a change that would create fifteen African seats in a parliament of sixty-five, with the prospect of more as the number of Africans qualifying to vote (on an education and property franchise) grew larger.[54] (In return, London gave up its reserve powers over local legislation that applied to Africans only.) But these were deceptive successes. The reality was that, after mid-1961, the British lost almost all power to reshape Central Africa's politics.

There were several reasons for this. There was almost no chance of persuading most whites that a federation based on black majority rule in two of its three units was anything other than a reckless experiment that was certain to fail. Any doubts on this score were erased most of all by the violent chaos in the Congo, whose sudden independence in June 1960 was rapidly followed by an army mutiny, a massacre of whites and the collapse of central authority. The flood of white refugees that passed through federal territory was seen as a portent of the Rhodesias' fate if white power were surrendered. But it was equally true that few blacks were willing to accept a federal system in which whites retained any real power. The Federation was too deeply identified with white control of the land, with the privileges of white labour (in the heavily unionised Copperbelt), with restricted opportunities for literate blacks (in public services) and the undermining of traditional authority in the countryside. African leaders who took the federal shilling were dismissed as stooges. Instead, in Nyasaland and Northern Rhodesia, political movements that opposed federation exploited the end of emergency rule to mobilise mass followings of daunting size. The compromise constitution for Northern Rhodesia announced in June 1961 was denounced by UNIP, the United National Independence Party led by Kenneth Kaunda (the son of the first African missionary in Northern Rhodesia), and greeted by a wave of increasingly violent disturbances. This was the test of London's commitment to a revised federation. But the prospect of being drawn into a new Central African emergency had even less charm in August 1961 than two years before. London had its hands full with the defence of Kuwait (against the threat of an Iraqi invasion). It had little faith that its colonial authorities could police the Copperbelt townships and regain control of the countryside from the African leaders. In December 1961, the June constitution was scrapped; the following March saw a modified version with a clear black majority. By the end of the year, elections in Northern and Southern Rhodesia had produced black and white governments who demanded secession. It only remained to divide up the spoils. The Federation had lasted ten years.

'One's final impression is that the future of the Federation will depend . . . on an act of will', wrote one of Macmillan's closest aides during a visit to the Federation in October 1959. 'We must say – loudly, clearly, convincingly and repeatedly – that we intend it shall survive and succeed; and we must do something – something simple and striking – to show that we mean what we say.'[55] But, by late 1960, the price of 'something simple and striking' had risen too high. 'The Prime Minister and Colonial Secretary then said that they did not want an Algeria. That was the crux of the matter', noted Macmillan's private secretary in November 1960.[56] The diplomatic, military and political cost of an 'act of will' was now too great. London lacked the means to coerce white-ruled Southern Rhodesia or the African movements in the two protectorates. Military intervention had been discussed in June 1961 when London had feared that Welensky might take control of Northern Rhodesia by force. It was ruled out as impracticable.[57] The independence of Northern Rhodesia (as Zambia) and Nyasaland (as Malawi) may have been a release. But the Federation's collapse was still a disaster for Britain. It left behind the insoluble problem of Southern Rhodesia. By that time, of course, Macmillan's fond hopes of preserving British influence in the rest of Southern Africa – the aim of his visit to South Africa in January 1960, and of the appeal contained in his famous 'Wind of Change' speech to the South African Parliament – were also in ruins. In 1961, South Africa became a republic: in political terms an isolationist move. When it sought 'readmission' to the Commonwealth (as convention required), there was fierce opposition from its Asian and African members. Macmillan's desperate efforts to find a compromise formula won little support and the South Africans withdrew in May 1961. What remained of the tense and uneasy 'special relationship' between London and Pretoria quickly evaporated.[58]

Designs and defeats

In Africa, as in the Middle East, the British had found that in giving up their authority they had also surrendered their influence. As the continent was drawn into the global Cold War, the limits of British capacity – ideological and material – became more and more glaring. The presumption that a self-governing Africa would remain a huge sphere where British influence was preponderant had ceased to be credible by the end of 1963. By that time, London was hustling its remaining dependencies towards the threshold of sovereignty as fast as it could: in the Caribbean via the failed experiment of a West Indies Federation. It had scrambled out of Cyprus in 1960, clutching its 'sovereign base areas' after a long guerrilla struggle from which no exit seemed likely and which was tying down some 27,000 troops. The settlement that allowed the British to leave was framed not in Whitehall but between Greece and Turkey at Zurich, and sprang from their fear of a communal conflict between Greek and Turkish Cypriots.[59] The biggest commitments to which London was still tied lay on the maritime edge of the Arab Middle East (in the protectorates and trucial states of the Persian Gulf and in South Arabia and Aden) and in Southeast Asia. Here the British hoped to secure the future of successor states where they still had interests in oil, investment and trade. Strategically, they could be viewed as a remnant of the Anglo-Australian connection, long seen in London as a valuable adjunct to Britain's world status. But, by 1963, both were becoming much more costly and burdensome.

If by that date they were beginning to look like the redundant accessories of a now bankrupt enterprise, the change had been sudden. In the late 1950s it still seemed just possible that British world power would gain a new lease of life. The architect of this last, neo-imperial phase was Harold Macmillan. Macmillan had become prime minister in January 1957 in succession to Eden partly because he seemed more deeply imbued with the Churchillian ethos of British great power than his main rival, R. A. Butler, a doubter over Suez. Indeed, throughout his six-year premiership, he dominated British foreign policy as completely as Churchill, his model in this as in other respects. Macmillan set out to exude a breezy self-confidence and dispel the gloom and division that followed Eden's catastrophe. His immediate aim was to repair the damage Suez had done to Anglo-American relations and rebuild the personal friendships shattered by Eden's bitter quarrel with Dulles, the American Secretary of State, and his 'breach of faith' with Eisenhower. He was also keen to smooth over the angry reaction to Suez in parts of the Commonwealth, and embarked on a tour of Commonwealth capitals. As Chancellor of the Exchequer at the time of Suez, Macmillan had had a harsh education in the weakness of sterling. Well before the crisis broke, he had mused on the perils of a long confrontation. 'It is absolutely vital to humiliate Nasser... We must do it quickly or our M[iddle] East friends... will fall. We must do it quickly, or we shall ourselves be ruined.'[60] Macmillan was keen to restore sterling's status as an international reserve currency by making the pound freely convertible. To strengthen the export economy, he pressed on with the struggle to cut defence spending ('It is defence expenditure that has broken our backs', he had told Eden in March 1956),[61] and the demands it imposed on the wider economy, not least through conscription. He was anxious to reassert Britain's authority in Europe – the aim behind 'Plan G' whose formulation had coincided with the intense preoccupation with Suez in late 1956. 'The inner balance of Europe is essential to the balance of world power', he declared as an axiom in March 1953.[62] Finally, Macmillan turned a critical eye on the vast tail of dependencies that Britain still dragged in its wake. It is easy to exaggerate both the degree of Macmillan's detachment from the old 'colonial mission' and the coherence of his ideas about profit and loss on the colonial account. But there is little doubt that he saw (or soon began to see) that too little progress towards colonial self-rule would be a huge hostage to fortune as the scope of East–West competition grew wider. For that was the prism through which he now came to view the future of British world power.

From this list of intentions, we can infer the rudiments of a larger 'plan'. Macmillan was anxious to stabilise Britain's external position and thought he could do so. In the phase of geopolitical rivalry that he saw opening up, the search for influence in the 'uncommitted' world had become the vital arena. Here Britain enjoyed a major advantage if its Commonwealth and colonial 'assets' could be sensibly managed. Its role as the co-architect of the West's world policy would become more important. Its claim to special status within the Western alliance would be enhanced. The imperial 'legacy', artfully repackaged as the great work of nation-building, could be turned to account at home and abroad. The Conservatives' appeal as the party of 'greatness', badly damaged by Suez, could be resurrected and its disgruntled 'imperialists' reconciled. Meanwhile, economic expansion, low unemployment and the widening of 'affluence' would heal the scars of depression and reposition Conservatism in domestic politics. As the champion of the welfare state and of a 'property-owning democracy', its electoral position would be hard to assail. With its home base secure, a Conservative government could avoid the disasters to which (so it seemed) the French had succumbed. It could reject both imperial intransigence (of the kind that had trapped the French in Algeria) and a headlong retreat into an inward-looking Europe (the gross defect of the EEC project). It was a seductive vision and Macmillan (for all his mask of worldly-wise cynicism) was a man less of vision than of visions.

At first, things went well. Macmillan quickly restored good relations with Eisenhower with whom he maintained a close and frequent correspondence.[63] At the conference in Washington in October 1957, he scored two hugely gratifying successes. The Americans withdrew the restriction on the sharing of nuclear knowledge in force since the McMahon Act in 1946. Eisenhower agreed to a 'Declaration of Common Purpose' which proclaimed the principles of inter-dependence and partnership, the combining of resources and the sharing of tasks, as the bases of Anglo-American relations – a 'declaration of inter-dependence' as Macmillan described it to an admiring Cabinet.[64] Touring the Commonwealth was a definite signal that Britain's role as its 'leader' was taken seriously in London, and gave Macmillan the chance to exert his personal influence on its most prominent figures. The formal transfers of power in Ghana and Malaya in 1957 passed off smoothly, and the joint Anglo-American intervention in Lebanon and Jordan in 1958 softened the blow of the Iraq revolution which erased (literally) Britain's most powerful friends in the Arab world. The defence white paper of 1957, marking a shift to missile-based deterrence, promised large savings in manpower and money, lifting the burden on the civilian economy. The dash to convertibility at the end of 1958 heralded the transition from the post-war 'siege economy' towards Britain's (and London's) old place as a pivot of the global economy.

But, as Macmillan himself periodically sensed, the material base for his grand superstructure was dangerously fragile and liable to capsize. By the late 1950s, the British no longer possessed a world-system but only its shadow. Without India or the commercial empire once ruled from the City, without their old claim on the 'white dominions', or effective command of the 'imperial oasis' in the Arab Middle East, London peered out on an empire whose assets had been stripped. The desperate effort to retain a Middle East satrapy had died with a whimper: what was left was the rind. The brief post-war hope that Britain's African colonies would become a new India was already flickering out and would soon be extinguished. The burden of world power had thus been thrown back upon Britain itself: the costs of world influence would have to be met there. Everything rested on Britain's economic revival and on exploiting the leverage that the British enjoyed as a great power in Europe and as America's principal ally.

The strain was soon felt. Macmillan had intended that 'interdependence' would mean the coordination of policy between London and Washington, in which the British provided the know-how and the Americans supplied (most of) the military strength. The West's defence of its worldwide interests against the communist threat would be jointly managed by its two 'trustees'. It would revive the elements of the wartime alliance in which the commands were shared out but the resources were pooled.[65] By the late 1950s, however, the gross disparity in military power (the United States spent ten times as much on defence as the British), the growth of American overseas interests, and the Americans' confidence in their own expertise (through a huge expansion in their diplomatic and intelligence machinery) made this expectation unreal. The American reaction to the threatened advance of Soviet influence was not to defer to British advice. Even in Black Africa, where American involvement had been small and came late, there was a rapid response to the signs of political change: the visit by Vice-President Nixon in 1957 was followed by the quintupling of economic aid between 1958 and 1963.[66] The Americans were impatient with the crab-like progress towards majority rule in Britain's African colonies. They were extremely mistrustful of British attempts to solve the chaos in the Congo (with its worrying scope for Soviet intrusion) by a federal scheme that preserved much of Katanga's autonomy. In late 1962, they broke with the British to back Katanga's reconquest by a UN military force. And, on an old battleground of Anglo-American diplomacy, they simply imposed their will: in March 1961, after dogged resistance, Macmillan was forced to agree to send British troops to Laos as part of a joint intervention. He was saved from the furore at home when President Kennedy reversed the decision.[67] But he might have reflected on how different things had been only seven years earlier when Eden had coolly resisted intense American pressure to fight a war in Vietnam.

But it was 'summit diplomacy' that burst the bubble of Macmillan's pretensions. In another echo of Churchill, Macmillan attached enormous importance to a face-to-face meeting between the Soviet and Western leaders. He had rushed to Moscow in February 1959 in an effort to relieve the high tension over Berlin which Khrushchev had threatened to cut off from the West. He waged a furious campaign against American scepticism: 'We must have a summit', he told his Foreign Secretary, Selwyn Lloyd.[68] He was enraged when Eisenhower and Khrushchev decided that they would hold separate talks: the 'UK had better give up the struggle and accept . . . the position of a second-rate power', was his bitter reaction.[69] The 'summit', in fact, was a crucial part of Macmillan's grand scheme. Regular meetings of the American, Soviet, British and French leaders would choke off the trend towards bi-polar diplomacy, and entrench British (and French) influence at a global 'top table'. But the summit when it finally came in May 1960 was a diplomatic disaster. It was wrecked at the outset by the dramatic shooting down of an American spy-plane, the famous U-2, over Soviet airspace. Amid the furious row that erupted between Khrushchev and Eisenhower, Macmillan's entreaties for the talks to go on fell on deaf ears. The summit collapsed. It was the moment, recorded Macmillan's private secretary, when he 'suddenly realised that Britain counted for nothing'.[70]

It may have been also the moment when the weakness of Britain's position in Europe began to seem serious. The British were infuriated by De Gaulle's refusal to discuss the merger of the impending European Economic Community – 'the Six' – with a larger and looser 'Free Trade Area' of which Britain would be part. In January 1959, the EEC was duly inaugurated. Most British opinion, including within Macmillan's own party and among his Cabinet colleagues, regarded exclusion as a price worth paying to keep the trade with the Commonwealth, and continue the heavy reliance on Commonwealth foodstuffs. But, when Macmillan ruminated on the consequences of May 1960, it was obvious to him that continued exclusion would damage Britain's prospects of economic revival. Still more pressing was the fear that Britain would be squeezed between a European bloc of which France was the leader, and an American superpower veering erratically between special treatment for Britain and disregard of its interests. In July 1961, Macmillan wrung from his colleagues approval for the attempt to enter the EEC – provided Commonwealth interests were not sacrificed in the effort.[71] The British embarked upon the arduous struggle for terms that would safeguard key Commonwealth interests. After a year of exhausting diplomacy, De Gaulle intervened. At an Elysée press conference, Britain's entry was vetoed. Macmillan was shattered. 'All our policies at home and abroad are in ruins', was his private lament.[72]

To its supporters in Britain a European future had been the solution to British decline. The European market would be the tonic required by a flagging economy. European capital, managed from London, would restore the City's pre-eminence in global finance. Britain's place at the centre of European politics would ensure that the continent faced outwards not in, and took its full share in the West's global commitments. This was the key argument in Macmillan's so-called 'Grand Design' and in the case he put to the Cabinet for a British application.[73] London's key role in this European effort would make it the pivot of the Atlantic alliance and invest the 'special relationship' with a whole new importance. With the 'home base' thus strengthened, the British could use their Commonwealth links to greater advantage in the struggle to influence the 'uncommitted world'. The crushing defeat that Macmillan's plan suffered is usually attributed to Britain's 'missing the bus' of European unity in 1955–8. But this is much too anglocentric a view. It was really the consequence of a diplomatic revolution in Europe. The arrival in power of General De Gaulle in May 1958 transformed the balance of Anglo-French power. This was not because France had become stronger than Britain, though its economic growth was much faster. It was still deeply embroiled in the Algerian struggle that threatened De Gaulle's survival, political and physical. But De Gaulle was determined to restore France's greatness on a European platform, a project that was bound to be at Britain's expense. His rapprochement with West Germany was the vital foundation. De Gaulle achieved this in part by exploiting British mistakes: Macmillan's apparent reluctance to stand firm on Berlin in 1958–9; his courting of Khrushchev and zeal for summit diplomacy; the empty threats directed at Bonn when 'Plan G' was resisted (that the British would withdraw their forces in Germany); and his contemptuous dismissal of the 'half-crazy Adenauer'. From Bonn's point of view, Macmillan became an unreliable ally: De Gaulle was the stalwart against the Soviet peril. It was this grand realignment that enabled De Gaulle to resist British pressure for a free trade agreement, to dismiss their request for EEC membership and to face down the dismay of his other EEC partners.[74] The 'inner balance' of Europe had turned against Britain.

It may not be fanciful to see in this episode a futile last bid to revive a British world-system. Its failure demolished what remained of the post-war assumption that Britain could remain indefinitely as the 'third world power', head and shoulders above any other contender. By the time that Macmillan resigned as prime minister in October 1963, such vaunting ambition seemed simply absurd. The weakness of sterling had not gone away. By 1962, even a Conservative chancellor was longing to jettison the pound's 'reserve currency' status. Britain's 'knife-edge' economy, as Macmillan had called it, now seemed in need of a structural change. With the scrapping of 'Blue Streak' in 1960, the British abandoned the effort to make their own nuclear weapons in a partnership with Australia. Britain would depend on the United States after 1965, remarked the Australian deputy prime minister, 'Black Jack' McEwen, to the Naval emissary sent to bring the bad news. 'We must now face a future', he told his Cabinet colleagues, 'when the United Kingdom, because of its small size, must drop out of the race and rely on another power.'[75] The British now depended on America's willingness to indulge their claim to be an 'independent' nuclear power, first with 'Skybolt', and, when that was aborted in 1962, with the 'Polaris' system. But there could be little pretence that they enjoyed 'interdependence'. 'As much the weaker partner, dependent on overseas trade and with worldwide responsibilities, we find American support for our overseas policies virtually indispensable', remarked R. A. Butler, now Foreign Secretary, in September 1964, in the last weeks of a Conservative government that had ruled since 1951. 'They find our support for theirs useful and sometimes valuable.'[76]

The status barrier, 1964–1968

After his crushing defeat at the hands of De Gaulle, Macmillan's prestige was in tatters. His retirement through ill-health in October 1963 was a happy release. In the general election that followed a year later, the Conservative government under Macmillan's successor, Sir Alec Douglas-Home, the former Foreign Secretary, was ejected from power, though by the slimmest of margins. A new Labour government, with Harold Wilson as Prime Minister, came into office. Since much of Wilson's rhetoric, as the party's new leader in succession to Hugh Gaitskell, had dwelt on the need to modernise Britain and poured scorn on the illusion that British governments possessed an independent nuclear deterrent, it might have been expected that an aggressive new realism would infuse British policy. The rapid handover of power in the colonial territories that remained enjoyed all-party support. But there was no such consensus on whether Britain should give up its claim to world power, or whether 'modernisation' required the abandonment of 'obsolete' military burdens in the world east of Suez. In fact, it soon became clear that the new Labour Cabinet would not sound the retreat. The 'world role' would continue. What one Labour minister sardonically termed 'breaking through the status barrier... as difficult to break through as the sound barrier: it splits your ears and is terribly painful when it happens',[77] seemed too risky and painful. What happened instead was a morale-sapping struggle to square the costs of that status with the brutal demands of economic recovery. Under this pressure, what was still left of the 'imperial' world-view began to wither away. Even so, it required an intense economic and political crisis to smash it completely.

Indeed, from the moment it took office, the Labour government found itself in a vice of economic misfortune. The fundamental problem it faced was all too familiar: the relative slowness of the British economy to adapt to the competitive demands of world trade. Without the old cushion of a large invisible income, success now depended upon the export performance of the engineering, electrical and chemical industries. In turn they had to match the productivity gains (or lower labour costs) of their foreign competitors. But to complicate matters, the economic climate in Britain was shaped by two immensely powerful constraints. The first was the commitment of both major parties to maintain 'full employment' – broadly defined as under 500,000 out of work (around 300,000 was considered to represent those between jobs) – by avoiding restraints upon purchasing power that drove it any higher. The effect was to keep wages relatively high (or prevent them from falling) and strengthen organised labour. The second great constraint was to maintain the fixed value of sterling (at $2.80). If the balance of payments moved into deficit, foreign holders of sterling began to sell off, and sterling's price fell, and the London authorities were forced to take action. To attract holders back, they would raise the 'Bank rate' in London (making credit at home more expensive) and borrow abroad to shore up their reserves, thus incurring new debts. What made this more urgent was the need to reassure those overseas countries (including Kuwait and the colony of Hong Kong) whose foreign currency reserves were held in sterling and banked in London that their deposits were safe. The danger was that the (political) imperative to delay any slowdown in the domestic economy (and thus raise unemployment) would conflict with the (economic) imperative to keep sterling strong by early action on the Bank rate. Once sterling's convertibility was restored in 1958, this delicate balancing act became more and more critical.

It was precisely the effects of such a 'political' delay that Labour inherited in 1964. The result was a huge payments deficit and emergency action to bring it under control. But the problem persisted. There were large deficits, and the associated sterling crises in 1965, 1966, 1967 and 1968. The search for a way out of this economic labyrinth dominated government policy. No Labour leader could afford to ignore the reputation for economic mismanagement that had been fastened upon the post-war Labour government and its ill-fated precursor in 1929–31: a disaster for sterling would wreck him as well. Equally, no Labour government could afford to let unemployment creep up, or abandon the claim that it would stimulate 'growth', the new holy grail of economic endeavour. Between these two jaws of political fate, Harold Wilson and his colleagues squirmed and wriggled. One solution to their difficulties might have been to devalue the pound (or even let it 'float') and give up its role as a 'reserve currency' with its own 'sterling area'. But this was ruled out – until the last possible moment. Devaluation bore the taint of misconduct and failure. It might lead overseas holders of sterling to bail out completely. It might damage the prospects of the City's revival as a great centre of finance. If the sterling area fell apart, the effects on British trade might also be serious, since some of it benefited from doing business in sterling, and this was hardly the time to risk a downturn in exports. Nor did the experts agree on how beneficial devaluing sterling would be, or what new rate should be set.[78] On the other hand, Labour ministers were deeply reluctant to rein back their plans for more public investment. Between 1963–4 and 1966–7, their expenditure rose by one-sixth in real terms (over 16 per cent), and by nearly 13 per cent in 1966–7, so that in the course of four years there was a 6 per cent rise in the proportion of GDP taken by public expenditure.[79] A high tide of employment helped sweep them to victory in the 1966 general election; and, amid the warnings and woes of 1967, they eased the constraints on domestic consumption.[80] It was a volatile mixture.

Labour's leaders still yearned – amid these huge economic anxieties – to be seen as a power in the world, and to maintain Britain's 'traditional' place on the 'management committee' of global affairs, at the so-called 'top table'. There were several reasons for this. Disavowing Britain's claim to be a world power (even the failure to avow it with conviction) was not easily done. Despite the damage of Suez and De Gaulle's brutal '*Non*', many bastions of empire still spangled the map to produce the illusion of power. The press and public opinion could not be expected to discount them completely. The idea of the Commonwealth as a vehicle of post-imperial world influence had been fiercely promoted: it was hard to repudiate. It had helped to anaesthetise British public opinion against the pain of decline; the patient might howl if it were taken away. The wafer-thin mandate that the Labour party had gained in October 1964 was thought to reflect the electorate's doubt that it could bend Churchill's bow and keep Britain 'great'. To confirm this suspicion might be electorally fatal. Nor was the new Prime Minister, once established in office, reluctant to strut the world stage, and reap the prestige that a high-profile performance could bring. There were also practical reasons to keep up the appearance of world power. With so much unfinished colonial business from Hong Kong to the Falklands, where predatory neighbours harboured expansive ambitions, great-power prestige was a valuable asset, and perhaps even vital to a dignified exit. Renouncing the claim to world power might soften De Gaulle's opposition to Britain's entering the European Common Market – though taking his words at face value had rarely brought anyone luck – but would weaken the case for getting favourable terms. Above all, as most British leaders understood very well, much of their leverage in a superpower world derived from their claim to have close relations with Washington. But American favour depended in large part on the British ability to add influence and muscle to the global containment of communism by their long-standing connection with Australia and South Africa, and by their military presence in the Middle East and Southeast Asia.[81] It was by this curious route that a strange paradox had arisen. The subsidiary spheres of the old British system, the vulnerable outposts of their Indian sub-empire in the Persian Gulf and Malaya, had now become the chief theatres where British military power was deployed as 'vital' British interests. To gloss over this, and to give their ragbag of commitments a patina of logic, British leaders fell back on an elegant phrase. The aim of their policy, they began to insist, was to maintain Britain's 'world role'. Like all the best arguments, it was perfectly circular. Upholding the 'world role' was why Britain had to be there (anywhere). Unless it was there (anywhere), it could not play a 'world role'.

But even a 'world role' had a material cost. It was measured in defence spending and development aid, and more indirectly by the export of capital. Although British foreign investments were desperately modest compared with their total in 1913, and income from abroad at 1.4 per cent of GDP was less than one-sixth of the earlier figure,[82] they had begun to recover. Rebuilding Britain's overseas property empire, and enlarging its invisible income, were seen in the City as the only road back to its old global role and the rewards it had earned. Even before 1964, the export of capital had been closely controlled (to limit its impact on the balance of payments) and most had been steered towards sterling area economies – especially Australia. The shock of two crises in 1964 and 1965 brought a radical rethink. One way of squaring the circle of domestic employment and currency weakness was to redirect British savings into investment at home. Labour's 'National Plan' in September 1965 signalled this change of priorities.[83] It was followed nine months later by a 'voluntary programme' to restrain British investment in the main sterling recipients, Australia, New Zealand, South Africa and the Irish Republic. In 1965, remarked a later Treasury memorandum, the aim was to bring about 'a permanent shift of emphasis away from investment abroad in favour of investment at home'.[84] Scrapping the time-honoured doctrine that the export of capital was a key function of the British economy and one of the pillars of British prosperity showed how far official thinking had moved in barely six years since the Radcliffe Report of 1959 towards something close to a siege mentality. But the second decision in 1965 had even more dramatic (if unintended) consequences.

This was the insistence that defence spending should be fixed at a ceiling of £2,000 million a year, to reduce its very high share

(7 per cent) of GDP and to save on foreign exchange. The logic of this, senior ministers agreed in June 1965, was that the cost of Britain's world role east of Suez must be sharply reduced. A small military presence should be kept in the Middle East and in Northern Australia, while retaining island bases in the Indian Ocean would allow the projection of force if the need should arise. But, once the 'confrontation' with Indonesia (which had opposed the creation of the Malaysian Federation) was over, the British should leave Southeast Asia, including Singapore.[85] It was an attractive solution. It would avoid a risky commitment on the mainland of Asia in a region where 'neutralisation' seemed the most to be hoped for. But it could still be asserted that Britain was playing its part in global affairs. Under fierce American (and Australian) pressure, this plan was shelved, and the promise was made (in the defence white paper of 1966) to remain in Malaysia and Singapore for the foreseeable future.[86] It did not last long. A huge sterling crisis in June 1966 forced another sharp turn. Now it was said that the number of troops in Southeast Asia would be reduced ('confrontation' had ended). The British would stay but no further commitments on the same scale could be made.[87] To one critical minister, the discussion of policy was 'a futile attempt to remain Great Britain, one of the three world powers, while slicing away at defence'.[88] In any event, this new formulation was quickly abandoned. A backbench revolt changed ministers' minds. With a pay freeze at home and rising unemployment, the cost of defence became an irresistible target. In April 1967, the Cabinet agreed to withdraw in two stages from Singapore and Malaysia, reducing the British presence by half by 1970–1, and leaving completely by 1975–6. Britain would retain the means to return if need be, but from a base in Australia, if the Australians agreed.[89] This time there was little reaction from Washington. A more urgent concern was withdrawing from Aden which the British had made part of a 'South Arabian Federation'. By mid-1967, the federal government's authority had collapsed. Faced with a street war against rival nationalist groups to keep control of a base which they had already decided to leave, the British threw in the towel and abandoned the colony in November 1967.

Three years of argument had brought an uneasy compromise. A term had been set to Britain's military presence in Singapore and Malaysia, still nearly a decade away, with a partial withdrawal by 1971. Meanwhile, the British would keep up their guard in the Persian Gulf, where a string of Gulf statelets from Kuwait to Oman still needed protection. The 'world role' lived on, but its lifetime was short. For, in November 1967, the weakness of sterling, aggravated by the effects of the Arab-Israeli war, reached a new crisis. With a huge payments deficit, and large debts already, propping up sterling by further borrowing abroad was no longer possible. Faced with disaster, the tenacious resistance of Harold Wilson and his Chancellor of the Exchequer, James Callaghan, to devaluing sterling was broken at last. But the relaunch of sterling at a new lower parity ($2.40) required a package of measures to restore foreign confidence in Britain's finances – and avert a further sharp fall. With social expenditure taking the brunt of the cuts in government spending, a furious argument broke out in the Cabinet over the timing of British withdrawal from its commitments east of Suez. The outcome was a triumph for the new Chancellor of the Exchequer, Roy Jenkins, on whose success in retrenchment the survival of sterling (and of the government) now seemed to hang. Against fierce opposition, he imposed a new timetable. The British would withdraw completely by 1971. Not only that, they would also abandon their Persian Gulf role, solemnly reaffirmed to the anxious Gulf rulers less than two months before. This dramatic farewell to Britain's world role, and its imperial tradition in Asia, was announced in Parliament on 16 January 1968.

It seems likely, in retrospect, that, while Harold Wilson and his senior ministers had acknowledged in mid-1965 the need to scale down the forces stationed east of Suez, and withdraw altogether from the mainland of Asia, they intended to do so at a relatively leisurely pace. By offering to contribute (modestly) to regional defence in Southeast Asia, they would appease their American ally, and could continue to claim that Britain's world role was safe in their hands. But everything went wrong. Facing a huge new war in Vietnam, the Americans dismissed this scheme with contempt. When London reversed course, its promise to stand firm collided with a new crisis in the fortunes of sterling and the backbench demand that defence share the pain of expenditure cuts. Yet the brutal finality of the January statement was not simply the product of the need to cut costs: bringing forward the date promised marginal gains; leaving the Gulf, virtually none at all.[90] Much more important was Roy Jenkins' determination to force through a change in Britain's external direction away from the relics of empire and towards a future in Europe. It was also essential to buy off those (on the Left) most fiercely opposed to the austerity programme for sterling's recovery that he meant to impose. But, if the result was the unexpectedly sudden denial that Britain could hold its old place in the world, the public reaction was surprisingly muted. Pricking the bubble of Conservative outrage in the Commons debate, Wilson quoted the views of the Opposition defence spokesman uttered twelve months before. 'The "world role" East of Suez', Enoch Powell had remarked in the *Spectator* magazine, 'was a piece of humbug.'[91] In fact, Conservative (and conservative) opinion had already begun to edge its way back from the idea of the Commonwealth as a key British interest and a pivot of policy.

The main reason for this was what became known as the 'Rhodesian problem'. As we have seen, dissolving the Central African Federation in 1963 had left a difficult legacy. Two of its territories (Zambia and Malawi) were given independence in 1964 as black majority states. But, in Southern Rhodesia (which adopted the shorter name 'Rhodesia'), a white minority still ruled under the 1961 constitution that London had approved. The constitution was 'colour-blind': unlike in South African, blacks could vote but only if they met stringent qualifications in education and property. Hence the prospect of a black majority among voters, let alone in the parliament, lay in the indefinite (but far-distant) future. Nevertheless, the colony's white leaders insisted that, since they had been almost completely self-governing since the 1920s, their claim to independence was as strong as (they *meant* much stronger than) that of the African colonies where self-rule had arrived in a rush with minimal warning. They were also convinced that at the break-up of the federation they had been promised independence by R. A. Butler, then the Secretary of State for Central Africa, in a verbal undertaking 'in a spirit of trust'. (No documentary evidence has turned up, but the utter conviction of Winston Field, then Rhodesian premier, and Ian Smith, his deputy, that the promise had been made was an awkward political fact.[92]) London's main difficulty lay in the international political climate of 1964–5. With the rapid conversion of almost all of Black Africa into sovereign states, and the near universal hostility towards *apartheid* South Africa, British complicity in creating a second independent 'settler' regime was almost unthinkable. Yet the British had no hope of persuading the whites in Rhodesia that an early take-over by African nationalist leaders would not quickly lead to the murderous chaos that they saw in the Congo. This was the dilemma that Labour inherited from the Conservative government, which had carefully prevaricated. What made it worse was that, short of withholding 'legitimate' independence, Harold Wilson and his colleagues had very few means of applying pressure on the whites who controlled internal security and had their own (small) army.

In the year of arduous negotiation that preceded 'UDI' – the Rhodesians' 'unilateral declaration of independence' on 11 November 1965 – both sides tried to wear each other down. The key issue was how far the 1961 constitution should be revised to make it acceptable to the Rhodesian African nationalists. The British idea was that a new royal commission (like the Monckton Commission) should decide what was acceptable and make recommendations. But, to Ian Smith and his Cabinet (Smith was now prime minister), to hand over their constitutional right to self-government (though not independence) to a British-appointed commission would be to sign their political death-warrant. The commission might dissolve their constitutional authority as Monckton had dissolved that of the federal government. In the confusion that followed, anything might happen.[93] But, if Smith could not budge London from its demand for a commission, Wilson for his part made a crucial admission – that Britain would not use military force to impose a solution. It may have been made to convince the African leaders to accept terms they disliked. It may have reflected a common assumption that the British armed forces would have refused to fire on white 'kith and kin'. Or it may have been the realistic appraisal that taking over Rhodesia by force would have been to incur a large open-ended commitment, military and political.[94] Since this was precisely the moment when reducing its post-imperial hostages to fortune had become London's main external priority, to make such a dangerous exception would have been very odd.

The result, nevertheless, was a diplomatic fiasco. When UDI was declared, London replied with a broadside of bombast. It soon became clear that its threats and sanctions had very little effect, largely because the economic coercion of Rhodesia required the unlikely cooperation of its white neighbour, South Africa. What UDI did reveal was the embarrassing impotence of the Labour government in London, whose 'world-role' fell short of dealing with 'rebels' in its constitutional backyard. Worse still, it exposed it to a torrent of criticism – turning into abuse – from Britain's Commonwealth 'partners'. At the Commonwealth prime ministers conferences – once the arena where British world-leadership was reassuringly paraded – Harold Wilson and his colleagues now found themselves in the dock, charged with betrayal of Commonwealth ideals, harangued on the need to show courage and take action. After two ill-fated attempts at a compromise settlement in 1966 and 1968 (the 'Tiger' and 'Fearless' talks at sea off Gibraltar), Wilson abandoned hope of a deal.[95] But the effect was not simply to embarrass his government and expose its shortcomings. The spectacle of Commonwealth countries, whose political record fell far short of ideal, pressing for military action and denouncing British 'complicity' in a racist regime, transformed British public attitudes to the Commonwealth idea, and nowhere more than in the Conservative party, where grass-roots sympathy for the Rhodesian whites was especially strong.[96] Reinforced by the declining importance of Commonwealth trade and investment, and the association of the Commonwealth with black immigration into Britain (1968 was the year of Enoch Powell's speech on the 'rivers of blood'), it helped to erase with extraordinary speed the long-standing connection between patriotic feeling in Britain and loyalty to the Commonwealth as the offspring of empire.

The dramatic announcement on withdrawal from east of Suez thus coincided with a wider shift in the thinking of both political 'insiders' and public opinion at large. But, without the 'world role', the cherished illusion of close Anglo-American partnership and the claim to Commonwealth leadership, almost nothing was left of the Churchillian statecraft to which all post-war governments had tried to adhere, let alone of the late-Victorian *Weltpolitik* on which it was based. The policy-makers cast around in confusion. Official committees debated which British interests deserved recognition. An inane map was devised in the Foreign Office purporting to show on an imaginary scale which countries were important to Britain. Predictably, the United States and Europe were huge. Revealingly, the Falkland Islands, scene of Britain's last and most dangerous colonial war (in 1982), were omitted completely.[97] Salisbury (who knew a thing or two about cartographic delusions) would have put it in the waste-paper basket. In this maelstrom of uncertainties, official opinion fell back on two axioms. The first was that economic recovery was the root of all policy; the second that the only future for Britain lay in joining the European Community, at whatever the cost. The Labour government had made a second abortive application in 1967, dismissed with a shrug from De Gaulle. It fell to their Conservative successors, once De Gaulle had left power (and also the world), to win this ultimate prize. In the Heath government's white paper proclaiming Britain's new course, few tears were shed over all that was left of the old British connections. The Commonwealth, it said, did not 'offer us, or indeed wish to offer us alternative and comparable opportunities to membership of the European Community. The member countries of the Commonwealth are widely scattered in different regions of the world and differ widely in their political ideas and economic development. With the attainment of independence their political relations with the United Kingdom have greatly changed and are still changing.'[98] As a comprehensive repudiation of the old British 'system', that would be hard to improve on. With the white paper's publication in 1971, the imperial idea finally ceased to be a political force. It sailed away to the Coast of Nostalgia.

CONCLUSION

The argument of this book has been that the fate of the world-system in which the British Empire was embedded was largely determined by geopolitical forces over which the British themselves had little control. The distribution of wealth and power within and between the two ends of Eurasia, in East Asia and Europe, created the openings and then closed off the freedoms that the British had exploited with striking success since the early nineteenth century. Once the politics and economics of both these great regions had turned against them, and wrecked the fine balance of naval and military power on which the defence of their interests depended, they had little chance of surviving at the head of an independent world-system. Perhaps they might have hoped to ride out the storm. But the strategic catastrophe of 1938 to 1942, and its devastating impact on the central elements of their system, were together so crushing that recovery (after 1945) was merely short-lived remission.

Of course, the British were not just victims of blind fate, benign or malign. They had taken a hand in prompting the geopolitical changes from which they had gained, although (as at Trafalgar) perhaps more to ward off an imminent danger than to create a main chance. The peculiar trajectory of the British economy before 1800, and the accompanying emergence of a 'polite and commercial society', were essential foundations. By then, British commerce was geared to the long-distance traffic that had roused Adam Smith's ire, and the long credit advances required by the cycle of commodity trades, including the slave trade. The infrastructure to exercise maritime power in almost every part of the world was already in place, including the systematic compilation of navigational data. The British consumer was already addicted to a range of exotic new tastes, both cultural and physical, and easily tempted with more. Economic and religious transformation had created a restless, competitive, pluralistic and (amongst a critical number) guilt-ridden society, harbouring rival visions of empire and of Britain's true place in a world needing redemption. It had the means and the motive to widen the bridgeheads already established in the world beyond Europe, and to send in new 'landings' for commerce, conversion and colonisation. All that was needed was the (vague) promise of gain in new regions opened up to commercial or spiritual enterprise. In the 1820s and 1830s, a torrent of travellers' 'narratives', seductive prospectuses, missionary reports and settler propaganda proclaimed a world that was ready for a British invasion.

Nineteenth-century British leaders shared much of the intoxication that these visions had stirred among the key interest groups behind Britain's global expansion. Yet they were generally cautious about the government's part. They commanded a strong and well-funded state apparatus, but were wary that public opinion might turn against an unlucky venture abroad. They subscribed to 'Gladstonian' finance which implied a steady reduction of the government's share of the national income, and a negative view of costly long-term commitments. Hence they preferred to avoid direct confrontation with large or resilient states in Europe or Asia and intuitively grasped the signal advantage of an 'intermediate' situation, neither fully 'continental', nor entirely peripheral to the rest of Eurasia. They saw – or sensed – that this geostrategic prudentialism was vital to the stability of Britain's global connections, because these depended so much upon cooperation and partnership, not coercion and conquest. The settlement colonies, effectively self-governing from the 1830s and 1840s, could not be *conscripted* into imperial wars, or made to pay for their strategic defence – it was hard enough to extract any real contribution to wars fought on their soil and in defence of their (settler) interests. India, which could, was viewed contradictorily as an economic and military asset, and as a strategic and political risk. Its loyalty and quiescence could never be taken for granted after 1857. The dense web of commercial connections was best left to itself under the regime of free trade, thought most British leaders. They knew that commercial success, and the commanding role of the City, depended on 'confidence' – not least foreign confidence in British public finances. They were ready to throw in their diplomatic resources, and sometimes the navy, to persuade 'recalcitrant' states to open their markets, although rarely in cases where they would meet strong resistance or risk a dispute with another great power. They pressed British officials in India and elsewhere to enlarge the consumption of British manufactures by heavy spending on railways (and heavy borrowing from London). But they were usually reluctant to champion particular companies (unless they could serve a larger objective) and suspected the motives of British merchants and capitalists as much as they did those of settlers, planters and missionaries (a missionary, quipped Lord Salisbury, was 'a religious Englishman with a mission to offend the religious feelings of the natives').[1] So British 'policy' was often in a state of unease between the need to defend 'British interests' abroad and official suspicion that the effort to do so would bring loss and embarrassment.

In the long nineteenth century, this hand-to-mouth practice had favoured the growth of a decentralised system. It was glued together by a mixture of commercial self-interest, ethnic solidarity, ideological sympathy and the common dependence of Indian Civilians and settlers on London's reserve bank of military force. It permitted the florescence of colonial societies largely left free to manage their local affairs: even the Indian Civilians enjoyed much of this freedom. Despite the feeling of strain in the last decades of the century (the subject of professional exaggeration by soldiers, sailors and diplomats), Britain's long lead in extra-European expansion allowed it to ride out the squalls of imperialist rivalry up to 1914. The prospects of a continental coalition against them (the great British fear) receded to vanishing point. The First World War marked a critical shift, though its full meaning was veiled. The huge war contributions of the dominions and India affected their 'British connections' after 1918: encouraging dominion 'isolationism' and Indian resentment at an imposed 'war economy' so poorly requited by political change. Britain's revenge on the Turks, evicting the Sultan from his centuries-old capital, roused the fury of Muslims in India, exploited by Gandhi in the 'non-cooperation' campaign. Indian politics were radicalised by religious emotion – a syndrome that endured. Britain's large war debts, the drain of dollar securities, and the general disruption of markets and currencies, destroyed vital parts of the global economic regime on which London, and Britain, had thrived. The general economic collapse of 1929–32 seemed to bury the old landscape of free trade imperialism, the commercial foundation of British world power. Protection, barter and blocs arrived to replace it.

Despite this deepening gloom, the inter-war years conveyed an ambivalent message. Cassandras foretold an ever steeper path of decline. A failure of will had cost the British their dominion in India, declared one ex-official in a widely read book. To Churchill (and others), the appeasement of nationalism was a betrayal of trust ('the great liner is sinking in a calm sea...but the captain, and the officers and the crew are all in the saloon dancing to the jazz band').[2] To a vociferous body of 'Die Hards' (and their less vocal supporters inside and outside the government), the same symptoms of weakness were alarmingly visible in many other parts of the system, especially in Ireland, Egypt and China. But, to much seasoned opinion, this was simply hysterical, the over-reaction of old men in a hurry. An impressive array of authorities rejected the view that the fundamentals had changed. Milner and Curzon, MacDonald and Baldwin, Simon and Halifax, Hailey and Lampson, among many others, acknowledged that the old methods of imperial command could no longer be used. But they insisted that Britain still enjoyed the ability to manage what mattered: those aspects of politics that affected the stability of its system as a whole. To their nationalist opponents before the Second World War, this machiavellian capacity seemed frustratingly real.

This confident view now looks strangely myopic. But there was much to encourage it. Despite economic hard times, Britain was not obviously weaker in the inter-war years than before 1914. The British had paid out the premium for more strategic insurance in the ex-Ottoman Middle East: a 'great glacis of desert and Arabs' (in Attlee's later phrase[3]) to protect their imperial communications by both sea and air. They had appeased Indian nationalism, but also divided it by Byzantine manoeuvres, leaving themselves free to command India's most vital resource – its military manpower. The white dominions acknowledged, with varying degrees of enthusiasm, that their British connection lay at the centre of their external relations, and, in three of the five, that their British identity was the cardinal fact of their national existence. Of the trade and monetary blocs into which the world was divided after 1931, the combined sterling bloc and imperial preference system seemed the best placed to restore its members' prosperity and escape economic disaster. If British power was constrained, so was that of other great states. Indeed, the deep mutual suspicions that divided all the other great powers seemed to suggest that, in relative terms, the British system still enjoyed considerable room for manoeuvre. In a fragmenting world, drifting towards autarky, the rapid implosion of the British world-system was among the least likely scenarios.

In fact, a total collapse was only barely averted between 1938 and 1942. The economic, political and ideological revolutions set off by the war and supercharged by depression convulsed much of Eurasia after 1930. To an extent that many contemporaries found hard to discern, they created a vortex of geopolitical change and destroyed almost all means of arresting its progress. At both ends of Eurasia, the local power balances on which the British relied broke down almost completely amid bitter mutual mistrust. Anglo-American friendship, which might have taken their place (and to which some British looked), survived in the circles of naval officers and financiers. But its formal (and effective) expression as a diplomatic alignment was blocked by disputes over debts, and the antipathy of important American interests towards the British world-system. The ethos of empire and its protectionist practice (through the Ottawa duties and the cooperation of sterling economies) were bound to stick in their craw. As a result, the *status quo* in world politics was defended inadequately by two reluctant associates, the British and the French, each of which doubted the other's good faith and military means. This proved no real protection against a violent geopolitical storm whose lightning assaults and sudden change of direction baffled most onlookers. With France's sudden collapse in June 1940, the central assumption of British grand strategy – that the line against Germany would be held on the mainland of Europe – disappeared like a dream. Perhaps only the failure of their three main assailants to combine more effectively (a function in part of *their* mutual suspicions) gave the British the time to rally American help, and for that help to arrive before it was too late.

The British system survived. But the cost of staying alive was enormous and the collateral damage irreparable. The British were forced to accept the early independence of India, both 'premature' (as they saw it) and partitioned. Any part India might play in their post-war recovery was soon written off. The loss of the vast bulk of their non-sterling assets (dollars above all) wrecked their balance of payments, forced a retreat to a closed sterling zone, and (by throwing the full burden of paying for imports on a steam-age economy near the end of its tether after six years of war) gravely damaged the prospects of industrial modernisation. It also transformed the terms of Anglo-American relations making the British dependent upon American aid as well as support for their currency – although this was offset in part by the value of Britain's contribution in a widening Cold War. Even so, to survive as a world power at all, the British were forced into much heavier intervention in their tropical empire, with its skeletal states; to risk a deeper involvement in the volatile Middle East just at the time when their influence was waning; and to impose an unprecedented burden of military spending on their peace-time economy. In a different geopolitical setting, they might just have remained the 'third world power' and exploited American help to recoup some of their pre-war position. But the scale of the Soviet victory in Europe and Mao's triumph in China – the climax of Eurasia's twentieth-century revolutions – ended all prospect of this. The Cold War did not end, as Churchill had hoped, in a three-power agreement. Instead, what remained of the British world-system was harnessed to the task of Western 'containment', until the strain on British resources enforced a final surrender in the late 1960s.

Of course, the roller-coaster of geopolitical fortune can form only part of the story. It provided the setting for the upsurge of private expansionist energies, the spawning of multiple 'British connections', the fusing of British and local resources (willing or coerced) in an endless variety of regional cases. It promised at one time the eventual formation of a globe-spanning 'British world'. Ethnic populations of British Isles origins, the mercantile classes in Britain's commercial and cultural spheres, and colonial elites in Asia and Africa: all might have found in the liberal imperialism of British free trade the ideal global regime within which to pursue their own state-building objects. To leaders as different as Surendranath Banerjea, the Yoruba Samuel Johnson, the Xhosa John Tengo Jabavu and the Afrikaner Jan Christiaan Smuts, this was the true meaning of Britain's world mission. This vision assumed that Britain would remain strong enough to withstand hostile exogenous pressures without visible strain. But, for all its appeal, such a global 'commonwealth' under British protection was never more than a pipe-dream. The great power arena was always too dangerous (this was London's view) to risk the representative politics for which Indian nationalists were calling before 1914. Ethnic solidarities (among whites and non-whites) sabotaged the appeal of pan-imperial citizenship or imposed on it a narrowly racial meaning. 'Garrison' interests in the Civilian Raj and the colonial dependencies successfully excluded local native elites from political power and drove them towards an ethnic-nationalist programme. The wealth and cultural prestige of late-Victorian Britain, largely founded upon London's centripetal attractions, flagged in the wake of world war and depression. And, amid the huge general crisis that embroiled most of Eurasia after 1917, the appeal of British 'modernity' on which the Victorians had relied first came under siege and then faded away. When Whitehall rolled up the map of the world in the late 1960s, the substance of world power had already shrivelled up, leaving only the ghost of the British world-system. It only remained to acknowledge its passing.

NOTES

Preface and acknowledgments

1. A. Smith, *The Wealth of Nations* [1776] (Everyman edn, 1910), p. 430.

2. J. A. Gallagher, *The Decline, Revival and Fall of the British Empire* (Cambridge, 1982), p. 73.

3. J. Gallagher and R. Robinson, 'The Imperialism of Free Trade', *Economic History Review* New Series, 6, 1 (1953), pp. 1–15.

4. P. Cain and A. G. Hopkins, *British Imperialism 1688–2000* (new edn, 2002); J. Darwin, 'Imperialism and the Victorians', *English Historical Review* 112, 447 (1997), p. 616.

5. See C. Bridge and K. Fedorowich (eds.), *The British World: Diaspora, Culture and Identity* (2003), 'Introduction', for an excellent statement of this.

Introduction

1. For an authoritative account of early usage of the term, see A. Parchami, 'The Pax Romana, Britannica and Americana: A Conceptual and Historiographical Study' (Oxford, DPhil thesis, 2006).

2. The classical account of this process is P. J. Cain and A. G. Hopkins, *British Imperialism*, 2 vols. (1993). For the emphasis on the speculative and often fraudulent dimension of the City's foreign

investment, see I. R. Phimister, 'Corners and Company-Mongering: Nigerian Tin and the City of London', *Journal of Imperial and Commonwealth History*, 28 (2000), 23.

3. See S. J. Potter, *News and the British World: The Emergence of an Imperial Press System 1876–1922* (Oxford, 2003).

4. The classic account is in S. B. Saul, *Studies in British Overseas Trade* (Liverpool, 1960).

5. For the 'Black Indies', see W. S. Jevons, *The Coal Question: An Inquiry Concerning the Progress of the Nation, and the Probable Exhaustion of Our Coal Mines* (1865).

6. Calculated by M. G. Mulhall, *Dictionary of Statistics* (1892), p. 545.

7. University of Texas at Austin, Harry Ransome Center for the Humanities, J. L. Garvin Papers: Milner to J. L. Garvin, 27 May 1917.

8. For the most influential exposition of this, see R. Robinson and J. Gallagher, *Africa and the Victorians* (1961), esp. pp. 471–2.

9. This is the argument of A. L. Friedberg, *The Weary Titan: Britain and the Experience of Relative Decline, 1895–1905* (Princeton, 1988).

10. See J. Ferris, '"The Greatest Power on Earth": Great Britain in the 1920s'; B. McKercher, '"Our Most Dangerous Enemy": Great Britain Pre-eminent in the 1930s'; and G. Martel, 'The Meaning of Power: Rethinking the Decline and Fall of Great Britain', all in *International History Review*, 13 (1991).

11. The grand argument of J. Gallagher, *The Decline, Revival and Fall of the British Empire* (Cambridge, 1982).

12. For an example of this genre, see A. McClintock, *Imperial Leather: Race, Gender and Sexuality in the Colonial Contest* (1995).

13. B. Porter, *The Absent-Minded Imperialists: Empire, Society and Culture in Britain* (Oxford, 2004).

14. P. J. Jupp, *British Politics on the Eve of Reform* (1998), p. 338. Sales of the leading London newspapers rose from 16 million per year in 1837 to 31.4 million in 1850. See J. White, *London in the Nineteenth Century* (2007), p. 230.

15. For this lament, see P. A. Buckner (ed.), *Canada and the British Empire* (*Oxford History of the British Empire* Companion Series) (Oxford, 2008), Introduction.

16. R. E. Robinson, 'The Non-European Foundations of European Imperialism: Sketch for a Theory of Collaboration', in R. Owen and B. Sutcliffe (eds.), *Studies in the Theory of Imperialism* (1972).

17. Gallagher, *Decline, Revival and Fall*, p. 75.

18. See S. Ward, *Australia and the British Embrace* (Melbourne, 2001).

19. For the best accounts of this period, see C. A. Bayly, *Imperial Meridian* (1989); and the three Presidential Addresses by P. J. Marshall on 'Britain and the World in the Eighteenth Century', *Transactions of the Royal Historical Society*, 1998, 1999, 2000. For a longer perspective, see B. Simms, *Three Victories and a Defeat: The Rise and Fall of the First British Empire, 1714–1783* (2007).

20. B. R. Mitchell, *Abstract of British Historical Statistics* (Cambridge, 1971), p. 130.

21. The closing lines of the *Wealth of Nations*.

Chapter 1

1. C. W. Dilke, *Greater Britain* (1869).

2. For Naoroji's views, see chapter 5.

3. PP 1867–8 (197) VI.789, Select Committee on Duties Performed by the British Army in India and the Colonies: *Report, Proceedings*.

4. Reflected in the appointment of the Royal (Carnarvon) Commission on Colonial Defence 1879–82. Its report (TNA, CAB 7/2–4) was left unpublished.

5. PP 1837 (425) VII.1, *Report of Select Committee on Aborigines in British Settlements*, p. 3.

6. For Canning's views and policy, P. J. V. Rolo, *George Canning: Three Biographical Studies* (1965), pp. 223–33.

7. C. K. Webster, *The Foreign Policy of Palmerston 1830–1841* (1951), II, p. 832: Grey to Palmerston, 23 April 1833.

8. E. D. Steele, *Palmerston and Liberalism, 1855–1865* (Cambridge, 1991), p. 293.

9. Webster, *Palmerston*, I, p. 390.

10. C. S. Parker, *Sir Robert Peel*, 3 vols. (2nd edn, 1899), III, p. 405: Wellington to Peel, 22 September 1845.

11. Webster, *Palmerston*, II, p. 848: Palmerston to Melbourne, 26 October 1840.

12. Parker, *Peel*, III, p. 208: Peel to Wellington, 9 August 1845.

13. Webster, *Palmerston*, II, p. 842: Palmerston to Melbourne, 8 June 1835.

14. For a brilliant survey, see A. Rieber, 'Persistent Factors in Russian Foreign Policy', in H. Ragsdale (ed.), *Imperial Russian Foreign Policy* (Cambridge, 1993).

15. Webster, *Palmerston*, II, pp. 738–9: Palmerston to J. C. Hobhouse, 14 February 1840.

16. The French expeditionary force was twice the size of the British.

17. Henry Clay, *Speech in Defence of the American System against the British Colonial System* (Washington, 1832), p. 26. Clay had been Secretary of State in 1825–9, and was a senator in 1831–42.

18. *Ibid.*, p. 18.

19. D. W. Meinig, *The Shaping of America: Volume 2: Continental America, 1800–1867* (1993), p. 155. Meinig's is a brilliant analysis of the geopolitical issues.

20. Henry C. Carey, *The Past, the Present and the Future* (1847). Quoted in D. Ross, *The Origins of American Social Science* (Cambridge, 1990), p. 46.

21. R. Bullen, *Palmerston, Guizot and the Collapse of the Entente Cordiale* (1974), pp. 38–41; J. S. Galbraith, *The Hudson's Bay Company as an Imperial Factor* (Berkeley, 1957), pp. 246, 261.

22. Southampton University Library Palmerston Papers PP/LE/230 (consulted online), Palmerston to Sir G. C. Lewis, 26 August 1861. 10,000 soldiers were to be sent.

23. For New York, see R. G. Albion, *The Rise of New York Port* (New York, 1939).

24. See S. Bruchey, *Cotton and the Growth of the American Economy 1790–1860* (New York, 1967).

25. The presence of the other Western powers in East Asia, remarked Disraeli, meant that 'a system of political compromise has developed itself like the balance of power in Europe'. See W. C. Costin, *Great Britain and China, 1833–1860* (Oxford, 1937), p. 228.

26. See L. Bethell, *The Abolition of the Brazilian Slave Trade* (Cambridge, 1970).

27. See PP 1843 (596) XXXV.607, *Correspondence and Return relating to Military Operations in China.*

28. See the *Appeal on Behalf of British Subjects Residing in and Connected with the River Plate against Any Further Violent Intervention by the British and French Governments in the Affairs of the Country* (1846).

29. PP 1849 (56) XXXII, *Return of Numbers on 25 January in . . . 1829, 1835, 1840 and 1847*, p. 93.

30. See PP 1843 (140), *Return of Numbers . . . Serving in Great Britain, Ireland and the Colonies 1792, 1822, 1828, 1830, 1835, 1842.*

31. PP 1834 (570) VI, *Report of Select Committee on Colonial Military Expenditure*, Q.2152 (Sir Rufane Donkin).

32. *Ibid.*, Q. 1873 (Sir Lowry Cole).

33. J. Belich, *The New Zealand Wars* (Auckland, 1986), ch. 3.

34. R. Graham, *Britain and the Onset of Modernization in Brazil 1850–1914* (Cambridge, 1972), pp. 107–8; Bethell, *Brazilian Slave Trade*; R. Miller, *Britain and Latin America in the Nineteenth and Twentieth Century* (1993), pp. 48–59.

35. J. Rutherford, *Sir George Grey* (1961), pp. 470ff.

36. *Parl.Deb.*, Third Series, Vol. XLIX, 1391 (6 August 1839).

37. R. Cobden, *England, Ireland and America* (1836), p. 11.

38. J. H. Clapham, *An Economic History of Modern Britain: The Early Railway Age 1820 -1850* (Cambridge, 1939), p. 211.

39. S. D. Chapman, *Merchant Enterprise in Britain from the Industrial Revolution to the First World War* (Cambridge, 1992), p. 161.

40. N. Buck, *The Development of the Organisation of Anglo-American Trade 1800–1850* (New Haven, 1925), pp. 172–3.

41. J. Stuart and D. McK. Malcolm (eds.), *The Diary of Henry Francis Fynn* (Paperback edn, Pietermaritzburg, 1986), pp. 40–1.

42. See John Langdon, 'Three Voyages to the West Coast of Africa 1881–1884', in B. Wood and M. Lynn (eds.), *Travel, Trade and Power in the Atlantic 1765–1884* (Cambridge, 2002).

43. Chapman, *Merchant Enterprise*, p. 69.

44. Graham, *Britain and Brazil*, ch. 3.

45. The classic account is M. Greenberg, *British Trade and the Opening of China 1800–1842* (Cambridge, 1951).

46. See D. G. Creighton, *The Commercial Empire of the St Lawrence* (1937).

47. See PP 1862 (380) XXXIV.881, *Return of Applications by Commercial Interests for Ships of War to be Sent to Foreign Stations for Protection of British Interests or Commerce*. In the five years (1857–62) covered, there were 102 applications.

48. C. W. Newbury, *British Policy Towards West Africa: Select Documents 1786–1874* (Oxford, 1965), p. 120: Lord Palmerston, Minute, 22 April 1860.

49. PP 1867 (178) XLIV.721, *Return of Number of Vessels-of-War Employed on Foreign and Colonial Service*, p. 5.

50. E. G. Wakefield, *England and America* (New York, 1834).

51. From around 10,000 chests in 1830–1 to over 80,000 by the early 1860s. See PP 1865 (94) XL.83, *Return of Opium Exported to China from Central India via Bombay and Bengal, 1830–1864*.

52. PP 1859 (2571) XXXIII.1, *Correspondence Relative to Lord Elgin's Special Missions to China and Japan, 1857–59*, Clarendon to Elgin, 20 April 1857.

53. B. R. Mitchell, *Abstract of British Historical Statistics* (Cambridge, 1971), p. 47.

54. C. Erickson, *Leaving England*, p. 184.

55. W. S. Shepperson, *British Emigration to North America: Projects and Opinions in the Early Victorian Period* (Oxford, 1957), p. 201.

56. P. Burns, *Fatal Success: A History of the New Zealand Company* (Auckland, 1989).

57. See *Correspondence with the Secretary of State relative to New Zealand*, published in *The Times*, 21 April 1840.

58. *The Times*, 3 February 1838.

59. R. G. Wood, *From Plymouth to New Plymouth* (Wellington, 1959).

60. For the Kaipara, see B. Byrne, *The Unknown Kaipara: Five Aspects of its History, 1250–1875* (Auckland, 2002); W. Rayburn, *Tall Spars, Steamers and Gum: A History of the Kaipara from Early European Settlement, 1854–1947* (Auckland, 1999).

61. Mitchell, *Abstract*, p. 47.

62. *Parl.Deb.*, Third Series, Vol. 121, col. 956 (21 May 1852).

63. *Ibid.*, Vol. 179, cols. 911–14 (26 May 1865). Cardwell was Colonial Secretary.

64. E. Elbourne, 'Religion in the British Empire', in S. Stockwell (ed.), *The British Empire: Themes and Perspectives* (2008), p. 139.

65. I. Bradley, *The Call to Seriousness* (1976), p. 90.

66. A. Aspinall (ed.), *English Historical Documents 1783–1832* (1959), p. 662: 'Receipts of the Principal Religious Charities in London', *The Scotsman*, 21 July 1821.

67. E. Stock, *The History of the Church Missionary Society*, 3 vols. (1899), vol. 1, p. 243.

68. Stock, *Church Missionary Society*, vol. 1, p. 485.

69. C. P. Groves, *The Planting of Christianity in Africa*, 3 vols. (1948–60), p. 267.

70. See M. Mackinnon (ed.), *New Zealand Historical Atlas* (Auckland, 1997), Plate 36.

71. Groves, *Planting of Christianity*, vol. 2, pp. 49, 36.

72. A. J. Broomhall, *Hudson Taylor and China's Open Century*, vol. I, *Barbarians at the Gates* (1981), chs. 3, 4.

73. *Ibid.*, p. 278.

74. Broomhall, *Hudson Taylor*, vol. II, *Over the Treaty Wall* (1982), p. 161.

75. Stock, *Church Missionary Society*, vol. I, p. 490.

76. Bradley, *Call*, p. 141.

77. *Ibid.*, p. 78.

78. *The Times*, 15 February 1858.

79. www.livingstoneonline.ucl.ac.uk, Livingstone to Lord Palmerston, 13 May 1859.

80. J. Belich, *Making Peoples: A History of the New Zealanders* (1996), p. 168; for the request by the chiefs of Bonny in 1848, see J. F. A. Ajayi, *Christian Missions in Nigeria 1841–1891* (Ibadan, 1965), p. 56.

81. Ajayi, *Missions*, p. 29.

82. A. C. Ross, *John Phillip (1775–1851): Missions, Race and Politics in South Africa* (Aberdeen, 1986), p. 167: Phillip's journal for 28 March 1842.

83. *Ibid.*, pp. 141, 221.

84. See A. Porter, 'An Overview: 1700–1914', in N. Etherington (ed.), *Missions and Empire* (Oxford, 2005), p. 51.

85. Memorial by Aborigine Protection Society to Lord Glenelg (the Colonial Secretary), 3 February 1838. See 'Early Canadiana Online' at www.canadiana.org.

86. H. M. Wright, *New Zealand 1769–1840: Early Years of Western Contact* (Cambridge, MA, 1959), p. 109.

87. See M. Fairburn, *The Ideal Society and its Enemies: The Foundations of Modern New Zealand Society* (Auckland, 1989), Part One.

88. K. T. Hoppen, *The Mid-Victorian Generation 1846–1886* (Oxford, 1998), p. 381.

89. G. Wynn, 'Industrialism, Entrepreneurship and Opportunity in the New Brunswick Timber Trade', in L. R. Fischer and E. W. Sager (eds.), *The Enterprising Canadians: Entrepreneurs and Economic Development in Eastern Canada, 1820–1914* (St John's, 1979), p. 12.

90. See *Dictionary of Canadian Biography* (online version).

91. See G. Tulchinsky, 'The Montreal Business Community, 1837–1853', in D. S. Macmillan (ed.), *Canadian Business History: Selected Studies 1497–1971* (Toronto, 1972), pp. 125–43.

92. See *Australian Dictionary of Biography* (online version) for details.

93. See J. McAloon, 'Resource Frontiers, Environment and Settler Capitalism: 1769–1860', in E. Pawson and T. Brooking (eds.), *Environmental Histories of New Zealand* (Melbourne, 2002), pp. 52–66; D. A. Hamer, 'Wellington on the Urban Frontier', in D. A. Hamer and R. Nicholls (eds.), *The Making of Wellington* (1990), p. 247; J. H. Millar, *The Merchants Paved the Way* (Wellington, 1956), pp. 37–8.

94. R. C. J. Stone, *Makers of Fortune: a Colonial Business Community and its Fall* (Auckland, 1973), p. 9.

95. See M. D. N. Campbell, 'The Evolution of Hawke's Bay Landed Society' (PhD, Victoria University Wellington, 1972), pp. 57–8.

96. Graphically described in K. Sinclair, *The Origins of the Maori Wars* (Wellington, 1957), pp. 58–9.

97. For an excellent description of commando expansion, see P. Delius, *The Land Belongs to Us: The Pedi Polity, the Boers and the British in the Nineteenth Century Transvaal* (Johannesburg, 1983), pp. 30–40, ch. 6.

98. See J. Carruthers, 'Friedrich Jeppe: Mapping the Transvaal c. 1850–1899', *Journal of Southern African Studies* 29, 4 (2003), 959.

99. See L. Subrahmanian, 'Banias and the British: The Role of Indigenous Credit in . . . Imperial Expansion in Western India', *Modern Asian Studies*, 21 (1987), 473–510.

100. D. Kumar (ed.), *Cambridge Economic History of India*, vol. II, *c.1757–c.1970* (Cambridge, 1982), p. 916.

101. See D. Kolff, *Naukat, Rajah and Sepoy* (Cambridge, 1990), pp. 180ff.

102. M. Yapp, *Strategies of British India* (Oxford, 1980), p. 175, for the 'horseshoe'.

103. *Parl. Deb.*, vol. 120, cols. 647ff (5 April 1852).

104. *Ibid.*, col. 651.

105. See PP 1857–8 (59), *Return of Number of Cadetships Conferred by the East India Company and the President of the Board of Control, 1840–57*, p. 2.

106. *The Times*, 6 August 1853.

107. PP 1847–8 (511) IX.1, *Report of Select Committee on the Growth of Cotton in India*, p. 307; Speech by John Bright at the Manchester Chamber of Commerce, 20 June 1853, in *The Times*, 22 June 1853.

108. See A. J. Baster, *The Imperial Banks* (1929), pp. 101–3.

109. See C. A. Bayly, *Empire and Information: Intelligence Gathering and Social Communication in India, 1780–1870* (Cambridge, 1996), ch. 9.

110. For the Mutiny, see C. A. Bayly, 'Two Colonial Revolts: The Java War 1825–1830, and the Indian "Mutiny" of 1857–59', in

C. A. Bayly and D. H. Kolff (eds.), *Two Colonial Empires: Comparative Essays on the History of India and Indonesia in the Nineteenth Century* (The Hague, 1986), pp. 111–35; S. David, *The Indian Mutiny* (2002); F. Robinson, 'The Muslims of Upper India and the Shock of the Mutiny', in his *Islam and Muslim History in South Asia* (New Delhi, 2000), pp. 138–55.

111. PP 1867 (478) VII.197, 553, *Select Committee to Inquire into the Duties of the British Army in India and the Colonies: Report, Proceedings, Minutes of Evidence*, p. 327: Minute by Lord Dalhousie, 13 September 1854.

112. Graham, *Britain and the Modernization of Brazil*, chs. 1–3.

113. See P. Gootenburg, *Between Silver and Guano: Commercial Policy and the State in Postindependence Peru* (Princeton, 1989).

114. Chapman, *Merchant Enterprise*, pp. 203–4.

115. C. Trocki, *Singapore: Wealth, Power and the Culture of Control* (2006), pp. 14–15.

116. Trocki, *Singapore*, p. 24.

117. Opium made up 33 per cent of Chinese imports in 1868, cotton goods 29 per cent: F. E. Hyde, *Far Eastern Trade 1860–1914* (1973), p. 217; for legalisation, see S. T. Wang, *The Margary Affair and the Chefoo Agreement* (Oxford, 1940), p. 120.

118. N. Pelcovits, *The Old China Hands and the Foreign Office* (New York, 1948), pp. 35, 42.

119. Pelcovits, *Old China Hands*, p. 42.

120. Y. P. Hao, *The Commercial Revolution in Nineteenth-Century China* (1986), p. 355.

121. See PP 1877 (5), *Report and Statistical Tables Relating to Emigration and Immigration, 1876*, Table XIII.

122. Dilke, *Greater Britain* (1869), p. vii.

123. For the debate on the motives behind Peel's decision to repeal the Corn Laws, see B. Hilton, 'Peel: A Reappraisal', *Historical Journal*, 22 (1979); B. Hilton, *The Age of Atonement: The Influence*

of Evangelicalism on Social and Economic Thought 1785–1865 (Oxford, 1988); A. C. Howe, 'Free Trade and the City of London c.1820–1875', *Economic History Review*, New Series, 77, 251 (1992); C. Schonhardt-Bailey, *From the Corn Laws to Free Trade: Interests, Ideas and Institutions in Historical Perspective* (Cambridge, MA, 2006).

124. From under £4 million to £58 million. Mitchell, *Abstract*, pp. 333–4.

125. J. A. Froude, 'England and Her Colonies', *Fraser's Magazine*, January 1870, p. 16.

126. Goldwin Smith, *The Empire* (1863).

127. PP 1866 (3683) XXX, *Royal Commission into the Origins, Nature and Circumstances of the Disturbances in . . . Jamaica: Report*, p. 41.

128. R. Cobden, 'How Wars Are Got up in India', in *Political Writings of Richard Cobden*, 2 vols. (1868), vol. 2, pp. 105ff.

129. Bodl. Mss Clarendon dep.c 85: Bowring to Clarendon, 18 January, 10 March, 9 April 1858.

130. H. T. Manning, *British Colonial Government after the American Revolution 1782–1820* (New Haven, CT, 1933), p. 361.

131. J. S. Mill, *Representative Government* (1861), ch. 18.

132. For a detailed reconstruction of British attitudes, focused on Birmingham, the Baptists and Jamaica, C. Hall, *Civilising Subjects: Metropole and Colony in the British Imagination 1830–1867* (2002), Part Two.

133. *Parl. Deb.*, Third Series, vol. 190, col. 394 (28 November 1867).

134. PP 1872 (C.493) XXXVII.383. *Memorandum by Commander-in-Chief on the Secretary of State's Proposals for Organization of Military Land Forces*, p. 7.

135. See C. Jones, 'Business Imperialism and Argentina 1875–1900: A Theoretical Note', *Journal of Latin American Studies*, 12, 2 (1980), 437–44.

Chapter 2

1. A. J. H. Latham and L. Neal, 'The International Market in Wheat and Rice, 1868–1914', *Economic History Review*, New Series, 36, 2 (1983), 260–75.

2. BLIOC, Curzon Papers, Mss Eur. F 111, Lord George Hamilton to Curzon (India), 2 November 1899.

3. M. Swartz, *The Politics of British Foreign Policy in the Age of Disraeli and Gladstone* (1985), p. 13.

4. C. H. Pearson, *National Life and Character* (1893); B. Kidd, *Social Evolution* (1894); A. Mahan, *The Problem of the Pacific* (1900); J. Bryce, *The Relations between the Advanced and Backward Peoples* (Oxford, 1902); H. Mackinder, 'The Geographical Pivot of History', *Geographical Journal*, 23, 4 (1904), 421–37.

5. Sandford Fleming, quoting Parkin at the Colonial Conference, held in Ottawa in 1894. *Proceedings of the Colonial Conference* (Ottawa, 1894), p. 89.

6. Mackinder, 'Geographical Pivot', p. 422.

7. Kidd, *Social Evolution*, p. 339.

8. Pearson, *National Life*, p. 13. For Pearson's career, see J. Tregenza, *Professor of Democracy: The Life of C. H. Pearson* (Melbourne, 1968).

9. Pearson, *National Life*, pp. 84–5.

10. Kidd, *Social Evolution*, p. 50.

11. J. Bryce, 'The Roman Empire and the British Empire in India', in *Studies in History and Jurisprudence* (Oxford, 1901), pp. 1–2.

12. *Ibid.*, pp. 6–7.

13. *Ibid.*, p. 36.

14. See A. Lyall, 'The Religious Situation in India', *Asiatic Studies* 1 (1899), 320–3.

15. See T. Raychaudhuri, *Europe Reconsidered: Perceptions of the West in Nineteenth-Century Bengal* (Oxford, 1989).

669 / Notes to pages 68-73

16. S. Teng and J. K. Fairbank (eds.), *China's Response to the West* (Cambridge, MA, 1979), p. 152.

17. E. W. Blyden, *Christianity, Islam and the Negro Race* (1887), pp. 20, 65, 387.

18. See A. Hourani, *Arabic Thought in the Liberal Age 1798–1939* (1962).

19. The classic study is B. H. Sumner, *Russia and the Balkans 1870–1880* (Oxford. 1937).

20. For this estimate, see R. W. Seton-Watson, *Disraeli, Gladstone and the Eastern Question* (1935), pp. 560–1.

21. See Swartz, *The Politics of British Foreign Policy*, p. 101.

22. G. Waterfield, *Layard of Nineveh* (1963), p. 442: Salisbury to Layard, April 1880.

23. See A. Schölch, *'Egypt for the Egyptians': The Socio-Political Crisis in Egypt 1879–1882* (1981).

24. See J. R. I. Cole, *Colonialism and Revolution in the Middle East: The Social and Cultural Origins of the 'Urabi Movement'* (Princeton, 1993).

25. See Baron Meyendorff (ed.), *Correspondance diplomatique de M. de Staal 1884–1900* (Paris, 1929), vol. 1, p. 30: Instruction to De Staal (Russian ambassador in London), 8 June 1884.

26. See D. A. Farnie, *East and West of Suez: the Suez Canal in History* (Oxford, 1969), esp. p. 294; and A. G. Hopkins' scintillating critique in 'The Victorians and Africa: A Reconsideration of the Occupation of Egypt, 1882', *Journal of African History*, 27, 2 (1986) 363–91.

27. Robinson and Gallagher, *Africa and the Victorians*, p. 111.

28. For Egyptian hostility towards Europeans in these two towns in the 1870s, see Cole, *Colonialism and Revolution*, p. 203.

29. H. C. G. Matthew, *The Gladstone Diaries (1881–1883)*, vol. X (Oxford, 1990), p. 327: Gladstone to Ripon (India), 6 September 1882.

30. B. Holland, *The Life of Spencer Compton Eighth Duke of Devonshire* (1911), vol I, p. 295.

31. Seton-Watson, *Eastern Question*, p. 236: Disraeli to the Queen, 3 November 1877.

32. See Farnie, *East and West of Suez*, ch. 14.

33. *Ibid.*, ch. 12.

34. *Ibid.*, p. 265.

35. The classic account is P. M. Holt, *The Mahdist State in the Sudan 1881–1898* (Oxford, 1958).

36. See R. C. Mowat, 'From Liberalism to Imperialism: The Case of Egypt, 1875–1887', *Historical Journal*, 16, 1 (1973), 109–24.

37. P. G. Halpern, *The Mediterranean Naval Situation 1908–1914* (Cambridge, MA, 1971), p. 2.

38. For the diplomacy of the Berlin conference, see S. Forster, W. Mommsen and R. E. Robinson, *Bismarck, Europe and Africa* (Oxford, 1988).

39. For Cromer's 'reign' in Egypt, see R. Owen, *Lord Cromer* (Oxford, 2004); R. L. Tignor, *Britain and the Modernization of Egypt 1882–1914* (Princeton, 1966); A. Milner, *England and Egypt* (1892); and his own magnificent two-volume apologia, *Modern Egypt* (1908).

40. *Essays by the Late Marquess of Salisbury* (1905), p. 55 (originally published in 1862).

41. Swartz, *British Foreign Policy*, p. 25.

42. *Essays*, p. 12

43. *Ibid.*, p. 53.

44. The best recent analysis of Salisbury's foreign policy can be found in E. D. Steele, *Lord Salisbury: A Political Biography* (1999).

45. For the pattern of French conquest, see A. S. Kanya-Forstner, *The Conquest of the Western Sudan* (Cambridge, 1969); M. Klein, *Slavery and Colonial Rule in French West Africa* (Cambridge, 1998).

46. Quoted by D. Gillard, 'Salisbury', in Wilson, *Foreign Secretaries*, p. 122.

47. E. T. S. Dugdale (ed.), *German Diplomatic Documents 1871–1914* (1929), vol. II, pp. 403–4: Hatzfeldt to Holstein, 21 January 1896.

48. See J. A. S. Grenville, *Lord Salisbury and Foreign Policy* (1964), ch. 6.

49. See G. N. Curzon, *Problems of the Far East* (1894).

50. Lo Hui-min (ed.), *The Correspondence of G. E. Morrison*, 2 vols. (Cambridge, 1976), vol. I, pp. 35, 40: Chirol to Morrison, 26 May, 11 August 1898.

51. L. K. Young, *British Policy in China 1895–1902* (Oxford, 1970), p. 70.

52. *Ibid.*, pp. 92ff.: Salisbury to MacDonald, 23 May 1900. See also T. G. Otte, 'The Boxer Uprising and British Foreign Policy: The End of Isolation', in R. Bickers and R. G. Tiedemann (eds.), *The Boxers, China and the World* (2007), pp. 157–77; and his longer study, *The China Question: Great Power Rivalry and British Isolation* (Oxford, 2007).

53. Anon., *Blackwood's Magazine*, 168 (December 1900).

54. See R. Kubicek, *The Administration of Imperialism* (Durham, NC, 1969).

55. See R. J. Blyth, *The Empire of the Raj: India, Eastern Africa and the Middle East, 1858–1947* (2003).

56. A. P. Kaminsky, *The India Office 1880–1910* (Westport, CT, 1986), p. 107.

57. For the debate on this question, see J. MacKenzie (ed.), *Imperialism and Popular Culture* (Manchester, 1983); B. Porter, *The Absent-Minded Imperialists: What the British Really Thought About Empire* (Oxford, 2004); A. Thompson, *The Empire Strikes Back* (2006).

58. Its classic expression is in R. Robinson and J. Gallagher, *Africa and the Victorians: The Official Mind of Imperialism* (1961).

59. For some discussion of the debate, see J. Darwin, 'Imperialism and the Victorians', *English Historical Review*, 112, 447 (1997), 614–42.

60. See P. Cain and A. G. Hopkins, *British Imperialism* (2nd edn, 2000).

61. Lugard to his brother, 29 August 1895, in M. Perham, *Lugard: The Years of Adventure 1858–1898* (1956), p. 555.

62. K. Wilson, 'Drawing the Line at Constantinople', in K. Wilson (ed.), *British Foreign Secretaries and Foreign Policy: From the Crimean War to the First World War* (1986), p. 202: Salisbury to Randolph Churchill, 1 October 1886.

63. Darwin, 'Imperialism and the Victorians', p. 628.

64. Bodl. Mss Selborne Box 5, Salisbury to Selborne, 26 August 1897.

65. Salisbury's remark, Robinson and Gallagher, *Africa and the Victorians*, p. 454.

66. Rhodes House Library, Mss Afr.S 1525, John Holt Papers Box 3/7, George Goldie to George Miller, 13 November 1887.

67. J. Flint, *Sir George Goldie and the Making of Nigeria* (1960), p. 275: Goldie to Colonial Office, 21 July 1897.

68. Flint, *Goldie*, p. 258; for the blitz of articles launched by Lugard in the British press in 1895–6, Perham, *Lugard: The Years of Adventure*, p. 544.

69. Flint, *Goldie*, p. 207.

70. Bodl. Mss Milner 3, Milner to Clinton Dawkins, 1 March 1895.

71. Bodl. Mss Milner 3, Dawkins to Milner, 18 February 1895.

72. Bodl. Mss Milner 3, Dawkins to Milner, 17 July 1896.

73. Salisbury's essay was reprinted in P. Smith, *Lord Salisbury on Politics* (Cambridge, 1972).

74. H. Spencer, *The Man Versus the State* (1884).

75. D. A. Hamer, *John Morley: Liberal Intellectual in Politics* (Oxford, 1968), p. 162.

76. R. F. Foster, *Lord Randolph Churchill* (Oxford, 1981), p. 319.

77. P. Marsh, *Joseph Chamberlain: Entrepreneur in Politics* (New Haven, 1994), p. 191.

78. W. S. Churchill, *Lord Randolph Churchill* (new edn,1951), pp. 375–6.

79. *Ibid.*, p. 521.

80. Kubichek, *Administration of Imperialism*, p. 76.

81. See J. A. Hobson, *Imperialism: A Study* (1902).

82. G. R. Sloan, *The Geopolitics of Anglo-Irish Relations in the Twentieth Century* (1997).

83. P. Marsh, *The Discipline of Popular Government* (1978), p. 303: Salisbury to Cranbrook, 19 October 1900.

84. For a classic expression, see F. W. Hirst, 'Imperialism and Finance', in *Liberalism and the Empire: Three Essays* (1900), p. 75.

85. A. M. Gollin, *Proconsul in Politics* (1964), p. 106: Milner to Amery, 1 December 1906; B. Porter, *The Absentee-Minded Imperialists: Empire, Society and Culture in Britain* (Oxford, 2004).

86. See A. S. Thompson, *Imperial Britain: The Empire in British Politics c. 1880–1922* (2000), esp. chs. 1, 2, 3. See also his important study, *The Empire Strikes Back: The Impact of Imperialism on Britain since the Mid-Nineteenth Century* (2005).

87. T. W. Freeman, *A Hundred Years of Geography* (1961), pp. 58–9.

88. J. MacKenzie, 'The Provincial Geographical Societies in Britain, 1884–1914', in M. Bell, R. Butlin and M. Heffernan (eds.), *Geography and Imperialism 1820–1940* (Manchester, 1995).

89. C.4715 (1886), Royal Commission on Trade and Industry, *Second Report*, Appendix Part One, p. 408.

90. *Ibid.*, p. 402.

91. *Ibid.*, p. 406.

92. B. R. Mitchell, *Abstract of British Historical Statistics* (Cambridge, 1971), pp. 47, 50.

93. For this estimate, see A. N. Porter, 'Religion and Empire: British Experience in the Long Nineteenth Century', *Journal of Imperial and Commonwealth History*, 20, 3 (1992), 15–31.

94. See the studies in M. Harper (ed.), *Emigrant Homecomings: The Return Movement of Migrants 1600–2000* (Manchester, 2007).

95. H. A. L. Fisher, *James Bryce* (1927) vol. I, p. 172.

96. A. Seal, *The Emergence of Indian Nationalism* (Cambridge, 1968), pp. 21–2.

97. See J. R. Seeley, *The Expansion of England* (1883); J. A. Froude, *Oceana, or England and Her Colonies* (1886); C. W. Dilke, *Greater Britain* (1869).

98. C. W. Dilke, *The Present Position in European Politics* (1887), p. 360.

99. See S. Potter, *News and the British World: The Emergence of an Imperial Press System 1876–1922* (Oxford, 2003).

100. For Lord Strathcona, Canadian High Commissioner in London 1896–1914, see B. Willson, *The Life of Lord Strathcona and Mount Royal* (1915), chs. 21ff. Strathcona was Canada's most prestigious businessman.

101. See C. Kaul, *Reporting the Raj: The British Press and India 1880–1922* (Manchester, 2003).

102. S. D. Chapman, *Merchant Enterprise in Britain: from the Industrial Revolution to World War I* (Cambridge, 1992), p. 203.

103. W. Cronon, *Nature's Metropolis: Chicago and the Great West* (New York, 1991), p. 126.

104. For an evocative account, see R. Jefferies, 'A Wheat Country', in his *Hodge and His Masters* (1880).

105. For the peerage (who did better), see A. Adonis, *Making Aristocracy Work: The Peerage and the Political System in Britain 1884–1914* (Oxford, 1993), pp. 244–5. For the gentry, see D. Cannadine, *The Decline and Fall of the British Aristocracy* (1990), p. 126.

106. J. M. Crook, *The Rise of the Nouveaux Riches* (1999), p. 12.

107. See J. MacKenzie, *The Empire of Nature: Hunting, Conservation and British Imperialism* (Manchester, 1988).

108. Crook, *Nouveaux Riches*, chs. 1, 2, 4.

109. H. G. Wells, *The New Machiavelli* (1911), p. 59.

110. See R. McKibbin, 'Why Was There No Marxism in Great Britain', *English Historical Review*, 99, 391 (1984), 297–331.

111. See G. Stedman-Jones, *Outcast London: A Study in the Relationship between Classes in Victorian Society* (Oxford, 1971), ch. 6. 'The theory of urban degeneration'.

112. A persistent theme in Froude, *Oceana*.

113. See G. R. Searle, *Corruption in British Politics 1895–1930* (Oxford, 1987).

114. J. Harris, *Private Lives, Public Spirit: Britain 1870–1914* (Oxford, 1993), p. 12.

115. M. Pugh, *The Tories and the People* (Oxford, 1985), pp. 87–92.

116. Quoted in E. D. Steele, 'Imperialism and Leeds Politics c.1850–1914', in D. Fraser (ed.), *History of Modern Leeds* (Manchester, 1980), pp. 344–5.

117. G. Chisholm, *Handbook of Commercial Geography* (7th edn, 1908), p. 58.

118. H. Mackinder, *Britain and the British Seas* (1902), p. 4.

119. *Ibid.*, p. 11.

120. *Ibid.*

121. W. C. Hutchinson (ed.), *The Private Diaries of Sir Algernon West* (1922), p. 259: Ripon to Sir A. West, 26 January 1894.

122. Quoted in W. H. Parker, *Mackinder: Geography as an Aid to Statecraft* (Oxford, 1982), p. 61.

123. See C. Erickson, *Leaving England* (Ithaca, 1994), ch. 3; H. L. Malchow, *Population Pressures: Emigration and Government in Late Nineteenth-Century Britain* (Palo Alto, 1979).

124. A. J. Hammerton, *Emigrant Gentlewomen: Genteel Poverty and Female Emancipation 1830–1914* (1979).

125. G. Wagner, *Children of the Empire* (1982).

126. Cmd. 7695, *Report of the Royal Commission on Population* (1949), ch. 12.

127. The classic account is J. Roach, 'Liberalism and the Victorian Intelligentsia', *Cambridge Historical Journal*, 13, 1 (1957), 58–81.

128. This transition is explained in E. T. Stokes, *The English Utilitarians and India* (Oxford, 1959).

129. The key concept in Kidd, *Social Evolution*.

130. Hobson's 'anti-imperialism' did not permit the 'closed economy'.

131. Mackinder, *Britain and the British Seas*, pp. 348–9.

132. Rhodes House Library, Mss Afr s.228, C. J. Rhodes Papers, C 27, Milner to Rhodes, 6 August 1898.

133. B. Schwertfeger (ed.), *Zur Europaischen Politik 1897: Unveroffentliche Dokumente*, vol. I, *1897–1904* (Berlin, 1919), p. 32: Memo by Belgian Foreign Office, 13 June 1898.

134. See N. Blewett, 'The Franchise in the United Kingdom 1885–1918', *Past and Present*, 32 (1965), 27–56; K. T. Hoppen, *The Mid-Victorian Generation 1846–1886* (Oxford, 1998), pp. 265–6. The percentage was lower in Scotland and Ireland.

135. R. Shannon, *The Age of Salisbury* (1996), pp. 553, 556.

136. See D. A. Hamer, *Liberal Politics in the Age of Gladstone and Rosebery* (Oxford, 1972), ch. 11.

137. Schwertfeger, *Europaischen Politik*, p. 44: Memo by Belgian Foreign Office, 29 August 1898.

138. See below ch. 6.

139. Speech at the Royal Colonial Institute, 31 March 1897. See Robinson and Gallagher, *Africa and the Victorians*, p. 404.

Chapter 3

1. I have adapted this term from W. K. Hancock, who derived it from Adam Smith's 'great mercantile republic'.

2. PP 1898 (344), *Return of Public Income and Expenditure... 1869–1898*, pp. 10, 20, 21.

3. For a vigorous exposition of this, see D. C. North, 'Conference Summary', in L. R. Fischer and E. W. Sager (eds.), *Merchant Shipping and Economic Development in Atlantic Canada* (St John's, Newfoundland, 1982). See generally, D. C. North, *Understanding the Process of Economic Change* (Princeton, 2005).

4. F. Knight, *Risk, Uncertainty and Profit* (Boston, 1921), p. 268.

5. Figures from W. Woodruff, *The Impact of Western Man* (1966), p. 253.

6. D. Headrick, *Tentacles of Progress: Technology Transfer in the Age of Imperialism, 1850–1914* (1988), p. 105.

7. Woodruff, *Impact*, p. 289.

8. *Ibid.*, p. 313.

9. R. C. O. Mathews, C. H. Feinstein and J. C. Odling-Smee, *British Economic Growth, 1856–1973* (Stanford, CA, 1982), p. 433. The figure for 1964 was 16.3%.

10. B. R. Mitchell, *An Abstract of British Historical Statistics* (Cambridge, 1971), p. 334.

11. R. C. Michie, *The City of London* (1992), p. 72. For an account stressing the diverse interests in the City, see M. J. Daunton, 'Financial Elites and British Society, 1880–1950', in R. C. Michie (ed.), *The Development of London as a Financial Centre*, 4 vols. (2000), vol. II, pp. 355–6.

12. Woodruff, *Impact*, p. 257.

13. Mitchell, *Abstract*,

14. M. Edelstein, *Overseas Investment in the Age of High Imperialism* (1982), p. 48.

15. C. H. Feinstein, 'Britain's Overseas Investments in 1913', *Economic History Review*, New Series, 43, 2 (1990), 288–95.

16. Woodruff, *Impact*, p. 154.

17. Michie, *City*, p. 112.

18. *Ibid.*, p. 113.

19. *Ibid.*, p. 114.

20. D. Kynaston, *The City of London: Golden Years, 1890–1914* (1995), p. 262.

21. A classic example was the firm of Brown, Shipley and Co. See A. Ellis, *Heir of Adventure: The Story of Brown, Shipley and Co., 1810–1960* (privately printed, n.d.).

22. For Rothschilds, see N. Ferguson, *The World's Banker: The History of the House of Rothschild* (1998); for Barings, see P. Ziegler, *The Sixth World Power: A History of One of the Great Banking Families, the House of Barings, 1762–1929* (1988).

23. See S. G. Checkland, 'The Mind of the City 1870–1914', *Oxford Economic Papers*, New Series, 9, 3 (1957), 261–78.

24. For a recent study, see R. C. Michie, *The London Stock Exchange* (Oxford, 2001).

25. Michie, *City*, p. 134.

26. J. A. Hobson, *The Evolution of Modern Capitalism* [1894] (rev. edn, 1926), p. 246. For Hobson's views, see P. Cain, *Hobson and Imperialism: Radicalism, New Liberalism and Finance, 1887–1938* (Oxford, 2002).

27. C. Harvey and J. Press, 'Overseas Investment and the Professional Advance of British Metal Mining Engineers, 1851–1914', *Economic History Review*, New Series, 42, 1 (1989), 67–8; 'The City and International Mining, 1870–1914', *Business History* 32, 3 (1990), 98–119; J. J. van Helten, 'Mining, Share Mania and Speculation: British Investment in Overseas Mining 1880–1913', in J. J. van Helten and Y. Cassis, *Capitalism in a Mature Economy* (1990).

28. For a graphic description of the speculative and disinformational tendencies to be found in the City, see I. R. Phimister, 'Corners and Company-Mongering: Nigerian Tin and the City, 1909–1912', *Journal of Imperial and Commonwealth History*, 28, 2 (2000), 23–41.

29. Checkland, 'The Mind of the City', pp. 265, 270, 278. For the outlook of bankers, see Y. Cassis, 'The Banking Community of London, 1890–1914: A Survey', *Journal of Imperial and Commonwealth History*, 13, 3 (1985), 109–26.

30. Thus Salisbury dismissed the suggestion for diplomatic pressure on Argentina at the time of the Barings crisis in 1890 as 'dreams'. H. S. Ferns, *Britain and Argentina in the Nineteenth Century* (Oxford, 1960), p. 468.

31. G. R. Searle, *Corruption in British Politics 1890–1930* (Oxford, 1987), p. 13.

32. See *Imperialism: A Study* (1902).

33. Kynaston, *Golden Years*, p. 383.

34. *Ibid.*, p. 385.

35. J. F. Gilpin, *The Poor Relation Has Come into Her Fortune: The British Investment Boom in Canada, 1905–15* (1992), p. 11.

36. The classic expression of this is N. Angell, *The Great Illusion* (1909).

37. For India's place in Britain's multilateral payments system, S. B. Saul, *Studies in British Overseas Trade 1870–1914* (Liverpool, 1960), chs. 3, 8; B. R. Tomlinson, *The Political Economy of the Raj 1914–1947* (1979), ch. 1.

38. A. J. Sargent, *Seaways of the Empire* (1918), ch. 1.

39. 'England . . . is the telegraph exchange of the world. Every great line of telegraph communication centres in this country', remarked the head of the Post Office telegraph department in 1893. R. W. D. Boyce, 'Imperial Dreams and National Realities: Britain, Canada and the Struggle for a Pacific Telegraph Cable, 1879–1902', *English Historical Review*, 115, 460 (2000), 57.

40. See the account in J. Schneer, *London 1900: The Imperial Metropolis* (New Haven, 1999).

41. For a superb study, see J. Forbes Munro, *Maritime Enterprise and Empire: Sir William Mackinnon and His Business Network, 1823–1893* (Woodbridge, 2003).

42. By the time of Mary Kingsley's visit in 1893, there was a weekly steamship service from Britain to the West Africa 'Coast'. See M. Kingsley, *Travels in West Africa* [1897] (4th edn, 1982), Appendix 1.

43. A recent account of this transaction is in A. Amanat, *Pivot of the Universe: Nasir al-Din Shah Qajar and the Iranian Monarchy 1831–96* (1997), pp. 424–5.

44. A classic study is M. Lynn, *Commerce and Economic Change in West Africa: The Palm Oil Trade in the Nineteenth Century* (Cambridge, 1997); see also C. Jones, '"Business Imperialism" in Argentina: A Theoretical Note', *Journal of Latin American Studies*, 12 (1980), 440ff.

45. R. Austen, *African Economic History* (1987), p. 275.

46. *Ibid.*, p. 114.

47. K. O. Dike, *Trade and Politics in the Niger Delta 1830–1885* (Oxford, 1956), is the classic study.

48. J. D. Hargreaves, *Prelude to the Partition of West Africa* (1966), pp. 35–7.

49. M. Lynn, 'The Imperialism of Free Trade: The Case of West Africa c.1830–c.1880', *Journal of Imperial and Commonwealth History*, 15, 1 (1986), 22–40.

50. From £29 per ton in 1881 to just over £19 in 1888. J. D. Hargreaves, *West Africa Partitioned*, vol I, *The Loaded Pause, 1885–1889* (1974), p. 252.

51. Goldie's eccentric personality is sketched in D. Wellesley, *Sir George Goldie: A Memoir* (1934), and his early career in J. Flint, *Sir George Goldie and the Making of Nigeria* (1960).

52. Flint, *Goldie*, p. 326.

53. *Ibid.*, Appendix 2.

54. Bodl. RHL Mss Afr. S.1525, John Holt Papers, Box 4.

55. M. Perham, *Lugard: The Years of Adventure 1858–1898* (1956), p. 544.

56. Bodl. RHL Mss Afr. S.88, Scarbrough Mss 4: Lugard to Royal Nigeria Company Council, 6 February 1897. If their losses had been heavier, he told his main business partner, 'we should not have had enough troops left for the work'. Goldie to John Holt, 9 January 1897, Bodl. RHL Mss Afr. S.1525, John Holt Papers Box 3.

57. Perham, *Lugard 1858–98*, p. 168.

58. The best account is now J. Forbes Munro, *Maritime Enterprise and Empire: Sir William Mackinnon and His Business Network 1823–1893* (Woodbridge, 2003).

59. C. P. Groves, *The Planting of Christianity in Africa*, 4 vols. (1948–58), vol. II, pp. 189–93. For Livingstone's impact in Britain, see chapter 1 above.

60. Bodl. RHL Mss Afr. 229, Rhodes Papers (Le Sueur): G. Portal to F. Rhodes, 23 May 1890.

61. Bodl. RHL Mss Afr. S.106, Gerald Portal Papers: Portal (Zanzibar) to Lord Salisbury, 15 August 1892; Mss Afr. S.113, Portal Papers, Salisbury to Portal, 11 September 1892.

62. Munro, *Maritime Enterprise*, p. 476.

63. See chapter 6 below.

64. R. Owen, *The Middle East and the World Economy 1830–1914* (1981), pp. 192–9.

65. See the views of the financier Ernest Cassel, in Kynaston, *Golden Years*, p. 513.

66. D. A. Farnie, *East and West of Suez: The Suez Canal in History* (Oxford, 1969).

67. See G. Baer, *A History of Landownership in Modern Egypt* (1962).

68. See J. I. Cole, *Colonialism and Revolution in the Middle East: Social and Cultural Origins of Egypt's 'Urabi Movement* (Cairo, 1999).

69. R. Owen, *Lord Cromer* (Oxford, 2004), chs. 10, 11.

70. Baer, *Landownership*, p. 67.

71. For this estimate, see Map 6, p. 118 above.

72. For the Egyptian economy, see Owen, *Middle East*, ch. 9.

73. J. Osterhammel, 'British Business in China, 1860s to 1950s', in R. P. T. Davenport and G. Jones (eds.), *British Business in Asia since 1860* (Cambridge, 1989).

74. I. Bird, *The Yangtse Valley and Beyond* (1899), pp. 64ff.

75. For French calculation along these lines, see M. Meuleau, *Des pionniers en extrême-orient: histoire de la Banque de l'Indochine 1875-1975* (Paris, 1990), p. 187.

76. Lo Hui-min (ed.), *The Correspondence of G. E. Morrison*, 2 vols. (Cambridge, 1976), vol. I, p. 22: Morrison to J. O. P. Bland, 17 January 1898.

77. R. A. Dayer, *Finance and Empire: Sir Charles Addis, 1861-1945* (1988), p. 37.

78. C.-K. Leung, *China: Railway Patterns and National Goals* (Hong Kong, 1986), Appendix 1.

79. University of Toronto, Thomas Fisher Rare Books Library, J. O. P. Bland Mss (Microfilm) reel 1: Bland to Burkhill, 13 April 1903 (I owe this to Robert Bickers).

80. F. H. H. King, *The Hong Kong Bank in the Period of Imperialism and War, 1875-1918* (Cambridge, 1988), pp. 345-6, 378, 404.

81. *Morrison Correspondence*, vol. I, p. 241: Morrison to Bland, 9 December 1903.

82. N. Pelcovits, *The Old China Hands and the Foreign Office* (New York, 1948), p. 270; L. K. Young, *British Policy in China 1895-1902* (Oxford, 1970), p. 170.

83. King, *Hong Kong Bank*, pp. 4–11.

84. *Ibid.*, p. 263.

85. R. A. Dayer, *Finance and Empire: Sir Charles Addis 1861–1945* (1988), p. 57.

86. J. O. P. Bland Mss, Reel 15, Addis to Bland, 28 March 1906. At this stage, Addis was the London manager of the Hong Kong Bank and in close touch with the Foreign Office.

87. King, *Hong Kong Bank*, p. 432.

88. For a contemporary lament along these lines, see J. O. P. Bland, *Recent Events and Present Policies in China* (1912).

89. Dayer, *Finance and Empire*, p. 63.

90. King, *Hong Kong Bank*, p. 517.

91. For the general setting, see L. Bethell (ed.), *Spanish America after Independence c.1820–c.1870* (Cambridge, 1987), chs, 1, 2; Tulio Halperin Dongi, *The Contemporary History of Latin America* (new edn, 1993), ch. 4, offers a brilliant survey.

92. See F. B. Pike, *Spanish America 1900–1970: Tradition and Social Innovation* (New York, 1973), pp. 15–18; J. Moya, *Cousins or Brothers: Spanish Immigration to Buenos Aires 1850–1930* (1998), pp. 50–1.

93. For this argument, see D. C. M. Platt, 'Dependency and the Historian: Further Objections', in C. Abel and C. M. Lewis (eds.), *Economic Imperialism and the Latin American State* (Cambridge, 1985), p. 36.

94. Mitchell, *Abstract*, pp. 322–23.

95. For this figure, see I. Stone, 'British Long-Term Investment in Latin America, 1865–1913', *Business History Review*, 42, 3 (1968), 311–39. In his *The Global Export of Capital from Britain 1865–1914* (Basingstoke, 1999), p. 351, the figure for 'capital called' (i.e. raised publicly on the Stock Exchange) is c.£800 million.

96. See D. C. M. Platt (ed.), *Business Imperialism: An Inquiry Based on British Experience in Latin America* (Oxford, 1977).

97. Bodl. Mss Bryce 267. This was Bryce's draft of his subsequent book on his Latin American travels.

98. See R. Graham, *Great Britain and the Onset of Modernisation in Brazil* (Cambridge, 1968), pp. 90–1.

99. See D. Joslin, *A Century of Banking in Latin America* (1963), pp. 39–42.

100. H. Blakemore, *British Nitrates and Chilean Politics, 1886–1896: Balmaceda and North* (1974).

101. For Pearson, see D. J. Jeremy (ed.), *Dictionary of Business Biography* 5 vols. (1984–6); G. Jones, 'Weetman Pearson', *Oxford Dictionary of National Biography*; F. Katz, *The Secret War in Mexico* (Chicago, 1981).

102. For the Bolivar Railway, see L. V. Dalton, *Venezuela* (1912), pp. 172, 255.

103. D. C. M. Platt, *Latin America and British Trade* (1972), p. 298.

104. See R. Miller, 'The Grace Contract: British Bondholders and the Peruvian Government, 1885–1890', *Journal of Latin American Studies* 8, 1(1976), 73–100.

105. M. Zeitlin, *The Civil Wars in Chile* (Princeton, 1984), p. 80.

106. P. R. Calvert, *The Mexican Revolution of 1910–1914: The Diplomacy of Anglo-American Conflict* (Cambridge, 1968), p. 20.

107. P. Winn, 'Britain's Informal Empire in Uruguay in the Nineteenth Century', *Past and Present*, 73 (1976), 112.

108. Platt, *British Trade*, p. 294.

109. Winn, 'Informal Empire', p. 112.

110. Graham, *Brazil*, p. 66.

111. Carlos F. Diaz Alejandro, *Essays in the Economic History of the Argentine Republic* (1970), ch. 1.

112. United States Department of Commerce, *Railways in South America*, 2 vols. (Washington DC, 1926), vol. I, p. 13.

113. Platt, *British Trade*, pp. 288–9.

114. Department of Commerce, *Railways*, vol. I, p. 35.

115. *Ibid.*, p. 60.

116. W. P. McGreevey, *An Economic History of Colombia 1845–1939* (Cambridge, 1971), p. 97.

117. Bodl. Mss Milner 2: Dawkins to Milner, 4 January 1892.

118. *Ibid.*: Dawkins to Milner, 30 July 1893.

119. Graham, *Brazil*, pp. 102–5.

120. Ferns, *Britain and Argentina*, pp. 446ff.; Kynaston, *Golden Years*, ch. 21.

121. Zeitlin, *Chile*, p. 99.

122. Mss Milner 2, Dawkins to Milner, 16 October 1893.

123. Ferns, *Britain and Argentina*, p. 468.

124. For the concept of 'structural power', see S. Strange, *States and Markets* (1988), ch. 2; A. G. Hopkins, 'Informal Empire in Argentina', *Journal of Latin American Studies*, 26 (1994), 469–84.

125. Zeitlin, *Chile*, p. 116.

126. Kynaston, *Golden Years*, p. 85.

127. Graham, *Brazil*, pp. 103–5; N. Ferguson, *The World's Banker: A History of the House of Rothschild* (1998), pp. 869–71.

128. Joslin, *A Century of Banking*, p. 111.

129. Bodl. Mss Milner 2, Dawkins to Milner, 4 January 1892.

130. Calculated from Sargent, *Seaways*.

131. *Ibid.*, p. 104. Eighty-five per cent of outward cargoes to Brazil were coal.

132. C. R. Enock, *The Republics of Central and South America* (1913), p. 497.

133. J. R. Scobie, *Argentina: A City and a Nation* (1971), p. 32.

134. Moya, *Cousins or Brothers*, p. 173.

135. M. Wilkins, *A History of Foreign Investment in the United States to 1914* (Cambridge, MA, 1989), p. 157.

136. Calvert, *Mexican Revolution*, p. 22: Minute by Sir Edward Grey, 23 August 1910.

137. Jones, 'Business Imperialism and Argentina', p. 440.

138. Moya, *Cousins or Brothers*, p. 364.

139. Enock, *Republics*, p. 497.

140. R. Bickers, 'Shanghailanders: The Formation and Identity of the British Settler Community in Shanghai, 1843–1937', *Past and Present*, 159, (1998), 179–80.

141. J. Barnes and D. Nicholson (eds.), *The Leo Amery Diaries*, Vol. I, *1896–1929* (1980), p. 47: L. S. Amery to Milner, 20 June 1903.

142. See T. O. Ranger, *Revolt in Southern Rhodesia 1896–97* (1967), chs. 2, 3; I. R. Phimister, *Wangi Kolia: Coal, Capital and Labour in Colonial Zimbabwe 1894–1954* (Johannesburg, 1994).

Chapter 4

1. See J. S. Martell, 'Intercolonial Communications, 1840–1867', in G. A. Rawlyk (ed.), *Historical Essays on the Atlantic Provinces* (Toronto, 1967), p. 177.

2. Earl Grey, *The Colonial Policy of Lord John Russell's Administration* [1853] (repr. New York, 1971), pp. 34–5.

3. See J. Mouat, 'Situating Vancouver Island in the British World, 1846–49', *BC Studies*, 145 (2005), 25.

4. Thus the powerful voice of the railway promoter Edward Watkin in 1861 proclaimed Canada's future as 'a great British nation . . . extending from the Atlantic to the Pacific'. A. A. Den Otter, *The Philosophy of Railways: The Transcontinental Railway Ideal in British North America* (Toronto, 1997), p. 113.

5. An idea most fully developed in J. A. Froude, *Oceana* (1887).

6. That it sold 80,000 copies in its first three years may be an indication of this. See J. Parry, *The Politics of Patriotism: English Liberalism, National Identity and Europe, 1830–1886* (Cambridge, 2006), p. 342.

7. There were several variants to describe Canada's links with Britain: this was the commonest.

8. Speech in Canadian Parliament, 8 February 1865, in P. B. Waite (ed.), *The Confederation Debates in the Province of Canada, 1865* (Toronto, 1963), p. 79.

9. See G. F. G. Stanley, *The Birth of Western Canada: A History of the Riel Rebellions* [1936] (Toronto, 1961).

10. See W. L. Morton, *Manitoba: A History* (Toronto, 1957).

11. See M. L. Hansen and J. B. Brebner, *The Mingling of the Canadian and American Peoples* (1940), vol. I, pp. 183–4.

12. See G. Stewart, *The Origins of Canadian Politics* (Vancouver, 1986). The classic study of Macdonald remains D. Creighton, *John A. Macdonald: The Young Politician* (Toronto, 1952) and D. Creighton, *John A. Macdonald: The Old Chieftain* (Toronto, 1955).

13. See R. W. Cox, 'The Quebec General Election of 1886' (Master's thesis, McGill University, 1948).

14. See P. Crunican, *Priests and Politicians: Manitoba Schools and the Election of 1896* (Toronto, 1974), pp. 310–16.

15. Goldwin Smith, *Canada and the Canadian Question* (1891).

16. O. A. Howland, *The New Empire: Reflections upon its Origins and Constitution and its Relation to the Great Republic* (Toronto, 1891).

17. Howland, *New Empire*, p. 363.

18. *Ibid.*, p. 360.

19. *Ibid.*, pp. 424, 513.

20. In a speech at Montreal in 1875. 'A British subject I hope to die' was his actual phrase. See Creighton, *John A. Macdonald: The Old Chieftain*, p. 206.

21. 'The example which he gave to the whole world shall live for ever', said Laurier on Gladstone's death in 1898. Speech in Canadian House of Commons, 26 May 1898, NAC, Mss Laurier (microfilm) C-1178.

22. Howland, *New Empire*, p. 363.

23. M. Evans, *Sir Oliver Mowat* (Toronto, 1992), pp. 201–2, 261ff.

24. See P. Currie, 'Toronto Orangeism and the Irish Question, 1911–1916', *Ontario History*, 87, 4 (1995), 397–409. The strength of Orangeism is referred to frequently in Laurier's political correspondence.

25. For Willison, see A. H. U. Colquhoun, *Press, Politics and People: The Life and Letters of Sir J. Willison* (Toronto, 1935).

26. D. J. Hall, *Clifford Sifton* (Toronto, 1981), vol. I, p. 95.

27. In 1901, 91 per cent of its population was of British origin; in 1911, 28 per cent were British born. M. Careless, *Toronto to 1918* (Toronto, 1984), pp. 158, 202.

28. C. Oreskovitch, *Sir Henry Pellatt: King of Casa Loma* (Toronto, 1982).

29. M. Bliss, *A Canadian Millionaire: The Life and Times of Sir Joseph Flavelle 1858–1939* (Toronto, 1978).

30. See Sir R. Falconer (president 1907–32) to Sir J. Flavelle, 23 October 1913, Colquhoun, *Willison*, p. 186.

31. See R. Fleming, *The Railway King of Canada: The Life of Sir William Mackenzie* (Vancouver, 1991).

32. Careless, *Toronto*, p. 150. For Walker's views on the role of the banks in making a 'national' economy, see his speech at Saratoga in 1895. University of Toronto, Thomas Fisher Rare Book Library, Mss B. M. Walker, Box 6.

33. Mss Walker Box 7, Glazebrook to Milner, 12 April 1906.

34. Mss Laurier C 769, Wilfrid Laurier to J. Cameron, 14 October 1899. Cameron was editor of the London *Advertiser* in Western Ontario.

35. Mss Laurier C 769, Cameron to Laurier, 12 October 1899.

36. NAC Mss Henri Bourassa (microfilm) M-722, Bourassa to Laurier, 18 October 1899.

37. *La Presse*, 14 October 1899, cited in D. Morton, 'Providing and Consuming Security in Canada's Century', *Canadian Historical Review*, 81, 1 (2000), 11.

38. Mss Bourassa M-721: N. A. Belcourt to Bourassa, 21 October 1899.

39. Mss Bourassa M-722: Laurier to Bourassa, 2 November 1899.

40. Some 7,000 Canadian volunteers served in the Boer War.

41. For the Quebec *nationaliste* alarm, see R. C. Brown and R. Cook, *Canada 1896–1921* (Toronto, 1974), pp. 136–9.

42. Mss Laurier C-1178, Speech 17 February 1890.

43. Colquhoun, *Willison*, pp. 131, 137, 148.

44. Brown and Cook, *Canada 1896–1921*, p. 168.

45. R. Cook, *The Politics of John W. Dafoe and the Free Press* (Toronto, 1963), p. 37.

46. See J. Levitt, *Henri Bourassa and the Golden Calf* (Ottawa, 1969), pp. 8–11, 64ff.

47. C. Murrow, *Henri Bourassa and French Canadian Nationalism* (Montreal, 1968).

48. Some 1.5 million immigrants arrived between 1900 and 1914.

49. P. F. Sharp, *The Agrarian Revolt in Western Canada* (Minneapolis, 1948), pp. 22–3, 25, 28.

50. Sharp, *Agrarian Revolt*, p. 75.

51. Mss Laurier C-899: Laurier to J. F. Clark, 5 February 1911.

52. For this view, NAC, MG 27 11 D 10 A: Mss F. D. Monk, vol. I, Bourassa to F. D. Monk, 28 February 1911.

53. Hall, *Clifford Sifton*, vol II, p. 229.

54. R. D. Cuff, 'The Toronto Eighteen and the Election of 1911', *Ontario History*, 57, 4 (1965), 169–80; for Lash's fierce criticism, Mss Laurier C 899, Lash to Laurier, 10 February 1911.

55. *Montreal Star*, 4 February 1911, Copy in Mss Laurier C 899.

56. NAC, Mss Clifford Sifton (microfilm) C 590, T. W. Crothers to C. Sifton, 25 September 1911.

57. Mss Walker Box 9, W. L. Grant to Walker, 15 November 1911.

58. Mss Walker Box 32, Address to Canadian Women's Club, Toronto, 7 March 1911.

59. Mss Sifton H-1014, Statement by Sifton, 22 September 1911.

60. Mss Laurier C 907, Laurier to Botha, 8 November 1911.

61. Mss Laurier C 907, Botha to Laurier, 29 September 1911.

62. On which Carl Berger's classic study concentrates. See C. Berger, *The Sense of Power: Studies in Canadian Imperialism* (Toronto, 1970).

63. E. Shann, *An Economic History of Australia* (Cambridge, 1930), p. 234. Shann was a free trader of conservative outlook.

64. N. G. Butlin, *Investment in Australian Economic Development 1861–1900* (Cambridge, 1964), p. 9.

65. T. A. Coghlan, *Labour and Industry in Australia* (Oxford, 1918), vol. IV, p. 1234.

66. Ross Fitzgerald, *A History of Queensland from the Dreaming to 1915* (paperback edn, St Lucia, 1986), p. 179.

67. G. Blainey, *The Rush that Never Ended* (paperback edn, Carlton, Vic., 1969), chs. 14, 20.

68. See G. Davison, *Marvellous Melbourne* (Melbourne, 1978).

69. G. Blainey, *The Tyranny of Distance* (paperback edn, South Melbourne, 1966), p. 259.

70. Coghlan, *Labour and Industry*, vol. IV, p. 2317.

71. Blainey, *Tyranny*, p. 279.

72. Just 3 per cent of inter-continental migrants in 1815–1920 were attracted to Australia and New Zealand. B. Dyster and D. Meredith, *Australia in the International Economy in the Twentieth Century* (Cambridge, 1990), p. 20.

73. Butlin, *Investment*, p. 6.

74. See J. W. McCarty, 'Australian Regional History', *Historical Studies*, 18, 70 (1978), 88–105.

75. P. Loveday and A. W. Martin, *Parliament, Faction and Party 1859–1889* (Melbourne, 1966), pp. 152–3.

76. Coghlan, *Labour and Industry*, vol. III, p. 1649.

77. K. Buckley and T. Wheelwright, *No Paradise for Workers* (Melbourne, 1988), p. 196.

78. Fitzgerald, *Queensland*, p. 319; M. McKenna, *The Captive Republic: A History of Republicanism in Australia 1788–1996* (Cambridge, 1996), pp. 178–9.

79. Fitzgerald, *Queensland*, p. 317.

80. Buckley and Wheelwright, *No Paradise*, pp. 137–8.

81. Buckley and Wheelwright, *No Paradise*, p. 196; R. Markey, *The Making of the Labor Party in New South Wales* (Kensington, NSW, 1988).

82. F. K. Crowley (ed.), *A New History of Australia* (Melbourne, 1974), pp. 240–1; Buckley and Wheelwright, *No Paradise*, p. 214; P. Grimshaw *et al.* (eds.), *Creating a Nation 1788–1990* (Melbourne, 1994), p. 188.

83. McKenna, *Republic*, p. 153; Markey, *Labor Party*, pp. 296, 304–5.

84. Coghlan, *Labour and Industry*, vol. IV, p. 2318.

85. Howland, *New Empire*, p. 363.

86. For Australian sub-imperialism, see R. C. Thompson, *Australian Imperialism in the South Pacific* (Melbourne, 1980).

87. See memo for prime minister Deakin, 6 March 1907: 'Uninterrupted sea communications is a *sine qua non* for Australia... Australia, whenever her coasts are closed, must "stop work".' N. Meany (ed.), *Australia and the World* (Melbourne, 1985), p. 165.

88. C. E. Lyne, *The Life of Sir Henry Parkes* (London, 1987), p. 492.

89. *Ibid.*, p. 495.

90. *Ibid.*, p. 494. For Parkes' equation of federation and imperial unity, see his speech at the Australasian federation conference at Melbourne in 1890, in C. M. H. Clark (ed.), *Select Documents in Australian History 1851–1900* [1955] (paperback edn, London, 1977), pp. 475–6.

91. It was a time, remarked the Melbourne *Age*, for 'large aggregations'. H. Irving, *To Constitute a Nation: A Cultural History of Australia's Constitution* (Cambridge, 1997), p. 29.

92. L. Trainor, *British Imperialism and Australian Nationalism: Manipulation, Conflict and Compromise in the Late Nineteenth Century* (Cambridge, 1994), p. 141 n.45. Deakin became the leading political figure in Victoria; Barton was influential in New South Wales. Both were to be federal prime ministers.

93. Irving, *Nation*, pp. 64ff.

94. *Ibid.*, pp. 204–5.

95. *Ibid.*, p. 160. Kingston was premier of South Australia.

96. Trainor, *British Imperialism*, p. 158.

97. See W. G. Osmond, *Frederic Eggleston: An Intellectual in Australian Politics* (Sydney, 1985), p. 53, for Deakin's hopes for an educated, professional elite. Acording to C. M. H. Clark in *A History of Australia*, vol. V, *1888–1915* (Melbourne, 1981), p. 293, Deakin was an Anglican who thought that empire stood between Australia and revolution. In fact, by contemporary British standards, Deakin was a radical who found Charles Dilke the most sympathetic of British politicians.

98. For Labor suspicions, see Clark, *Select Documents*, p. 494.

99. G. Davison, 'Sydney and the Bush: An Urban Context for the Australian Legend', *Historical Studies*, 18, 71 (1978), 191–209.

100. The Sydney *Bulletin* was established in 1880 as a weekly, and achieved a circulation of 80,000 by 1890. Apart from its racial-radical-republican politics, it made a point of publishing the work of local writers. Its editor from 1886 to 1902 was the republican J. F. Archibald. See G. Serle, *From Deserts the Prophets Came: the Creative Spirit in Australia 1788–1972* (Melbourne, 1973), pp. 60–1.

101. Irving, *Nation*, p. 132.

102. For the link between racism and egalitarianism, see Terry Irving, 'Labour, State and Nation-building in Australia', in S. Berger and A. Smith (eds.), *Nationalism, Labour and Ethnicity 1870–1939* (Manchester, 1999), p. 214.

103. C. N. Connolly, 'Class, Birthplace, Loyalty: Australian Attitudes to the Boer War', *Historical Studies*, 18, 71 (1978), 221.

104. See, for example, the opinions of J. F. Archibald and Rolf Boldrewood in I. Turner (ed.), *The Australian Dream* (Melbourne, 1968), pp. 270, 142.

105. For the panic over a declining birth-rate, which led to the appointment of a Royal Commission, see C. L. Bacchi, 'The Nature-Nurture Debate in Australia 1900–1914', *Historical Studies*, 19, 75 (1980), 200.

106. Connolly, 'Class, Birthplace, Loyalty', pp. 213–17.

107. From Deakin (see J. A. La Nauze, *Alfred Deakin* (Melbourne, 1965), vol. II, p. 482) to the *Bulletin* (Meany (ed.), *Australia*, p. 145).

108. See chapter 7.

109. Australia, it was remarked in the Colonial Office, was 'ill-qualified to deal with native questions'. Meany (ed.), *Australia*, pp. 192ff.

110. For the angry reaction of the (London-based) Australian Mercantile Land and Finance Company (employing a capital of around £2.3 million) to the absentee land tax imposed by the Labor

government in 1910, see J. D. Bailey, *A Hundred Years of Pastoral Banking* (Oxford, 1966), p. 200.

111. L. V. Harcourt (Secretary of State for the Colonies) to Sir A. Bigge, 28 December 1910. Bodleian Library, Mss L. V. Harcourt 462. Sir Arthur replied that Fisher could attend the coronation in ordinary dress but would have to wear court dress at any court function.

112. New Zealand's population in 1854 was 33,000; in 1864, 172,000; in 1871, 267,000; in 1878, 471,000; in 1891, 624,000; in 1911, 1,006,000.

113. The classic account is Andrew Hill Clark, *The Invasion of New Zealand by People, Plants and Animals* [1949] (Westport, 1970).

114. See K. Sinclair, *A Destiny Apart* (Auckland, 1987), p. 108.

115. William Pember Reeves, *The Long White Cloud: Ao Tea Roa* (London, 1898), p. 5. This was the most widely read and influential history of New Zealand until the 1950s. See E. Olssen, 'Where to from Here?', *New Zealand Historical Journal*, 26, 1(1992), 57.

116. See F. E. Maning, *Old New Zealand: A Tale of the Good Old Times* (1863). For a modern use of the term, see J. Belich, *Making Peoples: A History of the New Zealanders* (London, 1996), pp. 187ff.

117. See P. Burns, *Fatal Success: A History of the New Zealand Company* (Auckland, 1989); P. Adams, *Fatal Necessity: British Intervention in New Zealand 1830–1847* (Auckland, 1977).

118. What the Maori chiefs thought they had agreed to has become the central controversy in the history of colonial New Zealand. See Claudia Orange, *The Treaty of Waitangi* (Auckland, 1987).

119. See M. Mackinnon (ed.), *New Zealand Historical Atlas* (Auckland, 1997), Plate 12, for the probable extent of grassland in 1840.

120. For the growth (and later decline) of a Maori trading and agricultural economy near Auckland, see P. Monin, 'The Maori Economy of Hauraki 1840–1880', *New Zealand Journal of History*, 29, 2 (1995), 197–210.

121. K. Sinclair, *The Origins of the Maori Wars* (Wellington, 1957), pp. 75ff.

122. Sinclair, *Origins*, pp. 239–42. For the eagerness in the Colonial Office to avoid becoming New Zealand's 'tributary', see E. Cardwell to Governor Sir G. Grey, 26 September 1864, in F. Madden (ed.), *Select Documents*, vol. IV, *Settler Self-Government 1840–1900* (Westport, 1990), pp. 510–11.

123. J. Belich, *The New Zealand Wars* (Penguin edn, 1988), p. 309.

124. *Ibid.*, p. 310.

125. J. McAloon, 'The Colonial Wealthy in Canterbury and Otago: No Idle Rich', *New Zealand Journal of History*, 30, 1 (1996), 58–60.

126. A large wooden panel showing the dense network of coastal routes established by the USC can be seen in the Museum of Transport in Dunedin.

127. M. D. N. Campbell, 'The Evolution of Hawke's Bay Landed Society 1850–1914' (PhD thesis, Victoria University Wellington, 1972), pp. 57ff., 373; R. Arnold, *New Zealand's Burning: The Settler World of the 1880s* (Wellington, 1994), p. 30.

128. See G. H. Scholefield (ed.), *The Richmond-Atkinson Papers* (Auckland, 1960).

129. Arnold, *New Zealand's Burning*, pp. 117ff.

130. For example, the Manawatu round Palmerson North (see D. A. Hamer, 'Wellington on the Urban Frontier', in D. A. Hamer and R. Nicholls (eds.), *The Making of Wellington 1800–1914* (Wellington, 1990), pp. 247–52) and the 'Seventy Mile Bush' in Hawke's Bay.

131. Arnold, *New Zealand's Burning*, pp. 133–4, 138. R. J. C. Stone, *Makers of Fortune: A Colonial Business Community and its Fall* (Auckland, 1973); R. J. C. Stone, *The Father and His Gifts* (Auckland, 1987).

132. See R. Dalziel, *Julius Vogel: Business Politician* (Auckland, 1986).

133. *Ibid.*, p. 81.

134. Railway mileage stood at 50 in 1870 but had reached 1,613 by 1886.

135. Dalziel, *Vogel*, p. 179.

136. *Ibid.*, p. 190.

137. W. H. Oliver and B. R. Williams (eds.), *The Oxford History of New Zealand* (Oxford, 1981), pp. 210ff.

138. For Reeves' political career, see K. Sinclair, *Willliam Pember Reeves* (Oxford, 1965).

139. Tom Brooking, *'Lands for the People'?* (Dunedin, 1996), pp. 131–41.

140. K. Sinclair, *A History of New Zealand* (Harmondsworth, 1959) (since its publication, the most influential single-volume history).

141. See W. H. Oliver, 'Reeves, Sinclair and the Social Pattern', in P. Munz, *The Feel of Truth* (Wellington, 1969), pp. 163–78.

142. Oliver, 'Social Pattern', p. 170.

143. Cf. Sinclair, *New Zealand*, pp. 185, 296.

144. See E. Olssen, 'Towards a New Society', in Oliver and Williams (eds.), *Oxford History*. W. H. Oliver, 'Social Welfare: Social Justice or Social Efficiency', *New Zealand Journal of History*, 13, 1 (1979), 25–33.

145. A phrase attributed to Seddon.

146. See J. Stenhouse and B. Moloughney, '"Drug-Besotted Sin-Begotten Sons of Filth": New Zealanders and the Oriental Other', *New Zealand Journal of History*, 33, 1 (1999), 43–64.

147. C. G. F. Simkin, *The Instability of a Dependent Economy: Economic Fluctuations in New Zealand 1840–1914* (Oxford, 1951), p. 174. In 1911, wool exports were worth £6.5 million; and meat, butter and cheese exports £6.3 million.

148. Simpkin, *Instability*, p. 175.

149. See M. King, *Frank Sargeson: A Life* (Auckland, 1995), ch. 7. The classic account in fiction is J. Mulgan, *Man Alone* (1939).

150. M. Fairburn, 'The Rural Myth and the New Urban Frontier: An Approach to New Zealand Social History', *New Zealand Journal of History*, 9, 1 (1975), 3–21.

151. Reeves, *Long White Cloud*, p. 407.

152. For the persistence of this outlook up to 1940, see C. Hilliard, 'Stories of Becoming: The Centennial Surveys and the Colonization of New Zealand', *New Zealand Journal of History*, 33, 1 (1999), 4.

153. Dalziel, *Vogel*, p. 276.

154. D. K. Fieldhouse, 'New Zealand, Fiji and the Colonial Office 1900–1902', *Historical Studies*, 8, 30 (1958), 114.

155. R. J. Burdon, *King Dick* (London and Wellington, 1955), p. 211.

156. *New Zealand Parliamentary Debates*, vol. 110, pp. 75–6 (28 October 1899).

157. *Ibid.* p. 77.

158. Brooking, *'Lands for the people'?*, p. 217; Madden, *Select Documents*, vol. V, *The Dominions and India since 1900* (Westport, 1993), pp. 16–17.

159. Though some MPs resisted the idea of a military contribution to the Boer War. See *New Zealand Parliamentary Debates*, vol. 110, p. 82 (Carson, Taylor).

160. Any differences with the Crown since 1840, remarked Honi Heke, MP for the Northern Maori, 'have not interfered with our duty to the Crown': *New Zealand Parliamentary Debates*, vol. 110, 28 October 1899.

161. For important statements of this, see P. A. Buckner, 'Whatever Happened to the British Empire', *Journal of the Canadian Historical Association*, 4 (1993), 1–31; P. A. Buckner and C. Bridge, 'Reinventing the British World', *The Round Table*, 368 (2003), 77–88; C. Bridge and K. Fedorowich, 'Mapping the British World', in C. Bridge and K. Fedorowich (eds.), *The British World: Diaspora, Culture and Identity* (2003), pp. 1–15.

162. J. R. Seeley, *The Expansion of England* (1883), p. 75.

163. For Seeley's opposition to Irish Home Rule, see J. Roach, 'Liberalism and the Victorian Intelligentsia', *Historical Journal* (1957), 58–81.

164. See A. Jones and B. Jones, 'The Welsh World and the British Empire c.1851–1939: An Exploration', in Bridge and Fedorowich (eds.), *The British World*, pp. 57–81.

165. See D. MacKay, *The Square Mile: Merchant Princes of Montreal* (Vancouver, 1987).

166. K. Fedorowich, 'The British Empire on the Move, 1760–1914', in S. Stockwell (ed.), *The British Empire: Themes and Perspectives* (Oxford, 2008), p. 85.

167. See B. S. Elliott, 'Emigration from South Leinster to Eastern Upper Canada', in D. H. Akenson (ed.), *Canadian Papers in Rural History*, vol. VIII (Gananoque, Ontario, 1992), pp. 277–306.

168. Fedorowich, 'British Empire on the Move', p. 83.

169. For D'Arcy McGee, see *Dictionary of Canadian Biography* (online version); for Gavan Duffy and Coghlan, see *Oxford Dictionary of National Biography*.

Chapter 5

1. Indian exports were worth Rupees 329 million (1860) and Rs 2,490 million (1913). D. Kumar (ed.), *Cambridge Economic History of India* (Cambridge, 1982), vol. II, pp. 833–4, 837

2. S. B. Saul, *Studies in British Overseas Trade* (Liverpool, 1960), p. 62.

3. Railway mileage in India: 20 (1853), 4,771 (1870), 15,842 (1890), 23,627 (1900). See I. J. Kerr, *Building the Railways of the Raj 1850–1900* (Delhi, 1997), pp. 211–12.

4. PP LVIII, 847 (1900): East India (*Return of Wars and Military Operations Wars on or beyond the Borders of British India*), pp. 2–15; *ibid.* (1908), p. 1.

5. See M. Adas, *The Burma Delta* (Madison, 1971).

6. See Claude Markovits, 'Indian Merchant Networks', *Modern Asian Studies*, 33, 4 (1999), 883–911 at 892.

7. C. Markovits, 'Indian Communities in China', in R. Bickers and C. Henriot (eds.), *New Frontiers: Imperialism's New Communities in East Asia, 1842–1953* (Manchester, 2000), pp. 55–74.

8. W. S. Churchill, *My African Journey* (1908), ch. 3, for Churchill's opinions.

9. PP 1893–4, LXV, 16, *Report of Committee on Indian Currency*.

10. *Cambridge Economic History of India*, vol. II, p. 940.

11. B. R. Tomlinson, *The Political Economy of the Raj 1914–1949* (1949), p. 19.

12. Cd. 131 (1900), *Report of the Royal Commission on the Administration of the Expenditure of India* (the 'Welby Report'), vol. I, p. 79.

13. Lord Curzon, *Speeches in India* (Calcutta, 1900), vol. I, p. xiii.

14. *Ibid.*, p. xi.

15. Salisbury to Sir Henry Northcote (Bombay), 8 June 1900. R. L. Greaves, *Persia and the Defence of India 1884–1892* (1959), p. 16.

16. Consulates paid for by the Indian government were set up at Mohammerah (1890), Kerman (1895), Seistan (1899), Shiraz (1903), Bandar Abbas (1904) and the Makran (1905).

17. Despatch from GoI to Secretary of State for India, 2 November 1892. PP 1893–4 LXIII, *Further Papers Respecting Proposed Changes in the Indian Army System*, C. 6987 (1893), pp. 5–9.

18. Welby Report, pp. 126–7.

19. Lord Rosebery had insisted on this in 1895. Welby Report, vol. I, p. 116.

20. Lord George Hamilton to Elgin, 12 August 1897. P. L. Malhotra, *The Administration of Lord Elgin in India* (New Delhi, 1979), p. 159.

21. The number of letters and postcards exchanged between Britain and India, reported the Islington Commission, rose from 8.5 million in

1901–2 to 27 million in 1911–12: *Report of Royal Commission on Public Services in India*, Cd 8382 (1917), p. 12.

22. See T. Raychaudhuri, *Europe Reconsidered* (Delhi, 1988), especially the essay on Bhudev Mukhopadhyay.

23. J. B. Fuller, *The Empire of India* (1913), p. 275. Fuller's figure is 687.

24. B. Cohn, 'The Census, Social Structure and Objectification in South Asia', in his *An Anthropologist among the Historians* (Delhi, 1987).

25. See E. Gellner, *Nations and Nationalism* (1983).

26. As an embattled Indian Secretary complained: Viscount Morley, *Recollections* (1914), vol. II, pp. 211, 256.

27. For this evolution, see E. Stokes, *The English Utilitarians and India* (1959), Part IV, ch. 3; J. Roach, 'Liberalism and the Victorian Intelligentsia', *Cambridge Historical Journal*, 13, 1 (1957), 58–81.

28. A term only applied much later to 'Eurasians' of mixed Indian and European parentage.

29. 3rd edn (1894). Chesney had been Secretary in the military department of the Indian government, and a member of the Viceroy's Council. He was MP for Oxford 1892–5.

30. *Indian Polity*, p. 389.

31. *Ibid.*, p. 390.

32. Hunter to A. P. Watt, 10 June 1897. F. H. Skrine, *The Life of Sir William Wilson Hunter* (1901), p. 468.

33. W. W. Hunter, *History of British India* (1899), vol. I, introduction.

34. Welby Report vol. I, p. 111.

35. Speech in House of Common, 8 August. F. Madden and D. K. Fieldhouse (eds.), *The Dependent Empire and Ireland: Select Documents in the Constitutional History of the British Empire and Commonwealth*, vol. V (Westport, CT, 1991), p. 114.

36. For Lord Salisbury's view, Madden, *Select Documents*, vol. V, p. 99, n. 1.

37. It was likely to alienate the Raj's closest Indian allies.

38. H. H. Risley, *The People of India* [1908] (2nd edn, 1915), p. 283 (Risley was the Indian government's census expert).

39. A. Seal, *The Emergence of Indian Nationalism* (Cambridge, 1968), pp. 246ff.

40. Bengal District Administration Report (1913), cited in J. H. Broomfield, *Mostly about Bengal* (New Delhi, 1982), p. 4.

41. See T. Raychaudhuri, *Europe Reconsidered* (New Delhi, 1988).

42. R. C. Palit (ed.), *Speeches by Babu Surendra Nath Banerjea 1876–1880* (Calcutta, 1891), vol. I, p. 8.

43. Palit, *Speeches*, vol. I, p. 223.

44. Palit, *Speeches* (Calcutta, 1894), vol. II, p. 60 (14 January 1884).

45. *Ibid.*, vol, I, p. 119.

46. J. R. B. Jeejeebhoy (ed.), *Some Unpublished and Later Speeches of Sir Pherozeshah Mehta* (Bombay, 1918), p. 30.

47. B. R. Nanda, *Gokhale* (New Delhi, 1977), p. 125.

48. *Ibid.*, pp. 22ff.

49. 'An Appreciation by Babu Aurobindo Ghose', in *The Writings and Speeches of B. G. Tilak* (Madras, 1919), p. 6.

50. R. I. Cashman, *The Myth of the Lokmanya* (Berkeley, 1975), pp. 54–6.

51. Described cautiously by Gandhi as a 'misguided patriot', and later by J. Nehru as a 'predatory adventurer'. Cashman, *The Lokmanya*, pp. 121–2.

52. I have adopted this term from Irish history. See E. Curtis, *A History of Ireland* (1936), ch. 10.

53. See chapter 2 above.

54. Seal, *Indian Nationalism*, p. 179.

55. Palit (ed.), *Speeches* (Calcutta, 1896). vol. V.

56. *Ibid.*

57. Macdonnell to (Viceroy) Elgin, 16 July 1897. Bodl. Mss Eng. Hist. c.353.

58. Chesney, *Indian Polity*, p. 385.

59. Skrine, *Hunter*, p. 388.

60. See D. Rothermund, 'Emancipation or Reintegration: The Politics of Gopal Krishna Gokhale and Herbert Hope Risley', in D. A. Low (ed.), *Soundings in Modern South Asian History* (1968), pp. 131–58.

61. See Imran Ali, *The Punjab under Imperialism 1885–1947* (Princeton, 1988).

62. D. Gilmartin, *Empire and Islam: Punjab and the Making of Pakistan* (1988), pp. 13–24; P. M. H. van den Dungen, *The Punjab Tradition* (1972).

63. G. Johnson, *Provincial Politics and Indian Nationalism* (Cambridge, 1973), p. 64.

64. See Macdonnell to Elgin, 16 July 1897, Bodl. Mss Eng. Hist. c.353: the question was whether recent unrest amounted to 'a general movement of the country against us'.

65. D. Dilks, *Curzon in India* (1969), vol. I, pp. 64–5.

66. S. Gopal, *British Policy in India 1858–1905* (Cambridge, 1965), p. 255.

67. Lord Ronaldshay, *The Life of Lord Curzon* (1928) vol. II, p. 89.

68. Thomas R. Metcalf, *Ideologies of the Raj* (Cambridge, 1995), pp. 151ff.

69. For a summary, see *Report of Calcutta University Commission* (1919), vol. I, pp. 65ff.

70. Risley to Curzon, 7 February 1904, D. Banerjee, *Aspects of Administration in Bengal 1898–1912* (New Delhi, 1980), p. 61.

71. Curzon to Secretary of State for India, 17 February 1904. Banerjee, *Aspects*, p. 61.

72. Curzon to Secretary of State for India, 2 February 1905, F. Madden and J. Darwin (eds.). *The Dominions and India since 1900: Select Documents in the Constitutional History of the British Empire and Commonwealth* (Westport, CT, 1993), pp. 660–1.

73. R. Guha, 'Discipline and Mobilize', in P. Chatterjee and G. Pandey (eds.), *Subaltern Studies* (1992), vol. VII, pp. 76–90. Even Banerjea urged social boycott to coerce backsliders.

74. Curzon to Selborne, 21 May 1903. Bodl. Mss Selborne 10: 'I spoke on behalf of a unanimous Cabinet of my own with a constituency of 300 millions behind.'

75. Curzon, *India's Place in the Empire* (1909), esp. pp. 7–9.

76. 'Strong currents of democratic feeling [are] running breast high in the House of Commons'. J. Morley, *Recollections* (1913) vol. I, p. 171.

77. Arthur Hirtzel's diary. S. Wolpert, *Morley and India 1906–1910* (Berkeley, 1967), p. 43.

78. Morley to Minto, 15 June 1906. Morley, *Recollections*, vol. I, p. 174.

79. B. R. Nanda, *Gokhale* (Delhi, 1977), p. 249. 'Mere animal gathering in India', said Tilak, 'would be of no avail'.

80. Morley to Minto, 2 August 1906. Morley, *Recollections*, vol. I, p. 181.

81. *Ibid.*

82. For the Arundel Committee report, 12 October 1906, Morley Collection, BLIOC, Ms Eur. D 573/32.

83. The Government of India's 'reforms despatch', 21 March 1907, is printed in *ibid*.

84. *Ibid.*

85. See his speech at Calcutta, 2 January 1907, 'Tenets of a New Party'. *Writings and Speeches*, pp. 56–65.

86. *Ibid.*

87. R. K. Ray, *Social Conflict and Political Unrest in Bengal 1875–1927* (Delhi, 1984), pp. 154ff; Guha, 'Discipline and Mobilize', pp. 76–90.

88. See P. Heehs, *The Bomb in Bengal* (Delhi, 1993).

89. Motilal Nehru to Jawaharlal Nehru, 17 May 1907. R. Kumar and D. N. Panigrahi (eds.), *Selected Works of Motilal Nehru* (Delhi, 1982), vol. I, pp. 124–5.

90. Motilal Nehru to Jawaharlal Nehru, 23 April 1908, *Selected Works*, vol. I, p. 137.

91. Nanda, *Gokhale*, p. 311.

92. Morley to Minto, 17 June 1908. Nanda, *Gokhale*, p. 297.

93. A. P. Kaminsky, *The India Office 1880–1910* (1986), p. 145.

94. *Ibid.*, p. 144.

95. Wolpert, *Morley*, p. 191.

96. Minto to Lansdowne, 18 March 1909. Nanda, *Gokhale*, p. 318.

97. For the electoral system, see Banerjee, *Aspects*, p. 129. For Congress and the elections of 1912–13, see Broomfield, *Mostly about Bengal*, pp. 55–78.

98. Motilal Nehru to Jawaharlal Nehru, 30 August 1909, *Selected Works*, vol. I, p. 17.

99. Motilal Nehru to Jawaharlal Nehru, 29 April 1910, *Selected Works*, vol. I, p. 145.

100. For the 1910 Press Act, see N. Barrier, *Banned!* (Columbia, MO, 1974).

101. *Summary of the Administration of the Earl of Minto in the Home Department 1905–1910* (Simla, 1910), p. 19.

102. R. Popplewell, *Intelligence and Imperial Defence: British Intelligence and the Defence of the Indian Empire 1907–1924* (1993), pp. 51ff. For a sceptical view of its value, See R. Chandavarkar, *Imperial Power and Popular Politics* (Cambridge, 1998), pp. 208–9.

103. Sir R. Craddock to Sir J. Meston, 5 January 1913, BLIOC Mss Eur. F 136/3.

104. C. A. Bayly, *The Local Roots of Indian Politics* (Oxford, 1975), pp. 199–200.

105. For Minto's 'non-interference' speech at Udaipur, 3 November 1909, see Madden and Darwin, *Select Documents*, vol. VI, pp. 801–2.

106. Hardinge to Crewe, 25 August 1911 (the 'Delhi Despatch'). C. P. Ilbert, *The Government of India* (3rd edn, Oxford, 1916), Appendix III.

107. PP 1908 XLIV, *Report of the Royal Commission on Decentralisation in India*, vol. I, pp. 301ff. For Meston's views, see *Report*, vol. X, pp. 820–7.

108. See Delhi Despatch, Ilbert, *India*, Appendix III.

109. V. S. Srinivasa Sastri, *Speeches and Writings* (Madras, n.d.), p. 4.

110. President's speech, Bankipore, 1912. *Congress Presidential Addresses*, Second series (Madras, 1934), p. 67.

111. *Ibid.*

112. President's speech, Karachi, 1913. *Presidential Addresses*, p. 151.

113. *Ibid.*, p. 152.

114. President's speech, 1914. *Presidential Addresses*, p. 171.

115. 'The Two Empires', *The Times*, 24 May 1911. *India and the Durbar: A Reprint of the Indian Articles in the 'Empire Day' Edition of The Times* (1911), pp. 2–3.

116. Speech by Lord Hardinge in the Indian Legislative Council, 17 September 1913. *Speeches of Lord Hardinge of Penshurst 1913–1916* (Madras, n.d.), p. 16.

117. *Ibid.*, pp. 20–1.

118. *Presidential Addresses*, pp. 58–9.

119. Motilal Nehru, evidence to Royal Commission on Public Services in India, Lucknow, 4 April 1913. *Selected Works*, vol. I, p. 256.

120. *Ibid.*, p. 258.

121. See J. Zavos, *The Emergence of Hindu Nationalism in India* (New Delhi, 2000), chs. 3, 4.

122. 'Muhammadans are drifting... into the arena of political warfare', said Fazl Huq in April 1913. Broomfield, *Mostly about Bengal*, p. 93.

123. J. Pouchepadass, *Champaran and Gandhi* (New Delhi, 1999), ch. 6.

124. *Report of Calcutta University Commission*, vol. I, p. 27.

125. For the rising ambitions of 'rural-local bosses', see D. A. Washbrook, *The Emergence of Provincial Politics* (Cambridge, 1976), pp. 82ff.

Chapter 6

1. For a general account, see P. J. Van der Merwe, *Die Trekboer in die Geskiedenis van die Kaap*, trans. R. Beck (Ohio, 1995). An outstanding recent study is N. Penn, *The Forgotten Frontier* (Cape Town, 2005). The most brilliant introduction to South African history remains C. W. De Kiewiet, *History of South Africa: Social and Economic* (1941).

2. J. S. Marais, *Maynier and the First Boer Republic* (Cape Town, 1944), pp. 78–9.

3. See C. Hamilton (ed.), *The Mfecane Aftermath* (Johannesburg, 1995); J. Laband, *Rope of Sand* (Johannesburg, 1995), pp. 13–15; N. Etherington, *The Great Treks* (2001).

4. M. Legassick, 'The Northern Frontier to 1840', in R. Elphick and H. Giliomee (eds.), *The Shaping of South African Society 1652–1840* (2nd edn, 1989), pp. 390–6.

5. Sir P. Maitland to Lord Stanley, 1 August 1845, G. M. Theal (ed.), *Basutoland Records* [1883] (repr. Cape Town, 1964), vol. I, pp. 93–100.

6. Sir H. Smith to Earl Grey, 3 February 1848, *ibid.*, vol. I, p. 165.

7. Minute by Earl Grey, June 1848, K. N. Bell and W. B. Morrell (eds.), *Select Documents on British Colonial Policy 1830–1860* (Oxford, 1928), pp. 510–11.

8. For the conflict between the British and the Xhosa, see J. T. Peires, *The Dead Shall Arise: Nonqawuse and the Great Xhosa Cattle-Killing Movement of 1856–7* (1989); C. Bundy, *The Rise and Fall of the South African Peasantry* (2nd edn, 1988), ch. 2; J. Rutherford, *Sir George Grey 1812–1898: A Study in Colonial Government* (1961), chs. 20–9.

9. S. Trapido, 'Reflections on Land, Office and Wealth in the South African Republic, 1850–1900', in S. Marks and A. Atmore (eds.), *Economy and Society in Pre-industrial South Africa* (1980), pp. 350–9.

10. The Transvaal was barely a state before 1880: see J. A. I. Agar-Hamilton, *The Native Policy of the Voortrekkers* (Cape Town, 1928), p. 205.

11. C. J. Uys, *In the Era of Shepstone* (Lovedale, 1933), p. 77; C. W. De Kiewiet, *The Imperial Factor in South Africa* (1937), p. 29.

12. J. Benyon, *Proconsul and Paramountcy in South Africa 1806–1910* (Pietermaritzburg, 1980), pp. 144–5.

13. Uys, *Shepstone*, chs. 11, 12.

14. P. Delius, *The Land Belongs to Us* (Johannesburg, 1983), pp. 244–5.

15. D. M. Schreuder, *Gladstone and Kruger* (1969), pp. 164–5.

16. For the absorption of the Xhosa lands into Cape Colony, see C. C. Saunders and R. Derricourt, *Beyond the Cape Frontier* (1974).

17. For the Convention's terms, see Schreuder, *Gladstone and Kruger*, Appendix I.

18. *Ibid.*, p. 323.

19. *Ibid.*, ch. 6.

20. *Ibid.*, p. 422.

21. M. H. De Kock, *Economic History of South Africa* (Cape Town, 1924), pp. 242, 392, 398.

22. For Rhodes' career, see R. Rotberg, *The Founder: Cecil Rhodes and the Pursuit of Power* (Oxford, 1989).

23. H. Giliomee, 'The Beginnings of Afrikaner Nationalism 1870–1915', *South African Historical Journal*, 19 (1987); T. R. M. Davenport, *The Afrikaner Bond 1880–1911* (1966).

24. For Rhodes' sometimes fraught relations with Nathan Rothschild, his main backer in London, see N. Ferguson, *The World's Banker: The History of the House of Rothschild* (1998), pp. 881–94.

25. See C. W. Newbury, *The Diamond Ring* (Oxford, 1989).

26. J. S. Galbraith, *Crown and Charter: The Early History of the British South Africa Company* (Berkeley, 1974), chs. 2, 3, 4.

27. W. D. Mackenzie, *John Mackenzie: South African Missionary and Statesman* (1902), pp. 432–5.

28. *Ibid.*, p. 433.

29. 'As a purely Cape politician', Milner remarked of Rhodes in 1889, 'he was (is perhaps) Africander. As the author of enterprises that look far beyond the Cape and the Transvaal and reach to the Zambesi, and beyond the Zambesi, he must know (he is much too shrewd not to know) that without Imperial backing he is lost.' Mackenzie, *John Mackenzie*, pp. 433–4.

30. See M. Tamarkin, *Cecil Rhodes and the Cape Afrikaners* (1996).

31. See I. R. Phimister, 'Rhodes, Rhodesia and the Rand', *Journal of Southern African Studies*, 1,1 (1974), 74–90.

32. For Fitzpatrick's insistence on this as Rhodes' motive, see Fitzpatrick to his wife, 10 January 1896, A. H. Duminy and W. R. Guest (eds.), *Fitzpatrick, South African Politician: Selected Papers* (Johannesburg, 1976), pp. 29ff.; National English Literary Museum, Grahamstown, South Africa, Mss Percy Fitzpatrick A/L I: same to same, 7 January 1896.

33. See J. Butler, *The Liberal Party and the Jameson Raid* (Oxford, 1968), pp. 41, 275.

34. For a recent scholarly collection on the Raid, see the contributions of G. Cuthbertson and others in *The Jameson Raid: A Centennial Retrospect* (Johannesburg, 1996).

35. Selborne's memo, 26 March 1896, enclosed in Selborne to Salisbury, 30 March 1896. D. G. Boyce (ed.), *The Crisis of British Power: The Imperial and Naval Papers of the Second Earl of Selborne, 1895–1910* (1990), pp. 34–7.

36. A. Milner, *England and Egypt* (1892).

37. Milner to Selborne, 16 July 1897, Boyce (ed.), *Crisis*, p. 51.

38. Conyngham Greene to Selborne, 18 June 1897, Boyce (ed.), *Crisis*, pp. 52–3.

39. Bodl. Milner Mss 220: Milner to Goschen, 28 September 1897.

40. J. Chamberlain to Milner, 5 July 1897, C. Headlam (ed.), *The Milner Papers: South Africa 1897–1899* (1931), pp. 71–2.

41. Milner to Selborne, 2 June 1897, Headlam, *Milner Papers 1897–1899*, pp. 105–6.

42. *Ibid.*, p. 107.

43. Milner to Clinton Dawkins, 25 August 1897, Headlam, *Milner Papers 1897–1899*, p. 87.

44. *Ibid.*

45. Milner to Asquith, 18 November 1897, Headlam, *Milner Papers 1897–1899*, pp. 177–80.

46. Mss Fitzpatrick B/A I: J. D. Forster to Percy Fitzpatrick, 8 October 1897.

47. P. Lewsen (ed.), *Select Correspondence of John X. Merriman, 1890–1898* (Van Riebeek Society, 1963), p. 302.

48. J. X. Merriman to James Rose Innes, 26 January 1898, Lewsen, *Merriman 1890–1898*, p. 291.

49. Rhodes to Milner n.d. but March 1898, Headlam, *Milner Papers 1897–1899*, p. 154.

50. Mss Milner 219: Milner to J. Chamberlain, 22 March 1898.

51. Milner to Rhodes, 7 March 1898, Headlam, *Milner Papers 1897–1899*, pp. 152–4.

52. Rhodes House Library, Mss Rhodes C4: Grey to Rhodes, 11 June 1898.

53. Milner Mss 205: C. Greene to Milner, 27 May 1898.

54. Mss Rhodes C4: Wilson Fox to Rhodes, 1 July 1898.

55. Rotberg, *The Founder*, pp. 610–11.

56. *Ibid.*, pp. 615–16; L. Michell, *The Life of Cecil Rhodes* (1910), vol. II, p. 244.

57. For Rhodes' campaign in 1898–9, see James Rose-Innes to James Bryce, 25 July 1899, in H. M. Wright (ed.), *Sir James Rose-Innes: Select Correspondence (1884–1902)* (Van Riebeek Society, 1972), pp. 257ff.

58. J. P. Fitzpatrick, *The Transvaal from Within* (1899), pp. 267ff.

59. I. R. Smith, *The Origins of the South African War 1899–1902* (1996), p. 243.

60. Originally a telegram, Milner to Chamberlain, 4 May 1899. See Headlam, *Milner Papers 1897–1899*, pp. 349–53.

61. See A. Thompson, 'Imperial Propaganda during the South African War', in G. Cuthbertson, A. Grundlingh and M.-L. Suttie (eds.), *Writing a Wider War: Gender, Race and Identity in the South African War 1899–1902* (Athens, OH, 2002), pp. 303–27.

62. *The Times*, 2 May 1899.

63. Selborne to Milner, 25 June 1899, Boyce (ed.), *Crisis*, p. 83.

64. Mss Milner 220: Milner to Selborne 12 July 1899.

65. Selborne to Chamberlain, 3 July 1899, Boyce (ed.), *Crisis*, p. 88.

66. A. N. Porter, *The Origins of the South African War: Joseph Chamberlain and the Diplomacy of Imperialism* (Manchester, 1980), pp. 243–5.

67. W. K. Hancock and J. Van Der Poel (eds.), *Selections from the Smuts Papers* (Cambridge, 1966), vol. I, p. 82.

68. For Smuts' account, dated 14 September 1899 of his discussions with Conyngham Green, the British Agent in Pretoria, see *Smuts Papers*, vol. I, pp. 283–99; see also Smuts to J. H. Hofmeyr, 22 August 1899, *ibid.*, p. 301.

69. For this critical stage, see Smith, *Origins*, pp. 350–4. Once he grasped the meaning of Smuts' conditions, Chamberlain insisted in his Birmingham speech of 26 August 1899 that the question of who was the paramount power had to be settled. See *The Times*, 28 August 1899.

70. S. Marks and S. Trapido, 'Lord Milner and the South African State', *History Workshop*, 8 (1979), 50–80.

71. P. Harries, 'Capital, State and Labour on the 19th Century Witwatersrand: A Reassessment', *South African Historical Journal*, 18 (1986), 25–45; R. Mendelsohn, *Sammy Marks: The 'Uncrowned King of the Transvaal'* (Cape Town, 1991).

72. R. Robinson and J. Gallagher, *Africa and the Victorians* (1961), ch. 14.

73. For a deft portrait of Uitlander society and its divisions, see D. Cammack, *The Rand at War: The Witwatersrand and the Anglo-Boer War 1899–1902* (1990); E. Katz, *The White Death: Silicosis and the Witwatersrand Gold Miners 1886–1910* (Johannesburg, 1994), pp. 76–90.

74. Cammack, *The Rand at War*, pp. 10–15, 29–30.

75. See T. Gutsche, *Old Gold: The History of the Wanderers Club* (Cape Town, 1966), chs. 6, 7.

76. T. R. Adlam, 'Sunrise and Advancing Morn', in M. Fraser (ed.), *Johannesburg Pioneer Journals 1888–1909* (Van Riebeek Society, 1985), p. 85. The passage is in a letter from Adlam's father to his mother dated 13 June 1899.

77. Privately circulated from June, but not published until September.

78. J. S. Marais, *The Downfall of Kruger's Republic* (Oxford, 1961), p. 233.

79. See F. C. Mackarness to J. X. Merriman, 10 March 1899, in P. Lewsen (ed.), *Selections from the Correspondence of John X. Merriman* (Van Riebeek Society, 1966), pp. 19–20.

80. J. G. Lockhart and C. M. Woodhouse, *Rhodes* (1963), pp. 424ff.

81. Fitzpatrick to J. Wernher, 24 April 1899, Duminy and Guest (eds.), *Fitzpatrick Papers*, p. 208.

82. Fitzpatrick's speech, 13 March 1899, *Fitzpatrick Papers*, pp. 197–8.

83. Memo by J. C. Smuts, 4 September 1899, *Smuts Papers*, vol. I, pp. 313–29.

84. 'You know as well as I do', wrote Smuts at the end of the war, 'that this has been a civil war.' Smuts to T. L. Graham, 26 July 1902, *Smuts Papers* (Cambridge, 1966), vol. II, p. 115.

85. Royal Commission on the War in South Africa, *Report*, Cd. 1789 (1903), para. 152.

86. Bodl. Mss Selborne 12: Confidential report by Major E. Leggett, n.d. but July 1905.

87. See J. Krikler, *Revolution from Above, Revolution from Below: The Agrarian Transvaal at the Turn of the Century* (Oxford, 1993).

88. For a notorious case, see W. Nasson, *Abraham Esau's War: A Black South African War in the Cape, 1899–1902* (Cambridge, 1991). For Milner's reports on atrocities, see Headlam (ed.), *Milner Papers 1899–1905*, pp. 233–4. See also Cd. 821 (1901), *Correspondence relative to the Treatment of Natives by the Boers*.

89. For Kitchener's terms, see Mss Milner 235: Kitchener to Botha, 7 March 1901, enclosed in Milner to J. Chamberlain, 7 March 1901. The negotiations were published as Cd. 663 (1901), *Further Papers relating to Negotiations between Commandant Louis Botha and Lord Kitchener*.

90. For a recent assessment, see L. Scholtz, *Why the Boers Lost the War* (Basingstoke, 2005).

91. The detailed drafting of the terms is described in Headlam (ed.), *Milner Papers 1899–1905*, ch. IX. The crucial concession on the franchise had been made at Middelburg.

92. *Ibid.*, p. 410.

93. Mss Selborne 12: Milner to Selborne, 14 April 1905.

94. Mss Rhodes C 27: Milner to Rhodes, 30 January 1902.

95. See M. Fraser and A. Jeeves, *All That Glittered: Selected Correspondence of Lionel Phillips 1890–1924* (Cape Town, 1977), p. 115.

96. See J. Darwin, 'The Rhodes Trust in the Age of Empire', in A. Kenny (ed.), *The Rhodes Trust* (Oxford, 2002).

97. Mss Rhodes C 27: Milner to Rhodes, 30 January 1902.

98. Milner to J. Chamberlain, 6 February 1901, Headlam, *Milner Papers 1899–1905*, p. 201.

99. Milner hoped that, in five years' time, the British would enjoy a narrow majority among the 1.2 million whites. Headlam, *Milner Papers 1899–1905*, p. 280. In fact, the 1911 census showed that Dutch Reformed Church communicants (a good proxy for Afrikaners) formed over 54 per cent of the white population. See L. M. Thompson, *The Unification of South Africa* (Oxford, 1960), p. 488.

100. Milner to Sir Charles Crewe, 27 April 1904, Headlam, *Milner Papers 1899–1905*, pp. 508–9. Crewe was the leading loyalist politician in the Eastern Cape.

101. For this ambition, see Cory Library, Rhodes University, Grahamstown, Mss Edgar Walton 17/142, Crewe to Edgar Walton, 29 April 1904. Walton (like Crewe a newspaper proprietor) was the leading political figure of Port Elizabeth.

102. Headlam, *Milner Papers 1899–1902*, p. 322.

103. Mss Edgar Walton 17/142: Milner to Walton, 8 April 1903.

104. Mss Edgar Walton 17/142: Crewe to Walton, 29 April 1902; Milner to Walton, 5 May 1902.

105. Mss Edgar Walton 17/142: O. Lewis to Walton, 6 May 1902.

106. Fraser and Jeeves (eds.), *All That Glittered*, p. 123.

107. Milner to Lyttelton, 2 May 1904, Headlam, *Milner Papers 1899–1905*, p. 523. Lyttelton was Colonial Secretary succeeding Chamberlain.

108. For the labour question, see D. Yudelman, *The Emergence of Modern South Africa: State, Capital and the Incorporation of Organised Labour on the South African Gold Fields, 1902–1939* (Cape Town, 1984), ch. 2.

109. For Natal, see David Torrance, *The Strange Death of the Liberal Empire* (1996), p. 145. Thompson, *Unification*, remains the authoritative account of white politics after 1902.

110. Mss Fitzpatrick A/LB IV: Fitzpatrick to G. Cox, 3 May 1904.

111. Smuts to J. X. Merriman, 30 August 1906, *Smuts Papers*, vol. II, p. 298.

112. Fraser and Jeeves (eds.), *All That Glittered*, p. 145; Yudelman, *Emergence*, pp. 62, 65.

113. Mss Fitzpatrick A/LB I: Fitzpatrick to Julius Wernher, 5 June 1902.

114. See, for example, Smuts to J. X. Merriman, 13 March, 30 August, 23 December 1906, *Smuts Papers*, vol. II, pp. 242–3, 298, 309.

115. Mss Selborne 71: Selborne to Lionel Curtis, 11 November 1907.

116. Mss Selborne 9: Selborne to J. Chamberlain, 24 February 1908.

117. Mss Selborne 71: Selborne to Walter Long, 21 December 1907; to E. Pretyman, 13 January 1909.

118. For Selborne's ideas, see Torrance, *Strange Death*, pp. 180–92.

119. Mss Selborne 5: Selborne to (fourth) Marquess of Salisbury, 18 May 1907.

120. Mss Selborne 6: same to same, 22 August 1908; Fraser and Jeeves (eds.), *All That Glittered*, p. 172.

121. Torrance, *Strange Death*, pp. 155ff.

122. For Progressive divisions, see Jagger Library, University of Cape Town, Mss Patrick Duncan, D.16.1: Patrick Duncan to L. S. Amery, 29 June 1908.

123. For Fitzpatrick's initial opposition, see Fraser and Jeeves (eds.), *All That Glittered*, p. 172.

Chapter 7

1. PP 1904 Cd. 1789, Royal Commission on the War in South Africa [RCWSA], *Report* (1903), Appendix D, p. 225: Memo by Secretary of State for War, 1 June 1891.

2. This distribution is based on PP 1897 (349), *Statistical Report on the Health of the Navy: 1896*.

3. See A. Preston and J. Major, *Send a Gunboat* (1967).

4. RCWSA, *Report*, Appendix D, p. 289: Memo by Lord Lansdowne, 4 December 1896. There were also the Guards regiments.

5. See WO 33/256, 23 December 1902: 'The Cost of Principal British Wars 1857–1899'.

6. C. E. Callwell, *Small Wars: Their Principles and Practice* (3rd edn, 1906), p. 76.

7. RCWSA, *Report*, Appendix D, p. 213: Minute by Lord Wolseley, 22 February 1896.

8. W. R. Langer, *European Alliances and Alignments 1871–1890* (2nd edn, New York, 1950), p. 400: Salisbury to Queen Victoria, 10 February 1887.

9. Bodl. Mss Selborne Box 12: Milner to Lord Selborne, 31 January 1900.

10. PP 1904 Cd. 1790, RCWSA, *Evidence*, vol. 1, p. 175, Q.4134 (Sir E. Wood), 29 October 1902.

11. L. S. Amery, *The Times History of the War in South Africa* (1902), vol. II, p. 41.

12. M. Howard, *The Continental Commitment* (1974), p. 19.

13. D. G. Boyce (ed.), *The Crisis of British Power: The Imperial and Naval Papers of the Second Earl of Selborne, 1895–1910* (1990), pp. 105–6: Selborne to Hicks Beach, 29 December 1900.

14. Boyce, *Crisis*, pp. 124–6: Memo by Selborne, 4 September 1901.

15. Boyce, *Crisis*, p. 115: Selborne to Curzon, 10 April 1901.

16. G. Monger, *The End of Isolation* (1963), p. 64: Balfour to Lansdowne, 12 December 1901.

17. Boyce, *Crisis*, p. 154: Selborne to Curzon, 4 January 1903.

18. R. Williams, *Defending the Empire: The Conservative Party and British Defence Policy 1899–1915* (1991), ch. 4.

19. A. J. Marder, *Fear God and Dread Nought: The Correspondence of Admiral of the Fleet Lord Fisher of Kilverstone*, 2 vols. (1956); R. F. Mackay, *Fisher of Kilverstone* (Oxford, 1974).

20. Boyce, *Crisis*, p. 190: Cabinet memo by Selborne, 6 December 1904, 'Distribution and Mobilization of the Fleet'.

21. Marder, *Fear God*, vol. II, p. 59.

22. D. Gillard, *The Struggle for Asia 1828–1914* (1977), p. 176.

23. For a brilliant contemporary expression, see A. Colquhoun, *1912: Germany and Sea Power* (1909).

24. N. Tracy (ed.), *The Collective Naval Defence of the Empire, 1900–1940* (Navy Records Society, 1997), p. 92.

25. See D. C. Gordon, *Dominion Partnership in Imperial Defence* (Baltimore, 1965).

26. See I. L. D. Forbes, 'German Informal Imperialism in South America before 1914', *Economic History Review*, New Series, 31, 3 (1978), 396–8.

27. For a recent interpretation along these lines, see B. B. Hayes, *Bismarck and Mitteleuropa* (Toronto, 1994).

28. See I. N. Lambi, *The Navy and German Power Politics* (Boston, 1983), pp. 426–7.

29. For Russian expansion in Asia, see D. Geyer, *Russian Imperialism: The Interaction of Domestic and Foreign Policy 1860–1914* (Eng. trans., Leamington, 1987), ch. 9.

30. For a brilliant study, see A. Rieber, 'Persistent Factors in Russian Foreign Policy', in H. Ragsdale (ed.), *Imperial Russian Foreign Policy* (Cambridge, 1993).

31. Rieber, 'Factors', pp. 343ff.

32. Russian attempts to prevent the Austrian annexation of Bosnia ended in diplomatic humiliation.

33. See D. Lieven, *Russia and the Origins of the First World War* (1983).

34. D. Lieven, *Russia's Rulers under the Old Regime* (New Haven, 1989), p. 228.

35. Grand Admiral Von Tirpitz, *My Memoirs* (Eng. trans., 1919), pp. 178–9.

36. D. A. Yerxa, *Admirals and Empire: The United States Navy and the Caribbean 1898–1945* (Columbia, SC, 1991), p. 20. This was in February 1903.

37. See D. McCullough, *The Path between the Seas: The Creation of the Panama Canal 1870–1914* (New York, 1977).

38. See K. Bourne, *Britain and the Balance of Power in North America* (1967).

39. H. and M. Sprout, *Towards a New Order of Sea Power* (1944), p. 288.

40. See P. Calvert, *The Mexican Revolution 1910–1914: The Diplomacy of Anglo-American Conflict* (Cambridge, 1968); F. Katz, *The Secret War in Mexico* (Chicago, 1981), p. 68, for the scare of 10,000 Japanese invading the United States.

41. Yerxa, *Admirals and Empire*, ch. 2.

42. W. Tilchin, *Theodore Roosevelt and the British Empire* (New York, 1997), p. 236.

43. *Ibid.*, p. 237.

44. J. A. S. Grenville, 'Diplomacy and War Plans in the United States, 1890–1917', *Transactions of the Royal Historical Society* 5th Series, 11 (1961), 1–21.

45. P. P. O'Brien, *British and American Sea Power 1900–1936* (Westport, CT, 1998), chs. 3, 5.

46. G. P. Gooch and H. Temperley (eds.), *British Documents on the Origins of the First World War* 12 vols. (1927–38), vol. III, pp. 402–3: Memo by Eyre Crowe, 1 January 1907.

47. A. J. Marder, *From the Dreadnought to Scapa Flow:* vol. I, *The Road to War 1904–14* (Oxford, 1961), p. 322.

48. E. W. R. Lumby (ed.), *Policy and Operations in the Mediterranean 1912–1914* (Navy Records Society, 1970), pp. 62ff.: Committee of Imperial Defence, 117th meeting, 4 July 1912.

49. See Lumby, *Mediterranean*, pp. 24–30, for Churchill's memo, 'The Naval Situation in the Mediterranean', 15 June 1912, and pp. 32–3, for the Admiralty memo of 21 June 1912.

50. New Zealand National Archives, Wellington, Sir James Allen Papers, Box 14: Nelson *Evening Mail*, 29 November 1912.

51. New Zealand National Archives, Sir James Allen Papers Box 14: Speech at Vancouver, 15 May 1913.

52. Tracy, *Collective Naval Defence*, p. 198.

53. PP 1913 (30), *Return of Net Income and Expenditure of British India, 1901–1911*, pp. 475–7: net military expenditure of the Government of India, £20.6 million (1904–5), £19.1 million (1909–10), £19.5 million (1911–12). Between £4 million and £5 million was spent annually in Britain.

54. Gooch and Temperley, *British Documents*, vol. 10, p. 534: Grey to Goschen (Berlin), 13 June 1913.

55. *Ibid.*, ch. xcv.

56. See P. Lowe, *Great Britain and Japan 1911–1915* (1969).

57. D. Gillard (ed.), *British Documents on Foreign Affairs*, Part 1, Series B, *The Near and Middle East 1856–1914* (1984), vol. 14,

Persia, Britain and Russia 1907–1914, pp. 358–65: Townley
(Teheran) to Grey, 21 December 1913 encl. Smart (Tabriz) to
Townley, 18 November 1913.

58. Gooch and Temperley, *British Documents*, vol. 10, p. 38:
Hardinge (Viceroy of India) to Nicolson (Foreign Office), 29 March
1911.

59. Production of crude steel, 1910 (in metric tonnes): Britain:
6,476,000; Germany: 13,100,000; United States: 26,514,000. B. R.
Mitchell, *International Historical Statistics: Europe 1750–1988* (3rd
edn, 1992), p. 457; Mitchell, *International Historical Statistics: The
Americas 1750–1988* (2nd edn, 1993), p. 353.

60. R. C. Michie, *The City of London* (1992), p. 73.

61. See R. C. O. Matthews, C. H. Feinstein and J. C. Odling-Smee,
British Economic Growth 1856–1973 (Stanford, 1982), p. 440,
Figs. 14.7, 14.8.

62. W. Woodruff, *The Impact of Western Man* (1966), p. 313.

63. G. Chisholm, *Handbook of Commercial Geography* (7th edn,
1908), pp. 610–17.

64. B. R. Mitchell, *Abstract of British Historical Statistics*
(Cambridge, 1971), p. 219.

65. *Ibid.*, pp. 334–5

66. W. Schlote, *British Overseas Trade from 1700 to the 1930s* (Eng.
trans., Oxford, 1952), p. 126.

67. Matthews, Feinstein and Odling-Smee, *British Economic Growth*,
p. 433.

68. *Ibid.*, p. 164.

69. Mitchell, *Abstract*, p. 334.

70. *Ibid.*, p. 50.

71. Dominion of Canada Customs Department, *Report* (Ottawa,
1913), p. 9.

72. Woodruff, *Impact*, Table VII/17.

73. *Ibid.*, Table VII/14.

74. A. Sommariva and G. Tullio, *German Macroeconomic History 1880–1979* (1986), p. 47.

75. V. Bulmer-Thomas, *Economic History of Latin America since Independence* (Cambridge, 1994), p. 104.

76. Of France's total in 1913, 56 per cent was in Europe, 16 per cent in the Americas and 12 per cent in the Near East. See Rondo E. Cameron, *France and the Economic Development of Europe 1800–1914* (Princeton, 1961), p. 486.

77. M. Cowen, 'Capital, Nation and Commodities: The Case of the Forestal Land, Timber and Railway Company in Argentina and Africa', in Y. Cassis and J. J. Van Helten (eds.), *Capitalism in a Mature Economy* (1990), p. 192.

78. As in the case of the *Bagdadbahn*. See L. Gall, G. D. Feldman, H. James, *et al.*, *The Deutsche Bank 1870–1995* (Eng.trans., 1995), pp. 71–2.

79. A. I. Bloomfield, *Short-Term Capital Movements under the Pre-1914 Gold Standard* (Princeton, 1963), p. 46.

80. For an account of this mechanism, see J. B. Condliffe, *The Commerce of Nations* (1951), p. 397; P. M. Acena, J. Reis and A. L. Rodriguez, 'The Gold Standard in the Periphery: An Introduction', in P. M. Acena and J. Reis (eds.), *Monetary Standards in the Periphery: Paper, Silver and Gold 1854–1933* (2000), pp. 1–17.

81. See chapter 4 above.

82. M. H. De Kock, *Economic History of South Africa* (Cape Town, 1924), pp. 242, 249.

83. African mineworkers 1902/3: 77,000; 1913: 214,000. A. Jeeves, *Migrant Labour in South Africa's Mining Economy* (Kingston and Montreal, 1985), pp. 265–6. White mineworkers 1907: 18,600; 1913: 29,710. D. Yudelman, *The Emergence of Modern South Africa: State, Capital and Organised Labour 1902–1939* (Cape Town, 1984), p. 132.

84. M. Fraser and A. Jeeves (eds.), *All That Glittered: Selected Correspondence of Lionel Philipps 1890–1924* (Cape Town, 1977), p. 9.

85. J. Krikler, *White Rising: The 1922 Insurrection and Racial Killing in South Africa* (Manchester, 2005), ch. 1.

86. Yudelman, *Emergence*, p. 127. The Afrikaner proportion of the white workforce rose from 17.5 per cent in 1907 to 36.2 per cent in 1913. See Yudelman, *Emergence*, p. 132.

87. N. J. Butlin, *Australian Economic Development 1861–1900* (Cambridge, 1964), p. 436.

88. E. Shann, *Economic History of Australia* (Cambridge, 1930), p. 415.

89. A. R. Hall, *The London Capital Market and Australia* (Canberra, 1963), pp. 181–2.

90. D. B. Copland, 'The Finance of Industry, Banking and Credit', in Copland (ed.), 'An Economic Survey of Australia', *Annals of American Academy of Political and Social Science* (Philadelphia, 1931), p. 100.

91. C. G. F. Simkin, *The Instability of a Dependent Economy* (Oxford, 1951), pp. 176, 41.

92. *Ibid.*, p. 51.

93. J. B. Condliffe, *New Zealand in the Making* (1930), pp. 326–7; Simkin, *Instability*, p. 90.

94. For the gold exchange standard and its effects, see A. K. Bagchi, *The Presidency Banks and the Indian Economy, 1870–1914* (Calcutta, 1989), pp. 102ff.; B. R. Tomlinson, *The Political Economy of the Raj 1914–1947* (1979), pp. 18–23. The fund in London reached £25 million by 1912, about the same size as India's deficit with Britain.

95. D. Kumar (ed.), *The Cambridge Economic History of India*, vol. II, *c. 1757–1970* (Hyderabad, 1982), p. 837.

96. *Ibid.*, vol. II, pp. 873–4; Tomlinson, *Raj*, p. 16.

97. See C. J. Baker, *A Rural Economy, 1880–1955: The Tamilnad Countryside* (Oxford, 1984), pp. 107ff.; O. Goswami, *Industry, Trade*

and Peasant Society in the Jute Economy of Eastern India (Delhi, 1991), pp. 58–9.

98. Tomlinson, *Raj*, p. 29.

99. F. E. Hyde, *Far Eastern Trade 1860–1914* (1973), pp. 120, 126, 131–2.

100. Value of Gold Coast exports of cocoa 1900: £27,280; 1913: £2,489,218. Value of (all) Nigerian exports 1900: £2.08 million; 1913: £7.4 million. See A. MacMillan, *The Red Book of West Africa: Historical and Descriptive, Commercial and Industrial* (1920), pp. 161, 43.

101. I. R. Phimister, 'Corners and Company-mongering: Nigerian Tin in the City of London, 1909–1912', *Journal of Imperial and Commonwealth History*, 28, 2 (2000), 23–41.

102. See A. G. Hopkins, *Economic History of West Africa* (1973), ch. 6; W. I. Ofanagoro, *Trade and Imperialism in Southern Nigeria 1881–1929* (1979).

103. Despite the 60 per cent increase in government spending between 1895 and 1913, Lloyd George achieved consistent surpluses in 1910–14. See B. K. Murray, *The People's Budget* (Oxford, 1980), pp. 292–3.

104. S. J. Potter, *News and the British World: The Emergence of an Imperial Press System 1876–1922* (Oxford, 2003).

105. See J. E. Kendle, *The Round Table Movement and Imperial Union* (Toronto, 1975).

106. See H. Weinroth, 'British Radicals and the Agadir Crisis', *European Studies Review*, 3, 1 (1973), 54. For the decline of radical opposition to naval spending, see A. J. A. Morris, *Radicals Against War 1906–1914* (1972), p. 345.

107. Bodl. Mss Robert Brand Box 185: Milner to R. H. Brand, 20 April 1908.

108. *Ibid.*

109. Rhodes University, Grahamstown, Cory Library, Mss Edgar Walton 17/142: Hennessy to Walton, 14 March 1910. The

programme as adopted on 24 May 1910 is in the C. P. Crewe Papers, also in the Cory Library.

110. National English Literary Museum, Grahamstown, South Africa, Mss J. P. Fitzpatrick A/LB VIII: Fitzpatrick to Milner, 15 February 1909; Mss Fitzpatrick B/A V: Jameson to Fitzpatrick, 28 April 1910.

111. Mss Fitzpatrick A/LC IV: Fitzpatrick to Milner, 3 March 1911.

112. Mss Walton 17/142: *Eastern Province Herald*, 15 June 1910.

113. Mss Crewe: Walter Long to Crewe, 25 October 1912.

114. Mss Fitzpatrick B/A V: Milner to Fitzpatrick, 10 April 1911.

115. Mss Fitzpatrick A/LB VIII: Fitzpatrick to Milner, 15 February 1909.

116. PP 1913 (130), *Return of Indian Financial Statement and Budget for 1913–14 and ... Proceedings of Legislative Council*, p. 258 (24 March 1913).

117. D. Kimble, *The Political History of Ghana 1850–1928* (Oxford, 1963), ch. 11.

118. For an excellent description, see Akintola Wyse, *H. C. Bankole-Bright* (Cambridge, 1990).

119. TNA, CO 446/99, Governor Bell to Colonial Office, 30 August 1911.

120. PP 1919 (468), *Report by Sir F. Lugard*, 9 April 1919, para. 29.

121. For the 1907 constitution of the Gold Coast Aborigine Rights Protection Society, founded 1897, see F. Madden and J. Darwin (eds.), *The Dependent Empire 1900–1948: Select Documents in the Constitutional History of the British Empire and Commonwealth* (1994), vol. VIII, p. 614. For the views of a leading protagonist, see J. E. Casely-Hayford, *Gold Coast Native Institutions* (1903).

122. TNA, CO 583/80: Clifford to Milner, 3 December 1919.

123. For a recent survey, see S. Doyle, *Crisis and Decline in Bunyoro* (Oxford, 2006), ch. 3.

124. D. A. Low, 'Uganda: The Establishment of a Protectorate 1894–1919', in V. T. Harlow and E. M. Chilvers (eds.), *History of East Africa* (Oxford, 1965), vol. II.

125. G. H. Mungeam (ed.), *Kenya: Select Historical Documents 1884–1923* (Nairobi, 1978), pp. 458–62: Colonists' Association to Colonial Secretary (London), 23 August 1905.

126. R. G. Gregory, *India and East Africa: A History of Race Relations within the British Empire, 1890–1939* (Oxford, 1971).

127. Mungeam, *Kenya: Select Documents*, p. 477.

128. See A. Hourani, *Islam in European Thought* (Cambridge, 1990).

129. G. Bell, *The Desert and the Sown* (1907), p. 228.

130. R. Storrs, *Orientations* [1937] (definitive edn, 1943), p. 82.

131. A. T. Wilson, *South West Persia; A Political Officer's Diary* (1942), 15 September 1912.

132. Lord Cromer, *Modern Egypt* (1908), vol. II, pp. 170–1.

133. B. Fuller, *The Empire of India* (1913), pp. 170–1.

134. Quoted in Cromer, *Modern Egypt*, vol. II, p. 202.

135. M. Perham, *Lugard: The Years of Authority 1898–1945* (1960), p. 156.

136. A. Gailey, *Ireland the Death of Kindness: The Experience of Constructive Unionism 1895–1905* (Cork, 1987).

137. Library of Trinity College, Dublin, Mss Donoughmore K/10/21: Donoughmore to Sir W. Hely-Hutchinson, 30 January 1906.

138. P. Bew, *Conflict and Conciliation* (1987), p. 19.

139. *Ibid*.

140. Childers, *Framework*, p. 148.

141. Mss Donoughmore K/27/10: C. H. Clarke to Donoughmore, 27 November 1908; Bew, *Conflict*, p. 82.

142. T. Garvin, *Nationalist Revolutionaries in Ireland 1858–1928* (Oxford, 1987), p. 2.

143. *Ibid.*, p. 79.

144. M. Wheatley, 'John Redmond and Federalism in 1910', *Irish Historical Studies*, 32, 27 (2001), 354–63.

145. Childers, *Framework,* p. 104.

146. See Sir Gilbert Parker, 'Home Rule and the Colonial Analogy' (n. d.), copy in Mss Donoughmore K/27/15.

147. P. Buckland, 'The Southern Irish Unionists, the Irish Question and British Politics 1906–1914', in A. O'Day (ed.), *Reactions to Irish Nationalism* (1987), p. 381.

148. See A. Jackson, *The Ulster Party* (Oxford, 1989).

149. P. Jalland, *The Liberals and Ireland* (Brighton, 1980), p. 115.

150. N. Blewett, *The Peers, the Parties and the People: The General Elections of 1910* (1972), p. 407.

Chapter 8

1. D. French, *British Economic and Strategic Planning 1905–1915* (1982), p. 27.

2. For the best recent study, see A. Offer, *The First World War: An Agrarian Interpretation* (Oxford, 1989).

3. The best account is N. Stone, *The Eastern Front 1914–1917* (1975).

4. See B. Millman, *Pessimism and British War Policy, 1914–1918* (2001), pp. 12ff.

5. The best recent study is D. French, *The Strategy of the Lloyd George Coalition 1916–1918* (Oxford, 1995).

6. Bodl. Mss Milner 355: Milner to Lloyd George, 20 March 1918.

7. C. E. Callwell, *Field Marshal Sir Henry Wilson: His Life and Diaries*, 2 vols. (1927), vol. II, p. 76.

8. Bodl. Mss Milner 355: Milner to Wilson, 8 April 1918.

9. Callwell, *Wilson*, vol. II, p. 90.

10. Burton J. Hendrick, *The Life and Letters of Walter Hines Page* (1924), p. 391 (10 June 1918).

11. Bodl. Mss Milner (Additional) c696: Milner to Lloyd George, 9 June 1918.

12. *Ibid.*

13. Grey to Cambon, 16 May 1916, conveniently reprinted in W. Laqueur (ed.), *The Israel–Arab Reader* (3rd edn, New York, 1976), p. 13.

14. D. Vital, *A People Apart: The Jews in Europe 1789–1939* (Oxford, 1999), pp. 688–92; A. Verrier (ed.), *Agents of Empire* (1995), p. 210.

15. French, *Strategy of the Lloyd George Coalition*, p. 192.

16. Millman, *Pessimism*, p. 208.

17. J. Darwin, *Britain, Egypt and the Middle East* (1981), p. 156.

18. *Ibid.*

19. *Ibid.*, p. 158.

20. For British anxieties, see W. B. Fowler, *British–American Relations 1917–1918: The Role of Sir William Wiseman* (Princeton, 1969).

21. Fowler, *British–American Relations*, pp. 224–5.

22. E. Johnson (ed.), *Collected Works of John Maynard Keynes*, vol. XVI, *Activities 1914–1919, the Treasury and Versailles* (Cambridge, 1971), p. 23: Keynes' article in the *Morning Post*, 11 August 1914.

23. *Ibid.*, vol. XVI, *Activities*, pp. 110–11.

24. *Ibid.*, p. 125.

25. *Ibid.*, pp. 185ff.

26. J. Wormell, *The Management of the National Debt of the United Kingdom 1900–1932* (2000), p. 243; Johnson, *Collected Works*, vol. XVI, *Activities*, p. 224.

727 / Notes to pages 321–4

27. *Ibid.*, p. 244.

28. *Ibid.*, p. 250.

29. *Ibid.*, p. 268: Keynes to his mother, 24 December 1917.

30. By April 1917, the United States was an international creditor. See D. Kennedy, *Over Here: The First World War and American Society* (New York, 1980), p. 306.

31. Exports and re-exports in 1919, £385 million; 1913, £634 million. Both in 1913 prices. See A. W. Kirkcaldy (ed.), *British Finance during and after the War 1914–1921* (1921), pp. 364–8.

32. See R. Miller, 'British Trade with Latin America 1870–1950', in P. Mathias and J. A. Davis (eds.), *International Trade and British Economic Growth from the 18th Century to the Present Day* (Oxford, 1996), p. 137.

33. Kennedy, *Over Here*, p. 325.

34. *Ibid.*, p. 322.

35. Wormell, *National Debt*, p. 382.

36. *Ibid.*, p. 151.

37. Johnson, *Collected Works*, vol. XVI, *Activities*, p. 418.

38. Total government debt 1913: £625 million; 1920: £7809 million. See B. R. Mitchell, *Abstract of British Historical Statistics* (Cambridge, 1971), p. 403.

39. Wormell, *National Debt*, p. 151.

40. Mitchell, *Abstract*, pp. 334–35.

41. *Ibid.*, p. 476.

42. *Ibid.*, p. 491.

43. Wormell, *National Debt*, p. 299.

44. Bodl. Mss Robert Brand, Box 8: P. Duncan to Robert Brand, 8 February 1917.

45. Wormell, *National Debt*, p. 296.

46. Mss Robert Brand, Box 5B: R. Brand to E. S. Montagu, 18 July 1916.

47. Mss Robert Brand, Box 9: Note (n.d.) by Robert Brand.

48. Wormell, *National Debt*, pp. 151, 288.

49. PP 1917–18, XXIV, p. 12: Financial Statement by Finance Member, Government of India, 1 March 1917.

50. B. R. Tomlinson, *The Political Economy of the Raj 1914–1947* (1979), pp. 106–7.

51. PP 1917–18, XXIV, p. 101: Indian Legislative Council Proceedings, 7 March 1917.

52. Tomlinson, *Political Economy*, p. 109.

53. PP 1919, XXXVII, p. 4: Statement by Finance Member, 1 March 1919.

54. Kennedy, *Over Here*, p. 332.

55. *Ibid.*, p. 99.

56. *Ibid.*, p. 341.

57. *Ibid.*, p. 342.

58. H. Strachan, *The First World War*, vol. 1, *To Arms* (Oxford, 2001), p. 965.

59. Strachan, *First World War*, p. 908.

60. See J. M. Atkin, 'Official Regulation of British Overseas Investment 1918–1931', *Economic History Review*, 2nd series, 23 (1970).

61. R. Michie, *The London Stock Exchange* (Oxford, 1999), p. 181.

62. *Ibid.*, p. 173.

63. Mss Robert Brand 26: Notes for a Speech/Article on Anglo-Canadian Relations, ?1913.

64. The argument advanced by Ramsay MacDonald. See D. Marquand, *Ramsay MacDonald* (1977), p. 167.

65. See A. M. Gollin, *Proconsul in Politics* (1964), for the best discussion of this group.

66. J. M. McEwen (ed.), *The Riddell Diaries 1908–23* (1986), p. 186.

67. *Ibid.*, p. 219.

68. For a contemporary study of pre-war conditions, see J. Orr, *Report on Agriculture in Berkshire* (1916).

69. Mss Milner (Additional) c696: Milner to Lloyd George, 6 September 1918.

70. BLIOC, Curzon Papers, Mss Eur. F 112/122: Milner to Curzon, 23 January 1918.

71. C. Wrigley, *Arthur Henderson* (Cardiff, 1990), p. 113; Marquand, *Ramsay MacDonald*, p. 217.

72. D. Lloyd George, *War Memoirs*, 2 vols. (1936), vol. II, pp. 1595ff.

73. By comparison, 27 per cent of British adult males served overseas, 50 per cent were casualties, and over 900,000 were killed.

74. *Documents on Canadian External Relations*, vol. I, *1909–1918* (Ottawa, 1967), pp. 93–4: Prime Minister to Assistant High Commissioner, 30 October 1915.

75. *Ibid.*, p. 104: Prime Minister to Assistant High Commissioner, 4 January 1916.

76. *Ibid.*, p. 115: Borden to Perley, 24 February 1916.

77. A. F. Madden and J. Darwin (eds.), *Select Documents in the Constitutional History of the British Empire and Commonwealth*, vol. VI, *The Dominions and India since 1900* (Westport, CT, 1993), p. 42.

78. Mss Milner 361: Draft Report of Committee of Prime Ministers, 20 August 1918.

79. *Ibid.*

80. *Documents on Canadian External Relations*, vol. I, p. 218: Borden to Lloyd George, 29 October 1918; *ibid.*, p. 220: Hughes to Borden, 10 November 1918.

81. National Archives of Canada, J. W. Dafoe Papers, M-73 (microfilm): Wilfrid Laurier to J. Dafoe, 8 November 1912.

82. D. Morton, 'Providing and Consuming Security in Canada's Century', *Canadian Historical Review*, 81, 1 (2000), 11; this compared with some 18 per cent in its counterpart, the Australian Imperial Force.

83. See speech, 12 January 1910, National Archives of Canada, Borden Mss, C-412 (microfilm).

84. National Archives of Canada, Dafoe Papers, M-73: Sifton to Dafoe, 21 September 1914.

85. M. Westley, *Remembrance of Grandeur: The Anglo-Protestant Elite of Montreal 1900–1950* (Montreal, 1990), pp. 112ff.

86. J. M. Bliss, 'The Methodist Church and World War One', in C. Berger (ed.), *Conscription 1917* (Toronto, 1970), p. 40.

87. National Archives of Canada, Dafoe Papers M-73: Dafoe to T. Coté, 6 April 1916.

88. *Ibid.*, Dafoe to Coté, 1 January 1916.

89. B. G. Ferguson, *Remaking Liberalism: The Intellectual Legacy of Adam Shortt, O. D. Skelton, W. C. Clark and W. A. Mackintosh, 1890–1925* (Montreal and Kingston, 1993), p. 151.

90. National Archives of Canada, Henri Bourassa Papers M-721 (microfilm): Bourassa to C. H. Cahan, 3 October 1914.

91. *Ibid.*, Bourassa to J. S. Ewart, 18 September 1915.

92. National Archives of Canada, Wilfrid Laurier Papers C-908 (microfilm): Laurier to Senator Dandurand, 17 January 1915.

93. National Archives of Canada, Bourassa Papers M-721: Bourassa to W. D. Gregory, 24 November 1916.

94. National Archives of Canada, Clifford Sifton Papers H-1014 (microfilm): Sifton to Senator Bostock, 23 July 1917.

95. National Archives of Canada, Robert Borden Papers C-412 (microfilm): Meighen to Borden, 17 October 1916.

96. National Archives of Canada, Laurier Papers C-915 (microfilm): Laurier to Sir C. Russell, 27 December 1917.

97. National Archives of Canada, Borden Papers C-412: R. N. Gosnell to Borden, 20 December 1917.

98. National Archives of Canada, Laurier Papers C-915: Skelton to Laurier, 18 December 1917.

99. E. M. Andrews, *The Anzac Illusion* (Cambridge, 1993), p. 11: 146,602 in 1913.

100. R. Evans, *Loyalty and Disloyalty: Social Conflict on the Queensland Home Front, 1914–1918* (Sydney, 1987), p. 7.

101. Andrews, *Anzac Illusion*, pp. 28, 41.

102. J. McQuilton, *Rural Australia and the Great War* (Melbourne, 2001), p. 19.

103. *Ibid.*, p. 42.

104. The figures were 1,160,033 to 1,087,557.

105. 1,181,747 to 1,015,159.

106. D. Day, *John Curtin: A Life* (Sydney, 1999), p. 229.

107. Evans, *Loyalty*, p. 9.

108. *Ibid.*, p. 96.

109. Day, *Curtin*, p. 243.

110. Evans, *Loyalty*, p. 100.

111. S. Alomes, *A Nation at Last?* (North Ryde, NSW, 1988), pp. 67–8.

112. On 25 September 1914. New Zealand National Archives, Acc. 556, Sir James Allen Papers, Box 12.

113. *Ibid.*, Allen to T. Todd, 16 April 1915.

114. For Allen's speech in the New Zealand parliament, *The Dominion*, 9 August 1916, Allen Papers, Box 4.

115. James Belich, *Paradise Reforged* (2002), p. 111.

116. A. B. Keith, *War Government in the British Dominions* (1921), p. 97.

117. New Zealand National Archives, Allen Papers, Box 9: Allen to Massey, 8 November 1916.

118. University of Cape Town, Jagger Library, Patrick Duncan Papers, D.5.8: Duncan to Lady Selborne, 20 August 1914.

119. *Ibid.*, D.5.9: Duncan to Lady Selborne, 20 January 1915.

120. *Ibid.*, Duncan to Lady Selborne, 27 January 1915.

121. *Ibid.*, Duncan to Lady Selborne, 2 April 1915.

122. *Ibid.*, D.1.34: Sir Thomas Smartt to Duncan, 28 August 1915.

123. I. S. Uys, 'South Africans at Delville Wood', *South African Military History Journal*, 7, 2 (1986), 45–58; Keith, *War Government*, p. 107.

124. University of Cape Town, Jagger Library, Patrick Duncan Papers, A.1.2: Duncan to J. H. Hofmeyr, 10 March 1919.

125. M. Hasan (ed.), *Mohamed Ali in Indian Politics: Selected Writings* (New Delhi, 1987), vol. II, p. 115.

126. BLIOC, Chelmsford Coll., Mss Eur. E 264/2: Viceroy to Secretary of State for India, 27 May 1916.

127. Chelmsford Coll., Mss Eur. E 264/8: Viceroy to Secretary of State for India, 18 May 1917.

128. Madden and Darwin, *Select Documents*, vol. VI, pp. 678–9.

129. See clauses 12d and 16 of the Congress–League scheme, printed in L. Curtis, *Letters to the People of India on Responsible Government* (1918), appendix.

130. Trinity College, Cambridge, Edwin Montagu Papers: Montagu to Lloyd George, 27 June 1917.

131. E. S. Montagu, *An Indian Diary* (1930), p. 216.

132. *Ibid.*, p. 216.

133. Curtis, *Letters*, pp. 70–4.

134. Montagu, *Indian Diary*, p. 358: this was (Sir) William Marris, later governor of the United Provinces.

135. *Report of the Indian National Congress Special Session*, 29 August–1 September 1918.

136. *Ibid.*, p. 103: this was B. C. Pal of Bengal.

137. Montagu Papers: Montagu to Chelmsford, 27 April 1918.

138. Montagu Papers: Notes prepared on the Rowlatt Act, n.d.

139. *Collected Works of Mahatma Gandhi*, vol. XIV, pp. 486–7: Gandhi to S. Sastri, 18 July 1918.

140. Recruiting Appeal, 22 June 1918, in M. Desai, *Day to Day with Gandhi*, vol 1, November 1917 to March 1919 (Eng. trans., Benares, 1968). Desai was Gandhi's personal secretary.

141. F. Robinson, *Separatism among Indian Muslims* (Cambridge, 1974), p. 289.

142. Montagu Papers: draft, Montagu to Lloyd George, 27 June 1917.

143. W. E. Vaughan (ed.), *The New History of Ireland*, vol. VI, *Ireland under the Union*, Part 2 (Oxford, 1996), p. 218.

144. *Hansard*, HC Debs., 5s, 91, col. 446, 7 March 1917.

145. *Ibid.*, col. 477, 7 March 1917.

146. See R. B. McDowell, *The Irish Convention 1917–18* (1970).

147. Vaughan (ed.), *New History of Ireland*, vol. VI, Part 2, p. 607.

148. See E. O'Malley, *On Another Man's Wound* [1936] (paperback edn, 1979), ch. 6.

149. I. Bowman, *The New World: Problems in Political Geography* (1921).

Chapter 9

1. M. G. Fry, *Illusions of Security: North Atlantic Diplomacy 1918–1922* (Toronto, 1972), pp. 6ff.

2. For Smuts' urging along these lines, see his speech, 'The Commonwealth Conception', 15 May 1917, reprinted in J. C. Smuts, *Plans for a Better World* (1942), p. 42.

3. Fry, *Illusions*, pp. 8–9.

4. H. and M. Sprout, *Towards a New Order of Sea Power* (2nd edn, Princeton, 1946,) p. 285.

5. Foreign Office memorandum on the Neutralisation of the Rhineland, 7 April 1923, in W. N. Medlicott, D. Dakin and M. E. Lambert (eds.), *Documents on British Foreign Policy*, 1st series, vol. XXI (1978) p. 195.

6. House of Lords Record Office, Bonar Law Papers 111/12/40, Bonar Law to Curzon, 7 December 1922.

7. BLIOC, Curzon Papers, Mss Eur. F112/286, R. McNeill to Curzon, 28 January 1923.

8. The Anglo-American agreement was eventually signed on 18 June 1923. See A. Orde, *British Policy and European Reconstruction after the First World War* (Cambridge, 1990), pp. 233–7.

9. Memo by Austen Chamberlain, 4 January 1925. *Documents on British Foreign Policy*, 1st series, vol.XXVII (1986), p. 256.

10. Note by Hankey, 23 January 1925, *Documents on British Foreign Policy*, 1st series, vol. XXVII (1986), pp. 286–7.

11. Memo by H. Nicolson, 20 February 1925, circulated to Cabinet. *Documents on British Foreign Policy*, 1st series, vol. XXVII (1986), p. 316.

12. P. Towle, 'British Security and Disarmament Policy in Europe in the 1920s', in R. Ahmann, A. Birke and M. Howard (eds.), *The Quest for Stability* (1993), pp. 129–30.

13. Note by Chamberlain, 12 October 1925, *Documents on British Foreign Policy*, 1st series, vol. XXVII, p. 866.

14. I. Bowman, *The New World* (4th edn, New York, 1928), p. 745. Bowman played a leading part in founding the Council on Foreign Relations. For his career, see N. Smith, *American Empire: Roosevelt's*

Geographer and the Prelude to Globalization (Berkeley and Los Angeles, 2003).

15. Sprout and Sprout, *Sea Power*, p. 106.

16. Fry, *Illusions*, pp. 41–4.

17. *Ibid.*, pp. 50–61.

18. On 11 December 1919. Sprout and Sprout, *Sea Power*, p. 112.

19. See W. R. Louis, *British Strategy in the Far East 1918–1939* (Oxford, 1971), pp. 19–39; Memo by Sir B. Alston, 1 August 1920, in R. Butler, J. P. T. Bury and M. E. Lambert (eds.), *Documents on British Foreign Policy*, 1st series, vol. XIV (1966), pp. 83–5.

20. M. A. Barnhart, *Japan and the World since 1868* (1995), pp. 67–79.

21. Winston Churchill to Baldwin, 15 December 1924, in M. Gilbert (ed.), *Winston S. Churchill Companion*, vol. V, Part 1, *The Exchequer Years 1922–1939* (1979), p. 305.

22. See H. R. C. Greaves, *The League Committees and World Order* (1931).

23. For this consensus, see R. S. Sayers, *The Bank of England 1891–1944* (Cambridge, 1976), vol. I, p. 111.

24. D. Kynaston, *The City of London*, 5 vols. (1994–2001), vol. III, *Illusions of Gold 1914–1945*, p. 115.

25. W. Schlote, *British Overseas Trade from 1700 to the 1930s* (Oxford, 1952), p. 151. All in 1913 prices.

26. *Ibid.*, 1939 = 100.

27. See Mitchell, *Abstract*, pp. 334–5.

28. D. Hope, *A New History of British Shipping* (1990), p. 366.

29. *Ibid.*, p. 368.

30. *Ibid.*, p. 358.

31. For the Peninsular and Oriental Group, see S. Jones, *Trade and Shipping: Lord Inchcape 1852–1932* (Manchester, 1989). For the fate

of Harrison's, a Liverpool based line, see F. E. Hyde, *Shipping Enterprise and Management 1830–1939: Harrison's of Liverpool* (Liverpool, 1967).

32. See I. M. Drummond, *Imperial Economic Policy 1917–1939* (1974), pp. 26–7, 423, 429.

33. *Hansard*, 168 HC Deb., 5s, col. 482, 15 November 1923; for a recent discussion, see P. Williamson, *Stanley Baldwin* (Cambridge, 1999), p. 28.

34. J. M. Atkin, *British Overseas Investment 1918–1931* (New York, 1977), pp. 27–49.

35. *Ibid.*, p. 53.

36. *Ibid.*, p. 321.

37. I. Stone, *The Global Export of British Capital, 1865–1914* (1999), p. 411. The figure was £349 million.

38. R. Gravil, 'Anglo-American Trade Rivalry', in D. Rock (ed.), *Argentina in the Twentieth Century* (1975), p. 56.

39. A. Velasco (ed.), *Trade, Development and the World Economy: Selected Essays of Carlos Diaz-Alejandro* (Oxford, 1988), p. 238.

40. Robertson (British ambassador) to Craigie, 10 May 1929, R. Gravil, *The Anglo-Argentine Connection 1900–1939* (1985), p. 162.

41. E. K. S. Fung, *The Diplomacy of Imperial Retreat* (Hong Kong, 1991), pp. 37–54.

42. For a harsh contemporary view, see A. Loveday, *Britain and World Trade* (1931), p. 163.

43. A. Marrison, *British Business and Protection* (Oxford, 1996), p. 433.

44. J. Atkin, *Investment*, pp. 13–16.

45. See the jeremiad in G. Peel, *The Economic Impact of America* (1928), pp. 192–5.

46. Atkin, *Investment*, p. 311. They were estimated (by *The Economist*) at £100 million, compared with £836 million in 1913, not allowing for the 40 per cent fall in real value.

47. Eastern Committee, 42nd minutes, 9 December 1918, in J. Darwin, *Britain, Egypt and the Middle East: Imperial Policy in the Aftermath of War* (1981), p. 160.

48. For his views on Kurdistan, see Darwin, *Middle East*, p. 195.

49. See R. Pipes, *The Formation of the Soviet Union: Communism and Nationalism 1917–1923* (rev. edn, Cambridge, MA, 1964); R. Ullman, *Britain and the Russian Civil War* (1968).

50. For the origins of the Arab nationalist movement, see G. Antonius, *The Arab Awakening* (1938); A. Hourani, *Arabic Thought in the Liberal Age 1798–1939* (1962); P. S. Khoury, 'Continuity and Change in Syrian Political Life: The Nineteenth and Twentieth Centuries', *American Historical Review*, 96, 5 (1991), 1374–95

51. See resolutions of the General Syrian Congress, 2 July 1919, printed in Antonius, *Awakening*, pp. 440ff.

52. See Butrus Abu-Manneh, 'The Rise of the Sanjak of Jerusalem in the Late Nineteenth Century', in I. Pappé (ed.), *The Israel–Palestine Question* (1999), pp. 46–8.

53. For the Baghdad notables under Ottoman rule, see A. Hourani, 'Ottoman Reform and the Politics of Notables', in A. Hourani, P. S. Khoury and M. Wilson (eds.), *The Modern Middle East* (1993), pp. 83–109.

54. B. L. Add. Mss 52455, A. T. Wilson Papers: Civil Commissioner to Secretary of State for India, 29 July 1920.

55. Wilson Papers, 52459B: Wilson's draft reply to War Office, 3 September 1920.

56. Darwin, *Middle East*, pp. 66–79.

57. For the recruitment of traditional religious elites into a form of 'Kemalo-Islamism', see M. E. Meeker, *A Nation of Empire: The Ottoman Legacy of Turkish Modernity* (Berkeley and Los Angeles, 2002), p. 81.

58. For an account of the negotiations, see Darwin, *Middle East*, chs. 4, 5.

59. Curzon Papers, F 112/294: Note by Middle East Department, CO, 7 December 1922.

60. Bulent Gokay, *A Clash of Empires: Turkey between Russian Bolshevism and British Imperialism* (1997), pp. 155ff.

61. Although its existence was strongly suspected, no oil was found in Iraq until 1927. In 1920, Middle East oil made up 1 per cent of world production.

62. For a review of Anglo-Persian relations, see Harold Nicolson to Austen Chamberlain, 30 September 1926, *Documents on British Foreign Policy*, Series 1A, vol. II, pp. 812–20.

63. Bodl. Milner Mss 164: Memo by Lord Milner, n.d.

64. Curzon Papers F 112/208: Curzon to Milner, 3 January 1920.

65. *The Seven Pillars of Wisdom* was published for general circulation in 1935.

66. The title of the classic study by Elizabeth Monroe (1963).

67. *Collected Works of Mahatma Gandhi*, vol. XVII, p. 371: Gandhi to Home-Rule League, *Navajivan*, 2 May 1920.

68. R. Gordon, 'Non-cooperation and Council-Entry, 1919–1920', *Modern Asian Studies*, 7, 3 (1973), 458.

69. D. Page, *Prelude to Partition: The Indian Muslims and the Imperial System of Control 1920–1932* (Oxford, 1982), p. 33.

70. *Collected Works of Mahatma Gandhi*, vol. XVIII, p. 253: Speech at Calcutta Congress, 8 September 1920.

71. *Ibid.*, p. 350: Speech at Lucknow, 15 October 1920.

72. *Ibid.*, vol. XVIII, p. 270: 'Swaraj in One Year', *Young India*, 22 September 1920.

73. BLIOC, Sir F. Whyte Diaries, Mss Eur. D 761/VI, p. 24, 16 June 1923.

74. *Reforms Inquiry Committee, 1924: Views of Local Governments*, Cmd. 2361 (1925), p. 143: evidence of United Provinces Government.

75. R. Hunt and J. Harrison, *The District Officer in India 1930–1947* (1980), ch. 3.

76. See *Report of the Reforms Inquiry Committee, 1924*, Cmd. 2360 (1925), p. 102.

77. See *Report of Committee Appointed to Enquire into the Administration and Organisation of the Army in India*, Cmd. 943 (1920).

78. R. Kumar and H. D. Sharma (eds.), *Selected Works of Motilal Nehru* (New Delhi, 1986), vol. IV, p. 110: M. Nehru to M. R. Jayakar, 21 March 1925.

79. Page, *Prelude*, p. 127.

80. For the speech of C. R. Das at the 1924 Congress, see *Report of the 39th Congress at Belgaum, December 1924*, pp. 36–7.

81. Page, *Prelude*, p. 134.

82. Formally six, since Newfoundland enjoyed dominion status until its bankruptcy in 1933.

83. For the best study of King's policy, see P. Wigley, *Canada and the Transition to Commonwealth: British-Canadian Relations 1917–1926* (Cambridge, 1977).

84. D. Greasley and L. Oxley, 'A Tale of Two Dominions: The Macro-economic Record of Australia and Canada since 1870', *Economic History Review*, New Series, 51, 2 (1998), p. 305.

85. Queen's University, Kingston, Douglas Library, Charles G. Power Papers, Box 6: C. G. Power to E. Lapointe, 19 November 1925. For a similar view from a very different political quarter, see University of Manitoba, Elizabeth Dafoe Library, J. W. Dafoe Papers, Box 9: Clifford Sifton to J. W. Dafoe, 17 February 1921.

86. For King's early career, see H. S. Ferns and B. Ostry, *The Age of Mackenzie King: The Rise of the Leader* (1955).

87. See J. Macfarlane, *Ernest Lapointe and Quebec's Influence in Foreign Policy* (Toronto, 1999), pp. 11–12.

88. Dafoe Papers, Box 12: King to Clifford Sifton (proprietor of the *Manitoba Free Press*), 17 August 1923; Sifton to Dafoe, August 1923.

89. For King's unease at the 1923 Imperial Conference, see J. W. Dafoe's diary for September and October 1923, Dafoe Papers Box 1.

90. Dafoe Papers Box 11: D. B. McRae to Dafoe, 4 November 1926.

91. See S. Trofimenkoff, *Action française: French-Canadian Nationalism in the Twenties* (Toronto, 1975); L. Groulx, *Mes mémoires*, 4 vols. (Montreal, 1971).

92. Dafoe Papers Box 4: Dafoe to Clifford Sifton, 29 January 1923.

93. Dafoe Papers Box 6: Bourassa to Dafoe, 26 April 1928.

94. National Archives of Canada, Arthur Meighen Papers (microfilm) C-3439: L. Christie to Meighen, 17 February 1926. Meighen told Christie, 'On matters of external affairs I value your judgment more than that of anyone I know.' Meighen to Christie, 13 January 1926, in *ibid.*

95. S. Macintyre, *Oxford History of Australia:* vol. IV, *The Succeeding Age* (Oxford, 1986), pp. 227–8. Labour did better in the states.

96. S. Alomes, *A Nation at Last: The Changing Character of Australian Nationalism 1880–1988* (North Ryde, NSW, 1988), pp. 66–70.

97. See P. Spartalis, *The Diplomatic Battles of Billy Hughes* (Sydney, 1983), ch. 6.

98. *Ibid.*, p. 246.

99. *Ibid.*

100. House of Representatives, 30 September 1921. F. K. Crowley, *Documents in Australian History* (1973), pp. 349–51.

101. To parliament in June 1924. N. Meaney (ed.), *Australia and the World* (Melbourne, 1983), p. 347.

102. See his article 'The Status of the Australian States', *The Australian Geographer* 1,1 (1928), 28.

103. A stimulating discussion of these themes can be found in K. Tsokhas, *Making a Nation State: Cultural Identity, Economic*

Nationalism and Sexuality in Australian History (Melbourne, 2001), chs. 7, 8.

104. House of Representatives, 10 September 1919. Crowley, *Documents*, vol. I, p. 324.

105. House of Representatives, 3 August 1926. Meaney, *Australia and the World*, pp. 356–7.

106. Macintyre, *Succeeding Age*, p. 229.

107. D. Day, *John Curtin: a Life* (Sydney, 1999), p. 295.

108. Bruce in the Australian Parliament, 27 June 1924. Meaney, *Australia and the World*, p. 348.

109. See Isobel Hofmeyr, 'Building a Nation from Words: Afrikaans Language, Literature and Ethnicity 1902–1924', in S. Marks and S. Trapido (eds.), *The Politics of Race, Class and Nationalism in Twentieth-Century South Africa* (1987), pp. 95–123.

110. M. H. De Kock, *The Economic History of South Africa* (Cape Town, 1924), p. 455.

111. *Ibid.*, pp. 132–3: the value of agricultural production fell from £111 million in 1919–20 to £65.7 million in 1921–2.

112. *Ibid.*, pp. 253–4.

113. Rhodes University, Grahamstown, Cory Library, Sir Edgar Walton Papers 17/142: Sir T. Smartt to Sir E. Walton, 17 March 1922. The reference was to the Rand rising of 1914 and the Boer rebellion of 1914–15.

114. J. Van Der Poel (ed.), *Selections from the Smuts Papers*, vol. V, pp. 96–7.

115. See Smuts to Bonar Law, 20 November 1922, *Smuts Papers*, vol. V, pp. 147–8. Bonar Law had just become prime minister.

116. Smuts to Alice Clark, 9 April 1920, *Smuts Papers*, vol. V, p. 39.

117. Smuts to L. S. Amery, 25 November 1924, *Smuts Papers*, vol. V, pp. 238–9.

118. National English Literary Museum, Grahamstown, Percy Fitzpatrick Papers B/A IX: Smuts to P. Fitzpatrick, 15 February 1921. Fitzpatrick was a leading ex-Unionist.

119. The National party won 63 seats, the South African Party 53 and Labour 18 in a house of 135.

120. Fitzpatrick Papers A/LC IV: Fitzpatrick to Milner, 30 June 1924.

121. Fitzpatrick Papers A/LC I: Fitzpatrick to Amery, 30 June 1924.

122. University of Cape Town, Jagger Library, Patrick Duncan Papers, D.5.18.6: Duncan to Lady Selborne, 22 October 1924.

123. University of Stellenbosch Library, D. F. Malan Papers, 1/1/692: Hertzog to Malan, 21 November 1923.

124. For Balfour's role at the conference, see D. Judd, *Balfour and the British Empire* (1968), ch. 20.

125. C. M. Van Den Heever, *General J. B. M. Hertzog* (Eng. trans., Johannesburg, 1946), p. 213.

126. Balfour to Esher, 24 November 1926, Judd, *Balfour*, p. 337.

127. Wigley, *Canada and the Transition to Commonwealth*, p. 275.

128. See P. Canning, *British Policy towards Ireland 1921–1941* (Oxford, 1985).

129. See Tom Garvin, *1922: The Birth of Irish Democracy* (Dublin, 1996), chs. 2, 4. Garvin emphasises the abuse of local power by the IRA units.

130. F. Costello, *The Irish Revolution and its Aftermath 1916–1923* (Dublin, 2003), pp. 312–13.

131. For the significance of this claim for popular sovereignty, see L. Kohn, *The Constitution of the Irish Free State* (1934), p. 113–14.

132. Canning, *British Policy*, pp. 91–2.

133. See Mary E. Daly, *Industrial Development and Irish National Identity 1922–39* (Syracuse, 1992), ch. 2.

134. G. Keown, 'Taking the World Stage: Creating an Irish Foreign Policy in the 1920s', in M. Kennedy and J. M. Skelly (eds.), *Irish Foreign Policy 1919–1966* (Dublin, 2000), pp. 25–43; D. Keogh, *The*

Vatican, the Bishops and Irish Politics 1919–39 (Cambridge, 1986); D. Lowry, 'New Ireland, Old Empire and the Outside World 1922–1949: The Strange Evolution of a "Dictionary republic" ' in M. Cronin and J. M. Regan (eds.), *Ireland: The Politics of Independence 1922–49* (2000), pp. 164–216.

135. See D. O'Corrain (ed.), *James Hogan: Revolutionary, Historian and Political Scientist* (Dublin, 2001).

136. See John M. Regan, *The Irish Counter-Revolution 1921–36* (Dublin, 1999), ch. 11.

137. J. Campbell, *F. E. Smith, First Earl of Birkenhead* (1983), p. 793.

138. The classic account is M. Cowling, *The Impact of Labour* (Cambridge, 1970).

139. R. Skidelsky, *J. M. Keynes*, vol. II, *The Economist as Saviour* (1992), p. 133.

140. Skidelsky, *Keynes*, vol. II, p. 131; R. McKibbin, *Classes and Cultures: England 1918–1951* (Oxford, 1998), p. 115.

141. McKibbin, *Classes and Cultures*, p. 115.

142. P. Cain, *Hobson and Imperialism: Radicalism, the New Liberalism and Finance, 1887–1938* (Oxford, 2002), p. 199.

143. See F. Lee, *Fabianism and Colonialism: The Life and Political Thought of Lord Sydney Olivier* (1988).

144. Lee, *Fabianism and Colonialism*, ch. 5.

145. Lord Lugard, *The Dual Mandate in Tropical Africa* (1922).

146. J. Darwin, 'The Chanak Crisis and the British Cabinet', *History*, 65, 113 (1980), 32–48.

147. In a letter published in *The Times* and the *Daily Express*, 7 October 1922. See R. Blake, *The Unknown Prime Minister: The Life and Times of Andrew Bonar Law 1858–1923* (1955), p. 448.

148. For a magisterial study of MacDonald's career, see D. Marquand, *Ramsay MacDonald* (1977).

149. McKibbin, *Classes and Cultures*, p. 521.

Chapter 10

1. See A. Zimmern, *The Third British Empire* (Oxford, 1926).

2. See S. Constantine, 'Migrants and Settlers', in J. M. Brown and W. R. Louis (eds.), *Oxford History of the British Empire*, vol. IV, *The Twentieth Century* (Oxford, 1999), p. 165, Table 7.2.

3. Churchill College Archives, Lord Lloyd of Dolobran Mss, GLLD 17/15: Speech at Central Council of National Union, 4 December 1934, Press Cutting.

4. H. Kantorowicz, *The Spirit of British Policy* (1931), p. 507. The main aim of the book had been to demolish the 'myth of German encirclement' by a machiavellian British diplomacy.

5. Siegfried, *England's Crisis*, p. 231.

6. Memo by R. Craigie, 12 November 1928, quoted in B. L. McKercher, *The Second Baldwin Government and the United States, 1924–1929* (Cambridge, 1984), p. 174.

7. See D. A. Yerxa, *Admirals and Empire: The United States Navy and the Caribbean 1898–1945* (Columbia, SC, 1991), p. 95.

8. See McKercher, *Baldwin Government*, chs. 7, 8; O. Babij, 'The Second Labour Government and British Maritime Security', *Diplomacy and Statecraft*, 6, 3 (1995), 645–71; D. Marquand, *Ramsay MacDonald* (1977), pp. 504–14.

9. C. Tsuzuki, *The Pursuit of Power in Modern Japan 1825–1995* (Oxford, 2000), chs. 11, 12, 13, for a recent analysis.

10. For a contemporary account, see I. Bowman, 'A Modern Invasion: Mongolia and Manchuria', in his *The Pioneer Fringe* (New York, 1931).

11. Foreign Office Memo, 8 January 1930. *Documents on British Foreign Policy*, 2nd series, vol. VIII, pp. 18–19.

12. Bodl. Mss Dawson 76, Note by Geoffrey Dawson of talk with Sir John Simon, the Foreign Secretary, 14 March 1932. Dawson was editor of *The Times* in 1912–19 and 1922–41.

13. See Memo by C. Orde, 14 December 1933, *Documents on British Foreign Policy*, 2nd series, vol. XX (1984), pp. 119ff.; Lampson to Simon, 24 August 1933 (received 7 November), *Documents on British Foreign Policy*, 2nd series, vol. XI, pp. 558–97, esp. p. 592.

14. The Tshushima Strait lies between Japan and Korea.

15. The best account of the Sub-Committee's proceedings is now K. Neilson, 'The Defence Requirements Sub-Committee, British Strategic Foreign Policy, Neville Chamberlain and the Path to Appeasement', *English Historical Review*, 118, 477 (2003), 651–84.

16. See D. H. Cole, *Imperial Military Geography* (8th edn, 1935), pp. 148–50.

17. For this view in the Foreign Office, see G. Kennedy, *Anglo-American Strategic Relations in the Far East 1933–1939* (2002), p. 53.

18. For the First Sea Lord's memo of 14 March 1934, urging a two-power standard, see Kennedy, *Strategic Relations*, p. 140.

19. For Chamberlain's support for a non-aggression pact with Japan, see Kennedy, *Strategic Relations*, p. 176.

20. Neilson, 'Defence Requirements Sub-Committee', p. 677.

21. See Kennedy, *Strategic Relations*, chs. 2, 3.

22. *Ibid.*, pp. 186ff., 202.

23. For the Anglo-German Naval Agreement of June 1935, see J. Maiolo, *The Royal Navy and Nazi Germany 1933–1939* (1998).

24. CAB 4/23, Annual Review by Chiefs of Staff Sub-Committee, 29 April 1935, para. 19.

25. Minute, 25 February 1935, *Documents on British Foreign Policy*, 2nd series, vol. XIV, p. 166.

26. Minute, 8 June 1935, *Documents on British Foreign Policy*, 2nd series, Vol. XIV, p. 318.

27. Chatfield to Vansittart, 8 August 1935, *ibid.*, p. 465.

28. L. R. Pratt, *East of Malta, West of Suez: Britain's Mediterranean Crisis 1936–1939* (Cambridge, 1975), p. 23.

29. CAB 4/24, Chiefs of Staff Sub-Commiteee, Memo, 1 April 1936, p. 2.

30. CAB 4/24, Defence Requirements Sub-Committee, Third Report, 21 November 1935, p. 38.

31. Pratt, *East of Malta*, p. 47.

32. At the Imperial Conference in May 1937. See S. Roskill, *Hankey, Man of Secrets* (1974), vol. II, p. 282.

33. In November 1936, Germany and Japan had made their Anti-Comintern Pact.

34. In his lecture, 'Quo Vadimus' (1934), cited in D. Edgerton, *Warfare State: Britain, 1920–1970* (Cambridge, 2005), p. 56.

35. FO 371/20475, Chamberlain to Eden, 25 August 1936. For Hitler's reaffirmation of these policies in September 1936, see A. Tooze, *The Wages of Destruction* (2005), pp. 219ff.

36. G. Jones, *Merchants to Multinationals* (Oxford, 2000), p. 87.

37. Down from 3,057 million linear yards in 1913 to 375 million in 1936. G. E. Hubbard, *Eastern Industrialization and its Effect on the West* (2nd edn, 1938), p. 340.

38. Post-tax returns on capital slumped to less than 4 per cent. See Jones, *Merchants*, p. 95.

39. Averaging £33 million a year compared with £200 million (much more in real terms) before 1914. P. J. Cain and A. G. Hopkins, *British Imperialism* (1992), vol. II, p. 87.

40. For the contemporary view that Britain's population growth was over, see W. K. Hancock, *Survey of British Commonwealth Affairs: Problems of Economic Policy* vol. I, (1940), pp. 156–77.

41. Except in the Netherlands, Belgium, Britain and the Irish Free State. See W. A. Mackintosh, *The Economic Background to Dominion-Provincial Relations* ([1939] Toronto, 1978), p. 110.

42. Hubbard, *Eastern Industrialization*, p. 340.

43. For London's dealings with New Delhi, see I. M. Drummond, *The Floating Pound and the Sterling Area 1931–1939* (Cambridge, 1981), ch. 2; B. R. Tomlinson, 'Britain and the Indian Currency Crisis 1930–1932', *Economic History Review*, 2nd series 32 (1979), 88–9.

44. In Australia and New Zealand, at the lower level of 1.25:1.

45. See G. C. Peden, *The Treasury and Public Policy 1906–1959* (Oxford, 2000), p. 256: the Account was managed 'on a day to day basis by the Bank'.

46. For this analysis, see Drummond, *Floating Pound*, pp. 258–9.

47. See D. Kynaston, *The City of London*, vol. III, *Illusions of Gold* (2000), p. 361.

48. See R. Self (ed.), *The Neville Chamberlain Diary Letters*, vol. III, *The Heir Apparent 1928–1933* (2002), pp. 30–6.

49. Chamberlain had replaced Philip Snowden as Chancellor of the Exchequer.

50. Self (ed.), *Chamberlain Diary Letters*, vol. III, pp. 39–40.

51. For this estimate, see I. M. Drummond, *British Economic Policy and the Empire 1919–1939* (1972), p. 102.

52. For an example, see L. S. Amery's pamphlet, *Empire and Prosperity* (1930).

53. What British ministers thought they had got is summarised in their telegram to London, 14 August 1932, printed in I. M. Drummond, *Imperial Economic Policy 1917–1939: Studies in Expansion and Protection* (1974), pp. 290–5.

54. See Tim Rooth, *British Protectionism and the International Economy: Overseas Commercial Policy in the 1930s* (Cambridge, 1992), ch. 4.

55. *Ibid.*, pp. 146–56.

56. *Ibid.*, pp. 318–19.

57. P. J. Hugill, *Global Communications since 1844: Geopolitics and Technology* (Baltimore, 1999), p. 28.

58. Rooth, *British Protectionism*, p. 320.

59. League of Nations, *The Network of World Trade* (1942), p. 19. In 1938, Britain absorbed one-sixth of the world's imports, twice as much as the United States. See T. Rooth, 'Britain's Other Dollar Problem: Economic Relations with Canada 1945–1950', *Journal of Imperial and Commonwealth History*, 27, 1 (1999), 103.

60. See P. Clavin, 'Shaping the Lessons of History: Britain and the Rhetoric of American Trade Policy, 1930–1960', in A. Marrison (ed.), *Free Trade and its Reception 1815–1960: Freedom and Trade* (1998), pp. 287–307. For U.S. anxiety about British tariff barriers, see D. Irwin, 'From Smoot-Hawley to Reciprocal Trade Agreements: Changing the Course of Trade Policy in the 1930s' in M. Bordo, C. Goldin, E. White (eds), *The Defining Moment: The Great Depression and the American Economy in the Twentieth Century* (1998), pp. 335–43.

61. H. James, *The End of Globalization* (Cambridge, MA, 2001), p. 48.

62 The National Government won 62.9 per cent of votes and 554 seats in 1931; 54.8 per cent with 432 seats in 1935.

63. Wales, for example, lost 450,000 people by migration in 1921–39; and London gained 458,000 in 1931–9. See B. Thomas, *Migration and Urban Development* (1972), pp. 181–2.

64. See R. McKibbin, *Classes and Cultures: English History 1918–1951* (1998), p. 115.

65. For this, see *Ibid.*, p. 68.

66. For a superb analysis of Baldwin's style and rhetoric, see P. Williamson, *Stanley Baldwin: Conservative Leadership and National Values* (Cambridge, 1999).

67. See *The Economist*, 1 May 1937.

68. Newfoundland's status lapsed with bankruptcy in 1933; in Southern Rhodesia, despite wide internal self-government, the Imperial government retained reserved powers over 'native policy'.

69. For this complication, see the 'Report of the Conference on the Operation of Dominion Legislation and Merchant Shipping Legislation,1929, Part V', quoted in R. M. Dawson, *The Development of Dominion Status 1900–1936* (1936), pp. 381–9.

70. CAB 23/65, Cab. 51(30), 17 September 1930.

71. Bodl. Sankey Papers, Mss Eng. Hist. e285: Diary, 3 December 1931.

72. CAB 23/65, Cab. 51(30), 17 September 1930.

73. Bodl. Sankey Papers, Mss Eng. Hist. c547, Note by Sir M. Gwyer, June 1931.

74. *The Times*, 21 November 1931.

75. *Ibid.*

76. For the report on the debate, see *The Times*, 25 November 1931.

77. *The Times*, 20 November 1931.

78. Bodl. Sankey Papers, Mss Eng. Hist. c509, Notes on Cabinet meeting after Ottawa, 27 August 1932.

79. See P. Rich, *Race and Empire in British Politics* (Cambridge, 1986), pp. 69–84.

80. Churchill College, Cambridge, Lord Lloyd of Dolobran Papers, GLLD 17/62, D. O. Malcolm to H. V. Hodson, 6 July 1934. Malcolm was a director of the British South Africa Company and, like Amery, Curtis and Hodson, a Fellow of All Souls College, Oxford.

81. For Macmillan's disagreements with Curtis, see D. Lavin, *From Empire to International Commonwealth: A Biography of Lionel Curtis* (Oxford, 1995), pp. 235–9.

82. 329 Conservatives supported the bill, and 79 voted against. The bill was carried by 404 to 133.

83. See S. Ball, *Baldwin and the Conservative Party* (1988), p. 114.

84. See his speeches at Worcester, May 1933, *The Times*, 1 May 1933; at Manchester in June 1933, *The Times*, 30 June 1933; at the Conservative Central Council (i.e. the annual conference), 4 December 1934, press cutting in Lloyd Papers, GLLD 17/16.

85. Speech in House of Commons, March 1931, *The Times*, 12 March 1931.

86. *Ibid.*

87. P. Williamson and E. Baldwin (eds.), *Baldwin Papers: A Conservative Statesman 1908–1947* (Cambridge, 2004), p. 307.

88. As note 8 above.

89. For Reading's view that, without an agreed constitution, 'it will be a case of troops and money from here when we can spare neither', see his letter to MacDonald, 28 November 1931, Sankey Papers, Mss Eng. Hist. c539.

90. See the Union of Britain and India's pamphlet series: between May and August 1933, the UBI issued ten pamphlets and organised forty-three meetings; C. Bridge, *Holding India to the Empire: The British Conservative Party and the 1935 Constitution* (1986), pp. 100–1.

91. 'The House of Commons would misunderstand' a reference to dominion status, said Hoare, the Secretary of State for India, somewhat archly. See Cabinet Committee on India, 15 January 1935, copy in Sankey Papers, Mss Eng. Hist. c512. For the bargain with Austen Chamberlain, see Bridge, *India*, pp. 117–18.

92. See F. W. S. Craig, *British General Election Manifestos 1918–1966* (Chichester, 1976), p. 8.

93. Bodl. Mss Edward Grigg, Microfilm 1003, Neville Chamberlain to Edward Grigg, 30 September 1931. I owe this reference to Alex May.

94. For the usage of race, see the discussion of eugenic concerns in the 1930s in R. A. Soloway, *Demography and Degeneration: Eugenics and the Declining Birth-rate in Twentieth Century Britain* (1990).

95. Siegfried, *England's Crisis*, p. 207.

96. The phrase is J. C. Smuts': 'We of the Dominions are the Newer World.' Speech, 28 January 1930. See J. Van Der Poel (ed.), *Selections from the Smuts Papers* (Cambridge, 1973), vol. V, p. 450.

97. See W. J. Hudson and M. J. Sharp, *Australian Independence* (Melbourne, 1988), pp. 111–16. The National party opposition insisting on inserting a clause in the parliamentary resolution approving the bill that the Australian parliament, and not just the government, would have to agree to any request for legislation by the Imperial Parliament. See *The Times*, 18 July 1931.

98. Alexander Turnbull Library, J. G. Coates Papers, MS 1785/041, Note by A. G. Park, Secretary to New Zealand Treasury, 1 July 1931.

99. *The Times*, 13 September 1930. For an authoritative study, see C. D. Schedvin, *Australia and the Great Depression* (Sydney, 1970).

100. See his press statement, 25 September 1930, *The Times*, 26 September 1930.

101. John T. Lang, *Why I Fight* (Sydney, 1934), preface, pp. 54, 219.

102. *The Times*, 8 December 1931.

103. See S. Alomes, *A Nation at Last* (1988), pp. 74–98.

104. A. W. Martin, *Robert Menzies: A Life* (Melbourne, 1993), vol. I, p. 166.

105. *The Times*, 4 November 1932.

106. D. Day, *John Curtin: A Life* (2000), p. 346.

107. A trend broken off by the trade dispute of 1936. See P. Jones, 'Trading in a "Fool's Paradise"? White Australia and the Trade Dispute of 1936', in P. Jones and V. Mackie (eds.), *Relationships: Japan and Australia 1870s–1950s* (Melbourne, 2001), pp. 133–62.

108. Report on Mission to the East, *The Times*, 7 July 1934.

109. Quoted in I. Turner (ed.), *The Australian Dream* (Melbourne, 1968), p. 296.

110. Turner (ed.), *Australian Dream*, pp. 297–8.

111. Bodl. Sankey Papers, Mss Eng. Hist. c509, Notes on Cabinet meeting after Ottawa, 27 August 1932.

112. R. Self, *Neville Chamberlain* (2006), p. 84.

113. See copy in National Archives of Canada, R. B. Bennett Papers, microfilm, M 3176.

114. Copy in R. B. Bennett Papers, M 1271.

115. Queen's University, Kingston, Douglas Library, T. A. Crerar Papers, Box 98, Crerar to A. K. Cameron, 10 December 1941.

116. T. A. Crerar Papers, Box 98, Crerar to Cameron, 23 December 1932.

117. In the 1931 census, the three prairie provinces had a population of 2,353,529, of whom 1,195,084 were of British origin. *The Times*, 16 June 1933.

118. J. H. Thompson, *Forging the Prairie West* (Toronto, 1998), p. 133.

119. R. B. Bennett Papers, microfilm, M 1289, Second and Final Report of Parliamentary Committee on Radio Broadcasting, 1932.

120. National Archives of Canada, MG-32, B 5, Brooke Claxton Papers, vol. 19, Claxton to M. Lubbock, 12 November 1935. On Claxton's politics, see D. Owram, *The Government Generation: Canadian Intellectuals and the State 1900–1945* (Toronto, 1986), p. 224; D. J. Bercuson, *True Patriot: The Life of Brooke Claxton* (Toronto, 1993).

121. Brooke Claxton Papers, vol. 18, Claxton to W. D. Herridge, 26 December 1934.

122. See R. Cook, *The Politics of John W. Dafoe and the Free Press* (Toronto, 1963).

123. University of Manitoba, Elizabeth Dafoe Library, J. W. Dafoe Papers Box 2, Dafoe to J. S. Ewart, 9 January 1928.

124. Dafoe Papers, Box 1, Dafoe to W. Martin, 2 August 1932.

125. National Archives of Canada, J. W. Dafoe Papers, microfilm, M 74, Dafoe to A. Hawkes, 6 January 1928.

126. Brooke Claxton Papers, vol. 19, Claxton to K. Lindsay, 26 June 1934; Dafoe Papers Box 1, Dafoe to Lord Lothian, 10 October 1934.

127. A. R. M. Lower, 'Geographical Determinants of Canadian History', in R. Flenley (ed.), *Essays in Canadian History* (Toronto, 1939), p. 251.

128. Dafoe Papers, Box 1, Dafoe to H. F. Armstrong, 25 July 1935.

129. See the account of his interview with Grant Dexter in Dafoe Papers, Box 12, Dexter to Dafoe, 16 October 1932.

130. For this interpretation of Bennett's policy, see Dafoe Papers Box 1, Dafoe to Geoffrey Dawson, 19 October 1932. Dawson was a close ally of Baldwin.

131. For King's views, see J. Macfarlane, 'Double Vision: Ernest Lapointe, Mackenzie King and the Quebec Voice in Canadian Foreign Policy, 1935–1939', *Journal of Canadian Studies*, 34, 1 (1999), 94–5.

132. *The Times*, 3 April 1935.

133. L. Groulx, *Mes mémoires*, 4 vols. (Montreal, 1971), vol. II, p. 305.

134. See S. M. Trofimenkoff, *The Dream of Nation: A Social and Intellectual History of Quebec* (Toronto, 1983), chs. 14, 15; B. St Aubin, *Maurice Duplessis et son époque* (Montreal, 1979).

135. For a survey, see S. Marks and S. Trapido (eds.), *The Politics of Race, Class and Nationalism in Twentieth Century South Africa* (1987), chs. 1, 2.

136. University of Cape Town, Jagger Library, Patrick Duncan Papers, D 5.24.17, Duncan to Lady Selborne, 28 April 1932.

137. H. J. Schlosberg, *The King's Republics* (1929). Hertzog contributed a foreword.

138. *Ibid.*, pp. 49–50. Perhaps surprisingly, Schlosberg, *ibid.*, p. 43, denied the right of secession as this would mean abolishing the Crown.

139. Quoted in M. Roberts and A. E. G. Trollip, *The South African Opposition 1939–1945: An Essay in Contemporary History* (1947), p. 11.

140. See H. Giliomee, *The Afrikaners: Biography of a People* (2003), p. 397.

141. Jagger Library, H. G. Lawrence Papers, BC 640, Speech at Kalk Bay, 21 June 1927.

142. Speech at Pretoria, 30 April 1929, in J. Van Der Poel (ed.), *Selections from the Smuts Papers* (Cambridge, 1973), vol. V, p. 401.

143. See extract from Smuts' speech at Ermelo, January 1929, lovingly preserved in Stellenbosch University Library, D. F. Malan Papers, 1/1/822.

144. Duncan Papers D 5.24.11, Duncan to Lady Selborne, 17 May 1932.

145. Smuts to Heaton Nicholls, 14 November 1932, Van Der Poel (ed.), *Smuts Papers*, vol. V, p. 524.

146. J. Lewis. 'The Germiston By-Election of 1932', in P. Bonner (ed.), *Working Papers in South African Studies* (Johannesburg, 1981), vol. II, pp. 97–120.

147. Duncan Papers, D 5.26.9, Duncan to Lady Selborne, 12 April 1934; for Smuts' speech, 11 April 1934, see Van Der Poel (ed.), *Smuts Papers*, vol. V, pp. 582–96; for his estimate of its influence, see *ibid.*, p. 596, Smuts to M. C. Gillet, 15 April 1934.

148. Duncan Papers, D 5.26.23, Duncan to Lady Selborne, 1 August 1934.

149. See H. G. Lawrence Papers, BC 640, C.16.18.

150. H. G. Lawrence Papers, BC 640, C.16.4, *East London Daily Dispatch*, 2 April 1935, Speech by Major P. van Der Byl, an Afrikaner of impeccable 'empire' credentials.

151. Giliomee, *Afrikaners*, p. 409.

152. See Isobel Hofmeyr, 'Popularising History: The Case of Gustav Preller', *Journal of African History*, 29, 3 (1988), 521–35.

153. For an impression of this, see *South African Who's Who (Social and Business) 1931–1932* (Cape Town, 1931).

154. *The Times*, 12 December 1935.

155. See the proposals of Walter Nash, the finance minister, *The Times*, 18 June 1936, 4 December 1936, 16 January 1937.

156. See D. McMahon, *Republicans and Imperialists* (1982).

157. In India, Britain was moving from power to influence, declared Lord Halifax, Viceroy (as Lord Irwin) 1926–31. *The Times*, 22 July 1937.

158. Dafoe Papers, Box 2: Dafoe to J. S. Ewart, 9 January 1928.

159. Milner's Egyptian Diary, 5 December 1919, cited in Darwin, *Britain, Egypt and the Middle East*, p. 89.

160. B. R. Tomlinson, *The Political Economy of the Raj 1914–1947* (1979), p. 46. See also B. Chatterji, 'Business and Politics in the 1930s: Lancashire and the Making of the Indo-British Trade Agreement, 1939', *Modern Asian Studies*, 15, 3 (1981), 527–73.

161. For the fear that if the rupee was devalued the government of India would be unable to pay the Home Charges, see BLIOC, Reading Collection, Mss Eur. E 238/10, Memo by Secretary of State for India, October 1931.

162. Note by India Office official, December 1930. Tomlinson, *Political Economy*, p. 127.

163. For these recommendations, see *Report of Indian Statutory Commission*, vol. II, *Recommendations*, Parts 2, 4, 5.

164. The classic account is R. J. Moore, *The Crisis of Indian Unity* (Oxford, 1974).

165. S. and S. Bose (eds.), *Essential Writings of Netaji Subhas Chandra Bose* (Delhi, 1997), p. 211.

166. See W. M. Hogben, 'An Imperial Dilemma: The Reluctant Indianization of the Indian Political Service', *Modern Asian Studies*, 15, 4 (1981), 751–69.

167. Dafoe Papers Box 12, Willingdon to J. W. Dafoe, 17 January 1931. Willingdon complained that the ICS were 'hanging on desperately to their jobs'.

168. See D. Potter, 'Manpower Shortage and the End of Colonialism: The Case of the Indian Civil Service', *Modern Asian Studies*, 17, 1 (1973), 47–73.

169. D. Potter, *India's Political Administrators: From ICS to IAS* (Delhi. 1996), p. 40.

170. E. Blunt, *The Indian Civil Service* (1938), pp. 261–2.

171. See B. R. Nanda (ed.), *Selected Works of Govind Ballabh Pant* (Delhi, 1997), vol. VII, pp. 463-5, (Governor) Haig to (Viceroy) Linlithgow, 8 August 1937.

172. *Ibid.*, vol VIII, pp. 445-7, Haig to Linlithgow, 5 March 1938.

173. N. Charlesworth, 'The Problem of Government Finance in British India: Taxation, Borrowing and the Allocation of Resources in the Inter-War Period', *Modern Asian Studies*, 19, 3 (1985) 521-48.

174. See D. Omissi, *The Sepoy and the Raj* (1994), p. 160.

175. *Ibid.*, p. 187.

176. J. M. Brown, *Gandhi and Civil Disobedience 1928-1934* (Cambridge, 1977), pp. 83-4.

177. *All Parties Conference 1928* (Allahabad, 1928), pp. 100-24, 'Recommendations'; R. Kumar and H. D. Sharma (eds.), *Selected Works of Motilal Nehru* (New Delhi, 1993), vol. V, p. 308.

178. *Forty-Ninth Session of Congress* (Allahabad, n.d.), p. 26.

179. *Ibid.*, p. 28.

180. See *The Times*, 15 March 1937, for this verdict.

181. Speech by Lord Hailey, a former governor of the Punjab and the United Provinces, and one of the major ICS architects of the reforms. *The Times*, 29 May 1937.

182. See N. B. Khare, *My Political Memoirs* (Nagpur, 1959).

183. V. Damodaran, *Broken Promises: Popular Protest, Indian Nationalism and the Congress Party in Bihar, 1935-46* (Delhi, 1992); C. Markovits, 'Indian Business and the Congress, 1937-39', *Modern Asian Studies*, 15, 3 (1981), 514.

184. J. Sarkar, 'Power, Hegemony and Politics: Leadership Struggle in the Congress in the 1930s', *Modern Asian Studies*, 40, 2 (2006), 336.

185. D. Rothermund, *India in the Great Depression 1929-1939* (New Delhi, 1992), p. 209.

186. Markovits, 'Indian Business', p. 511.

187. See his Haripura address as Congress president in 1938. S. and S. Bose (eds.), *Essential Writings*.

188. Nehru to G. B. Pant, 25 November 1937, Rothermund, *Depression*, p. 249.

189. D. H. Cole, *Imperial Military Geography* (1935), ch. XI, pp. 290–4.

190. 'The Suez Canal of the Air: A Stay in Bahrein', *The Times*, 12 June 1935.

191. See D. K. Fieldhouse, *Western Imperialism in the Middle East 1914–1958* (Oxford, 2006), ch. 3; H. Batatu, *The Old Social Classes and the Revolutionary Movements of Iraq* (Princeton, 1978), Parts 1 and 2; D. Silverfarb, *Britain's Informal Empire in the Middle East: A Case Study of Iraq 1929–1941* (1986).

192. J. Kostiner, *The Making of Saudi Arabia 1916–1936* (Oxford, 1993), p. 140; C. Leatherdale, *Britain and Saudi Arabia 1925–1939: The Imperial Oasis* (1983), p. 126.

193. FO 371/ 20116, Minute on Anglo-Egyptian relations 1929–34, 9 August 1936.

194. FO 371/13841, Minute by J. Murray, 13 June 1929.

195. Middle East Centre, St Antony's College, Oxford, Killearn Collection: Lampson's diary, 18 April 1935.

196. See the account by T. Swedenburg, 'The Role, of the Palestine Peasantry in the Great Revolt of 1936–1939', in Ilan Pappé (ed.), *The Israel/Palestine Question* (1999), p. 143.

197. *Ibid.*, p. 144.

198. See Butrus Abu-Manneh, 'The Rise of the Sanjak of Jerusalem in the Late Nineteenth Century', in Pappé (ed.), *Israel/Palestine Question*, p. 46.

199. M. E. Yapp (ed.), *Politics and Diplomacy in Egypt: The Diaries of Sir Miles Lampson 1935–1937* (1997), p. 392 (11 December 1935).

200. See the Cabinet discussions on 6 and 20 May 1936 in FO 371/20106, 20108.

201. FO 371/20110, Conclusions of Cabinet Anglo-Egyptian Relations Committee, 15 June 1936.

202. *Ibid.*, 16 June 1936.

203. FO 371/20111, Memo by Foreign Secretary, 19 June 1936.

204. *Ibid.*

205. Cmd. 5308 (1936), Map to Illustrate the Treaty of Alliance with Egypt.

206. FO 371/22006, Lampson to Halifax, 30 June 1938.

207. FO 371/22006, Annual Report for 1937, 30 June 1938.

208. FO 371/20109, Lampson to Foreign Office, 28 May 1936.

209. S. J. Potter, 'The BBC, the CBC, and the Royal Tour of Canada, 1939', *Cultural and Social History*, 3 (2006), 432.

Chapter 11

1. A. Toynbee and F. Ashton-Gwatkin (eds.), *Survey of International Affairs: The World in March 1939* (1952), pp. 454–6.

2. For an up-to-date account, see A. Best, *British Intelligence and the Japanese Challenge in Asia, 1914–1941* (Basingstoke, 2002), chs. 6, 7.

3. Toynbee and Ashton-Gwatkin (eds.), *The World in March 1939*, pp. 454–6.

4. See R. Boyce, 'World Depression, World War: Some Economic Origins of the Second World War', in R. Boyce and E. M. Robertson (eds.), *Paths to War* (1989), pp. 55–95.

5. See A. Tooze, *The Wages of Destruction* (2006), for a brilliant description of the policies pursued by Schacht.

6. For the dilemmas and opportunities of Japanese economic policy in the 1930s, see C. Howe, *The Origins of Japanese Trade Supremacy* (1996), ch. 6.

7. H. James, *The End of Globalisation* (2001), p. 199.

8. M. J. Bonn, *The Crumbling of Empire* (1938), pp. 194–5.

9. For this analysis, see League of Nations, *The Network of World Trade* (1942), p. 95.

10. For the general setting, see M. Mazower, *Dark Continent: Europe's Twentieth Century* (1998), ch. 1.

11. If Hitler's New Order triumphed, 'we should be the blockaded party'. E. Staley, 'The Myth of the Continents' (first published in *Foreign Affairs*, April 1941) in H. Weigert and V. Stefansson (eds.), *The Compass of the World* (1943), p. 99.

12. J. Darwin, 'Imperialism in Decline?', *Historical Journal*, 23, 3 (1980), 673–7.

13. For a passionate (Indian) statement of this view, see K. M. Pannikar, *India and the Indian Ocean* (1945).

14. M. Ceadel, *Semi-Detached Idealists* (Oxford, 2000), p. 346.

15. See N. Angell, *The Defence of Empire* (1937).

16. University of Texas at Austin, Harry Ransome Humanities Centre, J. L. Garvin Papers: Lothian to J. L. Garvin, 29 October 1936, 18 November 1937; L. S. Amery to Garvin, 23 March, 10 June, 26 October 1936; Grigg to Garvin, 7 February 1938.

17. See E. H. Carr, *The Twenty Years Crisis* [1939] (new edn, 2001), p. lxxvi; C. Jones, *E. H. Carr and International Relations: A Duty to Lie* (Cambridge, 1998), p. 61.

18. For a brilliant discussion of this theme in Liddell Hart, see A. Gat, *Fascist and Liberal Theories of War* (Oxford, 2000), pp. 146–265.

19. CAB 27/599, Cabinet Memo by Anthony Eden, 11 February 1936, enclosing Note by Vansittart, 3 February 1936.

20. J. Neidpath, *The Singapore Naval Base and the Defence of Britain's Eastern Empire* (Oxford, 1981), p. 131.

21. CAB 24/270, Memo by Chancellor of Exchequer, 25 June 1937.

22. For Eden's views on Japan, see M. Murfett, *Fool-Proof Relations: The Search for Anglo-American Naval Co-operation during the Chamberlain Years* (Singapore, 1984), pp. 157–61.

23. For an early expression of his views on Japan, see Chamberlain to Simon, 1 September 1934, *Documents on British Foreign Policy*, 2nd series, vol. XIII, pp. 24–32.

24. For the pessimistic calculations of the Chiefs of Staff, see their memo, 'Military Implications of German Aggression against Czechoslovakia', March 1938. CAB 27/627. Intriguingly, the Chiefs of Staff did not consider the possibility of a Soviet alliance.

25. J. Maiolo, *The Royal Navy and Nazi Germany, 1933–1939* (Basingstoke and London, 1998), pp. 155–6.

26. W. Murray, *The Change in the European Balance of Power 1938–1939* (Princeton, 1984), pp. 247, 363.

27. Maiolo, *Royal Navy and Nazi Germany*, p. 156.

28. Except for the section given to Poland.

29. The authoritative study is S. Newman, *March 1939: The British Guarantee to Poland* (Oxford, 1976).

30. I. Cowan, *Dominion or Decline: Anglo-American Naval Relations in the Pacific 1937–1941* (Oxford, 1996), pp. 144–5.

31. CAB 27/627. Report by Chiefs of Staff Sub-committee on Far East Situation, 18 June 1939.

32. *Ibid.*

33. See P. Lowe, *Great Britain and the Origins of the Pacific War 1937–41* (Oxford, 1977), pp. 73–89.

34. Maiolo, *Royal Navy and Nazi Germany*, p. 183.

35. CAB 24/287, CP 149 (39), Note on Financial Situation, 3 July 1939.

36. CAB 23/100, Cabinet 36 (39), 5 July 1939.

37. *Canadian House of Commons Debates*, vol. 220, p. 2422, col. 2 (30 March 1939).

38. *Ibid.*, p. 2467, col. 2 (31 March 1939).

39. For the strength of 'Britannic' feeling in Ontario, see Terry Copp, 'Ontario 1939: The Decision for War', *Ontario History*, 86 (1974), 269–78.

40. 'We have ... been relegated to the role of a Crown Colony', raged Oscar Skelton, head of the External Affairs department, in his memorandum of 25 August 1939. J. Munro (ed.), *Documents on Canadian External Relations* (Ottawa, 1972), vol. 6, pp. 1247–9.

41. *Commonwealth Parliamentary Debates*, vol. 159, p. 198, col. 2 (9 May 1939). Quoted in speech by Sir H. Gullett, the external affairs minister.

42. R. G. Menzies, in *Commonwealth Parliamentary Debates*, vol. 159, p. 234, col. 1 (9 May 1939). For Menzies' statement of 6 September 1939, see *ibid.*, vol. 161, pp. 28–36.

43. *New Zealand Parliament Debates*, vol. 254, p. 20 (5 September 1939).

44. For Hertzog's views, see C. M. van den Heever, *General J. B. M. Hertzog* (English trans., Johannesburg, 1946), pp. 275–86.

45. University of Cape Town, Jagger Library, Patrick Duncan Papers E.10.19.1, 4, Duncan to Lady Duncan, 1, 4 September 1939.

46. See South Africa House of Assembly, *Debates*, vol. 36, 4 September 1939.

47. See the 'Neutrality Debate', 2 September 1939, in *Dail Eireann Parliamentary Debates*.

48. PP XX (1938–9), Cmd. 6121, *India and the War*, Appendix C, Resolution by All-India Congress Committee, 10 October 1939.

49. See the Nehru–Jinnah correspondence in J. Nehru, *A Bunch of Old Letters* (Bombay, 1958), pp. 392–4, 403–10.

50. See Chamberlain to Churchill, 16 September 1939; Churchill to Chamberlain, 18 September 1939; Military Co-ordination Committee, Minutes, 5 December 1939, in M. Gilbert (ed.), *The Churchill War Papers*, vol. I, *At the Admiralty* (1993), pp. 101, 111, 466.

51. *Fortune*, July 1940, p. 136.

52. Churchill to Roosevelt, 24 December 1939. Gilbert, *War Papers*, vol. I, p. 560.

53. *Fortune*, July 1940, p. 138.

54. Churchill to Wavell (Commander-in-Chief, Middle East), 26 January 1941, Gilbert, *Churchill War Papers*, vol. III, *The Ever-Widening War* (2000), p. 136.

55. Churchill to Margesson, 29 January 1941, Gilbert, *War Papers*, vol. III, p. 153.

56. J. Granatstein, *Canada's War: The Politics of the Mackenzie King Government 1939–1945* (Toronto, 1975), p. 25.

57. National Archives of Canada, Dafoe Papers M-79 (microfilm): T. A. Crerar to J. W. Dafoe, 10 June 1940; Queen's University Kingston, Douglas Library, T. A. Crerar Papers 119: Crerar to King, 23 February 1941.

58. National Archives of Canada, R. B. Bennett Papers M-3175 (microfilm), R. B. Hanson to R. B. Bennett, 17 September 1940.

59. National Archives of Canada, Mackenzie King Papers 4566 (microfilm), Mackenzie King to Churchill, 16 September 1940.

60. J. W. Pickersgill, *The Mackenzie King Record*, vol. I, *1939–1944* (Toronto, 1960), p. 203.

61. It was to be a *permanent* joint board.

62. Pickersgill, *Mackenzie King Record*, vol. 1, p. 204.

63. See R. Sarty, *Canada and the Battle of the Atlantic* (Montreal, 1998).

64. N. Meaney (ed.), *Australia and the World* (Melbourne, 1985), p. 459: R. G. Menzies to S. Bruce (Australian High Commissioner in London), 11 September 1939.

65. I. M. Cumpston, *Lord Bruce of Melbourne* (Melbourne, 1989), pp. 178, 181–4.

66. J. Grey, *A Military History of Australia* (Cambridge, 1999), p. 144.

67. D. Day, *John Curtin: A Life* (Sydney, 1999), p. 43.

68. J. Belich, *Paradise Reforged* (Auckland, 2001), p. 273; Grey, *Military History*, pp. 145–7.

69. Quoted in K. H. Bailey, 'Australia in the Empire', *Australian Outlook*, 14, 1 (1942), 13.

70. *The Economist*, 10 May 1941, p. 614.

71. See A. Grundlingh, 'The King's Afrikaners: Enlistment and Ethnic Identity in the Union of South Africa's Defence Force during the Second World War, 1939–45', *Journal of African History*, 40 (1999), 354.

72. J. Van Der Poel (ed.), *Selections from the Smuts Papers* (Cambridge, 1973), vol. VI, pp. 373–7: Smuts to F. H. Theron, 21 July 1942.

73. R. Hyam and P. Henshaw, *The Lion and the Springbok* (Cambridge, 2003), pp. 130–1.

74. M. Roberts and A. E. G. Trollip, *The South African Opposition 1939–1945* (1947), p. 159.

75. *Ibid.*, p. 174.

76. N. Prasad, *Official History of the Indian Armed Forces in the Second World War 1939–1945: The Expansion of the Armed Forces and Defence Organization* (Calcutta, 1956), pp. 54, 60.

77. Viceroy's statement, 8 August 1940. PP X (1939–40) Cmd. 6219, 'India and the War'.

78. See the development of Jinnah's views, in A. Jalal, *The Sole Spokesman: Jinnah, the Muslim League and the Demand for Pakistan* (Cambridge, 1985).

79. See I. Talbot, *Khizr Tiwana: The Punjab Unionist Party and the Partition of India* (Karachi, 2002), p. 134.

80. For this fear, see the Viceroy, Lord Linlithgow, to Hallett, 16 March 1942, N. Mansergh (ed.), *Constitutional Relations between Britain and India: The Transfer of Power 1942–47*, vol. I, *The Cripps Mission* (London, 1970), p. 430.

81. Amery to Linlithgow, 2 March 1942, Mansergh (ed.), *Constitutional Relations*, p. 295; Churchill to Linlithgow, Mansergh (ed.), *Constitutional Relations*, pp. 394–5.

82. War Cabinet Memo, 2 February 1942, Mansergh (ed.), *Constitutional Relations*, p. 112.

83. The authoritative account of the Cripps Mission is R. J. Moore, *Churchill, Cripps and India 1939–1945* (Oxford, 1979).

84. Until mid-June 1945. J. M. Brown, *Nehru* (2003), p. 139.

85. *The Economist*, 20 November 1937, 'British Capital Abroad', p. 359. For a higher estimate, M. Wilkins, *The History of Foreign Investment in the United States, 1914–1945* (2004), p. 72 (nearer 6%).

86. *The Economist*, 6 August 1938, p. 281.

87. *The Economist*, 20 November 1937, p. 363.

88. For the best account of Anglo-American commercial relations, see I. M. Drummond, *The Floating Pound and the Sterling Area, 1931–1939* (Cambridge, 1981).

89. D. Hall, *North American Supply* (1955), p. 269: down from $4,483 million to $2,167 million.

90. *The Economist*, 22 November 1941, p. 630.

91. J. M. Blum, *From the Morgenthau Diaries: The Years of Urgency 1938–41* (Boston, 1965), pp. 217–18.

92. The senator in charge of the lend–lease bill suggested a lien on Malayan rubber and tin.

93. R. Skidelsky, *The Life of J. M. Keynes: Fighting for Britain* (2000), ch. 4.

94. D. Moggridge (ed.), *The Collected Works of John Maynard Keynes: External War Finance* (Cambridge, 1979), p. 222: Keynes to Sir F. Phillips, 14 June 1942.

95. *Ibid.*, p. 233: Keynes to Sir H. Wilson, 9 June 1942.

96. *Fortune*, May 1942, pp. 59–60.

97. A. Warren, *Singapore, 1942* (2002), pp. 117–18.

98. Quoted in *The Economist*, 21 February 1942.

99. A. Danchev and D. Todman (eds.), *War Diaries 1939–1945: Field Marshal Lord Alanbrooke* (paperback edn, 2002), p. 229 (12 February 1942).

Chapter 12

1. Speech by Anthony Eden, 30 October 1942, *The Times*, 31 October 1942.

2. By 1944, the US was spending four times as much as Britain on armaments.

3. Speech by Smuts, 25 November 1943, *The Times*, 3 December 1943.

4. *British Documents on the End of Empire*: S. R. Ashton and S. E. Stockwell (eds.), *Imperial Policy and Colonial Practice 1925–1945*, Part 1 (1996), pp. 231–44: Memo by Post-Hostilities Planning Staff, 'The Security of the British Empire', 29 June 1945. CAB 81/46, PHP(45)29(0) Final.

5. To 29 per cent by 1943. W. K. Hancock and M. Gowing, *British War Economy* (1949), p. 354.

6. See *Ibid.*, ch. 18.

7. See J. M.Keynes, 'Our Overseas Financial Prospects', 13 August 1945, in D. Moggridge (ed.), *Collected Works of John Maynard Keynes*, vol. XXIV, *Activities 1944–1946* (Cambridge, 1979), pp. 398–414.

8. See Memo by Deputy Minister of Labour, 27 November 1943, National Archives of Canada, Mackenzie King Papers C-7054 (microfilm).

9. See M. Milner, *Canada's Navy: The First Century* (Toronto, 1999), pp. 119, 157.

10. Quoted in D. Day, *John Curtin: A Life* (Sydney, 1999), pp. 438–9.

11. *The Times*, 16 August 1943, 7 September 1943.

12. *The Times*, 7 September 1943.

13. E. Grigg, *The British Commonwealth: Its Place in the Service of the World* (1943), p. 164.

14. Copy in Brooke Claxton Mss, NAC MG 32 B-5, vol. 22.

15. W. L. Mackenzie King Diary, 15 May 1944, consulted online at http://king.collections.canada.ca.

16. Day, *Curtin*, p. 518.

17. *Ibid.*, p. 543.

18. *The Times*, 19 May 1942.

19. *The Times*, 3 December 1943.

20. J. Barnes and D. Nicholson (eds.), *The Empire at Bay: The Leo Amery Diaries 1929–1945* (1988), p. 947 (14 October 1943).

21. *The Times*, 9 September 1943.

22. Mackenzie King Diary, 5 May 1944.

23. *Ibid.*, 9 May 1944.

24. Speech, 27 August 1943. Brooke Claxton Mss, NAC MG 32 B-5, vol. 22.

25. Mackenzie King Diary, 4 May 1944.

26. Queen's University, Kingston, Douglas Library, C. G. Power Mss, Box 1: Political Jottings, July 1943.

27. C. G. Power Mss, Box 1: Memo by C. G. Power, 10 December 1944.

28. Mackenzie King Diary, 11 May 1944.

29. J. Ehrman, *Grand Strategy*, vol. VI (1956), p. 118.

30. Memo by H. Caccia, 26 October 1944. D. Ellwoood, *Italy 1943–1945* (Leicester, 1985), p. 118.

31. G. M. Alexander, *The Prelude to the Truman Doctrine: British Policy in Greece 1944–1947* (Oxford, 1982), p. 48.

32. R. Wilson, 'Economic Aspects of Arab Nationalism', in M. J. Cohen and M. Kolinsky (eds.), *Demise of the British Empire in the Middle East: Britain's Response to Nationalist Movements, 1943–1955* (1998), p. 67.

33. By 1948, it was nearly 40 per cent. W. B. Fisher, *The Middle East* (1950), pp. 242–4.

34. Thus the British ambassador in Cairo had been authorised to use force in April 1944 to prevent the dismissal of his favoured prime minister. See M. Kolinsky, 'Lampson and the Wartime Control of Egypt', in Cohen and Kolinsky (eds.), *Demise of the British Empire in the Middle East*, p. 108.

35. Quoted in J. Darwin, *Britain, Egypt and the Middle East: Imperial Policy in the Aftermath of War 1918–1922* (1981), p. 160.

36. Sir M. Hallet (Governor of the United Provinces) to Linlithgow (Viceroy), 9 March 1943. N. Mansergh (ed.), *Constitutional Relations between Britain and India: The Transfer of Power*, 12 vols. (London, 1970–83), vol. III, p. 778.

37. Linlithgow to Amery (Secretary of State for India), 19 July 1943. *Ibid.*, vol. IV, p. 53.

38. Amery to Churchill, 16 April 1943. *Ibid.*, vol. III, p. 895.

39. Wavell to Amery, 10 July 1944. *Ibid.*, vol. IV, p. 1075.

40. Wavell to Amery, 28 August 1944. *Ibid.*, vol. IV, p. 1228.

41. *Ibid.*, vol. IV, p. 165.

42. In his cabinet memo. 2 February 1942. *Ibid.*, I, pp. 110–12.

43. M. Perham, 'The Colonial Empire: Capital, Labour and the Colonial Colour Bar', *The Times*, 14 March 1942.

44. For a vehement attack on indirect rule, see W. M. Macmillan, *Africa Emergent* (1938).

45. *The Times*, 11 January 1943. Morrison was Home Secretary.

46. V. H. Rothwell, *Britain and the Cold War 1941–1947* (1982), p. 248.

47. *Ibid.*, p. 252.

48. For a brilliant description of Keynes' tortured negotiation, see R. Skidelsky, *John Maynard Keynes: Fighting for Britain 1937–1946* (2000), pp. 403–52. For an analysis that draws on the sceptical view from the Bank of England, see J. Fforde, *The Bank of England and Public Policy 1941–1958* (Cambridge, 1992), pp. 62–87.

49. HC Deb., 5th series, vol. 417, col. 442.

50. Speech in House of Lords, 18 December 1945. D. Moggridge (ed.), *Collected Works of John Maynard Keynes*, vol. XXIV, *Activities 1944–1946*, p. 620.

51. CAB 128/5, Cabinet 54(46), 3 June 1946.

52. CAB 128/7, Cabinet 55(46), 5 June 1946, Confidential Annex.

53. See R. Smith and J. Zametica, 'The Cold Warrior: Clement Attlee Reconsidered 1945–47', *International Affairs*, 61, 2 (1985), 237–52.

54. Conclusions of Prime Ministers' Meeting (46)5. See W. J. Hudson and W. Way (eds.), *Australia and the Post-War World: Documents 1947* (Canberra, 1995), p. 320.

55. Attlee's views can be traced in his memoranda on 'The Future of the Italian Colonies', 1 September 1945 and 2 March 1946; his letter to Bevin, 1 December 1946, and his minute to Bevin on 'Near Eastern Policy', 5 January 1947; all in R. Hyam (ed.), *British Documents on the End of Empire: The Labour Government and the End of Empire 1945–1951*, Part III, *Strategy, Politics and Constitutional Change* (1992), pp. 207–8, 213–15, 221–2, 223–6.

56. Minute by Bevin to Attlee, 9 January 1947. Hyam, *Labour Government*, Part III, p. 228.

57. Of the huge literature on the end of the Raj, the best survey is R. J. Moore, *Escape from Empire: The Attlee Government and the Indian Problem* (Oxford, 1983).

58. CAB 128/5, Cabinet 73(46) 25 July 1946.

59. M. J. Cohen, *Palestine and the Great Powers 1945–1948* (Princeton, 1982), is the standard account of the British withdrawal.

60. Fforde, *Bank of England*, pp. 101–2.

61. A. P. Dobson, *The Politics of the Anglo-American Special Economic Relationship, 1940–1987* (1988), pp. 109–13.

62. Canadian High Commissioner, London to Secretary of State for External Affairs, 8 April 1946. D. M. Page (ed.), *Documents on Canadian External Relations*, vol. 12 (1946) (Ottawa, 1977), p. 1242.

63. See J. Darwin, *Britain and Decolonization: The Retreat from Empire in the Post-War World* (1988), pp. 94–5.

64. P. Williams (ed.), *The Diary of Hugh Gaitskell* (1983), p. 54 (30 January 1948).

65. Bevin's Cabinet Memo, 19 October 1949. Hyam, *Labour Government*, Part 3, p. 382.

66. CAB 129/28, CP (48) 171, Memo by A. Creech Jones, 1 July 1948.

67. See *British Documents on the End of Empire*: J. Kent (ed.), *Egypt and the Defence of the Middle East*, 3 vols. (1998), 'Introduction', pp. liv–lv.

68. Alexander Turnbull Library, Wellington, Alister McIntosh Papers, MS 6759/050: Attlee to Fraser, 14 January 1948.

69. PREM 8/950: Sir N. Brook, Draft Report on Proceedings of Official Committee on Commonwealth Relations, 24 March 1948.

70. CAB 131/5, Cabinet Defence Committee, DO 19 (48), 18 September 1948.

71. G. C. Peden, *The Treasury and Public Policy 1906–1959* (Oxford, 2000), p. 407.

72. CAB 129/29, CP (48) 206, Prime Minister's Memo, 24 August 1948.

73. S. Constantine, 'Migrants and Settlers', in W. R. Louis and J. M. Brown (eds.), *The Oxford History of the British Empire: The Twentieth Century* (Oxford, 1999), p. 186.

74. P. W. Bell, *The Sterling Area in the Post-War World* (Oxford, 1956), p. 316–17.

75. R. Hyam and P. Henshaw, *The Lion and the Springbok* (Cambridge, 2003), pp. 135–6.

76. Peden, *Treasury*, p. 392.

77. See J. Tomlinson, 'The Attlee Government and the Balance of Payments, 1945–1951', *Journal of Twentieth Century British History*, 2, 1 (1991), 59.

78. J. Fred Rippy, 'Point Four Background: A Decade of Income from British Overseas Investment', *Journal of Business of the University of Chicago*, 26, 4 (1953), 231–7.

79. HC Deb., 5th series, vol. 450, col. 1318.

80. Alexander Turnbull Library, Wellington, Alister McIntosh Papers MS 6759/050, Prime Minister to Berendsen, Secret and Personal Telegram, 4 October 1947.

81. W. Reynolds, *Australia's Bid for the Atomic Bomb* (Carlton, Vic., 2000), p. 47.

82. Alexander Turnbull Library, Wellington, Chifley to Attlee, 22 January 1948, copy in Alister McIntosh MS 6759/050.

83. Alexander Turnbull Library, Wellington, Alister McIntosh Papers MS 6759/050: Report on Visit to Australia in Memo by McIntosh for Prime Minister Fraser, 1 March 1948.

84. I. McGibbon (ed.), *Undiplomatic Dialogue: Letters between Carl Berendsen and Alister McIntosh 1943–1957* (Auckland, 1993), p. 174.

85. It was approved by 568,427 to 160,998.

86. *New Zealand Parliamentary Debates*, vol. 277, p. 595 (21 August 1947).

87. A. W. Martin, *Robert Menzies: A Life* (Melbourne, 1993), vol. I, p. 166, quoting Menzies in 1935.

88. Martin, *Menzies* (Melbourne 1999), vol. II, p. 95.

89. See B. MacFarlane, 'Australian Post-War Economic Policy 1947–1953', in A. Curthoys and J. Merritt (eds.), *Australia's First Cold War 1945–1953* (1984), p. 41.

90. Martin, *Menzies*, vol. II, p. 222.

91. The commitment was eventually approved by the Australian cabinet in December 1951. See H. Donohue, *From Empire Defence to Long Haul: Post-War Defence and its Impact on Naval Force Structure and Planning 1945–1955* (Canberra, 1996), p. 111.

92. See D. Lowe, *Menzies and the 'Great World Struggle': Australia's Cold War 1948–1954* (Sydney, 1999), p. 96.

93. G. P. Grant, *The Empire, Yes or No* (Toronto, 1945).

94. National Archives of Canada. Brooke Claxton MS Mic. H-1422: *St Catherine's Standard*, 12 March 1948.

95. See P. Buckner, 'The Long Goodbye: English Canadians and the British World', in P. Buckner and R. D. Francis (eds.), *Rediscovering the British World* (Calgary, 2005), pp. 181–207.

96. National Archives of Canada, Mackenzie King MS C-11051: Mackenzie King to St Laurent, 3 October 1948.

97. J. Hilliker (ed.), *Documents on Canadian External Relations*, vol. 11 (Ottawa. 1990), pp. 1262–7: Memo by Senior Canadian Army Member, Permanent Joint Board of Defence, 2 August 1945.

98. B. W. Muirhead, *The Development of Post-War Canadian Trade Policy* (Montreal and Kingston, 1992), pp. 183–6.

99. Muirhead, *Trade Policy*, p. 43.

100. See Canadian High Commissioner in London to Secretary of State for External Affairs, 14 November 1949, H. Mackenzie (ed.), *Documents on Canadian External Relations*, vol. 15 (Ottawa, 1995), pp. 1318–20.

101. For two contemporary estimates, see Tom MacDonald, *Jan Hofmeyr: Heir to Smuts* (Cape Town, 1948); A. Keppel-Jones, *When Smuts Goes* (Cape Town, 1947).

102. See note 75 above.

103. DO 121/75, Memo, 'The Commonwealth Relationship: Constitutional Questions', February 1949, containing Congress Party Resolution, 16 December 1948.

104. PREM 8/950, Fifth Report of Official Committee, January 1949.

105. PREM 8/950, Report by Sir N. Brook on Consultations with Canada, Australia and New Zealand, 14 September 1948.

106. PREM 8/950, Cabinet Committee on Commonwealth Relations, 2nd Conclusions, 8 February 1949.

107. *Ibid.*

108. PREM 8/950, Listowel (Wellington) to Commonwealth Relations Office, 22 March 1949.

109. PREM 8/950, Attlee to Nehru, Top Secret and Personal, 20 March 1949.

110. PREM 8/950, Note by Sir N. Brook, 22 April 1949.

111. CAB 129/35, CP (49) 141, 21 June 1949, 'The Commonwealth Relationship: Republicanism in South Africa': Evelyn Baring to P. Noel-Baker, 7 June 1949.

112. PREM 8/950, Commonwealth Prime Ministers Meeting, 27 April 1949.

113. See M. Bassett and M. King, *Tomorrow Comes the Song: A Life of Peter Fraser* (Auckland, 2000), p. 325.

114. For Attlee's note on Commonwealth nomenclature, 30 December 1948, see Hyam, *Labour Government*, Part 4, pp. 178–80.

115. See *British Documents on the End of Empire*: Kent, *Egypt*, vol. I, p. 289: Bevin to Alexander, 13 September 1948.

116. FO 371/73465, Sir W. Strang to E. A. Chapman-Andrews (Cairo), 21 September 1949.

117. FO 371/73464, Minute by G. Clutton, 24 June 1949.

118. FO 371/69274: Note on 'Operation Bystander', by Colonel Jenkins, 14 July 1948.

119. CAB 131/9, DO (50) 40, Cabinet Defence Committee, 19 May 1950, Appendix 1.

120. CAB 131/11, DO (51) 12, 17 February 1951, Chiefs of Staff Memo, 17 February 1951.

121. *The Times*, 29 September 1950.

122. See e.g. CAB 129/36, CP (49) 176, Memo by Minister of Fuel and Power, 18 August 1949.

123. See Z. Mikdashi, *A Financial Analysis of Middle Eastern Oil Concessions 1901–1965* (New York, 1966), p. 110. Compare the figure of £36 million in tax in J. Bamberg, *History of the British Petroleum Company*, vol. II, *The Anglo-Iranian Years 1928–1954* (Cambridge, 1994), p. 325. The difference refers to the percentage of revenue attributable to the company's Iranian operations.

124. E. Abrahamian, *Iran Between Two Revolutions* (Princeton, 1982), ch. 5.

125. W. R. Louis, *The British Empire and the Middle East 1945–1951* (Oxford, 1984), p. 666.

126. Louis, *Middle East*, p. 688.

127. See Circular Dispatch from Secretary of State for the Colonies to the African Governors, 25 February 1947, in *British Documents on the End of Empire*: Hyam, *Labour Government*, Part I, pp. 119–29.

128. Governor Arden-Clarke to A. B. Cohen, 5 March 1951, *British Documents on the End of Empire*: Hyam, *Labour Government*, Part III, p. 65. For the motives behind constitutional change, see Cabinet Memo by A. Creech-Jones, 8 October 1949, *ibid.*, p. 47.

129. See D. Anderson, *Histories of the Hanged* (2005), ch. 1.

130. See T. N. Harper, *The End of Empire and the Making of Malaya* (Cambridge, 1999). chs. 2, 3, 4, offer a brilliant analysis.

131. CAB 129/26, CP (48) 91: Memo by P. Gordon Walker, March 1948.

132. National Archives of Australia, A4933, OCR, Chancellor of Exchequer to Treasurer, 15 January 1951, enclosed in 24th Report of Inter-departmental Dollar Committee.

133. *The Times*, 2 March 1951.

134. Fforde, *Bank of England*, p. 420.

135. See draft dated 18 January 1952 in Sir Alister McIntosh Mss, Alexander Turnbull Library, Wellington, 6759/063.

136. See Bell, *Sterling Area*, p. 382.

137. National Archives of Australia, A 11099, 1/16, Cabinet Notebooks 1952: Cabinet of 3 June 1952.

138. CAB 159/11, Joint Intelligence Committee (52) 2, 3 January 1952.

139. FO 371/90119, British Middle East Office to Foreign Office, 17 November 1951.

140. CAB 128/23, Cabinet (51) 20, 28 December 1951; (51) 21, 29 December 1951.

141. CAB 129/48, Cabinet (51) 40, Memo by Foreign Secretary, 6 December 1951.

142. Minute by Sir P. Dixon, 23 January 1952, FO 371/96920, in *British Documents on the End of Empire*: Kent, *Egypt*, Part 2, p. 320.

143. *Ibid.*

Chapter 13

1. See M. J. Daunton, *Just Taxes: The Politics of Taxation in Britain, 1914–1979* (Cambridge, 2001).

2. E. Shuckburgh, *Descent to Suez: Diaries 1951–56* (1987), p. 93. Shuckburgh was Eden's Private Secretary at the Foreign Office.

3. *British Documents on the End of Empire*: D. Goldsworthy (ed.), *The Conservative Government and the End of Empire 1951–1957* (1994), Part 1, *International Relations*, pp. 344–8: 'India and the Colonial Problem', a note by R. C. Ormerod, Commonwealth Relations Office, 7 July 1955.

4. See G. Kahin, *The Asian-African Conference at Bandung, Indonesia, April 1955* (Ithaca, NY, 1956).

5. W. R. Louis, 'Public Enemy Number One: Britain and the United Nations in the Aftermath of Suez', in W. R. Louis, *Ends of British*

Imperialism: The Scramble for Empire, Suez and Decolonization (2006).

6. *British Documents on the End of Empire*: A. J. Stockwell (ed.), *Malaya*, Part 2, *The Communist Insurrection 1948–1953* (1995), p. 330: Cabinet Memo by O. Lyttelton, 21 December 1951.

7. *British Documents on the End of Empire*: Goldsworthy (ed.), *The Conservative Government and the End of Empire 1951–1957*, Part 2, *Politics and Administration*, p. 188: Cabinet Conclusions, 12 February 1952.

8. *Ibid.*, p. 203: Cabinet Memo by O. Lyttelton, 4 September 1953.

9. See M. Lynn, '"We Cannot Let the North Down": British Policy and Nigeria in the 1950s', in M. Lynn (ed.), *The British Empire in the 1950s: Retreat or Revival* (2006), pp. 144–63.

10. *British Documents on the End of Empire*: Goldsworthy (ed.), *The Conservative Government and the End of Empire 1951–1957*, Part 2, p. 247: Sir E. Baring to Lyttelton, 29 October 1953.

11. See J. Darwin, *Britain and Decolonization: The Retreat from Empire in the Post-War World* (1988), pp. 202–6.

12. *British Documents on the End of Empire*: Goldsworthy (ed.), *The Conservative Government and the End of Empire 1951–1957*, Part 2, p. 23: Memo by Lord Swinton, 16 June 1954.

13. *Ibid.*, p. 30: Cabinet Memo by Lord Swinton, 11 October 1954.

14. *Ibid.*, Part 1, p. 99: Note on 'The Probable Development of the Commonwealth', June 1956.

15. *Ibid.*, p. 100.

16. See K. Larres, *Churchill's Cold War* (2002).

17. See *Fortune*, November 1952, 'The Colonial Big Five'.

18. See T. Shaw, *Eden, Suez and the Mass Media: Propaganda and Persuasion during the Suez Crisis* (1996), p. 197.

19. S. Howe, *Anti-Colonialism in British Politics 1918–1964: The Left and the End of Empire* (Oxford, 1993).

20. See S. Ward, *Australia and the British Embrace: The Demise of the Imperial Ideal* (Melbourne, 2001), ch. 1. For the economic strains, see D. Lee, 'Australia, the British Commonwealth and the United States, 1950–53', *Journal of Imperial and Commonwealth History*, 20, 3 (1992), 445–69.

21. J. Jupp, *From White Australia to Woomera* (Cambridge, 2002), p. 12.

22. See Megan Hutchings, *Long Journey for Sevenpence: Assisted Immigration to New Zealand from the United Kingdom, 1947–1975* (Wellington, 1999), pp. 45ff.

23. A. McIntosh to C. Berendsen, March 1949, I. McGibbon (ed.), *Undiplomatic Dialogue: Letters between Carl Berendsen and Alister McIntosh 1943–1952* (Auckland, 1993), p. 177.

24. Press Statement, 21 February 1952, Alister McIntosh Papers, Ms 6579/063, Alexander Turnbull Library.

25. M. Templeton, *Ties of Blood and Empire: New Zealand's Involvement in Middle East Defence and the Suez Crisis, 1947–1957* (Auckland, 1994), p. 183.

26. Holland's notes on Suez Crisis and New Zealand policy, 6 November 1956. Alister McIntosh Papers Ms 6759/079. For the private reservations in the New Zealand cabinet, see R. Pfeiffer, 'New Zealand and the Suez Crisis of 1956', *Journal of Imperial and Commonwealth History*, 21, 1 (1993), 126–52.

27. See Anna Green, *British Capital, Antipodean Labour: Working the New Zealand Waterfront 1915–1951* (Dunedin, 2001), p. 16.

28. 'The Boom That Made Canada', *Fortune*, August 1952, p. 91.

29. See P. Buckner, 'The Long Goodbye: English Canadians and the British World', in P. Buckner and D. Francis (eds.), *Rediscovering the British World* (Calgary, 2005), pp. 181–207. For Canada's increasing economic detachment, see T. Rooth, 'Britain's Other Dollar Problem: Economic Relations with Canada 1945–50', *Journal of Imperial and Commonwealth History*, 27, 1 (1999), 81–108.

30. See R. Hyam and P. Henshaw, *The Lion and the Springbok: Britain and South Africa since the Boer War* (Cambridge, 2003), ch. 10.

31. See D. Anderson, *Histories of the Hanged* (2006).

32. *British Documents on the End of Empire*: Goldsworthy (ed.), *The Conservative Government and the End of Empire 1951–1957*, Part 2, pp. 282–3: Cabinet Memo by Lord Ismay and O. Lyttelton, 9 November 1951.

33. R. C. O. Matthews, C. H. Feinstein and J. Odling Smee, *British Economic Growth 1856–1973* (Stanford, 1982), p. 128.

34. R. Michie, *The City of London: Continuity and Change 1850–1990* (1992), p. 113.

35. W. H. Branson, H. Giersch and P. G. Peterson, 'Trends in United States International Trade and Investment since World War II', in M. Feldstein (ed.), *The American Economy in Transition* (1980), p. 184.

36. See the briefing by Sir F. Brundrett, July 1956. Alister McIntosh Ms 6759/081, Alexander Turnbull Library.

37. N. Tiratsoo and J. Tomlinson, *The Conservatives and Industrial Efficiency, 1951–1964: Thirteen Wasted Years?* (1998), pp. 155ff.

38. See S. Strange, *Sterling and British Policy* (1971), pp. 4–5, for the definition of 'master currency', 'top currency' etc.

39. S. N. Broadberry, *The Productivity Race: British Manufacturing in International Perspective, 1850–1990* (Cambridge, 1997), pp. 94–6.

40. *The Economist*, 25 January 1958, p. 356.

41. For the origins of ROBOT, see J. Fforde, *The Bank of England and Public Policy 1941–1958* (Cambridge, 1992), ch. 6.

42. *Ibid.*, pp. 442–3.

43. For Eden's hostile reaction, see Shuckburgh, *Descent to Suez*, pp. 36–8.

44. For an authoritative account of the approach to convertibility, see Fforde, *Bank of England*, pp. 585–605.

45. *The Economist*, 3 January 1959, p. 12.

46. Broadberry, *Productivity Race*, pp. 94–6.

47. See J. Black, 'The Volumes and Prices of British Exports', in G. N. Worswick and P. Ady (eds.), *The British Economy in the 1950s* (Oxford, 1962), pp. 129–30.

48. See G. C. Peden, *The Treasury and British Public Policy 1906–1959* (Oxford, 2000), p. 450.

49. *British Documents on the End of Empire*: Goldsworthy (ed.), *The Conservative Government and the End of Empire 1951–1957*, Part 3, *Economic and Social Policies*, p. 122.

50. *Ibid.*

51. *Ibid.*, p. 126: Cabinet Conclusions, 14 September 1956.

52. *Ibid.*, p. 128.

53. *Ibid.*, p. 131.

54. *Ibid.*, p. 134: Joint Cabinet Memo, 6 November 1956.

55. For a critical view, see *The Economist*, 13 September 1958, p. 815: 'Which Gospel at Montreal?'.

56. Cmnd. 827 (1959), *Report of the Committee on the Working of the Monetary System*, p. 657.

57. *Ibid.*, p. 739.

58. Broadberry, *Productivity Race*, pp. 393ff.

59. For this view, see *The Economist*, 13 February 1960, p. 642.

60. *British Documents on the End of Empire*: J. Kent (ed.), *Egypt and the Defence of the Middle East*, Part 2, *1949–1953* (1998): Memo by Chiefs of Staff, 'Defence Policy and Global Strategy', 17 June 1952.

61. *British Documents on the End of Empire*: Kent (ed.), *Middle East*, Part 2, pp. 538–9: Cabinet Memo by Anthony Eden, 14 January 1953, annex.

62. *Ibid.*, pp. 346–8: Sir R. Stevenson to Eden, 25 February 1952.

63. *Ibid.*

64. *Ibid.*, pp. 355–6: Eden's Minute to Churchill, 10 March 1952.

65. *Ibid.*, p. 387: Memo by R. Allen, 1 May 1952.

66. No hint of the coup had reached British intelligence, noted the Joint Intelligence Committee. See CAB 159/12: JIC (52) 83, 30 July 1952.

67. FO 371/102796: Minute by R. Allen, 14 February 1953.

68. T. L. Hanes III, 'Sir Hubert Huddleston and the Independence of the Sudan', *Journal of Imperial and Commonwealth History*, 20, 2 (1992), 248–73.

69. For Neguib's outlook and attitudes, see General Neguib, *Egypt's Destiny* (1955).

70. FO 371/102803: Cresswell to Allen, 30 March 1953.

71. CAB 158/ 18: JIC (53) 50, 14 May 1953.

72. *British Documents on the End of Empire*: Kent (ed.), *Middle East*, Part 3, *1953–1956*, p. 147: Hankey to Eden, 23 November 1953. Hankey was the son of Lord Hankey, the former Cabinet Secretary who was a sharp critic of the evacuation policy. His appointment at the instigation of Churchill was regarded by some Egyptians as a wrecking move. See FO 371/102848: C. B. Duke (Cairo) to R. Allen, 23 July 1953.

73. *Ibid.*

74. FO 371/102823: Churchill's Minute, 11 December 1953.

75. *Ibid.*: Eden's Minute, 12 December 1953.

76. *British Documents on the End of Empire*: Kent (ed.), *Middle East*, Part 3, p. 156: Eden's Minute to Churchill, 1 December 1953.

77. FO 371/102824: Eden's Minute for Churchill, 21 December 1953.

78. CAB 129/61: Memo by Acting Foreign Secretary, 4 July 1953, C (53) 190. See also M. Thornhill, 'Britain, the United States and the Rise of an Egyptian Leader: The Politics and Diplomacy of Nasser's Consolidation of Power 1952–4', *English Historical Review*, 119, 483 (2004), 892–921.

79. *British Documents on the End of Empire*: Kent (ed.), *Middle East*, Part 3, p. 163: Eisenhower to Churchill, 21 December 1953.

80. *Ibid.*, p. 82: Eden's Cabinet Memo, 7 January 1954.

81. See *The Times*, 26 March, 29 March 1954.

82. CAB 129/69, Note by Minister of State, 'Egypt: Defence Negotiations', 6 July 1954, C (45) 220.

83. See the sardonic remarks of Charles Waterhouse in the House of Commons. *The Times*, 3 November 1954.

84. Which began as an Iraqi-Turkish agreement in February 1955.

85. CAB 158/18: Report by JIC, JIC (54) 72 (Final), 11 November 1954.

86. *British Documents on the End of Empire*: Kent (ed.), *Middle East*, Part 3, p. 437: Minute by E. Shuckburgh, 23 September 1955.

87. *Ibid.*, p. 447: Cabinet Conclusions, 4 October 1955.

88. Shuckburgh, *Descent*, p. 345.

89. *Ibid.*, p. 346.

90. The best accounts of the Suez crisis can be found in D. Carlton, *Anthony Eden* (1981); W. R. Louis and R. Owen (eds.), *Suez 1956: The Crisis and its Consequences* (Oxford, 1989); K. Kyle, *The Suez Conflict* (1989); and D. J. Dutton, *Anthony Eden: A Life and a Reputation* (1997). D. R. Thorp, *Eden: The Life and Times of Anthony Eden* (2003), offers a more sympathetic view of Eden than most. The best recent short account is in R. Hyam, *Britain's Declining Empire* (Cambridge, 2006).

91. In his poem, 'The Lesson'.

92. A. Nutting, *No End of a Lesson* (1967).

93. J. G. Ballard, *Miracles of Life* (2007), p. 21.

94. W. Webster, *Englishness and Empire* (Oxford, 2005), p. 140.

95. On this theme, see W. R. Louis, 'Public Enemy Number One: Britain and the United Nations in the Aftermath of Suez', in W. R. Louis, *Ends of British Imperialism* (2006), pp. 689–724.

96. Fforde, *Bank of England*, p. 544.

97. See D. Kunz, *The Economic Diplomacy of the Suez Crisis* (Durham, NC, 1991), p. 132.

98. Fforde, *Bank of England*, p. 555.

99. For Commonwealth reactions, see J. Eayrs (ed.), *The Commonwealth and Suez: A Documentary Survey* (1964).

100. For a recent account, see Barry Turner, *Suez 1956* (2006), which stresses the muddle and uncertainty of British operations.

101. See R. Worrall, 'Britain and Libya: A Study of Military Bases and State Creation, 1945–1956' (DPhil., Oxford University, 2007).

Chapter 14

1. For two recent surveys, see S. Howe, 'When If Ever Did Empire End? Internal Decolonization in British Culture since the 1950s', in M. Lynn (ed.), *The British Empire in the 1950s: Retreat or Revival* (2005); W. Webster, *Englishness and Empire 1939–1965* (Oxford, 2005).

2. *British Documents on the End of Empire*: D. Goldsworthy (ed.), *The Conservative Government and the End of Empire 1951–1957*, Part 2, (1994), pp. 202–4: Cabinet Memo by Colonial Secretary, 4 September 1953.

3. *British Documents on the End of Empire*: Goldsworthy (ed.), *The Conservative Government and the End of Empire 1951–1957*, Part 2, pp. 206–12: Cumming-Bruce to Laithwaite, 19 August 1955.

4. *British Documents on the End of Empire*: R. Hyam and W. R. Louis (eds.), *The Conservative Government and the End of Empire, 1957–1964, Part 1, High Policy, Political and Constitutional Change* (2000), p. 341: Memo by Colonial Secretary for Cabinet Colonial Policy Committee, 7 May 1957.

5. *Ibid.*, p. 356: Cabinet Memo, 20 October 1958.

6. *Ibid.*, p. 91: Cabinet Memo, 24 February 1960, Report of Officials' Committee on 'Future Policy Study 1960–1970'.

7. CO 554/2147, Carter to Axworthy, 10 May 1960; Colonial Secretary (Macleod) to Sir E. Windley (the Governor), 7 March 1961.

8. CO 554/1568, Minute by C. G. Eastwood, 11 March 1959.

9. See D. Anderson, *Histories of the Hanged* (2006).

10. CO 822/1200: Baring to Colonial Secretary, 7 March 1954.

11. CO 822/1200: Brief for Colonial Secretary, October 1954.

12. Multiracialism was abandoned as a constitutional principle in 1958.

13. *British Documents on the End of Empire*: Hyam and Louis (eds.), *The Conservative Government and the End of Empire 1957–1964*, Part 1, pp. 371–81: Memo by Colonial Secretary for Cabinet Colonial Policy Committee, 10 April 1959.

14. *Ibid.*, p. 383: Cabinet Colonial Policy Committee, Minutes, 17 April 1959.

15. FO 371/137970: Note by Foreign Office for Cabinet Africa (official) Committee, 'Africa: The Next Ten Years. Talks with the Americans', 12 October 1959.

16. Ten per cent of post-war investment in Africa had flowed to the Federation, *The Economist* reported in December 1958.

17. Welensky had been born in poverty in Southern Rhodesia but his career as a railwayman, trade unionist and politician had been built in Northern Rhodesia.

18. The best account of the Emergency is now C. Baker, *State of Emergency: Crisis in Central Africa, Nyasaland 1959–1960* (1997); see also J. Darwin, 'The Central African Emergency, 1959', *Journal of Imperial and Commonwealth History*, 21 (1993), 217–34.

19. Baker, *Emergency*, pp. 153–68.

20. The best biography of Macleod is R. Shepherd, *Iain Macleod* (1994).

21. *British Documents on the End of Empire*: Hyam and Louis (eds.), *The Conservative Government and the End of Empire 1957–1964*,

Part 1, p. 413: 'I do not believe that we should bow to expediency' and release Kenyatta, he told Macmillan in April 1961.

22. *Ibid.*, pp. 476–80: Memo by Colonial Secretary for Colonial Policy Committee, 12 November 1959.

23. *Ibid.*, p. 479.

24. *Ibid.*, p. 485: Macleod's Minute, 28 July 1960.

25. *Ibid.*, p. 494: Macleod to Turnbull (Governor of Tanganyika), 11 February 1961.

26. *Ibid.*, p. 497: Memo 27 February 1961.

27. CO 822/2262, Draft Memo for Colonial Policy Committee, January 1960; Colonial Secretary to Officer Administering the Government, 12 February 1960.

28. CO 822/2262: Minutes of Cabinet Colonial Policy Committee, 8 February 1960.

29. CO 822/2263, Minute by F. D. Webber, 15 July 1960.

30. CO 822/2264, Monson to Crawford (Governor of Uganda), 30 August 1961.

31. CO 822/2264, Coutts to Monson, 24 January 1962.

32. Shepherd, *Iain Macleod*, pp. 156–7.

33. CO 822/1427, Webber to Renison (Governor of Kenya), 1 December 1959.

34. *British Documents on the End of Empire*: Hyam and Louis (eds.), *The Conservative Government and the End of Empire 1957–1964*, Part 1, p. 180: Macleod to Macmillan, 31 May 1960.

35. CO 822/2235, Colonial Secretary to Governor of Kenya, 14 April 1961.

36. CO 822/2241, Colonial Secretary to Governor of Kenya, 9 May 1961, 19 May 1961.

37. *The Times*, 12 June 1961: Report by Africa Correspondent.

38. 16 May 1961.

39. *British Documents on the End of Empire*: Hyam and Louis (eds.), *The Conservative Government and the End of Empire 1957–1964*, Part 1, p. 529: Memo by Colonial Secretary for Cabinet Colonial Policy Committee, 30 January 1962. A draft of this can be found in CO 822/2238.

40. *Ibid.*, p. 531: Cabinet Memo by Colonial Secretary, 6 February 1962.

41. *Ibid.*

42. *British Documents on the End of Empire*: P. Murphy (ed.), *Central Africa, Part 1, Closer Association 1945–1958* (2005), p. 433: Note by B. Trend for Macmillan, 17 November 1958.

43. *Ibid.*, Part 2, *Crisis and Dissolution 1959–1965*, p. 131: Macleod to Macmillan, 3 April 1960.

44. The Nyasaland Emergency had been followed by those in Northern and Southern Rhodesia.

45. Macmillan to Welensky, 17 April 1959. Quoted in J. R. T. Wood, *The Welensky Papers* (Durban, 1982), p. 665.

46. Wood, *Welensky Papers*, p. 733.

47. *British Documents on the End of Empire*: Murphy (ed.), *Central Africa*, Part 2, p. 93: Macleod's Minute to Macmillan, 3 December 1959.

48. *British Documents on the End of Empire*: Murphy (ed.), *Central Africa*, Part 2, p. 182: Macleod's Minute to Macmillan, 29 November 1960.

49. Wood, *Welensky Papers*, p. 790.

50. *British Documents on the End of Empire*: Murphy (ed.), *Central Africa*, Part 2, p. 95: Macleod's Minute to Macmillan, 3 December 1959.

51. *Ibid.*, p. 131: Macleod (Zomba) to Macmillan, 3 April 1960.

52. Cmnd. 1148 (1960), *Report of the Advisory Commission on the Review of the Constitution of the Federation of Rhodesia and Nyasaland*, para. 27.

53. For Macleod's calculations, see *British Documents on the End of Empire*: Murphy (ed.), *Central Africa*, Part 2, pp. 232–35: Macleod to Sandys, 26 May 1961.

54. Cmnd. 1291 (1961). *Report of the Southern Rhodesian Constitutional Conference*, February 1961.

55. PREM 11/2784, Report by Burke Trend, 13 October 1959.

56. Shepherd, *Iain Macleod*, p. 212.

57. *British Documents on the End of Empire*: Murphy (ed.), *Central Africa*, Part 1, Introduction, p. lxxxvii.

58. *British Documents on the End of Empire*: Hyam and Louis (eds.), *The Conservative Government and the End of Empire, 1957–1964*, Part 2, pp. 455–62, for the valedictory report by Sir John Maud, 14 May 1963.

59. See R. F. Holland, *Britain and the Revolt in Cyprus 1954–1959* (Oxford, 1998), pp. 300–20.

60. Macmillan's diary, 15 September 1957. P. Catterall (ed.), *The Macmillan Diaries: The Cabinet Years, 1950–1957* (2003), p. 599.

61. Peden, *Treasury*, p. 501.

62. See P. Mangold, *The Almost Impossible Ally: Harold Macmillan and Charles De Gaulle* (2006), p. 79.

63. See E. B. Geelhoed (ed.), *The Macmillan–Eisenhower Correspondence, 1957–1965* (2005).

64. See N. Ashton, 'Harold Macmillan and the "Golden Days" of Anglo-American Relations Revisited, 1957–1963', *Diplomatic History*, 29, 4 (2005), 70. For the declaration, *British Documents on the End of Empire*: Hyam and Louis (eds.), *The Conservative Government and the End of Empire 1957–1964*, Part 2, p. 227.

65. For this suggestion, see Ashton, 'Harold Macmillan and the "Golden Days"', p. 699.

66. See W. A. Nielsen, *The Great Powers and Africa* (1969), chs. 8, 9 and Table 20.

67. For this episode, see Ashton, 'Harold Macmillan and the "Golden Days"', p. 710.

68. Mangold, *Impossible Ally*, p. 127.

69. *Ibid.*, p. 128.

70. *Ibid.*, p. 136.

71. *British Documents on the End of Empire*: Hyam and Louis (eds.), *The Conservative Government and the End of Empire 1957–1964*, Part 2, pp. 214–15, for the Cabinet discussion.

72. Macmillan's diary, 28 January 1963. Quoted in Mangold, *Impossible Ally*, p. 205.

73. *British Documents on the End of Empire*: Hyam and Louis (eds.), *The Conservative Government and the End of Empire 1957–1964*, Part 2, p. 198: Cabinet Conclusions, 26 April 1961.

74. See G. H. Souton, *L'alliance incertaine: les rapports politico-strategiques franco-allemands, 1954–1991* (Paris, 1996); P. M. H. Bell, *France and Britain 1940–1994: The Long Separation* (1997), pp. 176–8; C. Wurm, 'Two Paths to Europe', in C. Wurm (ed.), *Western Europe and Germany: The Beginnings of European Integration 1945–1960* (Oxford, 1995), pp. 186–8; W. Kaiser, 'Against Napoleon and Hitler: Background Influences in British Diplomacy', in W. Kaiser and G. Staerck (eds.), *British Foreign Policy 1955–1964: Contracting Options* (2000), pp. 122–3; Mangold, *Impossible Ally*, chs. 14–20.

75. National Archives of Australia, A1209/64, Special Committee on Blue Streak, 22 March 1960.

76. *British Documents on the End of Empire*: Hyam and Louis (eds.), *The Conservative Government and the End of Empire 1957–1964*, Part 2, p. 283: Cabinet Memo by Foreign Secretary, 2 September 1964.

77. R. H. S. Crossman, *Diaries of a Cabinet Minister* (1976), vol. II, p. 639 (7 January 1968).

78. A. Cairncross, *Managing the British Economy in the 1960s: A Treasury Perspective* (Basingstoke, 1996), pp. 92–5.

79. *Ibid.*, p. 172.

80. *Ibid.*, p. 178.

81. For the Middle East role, see G. Balfour-Paul, *The End of Empire in the Middle East: Britain's Relinquishment of Power in Her Last Three Arab Dependencies* (Cambridge, 1991); for Southeast Asia and the containment of Indonesia, see J. Subritzski, *Confronting Sukarno: British, American, Australian and New Zealand Diplomacy in the Malaysian–Indonesian Confrontation, 1961–1965* (2000).

82. R. C. O. Matthews, C. H. Feinstein and J. Odling-Smee, *British Economic Growth 1856–1973* (Stanford, 1982), p. 164.

83. Cmnd. 2764 (1965), pp. 6, 70–1.

84. *British Documents on the End of Empire*, Series A, Vol. 5: S. R. Ashton and W. R. Louis (eds.), *East of Suez and the Commonwealth*, Part III, *Dependent Territories, Africa, Economics, Race* (2004), p. 496: Treasury Memo, 26 April 1968.

85. The authoritative study of British policy is now Phuong Pham, 'The End of East of Suez: The British Decision to Withdraw from Malaysia and Singapore 1964 to 1968' (DPhil., Oxford, 2001), shortly to be published by Oxford University Press. See also J. Darwin, 'Britain's Withdrawal from East of Suez', in C. Bridge (ed.), *Munich to Vietnam: Australia's Relations with Britain and the United States since the 1930s* (Carlton, Vic., 1991), pp. 140–58.

86. Cmnd. 2901, *Statement on Defence Estimates*, 1966, p. 8.

87. Cmnd. 3203, *Statement on Defence Estimates*, 1967, p. 7.

88. Crossman, *Diaries of a Cabinet Minister*, vol. II, p. 86 (22 October 1966).

89. Cmnd. 3357, *Supplementary Statement on Defence Policy*, 1967, pp. 5ff.

90. The Gulf rulers offered to meet the costs of the British military presence. For the background, see S. C. Smith, *Britain's Revival and Fall in the Gulf: Kuwait, Qatar and the Trucial States 1950–1971* (2004).

91. *HC Debs.*, 5th series, vol. 756, col. 1991, 18 January 1968.

92. See J. R. T. Wood, *So Far and No Further!: Rhodesia's Bid for Independence during the Retreat from Empire 1959–1965* (Johannesburg, 2005), p. 167. Wood's account is based on both British and Rhodesian records, including the papers of Ian Smith.

93. *Ibid.*, ch. 26, for the Anglo-Rhodesian dispute over the role a commission might play.

94. For Minister of Defence Denis Healey's calculation two months after UDI, see his minute of 20 January 1966, *British Documents on the End of Empire*: Ashton and Louis (eds.), *East of Suez and the Commonwealth 1964–1971*, Part II, *Europe, Rhodesia and the Commonwealth*, p. 232.

95. For the negotiations, see E. Windrich, *Britain and the Politics of Rhodesian Independence* (1978).

96. Of the twenty-six Commonwealth member states in 1967, eleven were African and five Asian.

97. This map, labelled 'Secret', can be found in *British Documents on the End of Empire*: Ashton and Louis (eds.), *East of Suez and the Commonwealth 1964–1971*, Part II: *Europe, Rhodesia, Commonwealth*, following p. 100.

98. Quoted in J. Darwin, *Britain and Decolonisation* (1988), p. 324.

Conclusion

1. A. Roberts, *Salisbury: Victorian Titan* (1999), p. 42.

2. Churchill in the House of Commons, HC Deb., 5th series, vol. 247, col. 702 (26 January 1931).

3. H. Dalton, *High Tide and After: Memoirs 1945–1960* (1962), p. 105.

SELECT BIBLIOGRAPHY

This is not intended as a full bibliography of the sources used for this book (the detail of these can be found in the endnotes that accompany each chapter) let alone of the whole range of materials consulted, or available to an interested reader. Indeed, the sources for the study of British world power over a period of a century and a half are virtually limitless. Some idea of their scale can be gained from a glance at A. Porter (ed.), *Bibliography of Imperial, Colonial and Commonwealth History since 1600* (Oxford, 2002). This contains nearly 24,000 items, some of them running to dozens of volumes. A much shorter but very useful bibliography can be found in S. Stockwell (ed.), *The British Empire: Themes and Problems* (Oxford, 2008). J. Holland Rose, A. P. Newton and E. A. Benians (eds.), *The Cambridge History of the British Empire*, vol. 1 (1929) and vol. 2 (1940) both provide extensive bibliographies, including a guide to archival materials and parliamentary debates. What I have listed below are the main primary sources which I have used, a selection of the available printed sources, and a short list of what seem to me to be the most brilliant or insightful large views of the subject.

Unpublished primary sources

I made use of the following private papers collections. In the United Kingdom: Stanley Baldwin (Cambridge University Library), A. J. Balfour (British Library), Andrew Bonar Law (House of Lords Record Office), Robert Brand (Bodleian Library), Austen Chamberlain (Birmingham University Library), Viscount Chelmsford (British Library India and Oriental Collection), Arthur Creech Jones (Rhodes

House Library, Oxford), Lionel Curtis (Bodleian Library), 1st
Marquess Curzon (BLIOC), Geoffrey Dawson (Bodleian Library),
Edward Grigg (Bodleian Library: microfilm), John Holt and Co.
(Rhodes House Library, Oxford), Miles Lampson, later Lord Killearn
(Middle East Centre, St Antony's College, Oxford), George Lloyd
(Churchill College Archives, Cambridge), David Lloyd George (House
of Lords Record Office),Viscount Milner (Bodleian Library), E. S.
Montagu (Trinity College, Cambridge), Gerald Portal (Rhodes House
Library, Oxford), C. J. Rhodes (Rhodes House Library, Oxford),
Viscount Sankey (Bodleian Library), Earl Selborne (Bodleian Library)
and John Simon (Bodleian Library).

In the Irish Republic: Donoughmore Mss (Trinity College, Dublin).

In Canada: John Buchan (Douglas Library, Queen's University
Kingston), Henri Bourassa (National Archives of Canada),
Robert Borden (NAC), Brooke Claxton (NAC), T. A. Crerar
(Douglas Library, Queen's University), J. W. Dafoe (Elizabeth Dafoe
Library, University of Manitoba), Wilfrid Laurier (NAC), Mackenzie
King (NAC), Arthur Meighen (NAC), Charles G. Power (Douglas
Library, Queen's University), Clifford Sifton (NAC) and Byron E.
Walker (Thomas Fisher Rare Books Library, University of
Toronto).

In South Africa: Sir Patrick Duncan and H. G. Lawrence
(both in Jagger Library, University of Cape Town), D. F. Malan
(Stellenbosch University Library), Charles Crewe and Sir Edgar
Walton (both in Cory Library, Rhodes University Library,
Grahamstown) and J. P. Fitzpatrick (National English Literary
Museum, Grahamstown).

In New Zealand: Sir James Allen (New Zealand National Archives)
and J. G. Coates and Sir Alister McIntosh (both in Alexander
Turnbull Library).

In the United States: J. L. Garvin (Harry Ransome Humanities
Research Centre, University of Texas at Austin).

I have also made use of Official Records, principally Cabinet, Foreign
Office and Colonial Office records in the National Archives at Kew,
and Australian Cabinet records at the National Archives of Australia,
Canberra.

Printed sources

There is a huge array of printed sources to be mined or quarried. Among those that I have found most valuable are:

G. P. Gooch and H. Temperley (eds.), *British Documents on the Origins of the War 1898–1914*, 12 vols. (1927–38).

E. L. Woodward, R. Butler, D. Dakin and M. Lambert (eds.), *Documents on British Foreign Policy 1919–1939*, Three Series (1946–86).

A. F. McMadden and D. K. Fieldhouse (eds.), *Select Documents on the Constitutional History of the British Empire and Commonwealth*, 8 vols. (1985–2000), especially vols. 5, 6, 7, 8.

P. N. S. Mansergh (ed.), *Documents and Speeches on British Commonwealth Affairs 1931–1952*, 2 vols. (1953).

P. N. S. Mansergh, E. W. Lumby and E. P. Moon (eds.), *Constitutional Relations between Britain and India: The Transfer of Power, 1942–1947*, 12 vols. (1970–83).

The *British Documents on the End of Empire* series includes both 'general' volumes and 'country' volumes. I have made particular use of:

- R. Hyam (ed.), *The Labour Government and the End of Empire 1945–1951*, 4 vols. (1992).
- D. J. Goldsworthy (ed.), *The Conservative Government and the End of Empire 1951–1957*, 3 vols. (1994).
- R. Hyam and W. R. Louis (eds.), *The Conservative Government and the End of Empire 1957–1964*, 2 vols. (2000).
- S. R. Ashton and W. R. Louis (eds.), *East of Suez and the Commonwealth 1964–1971*, 3 vols. (2004).
- J. Kent (ed.), *Egypt and the Defence of the Middle East*, 3 vols. (1998).
- P. Murphy (ed.), *Central Africa*, 2 vols. (2005).

D. R. Murray and J. F. Hilliker (eds.), *Documents on Canadian External Relations* (Ottawa, 1972–).

F. K. Crowley (ed.), *Documents in Australian History* (1973).

G. Greenwood and C. Grimshaw (eds.), *Documents on Australian International Affairs 1901–1918* (West Melbourne, 1977).

N. Meaney (ed.), *Australia and the World: A Documentary History from the 1870s to 1970s* (Melbourne, 1985).

W. J. Hudson and W. Way (eds.), *Australia and the Post-War World: Documents 1947* (Canberra, 1995).

I. McGibbon (ed.), *Undiplomatic Dialogue: Letters between Carl Berendsen and Alister McIntosh 1943–1957* (Auckland, 1993).

C. Headlam, *The Milner Papers: South Africa 1897–1905*, 2 vols. (1931).

W. K. Hancock and J. Van Der Poel (eds.), *Selections from the Smuts Papers*, 7 vols. (Cambridge, 1966–73).

A. H. Duminy and W. R. Guest (eds.), *Fitzpatrick, South African Politician: Selected Papers 1888–1906* (Johannesburg, 1976).

M. Fraser and A. Jeeves (eds.), *All That Glittered: Selected Correspondence of Lionel Phillips, 1890–1924* (Cape Town, 1977).

M. E. Yapp (ed.), *Politics and Diplomacy in Egypt: The Diaries of Sir Miles Lampson 1935–1937* (Oxford, 1997).

R. C. Palit (ed.), *Speeches by Babu Surendra Nath Banerjea 1876–1880*, vols. 1–5 (Calcutta, 1891–6).

Writings and Speeches of B. G. Tilak (Madras, 1919).

V. S. Srinavasa Sastri, *Speeches and Writings* (Madras, n.d.).

Congress Presidential Addresses, Second Series (Madras, 1934).

M. Hasan (ed.), *Mohamed Ali in Indian Politics: Selected Writings*, vol. II (New Delhi, 1987).

R. Kumar and H. D. Sharma (eds.), *Selected Works of Motilal Nehru*, 6 vols. (New Delhi, 1992–5).

S. Gopal (ed.), *Selected Works of Jawaharlal Nehru*, First Series, 15 vols. (New Delhi, 1972–82).

The Collected Works of Mahatma Gandhi, 100 vols. (New Delhi, 1964–).

Of the ever-increasing volume of material now available online, *British Parliamentary Papers* for the nineteenth and twentieth century, the *Times Digital Archive*, giving access to *The Times* since its first publication, *The Mackenzie King Diaries*, the *Dictionary of Canadian Biography*, the *Australian Dictionary of Biography* and the *Oxford Dictionary of National Biography* were particularly useful.

Secondary works

The starting point for any serious study of the subject of this book is
J. Gallagher and R. Robinson, 'The Imperialism of Free Trade',
Economic History Review, New Series, 6, 1 (1953). The ideas and
arguments found there repay almost constant re-reading. They were
further developed in R. E. Robinson and J. Gallagher, *Africa and the
Victorians* (1961), R. Robinson, 'The Non-Imperial Foundations of
European Imperialism: Sketch for a Theory of Collaboration', in R.
Owen and B. Sutcliffe (eds.), *Studies in the Theory of Imperialism*
(1972) and J. Gallagher, *The Decline, Revival and Fall of the British
Empire* (Cambridge, 1982). Their application to India was proposed
in J. Gallagher, G. Johnson and A. Seal (eds.), *Locality, Province and
Nation* (Cambridge, 1973). An essential contrast to their emphasis on
the 'official mind' of the policy-makers can be found in P. Cain and
A. G. Hopkins, *British Imperialism: 1688–2000* (2nd edn, 2001).
Here it is the financial power of the City of London which exerts a
commanding influence over the pattern of British expansion. Although
the extent to which 'gentlemanly capitalism' was the dominant ethos
in both Whitehall and the City has been disputed, *British Imperialism*
provides an essential corrective to narrowly political or diplomatic
accounts of British world power, and to the view that its decline had
set in by 1914. The role of the City can be followed in R. C. Michie,
The City of London: Continuity and Change 1850–1990 (1992) and
(with brio) in D. Kynaston, *The City of London*, 4 vols. (1994–2001).
The most brilliant account of Britain's economic travails in the first
half of the twentieth century is R. Skidelsky, *John Maynard Keynes:
A Biography*, 3 vols. (1983–2000). K. H. O'Rourke and J. G.
Willliamson, *Globalisation and History: The Evolution of a
Nineteenth-Century Atlantic Economy* (1999), examines the growth
of an Atlantic economy on its way to being global. The most elegant
short survey of British sea-power remains G. Graham, *The Politics of
Naval Supremacy* (Cambridge, 1965); on the broader subject of
'imperial defence', there is now G. Kennedy (ed.), *Imperial Defence:
The Old World Order 1856–1956* (2008). Much the best survey of
the domestic impact of empire in Britain is A. S. Thompson, *The
Empire Strikes Back: The Impact of Imperialism on Britain from the
Mid-Nineteenth Century* (2005). One of the key themes of this book
has been the neglected significance of the settlement colonies/'white

dominions' for British world power, and the close identification of their 'British' populations with the fate of the British Empire. The revival of interest in the socio-cultural connections across this 'British World' can be followed in C. Bridge and K. Fedorowich (eds.), *The British World: Diaspora, Culture and Identity* (2003), and P. Buckner and R. D. Francis (eds.), *Rediscovering the British World* (Calgary, 2005). Two recent volumes in the *Oxford History of the British Empire* Companion Series, namely, P. Buckner (ed.), *Canada and the British Empire* (Oxford, 2008) and D. Schreuder and S. Ward (eds.), *Australia's Empire* (Oxford, 2008), reflect this new orientation. James Belich's two-volume history, *Making Peoples* (1996) and *Paradise Reforged* (2001), pioneered the reinterpretation of New Zealand history as a process of 'recolonisation', in which the cultural, economic and strategic ties with Britain were progressively *strengthened* from the late nineteenth century. I have not found much space for an explicit discussion of imperial culture in this book, but the reader will find much of the material for a cultural history of empire in John MacKenzie's hugely successful series, *Studies in Imperialism*, now approaching its hundredth volume. I have attempted throughout to set the fortunes of British expansion in a global context. C. A. Bayly, *Imperial Meridian: The British Empire and the World 1780–1830* (1988), offers a brilliant account of how this might be done for an earlier period, while his *Birth of the Modern World 1780–1914: Global Connections and Comparisons* (Oxford, 2004) is a panoramic interpretation of the long nineteenth century. In *After Tamerlane: The Global History of Empire* (2007), I attempted to sketch the Eurasian conditions in which British and other European imperialisms rose and then fell.

Readers in search of an alternative panoptic view of the places and periods covered in this book should turn to the *Oxford History of the British Empire*, vol. III, *The Nineteenth Century*, ed. Andrew Porter (Oxford, 1999) and vol. IV, *The Twentieth Century*, ed. Judith Brown and W. R. Louis (Oxford, 1999), or to Piers Brendon, *The Decline and Fall of the British Empire 1781–1997* (London, 2007).

INDEX

Printed in Great Britain
by Amazon

22500219R00453